Microsoft® SQL Server™ OLAP Developer's Guide

Microsoft®
SQL Server™ OLAP
Developer's Guide

William C. Amo

IDG Books Worldwide, Inc.
An International Data Group Company

Foster City, CA ◆ Chicago, IL ◆ Indianapolis, IN ◆ New York, NY

Microsoft® SQL Server™ OLAP Developer's Guide

Published by
M&T Books
An imprint of IDG Books Worldwide, Inc.
919 E. Hillsdale Blvd., Suite 400
Foster City, CA 94404
www.idgbooks.com (IDG Books Worldwide Web site)

ISBN: 0-7645-4643-0

Printed in the United States of America

10 9 8 7 6 5 4 3 2 1

1B/RY/QU/QQ/FC

Distributed in the United States by IDG Books Worldwide, Inc.

Distributed by CDG Books Canada Inc. for Canada; by Transworld Publishers Limited in the United Kingdom; by IDG Norge Books for Norway; by IDG Sweden Books for Sweden; by IDG Books Australia Publishing Corporation Pty. Ltd. for Australia and New Zealand; by TransQuest Publishers Pte Ltd. for Singapore, Malaysia, Thailand, Indonesia, and Hong Kong; by Gotop Information Inc. for Taiwan; by ICG Muse, Inc. for Japan; by Intersoft for South Africa; by Eyrolles for France; by International Thomson Publishing for Germany, Austria and Switzerland; by Distribuidora Cuspide for Argentina; by LR International for Brazil; by Galileo Libros for Chile; by Ediciones ZETA S.C.R. Ltda. for Peru; by WS Computer Publishing Corporation, Inc., for the Philippines; by Contemporanea de Ediciones for Venezuela; by Express Computer Distributors for the Caribbean and West Indies; by Micronesia Media Distributor, Inc. for Micronesia; by Chips Computadoras S.A. de C.V. for Mexico; by Editorial Norma de Panama S.A. for Panama; by American Bookshops for Finland.

For general information on IDG Books Worldwide's books in the U.S., please call our Consumer Customer Service department at 800-762-2974. For reseller information, including discounts and premium sales, please call our Reseller Customer Service department at 800-434-3422.

For information on where to purchase IDG Books Worldwide's books outside the U.S., please contact our International Sales department at 317-596-5530 or fax 317-596-5692.

For consumer information on foreign language translations, please contact our Customer Service department at 800-434-3422, fax 317-596-5692, or e-mail rights@idgbooks.com.

For information on licensing foreign or domestic rights, please phone +1-650-655-3109.

For sales inquiries and special prices for bulk quantities, please contact our Sales department at 650-655-3200 or write to the address above.

For information on using IDG Books Worldwide's books in the classroom or for ordering examination copies, please contact our Educational Sales department at 800-434-2086 or fax 317-596-5499.

For press review copies, author interviews, or other publicity information, please contact our Public Relations department at 650-655-3000 or fax 650-655-3299.

For authorization to photocopy items for corporate, personal, or educational use, please contact Copyright Clearance Center, 222 Rosewood Drive, Danvers, MA 01923, or fax 978-750-4470.

Library of Congress Cataloging-in-Publication Data
Amo, William C.
     SQL Server 7 OLAP developer's guied/William C. Amo.
     p. cm.
     ISBN 0-7645-4643-0 (alk. paper)
     1. SQL server. 2. Client/server computing 3. OLAP technology. I. Title.
QA76.9C55 A527   2000
005.75'85--dc21   00-026776

is a registered trademark or trademark under exclusive license to IDG Books Worldwide, Inc. from International Data Group, Inc. in the United States and/or other countries.

ABOUT IDG BOOKS WORLDWIDE

Welcome to the world of IDG Books Worldwide.

IDG Books Worldwide, Inc., is a subsidiary of International Data Group, the world's largest publisher of computer-related information and the leading global provider of information services on information technology. IDG was founded more than 30 years ago by Patrick J. McGovern and now employs more than 9,000 people worldwide. IDG publishes more than 290 computer publications in over 75 countries. More than 90 million people read one or more IDG publications each month.

Launched in 1990, IDG Books Worldwide is today the #1 publisher of best-selling computer books in the United States. We are proud to have received eight awards from the Computer Press Association in recognition of editorial excellence and three from Computer Currents' First Annual Readers' Choice Awards. Our best-selling *...For Dummies®* series has more than 50 million copies in print with translations in 31 languages. IDG Books Worldwide, through a joint venture with IDG's Hi-Tech Beijing, became the first U.S. publisher to publish a computer book in the People's Republic of China. In record time, IDG Books Worldwide has become the first choice for millions of readers around the world who want to learn how to better manage their businesses.

Our mission is simple: Every one of our books is designed to bring extra value and skill-building instructions to the reader. Our books are written by experts who understand and care about our readers. The knowledge base of our editorial staff comes from years of experience in publishing, education, and journalism — experience we use to produce books to carry us into the new millennium. In short, we care about books, so we attract the best people. We devote special attention to details such as audience, interior design, use of icons, and illustrations. And because we use an efficient process of authoring, editing, and desktop publishing our books electronically, we can spend more time ensuring superior content and less time on the technicalities of making books.

You can count on our commitment to deliver high-quality books at competitive prices on topics you want to read about. At IDG Books Worldwide, we continue in the IDG tradition of delivering quality for more than 30 years. You'll find no better book on a subject than one from IDG Books Worldwide.

John Kilcullen
Chairman and CEO
IDG Books Worldwide, Inc.

*Eighth Annual
Computer Press
Awards ≥1992*

*Ninth Annual
Computer Press
Awards ≥1993*

*Tenth Annual
Computer Press
Awards ≥1994*

*Eleventh Annual
Computer Press
Awards ≥1995*

Credits

ACQUISITIONS EDITORS
John Osborn
Judy Brief

PROJECT EDITORS
Jenna Wallace
Andy Marinkovich

TECHNICAL EDITOR
Ashvini Sharma

COPY EDITORS
Amy Eoff
Robert Campbell

MEDIA DEVELOPMENT SPECIALIST
Jason Luster

PERMISSIONS EDITOR
Lenora Chin Sell

MEDIA DEVELOPMENT MANAGER
Stephen Noetzel

PROJECT COORDINATORS
Linda Marousek
Louigene A. Santos
Danette Nurse

GRAPHICS AND PRODUCTION SPECIALISTS
Robert Bihlmayer
Jude Levinson
Michael Lewis
Dina F. Quan
Ramses Ramirez
Victor Pérez-Varela

BOOK DESIGNER
Jim Donohue

ILLUSTRATOR
Mary Jo Richards

PROOFREADING AND INDEXING
York Production Services

About the Author

William C. Amo is a database consultant specializing in Microsoft SQL Server. He has over 20 years of experience developing databases and database applications from mainframe to desktop. He is the author of *Transact-SQL: Programming Microsoft SQL Server 7.0* and the coauthor of *Access 97 Secrets* and *SQL Server 7 Secrets*, all three books published by IDG Books Worldwide.

Bill holds a Bachelor of Arts degree in computer science from the State University of New York at Potsdam and a Master of Science degree in computer science from Rensselaer Polytechnic Institute.

This work is dedicated to my family.
For my lovely wife, Marianne, whose love and support brought
this book to completion. You are my life forever.
For Kirsten, Bill, Dean, Jennifer, Willy, Zachary, and Matthew
for supporting this effort and the constant happiness you give me.

Preface

With the release of SQL Server 7.0, Microsoft delivered a new tool that enables developers of database-centric applications to provide their users with new insight into their data. This new tool is OLAP Services version 7.0, and it brings affordable, powerful data analysis to organizations of all sizes.

I have no doubt that this new technology will be well received by developers, who will quickly discover its ease of use and employ its rich programming environment to deliver powerful analysis tools to their user community.

Why I Wrote This Book

This book is targeted to the developer who has experience in developing SQL Server databases and database applications. Its intent is to discuss the various facilities OLAP Services makes available to developers for building OLAP applications.

The interactive tools OLAP Services offers for building and administering cubes are discussed in this book to provide you with a familiarity with how these tools work. But the focus of the book is on the technology underlying these tools.

I want to introduce you to the OLAP Services technology in sufficient depth to enable you to be productive programming your own custom OLAP applications and to put you in a position to grow with the product as new releases become available.

What You Need to Know

This book concentrates on programming OLAP Services. The book provides no discussion on the theory and practice of data warehousing or on the topic of Online Analytical Processing (OLAP) in general.

I recommend at least a conceptual knowledge of data warehousing as defined by Microsoft and a basic working knowledge of the Data Transformation Services (DTS) to transfer data from Online Transaction Processing (OLTP) data sources into a data warehouse.

An understanding of the basic principles of database design, especially as applied to databases used in online transaction processing applications, is helpful as background to an appreciation of data warehouses, data marts, and their role in online analytical processing.

It would be beneficial for you to have a good understanding of Transact-SQL and in particular those statements and operators used to yield aggregations, such as GROUP BY, COMPUTE, CUBE, and ROLLUP. Aggregated data such as that resulting from these statements and operators represents the core principle of cube technology.

At the time of this writing, the Microsoft Web site has two white papers available that you may find helpful as background material for this book.

◆ Microsoft SQL Server 7.0 Data Warehousing Framework: www.microsoft.com/SQL/bizsol/datawareframe.htm

◆ Microsoft SQL Server 7.0 OLAP Services Overview: www.microsoft.com/SQL/productinfo/olapoverview.htm

The sample OLTP database for this book comes from my previous book entitled *Transact-SQL: Programming Microsoft SQL Server 7.0* (ISBN 0-7645-8048-5 published by IDG Books Worldwide, Inc.). This database is the source for the data warehouse sample database developed in this book. Although the material in my Transact-SQL book is useful background, it is not required to have read that book to undertake the content of this book. The sample database from the Transact-SQL book can be found on the CD that accompanies this book, and information on the use of the sample database can be found in Chapter 2 of this book.

How This Book Is Organized

The book is organized into three parts. The first part covers introductory topics; it includes Chapters 1 through 6.

The second part of the book addresses the details of programming in the OLAP services environment and prepares you for the practical exercises found in Part III.

Part III applies the material from Part II in practical programming exercises and presents additional tutorials along the way.

Part 1: Overview of the Microsoft OLAP Environment

This part presents topics that introduce you to the OLAP Services and associated development tools and components. Chapter 1 introduces OLAP Services and defines terms used throughout the book.

Chapter 2 discusses the sample data warehouse used in this book and how to establish this database and its source OLTP database on your own server. Chapter 3 uses the OLAP Manager facility to build your first cube. This cube is used extensively in the book's examples.

Once data is loaded into a cube, it needs to be kept current with the data in its source data warehouse. Chapter 4 explains the various methods OLAP Services supports for keeping cubes up to date with changes in the data warehouse.

Chapter 5 presents the Decision Support Object model used by the OLAP Manager to build and administer server cubes. Using this object model, you can develop your own application for working with server-side cubes.

OLAP Services ships a new OLE DB provider that enables access by client-side applications to an OLAP server. This provider is named the PivotTable service and contains the capability of supporting a subset of server functionality to enable an application to define and access a local cube. The PivotTable service is introduced in Chapter 6 and accessed through the use of the ActiveX Data Objects Multidimensional (ADO MD), an extension to the familiar ADO object model that deals specifically with OLAP structures.

Part II: Examining the Microsoft OLAP Services Components

Each of the elements in Part I are treated in more detail in Part II. The goal of this part is to provide you with a detailed working knowledge of the OLAP Services programming elements to enable you to work with these elements to build both server-side and client-side OLAP applications.

Chapter 7 discusses the Multidimensional Expression (MDX) grammar for querying OLAP cubes. The chapter explains the various parts of an MDX statement including how they are constructed and used.

The Decision Support Object model is explored in Chapter 8, which covers each of the objects and their properties. Numerous code examples throughout the chapter illustrate how the object model is used in an application.

The OLAP Manager supports custom add-ins in much the same way that the Microsoft Management Console (MMC) supports add-ins. Chapter 9 discusses the required COM interfaces and methods you'll use to create your own add-in.

Chapter 10 continues the trek through MDX exploring the many functions supported by OLAP Services. Each function in the chapter is explained and its use illustrated with an example call.

The last chapter in Part II shows you how to use Microsoft Excel 2000 PivotTables and PivotCharts to report on OLAP data. Chapter 11 also introduces OLAP@Work for Excel, a powerful tool that integrates itself into Excel to enable you to create reports and analysis on your cubes. This software is found on the companion CD in the Third-Party Software folder.

Part III: Exercises in OLAP Services Programming

Part III uses the material presented in Part II to build practical OLAP applications. You'll step through the creation of a server-side application using DSO, a client-side application using the PivotTable service, and an OLAP Manager add-in that uses the DSO application.

Chapter 12 develops a DSO application packaged in a DLL that supports the reporting of all DSO object properties. This DLL is used by the OLAP Manager add-in developed in Chapter 14. This add-in enables an OLAP Manager user to report, either via form or paper, all properties of objects under a given OLAP server.

In Chapter 13, you use ADO MD to create a client-side application that uses MDX queries and navigation functions to drill up and down through a cellset providing users with a very powerful user interface for exploring their data.

Chapter 15 walks you through the DTS utilities for importing and exporting data into and out of a database. These utilities are very useful for moving data between your data warehouse and various source and target formats. This chapter is not an exhaustive treatment of DTS, but it provides you with enough information to effectively work with the utilities.

At the back of the book, you'll find many useful appendixes that cover the ADO and ADO MD objects models, the DSO object model, an MDX reference, the schema for the sample databases used in the book, and an OLAP Services function reference.

About the Companion CD-ROM

The inside back cover of this book contains a CD that holds the examples that I discuss in the text. All example code from each of the chapters is included in the corresponding chapter folder on the CD. All example Visual Basic projects discussed in Part III are also included.

Two folders on the CD contain trial versions of third-party software I think you'll find useful. One is OLAP@Work for Excel from OLAP@Work. This product, discussed in Chapter 11, is very useful for providing OLAP applications through Microsoft Excel.

The second third-party software product on the CD is AntQuery from Geppetto's Workshop. You'll find this product useful for developing MDX queries as well as supporting a number of other functions.

The files on the companion CD are not compressed, so you can access them directly from the CD.

All CD-ROM files are read-only. To work with the Visual Basic projects on the CD, you should copy the project files from the CD-ROM to your hard drive and then change the file attributes after copying. To change a file, right-click the filename or icon and select Properties from the shortcut menu. In the Properties dialog box, click the General tab and remove the checkmark from the Read-only check box.

How to Use This Book

The material is best understood by starting at the front with the introduction to the OLAP services environment and tools and proceeding through to the detailed discussion of programming in this environment found in Part II.

If you don't wish to complete the exercises in Part III, I recommend at least reading through it, since additional details in several areas are included that illustrate how the technology can be applied.

What the Icons Mean

Throughout the book, I've used *icons* in the left margin to call your attention to points that are particularly important.

I use this icon to indicate that the material discussed refers to material found in other chapters or appendixes.

I use Note icons to bring your attention to a particular point related to the main topic being discussed.

Tip icons indicate a method of performing some task or a technique that should yield more efficient results.

These icons indicate that an example file is on the companion CD. This CD holds the examples that I cover in the book, as well as trial copies of some very useful third-party software for OLAP developers.

I use Warning icons to bring your attention to actions that can have potential negative effects on your database system or applications.

Acknowledgments

There have been many hands in this project from start to finish but there are a few individuals who have been instrumental in its completion. I thank those who adopted the level of interest that I myself have in this book and helped me deliver its content to you.

John Osborn gave me the opportunity to write this book, and his interest, motivation, and energetic support of this effort kept me going forward. Andy Marinkovich and Jenna Wallace, Project Editors at IDG Books Worldwide, picked up the management of this project in mid-stream and saw it through to the end under rather difficult circumstances. Jessica Montgomery, Media Development Assistant at IDG Books, applied meticulous work on the development of the CD. Amy Eoff and Robert Campbell, Copy Editors at IDG Books, as always did an excellent job in editing the content. Ashvini Sharma, a member of the OLAP Services development team at Microsoft, conducted the review of the technical content and provided some welcomed guidance along the way.

All are true professionals that have been a joy to work with.

Contents at a Glance

Preface ix

Acknowledgments xiv

Part 1   **Overview of the Microsoft OLAP Environment**

Chapter 1   Introduction to Microsoft OLAP Services 3
Chapter 2   Building the Sample Data Warehouse 21
Chapter 3   A Tour of the OLAP Manager 41
Chapter 4   Maintaining OLAP Data 67
Chapter 5   Introduction to Decision Support Objects 83
Chapter 6   Getting Acquainted with the PivotTable Service. . . 111

Part II   **Examining the Microsoft OLAP Services Components**

Chapter 7   Introduction to Multidimensional Expressions . . . 143
Chapter 8   Building Applications with
                  Decision Support Objects 159
Chapter 9   Using OLAP Manager Add-Ins 195
Chapter 10   More MDX 211
Chapter 11   Exploring Microsoft Excel 2000 and OLAP 233

Part III   **Exercises in OLAP Services Programming**

Chapter 12   A Server Application Using
                  Decision Support Objects 247
Chapter 13   Client Applications Using the PivotTable Service. . 255
Chapter 14   Creating an OLAP Manager Add-In 267
Chapter 15   Exploring Data Transformation Services. 275

Appendix A: What's on the CD. 287

Appendix B: Sample Database Schemas 289

Appendix C: Decision Support Objects Reference. . 303

Appendix D: The MDX Statement and
                           Format String Specifiers 327

Appendix E: The ADO MD Object Model 333

Appendix F: OLAP Services Specifications 335

Appendix G: OLAP Services Function Reference . . 337

Index. 349

End-User License Agreement 358

CD-ROM Installation Instructions 362

Contents

Preface. ix

Acknowledgments xiv

Part 1   Overview of the Microsoft OLAP Environment

Chapter 1   Introduction to Microsoft OLAP Services. 3
                  Building the Data Warehouse 4
                  Exploring Dimensions, Facts, and Schemata 5
                  A Tour of Multidimensional Structures 7
                      Precalculated Aggregations 7
                      Exploring Cube Dimensions. 9
                      Defining Member Properties. 10
                      Virtual Dimensions. 10
                      The "All" Level 11
                      Working with Cells. 11
                      Using Virtual Cubes. 12
                      Selecting Cube Storage Modes 12
                      Partitioning Cubes 12
                  Reviewing GROUP BY and COMPUTE. 13
                  Exploring OLAP Object Models and APIs 17
                      The OLAP Manager and Add-Ins 17
                      Decision Support Object Model 18
                      The PivotTable Service. 18
                      Using ActiveX Data Objects Multidimensional(ADO MD). 19
                      Migrating the OLAP Services Repository 19

Chapter 2   Building the Sample Data Warehouse. 21
                  Introduction to the Mutual Fund Account OLTP Database. . . 21
                      Defining the Data Warehouse. 23
                      Using the DTS Export Wizard. 25
                  Using the DTS Package Designer 30

Chapter 3   A Tour of the OLAP Manager. 41
                  Starting OLAP Manager. 41
                  Creating an OLAP Database 42
                      Specifying the Data Source 43
                      Using the Cube Wizard. 44
                      Using the Cube Editor 50
                      Designing Storage and Populating the Cube 53
                      Browsing the Investments Cube. 56

Defining Member Properties 60

    Creating Virtual Dimensions 62

    Using Calculated Members 63

Chapter 4   **Maintaining OLAP Data** **67**

Considering the Warehouse Data 67

    Verifying Referential Integrity 68

    Ensuring Proper Indexes 68

A Review of OLAP Storage 68

    Dimension Storage 69

    Aggregation Storage 69

Developing a Maintenance Plan 70

    A Sample Change Scenario 70

    Handling Changes in the Sample Data Warehouse 71

Processing Cube Updates 71

    Running an Incremental Update 74

    Running the Refresh Method 78

    Running the Complete Process 79

    Updating Shared Dimensions 80

    Checking Update Results 81

Chapter 5   **Introduction to Decision Support Objects** **83**

Object Model Overview 84

    The MDStore Interface 85

    The Dimension Interface 89

    The Level Interface 94

    The Measure Interface 96

    The Command Interface 97

    The Role Interface 99

    Objects Accessed Directly 101

    Exploring DSO Enumerations 102

The DSO Repository 108

Chapter 6   **Getting Acquainted with the PivotTable Service** **111**

Using the ADO and ADO MD Object Models 111

    Connecting to an OLAP Catalog 113

    Examining Catalog Schema 115

    Examining OLAP Data 119

PivotTable Service SQL Support 124

    Flattening the Dataset from an MDX Query 126

Working with the Data Definition Language 127

    Creating Calculated Members 128

    Creating User-Defined Sets 130

    Dropping Sets and Members 133

    Creating a Cache 133

    Creating Local Cubes 134

Part II   **Examining the Microsoft OLAP Services Components**

Chapter 7   Introduction to Multidimensional Expressions..... 143
MDX Statements...................................... 144
Slicing a Cube 145
Understanding Sets and Tuples 147
Using the WITH Clause 148
Specifying Calculated Members 148
Specifying Sets...................................... 150
Specifying a Cache................................... 151
Using Functions 152
Built-In Functions 153
User-Defined Functions 154
Accessing Member Properties.......................... 157

Chapter 8   Building Applications with
Decision Support Objects.................... 159
Accessing the OLAP Server with clsServer.............. 159
Locking Objects 165
Temporary Objects 167
Creating a Cube with DSO........................... 167
Working with Partitions.............................. 174
Using the Partition Wizard............................. 176
Merging Partitions in OLAP Manager..................... 179
Using DSO to Create a Partition 180
Using DSO to Merge Partitions.......................... 181
Designing Aggregations and Processing................. 183
Exploring Cube Commands........................... 188
Implementing Security............................... 189
Implementing Cell-Level Security........................ 191

Chapter 9   Using OLAP Manager Add-Ins 195
Understanding OLAP Manager Add-Ins 195
Using the Microsoft OLAP Manager Add-Ins............. 196
Calculated Member Manager 196
Copy and Paste Objects Add-In 198
Archive and Restore Databases Add-In 198
Creating Your Own Add-Ins 201
Create an ActiveX DLL Project.......................... 201
Implement the IOlapAddIn Interface...................... 202
Register Your Add-In 209

Chapter 10   More MDX 211
Exploring MultiDimensional Expressions 211
Using Set and Tuple Expressions 212
Specifying Member Expressions......................... 219
Using Time Series Functions and Expressions 221
Using Conditional Expressions.......................... 222

Working with Empty Cells 223
Using Virtual Dimensions and Virtual Cubes. 225
Write-Enabling a Cube. 230

Chapter 11   **Exploring Microsoft Excel 2000 and OLAP** **233**
Creating a PivotTable Report on an OLAP Cube 233
Charting Your Data with PivotCharts 236
Performing What-If Analysis with OLAP@Work 238
Creating OLAP Cubes in Excel 2000 240

Part III   **Exercises in OLAP Services Programming   245**

Chapter 12   **A Server Application Using**
               Decision Support Objects **247**
How the DSO Inspector Works 247
Using the Inspector Object 248
Using the DSO Hierarchy Forms. 249
Inspecting the DataSource Connection Property. 251
Zooming a Property Value 251
Inspecting Registry Settings 252

Chapter 13   **Client Applications Using the PivotTable Service** . . **255**
Drilling Through Data 256
Drilling Operations by Member 256
Drilling Operations by Level. 258
A Client Application Using the Drilling Functions 259
Exploring the Time Series Functions. 262
Exploring the Numeric Functions 264

Chapter 14   **Creating an OLAP Manager Add-In** **267**
Building the PropertyInspector Add-In 268
Class Initialization 268
Coding Menu Items 268
Coding the ExecuteMenuItem Method 271
An Alternate Server Connection Method 272
Using Nodes. 272
Registering the PropertyInspector Add-In. 273
Debugging the Add-In 273

Chapter 15   **Exploring Data Transformation Services**. **275**
Data Transformation Services Overview 276
Using the DTS Import Wizard. 278
Using the DTS Export Wizard. 279
Using the dtswiz Utility 281
Using the dtsrun Utility 282
Using the DTS Task Kit 283

Appendix A: What's on the CD.................... 287

Appendix B: Sample Database Schemas 289

Appendix C: Decision Support Objects Reference .. 303

Appendix D: The MDX Statement and
            Format String Specifiers 327

Appendix E: The ADO MD Object Model.......... 333

Appendix F: OLAP Services Specifications........ 335

Appendix G: OLAP Services Function Reference... 337

Index 349

End-User License Agreement..................... 358

CD-ROM Installation Instructions 362

Part I

Overview of the Microsoft OLAP Environment

CHAPTER 1
Introduction to Microsoft OLAP Services

CHAPTER 2
Building the Sample Data Warehouse

CHAPTER 3
A Tour of the OLAP Manager

CHAPTER 4
Maintaining OLAP Data

CHAPTER 5
Introduction to Decision Support Objects

CHAPTER 6
Getting Acquainted with the PivotTable Service

Chapter 1

Introduction to Microsoft OLAP Services

IN THIS CHAPTER

- ◆ Discovering the reasons why data warehouses are built
- ◆ Acquiring an overview of the tasks required in building data warehouses
- ◆ Learning what an OLAP multidimensional structure is
- ◆ Exploring the terminology surrounding OLAP Services and multi-dimensional structures
- ◆ Finding out which object models are available for programmers coding OLAP applications

THE GOAL OF MICROSOFT OLAP Services, a component of Microsoft SQL Server 7.0, is to provide quick response to queries against data warehouse data. The performance of these queries, especially queries that request summary information, is enhanced by the precalculation of the summaries, known simply as *aggregations*, and the means of storing these summaries in structures that lend themselves to rapid access.

Microsoft OLAP Services supports a multidimensional data structure called a *cube* and a language that allows for easy navigation of this cube. These two features together with supporting services, wizards, and object models make up the OLAP environment. You as a programmer, and especially as an application or system support programmer working on an OLAP project, must have a good understanding of this environment, its architecture, its terminology, and its models to effectively build solid solutions.

In this chapter, we'll introduce the terminology you'll be working with in Microsoft OLAP Services along with a brief peek at the object models and APIs you'll use to code your applications. OLAP is concerned with data warehouse schemata and the data they hold, so that is where we will start our journey.

Building the Data Warehouse

Many books and papers are available today describing data warehouses. These sources describe how to design them, how to populate them with data, and how to use them to analyze their content. You will generally find that many of these sources, although agreeing in principle, define a data warehouse in different ways.

The definition that this book will adopt is this: a *data warehouse* is a database that can contain relational and multidimensional structures organized for fast query performance. The data contained in a warehouse usually represents business history — transactions over time — about some key interest of the business. For example, an insurance data warehouse may contain information about claims activity. A retail business warehouse may contain data about sales. A money management firm may build a warehouse containing information about investments in funds. This last example is the basis for this book's sample data warehouse. All examples in Part III will use this sample database.

The warehouse is a repository for data collected from many different operational databases, usually from Online Transaction Processing (OLTP) systems, and possibly external sources as well. The data collected into the warehouse is scrubbed and filtered to provide a consistent data store for further analysis. Some of this data may be stored as raw detail, much as it was captured from its source, or it may be stored in summarized form. Data loaded from such sources is usually taken at some predetermined point in time, a snapshot of the enterprise at that time.

The schema found in the source systems that feed the data warehouse is usually very different from the schema of the data warehouse itself. The warehouse schema, as you'll discover in the next section, serves the purpose of providing quick response to queries. Source systems including OLTP databases are usually designed to serve up performance in processing short transactions to either collect data or deliver data, possibly interfacing with more than one system and quite likely supporting numerous simultaneous connections.

You therefore have your first task defined for you, and that is to map the data you are interested in from the source database or data store into your data warehouse schema. In performing this mapping, you will most likely need to perform a number of other tasks. These include:

- Verification
- Extraction
- Scrubbing
- Transforming

Verification ensures that the data you are putting into your data warehouse, and therefore the data that is used in making decisions, is valid and correct within the domain that is defined for it.

Extraction, performed at some point in time, that point being carefully defined and coordinated with extractions from other sources, is the process of reading and filtering the data destined for the data warehouse or an intermediate data store that eventually feeds the warehouse.

Scrubbing involves making the data, collected from various sources, consistent for the intended use in the warehouse. This might involve making state abbreviations out of state name columns, formatting postal codes into consistent formats that support U.S. as well as international postal systems, formatting name columns to be consistent in the adoption and placement of name components and titles, and a number of other processes that involve common and custom data.

Transformation has the task of exploding a data item into multiple related items, collapsing multiple items into one, performing lookups and translating data items (also possible in scrubbing), making the case of an item consistent for the purposes of display or comparison, and calculating new values from existing data. The transformation task may additionally be responsible for loading the data warehouse or a portion of it with the data that has passed through all previous processing steps. Both extraction and transformation are excellent candidates for the Microsoft Data Transformation Service (DTS), as you will see in Chapter 2, when you build your sample data warehouse. This isn't of course the whole story when it comes to data warehouses, but it's enough of an overview to get you started into the world of OLAP Services programming. I'll use the acronym VEST (verification, extraction, scrubbing, and transformation) for the tasks we've just discussed and say that "when your data is VESTed, it is ready for OLAP." As you gain experience in data warehousing and OLAP Services, you'll discover that VEST is a very important acronym to understand and remember.

Exploring Dimensions, Facts, and Schemata

Two popular schemata found in data warehouses are the *star* schema and the *snowflake* schema. Each of these has a core fact table containing data items of interest in the analysis for which the warehouse is built. These data items might be transaction amounts such as an amount invested in a fund account in our sample money management business, an amount deposited into a savings account at a bank, or a claim amount at an insurance company. The values collected into the fact table are to be either directly or indirectly involved in the analysis.

Sometimes these values are aggregated to some level of rollup prior to being stored in the data warehouse. An example from the money management sample might be the aggregation of reinvested dividend transactions and investments into a fund. If your analysis does not require these two transaction types to be addressed separately and you always treat these transaction amounts as merely investments, then this preaggregation is warranted. In many cases, however, it is best to store the most detailed values you can acquire from the source systems. This practice generally provides the most value in the warehouse.

In addition to the values to be used for analysis, the fact table contains one or more foreign keys relating the fact table entries to the dimension tables. In your sample FundAcctsWH database, we have an Investments fact table containing four foreign keys relating an investment transaction to each of Office, Manager, Fund, and Account dimension tables. This star schema is shown in Figure 1-1. A fifth data item, the transaction date, represents an implied time dimension that will become evident when you use this schema to build a cube.

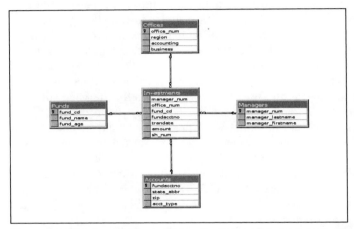

Figure 1-1: The star schema involving the Investments table in the sample data warehouse

Notice that with the star schema, no more than one join is required to access the dimension information for a given fact. In the snowflake schema, at least two joins would be required to access all dimension information. The reason for the additional join over the star schema is that the information for at least one dimension is held in two tables rather than one. The fact table in this schema holds the foreign keys to the primary dimensions and not to the dimensions accessed through the primary dimension tables.

'In your OLTP database for the FundAccts sample (see Appendix B for the complete schema of the FundAccts OLTP database and the FundAcctsWH data warehouse database), an account manager in the Managers table reports to a business office in the Offices table.

You could have left this relationship in the data warehouse and retrieved office information through the manager foreign key in the Investments fact table. In this case, you would have eliminated the office foreign key in the fact table and kept the manager foreign key. The result is the snowflake schema shown in Figure 1-2.

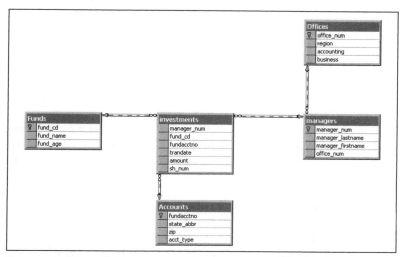

Figure 1-2: A snowflake schema representation of the Investments facts

Due to the requirement to perform fewer joins, the star schema is usually preferred over the snowflake schema for improved query performance.

A Tour of Multidimensional Structures

Another structure may be found in the data warehouse. This one is also built for query performance, contains quantitative values of interest to the analysis, and uses dimensions. It's called a *cube*, or multidimensional structure, and it has its data source in the star or snowflake structures we've just discussed.

In this section, we take a look at these multidimensional structures to gain an understanding of the terminology used in describing them. This knowledge is fundamental to the work we will do in upcoming chapters.

Precalculated Aggregations

Generally in your work with OLTP databases, you write Transact-SQL queries containing GROUP BY and COMPUTE clauses whenever you are required to display summarizations of the data by some category. You might be called upon to display total sales by region, or total investments by manager, or maybe average investments by fund by quarter.

You write these queries and store them as procedures in the database, or as script files or as strings in your application code. When necessary, you run these queries and display the results to the user. The amount of time the user has to wait for these results is dependent upon the amount of information to be processed by the query, the structure of the database the query is accessing, the information available to the query processor, the number of users logged into the database, and a number of other factors.

The summary queries have to be tuned within the database environment they are running in, and usually in OLTP there are trade-offs to be considered that do not lend to optimal query performance. Many times, an overnight reporting run is the best that can be achieved, and even that has a lot of competition to consider.

An alternative to providing the summarizations is to run the queries and store the results in a database separate from the OLTP database. This second database would be used only for providing the summary information to analysts and management and would be configured not for online transaction performance but for query performance. This alternative is the basis of OLAP and is supported in various ways in Microsoft OLAP Services.

In an OLAP environment, you concentrate on providing query performance against a set of data that supports some well-defined level of analysis. You require that the users of your analysis database define the information they need from the database and the summarizations they expect to see. You must then acquire this data from one or more sources along with any data needed to provide the necessary categorizations.

You need to store the lowest level of detail the user wants to see. In addition, to enhance the performance of the database, you should attempt to store precalculated summarizations when you can. If the user only needs to see total sales by region, for example, then there is no need for you to store individual sales transactions. On the other hand, if you do store individual sales transaction amounts, then you have the opportunity to answer many more queries than just total sales by region.

If you store individual sales amounts along with their attributes such as the store the sale was recorded in, the salesperson the sale is attributed to, the product or service that was sold, and other attributes, you are still faced with the question of how to provide optimal performance for the queries that want this data summarized. If you could store all possible ways of summarizing and presenting this data to the user, then a user could ask any question of the database and you would have the answer already calculated. All you would need to do is to present it. In many cases, however, storing *all* possible summarizations would take much more storage space and processing time than you would want to devote to it. You need to consider the value of the warehouse versus the cost of storage versus other opportunities where the investment might provide a better return. The idea of precalculated summarizations, however, is a valid one, especially if you consider the most frequent query requirements.

If your users will generally be asking about total sales by geographical category such as sales region, state, zip, then precalculating and storing sales by these categories will prove beneficial. For those summarizations that are requested less frequently, you would rely on processing the query on demand.

Your data warehouse, by definition, needs to be structured to provide good query performance, maintain the proper levels of data and aggregations of data to support the queries that will be submitted to it, and store the data within the resource constraints placed on it by management. So as we move forward into this book, keep in mind that the warehouse is supporting detail data and aggregations of data, whether those aggregations are sums, averages, or some other aggregate function applied over a given set of data.

Exploring Cube Dimensions

A *cube* consists of a collection of dimensions. Each dimension is a category of data within the domain of the business problem being supported by your multidimensional database. Cubes in Microsoft OLAP Services may contain from 1 to 64 dimensions.

A *dimension* is a collection of one or more hierarchies. A *hierarchy* is a parent-child relationship of multiple levels from some root level at the top of the hierarchy to one or more leaf levels at the bottom of the hierarchy. Each of these levels can be thought of as categorizations of data within the dimension. Each *member,* or level value, at a particular level in a hierarchy contains an aggregation value for the category represented by the level. The top or root of the hierarchy holds the least-granular aggregation, whereas the bottom or leaf levels hold the most-granular aggregations. An example will help sort this out.

A category that just about all business data relates to is time. There are invoice dates, transaction dates, closing dates, delivery dates, accounting periods, and so on. Consider your sample money management firm for a moment. Investors send an amount of cash to be invested in some fund. The firm records that investment amount in the system with a transaction date. This is the date the cash was invested in the specified fund.

The management of the money management firm wants to see how their clients invest over time. In providing this information, you use a time dimension containing a hierarchy of year, quarter within year, and month within quarter, three levels.

Members you find at the quarter level are Quarter 1, Quarter 2, Quarter 3, and Quarter 4. At the month level within Quarter 3, you find the July, August, and September members. Each of these members will contain an aggregation of the investment amounts realized in those categories. So in September you may see an aggregate sum of $350,000 across all clients. In the Quarter 3 member at the quarter level you may see $1,500,000 representing the rollup across all clients across all three months of the quarter for the year in which the quarter is located.

So far you know that a cube contains at least one dimension and that dimension contains at least one hierarchy made up of one or more levels. At each level, you can have multiple members, each member containing at least one data value via the intersection of the dimension member with the fact table keys. The fact table data value is known as a *measure* and is the quantitative information your analysis is seeking.

Other examples of dimensions might include office, store, or some other business entity, manager, product, and location or geography. In addition to the dimensions you normally include as part of your warehouse, you consider one other dimension that holds the actual numeric values or aggregations to be reported and analyzed. This dimension is called the *measures dimension*. These measures are sourced in the fact table of the data warehouse. There may be more than one measure for any given member. In the example looking at investment amounts over time, you could have included fund redemption amounts as well giving two measures for a member.

A member that is acquired directly from the data warehouse dimension tables is called an *input member*. Members that are derived from some expression involving other member values are known as *calculated members*. These members are calculated at run time and only the expression used to derive the member is stored in the multidimensional database. A calculated member can be specified for either dimension members or measure members.

A *data point*, known as a *cell*, in a cube is referenced by a set of coordinates that include the members of the dimensions. The amount invested by a client can be referenced by Measures.InvestAmount. This is a data item in the Measures dimension. This one-level reference, although valid, does assume default levels in the cube. In a cube having a time dimension and an office dimension, you would more likely see a reference like this to describe the invested amounts booked by the Connecticut office in August 1997:

```
Connecticut.1997.Qtr3.August.Measures.InvestAmount
```

Defining Member Properties

Levels within a hierarchy may have one or more *properties* associated with them. Different property sets may be associated with different levels of the same hierarchy. For example, in your Investments cube, you have an office dimension consisting of a hierarchy containing levels for regional office, accounting office, and business office. Each regional office member in the office dimension has an office ID just like other office levels, but unlike other levels, regional offices also have a region manager and a training manager.

As you can see from this example, both region manager and training manager are columns in the Offices dimension table. These columns can be used to develop member properties. In fact, member properties defined for a given dimension level must come from the same dimension table. When you get into building your Investments cube, you'll create a couple of properties for the Fund dimension and use these properties to create *virtual* dimensions.

Virtual Dimensions

Virtual dimensions do not require physical storage as do other dimensions. Dimensions can be *private* to the cube being defined, or they can be *shared* across multiple cubes in the database. Member properties associated with shared dimensions can be used to create a virtual dimension in a query.

If you define the Fund dimension as a shared dimension in the Investments cube, and you define a property named Age (meaning how long the fund has been in operation expressed to the nearest year) for the Fund members, a query can request investment amounts by Fund Age as if Age were a defined dimension in the cube.

> In the next chapter when we explore the OLAP Manager, you'll define the Age property for the Fund dimension and then use the Virtual Dimension Wizard to define a virtual dimension for this property.

The Age property has its source in the Age column of the Funds dimension table in the data warehouse. Multiple properties can be defined for a level, and different properties can be defined for different levels of a dimension hierarchy.

Does the Funds dimension have a hierarchy? Certainly not in the same sense that the Time dimension does or the Office dimension does, but it does have a hierarchy. The top level of the Funds hierarchy is called the "All" level, and the next level below that is the Fund level, each member at this level being a Fund name.

The "All" Level

The "All" level is the root level of a hierarchy that contains a member summarizing all members immediately subordinate to the root. It is the most-summarized (least granular) level of data for a given dimension.

In the Time dimension discussed earlier, the "All" level would hold the summarized value for All years. As you just saw in the Fund dimension, the "All" level represents All funds.

Working with Cells

A *cell* in a cube is the intersection of a set of members, each member being selected from each of the dimensions of the cube. So if a cube has three dimensions, the intersection of a selection of three members from these dimensions would constitute a cell in the cube. This cell would hold a value property containing the cell's data item. It may be an aggregated data value, a direct input data value from the data warehouse, a calculated value based on other cell values in the cube, or even null.

We look at cells and positions within cubes in much more detail when we discuss multidimensional expressions (MDX), a language for querying cubes, in Chapter 7 and again in Chapter 10 when we explore the PivotTable service. The OLAP Services setup installs a sample MDX application that can be used to explore this language and provides the Visual Basic source code that enables you to learn how such an application can be built.

Using Virtual Cubes

In a SQL Server database, you can create views involving one or more tables joined together to present a logical organization of data that behaves much like a table does. Once this view is defined, a user can query from it just as they would from a table. They don't see the complexity of the query behind the view; they only see the view name.

In OLAP, you can do much the same thing with cubes. Multiple cubes can be joined together to present a virtual cube from which queries can retrieve information. Here too, the user doesn't see the complexity of the joined cubes but only the virtual cube. Using virtual cubes in a database allows the user to access information across multiple cubes without the need to build and store those cubes in the database. This practice provides the needed information and at the same time saves disk space.

Virtual cubes can be used to provide a level of security as well. If a virtual cube is defined to include a selected subset of dimensions from the underlying base cubes, users granted access to the virtual cube will be restricted to the selected dimensions and prohibited from seeing the base cubes.

Selecting Cube Storage Modes

Microsoft OLAP Services supports the storage of multidimensional structures in three storage modes. A *Multidimensional OLAP (MOLAP)* stores cube data and cube aggregations in a multidimensional structure optimized for query performance and space. NULL values are not stored and the data is compressed for space optimization.

A storage mode that stores cube data and aggregate data in a relational structure is called *Relational OLAP (ROLAP)*. This mode uses standard relational technology for cube storage.

The third storage mode is called *Hybrid OLAP (HOLAP)* and uses a combination of MOLAP and ROLAP modes for cube storage. In this case the cube data is stored in the relational structures and the aggregates are stored in the multidimensional structures.

We explore these three modes later and see first-hand how they are stored physically.

Partitioning Cubes

If you are running SQL Server OLAP Services Enterprise Edition, you have the option of separating cube storage into one or more partitions. Each partition can use a different storage mode (ROLAP, MOLAP, HOLAP) and a different physical location.

Using partitions aids in the management and tuning of the cube. When certain aggregations of a cube are in more demand than others, you may find that partitioning the cube helps balance the access to the cube, giving better performance to all users. OLAP Services allows you to use different aggregations in each of the partitions if necessary. So within the same cube, you can provide various levels of granularity depending on usage requirements.

If it becomes necessary to bring partitions back together, you can merge any number of separate partitions back into one partition. Since the user doesn't see partitioning, but only the logical cube, there is no change in the user's view of the cube when partitions are either created or merged.

The interaction between a cube and the data warehouse is dependent upon the mode of storage selected for a cube partition. With MOLAP, the partition contains all aggregated values from the fact table in a separate storage space. The partition requires processing to update its structure before any changes made in the data warehouse can be seen in the cube. This storage mode provides the best query performance but at the price of additional storage beyond the data warehouse database to hold the structure.

Using a partition storage mode of ROLAP causes the aggregated values to be stored in data warehouse tables. For some queries, the data warehouse fact table may be accessed in addition to the aggregation tables. To ensure that the query returns correct results, you must process the cube whenever changes to the fact table are processed. If this synchronization is not done properly, a query can report the wrong aggregate values for a given set of detail from the updated fact table. This would be analogous to running a group by queries, saving the results into a table, running an update to the fact table, and then running a query that joins the two, returning both detail and aggregates. These results would of course be erroneous.

With a ROLAP partition, the cube structures are completely stored in the data warehouse database. No additional storage space beyond the warehouse is required, as it is under the MOLAP mode.

HOLAP storage mode uses an additional storage space for the aggregated values of the cube stored in MOLAP mode, although the fact table details remain in the data warehouse as in ROLAP mode. The same cautions that apply to ROLAP also apply to HOLAP. Updates to the fact table must be countered by processing the cube to update the aggregate values in the MOLAP structure. With HOLAP, query performance varies dependent upon the query. Queries accessing detail in the fact table will experience somewhat slower performance than queries, or parts of queries, that access the MOLAP multidimensional structures.

As always in database design, there is a trade-off here between storage space requirements and performance. The choice you make for your cube partitions will depend on your user requirements and the available system resource budget.

Reviewing GROUP BY and COMPUTE

To help bring some of this new terminology into better focus, we'll explore for a moment some Transact-SQL examples that use select statements with GROUP BY and COMPUTE clauses. Your knowledge and use of these statements will come in handy to check the results you get from OLAP queries, either from the book's examples or from your own projects. Submitting queries such as these into the data warehouse can provide a check and balance against OLAP queries into cubes.

ON THE CD These examples will query the Data Warehouse Investments fact table and involve joins to the Funds dimension table. In addition, we'll use Transact-SQL date functions on the transdate column of the Investments table to create rollups by various date components and funds. In all three examples, only a partial result set is shown. These scripts can be found on the CD in the Chapter 1 folder.

First, submit a simple GROUP BY query to display the sum of Investments amounts by related fund name. This query performs an equi-join between the Investments fact table and the Funds dimension table on the fund_cd column:

```
select fund_name as Fund,sum(amount) as 'Total Amount'
 from funds inner join investments on
  funds.fund_cd = investments.fund_cd
group by fund_name
order by fund_name
```

Fund	Total Amount
Brandywine	40000.0000
CGM Mutual	34000.0000
Fidelity Equity Income	122920.6500
Fidelity Magellan	36942.3400
Gabelli Growth	307982.9100
IDS Stock	700.0000
Janus	216687.9000
Janus Enterprise	20000.0000
Janus Mercury	120168.1300
Janus Twenty	85047.5700
Janus Venture	69025.5500
Lindner	120516.0500
Lindner Dividend	365668.9800
Lindner/Ryback Small-Cap	33000.0000
Meridian	63225.3900

Next, expand on the GROUP BY query by grouping on the quarter implied in the Investments table trandate column. By using the Transact-SQL datepart function, you can extract the quarter from the trandate and use it for grouping your results below the fund name grouping, giving you a sum of the investment amounts by fund by quarter:

```
select fund_name as Fund,
   datepart(qq,trandate) as Quarter,
```

```
  sum(amount) as 'Total Amount'
from funds inner join investments on
  funds.fund_cd = investments.fund_cd
group by fund_name,datepart(qq,trandate)
order by Fund,Quarter
```

Fund	Quarter	Total Amount
Brandywine	1	5000.0000
Brandywine	2	5000.0000
Brandywine	3	25000.0000
Brandywine	4	5000.0000
CGM Mutual	1	24000.0000
CGM Mutual	2	2000.0000
CGM Mutual	3	3000.0000
CGM Mutual	4	5000.0000
Fidelity Equity Income	1	20000.0000
Fidelity Equity Income	2	10000.0000
Fidelity Equity Income	3	92920.6500
Fidelity Magellan	1	22006.4000
Fidelity Magellan	2	12947.9400
Fidelity Magellan	4	1988.0000
Gabelli Growth	1	89432.9100
Gabelli Growth	2	57900.0000
Gabelli Growth	3	60700.0000
Gabelli Growth	4	99950.0000
IDS Stock	1	75.0000
IDS Stock	2	575.0000
IDS Stock	3	50.0000

The last example in this brief review incorporates the COMPUTE BY clause in the preceding query to yield the investment detail by fund and quarter with an additional line to report the total for the fund as requested in the COMPUTE clause:

```
select fund_name as Fund,datepart(qq,trandate) as Quarter, amount
from funds inner join investments on
  funds.fund_cd = investments.fund_cd
order by fund_name,datepart(qq,trandate)
compute sum(amount) by fund_name
```

Fund	Quarter	amount
Brandywine	1	5000.0000
Brandywine	2	5000.0000
Brandywine	3	25000.0000

```
Brandywine                4              5000.0000

                                         sum
                                         ============
                                         40000.0000


CGM Mutual                1              1000.0000
CGM Mutual                1             19000.0000
CGM Mutual                1              4000.0000
CGM Mutual                2              2000.0000
CGM Mutual                3              3000.0000
CGM Mutual                4              5000.0000

                                         Sum
                                         ============
                                         34000.0000
```

To see the effect of COMPUTE BY, compare the CGM Mutual quarter 1 total in the previous GROUP BY query with the results for the same fund and quarter in this query. In the previous query, you see the grouped sum for the fund and quarter, whereas in this COMPUTE BY query you see the fund and quarter detail with a sum for the fund across all quarters.

With a slight modification of the preceding query, you can display the fund and quarter detail with a summary line for fund and quarter together and a total summary line at the end of these combinations for the fund across all quarters. As you can see, this bottom total for the fund equals the total in the preceding query, which in turn equals the summary lines for the fund by quarters:

```
select fund_name as Fund,datepart(qq,trandate) as Quarter, amount
from funds inner join investments on
  funds.fund_cd = investments.fund_cd
order by fund_name,datepart(qq,trandate)
compute sum(amount) by fund_name,datepart(qq,trandate)
compute sum(amount) by fund_name


CGM Mutual                1              1000.0000
CGM Mutual                1             19000.0000
CGM Mutual                1              4000.0000

                                      sum
                                      =================
                                      24000.0000


CGM Mutual                2              2000.0000
```

```
                               sum
                               =================
                                        2000.0000

CGM Mutual              3                3000.0000

                               sum
                               =================
                                        3000.0000

CGM Mutual              4                5000.0000

                               sum
                               =================
                                        5000.0000

                               sum
                               =================
                                       34000.0000
```

Exploring OLAP Object Models and APIs

Now let's take a tour of the APIs and object models we explore in this book. Part II of this book will concentrate on the details of each of these topics, to be followed by examples of each one in Part III.

The OLAP Manager and Add-Ins

In Chapter 3, we explore the OLAP Manager tool. Using this tool and its associated wizards, you can quickly define the fact table and dimensions for a cube, populate the cube with data from the warehouse, define roles to enable access to the cube, and perform maintenance on the cube to keep it in synchronization with changes in the data warehouse.

The OLAP Manager is implemented as a Microsoft Management Console (MMC) snap-in. MMC is the standard Microsoft BackOffice console used to manage many of the BackOffice products, including the Microsoft SQL Server Enterprise Manager.

A custom snap-in can be developed as a stand-alone MMC application or as an extension to an existing snap-in. In Chapter 9 we explore snap-ins in more detail, and in Chapter 14, we build an extension to the OLAP Manager using the OLAP Add-In Manager interface.

Decision Support Object Model

The OLAP Manager implements its functionality through the use of Decision Support Objects (DSO). This object model can be used to control the OLAP server; create and populate cubes; define calculated members, virtual dimensions and virtual cubes; and manage cube security.

The Decision Support Objects model presents a hierarchy of collections starting with the root of the hierarchy, the OLAP Server. This hierarchy is exposed in the OLAP Manager tree view and includes collections for cubes, virtual cubes, dimensions, aggregations, and partitions. We explore this object model in Chapter 8 and build an application using DSO in Chapter 12.

The PivotTable Service

The Microsoft PivotTable Service performs dual roles. It is an OLE DB provider to an OLAP server and, as such, can be used to connect to an OLAP server and query cubes defined to the server. In this role, the PivotTable service is no different than the OLE DB provider used to access and work with a SQL Server installation, an exception being that the PivotTable service supports the OLE DB for OLAP extensions defined in the OLE DB 2.0 specification.

The second role of the PivotTable service is as a stand-alone OLAP server but with limited functionality. OLAP Services can be provided to desktop applications by the PivotTable service when not connected to an OLAP server.

Through this service, cubes can be created locally, populated, and queried. Much of the functionality provided by OLAP Services is supported by the PivotTable service in stand-alone mode. There are some differences and restrictions, however, and we learn more about these in Chapter 6. In Chapter 13 we build a PivotTable service application.

Multidimensional expressions, an extension of the OLE DB 2.0 specification, is the native language used by the PivotTable service to manipulate OLAP cubes. In addition, the PivotTable service defines a data definition language (DDL) to support building local cubes.

Using ActiveX Data Objects Multidimensional(ADO MD)

ActiveX Data Objects (ADO) exposes an object model that maps to an OLE DB provider's interfaces, objects, methods, and properties. ADO is a rather simple object model but provides powerful and easy-to-use access to databases and other stores supported by OLE DB providers.

ActiveX Data Objects Multidimensional (ADO MD) is an extension to ADO (you can use ADO in conjunction with ADO MD) that enables an application to access the objects defined by an OLE DB for OLAP provider (such as the PivotTable service).

In the ADO MD object model, the *cubedef* object is the metadata object describing a cube, the cube's schema. The cubedef defines the multidimensional structure consisting of hierarchies, levels, and members as we discussed earlier in this chapter. Each of these elements is a separate object accessible in the object model. All cubedef objects are children to a *catalog* object, the parent metadata object.

A *cellset* object represents the dataset returned from a query against a cube. The cellset contains *cell* objects, where each cell is the intersection of axis coordinates, and an *axes* collection of *axis* objects. Each axis object contains *positions,* where each *position* in the collection holds a collection of members from a set of dimensions.

 Each of these ADO MD objects contains a properties collection that defines the object properties. The objects are listed in Appendix E and discussed in Chapter 6.

Migrating the OLAP Services Repository

When Decision Support Objects are used to define a cube, the object model must store this metadata and make it accessible whenever the cube is accessed. DSO uses a repository as the storage structure.

 By default, the OLAP Services repository is installed as a Microsoft Access database. This database, **msmdrep.mdb**, can be migrated to a Microsoft SQL Server 7.0 database. We do this in Chapter 5 as we explore the metadata stored by DSO in the repository.

Summary

In this chapter we've discussed some of the reasons why you build data warehouses and some of the things you need to consider before starting the task. We discussed the star schema, consisting of a fact table and one or more dimension tables. Each dimension table key is found as a foreign key in the fact table. Both the key columns of dimension tables and the composite set of foreign keys in the fact table are indexed.

We took a look at OLAP Services and what it has to offer in support of analysis on the multidimensional data stored in the warehouse. We defined multidimensional data structures and discussed the terminology of these structures. We discovered that OLAP Services offers three modes of storage for OLAP data.

The ROLAP storage mode stores aggregations in relational tables in the data warehouse but uses the Warehouse fact table for detail data.

With the MOLAP storage mode, both fact table detail and aggregations are stored external to the data warehouse in special multidimensional structures. We learned that although this mode requires more disk space than other modes, it is generally the fastest performer.

A hybrid mode that uses the Warehouse fact table for detail data and external multidimensional structures for aggregations is known as HOLAP. This mode might be used to balance disk space resources to performance requirements for selected summary queries.

At the end of this chapter, the APIs and object models of Decision Support Objects (DSO), ActiveX Data Objects Multidimensional (ADO MD), OLAP Manager add-ins, and the PivotTable service were introduced. All of these will be discussed in more detail in Part II of the book, with Part III providing examples of each. All example code can be found on the CD that accompanies this book. See Appendix A for a description of the CD contents and how to install the sample files.

Chapter 2

Building the Sample Data Warehouse

IN THIS CHAPTER

◆ Learning about the sample mutual fund account database

◆ Building the sample data warehouse to be used in upcoming chapters

◆ Using Data Transformation Services (DTS) to export data to the data warehouse

◆ Learning how to create a data-driven query DTS package using the DTS Package Designer

◆ Exploring the sample Fund Accounts database introduced in my book *Programming Microsoft SQL Server 7.0 Transact-SQL* (published by IDG Books) and the sample data warehouse built from that database

BOTH THE FUND ACCOUNTS OLTP sample database – FundAccts – and the data warehouse we create in this chapter – FundAcctsWH – can be found on the CD that accompanies this book. Scripts describing the schema of these databases are discussed in Appendix B.

Introduction to the Mutual Fund Account OLTP Database

The example OLTP database is one that might be used by a money management firm to store account information for mutual fund investors. The schema for this database is shown in Figure 2-1.

Our example money management firm advises its clients where to invest their money and handles the purchasing, selling, and transfer of various mutual fund shares directly from the funds on behalf of the client. The FundAccts database is used to track the clients' portfolios.

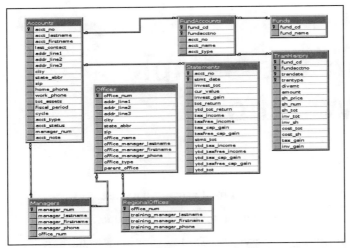

Figure 2-1: The mutual fund account example OLTP database schema (FundAccts)

The FundAccts database contains six tables that store information on the individual investors, the mutual funds they are invested in, the transactions against their mutual fund accounts, and the value of their portfolio.

A client is established in the Accounts table and may invest in one or more mutual funds. These funds are recorded in the FundAccounts table and linked via foreign key (acct_no) to the investor accounts in the Accounts table. The fund acctno column is the account number assigned by the fund to the client. All dividends and other transactions against a fund account carry this fundacctno when received by the money management firm and posted to the TranHistory table. A client may have more than one fund account with a particular fund.

Each record in the FundAccounts table is linked to its associated fund record in the Funds table to identify the characteristics of the fund, such as name, address, phone numbers, and so forth. However, the only information currently carried in the Funds table is the name of the fund.

A history of transactions against a client's fund accounts, such as buys, sells, dividend reinvestments, and so on, is recorded in the TranHistory table. Each of these transaction history records is linked to its associated fund account record in the FundAccounts table through the foreign keys, fund_cd and fundacctno.

The Statements table is used to store information sent to clients on the quarterly statements. The Statements table is linked to the InvSummary table by account number and statement date. Together, these two tables comprise an online record of a client's portfolio on any given statement date.

The Accounts table in this database contains a column named manager_num. This column is a foreign key into the Managers table. Each manager_num on an account row indicates the account manager who is managing the client's portfolio. The Managers table holds information about the account manager.

Each manager is associated with a business office. The office information – such as office location, contact phone number, and office manager name – is found in the Offices table. The office_type column in this table indicates one of three types of offices. The Business office type, denoted by a 'B' in the office_type column, is associated with the account managers. Every account manager reports to exactly one business office. Each business office reports to an Accounting office, denoted by 'A' in the office_type column. An accounting office may have multiple business offices reporting to it. At the top of the reporting hierarchy is the Regional offices denoted by 'R' in the office_type column.

Each office table row contains a parent_office column containing the office number (in the office_num column) of its parent office. Each business office has a parent accounting office and each accounting office has a parent regional office. The parent_office to office_num relationship is how the hierarchy is implemented within the Office table. We'll discuss this hierarchy a little later in the chapter when we consider the Offices dimension table in the data warehouse.

Information on regional offices is stored in the RegionalOffices table. In addition to managing accounting offices in their region, the regional offices are also responsible for training and thus have a training manager. At this time, the only information carried in the RegionalOffices table is the training manager contact information.

'Scripts containing the CREATE TABLE statements for the FundAccts database can be found in the Chapter02 folder on the CD. The data for these tables is in ASCII text files under the same name as the table they should be loaded into.

By the way, all data in the sample FundAccts and FundAcctsWH databases and ASCII text files is bogus. Data items such as mutual fund prices and ages are not necessarily actual values. All values and client accounts were created specifically for the example application in this book and my *Transact-SQL* programming book. Fund names in the Fund table are real fund names, but fund transaction amounts, such as a dividend recorded in the TranHistory table, are not necessarily actual amounts for the specified transaction date.

Defining the Data Warehouse

The data warehouse database for this sample money management firm is named FundAcctsWH. The schema for this database is shown in Figure 2-2.

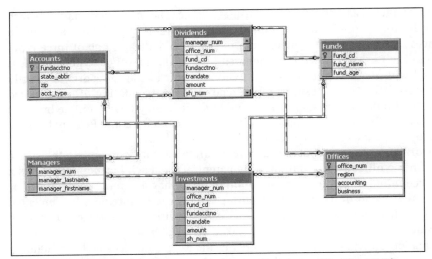

Figure 2-2: The schema for the fund accounts data warehouse (FundAcctsWH)

This data warehouse uses a star schema consisting of a fact table with four dimension tables. The fact table is named Investments and holds rows extracted from the OLTP database FundAccts..TranHistory table. The rows in the TranHistory table used to load the Investments table contain a trantype value of 'Invest', meaning that they are investments of cash by a client into a particular fund account. These transaction types define the domain for this fact table.

The measures that are stored in the Investments table are the amount column, which indicates the amount of cash invested, and the sh_num column, which indicates the number of shares purchased by the cash amount given the fund price on the transaction date.

The foreign keys for the Investments fact table are the primary keys for each of the four dimension tables: Managers, Offices, Funds, and Accounts. An additional column, trandate, is the transaction date for the investments transaction and will be used to create a fifth dimension, the Time dimension. Time is not stored in the data warehouse as a separate dimension table, although it could be. The Time dimension will be created in the cube definition only, as you will see in Chapter 3.

The Managers dimension table columns are extracted from the Managers table in the FundAccts database. This is nothing more than a simple extraction of these three columns: manager_num, manager_lastname, and manager_firstname.

The Offices table is a flattened representation of the office hierarchy found in the FundAccts..Offices table. Each office row in the FundAcctsWH..Offices table holds the office_num key of a Business office from the FundAccts..Offices table. In addition to this key, each row carries the office names of the accounting office the business office reports to and the regional office the accounting office reports to. The

Funds dimension table is an exact copy of the FundAccts..Funds table but with an additional column named fund_age. This column is not found anywhere in the FundAccts OLTP database because it comes from an external source. The fund_age column will be populated in the "Using the DTS Package Designer" section later in this chapter.

The Accounts dimension table is populated by a query joining the FundAccts..Accounts table and the FundAccts..FundAccounts table. The fundacctno and acct_type columns for the Accounts dimension are extracted from the FundAccts..FundAccounts table, and the remaining columns come from the Fundaccts..Accounts table. The FundAccounts table and Accounts table are related to each other on the acct_no column found in both tables.

ON THE CD   Chapter02 on the CD contains the CREATE TABLE scripts for the FundAccts and FundAcctsWH tables. The files containing these scripts are named FundAccts.sql and FundAcctsWH.sql, respectively.

Using the DTS Export Wizard

SQL Server 7.0 ships with a set of tools called the Data Transformation Services (DTS). These services enable the movement of data between different data sources with or without conversions to the data and/or the schema.

Any OLE DB provider, ODBC data source, or ASCII text file can participate in the transformation as either a source or a destination. DTS includes tools such as the DTS Import Wizard, the DTS Export Wizard, and the DTS Package Designer.

In this section, I will illustrate the use of the DTS Export Wizard to export the results of a query from the FundAccts database into the data warehouse Investments fact table.

The DTS Import and Export Wizards can be run from within the SQL Server Enterprise Manager or from the command line. We'll use the command line to start the Export Wizard.

To start the wizard, enter the following command line:

```
dtswiz /x /usa /p /sSecrets /dFundAccts
```

This command line launches the Export Wizard (with the /x argument) and displays its first dialog page. Click Next to advance to the second page, where we will choose which data source to export from. (See Figure 2-3.)

To export from the FundAccts database (already selected in the Database drop-down list), choose *Microsoft OLE DB Provider for SQL Server* from the Source drop-down list. Select the authentication method you wish to use at your server.

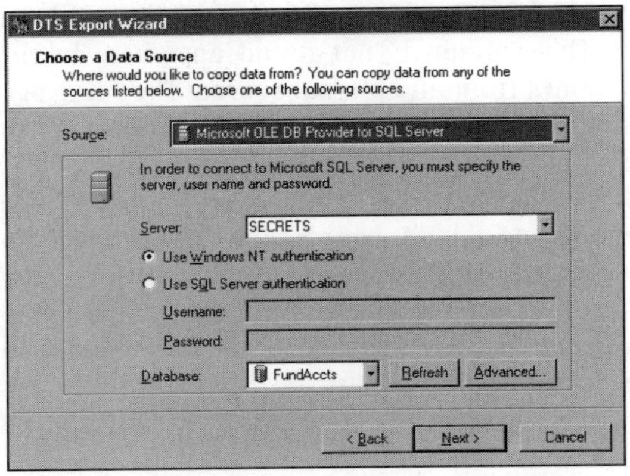

Figure 2-3: The Data Transformation Export Wizard Data Source page

The next page of the Export Wizard (shown in Figure 2-4) asks for a destination. Choose the FundAcctsWH data warehouse database as the destination and the authentication method for that database server, and click Next.

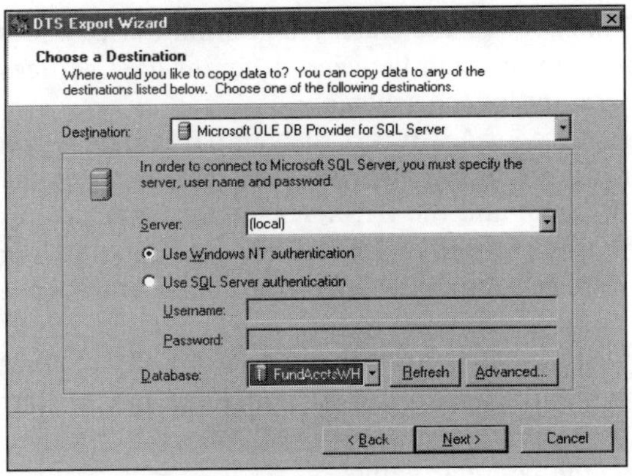

Figure 2-4: The DTS Export Wizard Destination page

Next, we specify either a table copy or a query copy. We'll select *Use a query to specify the data to transfer* to enable us to specify exactly what we want transferred. This page is shown in Figure 2-5.

The next page asks us to specify the query statement, as shown in Figure 2-6. This statement selects the necessary foreign key columns for the Investments fact table through inner joins to the dimension table sources in the OLTP database. In addition, the amount and sh_num (number of shares) columns from the TranHistory table are selected where the trantype column value is equal to 'invest'. For the Investments fact table we are only interested in client account investments.

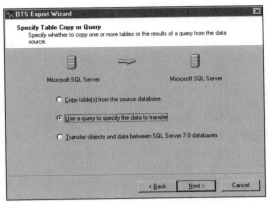

Figure 2-5: Specify the type of copy to be performed by the export.

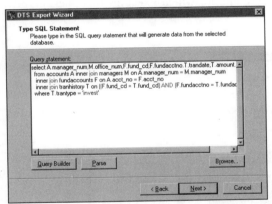

Figure 2-6: The Type SQL Statement page in the Data Transformation Export Wizard

On this page you have the option to parse the entered query to ensure it is valid, and to use the Query Builder to construct the query. In this case, the query was loaded from a file selected through the Browse button. Click Next to display the Select Source Table page. On the page shown in Figure 2-7, select the FundAcctsWH..Investments table as the destination. There are no transformations to define for this transfer, so we'll move on to the next page.

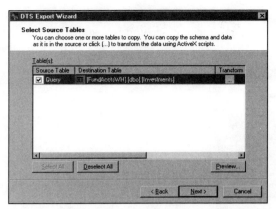

Figure 2-7: Select the Investments fact table in the FundAcctsWH data warehouse as the destination for the transfer.

The next wizard page enables saving the specifications we just made to the DTS package, which will be stored in the msdb database. As you can see in Figure 2-8, we have selected the Run immediately option, which executes this package after saving it to the database.

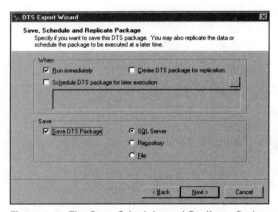

Figure 2-8: The Save, Schedule, and Replicate Package page of the Export Wizard

The next page of the wizard (shown in Figure 2-9) asks you to enter a name for the DTS package and an optional description. We've named this package DTS_Investments and selected Windows NT as the authentication method to be used to store the package.

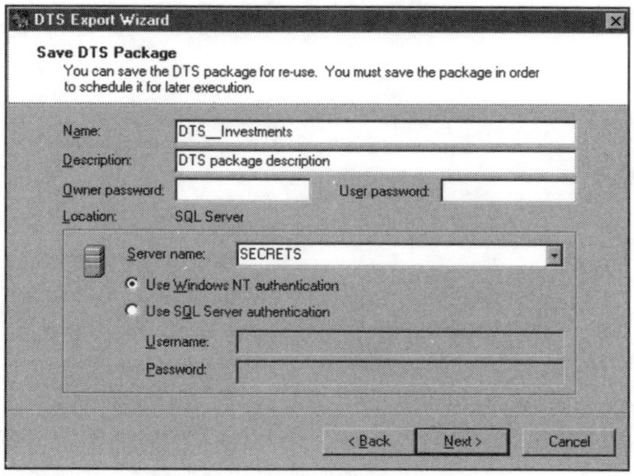

![The Save DTS Package page in the Export Wizard]

Figure 2-9: The Save DTS Package page in the Export Wizard

The last page of the Export Wizard shows a summary of the specifications we made. We can go back and change our choices or click Finish to run the package. This page is shown in Figure 2-10.

Figure 2-10: The DTS Completion page showing a summary of the choices we made in the Export Wizard

As the package runs, a Transferring Data dialog box is displayed that shows the progress of the transfer. At the end of the transfer, you'll get either a success message or an error message. If you receive an error message, go to the step with the error in the Transfer Status listbox and double-click the error to get more information. From there, you can go back to correct the error, or exit the wizard. The transfer shown in Figure 2-11 completed successfully, as did the Save Package step.

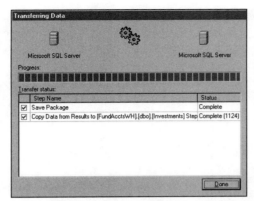

Figure 2-11: The completion of the transfer, indicating a successful package save and transfer

Using the DTS Package Designer

Now that we have the Investments fact table populated with investment transactions from the FundAccts database transhistory table, we can concentrate on populating the dimension tables.

The Accounts dimension table, just like the Investments table, is populated with the results from a query that joins the FundAccts..Accounts table with the FundAccts..FundAccounts table on the acct_no column.

The Managers dimension table is a copy of the necessary columns from the FundAccts..Managers table. Likewise, the Funds dimension table is populated by a copy from the FundAccts..Funds table. But rather than perform just a simple copy, let's add a little challenge here that will enable us to experiment with the DTS Package Designer tool.

As we learned in the "Defining the Data Warehouse" section earlier in this chapter, the Funds dimension table contains a column named fund_age that holds the number of years that the fund has been in operation. For the purposes of this exercise, we'll assume that the source of the fund_age data is external to the money management firm and comes to them via a standard comma-delimited ASCII text file. This text file contains records where the first column contains the fund code (fund_cd) and the second column contains the age of the fund (fund_age), but they do not contain fund names.

It will be our job to use this text file, match the fund_cd in column 1 to the fund_cd in the FundAcctsWH..Funds table, and update the fund_age column with the data in column 2 of the text file. We'll design a package that uses a Data Driven Update Query to accomplish the task.

In your SQL Server Enterprise Manager console, expand your SQL Server node by clicking the plus symbol next to the node to show the Data Transformation

Services folder. Right-click this folder and select New Package from the popup menu. This will display the Package Designer window.

The end result of our work here is shown in Figure 2-12. The package we will design contains a source connection to the ASCII text file, a destination connection to the FundAcctsWH database, and the data-driven query that will perform the transformation. The package contains a text notation and has been named FundAgeUpdate.

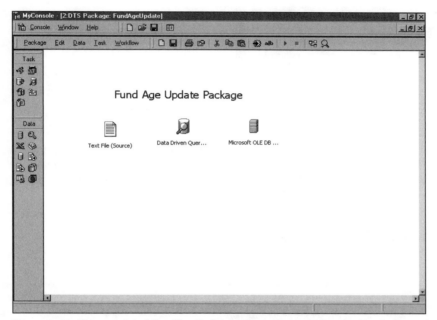

Figure 2-12: The completed FundAgeUpdate package for updating the Funds dimension table

We'll add the text file source connection first. On the Data bar at the left of the window, click the Text File (Source) icon. This will display the Connection Properties page shown in Figure 2-13.

ON THE CD   Click the browse button to the right of the File name: text box to browse for the Funds.txt file. This file is found on the CD in the Chapter02 folder.

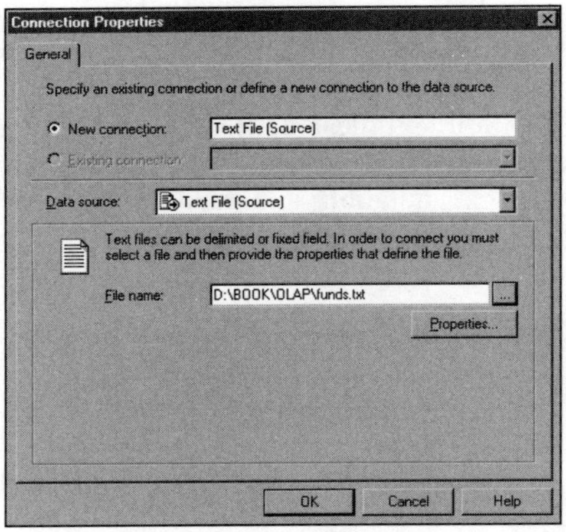

Figure 2-13: The Connection Properties for the Text File (Source) connection

If you wish to name the connection to something other than Text File (Source), enter the name in the New connection: text box. This name will display beneath the connection icon in the Package Designer window. When you click OK, the dialog shown in Figure 2-14 is displayed.

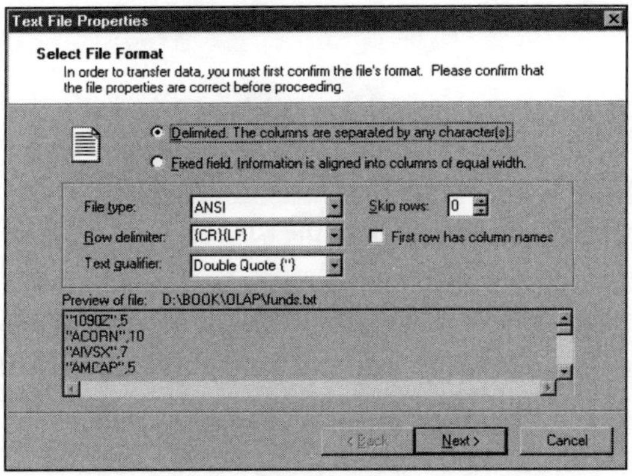

Figure 2-14: The Text File format dialog of the Text File connection

Accept the properties as displayed and click Next to display the Column Delimiter dialog shown in Figure 2-15. Our text file is using commas to delimit the column values on a row, so we choose the comma option and click Finish.

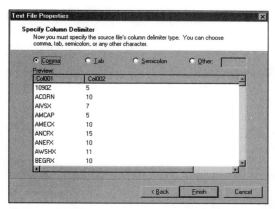

Figure 2-15: The Column Delimiter dialog of the Text File connection

Next we'll add the SQL Server connection to the FundAcctsWH database. This connection will use the Microsoft OLE DB Provider for SQL Server. This dialog, chosen from the Data bar, is shown in Figure 2-16.

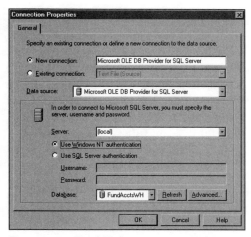

Figure 2-16: The SQL Server connection properties for the connection to the FundAcctsWH database

Here again, you can provide a name for the connection in the New connection: text box. Select the server you will use in the Server: drop-down list and the authentication you will use to connect to the server.

In the Database: drop-down list, select the FundAcctsWH database as our destination database. Click OK to dismiss this dialog and place a connection icon on the Package Designer window.

Click the Data Driven Query icon on the taskbar to display the properties dialog shown in Figure 2-17.

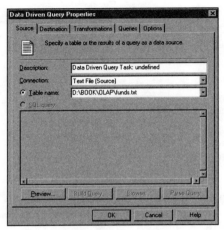

Figure 2–17: The Data Driven Query properties dialog

On the Source tab, enter a description for the task and then choose the Text File (Source) connection in the Connection: drop-down list. The Table name: will display the only table (file) defined for the source connection, our funds.txt file.

The Destination tab is shown in Figure 2-18. All we need to do on this tab is to select the Funds table from the Table name: drop-down list. Once selected, the columns of the Funds table are displayed.

Figure 2–18: The Destination tab of the Data Driven Query properties

On the Transformations tab, we'll select column mappings between the source text file columns and the columns of the Funds table. When you first come into the Data Driven Query properties, the Package Designer takes a guess as to what the mappings should be. You'll want to click the lines between the Source table and the Destination table to select the mapping, then right-click and select Delete from the popup menu to remove the mappings.

Next, select ActiveX Script in the New transformation: drop-down list. Now click the Col002 column in the Source table column list, drag it to the Destination table column list, and drop it on the fund_age column. This will map these two columns via an ActiveX script, which you enter into the dialog that displays when you drop the source column. This dialog is shown in Figure 2-19.

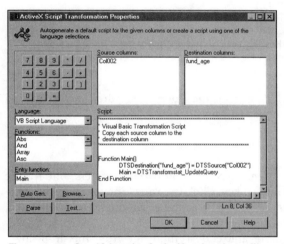

Figure 2-19: Specifying the ActiveX script that will control the column mappings between Col002 of the source text file and the fund_age column of the Funds table

The *Main* function shows the mapping we just designated via the drag/drop action. We won't be doing inserts into the Funds table as the Package Designer suggests, but we will be doing updates, so change line 2 of the script to read:

```
Main = DTSTransformstat_UpdateQuery
```

The query this line refers to will be specified on the Query tab. These two statements are all that is needed for this transformation, so click OK to dismiss the dialog.

Before we define the update query, drag the Col001 source column over to the Destination table and drop it on the fund_cd column to create a mapping between these two columns. This mapping should be a Copy Column transformation as indicated in the New transformation drop-down list. The results of our work up to this point are shown in Figure 2-20.

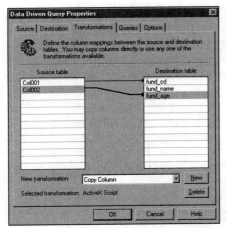

Figure 2-20: The Transformation tab showing the column mappings between source and destination

Click the Queries tab. Select Update from the Query type: drop-down list and type the following query into the query edit text box:

```
update funds set fund_age = ? where fund_cd = ?
```

This is a simple update query statement containing two parameters; one for the fund_age value and one for the fund_cd key. Click the Parse/Show Parameters button. This will cause two parameters to be displayed in the parameter mapping pane, but they are not the correct parameters we need.

Select the first Destination column and choose fund_age from the drop-down list. This is the column Parameter 1 is to map to. Now select fund_cd for the second parameter. These parameters map in order to the question marks in the query statement. The results are shown in Figure 2-21.

We won't specify any options for this data-driven query, but a few items on the Options tab are worth discussing for a moment. The Options tab is shown in Figure 2-22.

When you run large packages, you may encounter a number of errors. Rather than have DTS list all errors encountered for the entire package, you can stop the package execution after the number of errors you specify in Max error count.

If you want the errors to be logged, enter the name of a log file in the Exception file name text box. Using the Delimiters list boxes, you can control how this exception log is delimited.

When using a source in which the order of rows can be predicted, you have the option of specifying the starting row to be moved (First row) to the destination and the ending row (Last row) to be moved. These options can be helpful when you only need a portion of the source to be moved.

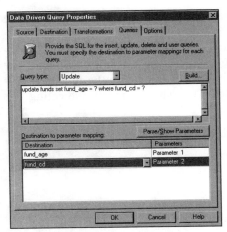

Figure 2-21: The update query to be used in the ActiveX script for the fund_age transformation

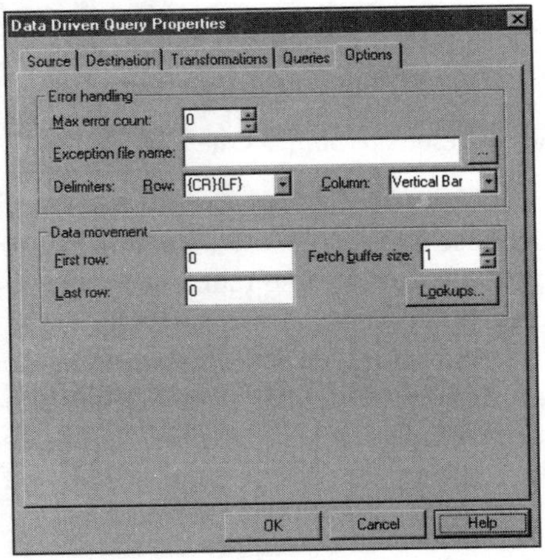

Figure 2-22: The Data Driven Query options

The Lookups button displays a dialog that enables you to build a parameterized lookup query for the transformation. This option can be used to translate values in the source prior to updating or inserting into the destination.

We're finished with this data-driven query, so click OK to dismiss the properties dialog and place the icon in the Package window. Arrange the icons in this window as you like by simple drag-and-drop operations. Place a text annotation in the window by choosing Add Text Annotation from the Package menu or clicking the Text Annotation toolbar button.

To run this package, choose Execute from the Package menu or click the Execute button on the toolbar. If DTS doesn't detect any errors in the package, you'll see a

Successfully Completed message; otherwise, you'll see the errors listed in the Executing Package dialog.

The Complete status in the Executing Package dialog shown in Figure 2-23 signifies that our update was completed. Verify the results by executing a select query on the Funds table in the FundAcctsWH database and compare the fund_age column values with the text file Col002 values. They should match, indicating our parameter specifications worked.

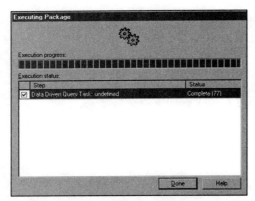

Figure 2-23: The Executing Package dialog showing the results of our package run

To save this package for future updates, choose Save on the Package menu to display the Save DTS Package dialog. Enter your choices for the name of the package, location, server, and authentication selections.

The population of the Offices dimension table requires us to devise a query to unravel the inherent office hierarchy found in the FundAccts..Offices table into a set of Offices dimension rows. Each row of this dimension table carries the office hierarchy in three columns: one for the Region, one for the Accounting office, and one for the Business office.

The query used for this task is shown here:

```
SELECT B.office_num,R.office_name As region,
            A.office_name As accounting,B.office_name as business
  FROM offices B INNER JOIN offices A
    ON A.office_num = B.parent_office
    INNER JOIN offices R
      ON R.office_num = A.parent_office
```

This query flattens the office hierarchy designated by the relationships among the office rows on the parent_office relator column. A business office, from which we are selecting the office_num, is related to its accounting office by containing the office_num of its accounting office in the parent_office column.

Accounting offices are related to regional offices by a similar relation. Each accounting office row contains the office_num of its regional office in the parent_ office column. By joining parent_office to office_num through each of the three copies of offices table we have in this query, we get a flattened representation of the hierarchy.

Running the preceding query in the FundAccts database yields the following results:

```
office_num        region            accounting        business
------------      ----------        -------------     ----------
101               NorthEast         Acct-510          Connecticut
234               NorthEast         Acct-550          New York
335               NorthEast         Acct-520          Vermont
245               NorthEast         Acct-550          Massachusetts
```

Exactly what we want for the data warehouse Offices dimension.

To load the FundAcctsWH..Offices table, we use the preceding query in DTS just as we did for loading the Investments and Accounts tables.

Summary

The Data Transformation Import and Export Wizards are great tools for obtaining quick results with easy-to-use point-and-click methods. With these tools, you can create data marts, create subsets for testing, move files, and more without hassle. It's a great alternative to using BCP.

Use of the DTS wizards and the DTS Package Designer should support just about any transformation task you will encounter in your work with a data warehouse. Custom queries, stored procedures, and ActiveX scripting are capabilities you'll find very useful in your work.

Of course, you have the option of creating your own customized procedures for transferring data, and you may find that these are just as easy and reliable as DTS. Nothing wrong with that approach. There are numerous examples of custom transfers in practice, especially considering that DTS arrived with SQL Server 7.0 and data warehouses have been in existence long before this arrival.

But DTS does offer a great deal of power and ease of use. We've only skimmed the surface in this chapter; there is much more to explore. You'll find some additional sample DTS packages on the CD in the DTSPackages folder.

The Databases folder on the CD contains the files for both the FundAccts database and the FundAcctsWH database. These files can be attached to your SQL Server by following the directions in the Readme.txt file also contained in the Databases folder. This is an alternative to building the data warehouse from scratch as discussed in this chapter and will prepare you for the remainder of the book's examples.

Chapter 3

A Tour of the OLAP Manager

IN THIS CHAPTER

- ◆ Learning how to create a cube using OLAP Manager wizards
- ◆ Using the Cube Editor to modify and maintain your cube
- ◆ Browsing your cube using the Cube Browser
- ◆ Discovering how to define member properties and virtual dimensions
- ◆ Adding calculated members to your cube using the Calculated Member Builder

IN THIS CHAPTER we'll explore the terminology of OLAP Services, introduced in Chapter 1, in a little more depth. In doing so, we'll gain some hands-on experience building a cube from the data in the FundAcctsWH data warehouse discussed in Chapter 2. A number of options are available for building cubes. Many of these options require that you write custom programs using either Decision Support Objects or the PivotTable Service, but there is a tool in OLAP Services that we can use that doesn't require us to write any code at all. That tool is called the OLAP Manager.

Starting OLAP Manager

OLAP Manager is a Microsoft Management Console application. To start OLAP Manager, select Programs on the Start bar, then select Microsoft SQL Server 7.0 OLAP Services and click OLAP Manager.

If you like, you can integrate SQL Server Enterprise Manager and OLAP Manager into one MMC application. To do this, launch the Enterprise Manager and then add the OLAP Manager snap-in to display both applications in the console tree. Another option is to start OLAP Manager and then add the Enterprise Manager snap-in.

The instructions that follow will create a shortcut on your desktop for a console that displays both the Enterprise Manager and the OLAP Manager. We'll start with an empty management console by launching MMC.

1. Right-click the Windows desktop and select New Shortcut from the menu.

2. In the *Create Shortcut Command line* textbox, enter the path to **mmc.exe** (usually c:\windows or c:\winnt). Click the Next button.

3. In the *Select a title for the program* textbox, enter the title of your choice.

4. Click the Finish button to create the shortcut on your desktop.

Double-click the new shortcut to launch MMC and follow these steps to add the snap-ins we'll be using:

1. From the Console menu, click Add/Remove Snap-in.

2. In the Add/Remove Snap-in dialog box, click the Add button to add a standalone snap-in.

3. In the Add Standalone Snap-in dialog box, select Microsoft SQL Enterprise Manager from the Available Standalone Snap-ins list and click the Add button.

4. Next select Microsoft SQL Server OLAP Services from the list and click Add again.

5. Click the Close button to close the Add Standalone Snap-in dialog box.

6. Click the OK button in the Add/Remove Snap-in dialog box to close it and add the selected snap-ins to the console.

You should see both Microsoft SQL Servers and OLAP Servers nodes under the Console Root folder in the console tree view. This configuration gives you convenient access to both database management and OLAP management facilities under one console.

Creating an OLAP Database

In this section we'll define an OLAP database named FundAcctSample under an OLAP server. On my machine, the OLAP server is named Secrets (named for another book project I worked on not long ago). In your installation, you may have more than one server to choose from. By default, only the current machine is shown, while others can be added. Also by default, only one database, "Foodmart," exists. You can see these servers by expanding the OLAP servers folder in the console tree. Anything under the OLAP servers folder is OLAP Manager domain. Follow these steps to create a database under your server:

1. When you click the server name, you should see a message box indicating that a connection is being made to the server.

2. Right-click the server node and select New Database from the shortcut menu. This will display the Database dialog box.

3. Enter the name **FundAcctSample** in the Database name textbox and then click the OK button.

When you expand the OLAP server node, you should now see the FundAcctSample database node. Expand this database to display the folders below it. You'll see the folders named Cubes, Virtual Cubes, and Library.

Specifying the Data Source

Next we need to define the data source for our new OLAP database. Expand the Library folder under the FundAcctSample database node and follow these steps:

1. Right-click the Data Sources folder and choose New Data Source from the shortcut menu. This will display the Data Link Properties dialog box.

2. On the Provider tab select *Microsoft OLE DB Provider for SQL Server* from the providers list.

3. Click the Connection tab and select the server on which you installed the FundAcctsWH sample database. Enter or select FundAcctsWH in the *Select the Database on the Server* drop-down combo box. This is the SQL Server database we'll use as our source for cube data. Choose the security mode you want to use to connect to the server and then click the OK button to dismiss the Data Link Properties dialog box. The Connection tab is shown in Figure 3-1 below.

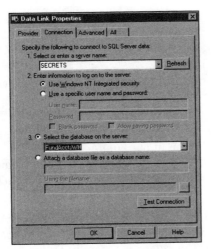

Figure 3-1: Enter connection information and the source database in the Data Link Properties dialog box.

Under the Library Data Sources node, you should now have a node labeled <your server name> - FundAcctsWH. On my machine this node reads, SECRETS – FundAcctsWH.

Using the Cube Wizard

Now we're ready to build our first cube. To do this we'll use the Cube Wizard, one of many wizards in OLAP Manager that help to build and manage OLAP databases. Right-click the Cubes folder under the FundAcctSample database node and choose New Cube from the shortcut menu. Here you have a choice of using the Cube Wizard or the Cube Editor to build your cube. We'll discuss the Editor a little later. For now, choose Cube Wizard from the shortcut menu, which will display the Welcome screen of the wizard.

Perform the following steps to specify the measures in your cube:

1. On the Welcome screen of the Cube Wizard, click the Next button. This action will display the *Select a fact table for your cube* screen as shown in Figure 3-2.

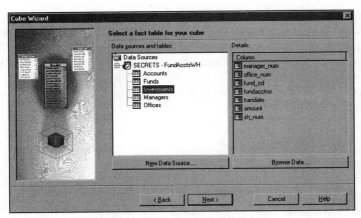

Figure 3–2: Select a fact table in the Cube Wizard.

2. Expand the FundAcctsWH node and choose the Investments table. Investments is the fact table we set up in our FundAcctsWH data warehouse. It enables analysis of investment transaction amounts and share amounts. Click the Next button to display the *Fact table numeric columns* screen shown in Figure 3-3.

3. Double-click the amount and sh_num columns to choose these columns as measures for the cube. Click the Next button to display the *Select the dimensions for your cube* screen. This screen is shown in Figure 3-4.

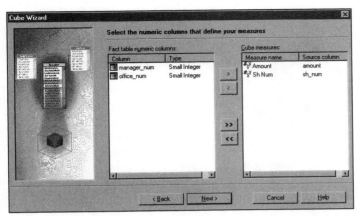

Figure 3-3: The Fact table numeric column screen in the Cube Wizard

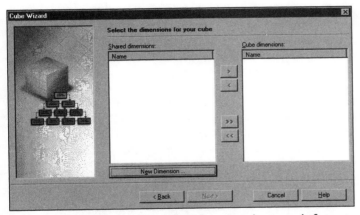

Figure 3-4: The Select the dimensions for your cube screen before we
specify dimensions for our cube

Next we'll define the dimensions for the Investments cube. We'll create a Time
dimension and a Fund dimension and add other dimensions a little later using the
Cube Editor. Follow these steps to define the dimensions:

1. Click the New Dimension button at the bottom of the wizard. This will display the opening screen of the Dimension Wizard as shown in Figure 3-5.

2. Select *A single dimension table (flat or star schema)* option and then click
   the Next button.

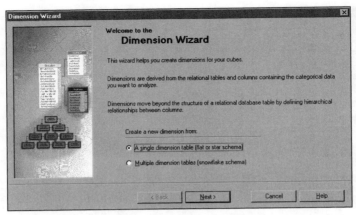

Figure 3-5: The first screen of the Dimension Wizard

3. Expand the FundAcctsWH node on the *Select the dimension table* screen shown in Figure 3-6 and click the Investments table. This is the same table we are using for our fact table. Our FundAcctsWH does not have a separate time dimension table for us to choose here. If we had built a separate table in the warehouse to hold time information, we could then choose that table in this step. However, the Dimension Wizard is capable of building a time breakdown from a single date-time data type column as we are doing here. This is sufficient for our application, therefore we don't need a special time dimension table in our warehouse. Click the Next button to display the *Select the dimension type* screen.

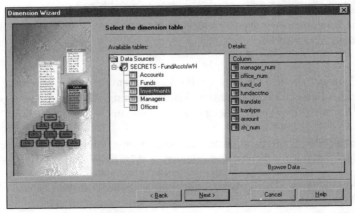

Figure 3-6: Choosing the dimension source table in the Dimension Wizard

The *Select the dimension type* screen is shown in Figure 3-7. On this screen, click the Time dimension option. The *trandate* column name should automatically appear in the Date column drop-down combo box since this is the only date-time data type column in the Investments table. Click the Next button.

Now, we need to define the levels of the time hierarchy we want to support in this dimension. From the *Select time levels* drop-down list shown in Figure 3-8, choose *Year, Quarter, Month* as the levels to be supported and then click the Next button.

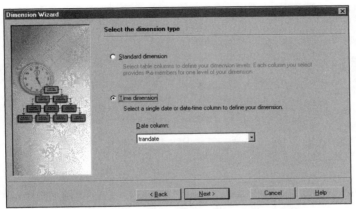

Figure 3-7: Select the dimension type in the Dimension Wizard.

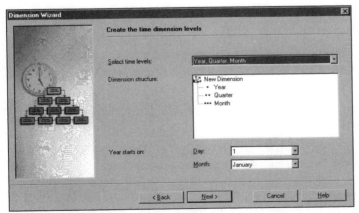

Figure 3-8: Select the levels of the time hierarchy to be supported in the time dimension.

The last screen of the Dimension Wizard is shown in Figure 3-9. Enter the name **Time** in the Name text box, clear the *Share this dimension with other cubes* checkbox and then click the Finish button to dismiss the Dimension Wizard and create the Time dimension. By clearing the *Share this dimension with other cubes* checkbox, we are specifying that the Time dimension be a private dimension for the cube we are building. When we create the Fund dimension, we will leave this checkbox checked.

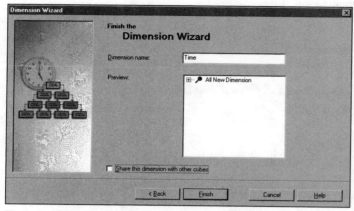

Figure 3-9: The final screen of the Dimension Wizard collects the name of the dimension and enables the choice of a private or shared dimension.

The *Select the dimensions for your cube* screen should now display the Time dimension in the right-hand pane labeled Cube Dimensions. Now let's go back into the Dimension Wizard to create our Fund dimension.

1. Click the New Dimension button.

2. Click *A single dimension table (flat or star schema)* and then click the Next button.

3. On the *Select the dimension table* screen, choose the Funds table and then click the Next button.

4. Double-click the FundName column in the Available Columns list. This is the only level we will use. FundName appears in the Dimension Levels list as shown in Figure 3-10. Click the Next button.

5. Type Fund in the Dimension Name text box and this time leave the *Share this dimension with other cubes* box checked so this dimension gets created as a shared dimension. The screen should look the one shown in Figure 3-11. Click the Finish button to create the Fund dimension.

You should see the Fund dimension appear in the Cube Dimensions list on the *Select the dimensions for your cube* screen as shown in Figure 3-12. The Fund dimension we just created does not appear in the Shared Dimensions list on this screen because it is not yet saved in the database. Future sessions of the Cube Wizard will show the Fund dimension as a shared dimension that is available for selection into cube definitions.

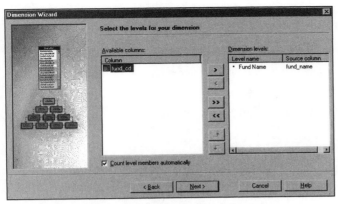

Figure 3-10: Defining the level for the Fund dimension

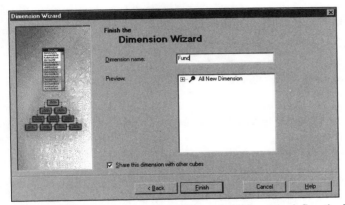

Figure 3-11: The last screen of the Dimension Wizard to define the Fund dimension

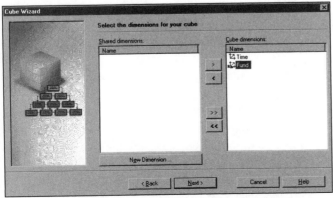

Figure 3-12: The Select the dimensions for your cube screen after adding the Time and Fund dimensions

So far we've specified the cube's fact table and two dimensions, a Time dimension consisting of Year, Quarter, and Month levels; and a Fund dimension consisting of one level – the fund name.

To complete the cube's specification, click the Next button to leave the *Select the dimensions for your cube* screen and display the screen shown in Figure 3-13.

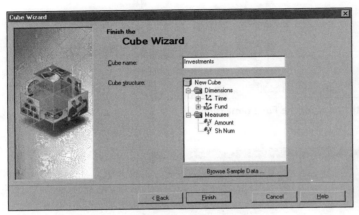

Figure 3-13: The final screen of the Cube Wizard

Click the Finish button to close the Cube Wizard and launch the Cube Editor.

Using the Cube Editor

Figure 3-14 shows our cube schema at this point in the development. The left pane of the editor displays the cube's dimensions, measures, and calculated members (which we haven't yet defined).

In the Editor, we're going to add the rest of the dimensions and add a role to the database. After this, we'll specify the storage mode for the cube, design aggregations, and then load the cube with data selected from the data warehouse.

Now we'll add the Office, Account, and Manager dimensions to the cube. These dimensions will be private to the Investments cube. Currently, no way exists to define a shared dimension using the Cube Editor.

Add the dimension tables to the schema window.

1. Choose Tables from the Insert menu.

2. In the Tables list, double-click the Offices table, the Accounts table, and the Managers table to add them to the schema. Click the Close button to dismiss the Select Table dialog.

3. Double-click the Region column in the Offices table in the schema pane. This will display the Map The Column dialog shown in Figure 3-15.

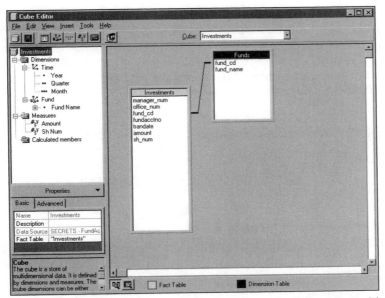

Figure 3-14: The Cube Editor after defining Time and Fund dimensions with the Cube Wizard

Figure 3-15: The Map The Column dialog in the Cube Editor

4. Click the Dimension option and then click the OK button.

5. In the Tree view pane, click the Region node and rename this node as Office. You should now see the Office node with Region as the first level under it.

6. Add the other office columns as lower levels beneath the Office dimension. To do this, drag the Accounting column from the Offices table in the schema pane and drop it on the Office node in the Tree view pane. Do the same for the Business column.

Expanding the Office node in the Tree view will now show Region, Accounting, and Business as the three levels of the Office hierarchy.

Now perform the steps above to define the Manager dimension consisting of Manager Lastname and the Account dimension consisting of State Abbr. Each of these dimensions will contain only a one-level hierarchy.

Our final result is shown in Figure 3-16. We have one fact table and five dimensions, four of which are displayed in the schema pane of the editor. The source for the Time dimension is the fact table itself.

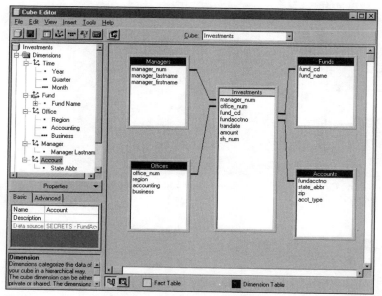

Figure 3-16: The final schema of the Investments cube

Before we design the aggregations for this cube, let's define a cube role that will enable users to query the cube. To do so, follow these steps:

1. Select Manage Roles in the Tools menu. This will display the Cube Roles dialog box.

2. Click the New Role button to display the *Create a Database Role* dialog box shown in Figure 3-17.

3. In the Role Name text box enter Managers, and in the Description text box enter Account Managers.

4. Click the Groups and Users button and select the groups and users that will need to access the cube. In Figure 3-17, I've selected three users in the Develop domain. All of these users are defined as NT security accounts on the server.

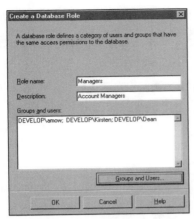

Figure 3-17: Creating the Managers role to enable access to the Investment cube

5. Click the OK button to create the role. The Managers role appears in the Cube Access list on the *Manage the cube roles* dialog box shown in Figure 3-18.

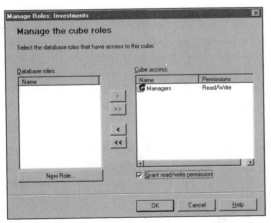

Figure 3-18: The Investments cube Access Roles dialog box after adding the Managers role

To save the work we've just completed, click *Save* in the File menu of the Editor.

Designing Storage and Populating the Cube

Now we need to define the storage mode we will use for this cube, calculate the aggregations that will be created for the cube according to the performance and resource options we select, and then populate the cube with data selected from the data warehouse.

To start off, launch the Storage Design Wizard by choosing Design Storage in the Tools menu. This will display the Welcome screen of the wizard. Click the Next button to select the type of data storage for the cube. This screen is shown in Figure 3-19.

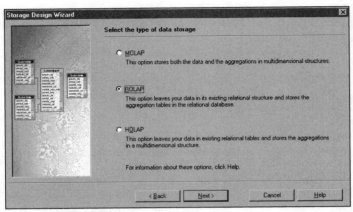

Figure 3-19: The Select the type of data storage screen in the Storage Design Wizard

For this cube, we'll use ROLAP mode to store the cube. This mode, as noted on the screen in Figure 3-19 and discussed in Chapter 1, stores the aggregations in relational tables in the data warehouse and leaves the detail data in the warehouse fact tables.

After you select the ROLAP option and click the Next button, you will see the Aggregation Options screen shown in Figure 3-20.

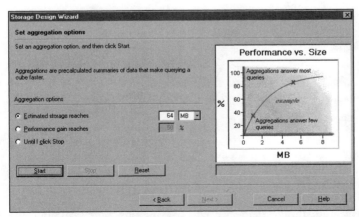

Figure 3-20: The Aggregations Options screen enables performance or resource constraints and limits to be specified before designing the aggregations.

The aggregation options are explained in Table 3-1.

TABLE 3-1 AGGREGATION OPTIONS IN THE STORAGE DESIGN WIZARD

Option	What It Does	Setting
Estimated storage reaches	OLAP services decides which aggregations to store given the maximum storage size allocation you enter for aggregation tables.	Enter the maximum storage size to be allocated in MB or GB.
Performance gain reaches	OLAP services calculates performance gain over maximum query time by storing aggregations in aggregation tables.	Performance gain in percent. (See explanation below.)
Until I click stop	Calculates aggregations to be stored until the user clicks the Stop button.	Monitor the Performance vs. Size graph and click the Stop button when the desired trade-off is reached.

The Performance Gain is calculated by the following expression:

```
Gain = 100 * (MaxQueryTime - TargetQueryTime) / (MaxQueryTime - MinQueryTime)
```

Using this calculation, if a non-optimized query is estimated to have a MaxQueryTime of 17 seconds and a MinQueryTime estimated to be 2 seconds with full aggregations, then a TargetQueryTime of 6 seconds would yield the following:

```
Gain = 100 * (17 - 6) / (17 - 2)
Gain = 100 * 11 / 15
Gain = 100 * .73
Gain = 73%
```

In Figure 3-20, I've chosen the *Estimated storage reaches* option and specified 64MB as a storage allocation maximum. Most likely, you will use this option more than the Performance gain reaches option since disk space can be better controlled and measured than minimum and maximum query times. If you choose to use the *Performance gain reaches option*, a recommended approach would be to use a setting of 20 to 30 percent; let the users run their queries for a time, and then redesign the aggregations using Usage Based Optimizations.

You can play with various options on this screen since the wizard is not actually building and storing aggregations at this point. It is merely designing the aggregations to be used. Figure 3-21 shows the results for our cube using a 64MB storage limit. As you can see in the figure, 22 aggregations were designed for the Investments cube requiring well below our specified maximum (thanks to the wonderful world of small sample databases).

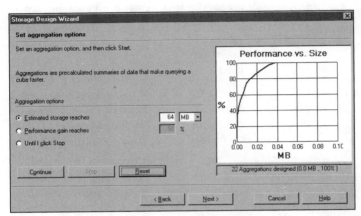

Figure 3-21: The results of calculating aggregations for the Investments cube

Click the Next button to move to the final screen in the Storage Design Wizard. This is where we will cause OLAP services to actually perform the aggregations and store them. Choose the Process Now option and then click the Finish button to start the process.

As the cube is processed, you'll see status information displayed in the Process window including start and stop times, and the steps as they run. If errors are detected, you'll see an error message displayed for the failed steps. Figure 3-22 shows the completed Process window for our cube. To view any of the Transact-SQL statements generated by OLAP Services and partially displayed in the process window, double-click the SQL icon in the window. This will display the full Transact-SQL statement in a window entitled *View Trace Line*.

Click the Close button on the Process window to dismiss this window and return to the Cube Editor. Choose Exit from the File menu to leave the Cube Editor and return to OLAP Manager.

Browsing the Investments Cube

Now we get to see the results of our work. Throughout the book we'll be accessing this cube and others as we explore the OLAP tools and APIs. But before we get to those, let's use the OLAP Manager's Cube Browser to check our results.

Right-click the Investments cube in the OLAP Manager Tree view and select Browse Data. The Browser window is displayed as shown in Figure 3-23.

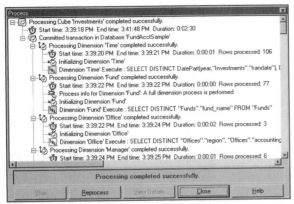

Figure 3-22: Process window showing completed steps for the Investments cube

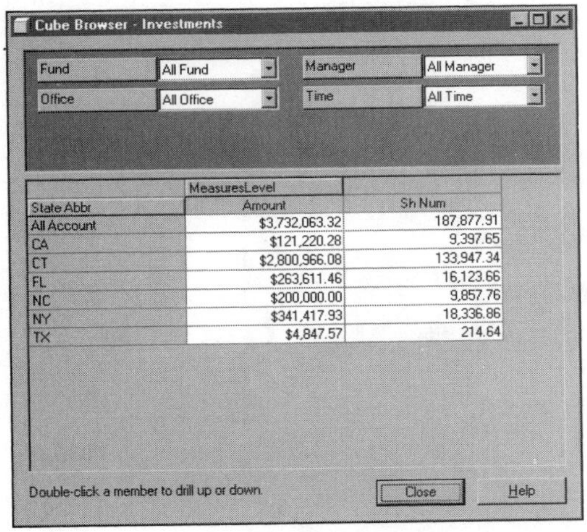

Figure 3-23: The Investments cube displayed in the Cube Browser

As shown in Figure 3-23, the measures for the Account dimension are displayed in the grid. Each of the other dimensions is displayed in the dimension pane at the top of the Browser and each is showing the All level for the dimension. This configuration indicates that any measure you choose in the grid is the sum at the intersection of All Funds, All Managers, All Offices, All Time, and the Account dimension member you choose. The entire firm is managing $3,732,063.32 in investments (actually this is the total investment amount seen in the TranHistory table and does not include dividend gains, redemptions, or fees). The number of shares purchased by this amount is nearly 187,878.

It is quite easy to see in this first view of our cube that most of the $3,732,063.32 is generated in the state of Connecticut. Since state abbreviations come from the Accounts table in the FundAccts OLTP database, these amounts reflect the contact address of our clients. So we would expect that most of our clients have Connecticut addresses or that our Connecticut clients are investing more heavily than other clients.

DRILL-DOWN IN A HIERARCHY

Notice in Figure 3-23 that each of the members in the Account dimension stands by itself. There is no further breakdown for any of the State Abbreviation members in the Account dimension. The amounts we see for these dimension members are at the lowest level within the dimension as it is currently defined. There is no further drill-down to lower levels to see how the amounts are distributed within the state. A possibility for drill-down within the Account dimension would be to see the state amounts by account type or maybe by zip code. In this cube, we haven't defined this capability.

However, we do have a dimension that does offer a drill-down capability, and that dimension is the Office dimension. To look at the Office dimension instead of the Account dimension, click on the Office label and drag it down to the State Abbr column in the grid and drop it. This action will replace the Account dimension members in the first column with the Office dimension members. This view is shown in Figure 3-24.

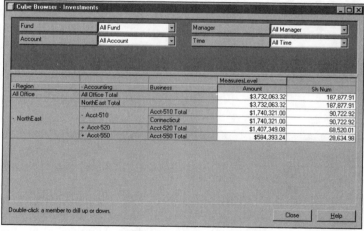

Figure 3-24: The Cube Browser showing the Office dimension hierarchy

Note in Figure 3-24 that a plus sign (+) next to the Office member indicates that by double-clicking on it, that member can be expanded to show levels below it. In the case of the Office dimension, the first level in the left-most column is the Regional office, the next column to the right shows the Accounting office, and finally the Business office is shown in the third column. Each column contains the members for the level and the total for the preceding level.

Because the Office dimension defines a hierarchy of office levels, we can drill-down within this hierarchy and watch the amount that aggregations change. In

Figure 3-24, we see that the Connecticut office has an amount of $1,740,321. Why does this amount differ from the amount shown in Figure 3-23 where CT has a value of $2,800,966.08?

The Account dimension view shows amounts associated with state abbreviations found in the contact address of client accounts. Any client with an address in the state of Connecticut would reflect their investment amounts on the CT line.

The Office dimension view shows amounts associated with the office to which the client's manager reports. Each client has one manager at any one point in time and that manager reports to one business office at a point in time. All client investment amounts related to the Connecticut office through the manager relationship would show up on the NorthEast.Acct-510.Connecticut line.

The fact that the amounts are different in these two views may indicate that some of the CT clients have managers reporting to offices other than Connecticut. We can find out if this is true by using a filter as discussed below.

USING FILTERS

If we were to look only at amounts for CT Accounts and look at those amounts by business office, we could determine if there are managers on CT accounts reporting to non-Connecticut offices.

To filter the measures so that only CT amounts are shown, click the Account drop-down list and expand the All Account node to display the Account members. Now select the CT member and the grid should change to show only the $2,800,966.08 amount.

Now expand each of the Office levels down to the Business Office level so that you can see amounts broken down by office. The view should look like the one shown in Figure 3-25.

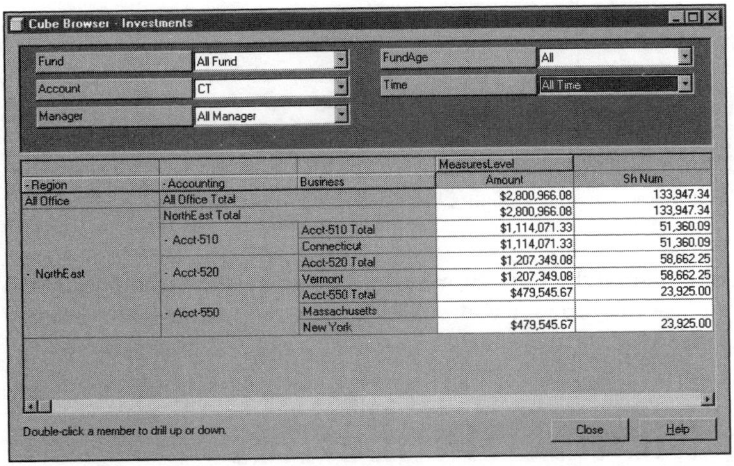

Figure 3-25: The Cube Browser filtered to display only the CT Account members

It is clear from Figure 3-25 that some CT accounts do have managers reporting to non-Connecticut offices because both the Vermont office and the New York office display amounts for the CT account member.

This is good so far. We can justify the amount differences between the CT Account view and the Connecticut Office view. Now for another question: Can we go further and find out which managers for CT accounts are reporting to Vermont and New York? The answer is yes, and we'll do this next.

ADDING A DIMENSION TO THE GRID

We need to break down the view of Figure 3-25 so that we can see the amounts for each office by manager. To do this, drag the Manager label to the grid and drop it on the grid itself instead of the Office column. This action will add the dimension to the grid instead of replacing a dimension.

If you now scroll the grid to display managers Stock and Yields, you will see that these are the managers on CT accounts reporting to the non-Connecticut offices. Manager Stock reports to the Vermont office, and manager Yields reports to the New York office. This view is shown in Figure 3-26.

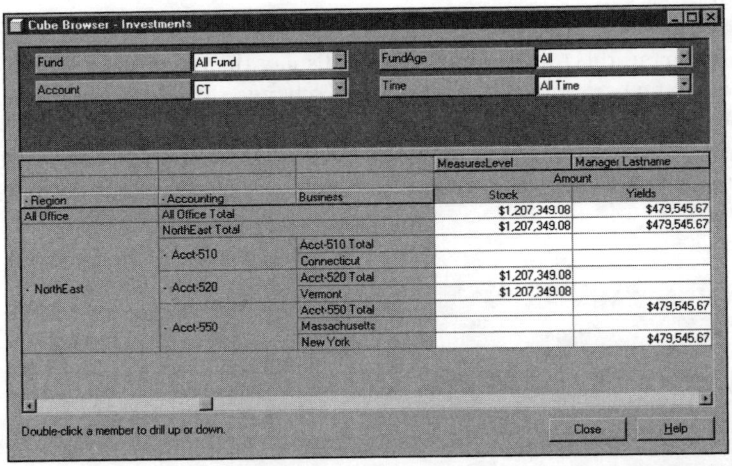

Figure 3-26: The Cube Browser showing amounts by two dimensions — Office and Manager

Now that we have explored the Cube Browser and know how to create views and filter the data, let's close the browser and enhance our Investments cube a bit by adding a member property, a virtual dimension, and a calculated member.

Defining Member Properties

You may have noticed in Figures 3-25 and 3-26 that I added a new dimension to the cube. This dimension is the FundAge dimension. Although you can't tell from the figures, this dimension is a virtual dimension. Virtual dimensions, discussed in the next section, are defined based on member properties, which we will add and discuss in this section.

Member properties provide additional attributes for a given member level in a dimension. In the case of our Investments cube, we will add a property to the Fund Name level within the Fund dimension. If there were other levels defined for this dimension, we could assign properties to them as well. To add the Fund Age property, follow these steps:

1. Expand the Library folder in the OLAP Manager Tree view.

2. Expand the Shared Dimensions folder. You should see the Fund dimension under this folder.

3. Right-click the Fund Dimension and select Edit from the shortcut menu. This will launch the Dimension Editor.

4. Expand the Fund Name node in the Dimension Editor to display the Member Properties folder.

5. Drag the fund_age column from the schema pane and drop it on the Member Properties folder to create the FundAge property.

To see the values for the FundAge member property, view the dimension members and select a member to see its associated FundAge property value in the Member Properties pane. Your view should look like the one shown in Figure 3-27.

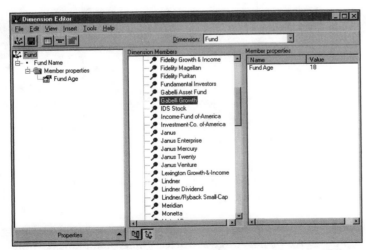

Figure 3-27: Viewing members and properties in the Dimension Editor window

Now that we have defined a member property for the Fund Shared dimension, we can create a virtual dimension on this property.

Creating Virtual Dimensions

A *virtual dimension* in a cube enables analysis on the member property on which the virtual dimension is based. In our sample, defining a virtual dimension on the FundAge property and adding that dimension to our cube enables queries to return results by age of fund.

Unlike the dimensions we've been working with so far, adding a virtual dimension to our cube will not increase the cube's size. The reason is that aggregations for virtual dimensions are calculated when needed for a query. They are not stored in the cube. Follow these steps to create the FundAge virtual dimension:

1. Right-click the Virtual Dimensions folder in the OLAP Manager Tree view. Select New Virtual Dimension from the shortcut menu to launch the Virtual Dimension Wizard.

2. Click the Next button to skip the Welcome screen.

3. In the *Select the member property for your virtual dimension* screen, expand the Fund node and select the FundName.FundAge property as shown in Figure 3-28. Click the Next button.

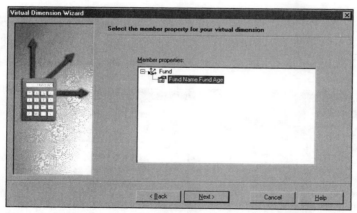

Figure 3-28: Selecting the member property for the virtual dimension

4. In the Virtual Dimension Name textbox, enter **FundAge** as the dimension name and then click the Finish button.

To add the new FundAge virtual dimension to the Investments cube, right-click the dimensions folder in the OLAP Manager tree and select Dimension Manager from the shortcut menu. Choose FundAge in the Dimension Manager and then save the cube. Virtual dimensions can only be added to a cube if the dimension containing the base member property is part of the cube. Since the FundAge member property is contained in the Fund dimension, and the Fund dimension is part of the Investments cube, we can add the FundAge virtual dimension to the cube as well.

Since FundAge aggregations are calculated only when needed for a query, there is no need to reprocess the cube to build new aggregations. We can immediately use the Cube Browser to view Amount and Sh Num aggregations by Fund Age.

Using Calculated Members

Members in a dimension — whether it be an ordinary dimension from a dimension table or a measure from the measures dimension — usually have their source in the data warehouse dimension and fact tables. These members are known as *input members*.

OLAP Services supports the definition of *calculated members*, which are dimension or measure members that derive their values from an expression executed at query time.Calculated member values are not physically stored in a cube, but the expressions used to arrive at the values are stored.

The source for calculated members is usually the values of other members used in simple expressions such as Amount / Sh Num, or used in any number of functions defined in function libraries.

OLAP Services supports a function library containing numerous functions in categories such as string functions, set functions, numeric functions, and special member and tuple functions specific to OLAP structures. These functions are listed in Appendix G of this book.

In addition to the built-in function library, OLAP Services supports the Microsoft Visual Basic for Applications Expression Services library (**VBA332.dll**), included with OLAP Services, and the Microsoft Excel worksheet function library if it is installed on the machine. Third-party libraries and your own custom libraries are also supported.

If you supply your own custom library, you must adhere to certain rules. Arguments to your functions must be either string or numeric data types, or variants containing string or numeric types. Arrays of these types are supported. The return values from your functions must be string or numeric data types or variants containing these types. I should also mention that the DLLs should support COM — this is how OLAP Services communicates with it.

Before using your own functions in calculated members, you must register the function library with OLAP Services. You can do this in the Calculated Member Builder dialog by clicking the Register button (see Figure 3-29). You can use any language — including Microsoft Visual Basic — that supports building ActiveX libraries. You can register the following file types:

◆ Type libraries with extensions *.olb, *.tlb, *.dll

◆ Executable files with extensions *.exe, *.dll

◆ ActiveX controls with extensions *.ocx

We'll build a calculated member in the measures dimension named Price which is derived from Amount / Sh Num. To create this member, follow these steps:

1. Right-click the Investments cube in the OLAP Manager Tree view and select Edit to display the Cube Editor.

2. In the Cube Editor, right-click the Calculated Members node and select New Calculated Member from the shortcut menu. This will display the Calculated Member Builder shown in Figure 3-29.

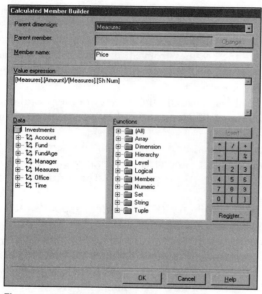

Figure 3-29: The Calculated Member Builder used to create the Price Calculated Member

3. In the Parent Dimension: drop-down list, select Measures. This is the dimension that will include the calculated member. Because we are adding a calculated measure, we select Measures from this list.

4. In the Member Name: text box, enter **Price**.

5. Expand the Measures node in the Data tree and drag the Amount node into the Value Expression text box and drop it.

6. Next, enter a / at the end of [Measures].[Amount] or click the / operator button.

7. Drag Sh Num from the Data tree and drop it after the / operator.

Because we are building a measure calculated member we do not use the Parent Member textbox. The Parent Member text box is used to specify a member within a multi-level dimension. If, for example, we were building a calculated member for the Office dimension, we could have specified the Region, Accounting, or Business level as a parent for the calculated member.

That's all we need for this calculated member expression. Before you leave the Calculated Member Builder, expand some of the Function nodes to see which functions are available to you for defining calculated members in your own cubes. When you are ready, click the OK button to close the Builder. Choose Save from the File menu in the Cube Editor to save your work and then exit the Editor to return to the OLAP Manager.

When you browse the Investments cube now, you will see another measure in the grid named Price displaying the quotient of Amount and Sh Num.

Summary

This chapter has given us an introductory tour of the OLAP Manager management console snap-in and guided you through the steps to build your first OLAP cube. The OLAP Manager offers a number of wizards to help make the job of building and maintaining cubes easier. Some of these wizards were introduced in this chapter. We started off using the Cube Wizard to guide us through the steps of defining the dimensions and fact table for the Investments cube. This wizard was also used to populate the cube with data from the data warehouse. We used the Dimension Wizard to define the dimensions for the cube. We learned about private dimensions defined for use only in a specific cube, and shared dimensions that can be used across multiple cubes. We saw that a cube can use ordinary dimensions, based on data warehouse dimension tables, and virtual dimensions based on member properties of shared dimensions.

The Storage Design Wizard is used to choose the mode of storage we want to use for the cube and to define the aggregations the cube will store. The design of aggregations is based on a trade-off between storage and performance, and the Storage Design Wizard gives us options for balancing this trade-off.

We used the Virtual Dimension Wizard to create a virtual dimension named FundAge. This dimension is based on the fund_age column in the Fund dimension table and was defined as a member property of that dimension. We learned that this dimension doesn't require any storage space in the cube because aggregations under this dimension are calculated at the time they are queried.

We used the Cube Browser to view the outcome of our work with the Investments cube. We saw how the dimensions can be organized to view the aggregations as needed and how to use the Browser to answer specific questions about the data. And finally, we learned about calculated members and created a member in the measures dimension named Price which was expressed as Amount divided by Sh Num. Calculated members can be defined for both measures and ordinary dimensions and are assigned to member levels in a dimension.

Now that we have defined a cube and populated it with data from the data warehouse, we need to address the issues of how to maintain the data in the cube. What happens to cube data when the data in the data warehouse changes? How do we reflect these changes in our cube? These are the issues we'll discuss next in Chapter 4.

Chapter 4

Maintaining OLAP Data

IN THIS CHAPTER

♦ Establishing referential integrity and indexes in the data warehouse

♦ Reviewing the OLAP partition storage modes

♦ Developing a maintenance plan to keep your cubes in synchronization with the data warehouse

♦ Learning the differences between an incremental update, a refresh, and a complete process

♦ Seeing how shared dimensions can be processed separately from the rest of the cube

SO FAR WE'VE EXPLORED the transition of data from our sample OLTP database, FundAccts, into our sample data warehouse, FundAcctsWH, and finally into our OLAP Investments cube.

As you've seen throughout this journey and perhaps from your own experience in working with data warehouses, there are a great number of issues and considerations to be dealt with when building and operating a data warehouse.

This chapter will focus on one of those issues and discuss methods you might use to deal with this issue. The issue we will address here is how to maintain the data in your data warehouse and in particular your OLAP Services cubes.

Considering the Warehouse Data

We spent some time in Chapters 1 and 2 discussing the architecture of the data warehouse and its derivation from the OLTP database. We also explored the movement of data into the data warehouse from various sources. In real life, there's a good chance you will have to deal with many sources for the warehouse data, whereas in our sample world, we only consider the FundAccts database and a few text files.

What we didn't spend much time on in previous chapters was the integrity of the data we are loading. The "V" in VEST, an acronym introduced in Chapter 1, stands for verification of the data. This means that data destined for the data warehouse and possibly for OLAP cubes needs to be verified to ensure that it correctly states its intended purpose, is reasonable within its domain, and is valid as to technical and business rules.

Verifying Referential Integrity

An important verification step for the star and snowflake schemata is to verify the referential integrity between the foreign keys in the fact table and the primary keys of the dimension tables they reference. It is important for the reasons that follow and because OLAP Services will not verify referential integrity when loading cubes.

In considering the cube that will be loaded from the star schema, such as our Investments cube, two important conditions involving referential integrity could cause problems for us. One is a missing entry in a dimension table for a particular foreign key in the fact table. The other is a missing entry in the fact table for a primary key in a dimension table. A fact table foreign key unmatched in a dimension table will cause the fact table row to be eliminated from processing by OLAP Services. Expected results involving a join under this condition will certainly fall short. Processing of the cube under this condition will most likely fail.

When a primary key in a dimension table is unmatched in a fact table, an empty cell can result in the cube, which in turn can cause erroneous results in analysis against the cube and possibly errors in calculated members.

Ensuring Proper Indexes

After creating the warehouse fact tables and dimension tables, create indexes on both tables so that OLAP Services can access these tables efficiently. The fact tables should have an index on the composite key made up of each of the dimension table foreign keys. Each of the dimension tables should contain a primary key index on the key of the dimension that is referenced by a foreign key in the fact table.

When using ROLAP or HOLAP storage modes, you should also place indexes on the dimension table keys. Using SQL Server's Index Tuning Wizard is a quick and easy method of ensuring that proper indexes are created.

These issues must be carefully considered in order to provide an update strategy that will yield consistent and complete OLAP structures. Additionally, as you will learn in this chapter, you must understand and choose the appropriate update method to keep your OLAP cubes in synchronization with the data warehouse.

A Review of OLAP Storage

Before we get into the discussion of updating cubes, it will help to review the storage modes for cubes that were presented in Chapter 1. Understanding how OLAP Services stores data will help you in determining which update methods you need to apply for various change scenarios in warehouse data.

Dimension Storage

Cube dimension data is stored in structures separate from the aggregations and fact data detail. This is always true no matter what the selected storage mode is. You can see these dimension files, under the Data folder, in the folder named for the OLAP database, the FundAcctSample folder for example. This dimension data storage being separate from the relational dimension tables implies that changes in the relational dimension tables need to be carefully managed with respect to the dimension structures. We'll discuss this further a little later in this chapter.

Aggregation Storage

Cube aggregations are stored in one or more partitions you define. There is always at least one default partition for a cube. Each partition uses one of the three storage modes, and it may be different from the modes of the other partitions. Cube data might be filtered to store a subset of the data in each partition. For the Investments cube, we might choose to partition by office or by time, storing a subset of the Office or Time dimension in one partition and a nonoverlapping subset in another partition. The partitioning filter decision will depend on business use of the cube, timing of updates, and data volume, to name a few possible factors. By default, one partition is created per cube. Users can define more if they feel this will be appropriate.

MOLAP (Multidimensional OLAP)	Partition stores all fact data detail and aggregations in its own file structure. The warehouse database is not accessed to answer queries against a MOLAP partition.
ROLAP (Relational OLAP)	Partition uses relational tables in the warehouse to store the aggregations. The fact table details remain in the warehouse fact table.
HOLAP (Hybrid OLAP)	Partition uses a MOLAP structure to store aggregations but leaves the fact table details in the warehouse fact table as a ROLAP partition does.

As you can see from these descriptions, changes in the warehouse fact table may or may not impact queries, depending on the storage mode chosen. With MOLAP, warehouse changes have no effect on queries until the MOLAP cube is reprocessed. With ROLAP and HOLAP, however, some queries requiring access to fact table detail will produce erroneous results until the warehouse fact table is synchronized with the cube partition. This risk is due to the aggregations in the cube aggregation tables not being synchronized with the warehouse fact table details.

Armed with this knowledge of OLAP storage modes, you can now develop a maintenance plan that will ensure that OLAP queries produce correct results.

Developing a Maintenance Plan

Your plan for updating the warehouse and its associated cubes should result from careful examination of various change scenarios in your organization. Together with your business user community, assemble a set of change scenarios that fully represent all change activity the warehouse will need to deal with.

For each scenario you identify, evaluate the impact of the change on your OLAP structures and especially on user queries and the business process using the warehouse. Let's look at an example.

A Sample Change Scenario

In our sample money management firm, account managers from time to time will move to other offices and take on responsibility for new clients and their portfolios. One scenario might be that manager 2321 (Porter Folio) in the Connecticut office, managing client 1 and client 2 portfolios, transfers to the New York office and picks up the clients, clients 56 and 57, of retiring manager 2877 (Bill Yields). Meanwhile, a new account manager, 2001 (Barbra Banks), joins the firm reporting to the Connecticut office and is assigned the client 1 and client 2 accounts.

- ◆ What is the impact on our Investments cube under this scenario?

- ◆ Should we change aggregations in the Investments cube such that client 1 and client 2 amounts are reflected under the New York office, or should they remain under the Connecticut office?

- ◆ Do the amounts in the cube under manager 2877 get transferred to manager 2321?

- ◆ Do the amounts in the cube under manager 2321 get transferred to manager 2001?

- ◆ At what point should changes in the OLTP database be reflected in the data warehouse and in cubes built from the warehouse data?

The answers may seem obvious, especially for an OLTP database where we are concerned with keeping the data as up to date as we can get it. But what about our historical snapshot stored in the warehouse? Should that reflect the "now" picture or the "then" picture? At what time, if any, does the picture change for the warehouse?

It is possible that the management of the firm wants to keep history as history. By that I mean that if a given amount is reported under the Connecticut office at a point in the past, say Quarter 1 of 1997, then that amount should *always* be reported unless it is in error. Historical transactions remain historical.

On the other hand, management could decide that changes in the OLTP database should be reflected in the warehouse and cubes at the time of the next scheduled warehouse update, thereby changing history to represent the current view of the business. By doing this, of course, we lose the historical view of the firm in the warehouse and its cubes.

Handling Changes in the Sample Data Warehouse

By close inspection of our sample warehouse design, you can see what the management decision was on this question. Our FundAcctsWH database has no provision for tracking account manager movement among offices and no provision for tracking client movement among states. We can only handle the current view of the business. The Investments table is the only object in the database capable of storing historical data, and that table is used for tracking changes to client portfolios.

To ignore manager and client movement altogether and only deal with new amounts becomes very complex and costly to implement and runs the risk of duplicate data reported in the warehouse cubes. We therefore have only one viable option with this design and that is to take whatever situation is found in the OLTP database and apply it to our warehouse database and cubes when updates are processed.

The questions must always be answered in the context of the business use of the warehouse and the cubes built from it. The answers will impact the timing of the update and the methodology we use to perform the update to the cubes in the warehouse. We must also consider the *types* of changes to be processed when selecting an update methodology. Let's look a little closer at the preceding scenario.

The assignment of the client 1 and client 2 accounts to manager 2001 in the Connecticut office does not impact the Investments cube aggregations for the Connecticut Office dimension member. The aggregations for the Manager dimension will change, however. The aggregations under manager 2321 will go down by the client 1 and client 2 amounts, while the new manager for these accounts will see an increase in aggregations. The account aggregations are not impacted under this scenario, because the clients have not moved to a new state.

Considering only the client 1 and client 2 accounts, we have a change in the Manager dimension aggregations for manager 2321 and a new Manager dimension member to be added to the cube for manager 2001. The Investments fact table, the Managers dimension table, the cube aggregation tables, and the cube Manager dimension table must all be updated.

So we know from this discussion that these changes should be applied to the warehouse and to the Investments cube to reflect the current view of the business. We know too what the impact on the aggregations in the cube is. The next questions are "When do we make the changes?" and "How do we make the changes?"

Processing Cube Updates

When we initially built the Investments cube with the OLAP Manager in Chapter 3, we executed a step called *Process the cube*. This step followed the storage design phase and involved processing the cube definitions, creating aggregation tables as well as dimension tables, and calculating and storing the cube aggregations with data extracted from the data warehouse.

This processing is one of three types of cube updating that OLAP Services supports. The *complete process* required for new cubes and certain data changes is the most time-consuming of the three. The other two update methods are named *incremental update* and *cube refresh*. A summary of these update methods and the data events that prompt their use is outlined in Table 4-1.

The Microsoft update method wizards use the term *process* to mean a complete rebuild of the cube including the processing of cube dimensions. In this book, I will use the term *complete process* for this method to provide a more descriptive indication of what the method does. You may find other documentation refer to this process as *full process*, especially in Decision Support Object documentation. Complete process and full process mean the same thing.

Whenever the structure of a cube changes, such as from adding a new ordinary dimension, the entire cube must be rebuilt by complete processing of the cube.

The timing of complete processing must be synchronized with user requirements for the cube data because the user session with OLAP server will be disconnected when processing is complete and the new cube is brought online to replace the original cube.

Once the cube is created, it is likely that complete processing will not be required often. Updates to data warehouse fact data will usually be handled by either the refresh method or the incremental update method. Timing of these updates is less of an issue than for the complete processing of a cube, but for large cubes, it is still an issue to be carefully addressed.

TABLE 4-1 UPDATE METHODS

Data Event	Update Method	User Impact
New data for existing dimension members; changes (+/–) to existing data (but refresh is better choice); no change in cube structure.	Incremental update	Users may query the cube while update runs; new data is accessible after update completes; no reconnect to OLAP server required.

Data Event	Update Method	User Impact
Existing data changed (such as rewriting history). Incremental update can handle this if source transactions are structured properly (see text); no change in cube structure; facts move from one dimension member to another.	Refresh	Users may query the cube while update runs; updated data is accessible after refresh completes; no reconnect to OLAP server required.
New cube; structure change in dimensions or measures (includes adding or removing a dimension); new members added/removed to/from a dimension.	Complete process	Users may query the cube while update runs; users are disconnected when update is complete and must reconnect to access changed cube.
Shared dimension structure changes such as a change in the fund dimension hierarchy; a level is added or deleted.	Rebuild the dimension structure	Applies to shared dimensions; all cubes using the dimension will be unavailable to users until the update is completed and the cubes using the dimensions are processed with complete process.

The last entry in Table 4-1 is one of two methods available for processing shared dimension changes. The *rebuild the dimension structure* method is used when either relationship changes have occurred between the levels of a dimension or a hierarchy is created or altered by adding or deleting a level. If the Office dimension were a shared dimension and we were to remove the accounting office level in the Office dimension, for example, we would need to use the rebuild method to process the change.

The other dimension update method is *incremental update,* which can be used to add new members to existing levels in a shared dimension.

Running an Incremental Update

The Chapter04 folder on the CD contains a script that will apply the necessary updates to the FundAcctsWH database for the scenario discussed in the earlier section "Developing a Maintenance Plan." The script file is named Ch04Transfer.sql.

This script will:

1. Insert manager 2001 into the Managers table.

2. Update the Investments table, replacing manager 2321 entries with manager 2001.

3. Update the Investments table, replacing manager 2877 entries with manager 2321.

4. Delete manager 2877 from the Managers table.

Before you run the incremental update, use the Cube Browser in OLAP Manager to view the aggregations for manager Folio and manager Yields. These amounts are shown in Figures 4-1 and 4-2.

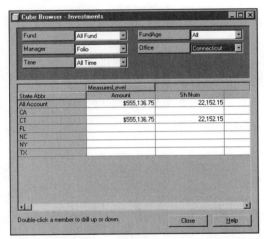

Figure 4-1: The amounts in the Investments cube for manager folio prior to transfer

You'll need these amounts to check your cube updates. After running the incremental update, we expect to see the cube reflect the original values shown in Figures 4-1 and 4-2 plus the changes we will apply to the Investments fact table. Now run the Ch04Transfer.sql script to update the warehouse.

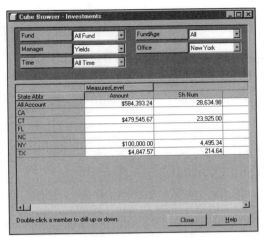

Figure 4-2: The amounts in the Investments cube for manager yields prior to transfer

 In the Ch04Transfer.sql file, you'll find that manager 2001 is given the name Barbra Banks. Try changing this name to Barbra Price. You'll discover that, after you update your cube with this Price Manager dimension member, your calculated member named Price no longer displays. Attempting to edit this calculated member will result in an error informing you that the member cannot be calculated. The reason is a SQL statement conflict between the Price manager member and the Price calculated member. A way to stay away from these conflicts when names are used in dimension members is to choose a unique naming scheme for your calculated members. You can see further evidence of conflicts by attempting to create a calculated member and name it Folio, the name of our sample manager. Again the error arises.

Inspection of Table 4-1 indicates that we need to run a complete process in order to realize both the fact table changes and the Manager dimension member addition and deletion.

To illustrate what happens under this scenario using the incremental update and refresh methods, we'll postpone the complete process for a moment and experiment with these other methods. Please realize that the incremental update we are about to run will yield results in the cube that are severely out of synchronization with the warehouse fact table. We are running this update to learn a few things about what it does and to learn what to watch out for when using this method.

INCREMENTAL UPDATE PROCEDURE

Run the incremental update using the following steps:

1. Right-click the Investments cube in the OLAP Manager tree view and select Process from the popup menu.

2. Choose the Incremental update option in the Process a cube dialog. Click OK.

3. The Data Source screen suggests the FundAcctsWH database and Investments fact table. Accept this source by clicking Next.

4. On the Create a Filter expression screen, you would ordinarily enter an expression here to update the cube fact table with selective data. You might use "Investments"."manager_num" = 2321 or some similar expression specified in terms of the fact table columns. This filter causes the update to process only this subset of the fact table. If we attempt to use "Investments"."manager_num" = 2001 here, the update will run but fail on the merge step because this new Manager dimension member is not processed by the incremental update and therefore not known. An attempt to merge the updates into the cube fails because we have a missing primary key in the cube's Manager dimension table for the 2001 foreign key in the cube's fact table.

5. Leave the Filter expression screen blank for now and click Next.

6. On the *Finish the Incremental Update Wizard* screen, click Finish to start the update. You'll see the Progress window record the steps as they occur.

WHAT THE INCREMENTAL UPDATE DOES

When the incremental update completes, browse through the SQL statements to see what the incremental update did. Here's a synopsis of how this method works.

Note that there is no clearing of the cube's aggregation tables. This update method is going to apply updates to what is already in the cube.

The aggregation steps select from the fact table specified in the wizard and insert results into a special update table created for this purpose. These tables will be used for the merge steps that follow.

The aggregations are joining the fact table rows to the warehouse dimension tables and applying the filter expression, if there is one, to the WHERE clause to select only this subset from the fact table.

Think about this aggregation step for a moment. It is reading the source fact table and selecting every row where equi-joins are true and the filter expression is true. Since we have no filter expression, all rows are considered. Right here you can see that we are headed for trouble. We're selecting rows and calculating aggregations for keys that are already present in the cube aggregation tables. We would expect that these aggregations will be merged into those already present in the cube and inflate the results. Let's continue.

The merge steps read the special update tables and do two things with them. First, any aggregate row in the update table that matches keys in the cube aggregation tables will result in the update aggregation being *added* to the aggregation already present in the cube aggregation table.

Second, a merge step does a left outer join between the update table and the cube aggregation table and inserts update aggregations where there is no matching key in the cube aggregation table.

To summarize the merge step, the update aggregations that match cube aggregation table keys are *added* to the data already in the cube and those that don't match are *inserted* into the cube. When you're done looking at the process results, dismiss the Process progress window and right-click the Investments cube to select Browse Data.

EXAMINING THE RESULTS

Select Folio in the Manager dimension and Connecticut in the Office dimension. We see that the original aggregations are still there even though we replaced 2321 (Folio) with 2001 (Banks). The incremental update didn't touch this aggregation in the cube.

Select Yields in the Manager dimension and All Offices in the Office dimension. Here again we still see the original aggregations for 2877 (Yields) even though we replaced these fact table rows with manager 2321. Note also that we removed manager 2877 from the warehouse Managers dimension table, yet he still shows up in the Cube dimension table.

Select Folio again in the Managers dimension and leave the Office dimension All Offices. Here you see basically the same results that Yields is showing. This is due to the new keys for Folio, a result of the transfer from Yields to Folio in the Investments fact table, being inserted into the cube aggregation tables by the incremental update merge steps. The result is a duplication of aggregations. Folio is showing the same aggregations as Yields plus Folio's original aggregations that are now under Banks in the fact table.

RECOVERING FROM THE INCREMENTAL UPDATE

Do we know what happened? It is exactly as we expected. The cube is inflated and out of synchronization with the warehouse fact table.

This is obviously not the outcome we are looking for. We now need to recover from this problem and get the correct results into the cube. To do this, we can run the refresh method, which we'll do in the next section. This will clear the cube aggregation tables, read the Investments fact table, calculate new aggregations, and insert them into the cube.

The refresh will get us the correct aggregations but not the correct overall results, because the issue of our new manager 2001 (Banks), added to the warehouse Managers dimension table, is not dealt with by the refresh method. More on this later.

How can we apply incremental updates safely without inflating the cube? We create a table with the same schema as the warehouse Investments fact table and apply to it all incremental update transactions destined for the fact table and cube. Use this table as the source for the incremental update. The sample warehouse database contains a table for this purpose named *InvestUpdate.*

Any new incremental update transaction from warehouse sources, our OLTP system for example, will be collected into the InvestUpdate table and applied to the fact table and cube on the update schedule.

When we run this update, we'll apply the InvestUpdate changes to the fact table and specify the InvestUpdate table as the source for the incremental update instead of the Investments fact table as we did before.

Doing this, we do not need a filter expression unless we want to apply a subset of the InvestUpdate table. Using the InvestUpdate table as the source for our incremental update will guarantee that we only apply changes and not aggregations already in the cube as we experienced in the earlier exercise. This technique works for new keys and existing keys and can be used safely. Be sure to clear the InvestUpdate table after applying the updates and before accepting new transactions.

 The special update tables created by the incremental update for merging are not deleted after the update completes. This can be good in that you can see what aggregations were created, but it also takes up space in the warehouse database that could be used for other purposes between scheduled updates. You may want to consider a DTS task to delete the rows in this table.

Running the Refresh Method

The refresh update method is a little less complicated than the incremental update. In refresh, the cube is first cleared of all aggregations by dropping the aggregation tables to prepare for the insertion of new aggregations.

The second refresh step calculates the new aggregations from the warehouse fact table and inserts them directly into the cube's aggregation tables. This method does not use temporary update tables as the incremental update does, because no merge step is done by the refresh method.

RUNNING THE REFRESH PROCEDURE

1. Right-click the Investments cube in the OLAP Manager tree view and select Process from the popup menu.

2. In the Process a Cube dialog, select the Refresh data option and then click OK.

3. The refresh method starts immediately, and you see the Process progress window displayed.

When the refresh completes, you can browse through the progress window and inspect the SQL statements used in the method. All steps after the drop table steps are inserts of aggregated data selected from the fact table. These inserts recreate the aggregation tables.

EXAMINING THE RESULTS

1. When you have finished viewing the SQL statements in the progress window, close the window and open the Cube Browser.

2. Select Folio in the Manager dimension. You'll see that he has the aggregations previously displayed for Yields. Now for the big test. Select Yields from the Manager dimension. There should be no aggregations at all for Yields.

Because the aggregation tables were dropped and recreated, the refresh process method inserts into the new aggregation tables whatever it finds in the fact table. In the case of our scenario, it found 2321 (Folio) with data previously under 2877 (Yields). Since we transferred this data, it did not find any data for 2877 and therefore the empty cells for this manager in the cube.

Other cube data is normal, no duplication and no inflation. There is still a problem, however. Notice here, as in the incremental update, that we are still able to select Yields in the cube's Manager dimension table even though he is no longer in the warehouse Managers dimension table. We don't see manager Banks in the cube's Manager dimension table either even though this manager was inserted into the warehouse Managers dimension table.

Refresh does not process cube dimensions. It only uses whatever dimension members it had before the refresh took place.

Running the Complete Process

We're finally ready to solve all of our problems involving this change scenario by running the complete process method. This will drop the entire cube, aggregations and dimensions, and rebuild it using the warehouse fact and dimension tables.

In doing this, we get the current state of the warehouse reflected in our Investments cube. Cube aggregations are in synchronization with the fact table, and cube dimensions are in synchronization with the warehouse dimension tables and with the fact table. Exactly what we want.

EXECUTING THE COMPLETE PROCESS

1. Right-click the Investments cube in the OLAP Manager tree view and select Process from the popup menu.

2. Select the Process option in the Process a Cube dialog and click OK.

3. The complete process starts immediately, and you see the Progress window displayed. When the process is completed, examine the SQL statements in the process steps. You'll notice that the entire cube is being rebuilt.

   Now you can open the Cube Browser and view Folio as you saw him after the cube refresh process, but unlike after the refresh, you don't see Yields in the Manager dimension members and you do see Banks.

4. Select Banks and verify that she has the aggregations previously held by Folio.

The complete processing has solved our problem. In this sample world, it was no trouble waiting a few minutes for this process to rebuild the cube. But in the real world, you may have to wait hours for this process, depending on the size of your cube.

Fortunately, you shouldn't have to do this often, because structure changes should be rare and new dimension members should also be rare. With some exceptions, dimensions are static entities in the warehouse design.

TIP   This leaves you with doing either incremental update or refresh processing much of the time. To make your life less stressful, take time to understand the change events in your application, be prepared to run the proper update method to handle those change events, and always check the results after completing the updates.

Updating Shared Dimensions

An alternative to completely processing the entire cube in change event scenarios such as the one we've been discussing is to define your dimensions as *shared dimensions*. Shared dimensions can be processed separately from the cube aggregation tables to enable member changes without the need to rebuild the complete cube, given that rebuilding may not be viable with large cubes.

Shared dimensions can be processed by rebuilding and by incremental update. To initiate dimension processing, right-click a shared dimension in the OLAP Manager tree view and choose Process from the popup menu.

When the structure of a shared dimension changes or the relationship between levels changes, you'll need to run a complete rebuild of the dimension. While this takes place, all cubes using the dimension will be unavailable to users until the update completes and the cube itself is processed to calculate new dimension paths and aggregations.

If only new members are added to the dimension, you can elect to incrementally update the dimension. Deleted members, such as our deletion of manager 2877 (Yields), are not processed by the incremental update.

Users may still query the cube while an incremental update runs against the dimension, and changes to the dimension become visible after the update completes.

In our scenario, defining a Manager dimension as a shared dimension would have helped. We could have processed the dimension with an incremental update and then refreshed the cube to pick up the other changes. The only problem left behind to address in this case would be that Yields is still resident as a manager member. Complete processing of either the cube, as we have done, or of the Manager dimension had it been shared, would solve the problem completely.

You may want to consider using shared dimensions for a cube because of this update capability, especially for dimensions that are identified as potential change event targets.

Checking Update Results

Once the update processing is completed, you'll need to run a few queries to check the results. For each change scenario identified in your analysis, or at least for each update method used, build one or more queries to verify synchronization between the data warehouse and the cubes.

These queries should at least spot-check the database and cubes to ensure correct results from the update processing. Some applications may require you to completely balance the warehouse before bringing it online. Run GROUP BY, CUBE, and ROLLUP queries on the data warehouse and compare the result sets with the same aggregations from queries run against the updated cubes in the Cube Browser or a custom application.

Custom queries for this purpose can be built using Decision Support Objects introduced in Chapter 5 or by using the PivotTable Service introduced in Chapter 6.

While processing cubes, you should ensure that no structure changes in the data warehouse are allowed to take place.

Summary

In this chapter, we've explored the handling of change events in the data warehouse. Changes in the warehouse source systems are inevitable. The manner in which these changes are brought into the data warehouse and the timing of the updates are critical to maintaining correct data for end-user analysis.

You learned that you should always include a phase in the analysis and design of data warehouses for identifying and evaluating change scenarios and how you will react to those changes to effect warehouse and cube updates. Each change event must be carefully studied to ensure you choose the proper update method and that cubes will remain in synchronization with the warehouse source tables.

Each of the update methods was explored to illustrate what can happen if the wrong update method is used on a cube and how we can recover from these errors.

The idea of using shared dimensions was discussed for dimensions that may be updated from time to time with new members. Shared dimensions can be processed separately from the cube aggregations to bring changes online quicker than with complete processing of the cube.

Chapter 5

Introduction to Decision Support Objects

IN THIS CHAPTER

- ◆ Learning what the Decision Support Object (DSO) model has to offer
- ◆ Previewing how to use the DSO model in your OLAP applications
- ◆ Exploring the DSO Interfaces and the classes that support them
- ◆ Looking at the DSO objects that are directly accessed
- ◆ Exploring the enumerations supported by DSO

WHEN THE REQUIREMENT arises to build an application that needs to access or control the OLAP server and to work with OLAP data stores, the Decision Support Object model is the technology you'll use.

Every function that we explored in Chapter 3, in using the OLAP Manager, can be supported by your own application using the DSO. This chapter will provide an overview of the DSO object model, introduce its components and their roles in the model, and discuss the properties of those classes.

In Chapter 8, we'll be exploring some of the objects, interfaces, methods, and properties of the model from a coding perspective in preparation for Chapter 12, where we'll build an application using DSO.

In addition to this overview, we'll learn about the repository that DSO uses to store OLAP metadata, the information that describes your OLAP stores.

You'll find the terms and language of OLAP Services that were introduced in Chapter 1 come to light here as we explore the object model. You'll see database objects, cube objects, dimension objects, and aggregations, to name a few. All of these are terms we've seen and worked with in previous chapters.

In fact, probably the best indication of the DSO object model and its hierarchy of objects and collections is found in the OLAP Manager tree view we used in Chapters 3 and 4. The objects you saw there and the functionality offered by the OLAP Manager menus are a good indication of the power that awaits you in this object model.

Object Model Overview

You have undoubtedly worked with component object models (COM) before in your programming experience. If you have worked with Microsoft Access databases, you most likely know about Data Access Objects (DAO). You know about the DBEngine, the database object and collection, the workspace object and collection, tabledefs, tables, querydefs, and so on. All of these objects offer properties and methods in the true spirit of objects that enable your application to access and manipulate Jet databases and to some extent SQL Server databases.

In regard to COM models, the Decision Support Object model is no different than DAO, OLE DB, ADO, or any other COM programming model. It obviously contains a different set of objects and collections than other models, but it remains within the well-known and comfortable framework of any COM model exposing collections, objects, properties, and methods. Throughout this book, we'll be using Microsoft Visual Basic 6.0 (with service pack 3) to illustrate DSO principles and to build DSO application samples.

A high-level view of the DSO is shown in Figure 5-1. As you see in this figure, the objects are quite familiar.

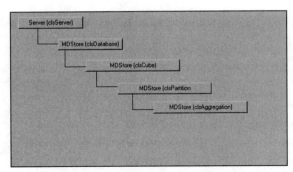

Figure 5-1: A high-level view of the Decision Support Object Model

The top node is the OLAP server object that we must establish a connection to in order to do our work. Beneath the server object is an OLAP database consisting of a physical cube and optionally a virtual cube, a view of other cubes in the database. A cube contains a collection of one or more partitions, each of which stores a set of aggregations. A container collection in DSO named *MDStores* holds references to each of the objects in this hierarchy. This container provides methods that enable you to add (*AddNew* method) and delete (*Remove* method) object members in the collection as well as locate (*Find* method) specific members. Each member object in the MDStores collection has a *ClassType* property that identifies the class from which the object was created.

The MDStores collection in the server object is a collection of database objects of ClassType *clsDatabase*. A database object holds an MDStores collection containing cube objects of ClassType *clsCube*. The MDStores collection of the cube object holds objects of type *clsPartition*, and the partition's MDStores collection holds *clsAggregation* ClassType objects.

The MDStores collection itself has a property named *ContainedClassType*, which indicates the type of objects contained in its collection. If this property is clsDatabase, then all object members in the MDStores collection are of ClassType clsDatabase.

Each of the objects in the hierarchy shown in Figure 5-1 implements an interface named *MDStore*. This interface is your gateway to the methods and properties offered by these objects.

The MDStore Interface

The MDStore interface is one of six interfaces supported among DSO objects. Table 5-1 lists these interfaces and the DSO objects that support them.

TABLE 5-1 DECISION SUPPORT OBJECT INTERFACES

Interface	Objects Implementing Interface
Command	clsCubeCommand clsDatabaseCommand
Dimension	clsAggregationDimension clsCubeDimension clsDatabaseDimension clsPartitionDimension
Level	clsAggregationLevel clsCubeLevel clsDatabaseLevel clsPartitionLevel
MDStore	clsAggregation clsCube clsDatabase clsPartition
Measure	clsAggregationMeasure clsCubeMeasure clsPartitionMeasure
Role	clsCubeRole clsDatabaseRole

When you use the DSO objects listed in Table 5-1 in a Visual Basic program, you declare a variable as the interface type, not the object type.

If we were to create a cube object in a database, for example, we would start with the following code:

```
Dim dsoMyCube As MDStore
. . .
Set dsoMyCube = dsoMyDatabase.MDStores.AddNew("ExampleCube")
```

Notice that we are declaring the dsoMyCube object variable as type MDStore, an interface data type. The code snippet assumes that a database object variable named dsoMyDatabase, another MDStore variable of ClassType clsDatabase, has already been declared and set by adding it to the MDStores collection of a clsServer object.

The MDStores collection in a clsDatabase object contains objects of ClassType clsCube. The ContainedClassType property of the clsDatabase MDStores collection would contain a value of clsCube. So we are guaranteed that an object added to this collection with its *AddNew* method will result in a clsCube object. This object reference is returned by AddNew and assigned into dsoMyCube. The program accesses the clsCube object through the MDStore interface.

We can now manipulate all properties, methods, and collections of clsCube using this dsoMyCube interface reference. For all intents and purposes, you may think of dsoMyCube as a clsCube object. It is an object that implements MDStore. Not all properties exposed by MDStore are implemented by all classes supporting MDStore. For a list of properties and their supporting classes, see Table 5-2.

Before coding DSO objects in a Visual Basic project, choose References from the Project menu and set a reference to <installation drive>\OLAP Services\Bin\ MSMDDO.DLL. This is the DSO in-process server DLL. After adding this reference, open the Object Browser and select DSO from the Library list.

You'll notice classes in the Classes list such as Cube, Database, Aggregation, and Partition. Selecting these classes displays nothing in the Members list box. Do not use these classes in your application. Use the MDStore interface class instead.

With the preceding reference set in a Visual Basic project, we can now write code such as the following:

```
Dim n As Integer
Dim dsoDatabase As MDStore

' Connect to the OLAP Server and set variable of type DSO.Server
MakeServerConnection
```

```
' Enumerate the databases known to the server and add their
' names to List1 list box
If Not mdsoServer Is Nothing Then
    For n = 1 To mdsoServer.MDStores.Count
        Set dsoDatabase = mdsoServer.MDStores(n)
        List1.AddItem dsoDatabase.Name
    Next n
End If
```

 The code examples in this chapter can be found in the Ch05 directory on the CD that accompanies this book. Open the Ch5.vbp Visual Basic project to review the code.

In the preceding code, we dimension a variable named dsoDatabase as an MDStore interface. We will use this variable as a reference to an object of ClassType clsDatabase. As the preceding caution states, we are *not* using DSO.Database as the type for the dsoDatabase variable.

The *MakeServerConnection* subroutine is defined as:

```
Public mdsoServer As DSO.Server

Dim dsoServer As DSO.Server
Set dsoServer = New DSO.Server

' Connect to OLAP server by setting the Connect property of the
' DSO.Server object equal to the name of the server entered by user
On Error GoTo MakeServerConnection_ErrHandler
dsoServer.Connect Me.txtServerName
' Save the reference to the server object
Set mdsoServer = dsoServer

...
```

After acquiring a connection to the server, the code loops through the items of the server's MDStores collection. As each item in the collection is visited, the dsoDatabase variable is set to reference the current database object in the collection.

Using the dsoDatabase reference, the code accesses the database *Name* property and adds it to a list box. If you run this code on a machine where OLAP Services has just been installed, you should see the FoodMart sample database that ships with SQL Server 7.0 displayed in the list. If you connect to the server where we created the FundAcctSample database in Chapter 3, you'll see this database name in addition to the FoodMart database.

TABLE 5-2 PROPERTIES OF MDSTORE INTERFACE CLASSES

Property	Supported by All Classes Except	Description
AggregationPrefix		Prefix for the MDStore aggregation
Analyzer	ClsAggregation clsDatabase	References the Analyzer object for the store
ClassType		Identifies the type of class
Description		Describes the store
EstimatedRows	ClsDatabase	Estimates of number of rows in the store
FromClause	ClsDatabase	SQL FROM clause for the MDStore object
IsDefault	ClsCube clsDatabase	Indicates if the store is the default store
IsReadWrite	ClsAggregation	Indicates if store is writable
IsTemporary	ClsDatabase	Indicates a temporary object
IsValid		Indicates a valid object
JoinClause	ClsDatabase	SQL JOIN clause for the MDStore object
LastProcessed		The date/time when the store was last processed
LastUpdated		A date specified by the user
Name		The name of the store
OlapMode		Identifies the storage mode of the store
Parent		The parent store object
Server		The server object reference
SourceTable	ClsDatabase	The source table name
SourceTableFilter	ClsAggregation clsDatabase	A SQL statement that selects records to include in the store
State	ClsAggregation	Indicates the processing state of the object on the server
SubClassType		Identifies the subclass type of the object

The Dimension Interface

As we've seen from our work with the Investments cube, the dimensions of a cube are used to organize and present the fact table information of the cube. When we used the Cube Browser in Chapter 3, we chose certain manager members from the Manager dimension and certain offices from the Office dimension to display investment sums and share sums as they pertain to the chosen manager and office. One example we looked at was the fact table aggregations by account state abbreviation for manager Folio in the New York office.

A dimension may exhibit a hierarchy of members. In the Investments cube, we have a three-level hierarchy in the Office dimension consisting of business offices within accounting offices and accounting offices within regional offices. The Time dimension is another example of a multilevel hierarchy in the Investments cube.

Dimensions are stored as collections within various objects of the DSO hierarchy such as the clsDatabase, clsCube, clsPartition, and clsAggregation objects. An expanded view of the DSO object hierarchy is shown in Figure 5-2.

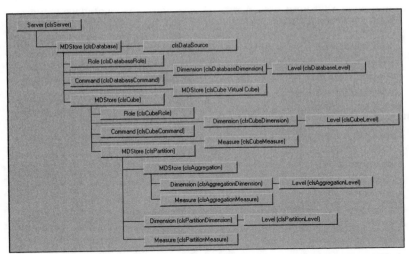

Figure 5–2: An expanded DSO Object Model showing additional interface and class types

A clsDatabase Dimensions collection holds the dimension definitions for the database and the data source for each dimension. In our FundAcctSample OLAP database, for example, inspection of the database object Dimensions collection would yield a *clsDatabaseDimension* object for the Manager dimension with a *SourceTable* property of Managers, another clsDatabaseDimension for Office with SourceTable of Offices, and so on for all dimensions in the database.

A clsCube Dimensions collection holds *clsCubeDimension* objects selected from the clsDatabase dimensions. These dimensions expose certain collections and properties through the Dimension interface but don't support any methods. The properties supported by Dimension interface classes are shown in Table 5-3.

Dimensions in a database may be *private* for use in a single cube or *shared* for use in multiple cubes. A private dimension name will contain the name of the cube it belongs to followed by a caret symbol (^) followed by the name of the dimension. Following this naming scheme, the Name of the Manager dimension in the Investments cube would be Investments^Manager.

Cube data is physically stored in one or more partitions that inherit certain default properties from the cube.

The Investments cube uses one partition at the moment. Each clsPartition object holds its own Dimensions collection containing *clsPartitionDimension* objects. The partition dimensions define the collections and properties of the dimensions within the cube partition and are inherited from the cube dimensions. Here, too, there are no methods supported by the clsPartitionDimension objects.

The aggregations of a partition, clsAggregation objects, contain the fourth Dimensions collection, which holds *clsAggregationDimension* objects. These dimensions are the same as the partition dimensions and describe the granularity or level of aggregation within each aggregation object.

You may have noticed after building the Investments cube in Chapter 3, which uses a ROLAP storage mode, that your FundAcctsWH data warehouse database contains a number of new tables. These tables have names like Investme_Investments1_Q3, Investme_Investments1_98, Investme_Investments1_A8, and so on. There is one table for each of the aggregations designed by the Storage Design Wizard. In the case of Chapter 3, there were 22 aggregations and hence 22 new tables. This count will vary depending on Storage Design Wizard settings and available resources.

These tables are the aggregation tables for the Investments cube. You can open a few of them in SQL Server Enterprise Manager and look at their contents. You'll see that they all have columns representing some combination of our cube dimensions. The schema for the Investme_Investments1_Q3 table in my FundAcctsWH database is shown in Figure 5-3.

Column Name	Datatype	Length	Precision	Scale	Allow Nulls	Default Value	Identity	Ident_
ManagerLastname_L6	varchar	70	0	0	✓			
Region_L8	varchar	50	0	0	✓			
Year_L12	smallint	2	5	0	✓			
Quarter_L13	smallint	2	5	0	✓			
SUM_Amount	money	8	19	4	✓			
SUM_ShNum	float	8	53	0	✓			

Figure 5-3: A table definition for the Investme_Investments1_Q3 aggregation table in the FundAcctsWH database

This aggregation table is storing the aggregations of Amount and Sh_Num by Manager, Regional Office, Year, and Quarter. The dimensions are Manager, Office, and Time. Two levels of the Time dimension hierarchy are used here. That's three out of five dimensions defined for the cube. The other two dimensions, Account and Fund, are not present in the table and are implied to be the (All) level.

Let's see how this table looks at the DSO metadata level. We'll use the following code to iterate through this aggregation and print some properties of the clsAggregationDimension objects contained in the Dimensions collection of this aggregation and some of the *Level* objects in the clsAggregationDimension *Levels* collection.

```
Set dsoDatabase = m_dsoServer.MDStores("FundAcctSample")
Set dsoCube = dsoDatabase.MDStores("Investments")
Set dsoPartition = dsoCube.MDStores(1)
For i = 1 To dsoPartition.MDStores.Count
  Set dsoAggregation = dsoPartition.MDStores(i)
  If dsoAggregation.FromClause = "Investme_Investments1_Q3" Then
      Debug.Print "Aggregation Name: "; dsoAggregation.Name
      Debug.Print "Aggregation Dimensions: "; dsoAggregation.Dimensions.Count
      For k = 1 To dsoAggregation.Dimensions.Count
          Set dsoDimension = dsoAggregation.Dimensions(k)
          Debug.Print "    Dimension Name: "; dsoDimension.Name
          Debug.Print "    Dimension FromClause: "; dsoDimension.FromClause
          For l = 1 To dsoDimension.Levels.Count
              Set dsoLevel = dsoDimension.Levels(l)
              Debug.Print "      Level Name: "; dsoLevel.Name
          Debug.Print "      Level MemberKeyColumn: "; _
              dsoLevel.MemberKeyColumn
          Debug.Print "      Level ColumnSize: "; dsoLevel.ColumnSize
          Next l
      Next k
  End If
Next i
```

The code does not show the connection to the OLAP Server. A For loop is coded to iterate through all of the aggregations in the partition, but for the sake of this discussion, only the aggregation stored in the Investme_Investments1_Q3 table is printed. Remove the *If dsoAggregation.FromClause = "Investme_Investments1_Q3" Then* statement to display this information for all aggregations or at least as much as your immediate window can hold.

The results of running this code look like this:

```
Aggregation Name: 11223
Aggregation Dimensions:  5
    Dimension Name: Fund
```

```
Dimension FromClause: Investme_Investments1_Q3
  Level Name: (All)
  Level MemberKeyColumn: All_L1
  Level ColumnSize:  0
Dimension Name: Investments^Account
Dimension FromClause: Investme_Investments1_Q3
  Level Name: (All)
  Level MemberKeyColumn: All_L3
  Level ColumnSize:  0
Dimension Name: Investments^Manager
Dimension FromClause: Investme_Investments1_Q3
  Level Name: (All)
  Level MemberKeyColumn: All_L5
  Level ColumnSize:  0
  Level Name: Manager Lastname
  Level MemberKeyColumn: ManagerLastname_L6
  Level ColumnSize:  70
Dimension Name: Investments^Office
Dimension FromClause: Investme_Investments1_Q3
  Level Name: (All)
  Level MemberKeyColumn: All_L7
  Level ColumnSize:  0
  Level Name: Region
  Level MemberKeyColumn: Region_L8
  Level ColumnSize:  50
Dimension Name: Investments^Time
Dimension FromClause: Investme_Investments1_Q3
  Level Name: (All)
  Level MemberKeyColumn: All_L11
  Level ColumnSize:  0
  Level Name: Year
  Level MemberKeyColumn: Year_L12
  Level ColumnSize:  10
  Level Name: Quarter
  Level MemberKeyColumn: Quarter_L13
  Level ColumnSize:  4
```

As you can see from the output, the Dimensions collection of this aggregation contains five clsAggregationDimension objects. The Fund dimension and the Investments^Account dimension (notice the naming scheme here for shared and private dimensions) only show the (All) level in their *Levels* collection. These are the implied levels in this aggregation table. The *ColumnSize* property of the (All) level (ColumnSize and ColumnType properties are used only in describing ROLAP stores) is 0, indicating that these (All) columns do not exist.

The other dimensions listed in the results show an (All) level and then at least one other level in addition to the (All) level. These additional levels in the dimension's Levels collection are the columns you see in the table definition shown in Figure 5-3. The Manager dimension, for example, shows a Level with *MemberKeyName* equal to *ManagerLastname_L6,* which is the name of the Manager dimension column in the Investme_Investments1_Q3 table.

A point to remember here when you create a cube using DSO: To ensure that the aggregation you're defining will aggregate to levels below the (All) level, which it does by default, you must add those levels into the Levels collection of the clsAggregationDimension object. Use the preceding results as a guide.

The aggregations representing (All) Managers, (All) Accounts, (All) Offices, (All) Funds, and (All) Time can be derived by selecting the Sum of the measures columns from *any one* of the aggregation tables. This Sum will be the same no matter which table you choose. If the Sum result is different for any one table, your cube has a major problem. To acquire a granularity below this (All)-dimensions level, an appropriate aggregation table must be chosen.

TABLE 5-3 PROPERTIES OF DIMENSION INTERFACE CLASSES

Property	Supported by All Classes Except	Description
AggregationUsage	clsAggregationDimension clsDatabaseDimension	Specifies how aggregations are designed
ClassType		Identifies the type of class
DataSource		The data source of the dimension
Description	clsAggregationDimension	Describes the dimension
DimensionType		Identifies the type of dimension
FromClause		SQL FROM clause for the dimension
IsShared		Indicates shared dimension
IsTemporary		Indicates temporary object
IsValid		Indicates valid dimension structure
JoinClause		SQL JOIN clause for the dimension

Continued

Table 5-3 PROPERTIES OF DIMENSION INTERFACE CLASSES *(Continued)*

Property	Supported by All Classes Except	Description
LastProcessed		The date/time when the dimension was last processed
LastUpdated		A date specified by the user
Name		The name of the dimension
OrdinalPosition		The position of the dimension relative to other dimensions in a collection
Parent		The parent dimension
SourceTable	clsAggregationDimension	The source dimension table name
State	clsCubeDimension clsPartitionDimension	Indicates the status of the dimension
SubClassType		Identifies the subclass type of the object

The Level Interface

As we saw from our exploration of clsAggregationDimensions, dimension objects contain a Levels collection. Each of the Level objects in these collections supports the Level Interface.

Level objects are used to describe a single hierarchy *within* a dimension, not *among* dimensions. All dimensions have at least one level in their hierarchy, and that level is the (All) level. The (All) level is the highest level of granularity within the dimension. Levels below the (All) level provide a finer granularity of aggregation. A multiple-hierarchy dimension is defined by two or more dimensions having the same prefix but different suffixes in the form <prefix name>.<suffix name>. A popular use of this capability is to represent a calendar hierarchy in a dimension named something like Time.Calendar, and a Fiscal hierarchy with the name Time.Fiscal. Each is defined as separate dimension hierarchies but they share the same prefix in their name.

In the Investme_Investments1_Q3 aggregation, the Investment^Time dimension is broken down to three levels. The lowest level represented in this dimension is the Quarter. So for this dimension in this aggregation (clsAggregationDimension), the aggregations for Amount and Sh_Num represent sums down to the quarter of any given year within (All) years present among the Time dimension members. A further breakdown of time to months within quarters is not available in this aggregation. We would need to look elsewhere to get aggregations for (All) Funds, (All) Accounts, Manager, Regional Office, Year, Quarter, Month.

Examining the aggregation tables in the warehouse (if using ROLAP partitions) may or may not turn up such a table. It depends on the aggregations designed by OLAP services. If our settings in the Storage Design Wizard resulted in OLAP services designing this combination of dimension levels, then we will most likely find a table containing the breakdown we seek. If, on the other hand, an aggregation for this combination was not designed, then we will not see a table for it.

So where does OLAP services get this level of detail when we ask for it? It is calculated on the fly from aggregations that do exist. This is the magic of the storage design algorithms used by OLAP services. It is not just a simple matter of calculating all possible combinations of dimension levels and storing them. The storage design algorithms must be smart and design aggregations that can yield results from a direct query against them and additionally support on-the-fly calculations, possibly using other tables, to yield results that are not stored.

There is a price to pay, of course. Calculated aggregations will be slower than stored aggregations. You'll need to experience the performance using a given aggregation design to know if it is acceptable or not. If it is not, then you have the option of redesigning the aggregations. Using the Usage-Based Optimization Wizard in OLAP Manager can help you adjust the aggregation design for a cube.

Classes supporting the Level interface are clsAggregationLevel, clsCubeLevel, clsDatabaseLevel, and clsPartitionLevel. You've already seen the clsAggregationLevel used to define the levels of a clsAggregationDimension.

The *clsCubeLevel* object describes the dimension levels in a cube. The cube dimensions and their levels are assigned from the collection of clsDatabaseDimensions and *clsDatabaseLevels*. The clsAggregationLevels and the clsAggregationDimensions they belong to are acquired for an aggregation from the clsCubeDimensions and clsCubeLevels. All Level objects are contained in the Levels collection of their parent dimension.

Table 5-4 lists the properties supported by Level Interface Classes.

TABLE 5-4 PROPERTIES OF LEVEL INTERFACE CLASSES

Property	Supported by All Classes Except	Description
ClassType		Identifies the type of class.
ColumnSize		The size of the aggregation column in the aggregation table.
ColumnType		The data type of the aggregation column.
Description		Describes the level.
EnableAggregations	ClsAggregationLevel clsDatabaseLevel	Specifies if aggregations are to be enabled for the level.

Continued

TABLE 5-4 PROPERTIES OF LEVEL INTERFACE CLASSES *(Continued)*

Property	Supported by All Classes Except	Description
EstimatedSize		The estimated number of members in level.
FromClause		SQL FROM clause for the level.
IsDisabled	ClsDatabaseLevel	Indicates if level is disabled and not visible to users.
IsUnique		Indicates if memberkeycolumn alone uniquely identifies level members or if other columns are needed to uniquely identify members.
IsValid		Indicates valid level structure.
JoinClause		SQL JOIN clause for the level.
LevelType		Identifies the type of level.
MemberKeyColumn		The name of the column containing member keys. May be an expression instead of column name.
MemberNameColumn		The name of the column or an expression containing member names.
Name		The name of the level.
Ordering		Specifies how the level is ordered.
OrdinalPosition		The position of the level relative to other levels in a collection.
Parent		The parent dimension.
SliceValue	ClsAggregationLevel clsDatabaseLevel clsCubeLevel	The level member name used to define partition slice.
SubClassType		Identifies the subclass type of the object.

The Measure Interface

The clsCube, clsPartition, and clsAggregation objects each contain a Measures collection. The objects in these collections implement the Measure interface, whose properties describe the numerical aggregations of fact table measures.

The clsCube Measures collection holds *clsCubeMeasure* objects. These objects represent a numeric measure in the cube's fact table. In our Investments cube, we have two measures, amount and sh_num, that will be described by clsCubeMeasure objects.

The Measures collection found in a clsPartition object will contain objects having ClassType *clsPartitionMeasure*. The properties of these objects describe the measures found in the partition.

The clsAggregation contains a collection of *clsAggregationMeasure* objects. The clsAggregationMeasures describe the measures in the parent aggregation that are aggregated across the dimensions, clsAggregationDimension, of the aggregation and cube.

Properties supported by Measure objects are shown in Table 5-5.

TABLE 5-5 PROPERTIES OF MEASURE INTERFACE CLASSES

Property	Description
AggregateFunction	The type of aggregation function used for the measure. Possible values are aggSum, aggCount, aggMin, and aggMax.
ClassType	Identifies the type of class.
Description	Describes the measure.
FormatString	The format used to display measure values.
IsInternal	Indicates if measure is used internally to calculate other measures.
FromClause	SQL FROM clause for the level.
IsValid	Indicates a valid measure object.
Name	The name of the measure.
OrdinalPosition	The position of the measure relative to other measures in a collection.
Parent	The parent MDStore object.
SourceColumn	The name of the fact table column being aggregated.
SourceColumnType	The data type of the SourceColumn.
SubClassType	Identifies the subclass type of the object.

The Command Interface

Objects supporting the Command Interface contain user-defined commands or series of commands that are executed on the OLAP client whenever the OLAP database or cube is accessed.

Commands that may be held in a Command interface object are library references such as user-defined or third-party function libraries, named sets of existing members, multidimensional expressions, and calculated members. The Price calculated member in the Investments cube is an example of a clsCubeCommand.

Two classes support this interface. The clsDatabase object contains a *Commands* collection that holds objects of ClassType *clsDatabaseCommand*. These commands are executed on access to the database.

The clsCube object contains a Commands collection of *clsCubeCommand* objects. These commands are executed on access to the cube.

When a command object parent, such as a clsCube object, contains more than one command in its Commands collection, the commands will be executed according to their order in the collection. Commands are added with the AddNew method of the Command collection.

Let's inspect the Investments cube commands with some code:

```
Dim i As Integer
Dim dsoDatabase As MDStore
Dim dsoCube As MDStore
Dim dsoCommand As DSO.Command

On Error GoTo ShowCommand_ErrHandler

MakeServerConnection

Set dsoDatabase = mdsoServer.MDStores("FundAcctSample")
Set dsoCube = dsoDatabase.MDStores("Investments")

For i = 1 To dsoCube.Commands.Count
    Set dsoCommand = dsoCube.Commands(i)
    List1.AddItem "Command Name: " & dsoCommand.Name
    List1.AddItem "  Command Type: " & dsoCommand.CommandType
    List1.AddItem "  Ordinal Position: " & dsoCommand.OrdinalPosition
    List1.AddItem "  Statement: " & dsoCommand.Statement
Next I
```

This code assigns a clsCubeCommand object from the Investment cube Commands collection to a variable dimensioned as type DSO.Command. Some of the command properties are then displayed in a list box. The result is shown here:

```
Command Name: Price
  Command Type: 1
  Ordinal Position: 1
  Statement: CREATE MEMBER Investments.Measures.[Price] AS
      '[Measures].[Amount]/[Measures].[Sh Num]', FORMAT_STRING = 'Standard'
```

As expected, we only see the one command defining our Price calculated member. The properties displayed by this code and other properties of the Command Interface are shown in Table 5-6.

TABLE 5-6 PROPERTIES OF COMMAND INTERFACE CLASSES

Property	Description
ClassType	Identifies the type of class.
CommandType	Identifies the command option.
Description	Describes the command.
IsValid	Indicates that the name and statement properties are either empty or valid.
Name	The name of the command.
OrdinalPosition	The position of the command relative to other commands in a collection. Commands are executed according to their position in the collection.
Parent	The parent MDStore object.
Statement	The command text.
SubClassType	Identifies the subclass type of the object.

The Role Interface

In Chapter 3 we established roles and user permissions for the Investments cube through the OLAP Manager's Manage Roles dialog. The results of these settings are stored in DSO objects supporting the Role interface. The two classes implementing the Role interface are used to maintain user groups and security for these groups. Members of a role are assigned common access privileges such as Read or Read/Write.

The *clsDatabaseRole* objects are found in the Roles collection of an MDStore of ClassType clsDatabase. These roles manage users of the database and can be assigned into the Roles collection of clsCube objects to control access to a cube. Roles in the Roles collection of a cube are of ClassType *clsCubeRole*. Both clsDatabaseRole and clsCubeRole contain a *UsersList* property that holds a semicolon-delimited string of user names. These users are members of the role, and all have the permissions stored in the role's Permissions property.

Permissions are assigned to the clsCubeRole only, not to the clsDatabaseRole. Permissions are Read Only or Read/Write and are set by the *SetPermissions* method of the clsCubeRole object. To grant Read/Write permissions to the members of the Analyst role, you would code:

```
Dim dsoDatabase As DSO.MDStore
Dim dsoCube As DSO.MDStore
Dim dsoCubeRole As DSO.Role

Set dsoDatabase = m_dsoServer.MDStores("FundAcctSample")
Set dsoCube = dsoDatabase.MDStores("Investments")
Set dsoCubeRole = dsoCube.Roles("Analyst")
dsoCubeRole.SetPermissions "Access", "RW"
```

To add a new role to the database, a Managers role, for example, we would code:

```
Dim dsoManagersRole As DSO.Role
...
Set dsoManagersRole = dsoDatabase.Roles.AddNew("Managers")
dsoManagersRole.UsersList = "Bill;Marianne"
dsoManagersRole.Update
```

We use the AddNew method of the Roles collection in the database to add a new role. This assigns an object of clsDatabaseRole to the dsoManagersRole variable.

We then set the users Bill and Marianne into this role by setting the role's UsersList property. Domain users will be of the form <domain name>\<user name> as in Develop\Bill in which Bill is a user in the Develop domain. The last statement uses the role's Update method to update the role into the repository. The repository is a storage unit for the DSO metadata and is discussed later in this chapter in the DSO Repository section. Properties of the Role interface are listed in Table 5-7.

TABLE 5-7 PROPERTIES OF ROLE INTERFACE CLASSES

Property	Supported by All Classes Except	Description
ClassType		Identifies the type of class.
Description		Describes the role.
IsValid		Indicates that the role structure is valid.
Name		The name of the role.
Parent		The parent MDStore object.
Permissions	ClsDatabaseRole	The access permissions to the cube.

Property	Supported by All Classes Except	Description
SubClassType		Identifies the subclass type of the object.
UsersList		A string of user names delimited by a semicolon. NT domain names are entered as "DomainName\ UserName."

Objects Accessed Directly

The Decision Support Object model exposes five classes that are not accessed through an interface. These classes are clsCubeAnalyzer, clsDatasource, clsMemberProperty, clsPartitionAnalyzer, and clsServer, and they are accessed directly.

The *clsCubeAnalyzer* is used to read information from a query log that describes the queries executed on the server. This class contains one method, OpenQueryLogRecordset, and no properties or collection.

The *clsPartitionAnalyzer* is used to analyze a partition and generate a collection of aggregations that can be built to improve query performance. The algorithm implemented here is the one used in the OLAP Manager Storage Design Wizard. As we saw in Chapter 3 when we used this wizard to design the aggregations for the Investments cube, there are certain design goals and constraints that you can enter to influence the choices the algorithm makes. This class will be explored in detail in Chapter 8.

The *clsDatasource* class describes the database that will act as the source for clsDatabase, clsCube, and clsPartition objects. These objects are used to connect to the data source when the OLAP server requires data for the parent object.

Objects of type *clsMemberProperty* hold collections and properties that describe a dimension level. These objects are held in the level's *MemberProperties* collection. Because cube and partition dimensions and levels are inherited from database dimensions, the member properties of cube and partition levels are read-only, whereas database level member properties are read/write.

The *clsServer* object is used to control the OLAP server. Through the methods of this class, you can start and stop or query the status of the OLAP server service (MSSQLServerOLAPService), create MDStore objects as children of the server object, check the state of the server, and manage the data stored in the server's databases. Many of the clsServer methods and properties will be explored when we discuss DSO further in Chapter 8.

Exploring DSO Enumerations

The DSO type library defines a number of enumerations that make coding a little easier. These enumerations, shown in Table 5-8, can be coded in conditional statements, case statements, and assignment statements as representations for their constant values.

```
Dim dsoAggMeasure As DSO.Measure
Dim s As AggregatesTypes
...
s = aggCount
...
If dsoAggMeasure.AggregateFunction = aggSum Then ...
```

In the preceding code, aggSum is one of the values associated with the AggregatesTypes enumeration used here in a conditional statement to test the AggregateFunction property of a clsAggregationMeasure (instantiation not shown) and an assignment to set a enumeration variable equal to 1.

TABLE 5-8 DSO ENUMERATIONS

Enumerator and Applies To	Values
CommandTypes CommandType	cmdUnknown = 0 cmdCreateMember = 1 cmdCreateSet = 2 cmdUseLibrary = 3
LevelTypes LevelType property	levRegular = 0 levAll = 1 levTimeYears = 20 levTimeHalfYears = 36 levTimeQuarters = 68 levTimeMonths = 132 levTimeWeeks = 260 levTimeDays = 516 levTimeHours = 772 levTimeMinutes = 1028 levTimeSeconds = 2052
OrderTypes Ordering property	orderName = 0 orderKey = 1

Enumerator and Applies To	Values
AggregatesTypes AggregateFunction	aggSum = 0 aggCount = 1 aggMin = 2 aggMax = 3
DimensionTypes DimensionType property	dimRegular = 0 dimTime = 1 dimQuantitative = 5
DimensionAggUsageTypes AggregationUsage property	dimAggUsageStandard = 0 dimAggUsageTopOnly = 1 dimAggUsageDetailsOnly = 2 dimAggUsageCustom = 3
SupportLevels	supportNoROLAP = 0 supportNoSQLNoTransactions = 1 supportSQL = 3 supportTransactions = 5 supportSQLTransactions = 7
OlapEditions Edition property of clsServer	olapEditionUnlimited = 0 olapEditionPivotOnly = 1 olapEditionNoPartitions = 2 olapEditionError = −1
ValidateErrorCodes	mderrNoError = −1 mderrUnknownError = 0 mderrNameNotSet = 1 mderrParentNotSet = 2 mderrMissingDataSource = 3 mderrCannotConnectToDataSource = 4 mderrCannotAccessDataSourceTables = 5 mderrInvalidSchemaLoopDetectedInTableJoins = 6 mderrInvalidSchemaBadSourceColumn = 7 mderrInvalidSchemaDatasource = 8 mderrInvalidSchemaIslandDetectedInTableJoins = 9 mderrConnectionStringNotSet = 10 mderrErrorBeginingDatasourceTransaction = 11 mderrUsersNotSet = 12 mderrStatementNotSet = 13 mderrMeasureMissingSourceColumn = 14 mderrMeasureInvalidColumnDataType = 15

Continued

TABLE 5-8 DSO ENUMERATIONS *(Continued)*

Enumerator and Applies To	Values
ValidateErrorCodes *(Continued)*	mderrAggColumnSizeNotSet = 16 mderrAggColumnTypeNotSet = 17 *mderrInvalidLevelMemberKeyColumnNotSet = 18* *mderrInvalidLevelMoreMembersThePreviousLevel = 19* *mderrInvalidLevelZeroMembersCount = 20* *mderrInvalidLevelBadTableInMemberKeyColumn = 21* *mderrInvalidLevelType = 22* *mderrInvalidLevelSourceMemberPropertyMissing = 23* *mderrDimensionTableNotSet = 24* *mderrInvalidDimensionZeroLevels = 25* *mderrInvalidDimensionAtLeastOneNonAllLevel = 26* *mderrInvalidVirtualDimension = 27* *mderrInvalidCubeZeroMeasures = 28* *mderrInvalidCubeZeroDimensions = 29* *mderrInvalidCubeBadFactTableSize = 30* *mderrInvalidVirtualCubeMeasure = 31* *mderrInvalidVirtualCubeDimension = 32* *mderrInvalidCubeBadFactTable = 33* *mderrInvalidCubeNoSourceForVirtualDimension = 34* *mderrInvalidCubeNoSourceLevelForVirtualDimension =35* *mderrTooManyMeasures = 36* *mderrInvalidPartZeroMeasures = 37* *mderrInvalidPartZeroDimensions = 38* *mderrInvalidPartBadFactTableSize = 39* *mderrInvalidPartBadFactTable = 40* *mderrInvalidAggregationPrefix = 41* *mderrOnlyOneWriteBackPartitionIsAllowed = 42* *mderrInvalidDatasetDefinition = 43* *mderrCubeToComplexForAggregationDesign = 44* *mderrAggPrefixNotSet = 45* *mderrNameAlreadySet = 46*
ErrorCodes	mderrCollectionReadOnly = –2147221503 mderrCollectionItemNotFound = –2147221502 mderrDimensionLockedByCube = –2147221501 mderrIllegalObjectName = –2147221500 mderrCannotDeleteLastPartition = –2147221499 mderrCannotRenameObject = –2147221498 mderrInvalidPropertySetting = –2147221497 mderrCannotDeleteDimension = –2147221496 mderrCannotDeleteLevel = –2147221495

Enumerator and Applies To	Values
ErrorCodes *(Continued)*	mderrCannotDeleteMemberProperty = −2147221494
	mderrCannotAddVirtualDimension = −2147221493
	mderrObjectChangedByAnotherApp = −2147221492
	mderrCannotSaveInsideTransaction = −2147221491
	mderrCannotCommitDatabase = −2147221490
	mderrCorruptedRegistrySettings = −2147221489
	mderrDimensionNotInUnderlyingCubes = −2147221488
	mderrMeasureDoesNotHaveValidSourceColumn = −2147221487
	mderrTooManyLevelsInDimension = −2147221486
	mderrCannotRemoveMeasureFromDefaultAggregation = −2147221485
	mderrCouldNotOpenServiceControlManager = −2147221484
	mderrCouldNotOpenService = −2147221483
	mderrCouldNotQueryTheService = −2147221482
	mderrBadParameterForServiceState = −2147221481
	mderrUnsuccesfullServiceOperation = −2147221480
	mderrDuplicateKeyInCollection = −2147221479
	mderrInvalidParent = −2147221478
	mderrCannotModifySharedObject = −2147221477
	mderrLockDescriptionTooLong = −2147221476
	mderrLockNetworkDown = −2147221475
	mderrLockNetworkPathNotFound = −2147221474
	mderrLockNetworkNameNotFound = −2147221473
	mderrLockFileCorrupted = −2147221472
	mderrLockFileMissing = −2147221471
	mderrLockNotEnoughMemory = −2147221470
	mderrLockSystemError = −2147221469
	mderrLockCannotBeObtained = −2147221468
	mderrLockObjectNotLocked = −2147221467
	mderrLockAccessError = −2147221466
	mderrNameCannotBeEmpty = −2147221465
	mderrNameCannotBeChanged = −2147221464
	mderrPropertyCannotBeChanged = −2147221463
	mderrPropertyCollectionCannotBeChanged = −2147221462
	mderrDefinitionCannotBeEmpty = −2147221461
	mderrDefinitionDoesNotContainNameAndValue = −2147221460
	mderrCorruptedProperty = −2147221459

Continued

TABLE 5-8 DSO ENUMERATIONS *(Continued)*

Enumerator and Applies To	Values
ErrorCodes *(Continued)*	mderrAggregationUsageNotCustom = –2147221458 mderrRegistryConnectFailed = –2147221457 mderrRegistryOpenKeyFailed = –2147221456 mderrRegistryQueryValueFailed = –2147221455 mderrRepositoryUpgradeFailed = –2147221454 mderrRepositoryConnectionFailed = –2147221453 mderrRepositoryIncompatible = –2147221452 mderrInvalidLockType = –2147221451 mderrCannotCloneObjectIntoItself = –2147221450 mderrUnexpectedError = –2147221449 mderrSourceDoesNotExist = –2147221448 mderrTargetDoesNotExist = –2147221447 mderrDifferentAggregationNumber = –2147221446 mderrDifferentAggregationStructure = –2147221445 mderrDifferentAggregationOLAPMode = –2147221444 mderrDifferentAggregationDatasources = –2147221443 mderrCannotCreatePartition = –2147221442
ServerStates State property	stateUnknown = 0 stateConnected = 1 stateFailed = 2
CloneOptions options for the Clone method	cloneObjectProperties = 0 cloneMinorChildren = 1 cloneMajorChildren = 2
ClassTypes ClassType property	clsServer = 1 clsDatabase = 2 clsDatabaseRole = 3 clsDatabaseCommand = 4 clsDatasource = 6 clsDatabaseDimension = 7 clsDatabaseLevel = 8 clsCube = 9 clsCubeMeasure = 10 clsCubeDimension = 11 clsCubeLevel = 12 clsCubeCommand = 13 clsCubeRole = 14 clsPartition = 19 clsPartitionMeasure = 20

Enumerator and Applies To	Values
ClassTypes ClassType property *(Continued)*	clsPartitionDimension = 21 clsPartitionLevel = 22 clsAggregation = 23 clsAggregationMeasure = 24 clsAggregationDimension = 25 clsAggregationLevel = 26 clsCubeAnalyzer = 28 clsPartitionAnalyzer = 29 clsCollection = 30 clsMemberProperty = 31
SubClassTypes SubClassType property	sbclsRegular = 0 sbclsVirtual = 1
OlapStateTypes State property	olapStateNeverProcessed = 0 olapStateStructureChanged = 1 olapStateMemberPropertiesChanged = 2 olapStateSourceMappingChanged = 3 olapStateCurrent = 4
OlapLockTypes LockType parm of the LockObject method	olaplockRead = 1 olaplockExtendedRead = 2 olaplockProcess = 4 olaplockWrite = 8
ProcessTypes Open parm of the Process method	processDefault = 0 processFull = 1 processRefreshData = 2 processBuildStructure = 3 processResume = 4 processSuspend = 5
OlapStorageModes OlapMode property	olapmodeRolap = 15 olapmodeMolapIndex = 0 olapmodeHybridIndex = 1 olapmodeAggsRolap = 3 olapmodeAggsMolapIndex = 0

You'll find the enumeration values shown in Table 5-8 helpful when attempting to interpret property values being displayed with Debug.Print statements, such as we did earlier in some of the code examples, or displayed in the repository, as you'll see in the next section.

The DSO Repository

DSO needs to support persistence of the metadata describing the OLAP objects you've been exploring in this chapter. This means it needs to store the properties and collections that you have specified for your server, databases, and cubes such that they can be made available at a later time.

The OLAP Services installation installs a Microsoft Access database in the <installation drive:>\OLAP Services\bin folder named **msmdrep.mdb**. This is the database DSO uses to store its metadata unless you migrate this repository to another platform such as SQL Server.

The **msmdrep.mdb** file is an Access 97 format database that you can open and browse. The schema you'll find in this database is surprisingly simple. It consists of two tables. The *OlapObjects* table shown in Figure 5-4 contains rows for the DSO objects you've defined, either through programming to the DSO object model or through the OLAP Manager. Most of the properties for these objects are stored in a memo field named *ObjectDefinition*.

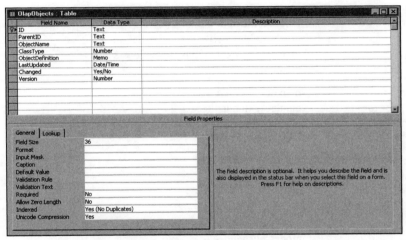

Figure 5-4: The table definition for the OlapObjects table in the msmdrep.mdb repository database

After opening the OlapObjects table, click in the ObjectDefinition field and then press Shift+F2 to display the field contents in a Zoom dialog box for easier viewing. This dialog box is shown in Figure 5-5.

The *OlapObjects_bak* table is used to manage changes in DSO objects. At this point in our trek through the book, you won't find any entries in this table for the Investments cube, because no changes have been made. There are plenty of changes recorded for the FoodMart database from Microsoft if you would like to see an example of what these look like.

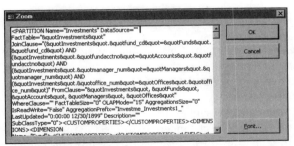

Figure 5-5: The ObjectDefinition column of the OlapObjects table showing the properties of the Investments partition

The *Server* table consists of one column, the ObjectDefinition column, containing properties of the Server object. If you wish to migrate the repository from Access 97 to SQL Server so that it can be better managed, follow these steps:

1. In the OLAP Manager tree view, right-click your OLAP server node and select Migrate Repository from the popup menu.

2. Choose or enter the name of a SQL server to store your repository. Click Next.

3. Choose either NT authentication or SQL Server authentication for the connection with the server. Click Next.

4. Choose the database you want to use for storing the repository tables. I have selected the msdb database. Click Finish to migrate the repository.

 If the database you chose in Step 4 already contains repository tables, you'll see a message asking you if you want to replace these tables. Be very careful in answering this prompt. Replacing the repository of another OLAP server will result in loss of metadata and cubes.

The migration results in an update to the system registry pointing the OLAP server to the new location of the repository. The old Access 97 repository database can be deleted at this point. If necessary, you can later migrate the repository to another database on the same server or to a remote server, but you cannot migrate back to an Access database.

 The structure of the OLAP repository is undocumented by Microsoft and may be changed at some point in the future, possibly to the use of the Microsoft Repository.

Summary

This chapter has introduced the Decision Support Object model, which exposes the OLAP server, its databases, and multidimensional structures. Using this object model, you can control the OLAP server service; create OLAP databases, dimensions, cubes, partitions, and aggregations; and set or query the metadata describing these objects.

The OLAP Manager we used to create our sample Investments cube provides an example of what can be done using this object model. The objects you see in the OLAP Manager tree view are representations of the objects discussed in this chapter. Using this model, you can develop your own OLAP server application.

Much of this chapter focused on introducing the classes and interfaces of DSO, what they do, and what properties they support. Some code samples were provided to show how these objects are used in Visual Basic code. Table 5-8 provides a list of enumerations supported by DSO. This table was built from the typelib information in msmddo.dll and shows the enumeration constants and their values. We discussed briefly the DSO repository where metadata is stored by DSO. We learned how to migrate this repository from its default Access 97 format into a SQL Server database.

Chapter 6

Getting Acquainted with the PivotTable Service

IN THIS CHAPTER

◆ Discovering what the PivotTable Service is and how it is used in client applications

◆ Learning the ActiveX Data Objects Multidimensional model

◆ Previewing multidimensional expressions (MDX) to query cubes

◆ Exploring the data definition language extension to OLE DB for OLAP used to create local cubes, user-defined sets, caches, and calculated members

◆ Learning how to get a flattened view of a multidimensional dataset

THE PIVOTTABLE SERVICE installed with the Client Component setup of Microsoft SQL Server OLAP Services plays dual roles in the OLAP environment.

The PivotTable Service is an OLE DB provider supporting the OLE DB for OLAP extensions specification found in OLE DB 2.0.

This enables a client application to communicate with an OLAP server. In this case, the PivotTable Service is acting as a client to OLAP server.

The second role played by the PivotTable Service is as a standalone in-process desktop OLAP server. In this role, the PivotTable Service is capable of providing online and local data analysis and access to OLAP data. Using this service, you can define and populate a cube locally on the client machine in a single cube partition. Calculated members, user-defined sets, and multidimensional expressions are supported on local cubes.

Using the ADO and ADO MD Object Models

With all OLE DB providers, you can write your programs directly using the provider's interfaces and methods. The PivotTable Service is no exception. But it is usually easier to code to a model that wraps the complexity of the OLE DB objects

111

into a simpler model representing much of the functionality required by applications. Microsoft provides such a front-end model called ActiveX Data Objects (ADO). ADO is a standard data model exposing objects such as Connection, Command, Recordset, Fields, Parameters, and Errors. The ADO model is shown in Figure 6-1.

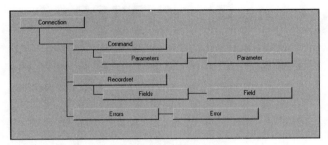

Figure 6-1: The ActiveX Data Objects model

To project an object model onto a multidimensional schema and work with data described by this schema, Microsoft released the ActiveX Data Objects Multidimensional (ADO MD) object model. This model exposes objects such as Catalog, CubeDef, Dimension, Hierarchy, Levels, Cellset, Axis, Position, and Members. This model is shown in Figure 6-2.

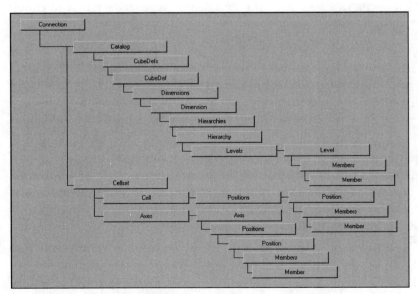

Figure 6-2: The ActiveX Data Objects multidimensional model

Whereas the ADO model is suited to working with tabular data formats, through the use of recordset objects, the ADO MD model is designed for working with multidimensional data retrieved through *cellsets*. You can develop applications using either of these models, but you'll generally find that using both ADO and ADO MD together enables you to author more robust applications. This is especially true using ADO 2.1 with its support for the Microsoft Data Shaping Service for OLE DB.

In working with the PivotTable Service in this book, we will spend much of our time developing with ADO and ADO MD. We will not discuss the direct use of the OLE DB API, because all of what this book intends to accomplish can be done using the ADO and ADO MD models. For information on programming directly to the OLE DB for OLAP API, see the OLE DB for OLAP 2.1 documentation in the oledb210.chm help file found in the msolap\documentation\oledb folder on the SQL Server 7.0 CD.

In this section, we use ADO and ADO MD to connect to an OLAP database and explore its schema through the ADO MD object model. The next section introduces multidimensional expressions and the use of these expressions to query cube data.

Connecting to an OLAP Catalog

Before your application can work with OLAP data or read its schema, you need to make a connection with an OLAP server. There are several ways you can do this.

The ADO object model exposes a *Connection* object through which you can establish a session with an OLAP server. Use the connection object *Open* method with the following arguments:

```
ConnectionObject.Open [ConnectionString], [UserID], [Password], [Options]
```

The *ConnectionString* argument provides the information as to which provider to use and which OLAP server to connect with. A ConnectionString may be specified as an argument in the Open method or by setting the ConnectionString property of the Connection object.

The *Provider=* parameter of the ConnectionString is supported by ADO and informs ADO which provider to load. To connect using the PivotTable Service, you need to specify msolap for this component:

```
Dim cnn As New ADODB.Connection
cnn.Open "Provider=msolap;Data Source=SECRETS;Initial Catalog= FundAcctSample;"
```

Both the *Data Source=* and *Initial Catalog=* parameters in the preceding example are connection parameters passed by ADO to the provider, in this case the PivotTable Service. Data Source identifies the server name, and Initial Catalog identifies the database.

For a connection to a local cube, you would use a ConnectionString like this:

```
Dim cnn As New ADODB.Connection

cnn.ConnectionString = "Provider=msolap;Location=C:\Dividends.cub;"
cnn.Open
```

In this example you are using the ConnectionString property of the Connection object, although you could have specified this ConnectionString in the Open method as we did in the first example.

The Data Source= and Initial Catalog= parameters are not required for a local cube file connection, because the PivotTable Service provider is acting as the OLAP server and you are connecting to the cube file specified in the *Location=* parameter. Location is the fully qualified path to the cube file. However, since OLAP services treats the Data Source= and Location= parameters as synonyms, you can use either to specify the local or remote data source.

Once you have a Connection object, you can assign it to the *ActiveConnection* property of the Catalog or Cellset objects in the ADO MD object model. Setting ActiveConnection on these objects enables them to communicate with the server.

```
Dim cat As New ADOMD.Catalog

Set cat.ActiveConnection = cnn
```

In the above example, notice that cat.ActiveConnection is preceded by a Set verb. If this verb is omitted, a new connection is implicitly created and used as the catalog's activeconnection causing performance problems. Using set prevents this and assigns the cnn connection to the activeconnection.

The preceding code assigns the open connection object, cnn, to the Active Connection property of a Catalog object in the ADO MD object model. This action enables you to inspect the Name property of the Catalog and its CubeDefs collection.

Another method of making a connection is to assign a connection string to the ActiveConnection property as shown here:

```
Dim cat As New ADOMD.Catalog

Set cat.ActiveConnection = "Provider=msolap;Data Source=SECRETS;Initial Catalog=
FundAcctSample;"
```

Using the preceding method of setting ActiveConnection, a Connection object is implicitly created for you and assigned to the ActiveConnection property of the

Catalog. This method of connecting can also be used with the Cellset object, as we'll see in the "Examining OLAP Data" section.

To close a connection and free its resources, use the *Close* method of the Connection object:

```
cnn.Close
```

Closing a connection sets the ActiveConnection of any open Catalog objects to Nothing. To close an implicit connection of a catalog, set its ActiveConnection property to Nothing:

```
Set cat.ActiveConnection = Nothing
```

You must close a Cellset with the Close method to release its implicit connection and resources. Attempting to set the Cellset ActiveConnection property to Nothing will result in an error.

Now that you have a connection with a server and a catalog, you can examine the catalog's schema.

Examining Catalog Schema

The ADO MD Catalog object and its dependencies expose the schema of multidimensional stores and their metadata.

The *CubeDefs* collection found in a Catalog contains a *CubeDef* object for each of the cubes in the catalog. A CubeDef contains a *Name* property that names the cube and a *Description* property that can be used to describe the cube. Other properties for the CubeDef can be found in the CubeDef *Properties* collection and are listed in Table 6-1. The properties in this collection are supplied by the MSOLAP provider.

TABLE 6-1 CUBEDEF PROPERTIES COLLECTION

Property	Description
Catalog_Name	The parent catalog for this cubedef
Created_On	Date/Time when the cube was created
Cube_GUID	The GUID of the cube
Cube_Name	Name of the cube
Cube_Type	Type of cube
Last_Data_Update	Date/Time of last data update

Continued

TABLE **6-1** **CUBEDEF PROPERTIES COLLECTION** *(Continued)*

Property	Description
Data_Updated_By	User ID of user doing last update
Description	Description of the cube
Last_Schema_Update	Date/Time of last schema change
Schema_Name	Name of schema owning this cubedef
Schema_Updated_By	User ID of the user making the last schema change

The CubeDef *Dimensions* collection holds *Dimension* objects describing the dimensions of the cube. Each Dimension object contains *Name, Description,* and *UniqueName* properties. The *Properties* collection holds the provider-supplied properties shown in Table 6-2.

TABLE **6-2** **DIMENSION PROPERTIES COLLECTION**

Property	Description
Catalog_Name	The parent catalog for this dimension
Schema_Name	Name of schema owning this cube
Cube_Name	Name of the cube
Dimension_Name	Name of the dimension
Dimension_Unique_Name	Unambiguous name of the dimension
Dimension_GUID	GUID of the dimension
Dimension_Caption	Display name of the dimension
Dimension_Ordinal	Ordinal position of the dimension in the collection
Dimension_Type	The type of dimension
Dimension_Cardinality	Number of members in the dimension
Default_Hierarchy	Name of the default hierarchy
Description	Description for the dimension
Is_Virtual	Indicates if the dimension is virtual

Each Dimension object contains a *Hierarchies* collection. Each *Hierarchy* object in this collection represents a hierarchy of dimension members that can be aggregated. A Hierarchy has *Name, Description,* and *UniqueName* properties and a *Properties* collection. The properties in this collection are listed in Table 6-3.

TABLE 6-3 HIERARCHY PROPERTIES COLLECTION

Property	Description
Catalog_Name	The parent catalog for this hierarchy
Schema_Name	Name of schema owning this cube
Cube_Name	Name of the cube
Dimension_Unique_Name	Unambiguous name of the parent dimension
Hierarchy_Name	Name of the hierarchy
Hierarchy_Unique_Name	Unambiguous name of the hierarchy
Hierarchy_GUID	GUID of the hierarchy
Hierarchy_Caption	Display name of the hierarchy
Dimension_Type	The type of dimension
Hierarchy_Cardinality	Number of members in the hierarchy
Default_Member	Name of the default member for the hierarchy
Description	Description for the dimension
All_Member	The highest level of aggregation in the hierarchy

In addition to the Properties collection, a Hierarchy object holds a *Levels* collection. In addition to the *Name, Description,* and *UniqueName* properties, each *Level* object has a Caption property and a Depth property.

The *Caption* property is the text to be displayed when displaying a Hierarchy Level or Level member. The *Depth* property indicates the number of levels in the hierarchy from the root of the hierarchy (Depth equals 0) down to the Level itself. The first level below the root would have a Depth of 1. The level below the first level would have a Depth of 2 and so on down the hierarchy.

Table 6-4 lists the properties found in the Level *Properties* collection.

TABLE 6-4 LEVEL PROPERTIES COLLECTION

Property	Description
Catalog_Name	The parent catalog for this hierarchy
Schema_Name	Name of schema owning this cube
Cube_Name	Name of the cube
Dimension_Unique_Name	Unambiguous name of the parent dimension
Level_Name	Name of the level
Hierarchy_Unique_Name	Unambiguous name of the parent hierarchy
Level_Unique_Name	Unambiguous name of the level
Level_GUID	GUID of the level
Level_Caption	Display name of the level
Level_Type	The type of level
Level_Cardinality	Number of members in the level
Level_Number	Distance between the root of the hierarchy and the level
Description	Description for the level

The *Members* collection of a Level object contains Member objects for each member at the specified level of a dimension hierarchy. The Properties collection of a member object contains only the *Expression* property. This property value is Null for input members. For calculated members, it contains the expression from which the member is derived.

If the member is a nonleaf member in the hierarchy, its *ChildCount* property indicates an estimate of the number of child members beneath the current member. To obtain an exact count of these members, access the Count property on the *Children* collection property. The *Children* property can be used to access each of the child members below a given Level member. At a leaf level of a hierarchy, this collection is empty.

The *LevelDepth* property of a member corresponds to the Depth property of the member's parent Level object. LevelDepth indicates the length of the path from the root level to the current member level where the root level depth is 0. The *LevelName* property identifies the name of the level to which the member belongs.

The *Type* property of a member indicates the type of member and can be one of the values shown in Table 6-5.

TABLE 6-5 TYPE PROPERTY OF A MEMBER OBJECT

Value	Description
AdMemberRegular (1)	A member representing an entity in the data warehouse
AdMemberMeasure (2)	A member of the measures dimension
AdMemberFormula (4)	A calculated member
AdMemberAll (8)	The member represents all members in the level
AdMemberUnknown (16)	Type cannot be determined

The objects discussed so far provide you with information about the multidimensional stores defined in an OLAP catalog but don't provide you access to the actual data stored in cubes. To access this data, you need to examine other objects of the ADO MD object model.

Examining OLAP Data

When you execute a query that returns data in the ADO DB object model, the result is a Recordset object. The Recordset is a cursor on the rows that the relational provider returned for the query you submitted. Recordset objects support properties and methods that enable you to access the data items of each row and the properties describing those data items. If you have opened the recordset with a type of cursor enabling updates, we can even make modifications to the data through the recordset object.

In the world of OLAP, your queries submitted to OLAP servers return datasets known to ADO MD as *cellsets*. A cellset represents the data returned from a multidimensional query and consists of a collection of cells selected from a cube or another cellset.

Typical steps used in creating and working with cellsets are:

1. Associate an ADO connection with a cellset object.

2. Define a multidimensional query and pass this query to OLAP Services in the cellset Open method.

3. Access a cell in the returned cellset using the cellset Item method.

4. Navigate the cellset using cell coordinates and ordinals.

5. Close the cellset using the Close method.

Let's examine each of these steps.

CELLSET CONNECTIONS

A cellset is connected with an OLAP server by setting the cellset ActiveConnection property. This is done in the same manner as you saw earlier for the Catalog connection.

The ActiveConnection property may be set to an active ADO DB connection object as in:

```
Dim cset as New ADOMD.Cellset

Set cset.ActiveConnection = cnn
```

The other method is to set the ActiveConnection equal to a valid connection string as in:

```
Dim cat As New ADOMD.Catalog

Set cset.ActiveConnection = "Provider=msolap;Data Source=SECRETS;Initial
Catalog= FundAcctSample;"
```

A third method for setting the ActiveConnection property is to inherit it from the ActiveConnection argument of the cellset Open method. We'll look at this method in the next section.

OPENING A CELLSET

The next step after setting the cellset connection is to develop a multidimensional query and open the cellset on this query.

Transact-SQL is a language familiar to all of us who develop SQL Server applications. It is the sole topic of my book *Programming Microsoft SQL Server 7.0 Transact-SQL* published by IDG Books Worldwide. This extension of the SQL-92 grammar is well suited to working with relational data found in a SQL Server database.

When it comes to working with multidimensional data stores such as cubes, OLE DB for OLAP defines a language called multidimensional expressions (MDX). MDX provides a syntax similar to Transact-SQL that enables cubes to be created and queried.

For the purposes of this cellset discussion, we'll use a simple MDX query that returns investment amounts by manager. Chapters 7 and 10 explore MDX in much more depth than what you'll see here.

The basic MDX syntax is defined as:

```
Select <axis_specification>
From <cube_name>
```

The <axis_specification> in the preceding syntax is defined as:

```
<set> ON <axis_name>
```

The axis names you use here are COLUMNS and ROWS. The investment amounts are to be returned as the column values of your cellset, whereas the manager names are returned as row headers. The cube you select this data from is the Investments cube as specified in the From clause. The MDX query looks like this:

```
Select {[Measures].[Amount]} On Columns,
{[Manager].Members} On Rows
From [Investments]
```

This MDX query is specified either in the cellset *Source* property or as the Source argument to the *Open* method.

```
Dim strmdx as String

strmdx = "Select {[Measures].[Amount]} On Columns,{[Manager].Members} On Rows
From [Investments]"

cset.Open strmdx
```

As mentioned earlier, the Open method can accept a connection object or connection string instead of setting the ActiveConnection property prior to using the Open method.

```
cset.Open strmdx,cnn
```

Now you're ready to explore the resulting dataset.

RETRIEVING CELLS

A cell within a cellset is the object you use to access the data and descriptions of the data. A cell is located at the intersection of coordinates or positions involving each of the cellset axes.

Because one or more dimensions can be projected onto a single axis, each position on an axis consists of an array of dimension members. The array contains one member from each dimension projected onto the axis. The member array is known as a *tuple*. The number of members in a tuple equals the number of dimensions projected onto the axis.

How many positions can we expect on an axis? If one dimension is projected on the axis, you get one position for each member selected from the dimension. If two dimensions are projected on an axis, the number of positions is the product of the dimension member counts. So if you project a dimension having 5 members and a dimension having 3 members, you see 15 positions, and each position has 2 members in its tuple.

The cellset *Item* method is used to access a cell within the cellset. The PivotTable Service currently supports two methods for addressing cells in the Item method. You can specify either an *ordinal position* within the cellset or an *axes position*. An ordinal number enables you to treat the cellset as an *n*-dimensional array where *n* is the number of axes in the cellset. An axes position is expressed as a position from each of the axes of the cellset.

Using an axes-positional notation, you access the third row of the first (and only) column in this sample cellset using:

```
Dim csetcell As ADOMD.Cell

Set csetcell = cset.Item(0,2)
```

Using axes positions, the column position (x-axis or axis 0) is specified first followed by the row position (y-axis or axis 1). To access the cell's value, you use either the *Value* property or the *FormattedValue* property of the cell.

```
Debug.Print csetcell.FormattedValue
```

To display the cell's coordinate members, you need to access the *Positions* collection of the cell and enumerate the members for each position. In this example query, you would expect to find two positions for a cell. Position(0) represents the Column axis and contains the member "Amount" from the Measures dimension. Position(1) represents the Row axis and contains the member corresponding to the dimension member being enumerated on this axis. In this example, you see a manager name from the Manager dimension.

To display these members, you use their *Caption* property as in the following code:

```
Debug.Print csetcell.Positions(1).Members(0).Caption
```

NAVIGATING THE CELLSET

As you discovered in the preceding discussion, you can navigate a cellset by using a familiar array-like indexing, specifying a coordinate for the column axis following by a coordinate for the row axis. The following code is extracted from the Ch06 project on the CD:

```
For n = 0 To cset.Axes(0).Positions.Count - 1
    For m = 0 To cset.Axes(1).Positions.Count - 1
        List1.AddItem cset.Item(n, m).Positions(0).Members(0).Caption & "("
            & cset.Item(n, m).Ordinal & ")"
        For k = 0 To cset.Item(n, m).Positions(1).Members.Count - 1
            List1.AddItem cset.Item(n, m).Positions(1).Members(k).Caption
        Next k
    List1.AddItem IIf(IsNull(cset.Item(n, m).Value), "Null", _
        cset.Item(n, m).FormattedValue)
        List1.AddItem ""
    Next m
Next n
```

The outermost loop of this code visits each position on the column axis (there are only two positions in the cellset) and loops through each position on the row axis with the inner loop. At each coordinate (n,m), the cellset Item method is used to display the member captions of the cell at the coordinate and the FormattedValue if there is a value or the word "Null" if no value exists in the cell.

Because the MDX query used in this sample projects two dimensions on the row axis, the innermost loop using index k is enumerating the members found at each row axis position. This loop displays the dimension members associated with the value of the cell.

Each cset.Item(n,m) in this code represents a cell in the cellset, and you can use this reference to access the cell properties. As long as you know the position bounds of the cellset, you can access any cell in the cellset in this manner.

The second method of cellset navigation involves the ordinal numbers of the cells and requires a bit of calculation to use them.

Each position on an axis is given an ordinal number relative to the axis. It is an index within the positions collection of an axis. Each cell in a cellset also has an ordinal number relative to the beginning of the cellset. Cells are numbered beginning with zero in a row-major order. The number of cellset ordinals is calculated as the product of positions of all axes in the cellset. If a cellset has a column axis containing 6 positions and a row axis containing 11 positions, then the number of ordinals (and cells) in the cellset is 66. The cell at cellset.Item(0,0) has an ordinal of 0, and the cell at cellset.Item(5,10) is 65. This numbering is evident in the results from the preceding code sample, where each cset.Item(n, m) cell's ordinal is displayed in parenthesis after the column member caption.

The cell ordinal of cellset.Item(n,m) in the preceding sample cellset is given by ((Upper Bound of n) x (m)) + n. So for cellset.Item(0,5), the cell ordinal would be 10 calculated as ((2) x (5)) + 0. The cell ordinal of cellset.Item(1,8) is 17. For cellset.Item(1,48), the result is 97.

The cell ordinal is then used with the cell Item method in place of the coordinate method you used previously. To see the formatted value of the cell having ordinal 54, you code:

```
cset.Item(54).FormattedValue
```

CLOSING THE CELLSET

When you have finished with a given cellset, your application should clean up the cellset and its related objects. To break the cellset connection, use the cellset *Close* method. This will release the data in the cellset and any related cell, position, or member objects assigned from the cellset. At this point, the cellset object is still in memory and can be reopened if necessary. To release the memory held by the cellset object, set the cellset variable to Nothing.

```
cset.Close
Set cset = Nothing
```

There are occasions when you will want to retrieve a flattened rowset from the PivotTable Service provider. In this way, you can view the multidimensional dataset as you would a relational recordset. One way to do this is to submit SQL to the PivotTable Service instead of MDX. We'll discuss the SQL supported by the PivotTable Service next.

PivotTable Service SQL Support

In addition to acting as a multidimensional data provider through the support of MDX, the PivotTable Service can act as a tabular data provider by supporting a subset of SQL. This tabular data support enables you to return flattened rowsets from a cube.

The SQL SELECT statement syntax supported by the PivotTable Service is shown here:

```
SELECT [DISTINCT] <select_list>
 FROM <from_clause>
 [WHERE <where_clause>]
 [GROUP BY <groupby_clause>]
```

The <select_list> may be composed of an asterisk (*) or a comma-delimited list of the following:

```
<column_reference> | <aggregate> |(<column_reference>) AS IDENTIFIER
```

The <aggregate> component is defined as:

```
<aggregate> ::= <aggregate_function> (<measure_name>)
```

The <aggregate_function> used here must be consistent with the Aggregate Function property of the measure referenced by <measure_name> and can be one of the following:

```
COUNT | MIN | MAX| SUM
```

The <column_reference> can be either a measure_name or a level_name. When a measure_name is used in the select list, an aggregate must also be specified.

If the WHERE clause is used, it must conform to the following rules:

```
<search_condition> AND <search_condition>
 | <search_condition> OR <search_condition>
 | (<search_condition>)
 |  (<column_reference>) = VALUE | VALUE = (<column_reference>)
```

If the GROUP BY clause is used, it must contain one or more of the following separated by commas in addition to an aggregate component on a measure:

```
(<level_name>)
```

In the earlier section titled "Opening a Cellset," you submitted a simple MDX statement that looks like this:

```
strmdx = "Select {[Measures].[Amount]} On Columns,{[Manager].Members} On Rows
From Investments"
```

 This query is found in the Ch06 project on the CD behind the Navigate Cellset button. Comment out the existing active query assignment and uncomment the preceding query assignment. Run the application and click the Navigate Cellset button.

The resulting dataset can be viewed much like a relational table with each row containing one column holding the aggregated Amount value for each Manager member. The difference between this dataset and a relational recordset lies in the structure used to represent the results. The multidimensional dataset requires a different method of interpretation than its recordset counterpart in the relational model.

Let's see what this same query would produce as a flattened rowset. The following query is submitted to the PivotTable Service from the SQL button in the Ch06 project on the CD:

```
strsql = "Select [Measures].[Amount],[Manager].[Manager Lastname]
  From Investments"
```

The result from this query produces something on the order of 1,000-plus rows where the MDX query produced only 7 cells. The difference is obvious. The SQL query causes the MSOLAP provider to access the detail data from the Investments table in the FundAcctsWH data warehouse, the source of the Investments cube.

Each detail amount found there is returned in our recordset. The returned cell values from the MDX query are aggregate values for each of the Manager members on the row axis.

To more closely reproduce the aggregated results, you need to use a Group By clause in the SQL statement and an aggregate on the measure:

```
strsql = "Select SUM([Measures].[Amount]),[Manager].[Manager Lastname]
  From Investments Group By ([Manager].[Manager Lastname])"
```

Running this query produces records for each non-null amount at the specified level (which excludes the (All) level). This result can now be compared to the MDX query result, and you'll find that the same amount aggregate values are displayed.

To restrict the recordset to display only amounts for manager 'Stock', use a Where clause as in:

```
strsql = "Select [Measures].[Amount],[Manager].[Manager Lastname]
    From Investments Where ([Manager].[Manager Lastname]) = 'Stock'"
```

or

```
strsql = "Select SUM([Measures].[Amount]),[Manager].[Manager Lastname]
    From Investments Where ([Manager].[Manager Lastname]) = 'Stock'
    Group By ([Manager].[Manager Lastname])"
```

Now let's look at another method of flattening that uses a mixture of ADO and ADO MD.

Flattening the Dataset from an MDX Query

Set up the Ch06 project Navigate Cellset button to run the following query. (The project is distributed with this query active, so if you haven't changed it, it's already set up.)

```
strmdx = "Select {[Measures].[Amount],[Measures].[Sh Num]} On Columns,
    Crossjoin({[Manager].members},{ [Account].members}) on rows From Investments"
```

When you run the application and click the Navigate Cellset button, you should see the members and measures values for all cells in the resulting cellset, starting with the Amount measure in position 0 of axis 0 enumerating all axis 1 positions and ending with the Sh Num measure in position 1 of axis 0 enumerating all axis 1 positions once again. There are a total of 98 cells displayed in the list box.

Now if you click the Flattened Dataset button, this same MDX query will be flattened by assigning the MDX query, normally assigned to the cellset *Source* property, to the Source property of an ADODB *Recordset* object and opening the recordset. The resulting records in the recordset are displayed in the list box. There are 49 records.

```
Dim rs As New ADODB.Recordset

strmdx = "Select {[Measures].[Amount],[Measures].[Sh Num]} On Columns,
    Crossjoin({[Manager].members},{ [Account].members}) on rows From Investments"

rs.Source = strmdx
```

```
rs.ActiveConnection = cnn
rs.Open     'Or specify the strmdx variable here instead of setting Source.
```

If you need both a cellset and recordset in your application, the cellset Source property can be assigned into the recordset Source property:

```
Dim rs As New ADODB.Recordset
Dim cset As New ADOMD.Cellset

strmdx = "Select {[Measures].[Amount],[Measures].[Sh Num]} On Columns,
    Crossjoin({[Manager].members},{ [Account].members}) on rows From Investments"


cset.Open strmdx


rs.Source = cset.Source
rs.ActiveConnection = cnn
rs.Open
```

Each record of the recordset holds both the Amount and Sh Num measures in addition to a field for each of the dimension members at the current position of the row axis (axis 1). Multiplying the number of records returned by the number of measures projected onto the column axis yields the number of cells displayed from the Navigate Cellset button.

As you can see, the flattened dataset resulting from this method is quite different from the results you get from using a SQL statement. Using SQL with MSOLAP, you need to be careful as to how you state the SQL statement to ensure you get what you want in the resulting recordset. With the method just illustrated using the Source property of the Recordset object, you get essentially the same result you would get from the MDX query returned in a cellset, only flattened into a recordset organization.

Study the results in the list box after clicking the Flattened Dataset button and pay close attention to how the field names are constructed for the dimension members. Knowing how OLAP Services constructs these field names will enable you to access the field values using the names of the fields rather than their index.

Working with the Data Definition Language

The PivotTable Service supports a data definition language (DDL) that supplements MDX to create local cubes, calculated members with session scope, user-defined sets with session scope, and cache with session scope.

Scope refers to the lifetime of the calculated member, set, or cache. In this section, you use DDL to create these items and give them a lifetime of the session in which they are defined. While the user remains connected with the OLAP server, these items can be referenced from within the user session and only by the user session defining them. Once the user breaks the session with the OLAP server, however, these items are released and no longer available.

 'In Chapter 7, we'll explore an even shorter lifetime for these items, one of only the duration of a given query.

Creating Calculated Members

Calculated members can be built using cube data, expressions, and functions that may be chosen from the built-in functions listed in Appendix G, from third-party function libraries, or from registered user-defined function libraries. In Chapter 3, you defined a calculated member in the Measures dimension named Price. Price is a simple expression that divides the sum of shares into the sum of invested dollars for each measure displayed (this expression is also known as the Net Asset Value or NAV). The resulting quotient is not stored in the cube, but the expression is, as we saw when we enumerated the commands collection of the Investments cube in Chapter 5. This type of calculated member is said to have global scope because it can be used in any query in any session.

Calculated members can also be defined for use by any query but only within the session defining the calculated member. This is done by using the CREATE MEMBER statement.

The syntax for the CREATE MEMBER statement is:

```
CREATE <optional-scope> MEMBER <cube-name>.<fully-qualified-member-name> AS
'<expression>' [.<property-definition-list>]
```

where <optional-scope> is:

```
<empty> | SESSION
```

and where <property-definition-list> is defined as:

```
<property-definition>  | <property-definition>. <property-definition-list>
```

and a <property-definition> is defined as:

```
<property-identifier> = <string> | <number>
```

Let's create a calculated member for the Investments cube that yields the average invested amount, across all client accounts (defined in our cube as roll-ups to client state), for each of the funds represented in the cube. To do this, you use the *Avg* function provided by Microsoft. Its syntax is:

```
Avg(<Set>[,<Numeric Expression>])
```

The Avg function will calculate the average of <Numeric Expression> over the tuples in the <Set> specified in the first argument. You are interested in obtaining the average Amount over the Account.Members for any given fund. You express this in code with the following calculated member:

```
CREATE MEMBER [Investments].[Measures].[Average Investment] As
  'AVG(GENERATE({[Fund].CurrentMember},EXCEPT({[Account].Members},
    {[Account].[All Account]})),[Measures].Amount)'
```

The CREATE MEMBER statement here names the member as [Average Investment] and places it in the Measures dimension. The cube qualification here is required. Following the member name, you specify the expression OLAP Services is to store for this member and use to calculate the member whenever you reference Average Investment in a query within your current session.

The set in the first argument of the Avg function just shown is a bit complex for us to dive into right now. We'll defer discussion of this until Chapter 7. The resulting set from this expression is the set of all accounts, excluding the *All Account* member, for the current fund in a query. The average amount is then calculated over the tuples in this set whenever Average Investment appears in a query.

In Visual Basic code (see the code behind the Create Member button in the Ch06 project), the CREATE MEMBER statement is submitted to OLAP Services via the connection object *Execute* method:

```
strmdx = "CREATE MEMBER [Investments].[Measures].[Average Investment] As
  'AVG(GENERATE({[Fund].CurrentMember},EXCEPT({[Account].Members},
    {[Account].[All Account]})),[Measures].Amount)'"

cnn.Execute strmdx, 0
```

Once this member is defined, you can refer to it anywhere in our current session with statements like this:

```
SELECT {[Measures].[Amount],[Average Investment]} ON COLUMNS,
{[Fund].Members} ON ROWS
FROM Investments
```

CONSIDERING EMPTY CELLS

As defined previously, the Average Investment does not consider empty cells in calculating the average. By default, all numeric functions, with the exception of the *Count* function, exclude empty cells. If you look at the resulting average for Brandy Wine for example, you'll see that the sum of the investments is $40,000 and the average investment over all accounts investing in this fund is $40,000, indicating that the average calculation found one account investing in this fund. Other accounts, those that did not invest in Brandy Wine, were not considered in the average calculation.

You'll also notice from the results that where there were no accounts at all investing in a fund, Acorn International for example, the average investment is displayed as –1.#IND. This results from an attempt to calculate an average on a Null value. I once worked with a colleague who referred to these values as "wonkies." Somehow, the word makes sense.

To force the average calculation to count null cells and replace the wonkies with zero, you can code the *CoalesceEmpty* function into the Avg expression like this:

```
CREATE MEMBER [Investments].[Measures].[Average Investment] As
'AVG(GENERATE({[Fund].CurrentMember},EXCEPT({[Account].Members},
 {[Account].[All Account]}))),CoalesceEmpty([Measures].[Amount],0))'
```

If you run the procedure behind the Create Member button using the preceding calculated member specification, you get an average investment of $6,666.67 for Brandy Wine instead of the previous $40,000. This is due to the CoalesceEmpty function forcing null amounts to zero, causing them to be counted. The amount $6,666.67 is the average investment over all accounts, regardless of whether an account invested in Brandy Wine or not.

So which way should you code the calculated member? It depends on how you want the average expressed. To obtain the average investment over those accounts actually investing in a fund, exclude the CoalesceEmpty function. To obtain the average investment over all accounts, whether they invested in a fund or not, use CoalesceEmpty.

If you elect to exclude the CoalesceEmpty function from the Avg expression, you are stuck with wonkies in our dataset. We'll deal with this issue next.

Creating User-Defined Sets

The *set* is an important concept in querying cubes. It defines the tuples that are to be accessed in the evaluation of a query or expression. Up until now, you have specified sets as tuples well known to OLAP Services within the context of a cube. The set {[Account].Members} is the set of all members in the Account dimension. The set {[Measures].[Amount],[Average Investment]} is the set consisting of an Amount from the Measures dimension and the Average Investment calculated member, also from the Measures dimension.

Sets are usually delimited by curly braces, {}. Although these delimiters are at times optional in MDX, I recommend using them to enhance readability and to reduce the risk of errors. If the syntax calls for a set, use the curly braces. An exception to this rule might be when you place a function that returns a set, such as Generate or CrossJoin, into a statement where a set is called for. In this case, the curly braces are not necessary but it doesn't hurt to use them.

You may find it helpful to define a set for use in your application. These sets are known as *named sets* or *user-defined sets* and can be placed anywhere a set is called for in a statement.

The syntax for creating user-defined sets is:

```
CREATE <optional-scope> SET <cube-name>.<set-name> AS '<set-expression>'
```

where <optional-scope> is specified as:

```
<empty> | SESSION
```

> In version 7.0, named sets are not exposed through the ADO schema rowsets. A client application must know that the sets exist for use in queries. This is likely to be fixed in future versions of OLAP services.

For the Average Investment calculated member expression, it would be nice to have a set that would contain only non-null members. Using such a set in the Avg function would result in calculations only where there are values. You would never see a wonkie in the result, because null sums would not be seen by the Avg function.

Conceptually, the preceding approach sounds as if it would solve your problem. But stop a minute and think about what is going on with calculated members. The expression as you've define it in the CREATE MEMBER statement is using the current member of the fund. When a query asks for [Average Investment] to be displayed in a dataset, the expression you have specified for the Average Investment calculated member is executed for each current fund, calculating an average over the accounts associated with the current fund in the dataset.

The Avg expression for the Average Investment calculated member refers to the current member of the Fund dimension. The current member is the Fund dimension member of the cell currently being evaluated for calculation of the average investment amount. The member value is dependent upon the query in which the calculated member is used. In this example, it is the query that dictates member selection, and these selected tuples define the values that your calculated member will work with. The best way to view this is to visualize the cellset resulting from the query as the controlling factor for selecting cells that will be seen by a calculated member expression.

You certainly could have written the Average Investment calculated member expression to calculate the average over all accounts, ignoring current position in any given query that uses the calculated member. This calculated member is still calculated at the time a query runs but has no relationship to any tuple members in the dataset. The displayed average investment in this case would just be the average over all accounts in the cube and would be the same value for any displayed tuple in the dataset. Although this type of calculated member expression may be helpful at times, you'll generally find that your calculated member expressions must be written to refer to current values from the query in some fashion, as you have done with Average Investment.

With this view in mind, you can look at your problem a little differently. If you leave the Average Investment calculated member expression alone and concentrate on filtering the data that will be exposed to the expression, the data from the query, then the expression will only see nonempty members. This is exactly what you want.

To build this special non-null member set, you use the following statement:

```
CREATE SET [Investments].[NONNULLAMOUNTS] AS
'FILTER({[Fund].MEMBERS},([MEASURES].AMOUNT > 0))'
```

Another method you can use to define the NONNULLAMOUNTS set that eliminates empty cells and admits all numeric values uses the IsEmpty function. This is illustrated below:

```
CREATE SET [Investments].[NONNULLAMOUNTS] AS
'FILTER({[Fund].MEMBERS},(NOT IsEmpty([MEASURES].AMOUNT)))'
```

With this set defined, you can now use it, not in the calculated member expression, but in the SELECT query.

```
SELECT {[Measures].[Amount],[Average Investment]} ON COLUMNS,
{[NONNULLAMOUNTS]} ON ROWS
FROM Investments
```

The result consists of all funds having at least one account invested in the fund. The Average Investment is then calculated with these values, and all the wonkies are gone.

Keep one point in mind when you work with numeric functions such as Avg: These functions are working within the context of the cube and not the data warehouse fact table detail. When you ask for average investment amounts as you have done here, the average is calculated using summary or aggregated values and a count of these values from the specified set. The answer would be different if you asked for the same average from the data warehouse. This is because data warehouse queries take an average over the transaction detail in the fact table using a different count from that used in the cube.

The Fund_Investments.sql and CGM_Investments.sql files in the Ch06 folder on the CD contain queries against the Investments fact table in FundAcctsWH. Run these queries in the Query Analyzer and compare the average of CGM Mutual investments to the average you saw from the MDX query. You should see different results because these queries are calculating an average over a different set of amounts.

It is important for you and your users to understand this difference. You will most likely end up incorporating a transaction count into your cube so that you can provide your users with either average. Having a count as a measure in your cube enables you to write expressions that calculate the average yourself rather than using the built-in Avg function.

Dropping Sets and Members

When a set or member is no longer needed in a session, you can drop it using a DROP statement. The syntax for this statement is:

```
DROP MEMBER <membername>[,<membername>. . .]
```

or

```
DROP SET <setname>[,<setname>. . .]
```

Creating a Cache

The CREATE CACHE statement enables you to cache a slice of a cube on the client. This cache is used to improve performance in your application. The CREATE CACHE syntax is:

```
CREATE <optional-scope> CACHE FOR <cube-name> AS
  '(<set-expression> [,<set-expression>...])'
```

where

```
<optional-scope> is <empty> | SESSION
```

The <set-expression> follows the rules for specifying sets, but each set expression must contain members from only one dimension and each set expression must refer to different dimensions. The Measures dimension is not allowed in the CRE-ATE CACHE statement.

If you were to execute one or more queries that required both the CT and NY members from the Account dimension, you could improve the performance of these queries by caching these members. To do this, you create a session cache as:

```
CREATE CACHE FOR [Investments] AS '(([Account].[All Account].[CT],
    [Account].[All Account].[NY]))'
```

Subsequent queries involving these Account members and executed within the same session as this CREATE CACHE statement result in the members being retrieved from cache rather than the cube.

Creating Local Cubes

The OLAP server cubes we explored in Chapter 5 using DSO cannot be built with the PivotTable Service. Whereas DSO fully supports the creation of a cube on an OLAP server, the PivotTable Service only supports the creation of local cubes.

Unlike server-based cubes, local cubes offer only two modes of storage, MOLAP and ROLAP. If you create a MOLAP local cube, all dimension members and measures data are stored locally in the cube structure. These cubes can be analyzed while disconnected from an OLAP server and data source. Creation time for MOLAP cubes may be longer than for ROLAP cubes, but query performance is enhanced.

Additional differences between local cubes and server-based cubes are that local cubes do not contain aggregation designs as server-based cubes do, and queries against local cubes are not multithreaded.

If you choose ROLAP storage mode, the dimension members are stored in the cube but the measures data remains in the data source. Querying local ROLAP cubes requires a connection to the cube's data source.

To create a local cube, the CREATE CUBE statement is used. The syntax of this statement is shown here:

```
CREATE CUBE <cube name> (
    DIMENSION <dimension name> [TYPE TIME], <hierarchy def> [<hierarchy def>...]
    [{, DIMENSION <dimension name> [TYPE TIME],<hierarchy def>
      [<hierarchy def>...]}...] ,
    MEASURE <measure name> <measure function def> [<measure format def>]
      [<measure type def>]
    [{, MEASURE <measure name> <measure function def> [<measure format def>]
      [<measure type def>] }...]
    [,COMMAND <expression>] [,COMMAND <expression>...] )
```

where:

```
<dimension name> is a legal name.
<hierarchy def> is [HIERARCHY <hierarchy name>,] <level def> [,<level def>...]
```

```
<level def> is LEVEL <level name> [TYPE <level type>] [<level format def>]
    [<level options def>]
<level type> is ALL | YEAR | QUARTER | MONTH | WEEK | DAY | DAYOFWEEK | DATE |
                HOUR | MINUTE | SECOND
<level format def> is FORMAT_NAME <expression> [FORMAT_KEY <expression>]
<level options def> is OPTIONS (<option>[,<option>][,<option>...)
<option> is UNIQUE | SORTBYNAME | SORTBYKEY
<measure function def> is FUNCTION <function name>
<measure format def> is FORMAT <expression>
<function name> is SUM | MIN | MAX | COUNT
<measure type def> is TYPE <supported OLEDB numeric types>
<supported OLEDB numeric types> is DBTYPE_I1 | DBTYPE_I2 | DBTYPE_I4 | DBTYPE_I8
| DBTYPE_UI1 | DBTYPE_UI2 | DBTYPE_UI4 | DBTYPE_UI8 | DBTYPE_R4 | DBTYPE_R8 |
DBTYPE_CY | DBTYPE_DECIMAL | DBTYPE_NUMERIC | DBTYPE_DATE
```

As an example of the use of CREATE CUBE, create a local cube named *Dividends*. This cube will have the same dimensions as the server-based Investments cube, but instead of the measures representing client investment amounts, the Dividends cube will represent client dividends received.

When a fund declares a dividend, the dividend is distributed to all holders of shares in the fund. The client's account receives the dividend amount times the number of shares owned as of the date of the dividend.

Within the sample mutual fund account system, dividends are recorded in the Tranhistory table according to the following transaction types:

ST CG D   Short-Term Capital Gain Dividend

Cap G D   Capital Gain Dividend

Inc Div   Income Dividend

Each of these transaction types represents a different tax treatment for the dividend. Transactions carrying these same codes but appended with the letter C indicate the dividend was distributed as cash and not reinvested into the client portfolio.

For the Dividends cube, you select only dividend transactions that were reinvested. These amounts are already stored in the Dividends fact table in the sample FundAcctsWH database, and this is the source you use for creating our Dividends cube. The Data Transformation Services package used to extract these records from the FundAccts database can be found in the Ch06 folder on the CD and also in the DTSPackages folder on the CD. The name of the package is DTS_Dividends.dts. If you built the FundAcctsWH database from scratch, you can run this package (after modifying it for your environment as discussed in the Readme file in the DTSPackages folder) to transfer the data and build the Dividends fact table.

The CREATE CUBE statement for the Dividends cube is shown here:

```
CREATE CUBE Dividends( DIMENSION [Account],LEVEL [All Account]  TYPE ALL,
    LEVEL [State Abbr] , DIMENSION [Fund],LEVEL [All Fund]  TYPE ALL,
    LEVEL [Fund Name] , DIMENSION [Manager],LEVEL [All Manager]  TYPE ALL,
    LEVEL [Manager Lastname] , DIMENSION [Time] TYPE TIME,
    HIERARCHY [TranDate], LEVEL [All Time]  TYPE ALL,
    LEVEL [Year]  TYPE YEAR, LEVEL [Quarter]  TYPE QUARTER,
    LEVEL [Month]  TYPE MONTH, DIMENSION [Office],
    LEVEL [All Office]  TYPE ALL, LEVEL [Region] ,
    LEVEL [Accounting] , LEVEL [Business] ,
    MEASURE [Amount] Function Sum Format 'Currency',
    MEASURE [Sh Num] Function Sum Type DBTYPE_DECIMAL);
```

This CREATE CUBE statement defines the cube's structure by specifying the dimensions and levels the cube is to have in addition to the measures for the cube. This cube looks exactly like the Investments cube except for the named Hierarchy, TranDate, you have inserted into the Dividends cube.

After defining the structure of the cube, you need to populate the cube with dimension members. Since you are defining a MOLAP cube, you also need to populate the cube with measures. Both of these tasks are achieved with the INSERT INTO statement. The syntax of INSERT INTO is:

```
INSERT INTO <target-clause> [<options-clause>] [<bind-clause>] <source-clause>
```

where:

```
<target-clause> is <cube-name> ( <target-element-list> )
<target-element-list> is <target-element>[, <target-element-list>]
<target-element> is [<dim-name>.[<hierarchy-name>.]]<level-name>
   | <time-dim-name>
   | [Measures.]<measure-name>
   | SKIPONECOLUMN
<level-name> is <simple-level-name> | <simple-level-time>.NAME |
   <simple-level-time>.KEY
<time-dim-name> is <dim-name-type-time> | <dim-name-type-time>.NAME |
   <dim-name-type-time>.KEY
<options-clause> is OPTIONS <options-list>
<options-list> is <option>[, <options-list>]
<option> is <defer-options> | < analysis-options>
<defer-options> is DEFER_DATA | ATTEMPT_DEFER
<analysis-options> is PASSTHROUGH | ATTEMPT_ANALYSIS
<bind-clause> is BIND (<bind-list>)
<bind-list> is <simple-column-name>[,<simple-column-name>]
<simple-column-name> is <identifier>
```

```
<source-clause> is SELECT <columns-list>
  FROM <tables-list>
  [ WHERE <where-clause> ]
  | DIRECTLYFROMCACHEDROWSET <hex-number>
<columns-list> is <column-expression> [, < columns-list> ]
<column-expression> is <column-expression-name>
<column-expression-name> is <column-name> [AS <alias-name>]
  | <alias name> <column-name>
<column-name> is <table-name>.<column-name>
  | <column-function> | <ODBC scalar function> | <braced-expression>
<column function> is <identifier>(. . .)
<ODBC scalar function> is {FN<column-function>}
<braced-expression> is (. . .)
<tables list> is <table-expression> [, <table-list>]
<table-expression> is <table-name> [ [AS] <table-alias>]
<table-alias> is <identifier>
<table-name> is <identifier>
<where clause> is <where-condition> [AND <where-clause>]
<where condition> is <join-constraint> | <application constraint>
<join-constraint> is <column-name> = <column-name>
  | <open-paren><column-name> = <column-name><close-paren>
<application-constraint> is (. . .) | NOT (. . .) | (. . .) OR (. . .)
<identifier> is <letter>{<letter>|<digit>|<underline>|<dollar>|<sharp>}. . .
```

To populate the Dividends cube described here with the CREATE CUBE statement selecting data from the Dividends fact table and related dimension tables in the FundAcctsWH database, you need to issue the following statement:

```
INSERT INTO Dividends( Account.[State Abbr], Fund.[Fund Name],
    Manager.[Manager Lastname], Office.[Region],
    Office.[Accounting], Office.[Business],
    Time.TranDate.[Year], Time.TranDate.[Quarter], Time.TranDate.[Month],
    Measures.[Amount], Measures.[Sh Num] )
SELECT Accounts.state_abbr AS Col1,
       Funds.fund_name AS Col2,
       Managers.manager_lastname AS Col3,
       Offices.region AS Col4,
       Offices.accounting AS Col5,
       Offices.business AS Col6,
       DatePart(year,Dividends.trandate) AS Col7,
       DatePart(quarter,Dividends.trandate) AS Col8,
       DatePart(month,Dividends.trandate) AS Col9,
       Dividends.amount AS Col10,
       Dividends.sh_num AS Col11
    From [Dividends], [Accounts], [Funds], [Managers], [Offices]
```

```
Where [Dividends].[fundacctno] = [Accounts].[fundacctno] And
    [Dividends].[fund_cd] = [Funds].[fund_cd] And
    [Dividends].[manager_num] = [Managers].[manager_num] And
    [Dividends].[office_num] = [Offices].[office_num];
```

In the preceding SELECT statement, you must match the order of columns in the select column list to the column specification in the INSERT INTO statement.

Now that you have the cube structure specified and the statement necessary to populate the cube with data, your next task is to submit these statements to the PivotTable Service.

Since you need to specify the cube file you are about to create as a data source but the cube file is not yet created, you need to open the connection with the PivotTable Service and create the cube at the same time. With DSO, you had an object hierarchy you could work with to create a cube on an active connection with the OLAP server. Using the PivotTable Service, you don't have that luxury when it comes to creating cubes.

The connection string you use to create your cube looks like this:

```
"Provider=msolap;Data Source=c:\Dividends.cub;SOURCE_DSN=FundAccts;"
```

The Data Source component of the connection string points to the path and filename of the Dividends cube. The connection string specifies a system DSN, named FundAccts, that uses the SQL Server driver and points to the source SQL Server where the FundAcctsWH database is managed. You'll need to establish this DSN on your machine before running the Ch06 create local cube sample found behind the Create Local Cube button in the Ch06 project on the CD.

Run the Create Local Cube sample in the Ch06 Visual Basic project. After it finishes, you should see the Dividends.cub file in your C: drive root folder or whichever folder you specified in the Data Source of your connect string.

Notice that nowhere in the previous CREATE CUBE statement or INSERT INTO statement did you specify which storage mode you wanted. Without any specification at all, the resulting cube storage mode is MOLAP. To create a ROLAP cube, you need to specify the OPTIONS DEFER_DATA clause in the INSERT INTO statement.

INSERT INTO STATEMENT OPTIONS

The options you use in the INSERT INTO statement affect the treatment of the SELECT statement and the resulting storage mode for the cube.

When you use the PASSTHROUGH option, the PivotTable Service makes no attempt at parsing the SELECT statement but instead passes the statement to the data source for execution. The use of this option depends on your choice for other options.

Without PASSTHROUGH, the PivotTable Service attempts to parse the query itself into a set of equivalent statements, which it then issues to the data source. These equivalent statements can at times result in more efficient queries against the data source.

Using DEFER_DATA, the PivotTable Service attempts to parse the query locally and execute it when retrieving data from the data source. This option results in a ROLAP storage mode. You cannot specify PASSTHROUGH with this option.

The ATTEMPT_DEFER option causes the PivotTable Service to attempt a parse of the SELECT statement, and if it is successful, the resulting behavior is that of DEFER_DATA. If the parse is not successful, the statement is passed to the data source as if PASSTHROUGH had been specified. If the statement is successfully parsed by the data source, the result is a MOLAP storage mode.

Your choice of these options of course depends on the volume of your data, the available local resources, and your user requirements.

LOCAL CUBES AND AGGREGATIONS

Another difference between OLAP server cubes and local cubes is that the PivotTable Service does not have any facilities to define, store, and manage aggregations. When you defined the Investments cube in Chapter 3 using the OLAP Manager, you went through an exercise of designing and building aggregations. Not so in the creation of your Dividends local cube. With the OLAP server cube, aggregation design dictates that a certain percentage of all possible aggregations for a given cube are precalculated and stored in the cube, ready for access by a user query. For those aggregations that are not stored, OLAP Services must access the detail fact table data and calculate the aggregation on the fly to satisfy a user request. The performance of this on-the-fly aggregation depends in part on the storage mode selected for the cube. With local cubes, all query requests are satisfied with on-the-fly aggregations and local MOLAP cubes should in most cases result in better performance over ROLAP.

Summary

We've explored the ADO MD object model and how it can be used in conjunction with the ADO object model in an OLAP application.

We saw how to establish a connection with an OLAP server, how ADO MD objects can be used to explore the schema of an OLAP catalog, and how to retrieve data through the use of cellsets. Various methods of cellset navigation were also explored.

The PivotTable Service support for SQL was discussed including how it can be used to produce a flattened dataset. This enables us to look at a multidimensional dataset as we would a relational recordset. The ADO recordset was used in another method of flattening a dataset that assigns an MDX statement to a recordset's Source property.

The data definition language extension to MDX was introduced where we created calculated members, sets, and cache to be used within the scope of an OLAP session. Our discussion of the calculated member looked at how an average can be calculated and some things to keep in mind when you deal with these types of calculations.

Last, we discussed the creation of local cubes using the PivotTable Service. We looked at how the CREATE CUBE statement is used to describe the local cube and how the INSERT INTO statement is used for populating the cube. Storage modes and options were explored in addition to some of the differences between local cubes created with the PivotTable Service and server cubes created with DSO.

Chapter 7 provides an introduction to MDX in sufficient detail to enable you to work through the examples found in the remainder of the book. In Chapter 10, we explore more of MDX, construct queries against the local Dividends cube we created in this chapter and against OLAP server cubes using the PivotTable Service.

Chapter 11 uses the PivotTable Service to access cubes from Excel 2000. In that chapter we explore the use of Pivot tables and Pivot charts for presenting OLAP data.

Part II

Examining the Microsoft OLAP Services Components

CHAPTER 7
Introduction to Multidimensional Expressions

CHAPTER 8
Building Applications with Decision Support Objects

CHAPTER 9
Using OLAP Manager Add-Ins

CHAPTER 10
More MDX

CHAPTER 11
Exploring Microsoft Excel 2000 and OLAP

Chapter 7

Introduction to Multidimensional Expressions

IN THIS CHAPTER

◆ Exploring the basic MDX statement structure

◆ Learning about slicer dimensions and expressions

◆ Discovering how to author and use your own function libraries

◆ Learning how to define calculated members with query scope

◆ Accessing member properties

MULTIDIMENSIONAL EXPRESSIONS (MDX) IS a language defined by OLE DB for OLAP for working with multidimensional data stores. The language consists of statements and clauses similar to Transact-SQL but specifically adapted to multidimensional terminology associated with the cube model.

An extension to the OLE DB for OLAP specification provides for data definition language (DDL) support in creating cubes, calculated members, sets, and cache, all of which was introduced in Chapter 6.

The MDX statement samples found in this chapter are located in ASCII files in the Chapter07 folder on the CD. These files have an .mdx extension. You can run these statements by copy and paste into a program similar to the Ch06 Visual Basic project we explored in the previous chapter, or you can open them in the MDX Sample Application installed with the OLAP client installation. This program is named MDXSampl.exe and can be found in the path <installation drive>:\OLAP Services\Samples\MdxSample\.

The MDX Sample Application is written in Visual Basic, and the full source code for this application can be found in the same folder as the executable. It's worth opening this project and browsing through the code to see how the application manages the datasets returned from a user query.

MDX Statements

A query against multidimensional data is expressed in the form of an MDX statement, and the results of the query are returned as a *dataset*. Datasets in ADO MD are known as *cellsets*. The simple form of an MDX statement looks like this:

```
Select <axis_specification> [, <axis_specification> . . .]
From <cube_name>
```

The <axis_specification> is defined as:

```
[NON EMPTY] <set> [<dimension_properties>] ON <axis_name>
```

The <axis_name> token may be any of the following:

```
COLUMNS | ROWS | PAGES | SECTIONS | CHAPTERS | AXIS(<index>)
```

The index mapping that can be used in place of the five axis names is:

AXIS(0) = COLUMNS

AXIS(1) = ROWS

AXIS(2) = PAGES

AXIS(3) = SECTIONS

AXIS(4) = CHAPTERS

When referring to axes in an MDX statement, you cannot skip an axis. You receive an error if you specify the COLUMN axis followed by the PAGES, axis skipping the ROW axis. You must use axis indexes in order from lowest to highest index specified in the statement.

The NON EMPTY specifier preceding the set specification removes empty tuples from the axis. For NON EMPTY to remove a tuple, all cells at the intersection of the tuple and all other tuples from other axes must be empty.

Given the Investments cube you created in Chapter 3, you can write an MDX statement as simple as:

```
Select {[Measures].Amount} ON COLUMNS
From Investments
```

This statement results in a dataset consisting of one cell. Did you expect to see several rows of Amounts returned as you would if you had entered the SQL equivalent query to retrieve Amount values from the Investments table?

The reason you only see one number in the result from this query is that OLAP Services is using members from dimensions that were not specifically assigned to an axis in the query as *slicer dimensions*, and it is filtering the data on the dimension default members. Slicer dimensions are projected onto the *slicer axis* of the dataset.

Slicing a Cube

Generally, a dimension's default member is the All member of the (All) level, if an (All) level exists. If the (All) level does not exist in a dimension, then some member from the first level of the dimension is chosen as the default. In the Investments cube, each of the dimensions contains an (All) level and an [All <dimension name>] member. The Account dimension, for example, has a default member named [All Account].

Slicer dimensions can be specified in a query using a WHERE clause. To obtain the same result as the preceding query, but by specifying the default members in a WHERE clause, you have:

```
Select {[Measures].Amount} ON COLUMNS
From Investments
Where
([Account].[All Account],[Manager].[All Manager],[Office].[All
Office],[Fund].[All Fund],[Time].[All Time])
```

If you execute the preceding query, you'll see that it does indeed return exactly the same result as our first example. The only difference is that this query specifically states the slicer dimensions whereas the first query obtained them by default.

A slicer specification in an MDX query WHERE clause is used to filter the cube data. When default members are not sufficient to produce the desired results or you need to specify specific slicer expressions in addition to the default members, you do so by adding a Where <slicer specification> to your query and providing the required filter dimension members.

If you want to select shares for the Connecticut business office and display them by manager and fund, you would code:

```
SELECT {[Manager].Members} ON COLUMNS,
{[Fund].Members} ON ROWS
FROM Investments
WHERE ([Sh Num],[Office].[Connecticut])
```

The preceding statement results in a dataset where the managers are returned on axis 0, the column axis, the funds are returned on axis 1, the row axis, and in each cell are the number of shares for the [Office].[Connecticut] member.

This statement has projected the Manager and Fund dimensions onto axes and specified a specific Measures member and Office member as slicer dimension. This leaves the Account dimension and Time dimension unaccounted for. Here again, OLAP Services uses the default members for these dimensions as slicers. Try the following statement to verify:

```
SELECT {[Manager].Members} ON COLUMNS,
{[Fund].Members} ON ROWS
FROM Investments
WHERE ([Sh Num],[Office].[Connecticut],[Time].[All Time],
[Account].[All Account])
```

You should see the same results as with the previous query. It makes sense, doesn't it? You are asking OLAP Services to retrieve data from a cube containing cells at the intersection of the members projected onto the axes of the cube. To access the cells, all coordinates must be specified. It's just like addressing an array in memory. You must code indexes for all dimensions of the array to get at a particular element of the array. It's no different with cubes.

When you need to access the slicer dimensions of a cellset in ADO MD, you can assign the *FilterAxis* property of the cellset to an Axis object and then navigate through the members of position 0. Using code similar to that found behind the cellset Cells button in the Chapter 6 Visual Basic project, you can list the slicer dimension members with:

```
Dim csetcell As ADOMD.Cell
Dim csetaxis As ADOMD.Axis
Dim csetpos As ADOMD.Position
Dim cellmember As ADOMD.Member
. . .
Set csetaxis = cset.FilterAxis
List1.AddItem csetaxis.Name & " = Cellset Axis"
For Each csetpos In csetaxis.Positions
    List1.AddItem "    " & csetpos.Ordinal & " = Axis Position Ordinal"
    For Each cellmember In csetpos.Members
        List1.AddItem "    " & cellmember.Caption & " = Position Member"
    Next
Next
```

The axis name displayed for the slicer axis is Axis(–1). Although it may seem that this axis would appear in the cellset axes collection, it does not. You need to use the FilterAxis property as done in the preceding example to access this axis, and the resulting axis is read-only.

Understanding Sets and Tuples

The *set* is an important concept in MDX. It is used in the axis specification of an MDX statement, in calculated members, and in many of the OLAP Services functions.

Sets consist of one or more *tuples,* which in turn contain one or more members from different dimensions. Sets are usually delimited by curly braces ({}).

 As we learned in Chapter 6, an axis contains a set of tuples where each tuple is known as a position or coordinate on the axis. A coordinate tuple contains one or more members, and each member is from one of the dimensions projected on the axis.

An MDX statement might express a set as a specific collection of tuples, a result of a function that returns a set, or even a set of sets. Examples of these expressions appear in this table:

Set Expression	Description
{[Account].Members}	Refers to the members of the Account dimension.
{CrossJoin ([Account].Members, [Fund].Members)}	Refers to a function that returns a set where each tuple the set consists of one member from the [Account] in dimension and one member from the [Fund] dimension. The number of sets returned is the product of the member counts in each of the dimensions specified.
{[Manager].[Yields], [Office].[Connecticut]}	The set consisting of two specific members, one from the Manager dimension and one from the Office dimension.
{[Fund].Members, [Time].Members}	The set consisting of two sets, one from the Fund dimension and the other from the Time dimension.

 As you develop MDX statements, it is helpful to design the sets for each axis in your cellset thinking about the tuples you want to see on the axis. In addition, read through the function list in Appendix G and familiarize yourself with the set category of functions and how other category functions use sets. We'll be exploring many of these in Chapter 10.

Using the WITH Clause

Chapter 6 introduced you to creating calculated members, sets, and cache having session scope. They live only for the duration of the user session in which they are created. These were all created using the MDX DDL extension language CREATE statement.

These same elements can be created for use in a specific MDX query. When the query completes and returns its dataset, the element is dropped and no longer available to other queries, even those executed within the same user session.

To create elements having query scope, you use the WITH clause followed by a keyword naming the element you are creating. This clause precedes the MDX SELECT statement. When you are creating more than one of these elements, you use the WITH keyword for the first element to be created and omit it for all subsequent elements, using only the keyword for the element to be created. If you were to create a SET followed by a calculated MEMBER followed by a CACHE in the same query, you use:

```
WITH SET <set specification>
    MEMBER <member specification>
    CACHE <cache specification>
SELECT . . .
```

The SELECT keyword is used to delimit the WITH clause. Now let's look at each element you can specify in the WITH clause.

Specifying Calculated Members

The <member_specification> syntax is used to define a calculated member or measure, and it breaks down as follows:

```
MEMBER <parent>.<member_name> AS '<value_expression>'
```

The <value_expression> value can include any functions that support MDX syntax. Here's the calculated member you created in Chapter 6:

```
CREATE MEMBER [Investments].[Measures].[Average Investment] As

'AVG(GENERATE({[Fund].CurrentMember},EXCEPT({[Account].Members},
    {[Account].[All Account]})),[Measures].Amount)'
```

Using CREATE, you are forced to prefix the name of the calculated member with the name of the cube the calculated member is associated with. Since the Average

Investment member has session scope, OLAP Services needs to know the cube this member will apply to.

Using a WITH clause, the calculated member is associated with the query, and therefore the cube is referenced in the query FROM clause, so here you needn't (and shouldn't) prefix a cube name to the member.

```
WITH MEMBER [Measures].[Average Investment] As
  'AVG(GENERATE({[Fund].CurrentMember},EXCEPT({[Account].Members},
   {[Account].[All Account]})),[Measures].Amount)'
```

The name of the calculated member is [Average Investment], and its parent is the [Measures] dimension. The expression that defines this member is given in quotes.

The Average Investment expression uses the *Avg* function, which calculates the average of an optional numeric expression over a set. The numeric expression used here is the Amount measure specified as the second argument to the Avg function.

The first argument to the Avg function, which needs to be a set, is specified as another function. This function is the *Generate* function, which returns a set generated by pairing each member in its first argument set with every member in its second argument set. This results in a set of tuples containing members from each of the arguments.

In the Generate function just described, the first argument set is the current member of the Fund dimension. The current member refers to the member at the current position in an iteration through the members of the Fund dimension.

The second argument of the Generate function is yet another function named *Except*. The Except function returns a set that is the difference between the sets specified in the first and second arguments. In the preceding case, you are asking for the difference between the set of all Account dimension members and the set consisting of the [All Account] member. Because [Account].Members returns all members including the [All Account] member, the difference between these set arguments is all Account members except the [All Account] member. You need to exclude this member so as not to inflate the average calculation, because the [All Account] member is the sum of all members in the Account dimension.

Assuming you are positioned on the Brandy Wine fund in the iteration through the Fund members, Generate pairs each member of the result difference set with the Brandy Wine and creates a set of tuples such as:

```
{(Brandy Wine,CT),(Brandy Wine,NY),. . . .}
```

The Avg function then calculates the average of the Amount values across the tuples using the count of the tuples as the divisor in the average formula. In building the return dataset, OLAP Services invokes this calculated member expression and returns the result in the dataset as [Average Investment] for the current position. The next position is then set, and the calculated member calculated for that position, using the position's current member and so on throughout the query processing.

Before we leave the MEMBER clause, there are two other parts to the clause that we need to look at. The first is the *solve order* specification. It is placed after the member expression like this:

```
WITH MEMBER [Measures].[Average Investment] As
  'AVG(GENERATE({[Fund].CurrentMember},EXCEPT({[Account].Members},
    {[Account].[All Account]})),[Measures].Amount)',
  SOLVE_ORDER = 1
```

The solve order specifies the order in which the calculated member will be solved when more than one calculated member is given. If not specified, the solve order is zero. The calculated member expression with the lowest solve order is solved first.

The second part that can be added to a MEMBER clause is a member property definition. This definition enables us to specify a *format string* to be applied to the calculated member you are creating. Adding this part to the MEMBER clause, you have:

```
WITH MEMBER [Measures].[Average Investment] As
  'AVG(GENERATE({[Fund].CurrentMember},EXCEPT({[Account].Members},
    {[Account].[All Account]})),[Measures].Amount)',
  SOLVE_ORDER = 1, FORMAT_STRING = '$###,##0.'
```

Using the preceding format string, the Average Investment is displayed rounded to the nearest whole dollar amount. The format string specifiers are listed in Appendix D in the MDX reference.

Specifying Sets

We saw in Chapter 6 that when the Avg function comes across a null sum for a given set, say {(Brandy Wine,<. . .>)}, for the first argument set, the resulting average is a wonky (–1.#IND). Filtering out the sets where this condition would arise eliminates the wonkies from our dataset. This is one place where a special Set comes in handy.

The <set_specification> syntax is used to define a set, and it breaks down as follows:

```
SET <set_name> AS '<set>'
```

The set we used in Chapter 6 to eliminate null sets from being exposed to the Average Investment calculated member expression is:

```
CREATE SET [Investments].[NONNULLAMOUNTS] AS
'FILTER({[Fund].MEMBERS},([MEASURES].AMOUNT > 0))'
```

To specify this set with query scope, you would code:

```
WITH SET [NONNULLAMOUNTS] AS
'FILTER({[Fund].MEMBERS},([MEASURES].AMOUNT > 0))'
```

The Filter function searches through the first argument set and returns those members satisfying the second argument search condition, in this case, those members in the Fund dimension where Amount is greater than zero (you're not including zero investments, only positive investments). The result of Filter is another set, but with amounts greater than zero and no nulls.

Following the WITH clause, the <set_name> value is used to reference the set. The entire MDX query now looks like this:

```
WITH SET [NONNULLAMOUNTS] AS
'FILTER({[Fund].MEMBERS},([MEASURES].AMOUNT > 0))'
    MEMBER [Measures].[Average Investment] AS
'AVG(GENERATE({[Fund].CurrentMember},EXCEPT({[Account].Members},
    {[Account].[All Account]})),[Measures].Amount)'
SELECT {[Measures].[Amount],[Average Investment]} ON COLUMNS,
{[NONNULLAMOUNTS]} ON ROWS
FROM Investments
```

In one statement you have filtered the Fund members to those having non-null amounts, defined an average calculation using those amounts, and specified a query to return the resulting averages by Fund. When the query completes, both the NONNULLAMOUNTS set and the Average Investment calculated member are released, not to become available again without respecifying them in another query or creating them with session scope.

Specifying a Cache

From the preceding discussion of calculated members, you can see that there is often an opportunity for improving the performance of a query. One option for improving performance is to use a cache.

The <cache_specification> syntax is used to populate a cache with a cube slice defined by sets of members. The syntax follows:

```
CACHE AS '(<set> [,<set>])'
```

The <set> value, in both the <set_specification> syntax and the <cache_specification> syntax, can include functions that support MDX syntax.

When you are using <set> within the <cache_specification> syntax, the following rules apply:

◆ Each <set> must contain members from only one dimension.

◆ Each member must be distinct.

◆ Each <set> must be from a different dimension.

◆ The <set> cannot contain measures.

The sets you specify in the CACHE clause used inside a WITH clause should contain members that you will reference in the associated query. When choosing these sets, be careful not to cache large amounts of data, because this can degrade performance rather than improve it.

Candidates for the query you built in the "Specifying Sets" section are Funds members and Account members. Since you know that these dimensions are not all that large, you may choose to set up a cache for both.

```
WITH CACHE AS '({[Account].Members},
  {[Fund].Members})'
```

Adding this clause to your query, you now have:

```
WITH CACHE AS '({[Account].Members},
  {[Fund].Members})'
    SET [NONNULLAMOUNTS] AS
'FILTER({[Fund].MEMBERS},([MEASURES].AMOUNT > 0))'
    MEMBER [Measures].[Average Investment] AS
'AVG(GENERATE({[Fund].CurrentMember},EXCEPT({[Account].Members},
    {[Account].[All Account]})),[Measures].Amount)'
SELECT {[Measures].[Amount],[Average Investment]} ON COLUMNS,
{[NONNULLAMOUNTS]} ON ROWS
FROM Investments
```

With such a small sample cube as you are using here, it is difficult to see the benefit of the cache. As with most performance tuning efforts, no one can tell you what setting or cache specification is going to work best in your installation. The best advice is for you to experiment yourself with various cache specifications on your own cubes and select the one providing the most gain.

Using Functions

Expressions used in MDX statements can refer to functions found in the OLAP Services function library, a third-party function library, or one that you custom build yourself.

In this section, we explore how these libraries can be built and registered with OLAP Services and how you can use their functions in MDX statements.

Built-In Functions

OLAP Services registers its own function library, the VBA332.DLL Visual Basic for Applications Expression Services library, and the Excel worksheet functions.

The table in Appendix G lists the OLAP Services functions, their syntax, and short descriptions of what they do. These functions are arranged by the categories listed in Table 7-1.

TABLE 7-1 FUNCTION CATEGORIES

Category Name	Description
Array	As of this writing, this category contains only one function. The SetToArray function converts one or more sets to an array with the number of dimensions equal to the number of sets specified.
Dimension	Functions in this set return dimensions.
Hierarchy	These functions return a hierarchy.
Level	These functions return levels.
Logical	This set consists of the IsEmpty function used to test an expression for the empty cell value.
Member	Functions in this set return members and are used for the most part in cube navigation.
Numeric	These functions perform some calculation over a set or expression. The Avg function we used in Chapter 6 is found in this category.
Set	These functions return sets or are used to perform some operation with a set. You'll find many of these functions used quite frequently in your work with MDX.
String	Many of the functions in this category return the name of a cube component.
Tuple	These functions return tuples.

User-Defined Functions

When the built-in functions or other function libraries fall short of supporting your application requirements or you want to implement a set of functions specific to your application domain, possibly a special set of financial functions or other processing functions, you have the option of authoring your own function library and using it in your MDX statements.

You can author your function library in any language that supports the development of Component Object Model (COM) ActiveX libraries. This includes of course Microsoft Visual Basic and Microsoft Visual C++. Any arguments or return values you specify for your functions cannot include user-defined types. Data types accepted as function arguments are string, numeric, array, or variant containing string or numeric types. Return values may be string, numeric, or variants containing string or numeric types.

After completing your library and before using its functions, you need to register the library, or any third-party library for that matter, with OLAP Services. When building calculated members in the OLAP Manager Calculated Member Builder, you can register a library for use in creating calculated members using the following steps:

1. In the Calculated Member Builder dialog, click Register.

2. In the Register Function Libraries dialog, click Add.

3. In the Open dialog, select the type library, executable, or ActiveX control file containing your library.

4. Click Close.

After you've completed these steps, the program IDs (project class names) in the libraries you added will appear in the Functions list box in the Calculated Member Builder.

If there are function name conflicts within the added libraries, OLAP Services resolves the conflict by selecting the function from the first library in the list.

To register a library for use in your program code, you can add a DSO cube command (clsCubeCommand) to a cube using the USE LIBRARY statement. The syntax of this statement is:

```
USE LIBRARY "<librarypath>" | <programID>
[,"<librarypath>" | <programID> . . .]
```

ON THE CD

If you were to install a user-defined library in a folder named Book\OLAP\ CD\Chapter07\OurLib.DLL, for example, you would use code like the example that follows to register this library for use with the Investments cube. This code is found behind the Register User-Defined Functions button in the Ch07 Visual Basic project on the CD:

```
Dim dsoServer As DSO.Server
Dim cmd As DSO.Command
Dim dsoDB As DSO.MDStore          'Database
Dim dsoCube As DSO.MDStore        'Cube
Dim dsoCmd As DSO.Command         'Command


On Error GoTo RegUDF_ErrHandler

Set dsoServer = New DSO.Server
dsoServer.Connect ("BAMO")

Set dsoDB = dsoServer.MDStores("FundAcctSample")

Set dsoCube = dsoDB.MDStores("Investments")

'  If a command exists in a cube, use the syntax below:
'    Set cmd = dsoCube.Commands("UDFLib1")
'  Else use the AddNew method to add the command
     Set cmd = dsoCube.Commands.AddNew("UDFLib1")

   'Used to remove libraries except for the OLAP Services library
'    cmd.Statement = "USE LIBRARY"

   'Used to register libraries
   cmd.Statement = "USE LIBRARY ""F:\Book\OLAP\CD\Chapter07\OurLib.DLL"""

   dsoCube.Update
```

Once the library is stored as an Investments cube command, it will be run whenever we access the cube. The USE LIBRARY command here enables us to reference functions contained in the library.

```
Dim cnn As New ADODB.Connection
Dim cset As New ADOMD.Cellset
Dim csetcell As ADOMD.Cell
Dim csetaxis As ADOMD.Axis
Dim csetpos As ADOMD.Position
Dim cellmember As ADOMD.Member
Dim n As Long, m As Long, 1 As Long, k As Long

Dim strmdx As String

On Error GoTo UDF_ErrHandler

List1.Clear
```

```
cnn.ConnectionString = "Provider=msolap;Data Source=BAMO;
    Initial Catalog= FundAcctSample;"
cnn.Open

' Following statement requires registration of OurLib.DLL
strmdx = "WITH MEMBER [Measures].[AdjustedAmount] AS
    '[Amount] + ClientAdjustment()'"
strmdx = strmdx & " Select {[Manager].Members} On Columns,
    {[AdjustedAmount]} On Rows From Investments"

Set cset.ActiveConnection = cnn

cset.Open strmdx

For n = 0 To cset.Axes(0).Positions.Count - 1
    For m = 0 To cset.Axes(1).Positions.Count - 1
        For l = 0 To cset.Item(n, m).Positions(0).Members.Count - 1
            List1.AddItem cset.Item(n, m).Positions(0).Members(l).Caption
                & "(" & cset.Item(n, m).Ordinal & ")"
        Next l
        For k = 0 To cset.Item(n, m).Positions(1).Members.Count - 1
            List1.AddItem cset.Item(n, m).Positions(1).Members(k).Caption
        Next k
        List1.AddItem IIf(IsNull(cset.Item(n, m).Value), "Null",
            cset.Item(n, m).FormattedValue)
            & " = Cell Value ( Cellset.Item(" & n & "," & m & ") )"
        List1.AddItem ""
    Next m
Next n

cset.Close
cnn.Close

Exit Sub
```

The MDX statement assigned to the strmdx string variable in the preceding code defines a calculated member with query scope. We look at these WITH statements a little later in this chapter. For now, note that this calculated member is using a function named ClientAdjustment, the return value of which is added to the Amount of the current member. The ClientAdjustment function is a simple function returning a constant numeric value of 500. So for every amount to be displayed in the dataset using this calculated member, 500 is added to the cell amount. The ClientAdjustment function can be found on the CD in the OurLib Visual Basic project in the Chapter07 folder.

The DSO code used to register a library can also be used to unregister a library. To remove the OurLib library, first set the command object

```
Set cmd = dsoCube.Commands("UDFLib1")
```

and then set the statement of the command as follows:

```
cmd.Statement = "USE LIBRARY"
```

After the cube is updated, the registered libraries will no longer be known to the cube and their functions can no longer be referenced. The built-in OLAP Services library will still be available, however.

Accessing Member Properties

The dimension properties clause in the axis specification enables you to access a dimension property such as the FundAge property you defined in Chapter 3.

The syntax for <dimension properties> is:

```
[DIMENSION] PROPERTIES <property>,<property>. . .
```

A <property> may be any of the following:

Property	Syntax
Dimension ID	<dimensionname>.ID
Dimension key	<dimensionname>.KEY
Dimension name	<dimensionname>.NAME
Level ID	<levelname>.ID
Level key	<levelname>.KEY
Level name	<levelname>.NAME
Member property	<levelname>.<memberpropertyname>

An example of using the PROPERTIES specification follows:

```
SELECT {[Manager].Members} ON COLUMNS,
{[Fund].Members} PROPERTIES [Fund].[Fund Age] ON ROWS
FROM Investments
WHERE ([Amount])
```

In the preceding statement, you are displaying the fund name and fund age properties on the rows axis intersecting with managers on the columns axis and displaying investment amounts in the cells. You are not able to see this result using the MDX Sample Application. You need to insert the statement into one of the Visual Basic projects on the CD, execute the statement, and display the row position member properties.

```
List1.AddItem "   " & cellmember.Properties(0).Name & " = " &
    cellmember.Properties(0).Value
```

Properties(0).Name displays Fund Age and the Properties(0).Value displays the Fund Age value for the current Fund member.

You may also use Properties as in the following expression:

```
WITH MEMBER [Measures].[FundAgeProp] As '[Fund].CurrentMember.Properties
("Fund Age")'
```

Summary

In this chapter, we've explored the basic parts of an MDX statement and how to use these to write a valid query. The syntax we discussed here is associated with the MDX Select statement.

We discovered that all cube dimensions are used by OLAP Services in a query whether we specify them or not. The dimensions we don't project onto an axis are used as slicer dimensions by OLAP Services. These filter the dataset to the dimensions on the slicer axis. This axis can be accessed in ADO MD by use of the cellset Filter property.

The WITH clause was explored for creating calculated members, sets, and cache having query scope. We saw how all three can be put together in a statement.

We learned about OLAP Services function libraries and how we can create our own library and use its functions in a calculated member. A simple example of a user-defined library can be found in the Ch07 folder on the CD in the OurLib.vbp project.

The last item we looked at was the use of member properties in a query and how you can access these properties in code.

Much more MDX will be explored in the chapters that follow, especially in Chapter 10, where we explore the use of case statements, IIF, and more functions from the OLAP Services library.

Chapter 8

Building Applications with Decision Support Objects

IN THIS CHAPTER

- ◆ Discovering how DSO can be used to design aggregations and process cubes

- ◆ Learning how to create a cube using DSO

- ◆ Using DSO to define cube commands

- ◆ Exploring the DSO methods for creating cube partitions

- ◆ Learning how to implement security at the database, cube, and cell levels

- ◆ Finding out how to control the OLAP server with the DSO server object

THE INTRODUCTION TO DECISION Support Objects in Chapter 5 concentrated on describing each of the objects in the Decision Support Object model, how these objects can be accessed through the use of interfaces, and the properties supported by each object.

In this chapter, we continue our exploration of DSO to include the server object, creating and processing cubes, calculated members, virtual dimensions, virtual cubes, partitions, and security. This chapter together with Chapter 5 provides the information you need to build a DSO application, which you will do later in Part III of the book.

Accessing the OLAP Server with clsServer

The clsServer object in DSO is used to control the OLAP server service (MSSQLServerOLAPService). This object is the root of the DSO object model and is required to make a connection and instantiate all other objects in the hierarchy. To use DSO in an application, you must be a member of the OLAP Administrators group on the server you are connecting to.

In Chapter 5, you used a routine named MakeServerConnection that established a connection with an OLAP server. The code found in MakeServerConnection is repeated here:

```
Public mdsoServer As DSO.Server

Dim dsoServer As DSO.Server
Set dsoServer = New DSO.Server

' Connect to OLAP server by setting the Connect property of the
' DSO.Server object equal to the name of the server entered by user
On Error GoTo MakeServerConnection_ErrHandler
dsoServer.Connect Me.txtServerName
' Save the reference to the server object
Set mdsoServer = dsoServer
```

The references in the Ch5 Visual Basic project include the Microsoft Decision Support Objects found in the OLAP Services Bin folder as MSMDDO.DLL.

The methods of clsServer are listed in Table 8-1.

TABLE 8-1 CLSSERVER METHODS

Method	Description
CloseServer	Releases all server resources acquired by the DSO server object. It is very important to use this method in your applications. Omitting it could cause resource problems.
Connect([*ServerName*])	Connects to an OLAP server service. The server name is specified to connect to a specific server or use *LocalHost* to connect to a server running on the same machine as your DSO application.
CreateObject(*ClassType*[, *SubClassType*])	Creates an object of *ClassType* and optional *SubClassType*.
LockObject(*object,LockType, LockDescription*)	Locks a specified object.
Refresh	Reads the repository and refreshes all objects.
UnlockAllObjects	Removes locks from objects.
UnlockObject(*object*)	Removes a lock from a specified object.
Update	Updates an object in the repository.

'DSO Enumerations for ClassType, SubClassType, and LockType are listed in Table 5-8 in Chapter 5.

If the name of the server to connect to is assigned to the clsServer.Name property, then no server name is required in the Connect method.

The *State* property of the server indicates the status of a connection. The enumerations for the server state are different than the OLAPStateTypes listed in Table 5-8. Those enumerations are for the State property of objects other than the server object. Here are the enumerations for the clsServer.State property:

Enumeration	Constant
stateConnected	1
stateFailed	2
stateUnknown	0

Whereas the State property indicates the status of a connection, the *ServiceState* property indicates the status of the OLAP server service. ServiceState is a read/write property that enables you to read the status of the server or start, stop, and pause the server.

The status of a server is interpreted by the values in Table 8-2.

TABLE 8-2 CLSSERVER SERVICESTATE VALUES

Example Constant & Value	Description
SERVICE_CONTINUE_PENDING (5)	Service Continue is pending.
SERVICE_PAUSE_PENDING (6)	Service Pause is pending.
SERVICE_PAUSED (7)	Service is paused.
SERVICE_RUNNING (4)	Service is running.
SERVICE_START_PENDING (2)	Service Start is pending.
SERVICE_STOP_PENDING (3)	Service Stop is pending.
SERVICE_STOPPED (1)	Service is stopped.

To start, pause, or stop the service, set these values into the ServiceState property:

Value	Meaning
1	Stop the service.
4	Start the service.
7	Pause the service.

Errors that may occur in connecting to a server or in using a DSO object can be determined by the *ErrorCodes* enumeration. The values for this enumerator are listed in Table 8-3.

TABLE 8-3 DSO ERRORCODES ENUMERATION

ErrorCode	Description
MderrAggregationUsageNotCustom	The EnableAggregations property cannot be set for dimension levels where the AggregationUsage property has a value other than 3.
MderrBadParameterForServiceState	Invalid service stsate parameter.
MderrCannotAddVirtualDimension	Source dimension for virtual dimension is not in the database.
MderrCannotCloneObjectIntoItself	Object cannot be cloned into itself.
MderrCannotCommitDatabase	Database cannot be created on the OLAP server.
MderrCannotCreatePartition	No system partition is available for the operation. User-defined partitions are available only when running the Microsoft SQL Server OLAP Services, Enterprise Edition.
MderrCannotDeleteDimension	Dimension cannot be deleted because it is being used by a cube, and the cube is not temporary.
MderrCannotDeleteLastPartition	Cannot delete the last partition in a cube.
MderrCannotDeleteLevel	Cannot delete a level being used in a virtual dimension.

ErrorCode	Description
MderrCannotDeleteMemberProperty	Cannot delete a member property being used in a virtual dimension.
MderrCannotModifySharedObject	Cannot change a shared dimension property being used in a cube.
MderrCannotRemoveMeasureFrom DefaultAggregation	Cannot remove a measure from an aggregation created by clsPartitionAnalyzer.
MderrCannotRenameObject	Renaming of object was not allowed by DSO.
MderrCannotSaveInsideTransaction	Object cannot be saved inside a DSO transaction. If objects are committed to the repository inside a transaction that was rolled back, the repository becomes out of sync with the OLAP server.
MderrCollectionItemNotFound	Item not found in collection.
MderrCollectionReadOnly	Objects cannot be added or removed from read-only collection.
MderrCouldNotLockObject	You attempted to lock an object already locked by another user session.
MderrCouldNotOpenService	The OLAP service could not be opened.
MderrCouldNotOpenService ControlManager	The OLAP service control manager could not be opened.
MderrCouldNotQueryTheService	The OLAP service could not be queried.
MderrDifferentAggregationDatasources	Only for ROLAP partitions. Source and target partitions have different relational data sources. Merge of partitions is not allowed.
MderrDifferentAggregationNumber	Source and target partitions have different number of aggregations. Merge of partitions is not allowed.
MderrDifferentAggregationOLAPMode	Source and target partitions have different storage modes. Merge of partitions is not allowed.
mderrDifferentAggregationStructure	Source and target partitions have different structures or storage modes. Merge of partitions is not allowed.

Continued

TABLE **8-3** DSO ERRORCODES ENUMERATION *(Continued)*

ErrorCode	Description
MderrDimensionLockedByCube	Dimension is locked because it is being used in a cube.
MderrDimensionNotInUnderlyingCubes	Dimension cannot be added to a virtual cube because it is not in any of the cubes on which the virtual cube is based.
MderrDuplicateKeyInCollection	An item in the collection has the same name as an item being added to the collection.
MderrIllegalObjectName	An illegal name cannot be assigned to an object.
MderrInvalidLockType	Invalid LockType argument value.
MderrInvalidParent	An object not in a collection has no parent.
MderrInvalidPropertySetting	Property value is not valid.
MderrLockAccessError	Unable to lock an object that is already locked by another user session. Or access denied when trying to lock an object.
MderrLockCannotBeObtained	Unable to acquire a lock from the server.
MderrLockDescriptionTooLong	Lock description exceeds maximum length.
MderrLockFileCorrupted	The server detected a corrupted lock file.
MderrLockFileMissing	The server cannot find lock file.
mderrLockNetworkDown	Network error detected.
MderrLockNetworkNameNotFound	Cannot find name on the network.
MderrLockNetworkPathNotFound	Cannot find network path.
MderrLockObjectNotLocked	Cannot unlock an object that is not locked.
mderrLockSystemError	A lock cannot be acquired due to an unknown error.
MderrMeasureDoesNotHaveValid SourceColumn	A measure cannot be added to a virtual cube when the name of the measure's source column is not in the correct format. The correct format being "[<underlying cube name>].[<measure name>]."
MderrNameCannotBeChanged	Only temporary objects can be renamed.

ErrorCode	Description
MderrNameCannotBeEmpty	An object cannot have an empty name.
MderrObjectChangedByAnotherApp	Object cannot be saved because it was not locked and was changed by another user session.
MderrObjectIsNotWriteLocked	Object cannot be updated because it is not write-locked.
MderrPropertyCannotBeChanged	Property cannot be changed in this context. Usually occurs if the parent of the member property is not a Database Level.
MderrRepositoryConnectionFailed	Cannot connect to repository. Object repository may be read-only.
MderrRepositoryIncompatible	Repository is incompatible with this version of DSO. Usually happens when you're opening repository using an older version of DSO and the repository was created using a newer version of DSO.
MderrSourceDoesNotExist	Source partition does not exist. Partitions cannot be merged.
mderrTargetDoesNotExist	Target partition does not exist. Partitions cannot be merged.
MderrTooManyLevelsInDimension	The maximum number of levels in a dimension is 63 plus the All level.
MderrUnsuccesfullServiceOperation	The OLAP server service is not running on the specified computer.

You probably noticed that some of the errors in Table 8-3 refer to object locking. From your work with SQL Server databases, you should understand locking as a concurrency control mechanism to ensure consistent and complete data in the database you are using. But what does locking mean in the world of OLAP server?

Locking Objects

Locking in the OLAP environment needs to be considered at two levels. One, the repository level, and two, the cube level.

When you work with DSO objects through the context of an OLAP server and wish to make object changes persistent, you issue an Update method on the object to write your changes into the repository. Since the repository is a database and shared among the users of the OLAP server you are connected to, there is a chance that change conflicts can occur, just as when you update any shared objects. To control these changes, OLAP Services implements a locking strategy that you can explicitly control using the *LockObject* and *UnlockObject* methods.

 Although locking can be implemented manually using these methods, it is almost never needed because DSO handles locking automatically.

The LockObject and UnlockObject methods apply to a number of objects and interfaces in the DSO model. The methods we concentrate on here are those that apply to clsServer and are found in Table 8-1.

The syntax for the LockObject method is:

```
LockObject(object,LockType,LockDescription)
```

The object argument is the object being locked, and *LockDescription* is a string that is returned to other sessions attempting to obtain a lock on the object while your lock is being held.

The *LockType* argument is one of four lock types enumerated by the OlapLockTypes enumeration. These locks are described in Table 8-4.

TABLE 8-4 DSO LOCK TYPES

OlapLockTypes Enumeration	Description
OlapLockExtendedRead	Object properties can be read by other users but not changed or processed.
OlapLockProcess	Other users can only read object properties until lock is released.
OlapLockRead	Other users can read properties from the repository but cannot change them.
OlapLockWrite	Other users cannot access the object properties.

The second lock you consider in OLAP Services pertains to write-enabled cubes. When a cube is enabled for writing, changes to the data in the cube are at risk of collision with another session and must be controlled. In this case, you're not concerned with metadata changes in the repository, but the integrity of the actual cube data.

Write-enabled cubes are an option when you are required to support what-if analysis for one or more cubes. This allows your users to make changes to the data and analyze the results. We defer discussion of this type of locking until we explore write-enabling a cube later in this chapter.

Temporary Objects

The MDStore and Dimension interface objects contain a property named *IsTemporary*. When you begin an object name with the tilde (~) character, the object named becomes a temporary object within your session. A temporary object cannot be saved into the repository and is not visible to other users of the database.

Temporary objects may be useful in a DSO application for holding copies of objects or some other utility function within your application. If you wish to save a temporary object into the repository and thus make it a permanent object in your database, remove the tilde character from the beginning of the object name and issue an Update method on the object. Issuing Update while the object name contains the tilde has no effect on the repository.

Creating a Cube with DSO

In Chapter 6 you created a local cube named Dividends. For comparison purposes, in this section you create the same cube only this time on an OLAP server and using DSO instead of the PivotTable service.

```
Dim dsoDatabase As DSO.MDStore
Dim mdsoServer As DSO.Server

Set mdsoServer = New DSO.Server

mdsoServer.Connect m_ServerName
Set dsoDatabase = mdsoServer.MDStores("FundAcctSample")
```

The home database for your Dividends cube is the FundAcctSample database you created in Chapter 3. Your first task in creating this cube is to connect to the OLAP server and set up a database object.

The variable m_ServerName in this code is expected to be set to the server where the FundAcctSample database is resident.

Now that you have an object of clsDatabase pointing to the FundAcct Sample database, you are ready to create your Dividends cube. To do this, you use a clsCube object, clsDatabaseDimensions, clsDatabaseLevels, and clsCubeMeasures. Here's the entire code utilizing your MakeServerConnection function borrowed from the Ch05 Visual Basic project. This code and the code discussed in the "Working with Partitions" section that follows can be found in the Ch08 project on the CD:

```
Dim dsoDatabase As DSO.MDStore
Dim dsoCube As DSO.MDStore
Dim dsoPart As DSO.MDStore
Dim dsoDataSource As DSO.DataSource
Dim dsoDimension As DSO.Dimension
Dim dsoLevel As DSO.Level
Dim dsoMeasure As DSO.Measure
Dim LQuote As String, RQuote As String

Me.MousePointer = vbHourglass

MakeServerConnection Me.txtServer.Text

Set dsoDatabase = mdsoServer.MDStores("FundAcctSample")

'<><><><><><><><><><><><><><><><><><><><><><><><><>
'          Create a DataSource
'<><><><><><><><><><><><><><><><><><><><><><><><><>

Set dsoDataSource = dsoDatabase.DataSources.AddNew("FundAcctsWH Connection")
dsoDataSource.ConnectionString = __
    "Provider=MSOLAP;Data Source=FundAcctsWH;Connect Timeout=15"
dsoDataSource.Update

'<><><><><><><><><><><><><><><><><><><><><><><><><>
'          Create a Cube
'<><><><><><><><><><><><><><><><><><><><><><><><><>

Set dsoCube = dsoDatabase.MDStores.AddNew("Dividends")
dsoCube.Description = "Dividends Cube"
dsoCube.OlapMode = olapmodeRolap
dsoCube.DataSources.Add dsoDatabase.DataSources("BAMO - FundAcctsWH")
LQuote = dsoCube.DataSources(1).OpenQuoteChar
RQuote = dsoCube.DataSources(1).CloseQuoteChar
dsoCube.SourceTable = LQuote & "Dividends" & RQuote
dsoCube.EstimatedRows = 2037

'<><><><><><><><><><><><><><><><><><><><><><><><><>
'          Create the database dimensions
```

```
'<><><><><><><><><><><><><><><><><><><><><><><><>

Set dsoDimension = dsoDatabase.Dimensions.AddNew("Dividends^Account")
Set dsoDimension.DataSource = dsoDatabase.DataSources("BAMO - FundAcctsWH")
LQuote = dsoDimension.DataSource.OpenQuoteChar
RQuote = dsoDimension.DataSource.CloseQuoteChar
dsoDimension.DimensionType = dimRegular
dsoDimension.FromClause = LQuote & "Accounts" & RQuote
Set dsoLevel = dsoDimension.Levels.AddNew("All Account")
dsoLevel.LevelType = levAll
dsoLevel.MemberKeyColumn = "All Accounts"
Set dsoLevel = dsoDimension.Levels.AddNew("State Abbr")
dsoLevel.LevelType = levRegular
dsoLevel.MemberKeyColumn = LQuote & "Accounts" & RQuote & "." & _
    LQuote & "state_abbr" & RQuote
dsoLevel.EstimatedSize = 6
dsoLevel.ColumnType = adChar
dsoLevel.ColumnSize = 2
dsoDimension.Update

Set dsoDimension = dsoDatabase.Dimensions.AddNew("Dividends^Manager")
Set dsoDimension.DataSource = dsoDatabase.DataSources("BAMO - FundAcctsWH")
LQuote = dsoDimension.DataSource.OpenQuoteChar
RQuote = dsoDimension.DataSource.CloseQuoteChar
dsoDimension.DimensionType = dimRegular
dsoDimension.FromClause = LQuote & "Managers" & RQuote
Set dsoLevel = dsoDimension.Levels.AddNew("All Manager")
dsoLevel.LevelType = levAll
dsoLevel.MemberKeyColumn = "All Managers"
Set dsoLevel = dsoDimension.Levels.AddNew("Manager Lastname")
dsoLevel.LevelType = levRegular
dsoLevel.MemberKeyColumn = LQuote & "Managers" & RQuote & "." & _
    LQuote & "manager_lastname" & RQuote
dsoLevel.EstimatedSize = 6
dsoLevel.ColumnType = adChar
dsoLevel.ColumnSize = 70
dsoDimension.Update

Set dsoDimension = dsoDatabase.Dimensions.AddNew("Dividends^Time")
Set dsoDimension.DataSource = dsoDatabase.DataSources("BAMO - FundAcctsWH")
LQuote = dsoDimension.DataSource.OpenQuoteChar
RQuote = dsoDimension.DataSource.CloseQuoteChar
dsoDimension.DimensionType = dimTime
dsoDimension.FromClause = LQuote & "Dividends" & RQuote
Set dsoLevel = dsoDimension.Levels.AddNew("All Time")
```

```
dsoLevel.LevelType = levAll
dsoLevel.MemberKeyColumn = "All Years"
Set dsoLevel = dsoDimension.Levels.AddNew("Year")
dsoLevel.LevelType = levTimeYears
dsoLevel.MemberKeyColumn = "DatePart(year,Dividends.trandate)"
dsoLevel.EstimatedSize = 33
dsoLevel.ColumnType = adDate
Set dsoLevel = dsoDimension.Levels.AddNew("Quarter")
dsoLevel.LevelType = levTimeQuarters
dsoLevel.MemberKeyColumn = "DatePart(quarter,Dividends.trandate)"
dsoLevel.EstimatedSize = 122
dsoLevel.ColumnType = adDate
Set dsoLevel = dsoDimension.Levels.AddNew("Month")
dsoLevel.LevelType = levTimeMonths
dsoLevel.MemberKeyColumn = "DatePart(month,Dividends.trandate)"
dsoLevel.EstimatedSize = 190
dsoLevel.ColumnType = adDate
dsoDimension.Update

Set dsoDimension = dsoDatabase.Dimensions.AddNew("Dividends^Office")
Set dsoDimension.DataSource = dsoDatabase.DataSources("BAMO - FundAcctsWH")
LQuote = dsoDimension.DataSource.OpenQuoteChar
RQuote = dsoDimension.DataSource.CloseQuoteChar
dsoDimension.DimensionType = dimRegular
dsoDimension.FromClause = LQuote & "Offices" & RQuote
Set dsoLevel = dsoDimension.Levels.AddNew("All Office")
dsoLevel.LevelType = levAll
dsoLevel.MemberKeyColumn = "All Offices"
Set dsoLevel = dsoDimension.Levels.AddNew("Region")
dsoLevel.LevelType = levRegular
dsoLevel.MemberKeyColumn = LQuote & "Offices" & RQuote & "." & _
    LQuote & "region" & RQuote
dsoLevel.EstimatedSize = 4
dsoLevel.ColumnType = adChar
dsoLevel.ColumnSize = 50
Set dsoLevel = dsoDimension.Levels.AddNew("Accounting")
dsoLevel.LevelType = levRegular
dsoLevel.MemberKeyColumn = LQuote & "Offices" & RQuote & "." & _
    LQuote & "accounting" & RQuote
dsoLevel.EstimatedSize = 4
dsoLevel.ColumnType = adChar
dsoLevel.ColumnSize = 50
Set dsoLevel = dsoDimension.Levels.AddNew("Business")
dsoLevel.LevelType = levRegular
```

```
dsoLevel.MemberKeyColumn = LQuote & "Offices" & RQuote & "." & _
    LQuote & "business" & RQuote
dsoLevel.EstimatedSize = 4
dsoLevel.ColumnType = adChar
dsoLevel.ColumnSize = 50
dsoDimension.Update


'<><><><><><><><><><><><><><><><><><><><><><><>
'        Assign dimensions to the cube
'<><><><><><><><><><><><><><><><><><><><><><><>

dsoCube.Dimensions.AddNew ("Dividends^Account")
dsoCube.Dimensions.AddNew ("Fund")
dsoCube.Dimensions.AddNew ("Dividends^Time")
dsoCube.Dimensions.AddNew ("Dividends^Office")
dsoCube.Dimensions.AddNew ("Dividends^Manager")


'<><><><><><><><><><><><><><><><><><><><><><><>
'        Create the cube measures
'<><><><><><><><><><><><><><><><><><><><><><><>
LQuote = dsoCube.DataSources(1).OpenQuoteChar
RQuote = dsoCube.DataSources(1).CloseQuoteChar
Set dsoMeasure = dsoCube.Measures.AddNew("Amount")
dsoMeasure.SourceColumn = LQuote & "Dividends" & RQuote & "." & _
    LQuote & "amount" & RQuote
dsoMeasure.SourceColumnType = dimCurrency
dsoMeasure.FormatString = "$#,##0;($#,##0)"
dsoMeasure.AggregateFunction = aggSum
Set dsoMeasure = dsoCube.Measures.AddNew("Sh Num")
dsoMeasure.SourceColumn = LQuote & "Dividends" & RQuote & "." & _
    LQuote & "sh_num" & RQuote
dsoMeasure.SourceColumnType = dimDecimal
dsoMeasure.AggregateFunction = aggSum


'<><><><><><><><><><><><><><><><><><><><><><><>
' Set the cube FromClause and JoinClause properties
'<><><><><><><><><><><><><><><><><><><><><><><>

dsoCube.FromClause = dsoCube.SourceTable & ", " & _
                     LQuote & "Accounts" & RQuote & ", " & _
                     LQuote & "Managers" & RQuote & ", " & _
                     LQuote & "Offices" & RQuote

dsoCube.JoinClause = _
```

```
            "(" & LQuote & "Dividends" & RQuote & "." & LQuote & _
            "manager_num" & RQuote & " = " & _
            LQuote & "Managers" & RQuote & "." & LQuote & _
            "manager_num" & RQuote & ")"
    dsoCube.JoinClause = dsoCube.JoinClause & " AND " & _
            "(" & LQuote & "Dividends" & RQuote & "." & LQuote & _
            "fundacctno" & RQuote & " = " & _
            LQuote & "Accounts" & RQuote & "." & LQuote & _
            "fundacctno" & RQuote & ")"
    dsoCube.JoinClause = dsoCube.JoinClause & " AND " & _
            "(" & LQuote & "Dividends" & RQuote & "." & LQuote & _
            "fund_cd" & RQuote & " = " & _
            LQuote & "Funds" & RQuote & "." & LQuote & "fund_cd" & RQuote & ")"
    dsoCube.JoinClause = dsoCube.JoinClause & " AND " & _
            "(" & LQuote & "Dividends" & RQuote & "." & LQuote & _
            "office_num" & RQuote & " = " & _
            LQuote & "Offices" & RQuote & "." & LQuote & "office_num" & _
            RQuote & ")"


    '<><><><><><><><><><><><><><><><><><><><><><><><>
    '  Save the cube definition in the repository
    '<><><><><><><><><><><><><><><><><><><><><><><><>


    dsoCube.Update
    dsoDatabase.Update
```

The first item of note about this code is that it creates a new datasource named FundAcctsWH Connection. Since you are using a database where you have previously created a datasource for the Investments cube, you could have merely used that datasource for your Dividends cube as well. The creation of the FundAcctsWH Connection datasource is redundant in this example, but at least you have an example of how a datasource is created using DSO. The next item of note is the naming of the database dimensions. The dimensions you are using here are the same dimensions used in the Investments cube. However, all but the Fund dimension in the Investments cube are private dimensions. They cannot be used by other cubes. You are therefore forced to redefine these dimensions and name them as private dimensions to the Dividends cube by prefacing the dimension name with the name of the cube and the caret (^) as in Dividends^Account.

The Fund dimension is an existing shared dimension in the database, and so you don't need to define it. In the section of the code where you assign dimensions to the cube, you only specify the dimension names; the dimension properties are picked up from the database dimensions.

In creating this cube, you are guaranteed to get one default partition named Dividends without coding for it. It is automatically created for you. In the next section of this chapter, we discuss how additional partitions can be created for a cube.

The *ColumnType* of a Level object and the *SourceColumnType* of a Measure accept values from the DataTypeEnum enumeration defined in the ADODB library. The values for this enumeration are listed in Table 8-5.

TABLE 8-5 DATATYPEENUM VALUES

Data Type	Value
Big Integer	AdBigInt
Binary	AdBinary
Boolean	AdBoolean
Char	AdChar
WChar	adWChar
Currency	adCurrency
Date	AdDate
Time	adDBTime
DateTime	adDBTimeStamp
Decimal	adDecimal
Double	adDouble
Integer	adInteger
Numeric	adNumeric
Single	adSingle
Small Integer	adSmallInt
BSTR	adBSTR
Tiny Integer	adTinyInt
Unsigned Big Integer	adUnsignedBigInt
Unsigned Integer	adUnsignedInt
Unsigned Small Integer	adUnsignedSmallInt
Unsigned Tiny Integer	adUnsignedTinyInt

The *ColumnType* property is read-only in cube levels, partition levels, and aggregation levels and read/write in database levels.

The *LevelType* property values are assigned from the LevelTypes enumeration. These values are listed in Table 8-6.

TABLE 8-6 LEVELTYPES VALUES

Level	Value
Top level of a dimension	levAll
A level not related to time	levRegular
Day level	levTimeDays
Half-year level	levTimeHalfYears
Hour level	levTimeHours
Minute level	levTimeMinutes
Month level	levTimeMonths
Quarter level	levTimeQuarters
Second level	levTimeSeconds
Week level	levTimeWeeks
Year level	levTimeYears

The *AggregateFunction* property of a measure defines how the measure should be aggregated into the aggregation tables. The options for this property are aggSum, aggCount, aggMin, and aggMax.

The code discussed so far defines a new cube on the server in terms of dimensions and measures, but there is still more to do. You need to address the cube security issues, the design of aggregations for the cube, and the population of the cube with data. We tackle these topics next.

Working with Partitions

As you saw in the preceding exercise and in Chapter 3, when you create a cube, you automatically get one partition. This is the default partition and is used by OLAP Services to store the cube's data. It is given the same name as the cube.

In large OLAP installations, it can be advantageous to store cubes in multiple partitions. Doing so enables you to better manage the cube to meet access requirements and performance targets. Partitions defined for a cube divide the cube's data such that no partition contains the same data as another partition. This division is totally under your control, and it is up to you to ensure that no overlap occurs.

Some partitions of a cube may be more heavily accessed than other partitions due to the data they are designed to contain. These partitions require a storage mode that will provide good query performance compared to partitions that will experience lighter access loads. To support this architecture, each partition of a cube may be defined to have a different storage mode: ROLAP, MOLAP, or HOLAP. This capability enables you to match the access performance of the cube to its intended use.

OLAP Services supports merging of partitions should the need arise to bring two or more partitions together as a single partition. Merging is supported as long as the partitions to be merged have the same storage mode and the same aggregation designs.

To use multiple partitions for a cube, you will need to be running SQL Server OLAP Services Enterprise Edition, which of course must be running on the Enterprise Edition of NT Server.

In designing partitions, you have three options to consider:

◆ Use the Partition Wizard and specify data slices.

◆ Use a single fact table filtered for each partition.

◆ Use a different fact table for each partition.

We'll step through the OLAP Manager Partition Wizard to define partitions for the Investments cube based on the business office members of the Office dimension. For comparison, we look at how this task is done using DSO.

Before you use the Partition Wizard, launch the MDX Sample Application and run a query against the Investments cube. You might want to display amounts by business office and year for example. Save these results and query so that you can check the results of your partitioning.

Partition Files

If you look in the folder where the FundAcctSample database is stored, you'll notice some files there with .prt extensions. These files are used by OLAP Services to manage a partition. There is one .prt file for each partition in the database.

The prt file holds information such as partition dimension information (not the dimension itself!), data slice and filter information, and other partition-specific data. These files are critical to the cube they are associated with but do not store aggregation or fact table data. Aggregations and fact table data are stored according to the storage mode for the partition, which may be a separate MOLAP file, a relational table in the source database, or a combination of these.

Using the Partition Wizard

In the OLAP Manager tree view, expand the cube where you will define new partitions. Right-click the Partitions folder and select New Partition from the shortcut menu. This displays the welcome screen for the Partition Wizard. Click Next to move to the first selection screen shown in Figure 8-1.

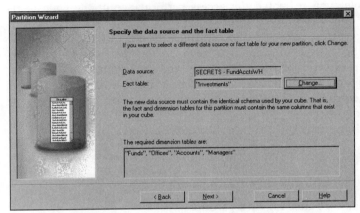

Figure 8–1: Select the data source and fact table for the partition.

Enter the warehouse database name and server in the Data source text box and then choose a fact table for the partition you are defining. The Fact table text box is prefilled with the name of the fact table for the selected cube. Click Next.

On the optional data slice screen, you can choose a dimension member. In Figure 8-2, I've selected the Connecticut member for this partition. This data slice specification will be paired with the filter we will define on the Advanced Settings dialog to select data for the partition. In this example, either the data slice specification or the filter would suffice. Both are not necessary because they specify the same selection of data.

When you merge partitions, the data slice is moved to the first common ancestor of the two slice members. The WHERE clauses are OR-ed together. Without a WHERE clause, you might get more data in the merged partition than you wanted.

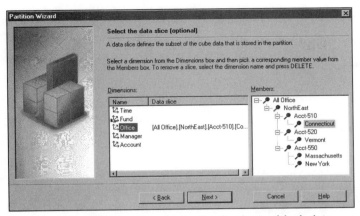

Figure 8-2: Specify the optional data slice for the partition's data.

Click Next to move to the Finish screen. On this screen, you can enter the name of the partition and how you want to handle the aggregation design. In Figure 8-3, I used the name of the data slice as the partition name and chose to copy the aggregation design from the Investments cube's default partition. The reason for this choice is to allow this partition to be merged with others you define for the cube. Merged partitions must have the same aggregation design. Had this merge requirement not been a factor or if the use of this partition dictated a different set of aggregations, possibly for performance reasons, you could choose one of the other options.

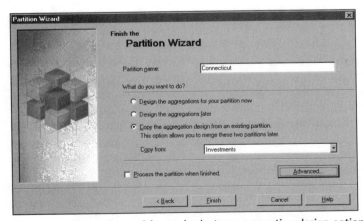

Figure 8-3: Name the partition and select an aggregation design option.

Before clicking Finish, click Advanced to display the Advanced Settings dialog shown in Figure 8-4.

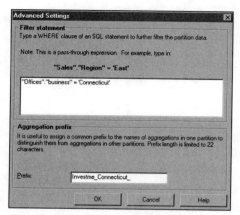

Figure 8-4: Enter a filter for the partition and an aggregation prefix.

On the Advanced Settings dialog, you can enter a filter that will be used in conjunction with the data slice, if one was selected. Figure 8-4 shows a Where clause specifying that only fact table entries having a joined Offices dimension row where the business column equals 'Connecticut' will be selected for the partition. This happens to be the same as the entered data slice and so is redundant, but it doesn't do any harm to leave it. The recommended practice is to specify a filter.

The suggested aggregation prefix shown at the bottom of the dialog is also accepted but could be changed if you desire. When you're finished with this dialog, click OK to return to the Finish screen of the wizard. Now click Finish to define the partition.

Follow these same steps to create partitions for each of the remaining business offices (Massachusetts, New York, and Vermont). When you are finished, select the Investments default partition and delete it. This partition is no longer needed, because all of the default partition data has been divided among the new partitions just defined. The OLAP Manager tree view pane should look like that depicted in Figure 8-5.

To complete the task, you need to process each of the partitions you just created. Since the aggregation designs have been copied from the Investments cube, you don't need to do any design steps and can just select process to fill the partitions with data.

After processing all of the partitions, go into the MDX Sample Application and enter or load the query you ran against the Investments cube default partition. You should see the same data as you saw before partitioning.

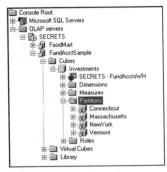

Figure 8-5: The tree view pane showing the partitions of the Investments cube

Merging Partitions in OLAP Manager

Two partitions can be merged together as long as the aggregation designs of both partitions are the same and they have the same storage mode.

To merge partitions using the OLAP Manager, right-click the partition you want to merge into another partition and choose Merge from the shortcut menu. The Merge Partitions screen is shown in Figure 8-6.

You may want to create a partition for the purpose of collecting other partitions together into one. In your Investments cube, for example, you created four partitions, one for each business office. If you want to merge these back together, you may want to create a partition named Investments as was your original default partition or some other name appropriate for the content. You would then merge the business office partitions into this new partition rather than into one of the existing partitions.

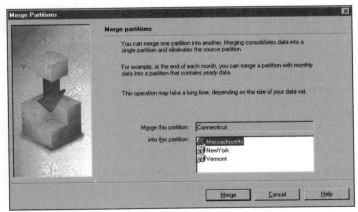

Figure 8-6: Selection of a target partition in the Merge Partitions screen

In the Merge Partitions screen, select the target partition for the selected partition displayed and click Merge. After the merge operation is complete, OLAP Services removes the source partition from the cube.

Using DSO to Create a Partition

Partitions in DSO are created via the AddNew method of the MDStores collection in a clsCube object. Assuming a cube object variable referencing the Investments cube, you would create a partition named Connecticut in the cube using this code:

```
Dim dsoPartition As DSO.MDStore

Set dsoPartition = dsoCube.MDStores.AddNew ("Connecticut")
```

Now that you have a partition object, you can set properties to define the same entries you made in the Partition Wizard.

```
dsoPartition.SourceTable = "Investments"
dsoPartition.SourceTableFilter = "Offices.business = 'Connecticut'"
dsoPartition.AggregationPrefix = "Investme_Connecticut_"
dsoPartition.OlapMode = olapmodeRolap
dsoPartition.Update
```

This partition is to have a ROLAP storage mode, and so you set the partition's *OlapMode* property to olapmodeRolap, one of the OlapStorageModes enumeration values specified in the DSO library. Other choices for this property are *olapmodeMolapIndex,* which yields a MOLAP partition containing fact table data and aggregations, and *olapmodeHybridIndex,* which results in HOLAP, where fact table data is in the source database and aggregation data is in the partition.

The datasource for the partition is inherited from the cube. At this point, however, you don't have any aggregations assigned to the new partition. If you were to process this partition right now, the processing would run very quickly because there are no aggregations in the partition's MDStores collection. Your next task is to copy the aggregation design from the Investments default partition into your new partition:

```
'<><><><><><><><><><><><><><><><><><><><><><><><>
' Set source and target partition object variables
'<><><><><><><><><><><><><><><><><><><><><><><><>

Set dsoPartition = dsoCube.MDStores("Investments")
Set dsoPartitionTgt = dsoCube.MDStores("Connecticut")

'<><><><><><><><><><><><><><><><><><><><><><><><>
'    Copy aggregations from default partition
```

```
'    to new partition.
'<><><><><><><><><><><><><><><><><><><><><><><><><>

For i = 1 To dsoPartition.MDStores.Count
    Set dsoAggregation = dsoPartition.MDStores(i)
    Debug.Print dsoAggregation.Name
    dsoPartitionTgt.MDStores.Add dsoAggregation
Next i


dsoPartitionTgt.Update
```

If you've been doing the exercises discussed up to this point in the chapter and you merged the partitions created with the Partition Wizard back into one partition named Investments (or you haven't created partitions and you still have the default Investments partition), then the preceding code assigning the source partition into the dsoPartition object variable will work. If you merged your partitions into some other partition, maybe the Vermont partition, then change the name in the preceding assignment to your source partition name.

The For loop is enumerating the aggregations of the source partition and assigning them to the new target partition using the Add method of the target partition's MDStores collection. After all aggregations have been copied from the source, the target partition is updated to save the designs in the repository.

At this point, you can process the new partition using the OLAP Manager or you can use DSO as discussed in the next section. To print the aggregations copied into the target partition, use the code found in the Ch08 project behind the Assign Aggregations button. The For loop following the partition update statement in the preceding code will print the aggregation name and dimension name for each of the aggregation dimensions in the aggregation. You can expand this code if you wish to also print the levels within each dimension.

Using DSO to Merge Partitions

When merging partitions with DSO, you set a partition object variable for the target partition and then specify the source partition name in the *Merge* method of the target partition:

```
Dim dsoDatabase As DSO.MDStore
Dim dsoCube As DSO.MDStore
Dim dsoPartitionTgt As DSO.MDStore
Dim dsoDimensionTgt As DSO.Dimension
```

```
Dim dsoLevelTgt As DSO.Level


On Error GoTo MergePartition_ErrHandler

Me.MousePointer = vbHourglass

'<><><><><><><><><><><><><><><><><><><><><><><><>
'          Connect to the server
'<><><><><><><><><><><><><><><><><><><><><><><><>

MakeServerConnection Me.txtServer.Text

'<><><><><><><><><><><><><><><><><><><><><><><><>
'          Set database and cube objects
'<><><><><><><><><><><><><><><><><><><><><><><><>

Set dsoDatabase = mdsoServer.MDStores("FundAcctSample")
Set dsoCube = dsoDatabase.MDStores("Investments")

'<><><><><><><><><><><><><><><><><><><><><><><><>
'          Set the partition slice values
'<><><><><><><><><><><><><><><><><><><><><><><><>

Set dsoPartitionTgt = dsoCube.MDStores("Connecticut")

Set dsoDimensionTgt = dsoPartitionTgt.Dimensions("Investments^Office")
For Each dsoLevelTgt In dsoDimensionTgt.Levels
    dsoLevelTgt.SliceValue = ""
Next

'<><><><><><><><><><><><><><><><><><><><><><><><>
'          Merge the partitions
'<><><><><><><><><><><><><><><><><><><><><><><><>

dsoPartitionTgt.Merge ("NewYork")
dsoPartitionTgt.Update
```

Prior to using the Merge method on the partition to bring the data together, you must set the data slices in the target partition to properly represent the data that will be contained in the partition after merging.

In the example shown here of merging the NewYork partition having the data slice [All Office].[NorthEast].[Acct-550].[New York] into the Connecticut partition having the data slice [All Office].[NorthEast].[Acct-510].[Connecticut], you would need to set the Vermont data slice to [All Office].[NorthEast]. Doing so, however, would not be sufficient to represent the partition data, because this slice specification would imply that all business offices should be contained in the partition, yet you have other partitions that contain Massachusetts and Vermont data. So if you choose to keep the slice values in the Connecticut partition, then you need to ensure that the SourceTableFilter properly states the data that you intend to put into the partition. There is another option, however.

Because the data slice specification is optional, you can remove all slice values from the Connecticut partition and just use the SourceTableFilter property of the partition to filter the data. This is the option taken in the preceding code.

TIP

Specifying the data slice is advantageous to query performance. The slice tells the server what the contents of a partition are to enable the server to process queries against the cube more efficiently.

ON THE CD

The Ch08 Visual Basic project contains code after the merge to print the merged SourceTableFilter property and to walk through the target partition dimensions and levels. Extract this code to display this information on pre-merged partitions so that you can see how the data slice looks in a partition.

Next we look at how you can create aggregations and process a partition using DSO.

Designing Aggregations and Processing

Your view of a cube partition thus far has involved objects such as the partition itself, the partition's dimensions and levels, filters, and data slices. In this section we discuss the aspects of the partition that involve performance, namely the partition's aggregations. We look at how they are designed, stored, and processed.

In the earlier exercise of creating a partition, you copied the aggregations from the default partition into the new partition with this code:

```
For i = 1 To dsoPartition.MDStores.Count
    Set dsoAggregation = dsoPartition.MDStores(i)
    Debug.Print dsoAggregation.Name
    dsoPartitionTgt.MDStores.Add dsoAggregation
Next I
```

The dsoPartition variable references the default partition where you obtain all the aggregations for your target partition. You did this for two reasons. One is that there are no requirements for your new partition to contain any aggregations different from the existing default partition. You would consider a different set of aggregation designs if your new partition were to have a higher demand for performance, dictating that you store more aggregated data to minimize your access to the source fact table to create aggregations that were not previously precalculated and stored.

The second reason for copying aggregations from the default partition was to enable merging partitions in the future. Only partitions with the same aggregation design can be merged.

Your target partition contains the same aggregations as your default partition. In the cube I have been working with on my machine, I have 22 aggregations designed. We'll now use these aggregation designs in processing the partition.

The dimensions in an aggregation are used a little differently that those in the partition or cube. In an aggregation, the dimensions are used to specify the granularity of the aggregation. To do this, the levels of the *AggregationDimension* object are set to specify the level of aggregation to be precalculated and stored. By default, the highest levels in the dimension are always calculated and do not require any specification in the aggregation dimension levels. To aggregate beyond this highest level, however, the levels need to be specified.

The best way to see how this scheme works is to inspect the aggregations directly. Open the Ch05 Visual Basic project and run the code behind the Show Aggregations button. This code walks through the aggregations of the default partition in the Investments cube and displays the dimensions and levels of each aggregation. To see all aggregations, remove the embedded filter limiting the aggregations displayed to the one containing the FromClause equal to "Investme_Investments1_Q3".

To design and process the aggregations currently stored in the partition, you can use the following code found behind the Process Partition button in the Ch08 project:

```
Dim dsoDatabase As DSO.MDStore
Dim dsoCube As DSO.MDStore
Dim dsoPartitionTgt As DSO.MDStore
Dim dsoAggregation As DSO.MDStore
Dim dsoPartAnalyzer As DSO.PartitionAnalyzer
Dim AggCount As Long, PctBenefit As Double, AccumSize As Double
Dim StopDesign As Boolean

On Error GoTo ProcessPart_ErrHandler
```

```
Me.MousePointer = vbHourglass

'<><><><><><><><><><><><><><><><><><><><><><><><>
'          Connect to the server
'<><><><><><><><><><><><><><><><><><><><><><><><>

MakeServerConnection Me.txtServer.Text

'<><><><><><><><><><><><><><><><><><><><><><><><>
'          Set database and cube objects
'<><><><><><><><><><><><><><><><><><><><><><><><>

Set dsoDatabase = mdsoServer.MDStores("FundAcctSample")
Set dsoCube = dsoDatabase.MDStores("Investments")

'<><><><><><><><><><><><><><><><><><><><><><><><>
'     Set target partition object variable
'<><><><><><><><><><><><><><><><><><><><><><><><>

Set dsoPartitionTgt = dsoCube.MDStores("Connecticut")

'<><><><><><><><><><><><><><><><><><><><><><><><>
'               Design aggregations
'<><><><><><><><><><><><><><><><><><><><><><><><>

Set dsoPartAnalyzer = dsoPartitionTgt.Analyzer

dsoPartAnalyzer.InitializeDesign

For i = 1 To dsoPartitionTgt.MDStores.Count
    Set dsoAggregation = dsoPartitionTgt.MDStores(i)
    dsoPartAnalyzer.AddExisitingAggregation _
       dsoAggregation, PctBenefit, AccumSize, AggCount
Next i

StopDesign = False

Do Until StopDesign
  If Not dsoPartAnalyzer.NextAnalysisStep(PctBenefit, AccumSize, AggCount) Then
     StopDesign = True
  Else
     'Check for desired limits
     If (AccumSize >= 64000000) Or (AggCount >= 22) Then
        StopDesign = True
```

```
      End If
    End If
Loop

dsoPartAnalyzer.CloseAggregationsAnalysis

'<><><><><><><><><><><><><><><><><><><><><><><>
'        Process the new partition
'<><><><><><><><><><><><><><><><><><><><><><><>

dsoPartitionTgt.Process processFull
```

You begin in the Design aggregations section by setting an object variable of type *PartitionAnalyzer*. This object property wraps the algorithm that calculates aggregation designs, and its methods enable you to prepare these designs prior to processing a cube partition.

The *InitializeDesign* method checks the structure of the partition and initializes objects required by the analysis.

Next add the existing aggregation designs found in the partition's MDStores collection to the analyzer's *DesignedAggregations* collection using the *AddExisiting Aggregation* method. This method returns the estimated percentage of performance improvement that the current collection of designed aggregations would yield, the estimated storage required by processing the current collection of designed aggregations, and the current count of designed aggregations assigned to the analyzer.

Once you've added all aggregations to the analyzer, you are ready to run the analysis. The analysis run using the *NextAnalysisStep* method yields a new aggregation design if the algorithm determines that an added design will be beneficial. The benefits thus calculated, for the entire DesignedAggregations collection, are returned to the variables passed into the method.

NextAnalysisStep *adds* aggregation designs to the aggregations you already placed into the collection with AddExistingAggregation. By checking the results of the returned variables against some predetermined goals, such as the ones stated in the code, you can control the number of designs added to the partition. This means that you can control the performance benefit of adding more designs and the amount of space required to hold the aggregations once you process the partition.

Keep in mind that because you already have a set of designed aggregations in the partition, you do not need to perform this analysis step unless you want to derive more aggregations. If you do the analysis and decide that a set of designed aggregations would better suit your needs, then you can replace the aggregations in the partition with those in the DesignedAggregations collection. This would require enumerating the DesignedAggregations collection and setting each aggregation found there into the partition's MDStores collection much as you did when copying the default partition aggregations. This code is not shown in the preceding code example.

While designing aggregations, you can limit the designs the analyzer considers by specifying Goal Queries. Each *GoalQuery* specifies a set of levels chosen from each of the dimensions of the partition.

The AddGoalQuery method specifies a set of levels by number in the order of the dimensions contained in the partition's Dimensions collection. The set of levels will contain the same number of digits as there are dimensions in the collection. An example of this method follows:

```
dsoPartAnalyzer.AddGoalQuery "1,1,1,3,1", 1
```

This statement adds a goal that specifies the All levels of all dimensions in the partition with the exception of the Office dimension, which specifies the business office level. This goal is weighted with a factor of 1, which weights the analysis to favor this query. The goal states that users will submit queries who want to see results aggregated to the All level of all dimensions but down to the business level for the Office dimension. The analyzer will take this goal into account when designing aggregations for the partition and create a set of DesignedAggregations that can quickly answer these queries in addition to meeting other design goals.

If you use the AddGoalQuery method to add a set of goals, follow the goals with a call to the *PrepareGoalQueries* method. PrepareGoalQueries sets up the analyzer to use the added goals in its analysis.

```
dsoPartAnalyzer.PrepareGoalQueries
```

Whether you design new aggregations or not, to process the partition, you use the partition's *Process* method. In the Process the new partition section in the preceding code example, you are using a complete process on the partition. The options for the Process Type argument are shown in Table 8-7.

TABLE 8-7 PROCESS TYPES

Process Type	Description
ProcessBuildStructure	Can be used on cubes only and causes the structure of the cube to be created without any data being populated into it.
ProcessDefault	Causes a refresh if the structure of the cube is up to date or a full process if the cube needs to be built.
ProcessFull	Rebuilds the structure if necessary and repopulates the data into the partition.
ProcessRefreshData	Refreshes the data in the partition but does not rebuild it.
ProcessResume	Server should resume responding to user queries against the partition or cube.
ProcessSuspend	Server should suspend responding to user queries against the partition or cube.

Refreshing data into a partition does not prevent users from querying the partition, but they cannot see any new data resulting from the refresh until the refresh commits its changes. Refer to Chapter 4 for more information on processing cubes.

Using the partition Process method causes only the referenced partition to be processed. You can choose to use this method on a cube object and cause all partitions of the cube to be processed. Another option available to you is to process the database, processing all cubes and partitions in it.

Aggregation design (or redesign) is undertaken for performance reasons. In fact, aggregation designs are the essence of cube technology. An alternative to designing aggregations as done in this section is to develop a design based on an initial estimate, run the system for awhile under normal usage, and then run Usage Based Optimization in the OLAP Manager to adjust your designs.

Exploring Cube Commands

A cube command object of class clsCubeCommand stores items such as calculated members, library references, and user-defined sets. Commands are added to a cube using the AddNew method of the Command collection.

```
Dim dsoCommand As DSO.Command
Set dsoCommand = dsoCube.Commands.AddNew("MyCommand")
```

In Chapter 3, you added a calculated member to the Investments cube named Price. In Chapter 7, you added a user-defined function library reference named UDFLib1. If you now enumerate the commands collection of the Investments cube using the Show Commands button in the Ch05 project, you get the following results:

```
Command Name: Price
  Command Type: 1
  Ordinal Position: 1
  Statement: CREATE MEMBER Investments.Measures.[Price] AS
'[Measures].[Amount]/[Measures].[Sh Num]', FORMAT_STRING = 'Standard'
Command Name: UDFLib1
  Command Type: 0
  Ordinal Position: 2
  Statement: USE LIBRARY "F:\Book\OLAP\CD\Chapter07\OurLib.DLL"
```

Commands may be stored at the cube and database object level, but currently only cube commands are committed to the server

These commands are executed on the PivotTable Service client when the object is accessed. In the case of your Investments cube as it now stands, the Price calculated member definition and the user-defined library USE LIBRARY statement is executed when you access the Investments cube. The calculated member expression is executed when the Price member itself is referenced. At the cube level, this calculated member has global scope across all sessions accessing the cube.

Implementing Security

Like SQL Server, OLAP Services supports a Microsoft Windows NT integrated security system enabling you to assign NT users and groups to access permissions. In order to enable access control, the OLAP server must be installed on an NTFS partition. This will allow the use of access control lists (ACLs) to manage access rights.

To authenticate a user, OLAP Services uses the Security Support Provider Interface (SSPI) to access NT security. The authentication scheme used is that of the NT LM Security Support Provider. To access an OLAP server, the NT logon user must first be authenticated by NT and be a member of the same domain as the user account used to install the OLAP server or be a member of a trusted domain. In my environment, I was the user who installed the OLAP server while logged on as a member of the DEVELOP domain. To access this server, a user must be a member of DEVELOP or a domain trusted by my domain server.

Because I installed the OLAP server under my account (DEVELOP/amow), I have Admin privileges on the server. When OLAP Services was installed on my server, it set up a group named *OLAP Administrators* and added my account to that group. This gives me all privileges (read-only, read/write, and admin). To use the OLAP Manager, as noted in Chapter 3, you must be a member of the OLAP Administrators group.

When OLAP Services processes a cube, it uses the account that the MSSQLServerOLAPService service is running under to access the source data. When installing my server, I set up my account rather than the *System Account* to be used for the service. I recommend you follow the same practice. Because I am also the dbo and owner of the database objects (that is, the dimension tables, the fact tables, and everything else in the warehouse database), the OLAP service is able to access the tables it needs to process the cube. If the tables were not owned by dbo or the account that the OLAP service is using, the cube process would fail with an "Invalid object name" error.

When you first created the Investments cube back in Chapter 3 using the OLAP Manager, you set up a role for managers and assigned users into it. This role was saved as a database role that can be assigned to any cube in the database.

The roles assigned to a cube are found in the Roles collection of the cube. In each cube role, you are mainly concerned with the three role properties: the Userlist, the Permissions, and the Name.

The Ch05 and Ch08 projects on the CD contain code to list existing roles along with these three properties for the Investments cube. The code to list these properties follows:

```
For Each dsoRole In dsoCube.Roles
    List1.AddItem dsoRole.Name
    List1.AddItem "  User List: " & dsoRole.UsersList
    List1.AddItem "  Permissions: " & dsoRole.Permissions("Access")
Next
```

The results are:

```
Managers
  User List: DEVELOP\amow; DEVELOP\Kirsten; DEVELOP\Dean
  Permissions: RW
```

As you can see from the output of this routine, a *UsersList* property contains a list of users in the form of <domainname>\<username> separated by a semicolon (the list shown here is from my machine, but obviously your user list will display the users you added from your own environment). This user list can be modified in database roles but not in cube roles.

The permissions assigned to the users in the UsersList of a role are found in the "Access" key of the *Permissions* property. The only permissions for this key are R to denote read-only access and RW to denote read/write access. We discuss read/write access permission when we explore write-enabled cubes in Chapter 10, but for now note that assigning read/write permission does not write-enable a cube. Assignment of these permissions can only be modified in the cube role, not the database role.

To create roles using DSO, you would use code like that found in the Ch08 project behind the Create Roles button. This code creates a role in the database, assigns a list of users to the role, assigns the database role to the Investments cube, and finally sets the permissions for the role:

```
'<><><><><><><><><><><><><><><><><><><><><><><>
'    Create a new role and set cell permission
'<><><><><><><><><><><><><><><><><><><><><><><>

Set dsoRole = dsoDatabase.Roles.AddNew("TeamA")
dsoRole.UsersList = "DEVELOP\Bill"

dsoRole.Update

Set dsoRole = dsoCube.Roles.AddNew("TeamA")
dsoRole.SetPermissions "Access", "R"
dsoRole.SetPermissions "CellRead", "IIF(Measures.CurrentMember.Name = _
    ""Amount"",1,0)"
```

`dsoCube.Update`

Permissions for a role are set using the *SetPermissions* method of the role object. Prior to SQL Server Service Pack 1, the only key that could be set with this method was the "Access" key. As noted when you listed the current permissions set with the OLAP Manager, you can set this key to either R or RW as a permission for the role.

You can remove a role from a cube, leaving the role defined in the database, or you can remove it from the database, automatically removing it from all cubes where it is assigned. A role is removed from the database or cube using the *Remove* method of the Roles collection.

Using roles and permissions, you can implement a level of security that controls who can access a given cube and how they may access it. The permission controls access to the entire cube.

Implementing Cell-Level Security

As of SQL Server 7.0 Service Pack 1, you can implement security at the cell level of a cube, providing a finer granularity of access control. This is what the second SetPermissions statement is doing in the preceding code.

The SetPermissions method of a role can now set security rules in the form of MDX statements into the Permissions property of a role. These security rules are evaluated each time a cell in the cube is accessed. When the security rule returns False, access to the cell is denied. In the case where a user is a member of multiple roles assigned to the cube, the least restrictive access permission is granted to the user.

Security rules are classified into the three categories listed in Table 8-8.

TABLE **8-8** SECURITY RULE CATEGORIES

Rule Category (Permissions Key)	Description
Readable cells (CellRead)	The cell value is returned whenever a security rule for one of the user's roles in the cube evaluates True. When all rules evaluate False, access to the cell value is prohibited.
Contingent Readable cells (CellReadContingent)	Used for calculated members. Cell value is returned if rule evaluates True and derived cells are accessible by the user. When all rules evaluate False, access to the cell value is prohibited.
Write-Enabled cells (CellWrite)	Cell values can be changed and committed if the cell security rule evaluates True; otherwise, the change fails.

By default, a failed rule will cause OLAP Services to return a #N/A for the cell Formatted Value property. This behavior can be changed for a session by providing a Secured Cell Value parameter in the connection string. The default setting for this parameter is 0, which yields the #N/A return for failed access. Other values for this parameter are as follows:

1	**Same as 0**
2	HRESULT is an error code. Used in calls to OLE DB for OLAP IMDDataset::GetCellData.
3	Null is returned in Formatted Value and Value properties.
4	Zero returned in Formatted Value and Value properties.
5	#SEC returned in Formatted Value and Value properties.

If you wanted a Null returned on failure instead of #N/A, you would specify the following connection string in your program:

```
Dim cnn As New ADODB.Connection
cnn.Open "Provider=msolap;Data Source=SECRETS; _
    Initial Catalog=FundAcctSample;Secured Cell Value=3"
```

To add Read permission on the Amount values in the Investments cube, you would add a security rule like the following to the role you added in the Ch08 project:

```
dsoRole.SetPermissions "CellRead", "IIF(Measures.CurrentMember.Name = _
    ""Amount"",1,0)"
```

After setting this rule and updating the cube, a TeamA role member would have access to the Amount value of a cell but not the Sh Num value. When running this code, you need to be logged into OLAP Services as a member of the OLAP Administrators group. To test the code, you can log in as one of the TeamA role members (but not a member of the OLAP Administrators group) and run the following query:

```
select
    { [Measures].[Amount], [Measures].[Sh Num] } on columns,
    { Manager.members} on rows
from Investments
```

The results should show Amounts but #N/A in Sh Num values because these are prohibited by the security rule added for TeamA. If you get Access Denied messages while attempting to access the Investments cube, make sure your logon account is *not* a member of the NT Administrators group on the server. This problem is recognized by Microsoft and will most likely be corrected in future service packs.

The security rule added to a role can include expressions more complex than that shown here. If you need to AND or OR several conditions together, you may do so and OLAP Services will accept it. The security rule may be any valid MDX expression.

At the time of this writing, a sample Visual Basic is available on the Internet at `msdn.microsoft.com/library/techart/sqlolapserv.htm` that provides an example of an OLAP Manager add-in to view and update cell security. This project is a good example of writing an add-in and using DSO in Visual Basic. These topics are discussed in more detail in Part III of this book.

Summary

The material in Chapter 5 and in this chapter will enable you to develop applications using the Decision Support Object model.

This chapter started off by exploring the clsServer object to include its methods, properties, connections, and error codes. We reviewed how to connect to an OLAP server and discussed briefly the topic of object locking.

We created the Investments cube in Chapter 3 using the OLAP Manager, and we created a local cube named Dividends in Chapter 6 using the PivotTable service. Here we used DSO to create the same Dividends cube on the OLAP server. In doing so, we created the cube, private dimensions, levels, and measures. These steps were very similar to those we used in Chapter 6.

The major differences between a local cube and a server cube lie in the ways we populate them with data. This chapter explored how to establish partitions for a cube if we are running under the Enterprise Edition of OLAP Services. We used various methods to create a partition including the OLAP manager and DSO. We also found out how to merge partitions back together using these same facilities.

We discussed how to use the DSO PartitionAnalyzer to design new aggregations for a cube and how to use existing aggregation designs. Once designs have been determined to meet our requirements, we then processed the cube using the Process method.

Cube command objects were investigated here for storing calculated members, library references, and sets. These commands are executed on the client whenever the cube is accessed.

The last topic explored in this chapter was OLAP security. We learned how to create a database role and assign users to it. We then assigned the database role to the Investments cube and assigned permissions using the SetPermissions method. We discussed the cell-level security features added to OLAP Services by SQL Server service pack 1 (SP1). Using DSO, we created a cell-level security rule for read-only access to the Amount measure.

In setting up an OLAP server, the practice used in this book is to use the data warehouse dbo security account for installing the OLAP Services and for running the MSSQLServerOLAPService service. The account used for installation is automatically added to the OLAP Administrators group; this is a requirement for performing any administrative task on the server, including processing cubes and using the OLAP Manager.

In Chapter 10, we explore two more topics involving DSO, the use of Virtual dimensions and cubes and write-enabled cubes.

Chapter 9

Using OLAP Manager Add-Ins

IN THIS CHAPTER

◆ Discovering what OLAP Manager Add-Ins are and how they can be used

◆ Learning how to use the Microsoft Manager Add-In Kit

◆ Exploring the methods and properties of the IOlapAddIn interface for building your own add-ins

THE MICROSOFT MANAGEMENT CONSOLE (MMC) that accompanies many of the BackOffice products and supports the SQL Server Enterprise Manager is becoming a significant tool in the Microsoft product strategy. The capability this tool offers to support a variety of custom administrative functions in a standardized fashion can be very beneficial to the DBA.

The OLAP Manager, following its SQL Server counterpart, the Enterprise Manager, is implemented as an MMC snap-in and provides numerous administrative functions for OLAP Services. OLAP Manager also supports extension add-ins; these can be acquired from third-party vendors or from Microsoft, as you'll see later in this chapter, or else you can author your own add-ins to handle some task specific to your installation.

In this chapter we explore OLAP Manager add-ins, including the Microsoft add-ins, and discover what steps you need to take to develop your own add-ins, which you'll do later in the book.

Understanding OLAP Manager Add-Ins

SQL Server 7.0 and OLAP Services use the Microsoft Management Console to deliver a consistent user interface for administration software. The SQL Server Enterprise Manager and the OLAP Manager you used in Chapter 3 fall into this category.

Microsoft Management Console publishes a number of COM interfaces that are provided for the purpose of controlling a standard user interface made up of a tree view, a results view (usually in the form of a list but ActiveX controls and HTML are also supported here), menus, and toolbars. A number of additional published COM interfaces are expected to be implemented by add-in programs and provide a means for MMC to communicate user actions to an add-in.

Two types of add-ins, also known as snap-ins by some developers, are supported by MMC. One type is a standalone add-in that interacts with MMC's COM interfaces to implement a custom user interface and added functionality. The second type is an extension add-in. This type of add-in extends a stand-alone add-in in some way, usually by providing additional features such as menus, toolbars, or property sheets. OLAP Services ships with an add-in program named OLAP Manager. This is a stand-alone MMC add-in that can be used to administer OLAP objects (as you saw in Chapter 3) and to manage other OLAP add-ins such as any custom add-ins provided by you or a third party. Management of OLAP add-ins is accomplished through the OLAP Add-In Manager.

To view the add-ins currently installed on the OLAP server, right-click an OLAP server node in the OLAP Manager tree view and select Properties from the shortcut menu. Select the Add-Ins tab to view the list of installed add-ins.

Using the Microsoft OLAP Manager Add-Ins

Microsoft has released the OLAP Manager Add-In Kit 1, which, at the time of this writing, can be downloaded from the Microsoft Web site at www.microsoft.com/sql/productinfo/OLAPaddin.htm. The download file is named addins.exe and is approximately 2MB in size.

To install these add-ins, you must be a member of the OLAP Manager Administrators group. The three add-ins supplied with this kit are described in the following sections.

Calculated Member Manager

The Calculated Member Manager Add-In enables you to create and edit calculated members in virtual cubes. Calculated members may be imported into a virtual cube from any of the base cubes, or they may be created from scratch.

Use the following steps to create a new calculated member in a virtual cube:

1. Right-click the virtual cube icon in the OLAP Manager tree view and select Manage Calculated Members. This displays the Calculated Member Manager window.

2. Click New Calculated Member on the File menu. This displays the Calculated Member Builder dialog.

3. In the Parent Dimension box, select the dimension to include the calculated member, or select Measures. If you select Measures or a one-level dimension, the Change button for Parent member is disabled.

4. Select the Parent member for the Parent dimension.

5. Enter a member name for the calculated member in the Member name text box.

6. Specify the expression used to generate the calculated member value in the Value expression box. Data and functions may be selected from the available lists to aid in building the expression.

7. Click OK to close the Calculated Member Builder dialog.

8. From the File menu, click the Save menu item to save the calculated member just created. You see these calculated members only through the Calculated Member Manager view.

To edit a calculated member in a virtual cube, use these steps:

1. Right-click the virtual cube and select Manage Calculated Members from the shortcut menu. This displays the Calculated Member Manager.

2. Right-click the calculated member you want to edit and select Edit Calculated Member from the shortcut menu to display the Calculated Member Builder.

3. In the Parent Dimension box, select the dimension to include the calculated member or select Measures.

4. Select the Parent member for the Parent dimension. Click Change to change the member being displayed.

5. Specify the expression used to generate the calculated member value in the Value expression box. Data and functions may be selected from the available lists to aid in building the expression.

6. Click OK to close the Calculated Member Builder dialog.

7. From the File menu, click the Save menu item to save the calculated member just created.

In addition to creating a calculated member, you can import members from any of the base cubes that make up a virtual cube. To import a calculated member, use these steps:

1. Right-click the virtual cube and select Manage Calculated Members from the shortcut menu to display the Calculated Member Manager.

2. Select Import Calculated Member from the File menu. This displays the Import Calculated Members dialog box.

3. Check the calculated member you want to import and then click OK.

4. Select Save from the File menu in the Calculated Member Manager.

It is possible to import a calculated member that references a measure, a dimension, or another calculated member that is not included in the virtual cube. When this occurs, the calculated member is flagged as an error and is not used until the error is corrected.

Copy and Paste Objects Add-In

The Copy and Paste add-in enables copy and paste of the metadata for certain objects within a database, between databases, or between servers.

When you are copying and pasting a cube, the dimensions, measures, and partitions of the cube are copied in addition to any shared dimensions and roles. Before using this add-in to copy and paste a virtual cube, you must ensure that the base cubes of the virtual cube already exist in the target database.

To copy and paste a virtual dimension, the shared dimension containing the member property used as a base for the virtual dimension must already exist in the target database.

If you copy a cube using a ROLAP partition, the add-in (msmdcp) warns you that the aggregations for the pasted partition will be shared with the original copied cube. To create non-shared aggregations for the pasted cube, assign a unique aggregation prefix to the cube through the Advanced options in the Partition Wizard and then process the cube. A future release of the Addins will correct this problem by automatically creating an aggregation prefix of the form <cube name>_<partition name> to avoid this problem.

Right-click a partition in the pasted cube and select Edit from the shortcut menu. Step through the screens of the Partition Wizard until you get to the Finish screen. The Advanced button on this screen enables you to assign a different aggregation prefix for the ROLAP aggregations. These prefix names must be 22 characters or less.

After assigning a unique prefix for the cube's aggregations, check the Process check box and then click Finish.

Archive and Restore Databases Add-In

This add-in enables you to archive an OLAP services database to a .cab file and then to later restore that database to its condition at the time of archive.

The archive file stores the content of the folder where the OLAP database resides. The name of the folder is the same as the name of the database and resides in the path OLAP Services\Data\ by default.

In addition to the database folder content, the archive file also stores the metadata for database objects read from the repository.

If a cube in the database is write-enabled, the write-back tables associated with the cube are not stored in the archive file. If possible, a separate backup of the write-back tables is recommended so that they may be recovered when the OLAP database is recovered.

Another item not stored in the archive file is the aggregation tables for ROLAP partitions. Because these tables are stored with the source detail data, neither they nor the detail are captured to the archive file.

When restoring an OLAP database from an archive file, consider the archive limitations. If any cube in the database is write-enabled and the original write-back tables are not recoverable, the cube must be processed to rebuild the write-back tables. This process loses any write-back data that was originally in the write-back tables when the database was archived.

The archive file content replaces any files in the database folder at the time of restore, and files added to the folder since the archive was taken will be deleted. In addition, the metadata in the archive file is restored to the repository, replacing any data that exists for the database being restored. Any changes made to database objects since the archive was taken will be lost.

When restoring ROLAP partitions, you must restore the aggregation tables associated with those partitions from a separate backup of the source database or rebuild them via cube processing.

ARCHIVING A DATABASE

To archive an OLAP database, follow these steps:

1. Right-click on a database in the OLAP Manager tree view and select Archive Database from the shortcut menu. This action displays the Archive Database dialog box.

2. Enter a filename and path for the archive .cab file. Click the Archive button. An Archive Database Progress dialog is displayed to indicate the progress of the archival process.

3. If you want to save the log generated by the archive, click the Save Log button and specify a path and filename for the log.

In addition to using the OLAP Manager to archive a database, you can use a command prompt window to execute msmdarch.exe. To use this method, open a command prompt window and enter the following command:

```
[<path to msmdarch.exe>]msmdarch /a servername "database path" "database name"
"archive path and filename" ["log file path and filename"]
```

The *servername* argument is the name of the server where the database is located.

The "*database path*" argument is the full path to the database folder without the database name.

The "*database name*" argument is the name of the database to be archived.

The "*archive path and filename*" argument is the path and filename of the archive file to be created.

The optional "*log file path and filename*" argument is the path and filename of the generated log file containing a log of the archive process. If this file already exists in the specified path, the new archive log is appended to it without warning.

RESTORING A DATABASE

To restore a database, follow these steps:

1. Right-click an OLAP server in the OLAP Manager tree view and select Restore Database from the shortcut menu. If restoring a database on a remote server, you need to enter the path to the database on the remote server where the restored database will be written.

2. In the Open Archive File dialog, select the archive file to be restored and click Open. This action displays the Restore Database dialog.

3. Click Restore. This displays a Restore Database Progress dialog.

4. If you want to save the restore log file, click the Save Log button and specify the path and filename for the log.

The msmdarch.exe program can be used to restore from an archive by supplying the /r command line switch. The syntax for restoring a database in this manner is:

```
[<path to msmdarch.exe>]msmdarch /r servername "database path" "archive path and
file name" ["log file path and file name"]
```

The only difference between the commands to restore and to create an archive is that the restore command uses the /r switch and does not specify a "*database name*" argument because this name is contained in the selected archive file.

 Do not attempt to rename a database by renaming the archive CAB file. The CAB file name has nothing to do with the restored database name.

Creating Your Own Add-Ins

In this section we discuss the methods, properties, and steps associated with creating an OLAP Manager add-in with Visual Basic. The material you learn here is applied in Chapter 14, where you build a custom add-in.

The basic steps involved in creating a custom add-in are:

1. Create an ActiveX DLL project and name it according to how you want your add-in to be known in the OLAP Manager.

2. Add the *OLAP Add-In Manager* reference and any other library reference your add-in will use.

3. Create a class that will implement the IOlapAddIn interface and supply your custom code for its methods.

4. Register your add-in DLL in the Registry so that the OLAP Add-In Manager can access it.

You will most likely want to use the Microsoft Decision Support Objects library or make a reference to a custom library that implements DSO such as the one you will build in Chapter 12.

The remainder of this section outlines the requirements for an add-in created with Microsoft Visual Basic.

Create an ActiveX DLL Project

To implement your add-in with Visual Basic, create an ActiveX DLL project and give the project a name you want for your add-in. This name appears in the add-ins list when users register your add-in with OLAP Manager.

Add a reference to the *OLAP Add-In Manager* library (DSSAddInsManager) in the file msmdadin.dll found in the OLAP Services\Bin folder. This library exposes the methods, properties, collections, and classes you need to communicate with the OLAP Add-In Manager. Add any additional references needed by your add-in.

In addition to the IOlapAddIn interface definition required to be implemented by your add-in, the OLAP Manager library defines OlapMenuItem and OlapTreeNode classes to enable your add-in to customize the user interface managed by the OLAP Manager.

Implement the IOlapAddIn Interface

For the class that implements the IOlapAddIn interface, set the Instancing property to MultiUse and code the Implements statement in the General Declarations:

```
Implements IOlapAddIn
```

The first method executed in your class that implements IOlapAddIn is the *Class_Initialize* method. This is where you have the opportunity to instantiate any helper objects for your application, initialize connections, and set up any forms you may need.

In addition to the methods declared in the IOlapAddIn interface (described in the next section), you must implement one property of this interface, the Name property, which provides the name of your add-in to the OLAP Add-In Manager. You are required to implement only the Property Get function.

```
Property Get IOlapAddIn_Name () As String
IOlapAddIn_Name = "NameofYourAddIn"
End Property
```

IOLAPADDIN METHODS

The methods of the IOlapAddIn interface that your class needs to implement are described here.

PROVIDECHILDNODES   The ProvideChildNodes method is used to add nodes beneath the OlapTreeNode passed into the method as the first argument. The syntax for this method's statement is:

```
ProvideChildNodes (Parent As OlapTreeNode, Children As OlapTreeNodes)
```

The second argument passed to this method is an empty OlapTreeNodes collection that is to be filled by your add-in. These child nodes are displayed by the OLAP Manager beneath the selected tree node and may be considered to be contained by the selected node.

PROVIDEMENUITEMS   ProvideMenuItems is called by OLAP Manager to acquire menu items for a specified tree node. The node for which menu items are to be supplied is passed into the method as the first argument. The statement syntax for this method is:

```
ProvideMenuItems (Node As OlapTreeNode, MenuItems As OlapMenuItems)
```

The menu items to be returned to OLAP Manager are added to the OlapMenuItems collection passed into the method as the second argument. This collection is discussed later in this chapter in the section "IOlapAddIn Objects and Collections."

EXECUTEMENUITEM   The *ExecuteMenuItem* method is called when a user clicks a menu item provided by your add-in with ProvideMenuItems. The code in your ExecuteMenuItems method should handle the processing appropriately for the menu item passed into the method.

The syntax for the ExecuteMenuItem function statement is:

```
Function ExecuteMenuItem (Node As OlapTreeNode, MenuItem As OlapMenuItem) As
RefreshTreeTypes
```

The first argument passed to ExecuteMenuItem is the node in the tree view with which the menu item is associated.

GETOBJECT   The *GetObject* method is called by OLAP Manager to acquire a reference to the object that is represented in the tree view by the node passed into the method as its first and only argument. The function statement is:

```
Function GetObject (Node As OlapTreeNode) As Object
```

PROVIDEHTML   When a user clicks a tree node in the tree view, the OLAP Manager attempts to display an HTML file in the result view in the right pane. To obtain the URL of the HTML file, OLAP Manager calls the ProvideHTML method in your add-in. The syntax for this method's statement is:

```
ProvideHTML (Node As OlapTreeNode, URL As String)
```

The node passed into ProvideHTML as its first argument is the node selected by the user. The URL passed into the method contains the current displayed HTML file, if any. After determining the HTML file to be displayed for the node, assign its URL to the second argument to be passed back to OLAP Manager.

This method provides your add-in with a great deal of power and flexibility in displaying information to the user. The full feature set of dynamic HTML and ActiveX scripting is available to you to enable the dynamic creation of HTML pages containing rich content.

MMC supports the object model and functionality of Internet Explorer 4.1 and above. If you are not already familiar with this technology, investing some time to learn it will go a long way toward creating some great add-ins.

PROVIDEICON   When OLAP Manager needs to display an icon for a given node in the tree view, the ProvideIcon method is called. The index of the icon requested by OLAP Manager is passed into the method as the first and only argument. This index is assigned by your add-in to each node added to the tree view with ProvideChildNodes. Each node contains two properties, for supplying indexes for a node-open icon and a node-closed icon. These properties are discussed in the "IOlapAddIn Objects and Collections" section, which follows.

```
Function ProvideIcon (Index As Integer) As stdole.OLE_HANDLE
```

It is up to your add-in to manage the icon indexes for the nodes so that you can properly interpret them when this method is called. You notice from the function statement that no reference to the node is passed into this method, so the index must be unique among the nodes you have provided to OLAP Manager.

'The return value from this method must be a handle to an icon resource in your add-in. The icon is read from a standard Visual Basic resource file compiled into your DLL. You'll see an example of how this works in Chapter 14, when you build a sample add-in.

IOLAPADDIN OBJECTS AND COLLECTIONS

Several of the methods discussed in the previous section use arguments that are either objects or collections or both. In this section, we discuss the properties and methods for these objects and collections.

OLAPMENUITEM OBJECT   For each OlapTreeNode in the tree view, OLAP Manager calls the ProvideMenuItems method in your add-in to fill an OlapMenuItems collection. This collection represents the shortcut menu displayed when a user right-clicks a node in the tree view.

Each item in the OlapMenuItems collection is an OlapMenuItem object that represents one selection in the shortcut menu. The properties of an OlapMenuItem object are shown in this table:

Property	Description
Caption	The text displayed for the menu item.
Disabled	Causes the menu item to be dimmed when set to True.
Flags	One or more OlapMenuFlags added with the + operator. See OlapAddIn Enumerations section for explanation.
HelpContextId	The help context ID for menu item help.

Property	Description
HelpFileName	The help file containing the HelpContextId.
Key	An identifier unique within the OlapMenuItems collection.
OwnerAddInName	The name of the add-in owning this menu item. This property is set by OLAP Manager.
ParentKey	The Key of the parent menu item if the menu item is a child menu item.

OlapMenuItem objects are created with the Add method of the OlapMenuItems collection.

OLAPMENUITEMS COLLECTION The OlapMenuItems collection contains two methods used to manage OlapMenuItem objects in the collection.

The *Add* method creates an OlapMenuItem object and adds it to the collection. The syntax for this method is:

```
Add (MenuType As OlapMenuTypes, Caption As String, Key As Long,
     ParentKey As   Long, Flags As OlapMenuFlags) As OlapMenuItem
```

The arguments of this method provide some of the properties of the OlapMenuItem being added. The returned OlapMenuItem object can be referenced to set other properties such as Disabled, HelpContextId, and HelpFileName.

The *Remove* method is used to remove an OlapMenuItem from the collection. The syntax for this method is:

```
Remove (Index)
```

The Index passed to the Remove method is either the ordinal position of the menu item to be removed or the Key of the item to be removed.

You can add and remove menu items for a node's menu at each call of ProvideMenuItems by OLAP Manager. To determine if the OlapMenuItems collection has been populated, access the Count property.

The *Count* property of the OlapMenuItems collection is a Long data type indicating the number of items in the collection. To access any item in the collection, use the Item property.

By passing either the ordinal position or the Key of a menu item to the collection's *Item* property, you can directly access the menu item in the collection. This enables you to change the item's properties for the current call to ProvideMenuItems.

OLAPTREENODE OBJECT   Each item or node in the OLAP Manager tree view is associated with an OlapTreeNode object. These objects are created with the Add method of the OlapTreeNodes collection when the OLAP Manager calls the ProvideChildNodes method. The nodes that OLAP Manager will display are returned in an OlapTreeNodes collection provided as the second argument of the ProvideChildNodes method.

The properties of an OlapTreeNode object are listed here:

Property	Description
Caption	The text displayed for the node
HelpContextId	The context ID identifying the help for the node
IconClosed	The icon to display when the node is collapsed
IconOpen	The icon to display when the node is expanded
LinkedObject	The add-in object that is associated with the node
OwnerAddInName	The name of the add-in that owns the node
Parent	The parent node of the node

The LinkedObject property enables you to associate an object in your application with a specific node. The same object can be associated with more than one node. It is up to your application to manage the use of this object. A suggested use for this property is to assign appropriate objects to handle different node types and to call a method of these objects to process the node selection by the user whenever OLAP Manager calls the ProvideHTML method.

OLAPTREENODES COLLECTION   The collection of OlapTreeNode objects supports the same two methods as the OlapMenuItems collection discussed previously. Adding an OlapTreeNode object to the collection using the *Add* method provides the Caption for the node and for the IconClosed and IconOpen icons.

```
Add (Caption As String, IconClosed As NodeIconIndex,IconOpen As NodeIconIndex)
As OlapTreeNode
```

The *Remove* method takes either an ordinal number identifying the position of the node to remove in the collection or the Caption for the node to remove.

The collection's *Count* property returns a total node count for the collection, and the *Item* property is used to access a node by either ordinal number or Caption.

IOLAPADDIN ENUMERATIONS

The OLAP Add-In Manager library defines the following four enumerations.

REFRESHTREETYPES   This enumeration enumerates values for modes of refreshing the tree view. The values for these modes are as follows:

Name	Description
reftreeNoRefresh	The tree view is not refreshed.
reftreeParentAndBelow	The current node parent and all child nodes of the parent are refreshed.
reftreeCurrentAndBelow	The current node and its child nodes are refreshed.
reftreeAllTree	All nodes of the tree view are refreshed.

One of these enumeration values is returned by the ExecuteMenuItem method to inform the OLAP Manager of how to refresh the tree view after your add-in has responded to user selection of a menu item.

OLAPMENUTYPES   The OlapMenuTypes enumeration enumerates values for types of menu items that can be associated with a node in the tree view. The values for these types are:

Name	Description
mnuSeparator	Indicates a separator bar in the menu
mnuStandard	Indicates a standard menu item in the menu

An OlapMenuType is required in the Add method of the OlapMenuItems collection to indicate the type of OlapMenuItem being added to the collection. The OlapMenuItems collection is an argument of the ProvideMenuItems method. The OlapMenuItem objects in this collection define a shortcut menu for a specified node in the tree view.

OLAPMENUFLAGS The OlapMenuFlags enumeration enumerates values for modes of menu items. The values for these modes are as follows:

Name	Description
mnuflagChecked	Places a check mark next to the menu item.
mnuflagDeleteKey	Enables the standard Delete menu item, Delete key, and Delete toolbar button.
mnuflagDisabled	The menu item is disabled but not grayed.
mnuflagDoubleClick	Not used.
mnuflagF1	Not used.
mnuflagGrayed	The menu item is disabled and grayed.
mnuflagInsertKey	Not used.
mnuflagNew	Places the menu item as a submenu item under the New menu item in the node's parent menu.
mnuflagPopup	Indicates that the menu item is to be the parent of submenu items.
mnuflagRegular	Places the menu item on the root menu of the node's menu.
mnuflagSeparator	Indicates that the menu item is a separator bar.
mnuflagSubmenu	Places the menu item as a child menu item of the parent popup item.
mnuflagTask	Places the menu item as a submenu item under the Task menu item in the node's parent menu.

These menu flags are optional arguments to the OlapMenuItems Add method. For any OlapMenuItem being added to the collection, you may specify one or more of these flags. To specify more than one flag, add the flags with the + operator. To specify a regular menu item that should be checked, code the following for the OlapMenuFlags argument of the Add method:

```
mnuflagRegular + mnuflagChecked
```

ERRDSSADDINERRORNUMBERS   This enumeration enumerates values for add-in errors. The values for these errors are as follows:

Name	Description
errCaptionRequired	Raised if one is adding a node or menu item to the OlapTreeNodes or OlapMenuItems collection without having specified a caption property
errInvalidMenuType	Raised if the menu type of a menu item being added to an OlapMenuItems collection is not a type listed in the OlapMenuTypes enumeration

For this release of OLAP Services, this enumeration is rather sparse. I expect to see this enumeration expanded in future releases.

Register Your Add-In

When a user wishes to add an add-in into the OLAP Manager, the OLAP Add-In Manager looks in the system Registry and builds a list of add-ins for the user to choose from. The Registry key the OLAP Add-In Manager searches is:

```
HKEY_LOCAL_MACHINE\SOFTWARE\Microsoft\OLAP Server\Olap Manager Info\Addins
```

Your custom add-in needs to be entered as a string value under this key. Enter the name you chose for your ActiveX DLL project. Setting this value to "True" causes OLAP Manager to load the add-in at start-up time.

Create a Registry key with the same name as the string value you just added under the Addins key. You need to add four string values under this key as listed here:

String Value Name	Setting
Class Name	The name of the class that implements IOlapAddIn
Name	The name displayed in the OLAP Manager Properties
Description Properties	The description of the add-in displayed in the OLAP Manager
Priority	The loading priority used by the OLAP Add-In Manager

Summary

This chapter has discussed the OLAP Manager add-in to MMC and how to use other add-ins that you may acquire from Microsoft or a third-party vendor.

We discussed the use of the three add-ins available from Microsoft in their OLAP Manager Add-In Kit 1, available from the Internet. This kit contains a Calculated Member Manager add-in, a Copy and Paste Objects add-in, and an Archive and Restore Database add-in.

The development of custom add-ins using Microsoft Visual Basic was discussed, including the implementation requirements for the IOlapAddin interface. The methods of this interface are called by the OLAP Add-In Manager, and your add-in is expected to implement these methods to enable communications with the OLAP Manager.

Finally, we discussed what Registry entries are necessary to inform the OLAP Add-In Manager that your add-in exists and is available for installation.

We explore more add-in programming in Chapter 14.

Chapter 10

More MDX

IN THIS CHAPTER

◆ Digging deeper into the MDX language and learning more about querying cubes

◆ Learning how to create virtual dimensions and virtual cubes

◆ Discovering how cubes can be write-enabled for what-if analysis

THIS CHAPTER CONTINUES THE exploration of MDX started in Chapter 7. Here, you sample some MDX expressions and functions (listed in Appendix G) and learn a little more about cube navigation.

You also see what virtual dimensions and virtual cubes are and how you can create them using the OLAP Manager and DSO.

Write-enabled cubes and write-back tables are also explored in preparation for Chapter 11, where you use Excel 2000 pivot tables to carry out some what-if analysis.

Exploring MultiDimensional Expressions

MDX statements involve writing expressions that operate on the basic elements of multidimensional structures. Those basic elements were introduced in Chapter 7 as the set, tuple, and member.

A *tuple* is a collection of members selected from different dimensions. When a tuple is placed on the axis of a cellset, its members specify one coordinate or position on the axis for the purpose of addressing a cell value in the cellset.

A *set* is a collection of tuples. Set expressions operate on this collection and its members to yield other sets. Set expressions are used to formulate one or more sets for use in producing a specific cellset.

The term *member* refers to a dimension value that can be chosen from any of the dimensions of the cube or from the measures dimension.

Coding MDX expressions requires a good understanding of hierarchy terminology. Figure 10-1 shows the Office dimension hierarchy found in the Investments and Dividends cubes.

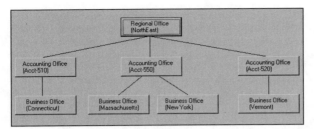

Figure 10-1: The Office dimension hierarchy in the FundAcctSample database

In Figure 10-1, the NorthEast regional office is at the root of the hierarchy and *parent* to the *child* accounting office members Acct-510, Acct-520, and Acct-550. Each of the accounting office-level members are *siblings* to each other, and each of them has child business office-level members.

Business offices Massachusetts and New York are siblings to each other but *cousins* to the Connecticut business office and to the Vermont business office. All members depicted in Figure 10-1 under the root are *descendants* of the NorthEast region member. The *ancestors* of the Connecticut business office are its parent, the Acct-510 accounting office, and the NorthEast regional office.

If there were another regional office member in the Office dimension, it too would have a hierarchy similar to the one shown in Figure 10-1. No matter which dimension hierarchy you encounter in a cube, the terminology for the relationships among its members is the same.

As you'll discover in this chapter and by inspection of the MDX function reference in Appendix G, there are numerous methods for navigating the levels of hierarchies to compare and analyze cube data.

Using Set and Tuple Expressions

Including all members of a dimension, hierarchy, or level is as easy as specifying the name of the dimension, hierarchy, or level followed by the keyword Members. You've used this syntax quite often in previous examples. If you want all of the members for the Manager dimension, you code:

```
[Manager].Members
```

This includes in the resulting set the name of every manager in the Manager dimension. The same set can be acquired by listing the members of the Manager Lastname level.

```
[Manager Lastname].Members
```

In the Office dimension, where you have a hierarchy of three levels defined, you can build a set of members from the Business office level using this statement:

```
Office.[Business].Members
```

<MEMBER>.CHILDREN

For any given member at a hierarchy level, you can get the members at the level below with:

```
Office.[Acct-550].Children
```

This syntax returns all business office members that are children of accounting office 550 and consists of the members Massachusetts and New York.

DESCENDANTS(<MEMBER>, <LEVEL>[, <DESC_FLAG>])

Using Children returns the members at the level immediately below the level containing the specified member. If you needed to return not only the children but members at any level below a specified member, you would use the *Descendants* function.

```
Descendants(Office.[NorthEast],Accounting,SELF)
```

Descendants returns members that are descendants of the first argument member at the level specified in the second argument. The third argument is a descendants flag that is used to include or exclude descendants before and after the second argument level. When this flag is SELF, the default, only members at the specified level are returned. When BEFORE or AFTER is used, members at the specified level plus members at the level before or after this level are also returned.

ORDER(<SET>, {<STRING EXPRESSION> | <NUMERIC EXPRESSION>}[, ASC | DESC | BASC | BDESC])

Members in a set can be ordered with the *Order* function. The order can be specified as hierarchized or nonhierarchized ordering. If you want to order the members of the Office hierarchy in the Investments cube first by level and then by investments amount, you would code:

```
Order(Office.Members, Amount, ASC)
```

The third argument orders the results in ascending (ASC) order, which is the default, or in descending (DESC) order of the second argument expression.

If you wanted to order by the investment amounts in the fourth quarter of 1987, you would code:

```
Order(Office.Members,([1987].[Quarter 4],Amount))
```

The results of this order expression placed into an MDX query are:

```
All Office     $3,732,163.32
NorthEast      $3,732,163.32
Acct-510       $1,740,346.00
Connecticut    $1,740,346.00
Acct-520       $1,407,374.08
```

```
Vermont        $1,407,374.08
Acct-550       $  584,443.24
Massachusetts $        25.00
New York       $  584,418.24
```

The amounts shown in these results are not those from Quarter 4 of 1987. They are the amounts for the displayed members for All Time, the same result you would get from just selecting Office.Members. The order of the results, however, are based on the actual amounts from Quarter 4 of 1987, which are:

```
Acct-510       $     8,496.98
Connecticut    $     8,496.98
Acct-520       $    17,000.00
Vermont        $    17,000.00
Acct-550       $    49,082.99
Massachusetts $
New York       $    49,082.99
```

The order of the results is amount within level of the office hierarchy. To return the preceding set in order according to the amounts without regard to hierarchy, use one of the "Break-hierarchy" specifiers BASC and BDESC as the third argument to the function. The expression using BASC and its results are:

```
Order(Office.Members,([1987].[Quarter 4],Amount),BASC)
```

```
Massachusetts $        25.00
Acct-510       $1,740,346.00
Connecticut    $1,740,346.00
Acct-520       $1,407,374.08
Vermont        $1,407,374.08
Acct-550       $  584,443.24
New York       $  584,418.24
All Office     $3,732,163.32
NorthEast      $3,732,163.32
```

Here again, the amounts displayed are in order according to the actual amounts from Quarter 4 of 1987.

HIERARCHIZE(<SET>)

The *Hierarchize* function orders a set according to its natural order in a hierarchy rather than by some specified expression as used in the Order function. Using this on the Office hierarchy, you have:

```
Hierarchize(Office.Members)
```

This expression returns all office members ordered within level by office name as shown here:

```
NorthEast        $3,732,163.32
Acct-510         $1,740,346.00
Connecticut      $1,740,346.00
Acct-520         $1,407,374.08
Vermont          $1,407,374.08
Acct-550         $  584,443.24
Massachusetts    $       25.00
New York         $  584,418.24
```

TOPCOUNT(<SET>, <COUNT>[, <NUMERIC EXPRESSION>])

In working with sets, we are often interested in some subset of members at the top or bottom of the set. For example, you might want only the top three business offices according to the investments managed. For this you can use the *TopCount* function:

```
TopCount(Office.[Business Office].Members,3,Amount)
```

Likewise, if you are interested in the three offices with the lowest amount of investments managed, you would code:

```
BottomCount(Office.[Business Office].Members,3,Amount)
```

These functions sort the set specified as the first argument by the expression in the third argument (breaking the hierarchy) and then return the number of members specified in the second argument.

Without the <numeric expression>, the function merely returns the first <count> members in the <set>.

TOPPERCENT(<SET>, <PERCENTAGE>, <NUMERIC EXPRESSION>)

TopPercent is a similar function to TopCount, but it returns a subset based on a percentage rather than a count. The following expression returns the business offices reflecting the top 10 percent of investments managed:

```
TopPercent(Office.[Business Office].Members,10,Amount)
```

The percentage is calculated by sorting the members on Amount and returning the minimal number of members from the top whose total amount is 10 percent of the amounts across all members. Replacing TopPercent with *BottomPercent* yields similar results, but members are selected from the bottom of the sorted list.

TOPSUM(<SET>, <VALUE>, <NUMERIC EXPRESSION>)

TopSum and *BottomSum* return members whose sum is at least the value given in the second argument. Here again, the minimal number of members from either the top or bottom of the list are chosen.

FILTER(<SET>, <SEARCH CONDITION>)

The *Filter* function operates much like a Where clause in a Transact-SQL statement. It limits the returned members to those that meet the criteria specified in the Filter expression.

```
Filter(Manager.Members,(Amount,[1989]) < (Amount,[1988]))
```

This filter returns the managers where the investment amounts under management in 1989 were less than those under management in 1988.

UNION(<SET1> <SET2>[, ALL])

The *Union* function combines the two sets specified as arguments and removes duplicates from the result. If the keyword All is specified as a third argument, then duplicates are retained.

```
Union(Office.[Acct-510].Children,Office.[Vermont])
```

This union results in a set containing all business offices under the 510 accounting office together with the Vermont business office.

DISTINCT(<SET>)

Duplicate members can be removed from a set by using the *Distinct* function. In the example that follows, the set specified would normally return one occurrence of New York and two occurrences of Massachusetts:

```
Distinct({Descendants(Office.[Acct-550],[Business]),Office.[Massachusetts]})
```

Using Distinct removes one of the occurrences of Massachusetts from the resulting set. You've probably noticed that many of the expressions discussed in this chapter support an optional ALL argument that enables duplicates to be returned when specified and eliminated when not specified.

INTERSECT(<SET1>, <SET2>[, ALL])

To find the intersection of two sets, use the *Intersect* function. This function returns a set of tuples that are common to both of the sets specified as arguments.

```
Intersect(Filter(Manager.Members,(Amount,[1989]) > (Amount,[1988])),
    {Manager.[Yields],Manager.[Folio]})
```

Because managers Yields and Stock are the only managers returned by the filter specified in this Intersect expression, the intersection of the filter set with the set consisting of managers Yields and Folio is Yields.

EXCEPT(<SET1>, <SET2>[, ALL])

The *Except* function returns the difference between the two sets specified as arguments. Tuples in the first argument set matched by tuples in the second argument set are removed, and the remaining tuples in the first argument set are returned.

```
Except(Manager.Members,Filter(Manager.Members,(Amount,[1987]) >
(Amount,[1986])))
```

In this example, the returned set consists of managers that do not have more managed amounts in 1987 than in 1986. This set contains Booker, Folio, Fundman, and Shares. When coding this expression, be sure that the first argument is a superset of the second argument.

CROSSJOIN(<SET1>, <SET2>)

The *Crossjoin* function produces the product of the two sets passed as arguments. Each tuple in the first argument set is paired with every tuple in the second argument set to produce the resulting set. If the first argument set has n tuples and the second argument set has m tuples, then the resulting set has n times m tuples.

```
Crossjoin(Manager.Members,Account.Members)
```

In this crossjoin, the Manager members count is 6 managers plus an All Manager member. The Account members count is 6 accounts plus an All Account member. The resulting crossjoined set therefore contains 49 tuples, with each tuple having one member from the Manager dimension and one member from the Account dimension.

EXTRACT(<SET>, <DIMENSION>[, <DIMENSION>...])

When you need to extract dimension members from a set, use the *Extract* function and specify the set as the first argument and the desired dimension as the second argument.

```
Extract(Crossjoin(Manager.Members,Account.Members),Account)
```

This example extracts the Account members from the crossjoin of managers and accounts. The expression that follows extracts the tuples ([CT]) and ([NY]) from the set coded into the first argument:

```
Extract({([Folio],[CT]),([Shares],[NY])},Account)
```

GENERATE(<SET1>, <SET2>[, ALL])

The *Generate* function applies the set expression, specified as the second argument, to each tuple in the set specified as the first argument and returns the union of the resulting sets.

```
Generate({Office.[Accounting].Members},{Office.CurrentMember.Children})
```

This expression returns the set of all business offices by applying the Children function to each of the members in the set of accounting offices and then returning the union of the results.

When you specify a set as the second argument that does not refer to the current member of the first argument set, then the results are the set of tuples of the second argument set repeated the "count of tuples in first argument set" times.

```
Generate({Office.[Accounting].Members},{[New York],[Vermont]},ALL)
```

There are three accounting offices, and so this Generate expression returns three occurrences of New York and three occurrences of Vermont.

Tuples are the elements of a set containing one or more members selected from the dimensions of the cube. A tuple can be coded into a set by placing members in parenthesis or by using any expression that returns a tuple.

Here's an example of hard-coded tuples in a set:

```
SELECT {(Office.[Connecticut],Manager.[Shares]),
  (Office.[New York],Manager.[Yields])} ON COLUMNS
FROM Investments
WHERE ([Amount])
```

The set projected onto the Columns axis in the preceding example contains two tuples. The first tuple specifies the Connecticut member from the Office dimension and the Shares member from the Manager dimension. The second tuple selects the New York office and the Yields manager. The result displays investment amounts at the intersection of each of the selected managers and offices.

<SET>.[ITEM](<STRING_EXPRESSION>|<INDEX>)

Set members can be specified in the same manner you would address an item in a Visual Basic collection. Using the *Item* function and either an index number or a key, you can directly access a member. Applying this to the set of offices in the Office dimension, you can walk through the office hierarchy in natural order by varying the index number.

```
Office.Members.Item(<index>)
```

An index of zero in this expression yields the All Office member, an index of 1 yields the NorthEast region member, an index of 2 the Acct-510 member, an index of 3, the Connecticut member, and so on through the hierarchy.

If you need to address a specific member such as the Connecticut member using this method, you would code:

```
Office.Members.Item("Connecticut")
```

Specifying Member Expressions

There are several expressions that enable you to refer to a member in a hierarchy in terms of the position of a given current member. We'll use these functions on the Office hierarchy.

<MEMBER>.PARENT

The following expression yields the Acct-510 member of the Accounting level:

```
Office.[Connecticut].Parent
```

Applying *Parent* to the Acct-510 member yields the NorthEast region member, and the parent of the NorthEast region is All Office. Attempting to return the parent of All Office results in a null set.

<MEMBER>.FIRSTCHILD AND <MEMBER>.LASTCHILD

The accounting office Acct-550 has two children, Massachusetts and New York. The *FirstChild* function returns the Massachusetts child member, and the *LastChild* function will return the New York child member.

<MEMBER>.PREVMEMBER AND <MEMBER>.NEXTMEMBER

The *PrevMember* function returns the member in the hierarchy occurring earlier at the same level as the specified member.

```
Office.[New York].PrevMember
```

This expression returns Massachusetts. Using Massachusetts as the member returns Vermont. If you specify a member at the Accounting office level, then the members returned are all members of the Accounting office level.

NextMember works the same as PrevMember but returns the member following the specified member in the hierarchy.

<MEMBER>.FIRSTSIBLING AND <MEMBER>.LASTSIBLING

The *Firstsibling* and *Lastsibling* functions return the first or last siblings of the specified member. "Sibling" of course implies that the returned member is of the same level as the specified member.

```
Office.[Massachusetts].Firstsibling
```

This expression returns Massachusetts, whereas specifying Lastsibling would return New York. Another way to look at these functions is that they return the first and last siblings of the parent of the member specified.

<MEMBER>.LEAD(<INDEX>)

The *Lead* function returns the member that is some number of positions away from the specified member along the specified member's dimension.

```
Office.[Massachusetts].Lead(1)
```

Specifying Lead(1) on the Massachusetts member yields New York. Specifying Lead(0) on Massachusetts yields Massachusetts. Using –1 as an index in the preceding example returns Vermont, and –2 returns Connecticut. Instead of using negative indexes, you can use the *Lag* function, which operates in the same manner as Lead.

<DIMENSION>.CURRENTMEMBER

As we've seen in several examples thus far, the *CurrentMember* function returns the current member of a dimension during an iteration across the dimension, such as that which occurs in the use of the Generate function.

ANCESTOR(<MEMBER>,<LEVEL>)

Ancestor returns the ancestor of the specified member at the specified level.

```
Ancestor(Office.[New York],[Accounting])
```

This function returns Acct-550 because this account is the parent of the New York business office at the Accounting level. Changing Accounting to Business in the preceding expression yields New York as the ancestor.

COUSIN(<MEMBER>,<ANCESTOR_MEMBER>)

Cousin returns the member in the same relative position under its ancestor specified by the second argument as the member specified by the first argument.

```
Cousin(Office.[Massachusetts],[Acct-510])
```

This expression returns Connecticut because the Connecticut member is in the same relative position under Acct-510 as Massachusetts is under Acct-550. If you change Massachusetts to New York in the preceding example, then you get a null set returned because there is only one business office under Acct-510 that does not correspond with the position held by New York under Acct-550.

Using Time Series Functions and Expressions

In performing analysis on a cube, you will undoubtedly be required to produce results in reference to time. You might be called upon to compare investment amounts for an account across years or quarters. You might want to know how investments are growing by month or how they have behaved year-to-date. Note that for using the time-related functions (like YTD()), and when skipping the time dimension information, make sure the dimension you think is the time dimension is actually marked as the time dimension. The name is not an indication to the MDX parser, but the type is.

This analysis can be achieved by using the time series functions we explore in this section. These functions are normally applied to a dimension of type time but can equally be applied to other dimensions as well.

PERIODSTODATE([<LEVEL>[,>MEMBER>]])

The *PeriodsToDate* function returns the number of periods within <level> up to and including <member>. The following example returns the four quarters of 1987:

```
PeriodsToDate(Year,Time.[1987].[Quarter 4])
```

The resulting set of members from the preceding expression is the same as entering the following *range* expression:

```
Time.[1987].[Quarter 1]:Time.[1987].[Quarter 4]
```

This example uses the *colon operator* to denote that your set should contain members from the Time dimension beginning with Quarter 1 in 1987 and ending with Quarter 4 inclusive.

When you need to query the year-to-date, quarter-to-date, month-to-date, or week-to-date periods, you can use the following functions as shortcuts to PeriodsToDate:

```
YTD(<member>)      Year-to-date
QTD(<member>)      Quarter-to-date
MTD(<member>)      Month-to-date
WTD(<member>)      Week-to-date
```

LASTPERIODS(<INDEX>[,<MEMBER>])

This function returns the number of periods starting with the period that lags the specified member by <index> – 1 up to and including the specified member.

```
LastPeriods(3,[1987].[Quarter 2])
```

This example returns the three periods starting with Quarter 4 of 1986 through Quarter 2 of 1987.

PARALLELPERIOD([<LEVEL>[,<INDEX>[,<MEMBER>]]])

ParallelPeriod takes the ancestor of the specified member at the level specified in the first argument, and returns the period parallel to the member under the ancestor's sibling that lags by <index>. The default for <index> is 1, and that for <member> is Time.CurrentMember.

```
ParallelPeriod([Quarter],3,[1987].[Quarter 4].[October])
```

This expression locates the sibling of the quarter-level ancestor of October in Quarter 4 of 1987, moves three quarters back, and returns the cousin of October 1987 in that quarter. The quarter three quarters back is Quarter 1, 1987, and the month returned is January.

OPENINGPERIOD([<LEVEL>[,<MEMBER>]])

The OpeningPeriod function returns the first period in the descendants of the specified member at the specified level.

```
OpeningPeriod([Quarter],[1986])
```

Quarter 1 is returned from the preceding expression because it is the first period at the Quarter level below 1986. *ClosingPeriod* called with the same arguments returns Quarter 4.

Using Conditional Expressions

MDX defines the conditional expressions IIF, simple case, and searched case. In the 7.0 version of OLAP Services, only the IIF expression is supported, but the syntax of all three expressions is discussed here.

IIF(<SEARCH_CONDITION>,<TRUE_PART>,<FALSE_PART>)

The IIF expression operates just like the IIF statement in Visual Basic. The condition specified in the first argument is tested and if the outcome is True, the result of the expression in the second argument is returned; otherwise, the result of the expression in the third argument is returned.

```
WITH MEMBER Measures.Weight AS
    'IIF(Manager.CurrentMember.Name = "Shares",Amount * 1.1,Amount * 1.05)'
SELECT Account.Members ON COLUMNS,
{CrossJoin(Manager.Members,{Measures.Weight})} ON ROWS
FROM Investments
```

Both the true_part and false_part must be of the same type, either both numeric or both string. In the preceding calculated member, IIF is checking the name of the Manager CurrentMember against the string "Shares". If the outcome is True, then 10 percent is added to the amount for the CurrentMember; otherwise, only 5 percent is added.

SIMPLE CASE EXPRESSION

The simple case expression evaluates the case operand according to one or more WHEN clauses and returns a result according to its value. The simple case expression that follows performs the same weighting as the IIF expression did:

```
WITH MEMBER Measures.Weight AS
    'CASE Manager.CurrentMember.Name
        WHEN "Shares" THEN Amount * 1.1
        ELSE Amount * 1.05
    END'
SELECT Account.Members ON COLUMNS,
{CrossJoin(Manager.Members,Generate({Manager.Members},{Weight}))} ON ROWS
FROM Investments
```

SEARCHED CASE EXPRESSION

A searched case expression is similar to the simple case, but in the searched case, the WHEN clause is a searched condition rather than a value expression.

```
WITH MEMBER Measures.Weight AS
    'CASE
        WHEN Manager.CurrentMember.Name = "Shares" THEN Amount * 1.1
        ELSE Amount * 1.05
    END'
SELECT Account.Members ON COLUMNS,
{CrossJoin(Manager.Members,Generate({Manager.Members},{Weight}))} ON ROWS
FROM Investments
```

All simple case expressions can be expressed as searched case expressions by specifying the simple case operand as the WHEN clause search condition.

Working with Empty Cells

If you can possibly design your cubes to have no empty cells in them, then by all means do so. You and your users will have a much easier time developing queries and performing analysis against cubes with no empty cells than against cubes such as our Investments cube, which has many empty cells. You've already discovered this fact when you developed a calculated member to compute an average back in Chapter 7.

But many cubes will have empty cells, and you need to understand what they can do to query results and how to work around them. In numeric calculations, for example, an empty cell can cause unpredictable results, such as what happens when you use an empty cell value as a divisor.

Empty cell values are handled by OLAP Services according to the following rules:

1. An empty cell value behaves like zero when used as a numeric operand to any of the numeric operators.

2. When involved in a string concatenation, empty cell values behave like an empty string.

3. When compared against numeric values using any of the comparison operators, an empty cell behaves like zero. When compared to strings, an empty cell value behaves like an empty string.

4. When an empty cell value is collated with numeric values, the empty cell value is placed before zero. When an empty cell value is collated with string values, the empty cell value is placed before the empty string.

You can test for an empty cell using the *IsEmpty* function. This function returns True if the cell is empty, and False otherwise. Use of this function in a calculated member, maybe in an IIF statement, enables you to develop work-arounds for empty cells.

The *CoalesceEmpty* function is used to replace an empty cell value with some other value, numeric or string. Using this function to return zero in place of empty cells in an expression, you would code:

```
CoalesceEmpty(Amount,0)
```

All numeric functions in MDX ignore empty cells. If a numeric function needs to include empty cells, then use the CoalesceEmpty function to convert the empty cells to a numeric value that is processed. The *Count* function is different. It supports an optional argument that enables empty cells to be included in the count. With the *IncludeEmpty* argument, Count counts empty cells; otherwise, it ignores them.

With empty cells in a cube, it is possible that an empty tuple may result in a set. This tuple has nothing but empty members in it. To remove empty tuples from a set, you specify the keywords NON EMPTY in the axis specification.

```
SELECT
    { [Measures].[Sh Num] } ON COLUMNS,
  NON EMPTY { Manager.members} ON ROWS
FROM Investments
```

Without NON EMPTY applied to the row axis, the preceding query returns empty tuples for managers Booker and Fundman. The query as written eliminates these empty tuples from the result. Be aware, however, that when using NON EMPTY, you may still encounter empty tuples if other tuples on an axis contain values.

Using Virtual Dimensions and Virtual Cubes

If you define member properties for a level, as you did in the Fund dimension in creating the Fund Age property, then you can use those properties to define *virtual dimensions* in a cube.

Using virtual dimensions, you can perform analysis based on the properties in addition to the physical dimensions. Any virtual dimensions you create in a database can be used in any cube that also includes the virtual dimension's physical shared base dimension. Virtual dimensions are shared dimensions consisting of an "All" level and a virtual level of member properties from the base dimension. In your FundAcctSample database, a virtual dimension created based on Fund Age could be used in either the Investments cube or the Dividends cube, in that both of those cubes include the Fund dimension.

Aggregations to satisfy queries for the virtual dimension are calculated when the dimension is accessed. For this reason, a virtual dimension does not take any space in the cube or require any processing time when the cube is processed. Virtual dimensions do, however, require additional time when used in a query because the aggregations must be done on the fly.

Virtual dimensions can be created by using the Virtual Dimension Wizard or through the use of DSO. To use the Virtual Dimension Wizard, right-click the Virtual Dimensions folder, located in the Library folder, and select New Virtual Dimension from the shortcut menu.

The screen shown in Figure 10-2 enables you to choose the member property for your virtual dimension. Your sample cube only has one member property, so choose it and then click Next to move to the Finish screen shown in Figure 10-3.

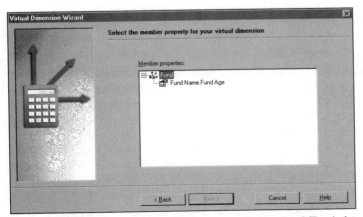

Figure 10-2: Selection of the member property for the AgeOfFund virtual dimension

On the Finish screen, enter the name AgeOfFund in the text box and then click Finish to create the virtual dimension.

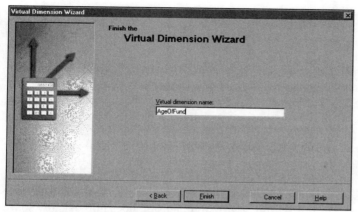

Figure 10-3: The Finish screen in the Virtual Dimension Wizard

Now that the virtual dimension is created, you can add it to the Investments cube. To do this, edit the cube, launch the Dimension Manager, select the AgeOfFund virtual dimension, and add it to the dimensions of the cube. After adding the virtual dimension, save the changes and process the cube.

Previous to adding the AgeOfFund dimension, you were not allowed to project the same dimension to different axes in a cellset. Attempting to do so results in an MDX error. But with your virtual dimension in place, you can run the following query without any problems:

```
SELECT {Fund.[Brandywine],Fund.[Gabelli Growth]} ON COLUMNS,
{AgeOfFund.Members} ON ROWS
FROM INVESTMENTS
```

The use of the AgeOfFund virtual dimension enables you to analyze the cube in terms of the physical dimensions of the cube and the Fund Age member property.

A *virtual cube* is a logical cube constructed from one or more physical cubes. In creating the virtual cube, you select the dimensions and measures that are available from the composite underlying physical cubes.

Due to the ability to pick and choose dimensions and measures to be included, the virtual cube can be used as a security mechanism to lock out users from access to sensitive data. If, for example, you want some users to have access to only the number of shares in a cube but not the invested amounts or the calculated prices, you would develop a virtual cube from the Investments cube and select only the sh num measure. You then create a role granting its members access to the virtual cube and denying access to the Investments cube.

In OLAP Manager, right-click the Virtual Cubes folder under the FundAcctSample database and select New Virtual Cube from the shortcut menu. Click Next on the Welcome screen to display the cubes selection screen shown in Figure 10-4.

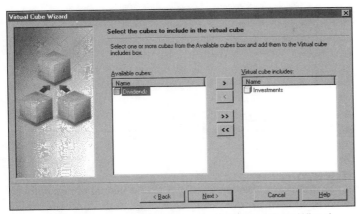

Figure 10-4: The cube selection screen in the Virtual Cube Wizard

Select the Investments cube from the Available cubes list and move it to the Virtual cube includes list. Then click Next to display the measures selection screen shown in Figure 10-5.

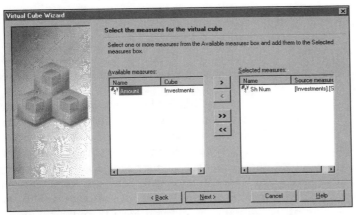

Figure 10-5: Selection of measures for the new virtual cube

Select Sh Num from the Available measures list and move it to the Selected measures list. Now click Next so that you can select the desired dimensions for the new virtual cube. The dimension selection screen is shown in Figure 10-6.

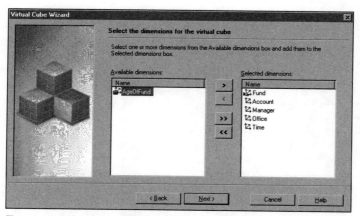

Figure 10-6: Selection of dimensions for the new virtual cube

Select all of the available dimensions except the AgeOfFund virtual dimension you created. Click Next to display the Finish screen and enter the name **VInvestments** in the Cube name text box and make sure the Process now option is selected.

Click Finish to process the virtual cube. If the underlying component cubes, in this case the Investments cube, require processing, this action causes those cubes to be processed. If they do not require processing, then OLAP Services only needs to record the metadata for the virtual cube.

Any users with an open session during the building of your virtual cube need to disconnect and reconnect before they will see VInvestments. Before testing your work, however, you need to do one more task.

Under the database Library folder, right-click the Roles folder and select New Role from the shortcut menu. Add a role named **VAnalyst** and add a user to this role. Now right-click the Roles folder under the VInvestments virtual cube and select Manage Roles. Select the VAnalyst role from the Database roles list and move it to the Cube access list.

Close out the Manage Roles dialog and exit OLAP Manager. Have the user you added to the VAnalyst role start a session with the OLAP server and attempt to access the Investments cube. Access is denied because the VAnalyst role members do not have access to the Investments cube. Now have the user access the VInvestments cube querying out the Amount measure. This time the user should get a bind error because no Amount measure is defined for the VInvestments cube. But when the user queries the Sh Num measure from VInvestments, results are returned successfully.

Nowhere in the definition of the virtual cube did you have the opportunity to select a calculated member. You do not want VAnalysts to have access to the Price calculated member. Price is defined by:

```
[Measures].[Amount]/[Measures].[Sh Num]
```

Because the VInvestments cube knows nothing about the Amount measure, Price cannot be calculated and therefore will not be available to queries. If Amount were available in VInvestments and cell-level security allowed access to it, then Price would also be available to VAnalysts.

Virtual dimensions and cubes can of course be created using DSO instead of the OLAP Manager. When creating a virtual dimension in DSO, you follow the same steps as for a regular dimension (remember to name the virtual dimension as shared), but when defining the levels of the virtual dimension, you need to set the SubClassType of the level to sbclsVirtual instead of sbclsRegular. Here's the code to define a virtual dimension level:

```
Set dsoLevel = dsoVirtualDim.Levels.AddNew("AgeOfFund", sbclsVirtual)
dsoLevel.MemberKeyColumn = "[Fund].[Fund Name].[Fund Age]"
dsoVirtualDim.Update
```

In defining a virtual cube with DSO, you again follow the same steps as for regular cubes. The difference here is that a virtual cube's MDStores collection contains cube objects instead of partition objects like a regular cube and the SubClassType of the virtual cube is sbclsVirtual instead of sbclsRegular. Let's look at the code:

```
Dim dsoVirtualCube As DSO.MDStore
Dim dsoMeasure As DSO.Measure

Set dsoVirtualCube = dsoDatabase.MDStores.AddNew("VInvestments",
    sbclsVirtual)
Set dsoMeasure = dsoVirtualCube.Measures.AddNew("Sh Num")
dsoMeasure.SourceColumn = "[Investments].[Sh Num]"

dsoVirtualCube.Dimensions.AddNew "Fund"
dsoVirtualCube.Dimensions.AddNew "Account"
dsoVirtualCube.Dimensions.AddNew "Manager"
dsoVirtualCube.Dimensions.AddNew "Office"
dsoVirtualCube.Dimensions.AddNew "Time"

dsoVirtualCube.Update
```

'Once this code has run, you can now process the cube just as you processed regular cubes back in Chapter 8. Then add the VAnalyst role to the database and to the virtual cube and you're ready to bring VInvestments online.

Write-Enabling a Cube

OLAP server cubes can be updated by users if you provide a role that has read/write permissions and write-enable the cube. Enabling a cube to be updated provides the users of the cube with the ability to perform what-if analysis on a cube and save the results of this analysis back to the cube to be shared with other users.

Local cubes cannot be write-enabled. What-if analysis is still possible on these cubes, but the changes made are not written back to the local cube and are never visible to other users.

'When you write-enable a cube, a special table is created by OLAP services. This table is called a *write-back table* and it holds all changes made to the cube. When users query a cube that is write-enabled, cellset data returned as a result of the query contains data merged from the cube and its write-back table. This merging of cube data with write-back data is transparent to the user. Appendix B contains a CREATE TABLE script describing the fields of a write-back table.

To write-enable the Investments cube using OLAP Manager, perform these steps:

1. Right-click the Investments cube and select Write-Enable from the short-cut menu.

2. Enter a name for the write-back table in the write-enable dialog or accept the name provided (WriteTable_Investments).

3. Select a Data Source for the write-back table.

4. Click OK to dismiss the dialog.

Updates to a cube are allowed only at the lowest level of dimensions where detail or *atomic* data resides. When a user makes a change to one of these cells and commits it to the write-back table, OLAP services stores the net difference between the original cell value and the user change. In this way, the original cell value is preserved in the cube.

The write-back data in the write-back table can be browsed by right-clicking the write-enabled cube in OLAP Manager tree view, selecting Write-Back Options, and then selecting Browse Write-Back Data.

The level of isolation supported by the PivotTable service for update transactions is *read-committed*. This means that any changes made by a user are not visible to other users until the change transaction is committed to the write-back table.

If you are running the Enterprise Edition of OLAP Services, then you can convert a write-back table to a partition. Doing so results in all read/write permissions being disabled and the write-back table being deleted.

To convert a write-back table to a partition, follow these steps:

1. Right-click the Investments cube and select Write-Back Options and then Convert To Partition.

2. Type a partition name in the Convert To Partition dialog.

3. Select the storage designs for the partition by using the Storage Design Wizard or copying designs from an existing partition. You also have the option of designing the aggregations later.

4. Click Advanced to specify a filter to filter write-back table data for the partition.

5. If you have designed or copied aggregation designs for the partition, you can elect to process the partition upon completion of the dialog. Click OK to dismiss the dialog.

In Chapter 11, you'll be testing this write-back feature by modifying data in an Excel 2000 PivotTable created from your Investments cube.

You need to be aware of several performance implications in using write-enabled cubes. Because write-back tables do not store aggregations until the table is converted to a partition, query performance against the write-enabled cube may be degraded. This is due to the need to integrate the write-back data into aggregations required to satisfy a query.

When a cell update is committed to the write-back table, both the client and server cache are flushed. Better performance can be achieved by grouping several changes within a single transaction.

Because the write-back table is stored in a relational database, you need to consider the performance of the relational engine and the database. The SQL Server 7.0 engine helps to improve the performance of insert activity to the write-back table (as with any table), but the number of concurrent users against this table, the condition of the physical storage for the table, and the overall load on the database are all factors to consider when attempting to optimize query performance against OLAP cubes.

Summary

In this chapter we explored MDX expressions and discussed the use of some of the functions listed in Appendix G. We learned dimension hierarchy terminology and which functions to use to access hierarchy members. We also explored the navigation of a time hierarchy to return a set of time periods.

The creation and use of virtual dimensions and virtual cubes was discussed, and we saw how to create these using OLAP Manager and DSO.

We discussed how a cube can be write-enabled so that users can perform what-if analysis on a cube and share this analysis with other users by committing their changes to a write-back table associated with the cube. We explore MDX further in the chapters that follow. In Chapter 13, we look at cellset navigation using drilling functions, and we look at a couple of Time Series functions in developing a client application with the PivotTable service.

Chapter 11

Exploring Microsoft Excel 2000 and OLAP

IN THIS CHAPTER

◆ Exploring the use of Excel PivotTables for reporting cube data

◆ Learning how to create a local cube from within Excel

◆ Discovering how to conduct what-if analysis by modifying cube data

FOR MANY ANALYSTS IN the business world today, Microsoft Excel is a familiar tool. Many business applications are developed that either are based on Excel or interact with Excel in some way, maybe to enter data, run Excel calculations, or produce reports and charts. Excel is a tool well adapted to analyzing numeric data.

Microsoft Excel has for many years had the capability to read and write external file formats, including access to SQL Server databases. With the release of Microsoft Office 2000, Excel can now access OLAP cubes, either cubes located on an OLAP server or local cubes located on a client machine. Local cubes can even be created by Excel for offline analysis when not connected to a server. Excel presents OLAP cube data as PivotTable or PivotChart reports.

This chapter presents a brief overview of how Excel can be used to report on OLAP data, how you can create local cubes that are subsets of OLAP server cubes, and how you can perform what-if analysis using the OLAP@Work Excel add-in found on the CD that accompanies this book.

A more in-depth exploration of using Excel and OLAP together can be found in the book entitled *Unlocking OLAP with SQL Server 7 and Excel 2000* by Wayne Freeze (ISBN 0-7645-4587-6) forthcoming in spring 2000 from IDG Books Worldwide.

Creating a PivotTable Report on an OLAP Cube

Creating PivotTables from OLAP cubes is quite easy in Excel 2000. The first step is to define a data source. You do this through the Microsoft Query. Follow these steps:

1. From the Data menu in Excel 2000, select Get External Data and click New Database Query.

2. In the Choose Data Source dialog, select the OLAP Cubes tab.

3. Highlight <New Data Source> and click OK.

4. In the Create New Data Source dialog, enter a name for your new data source. For this example, enter the name **Investments**.

5. In the Select an OLAP Provider drop-down list, select Microsoft OLE DB Provider for OLAP Services.

6. Click Connect to display the Multi-Dimensional Connection screen.

7. Choose the OLAP Server option and enter the name of your OLAP Server in the Server text box. Click Next.

8. Select the FundAcctSample database from the database list and click Finish.

9. Select the Investments cube from the drop-down list in Step 4 of the Create New Data Source dialog. Click OK.

10. With the Investments data source highlighted in the Choose Data Source dialog, click OK. This will launch the PivotTable and PivotChart Wizard.

The PivotTable and PivotChart Wizard shown in Figure 11-1 will help you define your PivotTable from the data in the Investments cube data source.

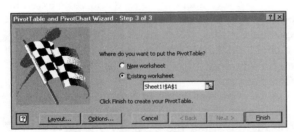

Figure 11-1: The PivotTable and PivotChart Wizard screen after establishing a data source

Follow these steps in the wizard to create the PivotTable:

1. Click Layout to display the Layout screen.

2. Click and drag the Manager field to the Column area of the layout diagram.

3. Next drag the Time field to the Row area of the diagram and drop it.

4. Now drag and drop the Amount, Sh Num, and Price fields to the Data area of the diagram.

5. Click OK to return to the wizard. Click Options and enter the name **Investments By Manager/Time** in the Name text box. Leave the other options at their default values.

6. Click OK and then click Finish to create the PivotTable.

The resulting PivotTable is shown in Figure 11-2.

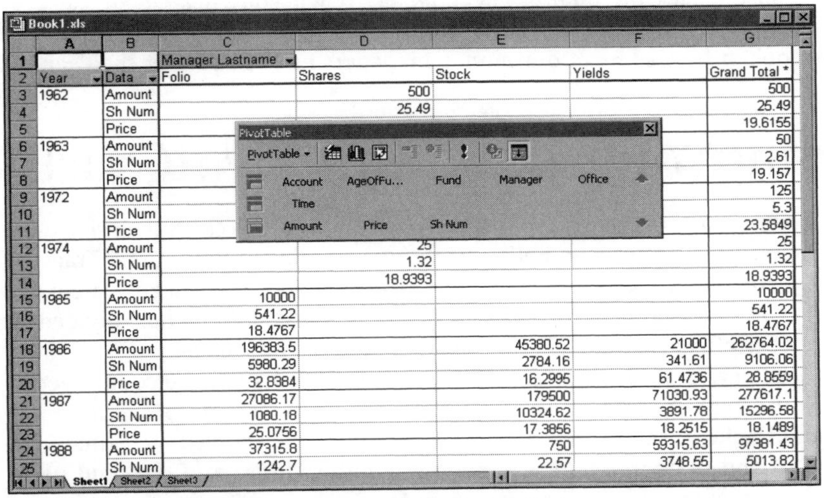

Figure 11-2: The Investments By Manager/Time PivotTable

To drill down into the Year dimension, click the arrow to the right of the Year header label. Click the + sign next to 1986 in the tree view, and then check the box next to each of the Quarters in the tree.

The PivotTable now shows the Amount, Sh Num, and Price for each of the Quarter levels in 1986 plus a total for each measure for the year, all by manager. At the very bottom of the PivotTable, you find totals for each measure across all years.

Note that unlike with PivotTables based on non-OLAP data, where you can view the detail that makes up a summary value, with OLAP data, the detail at the lowest level of a dimension hierarchy can be displayed only through drilling down through the hierarchy levels.

Whenever you change the layout of a PivotTable that is based on OLAP data to display different data, Excel refreshes the PivotTable. When using the PivotTable toolbar, note that dimension fields can only be placed on the column, row, or page area of the PivotTable. Likewise, measures can only be used as data fields.

Now drill down to the month level in Quarter 1 of 1986. This time, you will use a different method than the one you used before to display the Quarter level. Click in the Quarter 1 label cell and then click Show Detail on the PivotTable toolbar. This action displays the months level under Quarter 1. To collapse the months level, click Hide Detail on the toolbar.

To remove the Year level from the display, right-click the Year field label and choose Hide Levels from the shortcut menu. This removes the Year and leaves only the Quarters displayed on the rows. To return the Years to the display, right-click the Quarter label and choose Show Levels.

You will now do some charting of the data in the current PivotTable. Remove the quarter display for 1986 by clicking the arrow next to the Year field, expand the year 1986, and uncheck the quarter check boxes. When you click OK in the Year tree, you return to the view just showing the years.

Next we look at how some of our money managers have done over the years.

Charting Your Data with PivotCharts

The first manager you will chart is manager Folio. You want to chart the Price measure over time to determine how Folio has done managing his accounts. Tracking the price is a simplified method of tracking portfolio value. The price is calculated as the total of account investments (not including reinvested dividends) divided by the total number of shares held (also not including dividend shares).

Price is used here as a rough estimate of return. If Folio had one account over all these years and that account invested $100 in a fund priced at $10 a share, the account would hold 10 shares. If the price of the fund never moved over time from the initial $10 and the account never invested another dollar and the fund never earned a penny, we would see a flat line chart for Folio over time.

Now suppose that with this same investment scenario, at some point in your time line, the account invested another $100 but at a market price of $10.50 a share. The portfolio now shows $200 invested and 19.52 shares held for a price of $10.25, a $0.25 increase over the previous price of the portfolio, an upturn on a line graph. If, on the other hand, the market price of the fund were only $9.75, the number of shares purchased would be 10.26 and the portfolio price would yield $9.87, a decrease of $0.13 and a downturn on a line graph.

The only reason you are able to use portfolio price as a return indicator in your Investment PivotTable is that the share numbers and invested amounts are both void of reinvested dividends. If you allowed the number of shares to reflect reinvested dividends and held the amounts to only investor amounts, then the price calculation would not reflect portfolio value at all. Increasing shares while holding invested amounts steady would yield a decrease in portfolio price and a downward trend in portfolio value, although in reality the portfolio worth would be increasing.

The lesson in this discussion is that had you captured investment transactions from the OLTP database containing investment amounts and total shares instead of purchased shares, then your price calculated measure would be wrong. It is important to understand and carefully consider your data, the databases used as a source for your data warehouse, and the design of cubes and calculated members. Being careful to develop a good design and to understand the data you work with will save a great deal of time and money.

Now that you understand what you are looking at when you chart price over time for a given manager, let's find out how to do it.

The PivotTable and PivotChart are linked together. When you make a change in one, the change is reflected in the other. You're only interested in looking at Folio's performance, so you'll be modifying the data via the PivotChart. With the PivotTable displayed, click PivotChart Wizard on the PivotTable toolbar.

Click the down arrow on the Manager Lastname field button and uncheck all of the managers except Folio. On the Data field button, uncheck the Amount and Sh Num fields. The chart now displays only Folio, Price, and the Years of the Time dimension.

Change the chart type by right-clicking the chart area and selecting Chart Type from the shortcut menu. Select a line chart style that more clearly shows the trend of the price over time. Use a Line or Marked Line style of line chart for this purpose. Click OK to display the line chart. The result is shown in Figure 11-3.

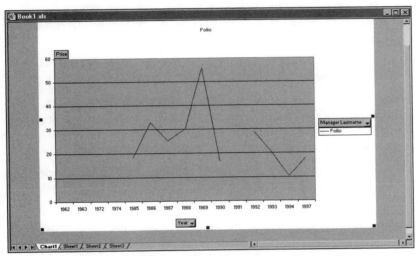

Figure 11-3: Line chart of price for Folio's accounts over time

To compare two managers, say Folio with Yields, simply select Yields from the Manager Lastname field box and you'll see the Price plot for both managers together over time. Based on your data, Yields has fallen way below Folio between 1987 and 1989 but then picked up again in 1990, but he is still far below his high back in 1986.

The PivotChart and PivotTable together make great tools for reporting your OLAP data and enabling your end users to compare various measures and dimensions of their choice. Another powerful end-user tool enables them to make changes to the displayed data and monitor the effects of those changes on the cube as a whole. Next we explore a third-party tool that supports this.

Performing What-If Analysis with OLAP@Work

If you haven't yet installed the OLAP@Work for Excel software from the accompanying CD, use the instructions found in the OLAP@Work folder and do so now. We'll be using this Excel add-in to discuss what-if analysis and write-back data in this section.

After installing OLAP@Work for Excel, go to the PivotTable you were working with in the previous section and select another sheet in the book or create a new sheet. You'll add an OLAP@Work for Excel report on this new sheet. Select cell A1.

1. From the OLAP@Work menu in Excel, select Query and then Create OLAP Report. This displays the OLAP@Work for Excel Wizard. Cell A1 is pre-filled in the text box and indicates where the report will be placed on the sheet. Click Next to display page 2 of the wizard.

2. In the OLAP Report Name text box, enter Manager Comparison. Leave all defaults checked and click Next.

3. On page 3 of the wizard, be sure the Create new report using Report Layout option is selected and then click Next. This will display a Login screen asking for your login information and the name of the OLAP server you want to access. After entering this information, click OK.

4. On the Select Cube from Database screen, expand the FundAcctSample database node and select the Investments cube. Click OK to display the OLAP@Work Report Layout screen.

5. Drag the Time field button and drop it on the Rows area. In the Properties of Time Dimension screen, copy all of the years displayed in the middle list box to the Report members list and then click OK to dismiss the screen and return to the layout screen.

6. Drag the Manager field button and drop it on the Columns area. Copy Folio and Yields to the Report members list in the Properties of Manager Dimension screen. Click OK to close this screen.

7. Now drag the Measures button to the Pages area and drop it. This will display the Properties of Measures Dimension screen. Select Price and Sh Num into the Report members list and click OK.

8. Click OK on the OLAP@Work Report Layout screen to create the report and chart. Position the chart to the right of the report so that you can see both on the sheet.

From the View menu, choose Toolbars and the OLAP@Work to display the OLAP@Work toolbar. Position this toolbar wherever you feel comfortable with it. Dock it or let it float.

Click a data cell on the report and then click Change the OLAP Page on the OLAP@Work toolbar. Click the Price entry in the Select Page dialog, click Select and then Finish. Both the report and the chart show the Price data.

To change the chart to a line style, right-click in the chart area and select Chart Type from the shortcut menu. Choose a Line chart type and click OK to see the line chart as we did in the Excel PivotChart. Note the difference in 1986 between the Price for Folio and the Price for Yields. You're going to now modify the Sh Num in 1986 and watch the effect on this price.

Change the OLAP Page to Sh Num. Select the cell at the intersection of 1986 and Folio. Click Modify cell value on the OLAP@Work toolbar. In the Enter a new value for selected cells dialog, enter 980.29 instead of the original 5980.29. Click OK to close this dialog. Now click Force a reallocation on the toolbar and choose Quick for the Allocation technique in the Allocation dialog. Click OK to close this dialog.

When the allocation is complete, you should see the screen shown in Figure 11-4.

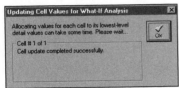

Figure 11-4: Cell value update completion screen for what-if analysis in OLAP@Work

Click OK to dismiss the Allocation complete screen and return to the report. Now switch back to the Price page by changing the OLAP page and selecting the Price page. Note the difference in the price in 1986 for Folio and the difference in the chart. Because we have reduced the shares for Folio in 1986, the calculated price has increased, a fact that is now reflected in the report and the chart.

You have just performed a simple what-if analysis on the OLAP Investment data. You have two options at this point. You can roll back the change, or you can commit the change to the cube (write it to the write-back table) so that all other users of the cube can see it.

To roll back the changes you just made back to the original values, click Rollback on the OLAP@Work toolbar. You see the 1986 Folio Sh Num revert back to 5980.29 and the price revert back to 32.84. These changes are reflected in the chart as well.

To commit the changes to the cube's write-back table, click WriteBack on the toolbar. Before you commit your changes to the write-back table, be sure you have a solid understanding of the OLAP@Work allocation techniques described in the "OLAP@Work Allocation Methods" sidebar.

Once committed to the write-back table, OLAP Services merges this data in with cube data when responding to a query against the Investments cube. In this way, any changes made to the cube through procedures like the one you just examined are seen by everyone accessing the cube.

OLAP@Work Allocation Methods

The allocation techniques offered on the Allocation dialog or the Change Pivot Table Values dialog specify different methods of applying a change to a cube. The three methods are:

Quick	Only the lowest-level descendants of the row, column, and page axes members and the first lowest-level descendant of each filter axis member are changed. To commit this type of allocation is not recommended. This provides quick allocation for what-if analysis but should be rolled back when analysis is completed.
Equal	Evenly distributes the difference between the new value and the old value to all cells below the changed cell. When an aggregated cell value is changed, the new value must be reflected down to the lowest level of all dimensions making up that cell, as if the lowest-level detail value had been changed. The change must then be brought up through all impacted aggregations to yield the same result as cube processing would yield. This allocation can take a considerable amount of time depending on the size of the cube, possibly much longer than a user is willing to wait.
Weighted	Calculates the percentage increase or decrease from the old value to the new value and applies that percentage to all lower-level cells. Note that with Equal allocation, cells with zero values will be changed to nonzero values; with Weighted allocation, zero values remain at zero. This allocation behaves like the Equal allocation with respect to the time it takes to allocate the change to a cube.

Creating OLAP Cubes in Excel 2000

One solution to enabling users to explore what-if analysis without concern for long-running allocations or destroying the integrity of the cube is to create local cubes populated with the data needed for the analysis.

A local cube can be created from an existing PivotTable. The local cube can then act as the data source for the PivotTable, and the OLAP@Work what-if analysis can be performed offline, while disconnected from the server cube.

To create a local cube from the PivotTable you created in the previous section, select the sheet containing our PivotTable and then follow these steps:

1. Select Client-Server Settings from the PivotTable menu on the PivotTable toolbar.

2. Select the option to create a local data file and click Create file.

3. In Step 2 of the Create Cube File Wizard, the Manager and Time dimensions are already selected. Click Next.

4. In Step 3, expand the Measures dimension and click the Amount member. All other members from the Manager and Time dimensions are selected according to the member selection we have included on the PivotTable. Click Next.

5. Step 4 prompts you for a folder in which to store the local cube file and the name of the cube file. Choose a folder and then enter **Investments.cub** in the File name text box. Click Finish to create the local cube.

The data source for the PivotTable is now pointing to the local cube you just created. Click OK to close the Client-Server Settings dialog and return to the PivotTable.

To perform OLAP@Work what-if analysis on the local Investments cube, insert a new sheet into the workbook, point to cell A1, and then choose Query and Create OLAP Report from the OLAP@Work menu.

1. On page 2 of the wizard, enter **Local Cube Report** as your report name, leave all default selections, and then click Next.

2. On page 3, select the Create new report option and then click Next to display the Login screen. This is where you divert from the report you created earlier. Instead of logging into the OLAP server, you select the local Investments cube as your data source for this report.

3. Click Edit at the bottom of the Login screen. On the OLAP Server Name dialog, click the Other option and be sure MSOLAP is specified as the server. Click Next.

4. On the Database Locations dialog, click the Cube Filename option and then the Browse button to locate the Investments.cub file. After selecting this file, click Next.

5. On the last dialog screen, enter a name, such as **Local**, to designate this data source. Click Finish to return to the Login screen. The name you just entered will appear in the Server box. Click OK to display the layout screen and lay out your report just as you did earlier.

When you drop the Measures button on the Pages areas during layout, you should select Amount and Sh Num for the report measures. Because Excel did not bring over your Price calculated measure into your local cube, you use OLAP@Work to easily create this measure for you.

1. Click Calc on the Properties of Measures Dimension screen. This displays the first screen of the Calculated Member Wizard.

2. On the Select Calculation Type screen, choose the Custom option and then click Next. (Be sure to go back to this screen later and explore the other powerful options available to you.)

3. On the Custom Calculation screen, enter the expression **[Measures].[Amount] / [Measures].[Sh Num]** or use the button on the side of the screen to choose these expression components. Enter **Price** as the name of the Calculated Member. Click Finish to return to the Properties of Measures Dimension screen. Price appears in the list of members selected for the report.

4. Click OK to return to the report layout screen and then click OK on that screen.

After the report is created, you can choose among the various pages you placed on the report to analyze the data. You can modify the data as you did earlier when connected to the OLAP server Investments cube. This time, however, the report is connected to your local cube, and so you can choose a different allocation technique and not be concerned about destroying the integrity of the main OLAP cube.

When you modify the Sh Num for Folio 1986 data, choose Equal as the Allocation technique this time. It will complete very quickly and yield the same results as you saw when you used the Quick allocation technique. The difference is in the definition of these two techniques. Using Equal, you have applied the difference between the old Sh Num value and the new Sh Num value to all descendant cells and adjusted all impacted aggregations in the local cube. The resulting local cube integrity is not in jeopardy, and you can safely commit this change to the local write-back table.

But wait! There is no write-back table associated with your local cube. The WriteBack button on the OLAP@Work toolbar is disabled. The reason is that local cubes cannot be write-enabled and therefore do not have write-back tables and do not accept permanent changes. Any change made during what-if analysis on a local cube is rolled back at the end of the session or whenever you manually roll back using the Rollback toolbar button.

Even though what-if modifications are not saved to the local Investments cube, the Price calculated measure you created with OLAP@Work is saved and appears the next time you open the report.

Using Excel 2000 and powerful tools such as OLAP@Work for Excel, your users can create some very useful reports and conduct some very detailed analysis with your OLAP data. It is well worth considering the integration of these tools into your OLAP solutions.

Summary

In this chapter we learned how to connect to an OLAP server from within Excel 2000 and query the Investments cube into an Excel PivotTable. We explored the options of the PivotTable toolbar and learned how to drill down into the Time dimension to expose more detailed cube data.

We created a PivotChart from the PivotTable and charted the trend in price of managed portfolios for two managers. We saw how the PivotTable and PivotChart are linked together so that changes in one affect display of the other.

To explore the write-back features of OLAP Services, we used the OLAP@Work for Excel product from the CD to quickly create an OLAP report and chart. We then performed what-if analysis with OLAP@Work to modify share holdings for a specified year and manager to discover the effects on price for the manager. We then learned about the options of rollback and write-back to either roll back or commit our changes to the cube's write-back table. OLAP@Work allocation methods were also discussed.

Last, we explored the creation of a local cube using Excel's Create Cube File Wizard and discussed the differences between OLAP server cubes and local cubes when it comes to what-if analysis and write-back options. After creating a local cube, we again used OLAP@Work for Excel to create a report based on the local cube and perform a what-if analysis on it.

We have only seen a brief overview in this chapter of the capabilities in using Microsoft Excel and tools like OLAP@Work for Excel to develop OLAP solutions for your users. Further exploration of these tools is encouraged to learn more of what these products can do. I think you'll soon discover how quickly you can put some powerful reporting and analysis capability into the hands of your end users.

Part III

Exercises in OLAP
Services Programming

CHAPTER 12
A Server Application Using Decision Support Objects

CHAPTER 13
Client Applications Using the PivotTable Service

CHAPTER 14
Creating an OLAP Manager Add-In

CHAPTER 15
Exploring Data Transformation Services

Chapter 12

A Server Application Using Decision Support Objects

IN THIS CHAPTER

- ◆ Exploring a server-side application using the Decision Support Object model
- ◆ Using the Inspector to explore any OLAP server

THIS CHAPTER DISCUSSES the DSO Inspector application found in the Chapter12 folder on the CD.

The Inspector enables you to display the properties of all objects conforming to the Decision Support Object (DSO) model on a given OLAP server. This project can easily be enhanced to provide object creation functionality such as that needed to create cubes, roles, and commands or to design aggregations and process cubes. All of the code necessary for these enhancements can be found in the Ch08 project in the Chapter08 folder on the CD.

There are two projects in the Chapter12 folder. The Ch12.vbp project contains the forms for displaying the DSO model, menu processing, and the code to call into an ActiveX DLL named DSOInspector to acquire the properties of the DSO objects selected by the user.

The DSOInspector.vbp project provides an Inspector object that implements several methods for querying properties of DSO objects into a list box that is then displayed by the Ch12 application.

The DSOInspector DLL is used again in Chapter 14 where we create an OLAP Manager add-in for producing reports of a server's metadata.

How the DSO Inspector Works

When you open the DSOInspector project, you'll find one class module named Inspector. If you look at the code for this class, you'll see that the *Initialize* subroutine calls a series of private subroutines in the module. These subroutines instantiate and load a number of private collections that are used to map certain property values to an enumeration name.

For example, the first routine called in Initialize, the *LoadClassTypesMap* sub-routine, loads a collection named *dsoClassTypesMap* that holds enumeration names for the ClassTypes enumeration. Each entry in the collection is a string containing the enumeration name and value. Every entry is keyed by the value of the enumeration so that a ClassType property value of an object supporting this property can be used to directly access the enumeration name.

A string value in one of these enumeration map collections is obtained by a property list method by calling one of the Get functions named for the property it supports. The *GetClassType* function, for example, accepts a key value as an argument and returns the corresponding string that names that value. These functions are currently used only from within the class but could be made public to expose them to an application using the Inspector object.

If you expand the Declarations list, you'll see the methods of the Inspector class used to list DSO object properties and two property procedures for supporting the *PropertyList* property. The PropertyList property uses a private variable of type List Box named *m_lstProps*. This property is set by an application to reference a list box within the application prior to making a call to an object property method. Every method in the Inspector class adds its object properties to this list box variable.

Using the Inspector Object

The references in the Ch12 project must be set to reference the DSOInspector DLL. Once this reference is set, the Inspector object hosted by that DLL can be used to access the server connection method and property list methods.

The first form to open in the Ch12 application, the DSO Inspector form shown in Figure 12-1, requires you to enter the name of an OLAP server. After entering the server name, click the Connect button to establish a connection with the server.

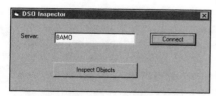

Figure 12-1: The initial DSO Inspector form used to connect to an OLAP server

The MakeServerConnection function used to make a connection with the OLAP server is the same routine we have used for all DSO samples in this book. Prior to calling MakeServerConnection, the code instantiates an Inspector object that will be used throughout the application.

```
Set insp = New DSOInspector.Inspector

If Not insp.MakeServerConnection(Me.txtServer.Text) Then
    cmdInspect.Enabled = True
```

```
Else
   MsgBox "Server connection failed", vbCritical, "Error"
End If
```

When a successful connection with the server is completed, the Inspect Objects button is enabled. Click this button to display the first page of the DSO model.

Using the DSO Hierarchy Forms

There are four forms in the application used to display various portions of the DSO model. The first form, DSO1 shown in Figure 12-2, enables you to inspect the properties of a clsDatabase object and all immediate dependents of the database object. DSO2 shows the hierarchy below the clsCube object. On the DSO3 form, you can explore the properties of a cube partition and its dependent objects, and finally DSO4 displays the clsAggregation and its dependents.

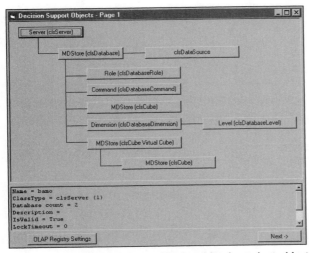

Figure 12-2: The clsDatabase object and its dependent object hierarchy shown on form DSO1

Server properties are listed by a call to the *GetServerProps* function. The code behind the clsServer button looks like this:

```
lstProps.Clear

Set insp.PropertyList = Me.lstProps

If insp.GetServerProps Then
   MsgBox "Server not initialized."
End If
```

Every button in the application has code similar to this. The property list box on all DSO forms is named lstProps. That list box is first cleared and then set into the *PropertyList* property of the Inspector object prior to calling a property function. You can cause the lstProps list box to be appended to simply by not calling the Clear method on the list box prior to calling one of the property list functions. All property list functions in the Inspector return zero on success, –1 if the required internal object variable is not valid, and an error code otherwise.

To choose a database object, right-click the clsDatabase button and select Choose Database from the shortcut menu. This displays a list of databases enumerated from the server's databases collection. The code to call into the Inspector object to list the databases and to change to the user-selected database is found in the *mnu_ChooseDB_Click* event subroutine:

```
Dim frmWrk As ObjList, selectedDB As String

Set frmWrk = ObjList
Set insp.PropertyList = frmWrk.lstObjects

If Not insp.GetDatabaseList() Then
   frmWrk.Show vbModal
   selectedDB = frmWrk.lstObjects.List(frmWrk.lstObjects.ListIndex)
   If insp.ChangeDatabase(selectedDB) Then
      MsgBox "Change database error."
   End If
Else
   MsgBox "Database list error."
End If

Unload frmWrk
Set frmWrk = Nothing
```

The list of databases obtained through *GetDatabaseList* is displayed in the *ObjList* form in the project. The list box of ObjList is used as the Inspector's PropertyList to collect the list of databases from the GetDatabaseList call.

Select one of the databases in the list and click OK. The selected database becomes the current database for the clsDatabase button by calling the *ChangeDatabase* function, passing it the selected database name from ObjList. After the Inspector changes its internal object pointers to reflect the new database object, you may inspect the newly selected database's properties just as you did the default. All other objects in the DSO model are selected in a similar way.

All dependent object variables are reset when a new database is selected. When an associated dependent object button, clsDataSource for example, is clicked, the object variable for the button has already been set to the default object, the first object in the DataSources collection of the current selected database object, and its properties are listed in the lstProps list box through a call to *GetDataSourceProps*.

Dependent objects may not be clicked until their parent objects have been clicked at least once to initialize object variables within the Inspector. You can of course change this behavior if you like by coding a routine in the DSOInspector project to set all object variables below a given parent instead of just the immediate dependent object variables.

Clicking a parent object establishes the default dependent object variables so that properties may be listed for them. Once set to the default object by the parent, dependent objects may be reset by choosing a different object from the collection corresponding to the button label.

Inspecting the DataSource Connection Property

The DataSource object contains a property named *Connection* that represents the connection to the relational DataSource through the provider specified in the *ConnectionString* property.

You can list the properties of the provider by inspection of the DataSource Connection. To do this, right-click the DataSource button and select List Connection Properties from the shortcut menu. The properties of the provider are displayed in the lstProps list box at the bottom of the form by the *GetConnectionProps* function. The code to list the connection properties is in the *mnu_ListConnectPropsDS_Click* event subroutine.

```
lstProps.Clear
Set insp.PropertyList = Me.lstProps

If insp.GetConnectionProps() Then
    MsgBox "Connection property error."
End If

Exit Sub
```

Zooming a Property Value

Some properties listed in the lstProps list box, such as the ConnectionString property, are much wider than the list box width, causing the property value to be truncated. To view the entire property value, select the property in the list box, right-click, and select Zoom from the shortcut menu.

A Zoom Property form is displayed showing the entire length of the selected property value.

Inspecting Registry Settings

In addition to supporting the listing of DSO object properties, the Ch12 application also supports the listing of system Registry entries for the OLAP services installation. The Registry keys and their values under the following Registry key are listed:

```
HKEY_LOCAL_MACHINE\SOFTWARE\Microsoft\OLAP Server\CurrentVersion
```

The Registry settings are provided by the *GetRegSettings* function located in the modCh12 module. All of the Registry key values are listed to the lstProps list box passed into the function.

To list the Registry settings, click the OLAP Registry Settings button on form DSO1. Unfortunately, many of these settings are currently undocumented by Microsoft. The settings that are documented are listed in Table 12-1.

TABLE **12-1** OLAP SERVER REGISTRY SETTINGS

Registry Setting (OLAP Manager)	Description
ReadAheadBufferSize	The size of the Read-Ahead buffer used by OLAP services when caching data from disk. Default is 4MB.
ProcessReadAheadSize (Read-ahead buffer size)	The size of the data buffer used by the Processor/Aggregator when processing a cube. Default is 4MB.
TempDirectory (Temporary file folder)	The directory used by the Processor/Aggregator to write temporary aggregations while processing a cube.
ProcessReadSegmentSize (Process buffer size)	The size of the data buffer in multiples of 64KB used when processing a cube.
BackgroundInterval	Sets the wakeup interval for the listener thread, which periodically checks the number of free server threads and creates threads as needed. Also used by the cache cleaner thread to find out when to wake up.
QueryLogSampling (Sample frequency)	Sets the sampling rate of queries to be written to the server query log. By default, every tenth query gets logged.
LowMemoryLimit (Minimum allocated memory)	Specifies a minimum allocation for OLAP services. The default is one-half the available memory.

Registry Setting (OLAP Manager)	Description
HighMemoryLimit (Memory conservation threshold)	Specifies a high-water mark for memory allocated to OLAP services. The Minimum allocated memory plus the Memory conservation threshold determine the total memory allocation for the server. Default is all available memory.
RootDir (Data folder)	The folder where database data files will be placed.
WorkerThreads (Maximum number of threads)	The number of threads allowed to a CPU. Default is twice the number of CPUs on the machine.

These properties can be viewed and edited in the OLAP Manager. To display the properties, right-click a server node in the tree view and select Properties from the shortcut menu. The properties sheet shown in Figure 12-3 is displayed.

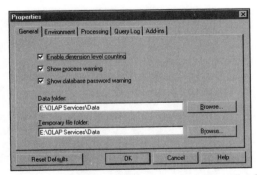

Figure 12-3: The properties sheet for editing the OLAP server properties

The various tabs of this property sheet categorize the server properties. The Add-Ins tab displays the OLAP Manager add-ins currently registered with the server. After you get through Chapter 14, where you build a sample OLAP Manager add-in and register it, you will revisit this tab to see your own add-in displayed.

Summary

This chapter discussed the DSO Inspector application that enables a user to list all of the properties of the DSO objects for a specified server.

The application is composed of two parts, an ActiveX DLL named DSOInspector and the Ch12 project that uses the Inspector object exposed by the DLL. Both of these components are implemented in Visual Basic 6.0.

The application provides users with an easy method of inspecting object properties and viewing the DSO model. The OLAP Server Registry settings are also available in the application to enable the viewing of the CurrentVersion Registry key under the OLAP Server key.

The DSOInspector DLL will again be used in Chapter 14 to enable a custom OLAP Manager add-in to create a report of server metadata.

Chapter 13

Client Applications Using the PivotTable Service

IN THIS CHAPTER

◆ Exploring the drilldown functions for navigating a cellset

◆ Developing MDX expressions using time series and numeric functions

◆ Discovering how the Microsoft Hierarchical FlexGrid control can be used in OLAP applications

IN CHAPTER 11 WE explored the use of Microsoft Excel and OLAP@Work for Excel as options for developing client-side applications that enable users to view and analyze cube data through PivotTables and PivotCharts.

Microsoft and third-party solutions are often cost-effective means of delivering powerful tools to your users that are easily installed and easy to use. But these tools may not always provide your users with everything they need or want in an application, especially if they demand a custom integration with their existing computing environment.

In those cases where users need more than what third-party software can provide, you need to develop an in-house solution that meets their demands. The answer may come in the form of VBA code embedded in an Excel spreadsheet, a custom ActiveX DLL called from VBA, or a C++ or Visual Basic standalone program. Whatever the choice of implementation, you at least need to deal with MDX, the PivotTable service, and presentation of cellsets.

This chapter provides an example of a stand-alone OLAP application that involves MDX queries against the Investments cube and the presentation of the results in a grid format that enables users to drill up and down through the time dimension to view cellset data.

We also continue our exploration of MDX with a look at the time series functions and numeric functions listed in the OLAP function reference in Appendix G.

Drilling Through Data

In developing user-interface applications for viewing OLAP data, you work with one or more MDX queries to access the required data from a cube or virtual cube. Once this data is acquired, you need to present it to users in a manner that they can easily grasp to quickly extract the information they need for their tasks. Having presented the data, a user needs the ability to query for more detail or ask for a higher level of aggregation starting from a given view of the data.

Submitting queries and filling a grid control with the results is an operation that can be easily dealt with. But how do you support the operations of drilling up to higher summary levels or down to lower detail levels? For these operations, MDX provides a set of functions that enable you to drill either up or down named sets by member or level.

The basic idea here is to define named sets for axes, based on data from a single dimension, that you present to the user and then by interpreting the user's navigation commands, submit drilldown or drillup queries against these named sets to acquire a new view of the data.

First, take a look at what these functions do and how to express them, and then apply some of them in a client application.

Drilling Operations by Member

These operations are used to drill through the members of a set consisting of tuples from a single dimension. The example queries for each function assume that two sets have been defined for the session. The statements for these sets are:

```
Create Set Investments.MgrSet As 'Manager.Members'
        Set Investments.TimeSet As 'Descendants(Time,Year)'
```

DRILLDOWNMEMBER(<SET1>,<SET2>[,RECURSIVE])

This expression drills down the members of <set1> that exist in <set2>. When a member in <set2> is found to exist in <set1>, then the member is drilled down to the next lower level. If the optional Recursive specifier is used in the expression, then <set2> is again checked against the outcome of the first operation on <set1> to drill down to lower levels.

```
SELECT {MgrSet} ON COLUMNS,
{DrillDownMember(TimeSet,{Time.[1987]})} ON ROWS
FROM Investments
```

This query results in the Time members at the Year level being returned on the Row axis with only 1987 drilled down to the Quarter level.

DRILLDOWNMEMBERTOP(<SET1>,<SET2>,<INDEX>[,[<NUMERIC_ EXPRESSION>][,RECURSIVE]])

This function works just like DrillDownMember but limits the number of children drilled down. Whereas the DrillDownMember function returns all children of the drilled-down member, DrillDownMemberTop only returns the top <index> children based on the <numeric_expression>. The following query returns the top quarter in 1987 based on Amount.

```
SELECT {MgrSet} ON COLUMNS,
{DrillDownMemberTop(TimeSet,{Time.[1987]},1,Amount)} ON ROWS
FROM Investments
```

The result of this query is Quarter 3 with $143,300 at the All Manager member.

DRILLUPMEMBER(<SET1>,<SET2>)

The DrillUpMember function drills up the members in <set1> that exist in <set2>. This function performs just like DrillDownMember with the exception that no optional Recursive specifier is available with DrillUpMember, because all descendants of a drilled-up member are removed, as opposed to just its children.

```
SELECT {MgrSet} ON COLUMNS,
{DrillUpMember({Time.[1987].[Quarter 3], _
Time.[1987].[Quarter 3].[July]},{Time.[1987].[Quarter 3]})} ON ROWS
FROM Investments
```

This query will only return one row for Quarter 3 of 1987.

TOGGLEDRILLSTATE(<SET1>,<SET2>[,RECURSIVE])

Each member in <set2> that exists in <set1> is checked to determine if the member is drilled up or drilled down. If the member is already drilled down (the *DrilledDown* property of the member's parent is True), a DrillUpMember(<set1>, {<set2_member>}) is applied. If the member is already drilled up (the DrilledDown property of the member's parent is False), then a DrillDownMember(<set1>, {<set2_member>}) is applied.

If Recursive is used in the ToggleDrillState function, then it is used in the resulting call to either DrillUpMember or DrillDownMember.

```
SELECT {MgrSet} ON COLUMNS,
{ToggleDrillState(TimeSet,{Time.[1987]})} ON ROWS
FROM Investments
```

If the 1987 member of TimeSet is drilled up when this query is run, then 1987 is drilled down to the Quarter level. If 1987 is already drilled down, the ToggleDrillState would cause it to be drilled up. Note that in the MDX Sample application, this query always results in 1987 being drilled down to display the quarters. This is because the query is being applied to the cube data. In a program, you can feed the result of this query back into the query again to see the effects of the toggle.

Drilling Operations by Level

These functions are used to drill at a specified level.

DRILLDOWNLEVEL(<SET1>[,<LEVEL>])

This function drills down the members in <set1> at the level specified by <level> to one level below <level>. If <level> is not specified, the lowest-level member of <set1> is used.

```
SELECT {MgrSet} ON COLUMNS,
{DrillDownLevel(TimeSet,Time.Year)} ON ROWS
FROM Investments
```

The above query drills down every member in the TimeSet to the Quarter level.

DRILLDOWNLEVELTOP(<SET1>,<INDEX>[,[<LEVEL>][,<NUMERIC_ EXPRESSION>]])

This function works like DrillDownLevel but includes only the top <index> children of the drilled-down level based on <numeric_expression>. The following query returns no more than the first two quarters in each year.

```
SELECT {MgrSet} ON COLUMNS,
{DrillDownLevelTop(TimeSet,2,Time.Year)} ON ROWS
FROM Investments
```

DRILLUPLEVEL(<SET1>[,<LEVEL>])

DrillUpLevel drills up the members that are below the specified <level>. If <level> is not specified, then the level that is one less than the lowest-level member in <set1> is used.

```
SELECT {MgrSet} ON COLUMNS,
{DrillUpLevel({Time.[1987],Time.[1987].[Quarter 3]},Time.Year)} ON ROWS
FROM Investments
```

This query returns only the 1987 row.

A Client Application Using the Drilling Functions

The Ch13.vbp Visual Basic project in the Chapter13 folder on the CD implements two of the drilling functions just discussed. This application performs the following tasks:

1. Creates two session-level sets for the columns and rows axes.

2. Uses the axes sets to query the Investments cube and fill a grid with cellset data.

3. Detects a double-click event and drills down on the member if the member is drilled up, or drills up on the member if the member is drilled down.

The one and only form in the project, frmCh13, is shown in Figure 13-1 as it looks after clicking the Query Cube button.

	All Manager	Booker	Folio	Fundman	Shares	Stock	Yields
1962	$500.00	Null	Null	Null	$500.00	Null	Null
1963	$50.00	Null	Null	Null	$50.00	Null	Null
1972	$125.00	Null	Null	Null	$125.00	Null	Null
1974	$25.00	Null	Null	Null	$25.00	Null	Null
1985	$10,000.00	Null	$10,000.00	Null	Null	Null	Null
1986	$262,764.02	Null	$196,383.50	Null	Null	$45,380.52	$21,000.00
1987	$277,617.10	Null	$27,086.17	Null	Null	$179,500.00	$71,030.93
1988	$97,381.43	Null	$37,315.80	Null	Null	$750.00	$59,315.63
1989	$188,260.90	Null	$27,800.00	Null	Null	$89,600.00	$70,860.90
1990	$152,185.94	Null	$2,000.00	Null	Null	$128,400.00	$21,785.94
1991	$255,763.29	Null	Null	Null	$48,621.12	$196,700.00	$10,442.17
1992	$1,009,798.79	Null	$97,389.18	Null	$349,785.19	$337,271.55	$225,352.87
1993	$1,069,089.05	Null	$116,477.83	Null	$517,242.76	$378,974.06	$56,394.40
1994	$398,602.80	Null	$30,784.27	Null	$268,835.18	$50,772.95	$48,210.40
1997	$10,000.00	Null	$10,000.00	Null	Null	Null	Null

Figure 13-1: The Ch13 application form displaying cellset data

Clicking the Query Cube button on the form executes the *QueryCube* function behind the form. This function opens a connection using the msolap provider and then creates the two axes sets through the following code:

```
strmdx = "Create Set Investments.MgrSet As 'Manager.Members'"
cnn.Execute (strmdx)


strmdx = "Create Set Investments.TimeSet As 'Descendants(Time,Year)'"
cnn.Execute (strmdx)
```

The MgrSet is used on the Columns axis, and the TimeSet is used on the Rows axis. Once these sets are created for the session, the QueryCube function then executes an initial query to populate the grid on the form with cellset data. The query is run with the following statements:

```
strmdx = "Select {MgrSet} On Columns ,{TimeSet} on rows From Investments"
cset.Open strmdx
```

To fill the cellset data into the grid, another function, named *FillView,* is used. This function accepts a cellset as its argument, fills the column and row labels with member names from the cellset axes, and then fills the grid with data by indexing each cell in the cellset. This FillView routine is the only routine in the application that fills grid values. It is used again for displaying user drilldown and drillup operations.

When the user double-clicks a row in the grid, the application processes either a drilldown or a drillup through the *grdView_DblClick* event procedure.

The problem to be solved is "How do we keep track of which members the user has drilled down and which members have been drilled up?" If the user double-clicks 1987 to drill down to the quarters level, the application has to create a cellset that contains all years as they appear in Figure 13-1 except for 1987, which needs to display the quarters below it.

After displaying the cellset reacting to the drilldown on 1987, the user may drill down on 1990 to see its quarters. After this, the user may drill down on one of the quarters below 1987 to see the month level. Each time the user drills up or down, the application must show the results of all previous operations plus the results of the current operation. This is known as *maintaining user state* and needs to be done as efficiently as possible.

Numerous designs can be developed to maintain the state of the grid and the user's interaction with it. The one used in the grdView_DblClick event is a design based on the fact that the number of members projected onto the Rows axis is known to be relatively small. Since there are only a small number of positions on the axis and only one member per position, the algorithm used to maintain user state in the cellset and displayed grid can use the *DrilledDown* property of each axis member to determine if the member is drilled down or not.

The algorithm used here simply inspects each member on the Rows axis and either includes it or excludes it from the member set in a query that uses the DrillDownMember function. The code in grdView_DblClick is attempting to build a string that looks like this:

```
DrillDownMember(TimeSet,{time_member,time_member,...})
```

Once this statement component is built to contain all members that should display as drilled down, the entire statement can then be inserted into the MDX query like this:

```
strmdx = "select {MgrSet} on columns,"
```

```
strmdx = strmdx & drillstr
strmdx = strmdx & " on rows From Investments"
```

In this code, the DrillDownMember statement is contained in the string variable drillstr. When concatenated into the surrounding MDX select statement, the statement is complete and ready to be executed.

Here are the steps used in the grdView_DblClick event procedure to build the drillstr string to be used to derive the next cellset to be displayed in the grid:

1. Iterate through all positions on Axes(1) and check the DrilledDown property of each member.

2. If a member's DrilledDown property is True, add the member to the drillstr.

3. After inspecting each position on the axis, inspect the current member selected by the user. If the member is not drilled down (DrilledDown = False) then a drilldown operation is to be carried out on it. The member is added to the drillstr string. If the member is to be drilled up, then it is already in the drillstr and we need to wrap a DrillUpMember function around the DrillDownMember function contained in drillstr. The member to be drilled up is the selected member, and it is appended to the DrillUpMember function string.

4. Wrap the resulting drill statement component into an MDX select statement.

5. Execute the MDX select statement and display the resulting cellset using the FillView function procedure.

The result of all this is an MDX query that looks like this:

```
select {MgrSet} on columns,DrillDownMember(TimeSet,{time_member,...})
    on rows From Investments"
```

to drill down or this:

```
select {MgrSet} on columns,
DrillUpMember(DrillDownMember(TimeSet,{time_member,...}),{time_member})
    on rows From Investments"
```

to drill up. Because TimeSet doesn't change but remains constant as Descendants(Time,Year), the queries you use to create your cellsets derived from TimeSet must provide the state of all user operations on the set. The procedure just discussed does so and without much difficulty.

Explore the application by drilling up and drilling down as you wish.

Exploring the Time Series Functions

In addition to using drilling functions to enable users to navigate through cube data, many business analysis applications will be required to display various relations among data across time. For these requirements, the Time Series functions discussed in this section can be used.

All of the functions in this section use the method of least squares in calculating the regression line given by the equation:

```
y = ax + b
```

where a is known as the *slope* and b the *intercept*.

These functions can be expressed in calculated members as in the following example:

```
WITH MEMBER Measures.LnSlope AS
  'LinRegSlope({LastPeriods(11)}, [Amount],[Sh Num])'
SELECT {LnSlope} ON COLUMNS,
{Descendants(Time.[1987],Month)} ON ROWS
    FROM Investments
```

Note from the discussion of calculated members back in Chapter 7 that you can specify more than one member in the WITH clause to allow for the use of multiple time series functions in the same query.

CORRELATION(<SET>,<NUMERIC_EXPRESSION1>[,<NUMERIC_ EXPRESSION2>])

The Correlation function uses <numeric_expression1> to evaluate <set> for y-axis values and <numeric_expression2> against <set> to obtain x-axis values. Once the set of (x,y) points is acquired, the correlation between the two series is calculated and returned. Zero values on both axes are included. If <numeric_expression2> is not present, then the set itself is used for x-axis values.

COVARIANCE(<SET>,<NUMERIC_EXPRESSION1>[,<NUMERIC_ EXPRESSION2>])

The (x,y) points are acquired here as they are for Correlation. The covariance, or the measure of the linear relation between the entity represented by the x-axis and the entity represented by the y-axis, is returned using the biased population formula, which is:

$$Covariance(P_1, P_2) = \frac{\sum (P_1 - \overline{P_1})(P_2 - \overline{P_2})}{N}$$

Covariance may be used to determine how the returns of one portfolio P_1 move in relation to the returns of another portfolio P_2. Calculating the Covariance(P_1,P_2) gives you an indication of how these returns move together.

The correlation coefficient is a more popular measure for this purpose and can be derived from the covariance by the formula:

$$CorrelationCoefficient = \frac{Covariance\ (P_1,P_2)}{Stdev(P_1)Stdev(P_2)}$$

To use the unbiased population formula using a divisor of (N–1), use the *CovarianceN* function.

LINREGINTERCEPT(<SET>,<NUMERIC_EXPRESSION1>[,<NUMERIC_ EXPRESSION2>])

LinRegIntercept calculates the linear regression line for the set of points (x,y) obtained as for Correlation and returns the intercept (b) of the regression line equation.

LINREGPOINT(<NUMERIC_EXPRESSION1,<SET>,<NUMERIC_ EXPRESSION2>[,<NUMERIC_EXPRESSION3>])

This function uses <numeric_expression2> to obtain y-axis values and <numeric_expression3> to obtain x-axis values from <set> to obtain a series of (x,y) points. The regression line equation is then determined from these points. The <numeric_expression1> value is then substituted into the equation for x and the resulting y value returned.

LINREGVARIANCE(<SET>,<NUMERIC_EXPRESSION1>[,<NUMERIC_ EXPRESSION2>])

This function calculates a regression line using (x,y) points obtained as for Correlation and then returns the variance of this line to the set of points.

LINREGSLOPE(<SET>,<NUMERIC_EXPRESSION1>[,<NUMERIC_ EXPRESSION2>])

LinRegSlope calculates the slope of the regression line fit to the series of points (x,y) obtained by applying the numeric expressions to <set> as was done for Correlation. If <numeric_expression2> is not present, then the <set> itself is used as the x-axis values; however, <numeric_expression2> is usually required.

LINREGR2(<SET>,<NUMERIC_EXPRESSION1>[,<NUMERIC_ EXPRESSION2>])

This function calculates the linear regression of a set of points and returns the *coefficient of determination*. The function obtains the (x,y) points as Correlation does and if <numeric_expression2> is absent, <set> itself is used for the x-axis values. The <numeric_expression2> is usually required.

After the set of points (x,y) is obtained, the equation for the best-fit line to these points is calculated using the least-squares method. The coefficient of determination describing the fit of the equation to the set of points is then calculated and returned.

Exploring the Numeric Functions

In many business applications, you need to provide your users with grand totals and other roll-ups. The numeric functions discussed here are some of the more common aggregation functions.

SUM(<SET>[,<NUMERIC_EXPRESSION>])

Sum returns the sum of <numeric_expression> over <set>. If you don't specify <numeric_expression>, then it is implied by the query in which Sum is used. In this case, the cell values returned in the cellset are summed for <set>.

AGGREGATE(<SET>[,<NUMERIC_EXPRESSION>])

This function selects the aggregate function in accordance with the context in which it is applied in a query. If a measure in a query is a summed amount, then Sum is applied. If a measure is a max or min value, then Max or Min is used.

COUNT(<SET>[,INCLUDEEMPTY])

The Count function counts the tuples in <set>. Empty cells are excluded by default. To include empty cells in the count, use the INCLUDEEMPTY flag.

AVG(<SET>[,<NUMERIC_EXPRESSION>])

This function, as you've seen in Chapter 6, computes the average of the tuples in <set> based on <numeric_expression>. The implied count required by the function does not include empty cells. To include empty cells, you can use the CoalesceEmpty function to translate empty cells to zero.

MEDIAN(<SET>[,<NUMERIC_EXPRESSION>])

This function returns the median <numeric_expression> in <set>.

MIN(<SET>[,<NUMERIC_EXPRESSION>])

Min returns the minimum <numeric_expression> in <set>.

MAX(<SET>[,<NUMERIC_EXPRESSION>])

Max returns the maximum <numeric_expression> in <set>.

VAR(<SET>[,<NUMERIC_EXPRESSION>])

Var returns the variance of <numeric_expression> over <set>. This function uses the unbiased population formula. To use the biased population formula, use the VarP function. The Variance function is an alias for Var. Variance can also be obtained as the square of the StdDev.

STDDEV(<SET>[,<NUMERIC_EXPRESSION>])

This function returns the standard deviation of <numeric_expression> over <set>. This function is an alias for Stdev, which uses the unbiased population formula. To use the biased population formula, use the StdevP function. The Stdev is the square root of the Var.

RANK(<TUPLE>,<SET>])

Rank returns the rank of <tuple> in <set>. The rank is based on 1.

VISUALTOTALS(<SET>,<PATTERN>)

The VisualTotals function totals the child members in <set> and returns the result with the label specified by <pattern>. The characters in <pattern> are taken literally except for the * character, which denotes the parent of the child members. To specify that an asterisk appear in the label, use two asterisks together (**).

```
SELECT {Measures.Amount} ON COLUMNS,
{VisualTotals({Time.[1987],Time.[1987].[Quarter 1],
    Time.[1987].[Quarter 3]},"Total for year *")} ON ROWS
FROM Investments
```

The label specified in the pattern in this query replaces the parent specified in the set as Time.[1987]. The result of this query is then:

```
Total for year 1987     $168,100.00
Quarter 1                    $24,800.00
Quarter 3                   $143,300.00
```

If the parent is not specified in the set, then the label specified by pattern is not displayed in the result.

ADDCALCULATEDMEMBERS(<SET>)

Although this function is not categorized as a numeric function, it may be useful in an application, and so you should understand it before leaving this chapter.

Normally, a set in an expression will not automatically include calculated members. To ensure that calculated members are represented in a set, use the AddCalculatedMembers function.

A simple example of this can be seen from executing the following:

```
SELECT {Measures.Members} ON COLUMNS,
{Time.[1987]} ON ROWS
FROM Investments
```

This statement returns Amount and Sh Num measures for 1987. To include the Price calculated member, use this statement:

```
SELECT {AddCalculatedMembers(Measures.Members)} ON COLUMNS,
{Time.[1987]} ON ROWS
FROM Investments
```

Summary

This chapter has discussed the use of the drilling operations that can be used in a query to drill down and drill up on a member or at a specified level. We examined functions for drilling by member and drilling by level.

We next looked at the sample application for this chapter and saw how it uses the drill functions to enable the user to drill down and up through a cellset through use of members selected from the Manager dimension and the Time dimension members. The concept of user state was explained, and you saw how the Ch13 application maintains user state in displaying cellset data.

Finally, we visited some other functions that a business application might use; these were categorized as time series functions and numeric functions.

Chapter 14

Creating an OLAP Manager Add-In

IN THIS CHAPTER

◆ Discovering how an OLAP Manager add-in is built

◆ Learning how to create shortcut menus for display in OLAP Manager

◆ Seeing how to register an OLAP Manager add-in and debug it in Visual Basic

THE SAMPLE APPLICATION FOR this chapter is found in the Ch13 folder on the CD. The Visual Basic project name is PropertyInspector.vbp.

The Property Inspector is an OLAP Manager add-in program that enables inspection of server metadata just as you saw in Chapter 12. In fact, this add-in borrows the DSO1 form from the Chapter 12 project for displaying the properties of server objects.

In the Chapter 12 application, you used the DSOInspector DLL to list the properties of DSO objects for a given server. The Property Inspector add-in also uses the DSOInspector DLL through the calls made from within the DSO1 form.

Both the DSO1 form and the DSOInspector DLL have been modified for use in this add-in. Since the add-in only displays the properties of the server, the databases, and the first-level objects below databases, the Next button on the DSO1 form is not necessary. This button has been converted to a Close button for this application.

The Chapter 12 application supported the display of OLAP Registry entries. That support has been removed in this add-in and replaced with a *Print Report* function that prints a simple report of a server's metadata.

The DSO1 form in the add-in is displayed as a modal form. Because of this, the zoom form used in Chapter 12 to zoom in on a property has been moved to the DSOInspector DLL to enable the modal DSO1 form to support zooming. It does this through a call to the *ZoomProperty* method in the DSOInspector.Inspector object.

The last change made to DSO1 is in the way it handles the listing of object collections such as databases and cubes. In Chapter 12, you used a separate form for listing these collections and enabling the user to select a new object from the list for inspection. In the add-in application, you display those collections in the list box at the bottom of the DSO1 form and allow selection from there.

Now let's see how the Property Inspector is implemented.

Building the PropertyInspector Add-In

The add-in is an ActiveX DLL built with Visual Basic. There are three required references for this project.

The first reference you need to add is the OLAP Add-In Manager. This is a reference to msmdadin.DLL found in the OLAP Services Bin folder. This DLL provides the type library for the *IOlapAddIn* interface that our add-in is required to implement.

The second reference you need to set is the Microsoft Decision Support Objects reference in msmddo.DLL, also located in the OLAP Services Bin folder. This provides the DSO type library just as you used in Chapter 12. You'll see why we need this library reference shortly.

The last reference you need is to your own DSOInspector.DLL. This is the DLL containing the Inspector object that handles listing all object properties.

In addition to the DSO1 form, there is a class module in this project named Inspector. This is the class that implements the IOlapAddIn interface required by the OLAP Add-In Manager. If you open the class module and look in the General Declarations, you find the following statement:

```
Implements IOlapAddIn
```

This statement provides the methods for the IOlapAddIn interface, which you can view by selecting IOlapAddIn from the Object list. Six methods and one property are defined in this interface.

Class Initialization

The first call made to the Inspector is a call to the class Initialize subroutine. This is where you instantiate your DSOInspector.Inspector object to be used throughout the lifetime of the add-in. As in Chapter 12, name this object variable *insp*.

```
Set insp = New DSOInspector.Inspector
```

Coding Menu Items

The add-in doesn't display any nodes in the OLAP Manager tree view but does display an Inspect menu item in the shortcut menu of a server node. To insert the menu item into the shortcut menu, code the *ProvideMenuItems* method, which has a function signature that looks like this:

```
Private Sub IOlapAddIn_ProvideMenuItems(CurrentNode As _
DSSAddInsManager.OlapTreeNode, MenuItems As DSSAddInsManager.OlapMenuItems)
```

The code in ProvideMenuItems is quite simple. All you need to do here is determine if the node passed to you is a server node and if it is, add your Inspect menu item to the *OlapMenuItems* collection passed into the method as the second argument. The code to do this follows:

```
If CurrentNode.LinkedObject.ClassType = clsServer Then
    MenuItems.Add mnuSeparator
    MenuItems.Add mnuStandard, "&Inspect...", 1, , mnuflagRegular
End If
```

The third argument used in the OlapMenuItems Add method here is a key that OLAP Manager passes back to you when the user selects this menu item. Because you only have one menu item in this add-in, a hard-coded 1 is used as the key. If more than one menu item were possible on a call from OLAP Manager, then it would be necessary to provide unique identifiers for the key argument so that you could react properly to the user's menu selection. We'll look at where this is used in a moment.

The last argument to the Add method is a flag that informs OLAP Manager of the type of menu item we are providing. These flags are defined in Chapter 9 under the section named *OlapMenuFlags*. The resulting menu item appears on the shortcut menu obtained by right-clicking a server node in the tree view. This menu is shown in Figure 14-1.

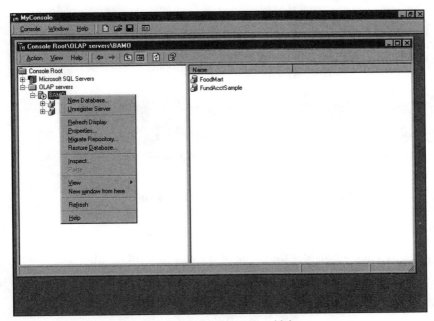

Figure 14-1: The Inspect menu item added by your add-in

To provide a popup menu with submenu items, you can use code similar to the following:

```
MenuItems.Add mnuStandard, "&Inspector", 1, , mnuflagPopup
MenuItems.Add mnuStandard, "&Inspect...", 2, 1, mnuflagSubmenu
MenuItems.Add mnuStandard, "&Report", 3, 1, mnuflagSubmenu
```

This code adds a parent menu item named Inspector and two submenu items beneath it. The fourth argument to the Add method adding the two submenu items specifies the ID of the parent node added with the first statement. The result is shown in Figure 14-2.

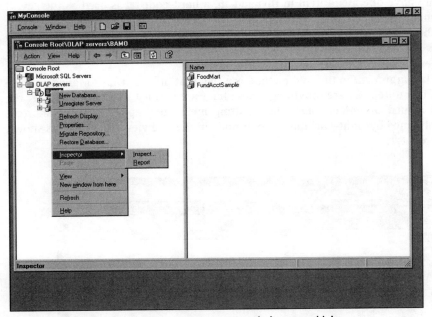

Figure 14-2: The result of using a popup menu style in your add-in

The Property Get procedure for IOlapAddIn_Name() is coded as:

```
IOlapAddIn_Name = "Property Inspector"
```

This property simply provides the name of the add-in to OLAP Manager.

Coding the ExecuteMenuItem Method

When a user selects our Inspect menu item, OLAP Manager calls the *ExecuteMenuItem* method defined as:

```
Private Function IOlapAddIn_ExecuteMenuItem(CurrentNode As _
 DSSAddInsManager.OlapTreeNode, MenuItem As DSSAddInsManager.OlapMenuItem) As _
 DSSAddInsManager.RefreshTreeTypes
```

This is where you need to decide which menu item the user chose and act on it. In this case, the choice is an easy one because you only have one menu item defined. Here's the code for the method:

```
If Not insp Is Nothing Then
    m_ServerName = CurrentNode.LinkedObject.Name
    If Not insp.MakeServerConnection(m_ServerName) Then
        Set frmDSO = New DSO1
        frmDSO.Show vbModal
        Set frmDSO = Nothing
    Else
        MsgBox "Connection with server failed.", vbCritical, _
               "Property Inspector Error"
    End If
Else
    MsgBox "Inspector not initialized.", vbCritical, "Property Inspector Error"
End If

IOlapAddIn_ExecuteMenuItem = reftreeNoRefresh
Exit Function
```

If you have a valid DSOInspector.Inspector object variable (insp), then you obtain the name of the server you need to connect to by accessing the *LinkedObject* of the *CurrentNode* passed into the method.

Using this server name, you make a call to the MakeServerConnection method in the Inspector, which creates a server object for the Inspector to use internally. If the connection succeeds, you then create a DSO1 form and show it modally. From this point, the user interacts with the DSO1 form to inspect the objects represented on the form just as was done in Chapter 12.

Once the form is closed, the form variable is set to nothing to free the resource and you exit the method.

An Alternate Server Connection Method

Another method is available for connecting to the server identified by the node if you care to make a slight modification.

The *CurrentNode.LinkedObject* property is a reference to a clsServer object, the server represented by the node the user has just right-clicked. You could modify the DSOInspector.Inspector to accept a clsServer object property and set its internal server object variable with the LinkedObject assigned to the property.

If this is done, be sure to test the server object *State* property to ensure that it is connected before using it to reference DSO properties.

```
If dsoServer.State = stateConnected Then
    'Use the variable
Else
    'Make a connection
End If
```

If this modification is made, a call to MakeServerConnection is not necessary unless the status of the server object indicates that it is not connected.

The rest of the IOlapAddIn interface methods can be nothing more than returns, because we are not using any views to be presented in the right-hand pane of the OLAP Manager and we are not providing any nodes for the tree view.

Using Nodes

If you are writing an add-in that needs to display nodes, you provide those nodes through the *ProvideChildNodes* method implementation.

This method is called by OLAP Manager when a node is selected or expanded. The signature for this function is:

```
Private Sub IOlapAddIn_ProvideChildNodes (ParentNode As _
    DSSAddInsManager.OlapTreeNode, OlapTreeNodes As _
    DSSAddInsManager.OlapTreeNodes)
```

The ParentNode is the node the user has selected or wants to expand. By inspection of this node, you can determine if you want to add child nodes to it or not. If you do add child nodes, they are added into the OlapTreeNodes collection passed into the method as the second argument.

The *Add* method of the OlapTreeNodes collection takes a caption as the first argument, an icon resource index for the icon displayed when the node is collapsed (closed) as the second argument, and an optional third argument that is the icon resource index for the icon displayed when the node is expanded (open).

Once you've added nodes to the tree view, OLAP Manager gives you the opportunity to add a menu for the node by calling the ProvideMenuItems method as discussed previously.

Registering the PropertyInspector Add-In

To inform the OLAP Manager that your add-in exists, you need to place a few keys into the system Registry. The keys are placed under the following HKEY_LOCAL_ MACHINE key:

```
Software\Microsoft\OLAP Server\Olap Manager Info\Addins
```

In the Addins key, place a new string value containing the name of your addin and set its value to True.

```
PropertyInspector              "True"
```

Next create a new key under the Addins key and name it with the same name as the preceding string value. To this key, add the following four string values:

```
ClassName = "PropertyInspector.Inspector"
Name = "Property Inspector"
Description = "OLAP Developer's Guide Ch14 Sample Add-In"
Priority = "2"
```

All of these values are found in the PropertyInspector.reg file in the Ch14 folder on the CD if you care to import this file into your Registry rather than enter the values by hand. The Addins value you added, however, is not in the reg file.

The *ClassName* value is the project name and class name that implements the IOlapAddIn interface.

The *Name* entry provides the name of the add-in that is shown on the Add-ins tab in the OLAP Manager Properties page.

Description provides a description of the add-in, and this too is shown on the Properties page.

The *Priority* entry is the loading priority used by OLAP Manager to load the add-in.

Once these entries are resident in the Registry, you can start your MMC console, right-click an OLAP server node, select Properties from the shortcut menu, and then click the Add-ins tab of the Property sheet. You should see the Property Inspector checked in the Available Add-ins list. Clicking this add-in entry will display the Description string Registry entry we made before. You're now ready to start using the Inspector from within OLAP Manager.

Debugging the Add-In

As you develop your add-ins, you will most likely want to or need to step through your add-in code as it is called by the OLAP Add-In Manager.

To do this, go to the Debugging tab on the Visual Basic Project Properties sheet and set the Start program option. The command line for the program to start should point to the MMC.EXE, and its argument should be the name of your custom console you created back in Chapter 3. My command line looks like this:

```
C:\WINNT\system32\mmc.exe "C:\WINNT\Profiles\Bill\Start Menu\Programs\
  My Administrative Tools\MyConsole.msc"
```

Setting this option will start the MMC console specified when you start debug in the Visual Basic IDE (you may need to minimize Visual Basic to enable the console to start up).

Set breakpoints in any of the methods of IOlapAddIn to monitor the calls made to your add-in.

An alternative method, if you prefer not to use the debugger, is the old standby method of placing MsgBox statements at strategic points in your code to monitor its progress. This is at times useful, but using the debugger is a quick way to find out what's going on inside.

Summary

As you can see from the sample add-in developed in this chapter, creating a custom add-in for OLAP Manager is not all that difficult.

Create an ActiveX DLL Visual Basic project, add a few references, implement the few methods of the required IOlapAddIn interface, register your DLL in the OLAP Manager Addins key, and you're in business.

Using the information you learned from creating the PropertyInspector Add-in in this chapter, you can develop your own add-in to create custom reports, enable maintenance tasks specific to your site, maintain security, or create a host of other applications using DSO or the msolap provider.

Chapter 15

Exploring Data Transformation Services

IN THIS CHAPTER

◆ Learning how to use the Data Transformation Services Task Kit 1 to perform processing on cubes and other OLAP objects

◆ Using the Import and Export Wizards to copy data from a source to a destination

◆ Executing DTS packages from command line utilities

DATA TRANSFORMATION SERVICES (DTS) are used to transfer data between heterogeneous data sources. As you discovered in Chapter 2, these services are extremely useful for extracting data for data warehouses and data marts as well as for simple transfer of data into and out of a test or production database.

DTS not only copies data from a source to a target but also offers a very powerful capability to transform the data during a copy operation. The data can be modified on the basis of extensive script processing that can include conditional tests and calculations based on lookups, and data can be transformed in size and type using a variety of methods.

The data processed by DTS can be obtained from any source for which an OLE DB provider is available. The tasks that DTS performs can easily be specified through various methods ranging from DTS wizards to the graphical DTS Designer and even through Visual Basic programming.

With the release of the Data Transformation Services Task Kit, it is now possible to create tasks that will process or update OLAP services cubes and databases. This chapter discusses the use of this task kit, the import and export wizards, and the command line methods for launching the wizards and running DTS packages. For a discussion of using the DTS Designer, see the section "Using the DTS Package Designer" in Chapter 2.

Data Transformation Services Overview

The Data Transformation Services components enable building packages that transfer data between a source and a destination. The packages that perform this transfer can range from a very simple copy of data to a very complex set of data processing tasks.

A DTS package defines a workflow including one or more tasks executed as a series of steps. Each task in the workflow specifies a unit of work to be performed in the transformation. A task is categorized as either a Data Pump task or an Object Transfer task.

A *DTS Data Pump* is an OLE DB provider that supports the import, export, and transformation of data between heterogeneous data sources. As data moves through the data pump, complex transformations and verifications may take place via ActiveX scripting. Using this method of transforming data, you gain full control over the data processed by the task. Columns can be computed, added, removed, and processed by custom external COM-based applications called from within the script.

A *DTS Object Transfer* task enables the transfer of any SQL Server database object and data to another SQL Server database. Any object in the database can be transferred.

In addition to using the DTS wizards and DTS Package Designer user interface for designing packages, you have the option of developing packages through COM programming using the DTS object model. A summary of the objects in the DTS object model is shown in Table 15-1.

TABLE 15-1 DATA TRANSFORMATION OBJECTS

Object	Description
Package	The main object acting as a container for all other objects used to define the data flow and transformation.
Tasks	A collection of task objects.
Task	Defines a unit of work within the transformation. A task may execute a SQL statement, execute an ActiveX script, run an external program, execute other packages, or use the DTS data pump against heterogeneous OLE DB data sources. Task objects can be typed as custom tasks as described by other entries in this table.
ActiveScriptTask	A task that runs an ActiveX script. This custom task may access DTS GlobalVariables.
DataDrivenQueryTask	A custom task that describes queries to be used at the destination for loading data. The query execution is based on transformed data.

Object	Description
DataPumpTask	A custom task that uses the DTS Data Pump to transform data.
Transformations	A collection containing Transformation objects.
Transformation	Describes the source and destination columns and the transformations that are to be carried out on them.
Columns	A collection containing Column objects. SourceColumns contain columns from the source, and DestinationColumns contain columns of the destination.
Column	Describes the source or destination column involved in a transformation.
ExecuteSQLTask	A custom task object that executes a SQL statement.
BulkInsertTask	Copies data from a text file to SQL Server. No transformations are carried out.
CreateProcessTask	Contains information for running an external program as a task.
TransferObjectsTask	Transfers SQL Server objects between SQL Server databases.
SendMailTask	Enables the sending of e-mail as a task.
Lookups	A collection of lookup objects in the DataPumpTask or DataDrivenQueryTask.
Lookup	Enables the execution of queries to retrieve data from a source other than the transformation source or destination.
Connections	A collection containing Connection objects.
Connection	Describes connections to OLE DB providers. Supports connection pooling and reuse.
Steps	A collection containing Step objects.
Step	Controls the flow of task execution. Can execute a task based on a conditional test. Steps may be executed in parallel where possible.
PrecedenceConstraints	A collection containing PrecedenceConstraint objects.
PrecedenceConstraint	Describes the order of step execution.
GlobalVariables	A collection of GlobalVariable objects.
GlobalVariable	Variant variable that can be shared by steps and ActiveX scripts.

Once a DTS package has been created, it can be stored in the Microsoft Repository, in a COM-structured storage file, or as local packages in the msdb database in SQL Server. The stored packages can be seen by expanding the Data Transformation Packages node under a SQL Server node in the Enterprise Manager tree.

Using the DTS Import Wizard

The Import Wizard is used to create a DTS package that will read and transform data from any OLE DB or ODBC data source ranging from ASCII text files to ODBC datasources to Access databases or Excel spreadsheets.

The data read from the source into a target table can be read through a query or copied in its entirety. During the copy operation, the data can be transformed according to specifications you apply through settings within the wizard or though scripting in an ActiveX script.

The following steps run the Import Wizard to import a file containing funds and their prices as of a specific date. The data in this file will be used to create a Prices table in the FundAcctsWH database.

1. In the SQL Server Enterprise Manager or your own custom MMC console, expand the Databases folder under a SQL Server node and select the database you wish to import data into.

2. Right-click and select All Task and then Import Data. This displays the welcome screen of the DTS Import Wizard.

3. Click Next to select a data source. In the Source drop-down list, select Text File, and in the File Name text box, enter the path to the price.txt file found on the companion CD in the Chapter15 folder. Click Next.

4. The Select File Format screen previews the price.txt file and asks you to enter some information about the file such as file type, the row delimiter used in the file, and the character used to qualify text strings in the file. You don't need to make any changes on this screen, so just click Next to specify the column delimiter.

5. On the Specify Column Delimiter screen, click the Comma option button, because this file uses commas to delimit column values. Click Next to choose a destination.

6. In the Destination drop-down list, select Microsoft OLE DB Provider for SQL Server. Choose the server in the Server drop-down list where you have installed the FundAcctsWH database and choose this database in the Database drop-down list. Select either Use Windows NT authentication or Use SQL Server authentication. If you choose Use SQL Server authentication, enter a valid username and password in the text boxes provided. Click Next.

7. The Select Source Tables screen shows the Price.txt file as the source and the price table (not yet created) as the proposed destination table. You need to specify some transformations for this import, so click the button in the Transform column.

8. On the Column Mappings tab of the Column Mappings and Transformations screen, the Create destination table option should be selected. Select the Destination column for the Col001 source column and enter the name **fund_cd**. In the Type column choose char from the list, and in the Size column enter 5 as the length of this column. Uncheck the Nullable check box. This specification matches the fund_cd column of the Funds table in this database. The Destination for Col002 should be <ignore> because the fund name is already resident in the Funds table. Col003 should map to a PriceDate column in the Destination and should be a datetime data type. The last column is the Price column and should have a money data type. No columns should be nullable. Click Edit SQL and then click Auto Generate to create a SQL statement using the column names you just entered. On the Transformations tab, the "Copy the source columns directly to the destination columns" option should be selected because you will not be performing any transformations on this data. Click OK to return to the Select Source Tables screen and then click Next.

9. On the Save, Schedule, and Replicate Package screen, check the Run Immediately check box to run this package now. If you want to save this package in SQL Server, check the Save Package check box and choose a destination for the package. Click Next.

10. On the Completing the DTS Wizard screen, read through the Summary to ensure DTS Import will do as you intended, and then click Finish.

After you click Finish, the wizard displays an Executing DTS Package window that shows the progress of the operation. When it is complete, you see a success message or an error message. If an error results, information on the specifics of the error can be viewed and you can click Back to go back and correct the error. After a successful execution, click Done to end the wizard. You should now have a Price table in the FundAcctsWH database.

Using the DTS Export Wizard

When you need to get data residing in a SQL Server database out to another SQL Server database, a desktop database, a text file, or a spreadsheet, the DTS Export Wizard presents an easy way of handling the task.

The same options you had in the Import Wizard are available in the Export Wizard as well. On the way out of the database, columns can be transformed through a variety of methods to get the result expected in the destination file.

Now that you've loaded data into the FundAcctsWH Price table, use the Export Wizard to get data back out to another text file. This time start the wizard from a different menu.

1. With a SQL Server node highlighted in the Enterprise Manager, select Data Transformation Services from the Tools menu and then click Export Data. This displays the welcome screen of the DTS Export Wizard. Click Next on this screen to move to the first data entry screen.

2. Since you're exporting from SQL Server, choose Microsoft OLE DB Provider for SQL Server from the Source drop-down list. In the Database drop-down list, select the FundAcctsWH database. Choose either Use Windows NT authentication or Use SQL Server authentication. After making these entries, click Next.

3. On the Choose a Destination screen, select Text File from the Destination drop-down list and enter the path for the file to receive the exported price data. Click Next.

4. On the Specify Table Copy or Query screen, click Use a query to specify the data to transfer. Click Next to enter the query.

5. Click Query Builder on the Type SQL Statement screen. This displays the Select Columns screen to enable the selection of columns to copy. Expand the price table in the tree to expose the column list.

6. Select all columns into the Selected Columns list. Click Next.

7. On the Specify Sort Order screen, move the fund_cd and PriceDate columns to the Sorting Order list box. These are your ORDER BY columns. Click Next.

8. On the Specify Query Criteria screen, click All Rows. Click Next to return to the Type SQL Query screen and then click Next on that screen.

9. On the Select Destination File Format screen, select the Price table as the Source table. Select the Delimited option and choose Comma as the Column Delimiter. Check the First row has column names check box. Click Transform.

10. On the Column Mappings and Transformations screen, select the Column Mappings tab and change the Type for PriceDate and Price to varchar with a length of 10.

11. On the Transformations tab, click the "Transform information as it is copied to the destination" option button. In the text box containing VBScript, locate the line for the PriceDate column and wrap a format function around it so that you can obtain a long date format in the output file. The statement for the PriceDate column should look like this:

```
DTSDestination("PriceDate") =
FormatDateTime(DTSSource("PriceDate"),vbLongDate)
```

Click OK and then click Next to move to the Save, Schedule, and Replicate Package screen.

12. Check the Run Immediately check box and then click Next to review your specifications for this package.

13. Click Finish to run the package and wait for the Successful completion message. Click Done to close the wizard.

Now open the text file you just created and take a look at the PriceDate column. You should see long date values here as a result of your date transformation using VBScript.

As you navigated through the wizard's dialogs, you probably got the feeling that there is a lot of power here. You're right, there is a lot of power here. DTS is a tool that I'm sure will be a welcome one in your toolbox.

Using the dtswiz Utility

The DTS import and export wizards can be started from a command prompt using the dtswiz utility.

The syntax of the dtswiz command line follows:

```
dtswiz [/f filename] [/i | /x] [/r providername]
 [/s servername] [/u loginid] [/p password] [/n]
 [/d databasename] [/y]
```

The switches are described in Table 15-2.

TABLE 15-2 COMMAND LINE SWITCHES FOR DTSWIZ

Switch	Description
/f filename	Name of a COM-structured storage file where the output package will be saved.
/i	Starts the import wizard.
/x	Starts the export wizard.
/r providername	The name of the provider used to connect to the data source or destination.
/s servername	Specifies the server name to import data to or export data from.
/u loginid	Login ID used to connect to SQL Server.

Continued

TABLE 15-2 COMMAND LINE SWITCHES FOR DTSWIZ *(Continued)*

Switch	Description
/p *password*	The password for the *loginid* specified with /u.
/n	Indicates a trusted connection.
/d *databasename*	The name of the database that data is imported into or exported from.
/y	Hides master, msdb, model, and tempdb from the list of databases for import or export.

Executing dtswiz launches the familiar Import or Export wizard you see from within the Enterprise Manager.

Using the dtsrun Utility

A DTS package stored in a COM-structured storage file, SQL Server msdb database, or Microsoft Repository can be run using the dtsrun command line utility.

The syntax of dtsrun is:

```
dtsrun [/? | /s servername /u username [/p password] | /e | /f filename /n
packagename [/m packagepassword] |
/g packageguidstring | [/v packageversionstring] [/!x]
[/!d] [/!y] [/!c]]
```

Table 15-3 describes the switches you can use with dtsrun.

TABLE 15-3 COMMAND LINE SWITCHES USED BY DTSRUN

Switch	Description
/?	Display these options.
/s *servername*	The name of the SQL Server to connect to.
/u *username*	The login ID used to connect to SQL Server.
/p *password*	The password associated with the login ID.
/e	Specify the use of a trusted connection.

Switch	Description
/n *packagename*	The name of a saved DTS package.
/m *packagepassword*	The password given to the DTS package (optional).
/g *packageguidstring*	The GUID of the saved DTS package.
/v *packageversionguidstring*	The version GUID assigned to the saved DTS package.
/f *filename*	The name of the structured storage file where the package is stored.
/!x	Causes the package to be retrieved from SQL Server and overwrites the filename specified with /f. Without this option, the package will be run instead of stored.
/!d	Causes the package to be deleted from SQL Server. The package is not executed.
/!y	Displays the encrypted command used to execute the package but does not run it.
/!c	Causes the command used to execute the package to be copied to the clipboard.

The dtsrun command can be used in a command file to run one or more packages. You may find this utility useful for bringing new data into the warehouse from an OLTP system or from external file feeds.

Using the DTS Task Kit

The Data Transformation Services Task Kit 1 enables you to create DTS packages that perform incremental updates or complete processing on OLAP databases, cubes, partitions, and dimensions. This kit is especially useful for developing packages that process OLAP objects after the transfer of new data into the data warehouse.

At the time of this writing, the DTS Task Kit was available for downloading at www.microsoft.com/sql/productinfo/DTSKit.htm. If this page is no longer available, search the Microsoft site for DTSTasks.exe.

After installing the task kit, open the SQL Server Enterprise Manager or your own console and right-click the Data Transformation Services folder and select New package from the shortcut menu. This will launch the DTS Package Designer window.

On the Task palette, locate the OLAP Services Processing Task and drop it on the workspace. This action will display the OLAP Services Processing Task dialog shown in Figure 15-1.

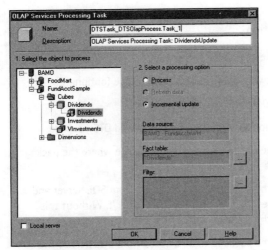

Figure 15-1: The OLAP Services Processing Task dialog

The dialog in Figure 15-1 shows the selections for processing an incremental update of the Dividends partition in the FundAcctsSample database. Depending on the object you select in the object tree, you have one or more of the processing options described in Table 15-4 to choose from.

TABLE 15-4 OLAP SERVICES PROCESSING TASK OPTIONS

Option	Description
Process	Perform a complete process on the selected object or dependent objects.
Refresh data	Reload existing data and recalculate aggregations. No new data added to the source is processed by this option, and no structural changes are processed.
Incremental update	Add new data and update aggregations. No structural changes are processed. When applied to dimensions, new members are added to the dimension.
Rebuild the dimension structure	Available for shared dimensions and virtual dimensions, this option performs a complete process on the dimension including the processing of structural changes in the dimension tables.

When running an incremental update, you need to ensure that the data source used for updating doesn't cause duplicate data to be applied to the target OLAP object. You have the option of specifying a fact table different from the default fact table as long as the table has the same structure as the default. If this new fact table source contains data that doesn't intersect with the data already in the target cube or partition, then the incremental update can be applied without risk.

If you use the default fact table for the data source, then you need to specify a filter in the processing task dialog to select data for updating that will not cause duplicates. The filter is the WHERE clause of a SQL SELECT statement but without the WHERE keyword. When you enter the filter expression, you should enclose the entire expression in parentheses so that it is properly interpreted when applied to the generated SELECT statement.

When rebuilding shared dimensions, the cubes that use the dimensions are unavailable to users. These cubes need to be processed before users can see the effects of the dimension changes. If the shared dimension structure is changed but not processed, it is processed as soon as one of the cubes or partitions using the dimension is processed.

When you are finished with the Processing Task dialog, click OK to dismiss the dialog. You can now add other tasks and connections if you wish to perform other processing in the package.

When the package design is complete, click Save from the Package menu. Enter a name for the package and the location where the package is stored.

Summary

Data Transformation Services is a powerful set of tools for converting and transferring data between heterogeneous sources and destinations. Data can be imported from any OLE DB or ODBC data source or text file into SQL Server tables with a few selections in the DTS Import Wizard. Likewise, data can be exported from a SQL Server table or query using the DTS Export Wizard.

Data transfer and transformations are specified in tasks contained in DTS packages. These packages can be built using the DTS Import or Export wizards, through the use of the DTS Package Designer, or though COM programming. Once created, the packages can be stored in a COM-structured storage file, in the Microsoft Repository, or in a SQL Server msdb database.

Stored packages can be retrieved and executed on demand or can be set up to run on some schedule. The command line dtsrun utility can be used to execute any package.

The DTS Task Kit enables a package to include tasks that process OLAP objects such as cubes, databases, and partitions. This capability is useful for automatic update of OLAP objects after transferring new data into the data warehouse facts and dimensions tables on which an OLAP cube is dependent.

Appendix A

What's on the CD

THE CD CONTAINS the sample code, scripts, and projects discussed in the book. These files are organized on the CD by chapter. Sample code discussed in Chapter 1, for example, will be found in the Chapter01 folder on the CD.

In addition to the chapter folders, four other folders hold files of interest. The Archive folder holds the archive of the sample OLAP database containing the two cubes discussed in the book. This database can be recovered using the Archive/Restore OLAP Manager Add-In discussed in Chapter 9. Read the Readme.txt file in the Archive folder for more information on the use of the archive file.

The Databases folder on the CD contains the files for the FundAccts OLTP database used as the source for the other database in the folder, the FundAcctsWH data warehouse database. The AttachFundAccts.sql script can be used to attach the FundAccts database to your SQL Server, and the AttachFundAcctsWH.sql script is used to attach the FundAcctsWH database. See the Readme.txt file in the Databases folder for more information.

The DTSPackages folder on the CD contains the Data Transformation Packages discussed in the book. These packages are used in part to build the FundAcctsWH data warehouse database. The Readme.txt file in this folder discusses how to change the connections in these packages to refer to the server where you will install the databases.

The ThirdParty folder on the CD contains two subfolders where you will find trial software for two very popular OLAP products. The Geppetto's Workshop folder contains a trial version of the AntQuery version 1.2 from Geppetto's Workshop. This is an excellent developer product that uses their AntMDX SDK and AntSQL SDK to generate MDX and SQL statements for querying cubes and both relational and multidimensional schemas. You can find more information on AntQuery and other Geppetto's Workshop products at their Web site at www.geppetto.com.

The OLAP@Work folder contains a trial version of OLAP@Work for Excel version 1.5 from OLAP@Work. This product is introduced in Chapter 11, where the use of Excel 2000, OLAP@Work, and Microsoft OLAP Services are used to provide end-user analysis of cube data in the form of PivotTable reports and charts. Information on OLAP@Work products including several excellent white papers can be found on the Internet at www.olapatwork.com.

Software Used for the Book's Projects

A list of the software versions used in this book follows:

Microsoft Windows NT version 4.0 with Service Pack 5 (SP5)

Microsoft Windows NT version 4.0 Enterprise Edition with Service Pack 5 (SP5)

Microsoft SQL Server 7.0 with Service Pack 1 (SP1)

Microsoft SQL Server 7.0 Enterprise Edition with Service Pack 1 (SP1)

Microsoft SQL Server OLAP Services 7.0 with Service Pack 1 (SP1)

Microsoft Visual Studio version 6.0 Enterprise Edition with Service Pack 3 (SP3)

Microsoft Excel 2000

OLAP@Work for Excel version 1.5

Appendix B

Sample Database Schemas

The FundAccts Database Schema

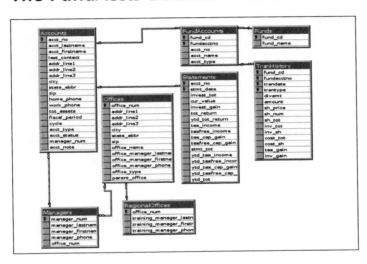

FundAccts OLTP Sample Database Scripts

```
ALTER TABLE [dbo].[FundAccounts] DROP CONSTRAINT FK_FundAccounts_Accounts
GO

ALTER TABLE [dbo].[Statements] DROP CONSTRAINT FK_Statements_Accounts
GO

ALTER TABLE [dbo].[TranHistory] DROP CONSTRAINT FK_TranHistory_FundAccounts
GO

ALTER TABLE [dbo].[FundAccounts] DROP CONSTRAINT FK_FundAccounts_Funds
GO

/****** Object:  Table [dbo].[Accounts]     Script Date: 10/30/99 8:29:00 AM
******/
```

```
if exists (select * from sysobjects where id = object_id(N'[dbo].[Accounts]')
and OBJECTPROPERTY(id, N'IsUserTable') = 1)
drop table [dbo].[Accounts]
GO


/****** Object:  Table [dbo].[AccountValues]     ******/
if exists (select * from sysobjects where id =
object_id(N'[dbo].[AccountValues]') and OBJECTPROPERTY(id, N'IsUserTable') = 1)
drop table [dbo].[AccountValues]
GO


/****** Object:  Table [dbo].[FundAccounts]     ******/
if exists (select * from sysobjects where id =
object_id(N'[dbo].[FundAccounts]') and OBJECTPROPERTY(id, N'IsUserTable') = 1)
drop table [dbo].[FundAccounts]
GO


/****** Object:  Table [dbo].[Funds]    ******/
if exists (select * from sysobjects where id = object_id(N'[dbo].[Funds]') and
OBJECTPROPERTY(id, N'IsUserTable') = 1)
drop table [dbo].[Funds]
GO


/****** Object:  Table [dbo].[Managers]    ******/
if exists (select * from sysobjects where id = object_id(N'[dbo].[Managers]')
and OBJECTPROPERTY(id, N'IsUserTable') = 1)
drop table [dbo].[Managers]
GO


/****** Object:  Table [dbo].[Offices]    ******/
if exists (select * from sysobjects where id = object_id(N'[dbo].[Offices]') and
OBJECTPROPERTY(id, N'IsUserTable') = 1)
drop table [dbo].[Offices]
GO


/****** Object:  Table [dbo].[RegionalOffices]    ******/
if exists (select * from sysobjects where id =
object_id(N'[dbo].[RegionalOffices]') and OBJECTPROPERTY(id, N'IsUserTable') =
1)
drop table [dbo].[RegionalOffices]
GO


/****** Object:  Table [dbo].[Statements]    ******/
if exists (select * from sysobjects where id = object_id(N'[dbo].[Statements]')
and OBJECTPROPERTY(id, N'IsUserTable') = 1)
```

```
drop table [dbo].[Statements]
GO


/****** Object:  Table [dbo].[TranHistory]    ******/
if exists (select * from sysobjects where id = object_id(N'[dbo].[TranHistory]')
and OBJECTPROPERTY(id, N'IsUserTable') = 1)
drop table [dbo].[TranHistory]
GO


/****** Object:  Table [dbo].[Accounts]    ******/
CREATE TABLE [dbo].[Accounts] (
        [acct_no] [varchar] (10) NOT NULL ,
        [acct_lastname] [varchar] (70) NOT NULL ,
        [acct_firstname] [varchar] (50) NULL ,
        [last_contact] [datetime] NULL ,
        [addr_line1] [varchar] (30) NULL ,
        [addr_line2] [varchar] (30) NULL ,
        [addr_line3] [varchar] (30) NULL ,
        [city] [varchar] (30) NULL ,
        [state_abbr] [char] (2) NOT NULL ,
        [zip] [varchar] (10) NOT NULL ,
        [home_phone] [varchar] (15) NULL ,
        [work_phone] [varchar] (15) NULL ,
        [tot_assets] [money] NOT NULL ,
        [fiscal_period] [char] (2) NOT NULL ,
        [cycle] [tinyint] NOT NULL ,
        [acct_type] [varchar] (6) NOT NULL ,
        [acct_status] [varchar] (8) NOT NULL ,
        [manager_num] [smallint] NULL ,
        [acct_note] [text] NULL
)
GO


/****** Object:  Table [dbo].[AccountValues]    ******/
CREATE TABLE [dbo].[AccountValues] (
        [acct_no] [varchar] (10) NOT NULL ,
        [stmt_date] [datetime] NOT NULL ,
        [invest_tot] [money] NOT NULL ,
        [cur_value] [money] NOT NULL
) ON [PRIMARY]
GO


/****** Object:  Table [dbo].[FundAccounts]    ******/
CREATE TABLE [dbo].[FundAccounts] (
        [fund_cd] [char] (5) NOT NULL ,
```

```
                [fundacctno] [char] (35) NOT NULL ,
                [acct_no] [varchar] (10) NOT NULL ,
                [acct_name] [varchar] (70) NULL ,
                [acct_type] [char] (4) NULL
        ) ON [PRIMARY]
        GO


        /****** Object:  Table [dbo].[Funds]      ******/
        CREATE TABLE [dbo].[Funds] (
                [fund_cd] [char] (5) NOT NULL ,
                [fund_name] [varchar] (45) NOT NULL
        ) ON [PRIMARY]
        GO


        /****** Object:  Table [dbo].[Managers]      ******/
        CREATE TABLE [dbo].[Managers] (
                [manager_num] [smallint] NOT NULL ,
                [manager_lastname] [varchar] (70) NOT NULL ,
                [manager_firstname] [varchar] (50) NOT NULL ,
                [manager_phone] [varchar] (15) NOT NULL ,
                [office_num] [smallint] NULL
        ) ON [PRIMARY]
        GO


        /****** Object:  Table [dbo].[Offices]      ******/
        CREATE TABLE [dbo].[Offices] (
                [office_num] [smallint] NOT NULL ,
                [addr_line1] [varchar] (30) NOT NULL ,
                [addr_line2] [varchar] (30) NULL ,
                [addr_line3] [varchar] (30) NULL ,
                [city] [varchar] (30) NOT NULL ,
                [state_abbr] [char] (2) NOT NULL ,
                [zip] [varchar] (10) NOT NULL ,
                [office_name] [varchar] (50) NOT NULL ,
                [office_manager_lastname] [varchar] (70) NOT NULL ,
                [office_manager_firstname] [varchar] (50) NOT NULL ,
                [office_manager_phone] [varchar] (15) NOT NULL ,
                [office_type] [char] (1) NOT NULL ,
                [parent_office] [smallint] NULL
        ) ON [PRIMARY]
        GO


        /****** Object:  Table [dbo].[RegionalOffices]      ******/
        CREATE TABLE [dbo].[RegionalOffices] (
                [office_num] [smallint] NOT NULL ,
```

```
        [training_manager_lastname] [varchar] (70) NULL ,
        [training_manager_firstname] [varchar] (50) NULL ,
        [training_manager_phone] [varchar] (15) NULL
) ON [PRIMARY]
GO


/****** Object:  Table [dbo].[Statements]    ******/
CREATE TABLE [dbo].[Statements] (
        [acct_no] [varchar] (10) NOT NULL ,
        [stmt_date] [datetime] NOT NULL ,
        [invest_tot] [money] NOT NULL ,
        [cur_value] [money] NOT NULL ,
        [invest_gain] [numeric](18, 0) NOT NULL ,
        [tot_return] [numeric](18, 0) NOT NULL ,
        [ytd_tot_return] [numeric](18, 0) NOT NULL ,
        [tax_income] [money] NOT NULL ,
        [taxfree_income] [money] NOT NULL ,
        [tax_cap_gain] [money] NOT NULL ,
        [taxfree_cap_gain] [money] NOT NULL ,
        [stmt_tot] [money] NOT NULL ,
        [ytd_tax_income] [money] NOT NULL ,
        [ytd_taxfree_income] [money] NOT NULL ,
        [ytd_tax_cap_gain] [money] NOT NULL ,
        [ytd_taxfree_cap_gain] [money] NOT NULL ,
        [ytd_tot] [money] NOT NULL
) ON [PRIMARY]
GO


/****** Object:  Table [dbo].[TranHistory]    ******/
CREATE TABLE [dbo].[TranHistory] (
        [fund_cd] [char] (5) NOT NULL ,
        [fundacctno] [char] (35) NOT NULL ,
        [trandate] [datetime] NOT NULL ,
        [trantype] [varchar] (10) NOT NULL ,
        [divamt] [money] NULL ,
        [amount] [money] NULL ,
        [sh_price] [money] NULL ,
        [sh_num] [decimal](18, 4) NULL ,
        [sh_tot] [decimal](18, 4) NULL ,
        [inv_tot] [money] NULL ,
        [inv_sh] [decimal](18, 4) NULL ,
        [cost_tot] [money] NULL ,
        [cost_sh] [money] NULL ,
        [tax_gain] [money] NULL ,
        [inv_gain] [money] NULL
```

```
) ON [PRIMARY]
GO


ALTER TABLE [dbo].[Accounts] WITH NOCHECK ADD
        CONSTRAINT [IX_Accounts] UNIQUE  CLUSTERED
        (
                [acct_no]
        )  ON [PRIMARY]
GO


ALTER TABLE [dbo].[Accounts] WITH NOCHECK ADD
        CONSTRAINT [PK_Accounts] PRIMARY KEY  NONCLUSTERED
        (
                [acct_no]
        )  ON [PRIMARY] ,
        CONSTRAINT [CK_Accounts] CHECK ([acct_type] = 'Tax' or [acct_type] =
'Nontax')
GO


ALTER TABLE [dbo].[AccountValues] WITH NOCHECK ADD
        CONSTRAINT [DF__AccountValues__invest_tot__3BFFE745] DEFAULT (0) FOR
[invest_tot],
        CONSTRAINT [DF__AccountValues__cur_value__3CF40B7E] DEFAULT (0) FOR
[cur_value]
GO


ALTER TABLE [dbo].[FundAccounts] WITH NOCHECK ADD
        CONSTRAINT [PK_FundAccounts] PRIMARY KEY  NONCLUSTERED
        (
                [fund_cd],
                [fundacctno]
        )  ON [PRIMARY]
GO


ALTER TABLE [dbo].[Funds] WITH NOCHECK ADD
        CONSTRAINT [PK_Funds] PRIMARY KEY  NONCLUSTERED
        (
                [fund_cd]
        )  ON [PRIMARY]
GO


ALTER TABLE [dbo].[Managers] WITH NOCHECK ADD
        CONSTRAINT [PK_Managers] PRIMARY KEY  NONCLUSTERED
        (
                [manager_num]
```

```
        )  ON [PRIMARY]
GO

ALTER TABLE [dbo].[Offices] WITH NOCHECK ADD
        CONSTRAINT [PK_Offices] PRIMARY KEY  NONCLUSTERED
        (
                [office_num]
        )  ON [PRIMARY]
GO

ALTER TABLE [dbo].[RegionalOffices] WITH NOCHECK ADD
        CONSTRAINT [PK_RegionalOffices] PRIMARY KEY  NONCLUSTERED
        (
                [office_num]
        )  ON [PRIMARY]
GO

ALTER TABLE [dbo].[Statements] WITH NOCHECK ADD
        CONSTRAINT [DF_Statements_invest_tot] DEFAULT (0) FOR [invest_tot],
        CONSTRAINT [DF_Statements_cur_value] DEFAULT (0) FOR [cur_value],
        CONSTRAINT [DF_Statements_invest_gain] DEFAULT (0) FOR [invest_gain],
        CONSTRAINT [DF_Statements_tot_return] DEFAULT (0) FOR [tot_return],
        CONSTRAINT [DF_Statements_ytd_tot_return] DEFAULT (0) FOR
[ytd_tot_return],
        CONSTRAINT [DF_Statements_tax_income] DEFAULT (0) FOR [tax_income],
        CONSTRAINT [DF_Statements_taxfree_income] DEFAULT (0) FOR
[taxfree_income],
        CONSTRAINT [DF_Statements_tax_cap_gain] DEFAULT (0) FOR [tax_cap_gain],
        CONSTRAINT [DF_Statements_taxfree_cap_gain] DEFAULT (0) FOR
[taxfree_cap_gain],
        CONSTRAINT [DF_Statements_stmt_tot] DEFAULT (0) FOR [stmt_tot],
        CONSTRAINT [DF_Statements_ytd_tax_income] DEFAULT (0) FOR
[ytd_tax_income],
        CONSTRAINT [DF_Statements_ytd_taxfree_income] DEFAULT (0) FOR
[ytd_taxfree_income],
        CONSTRAINT [DF_Statements_ytd_tax_cap_gain] DEFAULT (0) FOR
[ytd_tax_cap_gain],
        CONSTRAINT [DF_Statements_ytd_taxfree_cap_gain] DEFAULT (0) FOR
[ytd_taxfree_cap_gain],
        CONSTRAINT [DF_Statements_ytd_tot] DEFAULT (0) FOR [ytd_tot],
        CONSTRAINT [PK_Statements] PRIMARY KEY  NONCLUSTERED
        (
                [acct_no],
                [stmt_date]
        )  ON [PRIMARY]
```

```
GO

ALTER TABLE [dbo].[TranHistory] WITH NOCHECK ADD
        CONSTRAINT [PK_TranHistory] PRIMARY KEY  NONCLUSTERED
        (
                [fund_cd],
                [fundacctno],
                [trandate],
                [trantype]
        ) ON [PRIMARY]
GO

if (@@microsoftversion > 0x07000000 )
EXEC ('CREATE STATISTICS [_WA_Sys_zip_22AA2996] ON [dbo].[Accounts] ([zip]) ')
GO

 CREATE   INDEX [IDX_manager_num] ON [dbo].[Accounts]([manager_num]) ON [PRIMARY]
GO

ALTER TABLE [dbo].[FundAccounts] ADD
        CONSTRAINT [FK_FundAccounts_Accounts] FOREIGN KEY
        (
                [acct_no]
        ) REFERENCES [dbo].[Accounts] (
                [acct_no]
        ),
        CONSTRAINT [FK_FundAccounts_Funds] FOREIGN KEY
        (
                [fund_cd]
        ) REFERENCES [dbo].[Funds] (
                [fund_cd]
        )
GO

ALTER TABLE [dbo].[Statements] ADD
        CONSTRAINT [FK_Statements_Accounts] FOREIGN KEY
        (
                [acct_no]
        ) REFERENCES [dbo].[Accounts] (
                [acct_no]
        )
GO

ALTER TABLE [dbo].[TranHistory] ADD
        CONSTRAINT [FK_TranHistory_FundAccounts] FOREIGN KEY
```

```
        (
                [fund_cd],
                [fundacctno]
        ) REFERENCES [dbo].[FundAccounts] (
                [fund_cd],
                [fundacctno]
        )
GO
```

The FundAcctsWH Database Schema

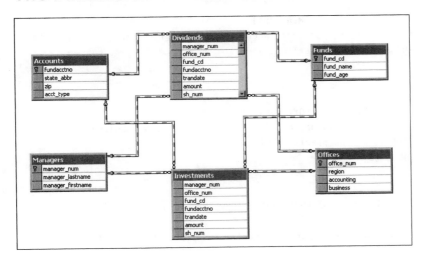

FundAcctsWH Sample Data Warehouse Database Scripts

```
/****** Object:  Table [dbo].[Accounts]    ******/
if exists (select * from sysobjects where id = object_id(N'[dbo].[Accounts]')
and OBJECTPROPERTY(id, N'IsUserTable') = 1)
drop table [dbo].[Accounts]
GO

/****** Object:  Table [dbo].[Dividends]    ******/
if exists (select * from sysobjects where id = object_id(N'[dbo].[Dividends]')
and OBJECTPROPERTY(id, N'IsUserTable') = 1)
drop table [dbo].[Dividends]
GO
```

```
/****** Object:  Table [dbo].[Funds]      ******/
if exists (select * from sysobjects where id = object_id(N'[dbo].[Funds]') and
OBJECTPROPERTY(id, N'IsUserTable') = 1)
drop table [dbo].[Funds]
GO


/****** Object:  Table [dbo].[Investments]      ******/
if exists (select * from sysobjects where id = object_id(N'[dbo].[Investments]')
and OBJECTPROPERTY(id, N'IsUserTable') = 1)
drop table [dbo].[Investments]
GO


/****** Object:  Table [dbo].[Managers]      ******/
if exists (select * from sysobjects where id = object_id(N'[dbo].[Managers]')
and OBJECTPROPERTY(id, N'IsUserTable') = 1)
drop table [dbo].[Managers]
GO


/****** Object:  Table [dbo].[Offices]      ******/
if exists (select * from sysobjects where id = object_id(N'[dbo].[Offices]') and
OBJECTPROPERTY(id, N'IsUserTable') = 1)
drop table [dbo].[Offices]
GO


/****** Object:  Table [dbo].[WriteTable_Investments]      ******/
if exists (select * from sysobjects where id =
object_id(N'[dbo].[WriteTable_Investments]') and OBJECTPROPERTY(id,
N'IsUserTable') = 1)
drop table [dbo].[WriteTable_Investments]
GO


/****** Object:  Table [dbo].[I_Investments_update_78]      ******/
if exists (select * from sysobjects where id =
object_id(N'[dbo].[I_Investments_update_78]') and OBJECTPROPERTY(id,
N'IsUserTable') = 1)
drop table [dbo].[I_Investments_update_78]
GO


/****** Object:  Table [dbo].[Investme_Investments1_7N]      ******/
if exists (select * from sysobjects where id =
object_id(N'[dbo].[Investme_Investments1_7N]') and OBJECTPROPERTY(id,
N'IsUserTable') = 1)
drop table [dbo].[Investme_Investments1_7N]
GO
```

```
/****** Object:  Table [dbo].[Accounts]     ******/
CREATE TABLE [dbo].[Accounts] (
        [fundacctno] [char] (35) NOT NULL ,
        [state_abbr] [char] (2) NOT NULL ,
        [zip] [varchar] (10) NOT NULL ,
        [acct_type] [char] (4) NULL
) ON [PRIMARY]
GO


/****** Object:  Table [dbo].[Dividends]     ******/
CREATE TABLE [dbo].[Dividends] (
        [manager_num] [smallint] NULL ,
        [office_num] [smallint] NULL ,
        [fund_cd] [char] (5) NOT NULL ,
        [fundacctno] [char] (35) NOT NULL ,
        [trandate] [datetime] NOT NULL ,
        [amount] [money] NULL ,
        [sh_num] [decimal](18, 4) NULL
) ON [PRIMARY]
GO


/****** Object:  Table [dbo].[Funds]     ******/
CREATE TABLE [dbo].[Funds] (
        [fund_cd] [char] (5) NOT NULL ,
        [fund_name] [varchar] (45) NOT NULL ,
        [fund_age] [int] NULL
) ON [PRIMARY]
GO


/****** Object:  Table [dbo].[Investments]     ******/
CREATE TABLE [dbo].[Investments] (
        [manager_num] [smallint] NOT NULL ,
        [office_num] [smallint] NULL ,
        [fund_cd] [char] (5) NOT NULL ,
        [fundacctno] [char] (35) NOT NULL ,
        [trandate] [datetime] NOT NULL ,
        [amount] [money] NULL ,
        [sh_num] [decimal](18, 4) NULL
) ON [PRIMARY]
GO


/****** Object:  Table [dbo].[Managers]     ******/
CREATE TABLE [dbo].[Managers] (
        [manager_num] [smallint] NOT NULL ,
        [manager_lastname] [varchar] (70) NOT NULL ,
```

```
            [manager_firstname] [varchar] (50) NOT NULL
) ON [PRIMARY]
GO


/****** Object:   Table [dbo].[Offices]     ******/
CREATE TABLE [dbo].[Offices] (
            [office_num] [smallint] NOT NULL ,
            [region] [varchar] (50) NOT NULL ,
            [accounting] [varchar] (50) NOT NULL ,
            [business] [varchar] (50) NOT NULL
) ON [PRIMARY]
GO
```

The following table is a sample of a write-back table that is generated by OLAP services to hold write-back data for a cube. This table is created when a cube is write-enabled.

```
/****** Object:   Table [dbo].[WriteTable_Investments]     ******/
CREATE TABLE [dbo].[WriteTable_Investments] (
            [MS_AUDIT_USER] [varchar] (32) NULL ,
            [MS_AUDIT_TIME] [datetime] NULL ,
            [FundName_L2] [varchar] (45) NULL ,
            [StateAbbr_L4] [varchar] (2) NULL ,
            [ManagerLastname_L6] [varchar] (70) NULL ,
            [Region_L8] [varchar] (50) NULL ,
            [Accounting_L9] [varchar] (50) NULL ,
            [Business_L10] [varchar] (50) NULL ,
            [Year_L12] [smallint] NULL ,
            [Quarter_L13] [smallint] NULL ,
            [Month_L14] [smallint] NULL ,
            [SUM_Amount] [money] NULL ,
            [SUM_ShNum] [float] NULL
) ON [PRIMARY]
GO
```

The following table is a sample of a table (one of many) that is generated by OLAP services during an incremental update process. These tables can be safely removed after processing is completed.

```
/****** Object:   Table [dbo].[I_Investments_update_78]     ******/
CREATE TABLE [dbo].[I_Investments_update_78] (
            [Region_L8] [varchar] (50) NULL ,
            [Accounting_L9] [varchar] (50) NULL ,
            [Business_L10] [varchar] (50) NULL ,
            [SUM_Amount] [money] NULL ,
```

```
            [SUM_ShNum] [float] NULL
) ON [PRIMARY]
GO
```

The following table is a sample of a table that is generated by OLAP services to store aggregated values for the Investments cube using a ROLAP storage mode. There are as many tables as there are designed aggregations for the cube.

```
/****** Object:  Table [dbo].[Investme_Investments1_7N]    ******/
CREATE TABLE [dbo].[Investme_Investments1_7N] (
        [Region_L8] [varchar] (50) NULL ,
        [Accounting_L9] [varchar] (50) NULL ,
        [Business_L10] [varchar] (50) NULL ,
        [SUM_Amount] [money] NULL ,
        [SUM_ShNum] [float] NULL
) ON [PRIMARY]
GO


ALTER TABLE [dbo].[Accounts] WITH NOCHECK ADD
        CONSTRAINT [PK_Accounts] PRIMARY KEY  NONCLUSTERED
        (
                [fundacctno]
        ) ON [PRIMARY]
GO


ALTER TABLE [dbo].[Funds] WITH NOCHECK ADD
        CONSTRAINT [PK_Funds] PRIMARY KEY  NONCLUSTERED
        (
                [fund_cd]
        ) ON [PRIMARY]
GO


ALTER TABLE [dbo].[Managers] WITH NOCHECK ADD
        CONSTRAINT [PK_Managers] PRIMARY KEY  NONCLUSTERED
        (
                [manager_num]
        ) ON [PRIMARY]
GO


ALTER TABLE [dbo].[Offices] WITH NOCHECK ADD
        CONSTRAINT [PK_Offices] PRIMARY KEY  NONCLUSTERED
        (
                [office_num]
        ) ON [PRIMARY]
GO
```

```
CREATE  UNIQUE  INDEX [IX_Investments] ON [dbo].[Investments]([manager_num],
[office_num], [fund_cd], [fundacctno], [trandate]) ON [PRIMARY]
GO

CREATE  INDEX [WriteTable_Investments1] ON
[dbo].[WriteTable_Investments]([FundName_L2]) ON [PRIMARY]
GO

CREATE  INDEX [WriteTable_Investments2] ON
[dbo].[WriteTable_Investments]([StateAbbr_L4]) ON [PRIMARY]
GO

CREATE  INDEX [WriteTable_Investments3] ON
[dbo].[WriteTable_Investments]([ManagerLastname_L6]) ON [PRIMARY]
GO

CREATE  INDEX [WriteTable_Investments4] ON
[dbo].[WriteTable_Investments]([Region_L8], [Accounting_L9], [Business_L10]) ON
[PRIMARY]
GO

CREATE  INDEX [WriteTable_Investments5] ON
[dbo].[WriteTable_Investments]([Year_L12], [Quarter_L13], [Month_L14]) ON
[PRIMARY]
GO

CREATE  INDEX [WriteTable_Investments0] ON
[dbo].[WriteTable_Investments]([FundName_L2], [StateAbbr_L4],
[ManagerLastname_L6], [Region_L8], [Accounting_L9], [Business_L10], [Year_L12],
[Quarter_L13], [Month_L14]) ON [PRIMARY]
GO

CREATE  INDEX [I_Investments_update_784] ON
[dbo].[I_Investments_update_78]([Region_L8], [Accounting_L9], [Business_L10]) ON
[PRIMARY]
GO

CREATE  INDEX [Investme_Investments1_7N4] ON
[dbo].[Investme_Investments1_7N]([Region_L8], [Accounting_L9], [Business_L10])
ON [PRIMARY]
GO
```

Appendix C

Decision Support Objects Reference

The clsDatabase Object

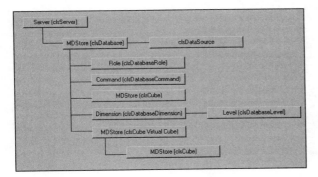

The clsCube Object

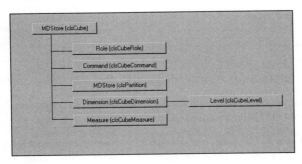

The clsPartition Object

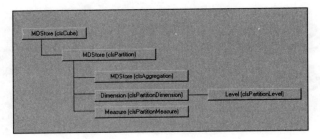

The clsAggregation Object

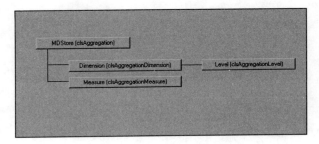

TABLE C-1 DECISION SUPPORT OBJECTS

Object Name	Description
ClsCubeCommand	Defines a user command such as a calculated member, named set, or library reference to be executed when the cube is accessed by an OLAP Services client.
ClsDatabaseCommand	Same as clsCubeCommand but executed when database is accessed. Currently not used by DSO.
ClsDatabaseDimension	Dimension objects of the database Dimensions collection. These can be private dimensions for a specific named cube (as in Investments^Manager) or shared dimensions to be assigned to any cube (no cube name or ^ in the dimension name, as in the shared Fund dimension).

Object Name	Description
clsCubeDimension	Dimension objects of the cube Dimensions collection added by referencing the dimensions of the database Dimensions collection.
clsPartitionDimension	Dimensions contained in a cube partition.
clsAggregationDimension	A designed aggregation dimension inherited from the aggregation's partition.
clsDatabaseLevel	A level of a database dimension. These levels are inherited by any cube to which the parent dimension is assigned.
clsCubeLevel	A level of a cube dimension inherited from a database dimension.
clsPartitionLevel	A level of a partition dimension containing slice values of the dimension.
clsAggregationLevel	A level of a dimension contained in a designed aggregation.
clsDatabase	The parent container object for OLAP objects such as cubes, dimensions, measures, partitions, aggregations, and virtual cubes.
clsCube	A multidimensional structure containing dimensions, measures, and partitions. Both regular and virtual cubes are supported in OLAP services.
clsPartition	Contains a portion of a cube's aggregations possibly stored in a separate location from other cube data and in a different storage mode from other partitions. Every cube has at least one partition.
clsAggregation	Defines measures aggregated over a specific set of dimensions.
clsCubeMeasure	A numeric value from a cube's fact table. Detail numeric values at the lowest level of a dimension are aggregated across higher levels of the dimension.
clsPartitionMeasure	Cube measures contained in a given partition of the cube.
clsAggregationMeasure	Cube measures in an aggregation.
clsDatabaseRole	A named collection of one or more users all having the same access rights.

Continued

Table C-1 DECISION SUPPORT OBJECTS *(Continued)*

Object Name	Description
clsCubeRole	A database role assigned to a specific cube, contains security information.
clsDatasource	Defines a connection to a data source such as the data warehouse database.
clsServer	Represents the OLAP server that manages OLAP databases and their contained objects.

Table C-2 PROPERTIES OF MDSTORE INTERFACE CLASSES

Property	Supported by All Classes Except	Description
AggregationPrefix		Prefix for the MDStore aggregation. If SourceTable is not specified, this will be used for the names of ROLAP aggregation tables.
Analyzer	clsAggregation clsDatabase	References the Analyzer object for the store.
ClassType		Identifies the type of class.
Description		Describes the store.
EstimatedRows	clsDatabase	Estimates number of rows in the store.
FromClause	clsDatabase	SQL FROM clause for the MDStore object.
IsDefault	clsCube clsDatabase	Indicates if the store is the default store.
IsReadWrite	clsAggregation	Indicates if store is writable.
IsTemporary	clsDatabase	Indicates temporary object.
IsValid		Indicates valid object.
JoinClause	clsDatabase	SQL JOIN clause for the MDStore object.

Property	Supported by All Classes Except	Description
LastProcessed		The date/time when the store was last processed.
LastUpdated		A date specified by the user.
Name		The name of the store.
OlapMode		Identifies the storage mode of the store.
Parent		The parent store object.
Server		The server object reference.
SourceTable	clsDatabase	The source table name.
SourceTableFilter	clsAggregation clsDatabase	A SQL statement that selects records to include in the store.
State	clsAggregation	Indicates the processing state of the object on the server.
SubClassType		Identifies the subclass type of the object.

TABLE C-3 PROPERTIES OF DIMENSION INTERFACE CLASSES

Property	Supported by All Classes Except	Description
AggregationUsage	clsAggregationDimension clsDatabaseDimension	Specifies how aggregations are designed.
ClassType		Identifies the type of class.
DataSource		The data source of the dimension.
Description	clsAggregationDimension	Describes the dimension.
DimensionType		Identifies the type of dimension.
FromClause		SQL FROM clause for the dimension.

Continued

TABLE C-3 PROPERTIES OF DIMENSION INTERFACE CLASSES (Continued)

Property	Supported by All Classes Except	Description
IsShared		Indicates shared dimension.
IsTemporary		Indicates temporary object.
IsValid		Indicates valid dimension structure.
JoinClause		SQL JOIN clause for the dimension.
LastProcessed		The date/time when the dimension was last processed.
LastUpdated		A date specified by the user.
Name		The name of the dimension.
OrdinalPosition		The position of the dimension relative to other dimensions in a collection.
Parent		The parent dimension.
SourceTable	clsAggregationDimension	The source dimension table name.
State	clsCubeDimension clsPartitionDimension	Indicates the status of the dimension.
SubClassType		Identifies the subclass type of the object.

TABLE C-4 PROPERTIES OF LEVEL INTERFACE CLASSES

Property	Supported by All Classes Except	Description
ClassType		Identifies the type of class.
ColumnSize		Size of the aggregation column in aggregation table.

Property	Supported by All Classes Except	Description
ColumnType		Data type of aggregation column.
Description		Describes the level.
EnableAggregations	clsAggregationLevel clsDatabaseLevel	Specifies if aggregations are to be enabled for the level.
EstimatedSize		Estimated number of members in level.
FromClause		SQL FROM clause for the level.
IsDisabled	clsDatabaseLevel	Indicates if level is disabled and not visible to users.
IsUnique		Indicates if memberkeycolumn alone uniquely identifies level members or if other columns are needed to uniquely identify members.
IsValid		Indicates valid level structure.
JoinClause		SQL JOIN clause for the level.
LevelType		Identifies the type of level.
MemberKeyColumn		Name of column containing member keys. May be an expression instead of column name.
MemberNameColumn		The name of the column or an expression containing member names.
Name		Name of the level.
Ordering		Specifies how the level is ordered.
OrdinalPosition		The position of the level relative to other levels in a collection.
Parent		The parent dimension.
SliceValue	clsAggregationLevel clsDatabaseLevel clsCubeLevel	The level member name used to define partition slice.
SubClassType		Identifies the subclass type of the object.

Table C-5 PROPERTIES OF MEASURE INTERFACE CLASSES

Property	Supported by All Classes Except	Description
AggregateFunction		The type of aggregation function used for the measure. Possible values are aggSum, aggCount, aggMin, and aggMax.
ClassType		Identifies the type of class.
Description		Describes the measure.
FormatString		The format used to display measure values.
IsInternal		Indicates if measure is used internally to calculate other measures.
FromClause		SQL FROM clause for the level.
IsValid		Indicates valid measure object.
Name		Name of the measure.
OrdinalPosition		The position of the measure relative to other measures in a collection.
Parent		The parent MDStore object.
SourceColumn		Name of the fact table column being aggregated.
SourceColumnType		Data type of the SourceColumn.
SubClassType		Identifies the subclass type of the object.

Table C-6 PROPERTIES OF COMMAND INTERFACE CLASSES

Property	Supported by All Classes Except	Description
ClassType		Identifies the type of class.
CommandType		Identifies the command option.

Property	Supported by All Classes Except	Description
Description		Describes the command.
IsValid		Indicates that the name and statement properties are either empty or valid.
Name		Name of the command.
OrdinalPosition		The position of the command relative to other commands in a collection. Commands are executed according to their position in the collection.
Parent		The parent MDStore object.
Statement		The command text.
SubClassType		Identifies the subclass type of the object.

TABLE C-7 PROPERTIES OF ROLE INTERFACE CLASSES

Property	Supported by All Classes Except	Description
ClassType		Identifies the type of class.
Description		Describes the role.
IsValid		Indicates that the role structure is valid.
Name		Name of the role.
Parent		The parent MDStore object.
Permissions	clsDatabaseRole	The access permissions to the cube.
SubClassType		Identifies the subclass type of the object.
UsersList		A string of user names delimited by a semicolon. NT domain names are entered as "DomainName\UserName."

TABLE C-8 DSO ENUMERATIONS

Enumerator and Applies To	Values
CommandTypes	cmdUnknown = 0
	cmdCreateMember = 1
CommandType	cmdCreateSet = 2
	cmdUseLibrary = 3
LevelTypes	levRegular = 0
	levAll = 1
LevelType property	levTimeYears = 20
	levTimeHalfYears = 36
	levTimeQuarters = 68
	levTimeMonths = 132
	levTimeWeeks = 260
	levTimeDays = 516
	levTimeHours = 772
	levTimeMinutes = 1028
	levTimeSeconds = 2052
OrderTypes	orderName = 0
Ordering property	orderKey = 1
AggregatesTypes	aggSum = 0
	aggCount = 1
AggregateFunction	aggMin = 2
	aggMax = 3
DimensionTypes	dimRegular = 0
	dimTime = 1
DimensionType property	dimQuantitative = 5
DimensionAggUsageTypes	dimAggUsageStandard = 0
	dimAggUsageTopOnly = 1
AggregationUsage property	dimAggUsageDetailsOnly = 2
	dimAggUsageCustom = 3
SupportLevels	supportNoROLAP = 0
	supportNoSQLNoTransactions = 1
	supportSQL = 3
	supportTransactions = 5
	supportSQLTransactions = 7

Enumerator and Applies To	Values
OlapEditions Edition property of clsServer	olapEditionUnlimited = 0 olapEditionPivotOnly = 1 olapEditionNoPartitions = 2 olapEditionError = -1
ValidateErrorCodes	mderrNoError = -1 mderrUnknownError = 0 mderrNameNotSet = 1 mderrParentNotSet = 2 mderrMissingDataSource = 3 mderrCannotConnectToDataSource = 4 mderrCannotAccessDataSourceTables = 5 mderrInvalidSchemaLoopDetectedInTableJoins = 6 mderrInvalidSchemaBadSourceColumn = 7 mderrInvalidSchemaDatasource = 8 mderrInvalidSchemaIslandDetectedInTableJoins = 9 mderrConnectionStringNotSet = 10 mderrErrorBeginingDatasourceTransaction = 11 mderrUsersNotSet = 12 mderrStatementNotSet = 13 mderrMeasureMissingSourceColumn = 14 mderrMeasureInvalidColumnDataType = 15 mderrAggColumnSizeNotSet = 16 mderrAggColumnTypeNotSet = 17 mderrInvalidLevelMemberKeyColumnNotSet = 18 mderrInvalidLevelMoreMembersThePreviousLevel = 19 mderrInvalidLevelZeroMembersCount = 20 mderrInvalidLevelBadTableInMemberKeyColumn = 21 mderrInvalidLevelType = 22 mderrInvalidLevelSourceMemberPropertyMissing = 23 mderrDimensionTableNotSet = 24 mderrInvalidDimensionZeroLevels = 25 mderrInvalidDimensionAtLeastOneNonAllLevel = 26 mderrInvalidVirtualDimension = 27 mderrInvalidCubeZeroMeasures = 28 mderrInvalidCubeZeroDimensions = 29 mderrInvalidCubeBadFactTableSize = 30 mderrInvalidVirtualCubeMeasure = 31 mderrInvalidVirtualCubeDimension = 32

Continued

TABLE **C-8** DSO ENUMERATIONS *(Continued)*

Enumerator and Applies To	Values
	mderrInvalidCubeBadFactTable = 33
	mderrInvalidCubeNoSourceForVirtualDimension = 34
	mderrInvalidCubeNoSourceLevelForVirtualDimension =35
	mderrTooManyMeasures = 36
	mderrInvalidPartZeroMeasures = 37
	mderrInvalidPartZeroDimensions = 38
	mderrInvalidPartBadFactTableSize = 39
	mderrInvalidPartBadFactTable = 40
	mderrInvalidAggregationPrefix = 41
	mderrOnlyOneWriteBackPartitionIsAllowed = 42
	mderrInvalidDatasetDefinition = 43
	mderrCubeToComplexForAggregationDesign = 44
	mderrAggPrefixNotSet = 45
	mderrNameAlreadySet = 46
ErrorCodes	mderrCollectionReadOnly = -2147221503
	mderrCollectionItemNotFound = -2147221502
	mderrDimensionLockedByCube = -2147221501
	mderrIllegalObjectName = -2147221500
	mderrCannotDeleteLastPartition = -2147221499
	mderrCannotRenameObject = -2147221498
	mderrInvalidPropertySetting = -2147221497
	mderrCannotDeleteDimension = -2147221496
	mderrCannotDeleteLevel = -2147221495
	mderrCannotDeleteMemberProperty = -2147221494
	mderrCannotAddVirtualDimension = -2147221493
	mderrObjectChangedByAnotherApp = -2147221492
	mderrCannotSaveInsideTransaction = -2147221491
	mderrCannotCommitDatabase = -2147221490
	mderrCorruptedRegistrySettings = -2147221489
	mderrDimensionNotInUnderlyingCubes = -2147221488
	mderrMeasureDoesNotHaveValidSourceColumn = -2147221487
	mderrTooManyLevelsInDimension = -2147221486
	mderrCannotRemoveMeasureFromDefaultAggregation = -2147221485
	mderrCouldNotOpenServiceControlManager = -2147221484

Enumerator and Applies To	Values
	mderrCouldNotOpenService = -2147221483 mderrCouldNotQueryTheService = -2147221482 mderrBadParameterForServiceState = -2147221481 mderrUnsuccesfullServiceOperation = -2147221480 mderrDuplicateKeyInCollection = -2147221479 mderrInvalidParent = -2147221478 mderrCannotModifySharedObject = -2147221477 mderrLockDescriptionTooLong = -2147221476 mderrLockNetworkDown = -2147221475 mderrLockNetworkPathNotFound = -2147221474 mderrLockNetworkNameNotFound = -2147221473 mderrLockFileCorrupted = -2147221472 mderrLockFileMissing = -2147221471 mderrLockNotEnoughMemory = -2147221470 mderrLockSystemError = -2147221469 mderrLockCannotBeObtained = -2147221468 mderrLockObjectNotLocked = -2147221467 mderrLockAccessError = -2147221466 mderrNameCannotBeEmpty = -2147221465 mderrNameCannotBeChanged = -2147221464 mderrPropertyCannotBeChanged = -2147221463 mderrPropertyCollectionCannotBeChanged = -2147221462 mderrDefinitionCannotBeEmpty = -2147221461 mderrDefinitionDoesNotContainNameAndValue = -2147221460 mderrCorruptedProperty = -2147221459 mderrAggregationUsageNotCustom = -2147221458 mderrRegistryConnectFailed = -2147221457 ojmderrRegistryOpenKeyFailed = -2147221456 mderrRegistryQueryValueFailed = -2147221455 mderrRepositoryUpgradeFailed = -2147221454 mderrRepositoryConnectionFailed = -2147221453 mderrRepositoryIncompatible = -2147221452 mderrInvalidLockType = -2147221451 mderrCannotCloneObjectIntoItself = -2147221450 mderrUnexpectedError = -2147221449 mderrSourceDoesNotExist = -2147221448 mderrTargetDoesNotExist = -2147221447

Continued

TABLE C-8 DSO ENUMERATIONS *(Continued)*

Enumerator and Applies To	Values
	mderrDifferentAggregationNumber = -2147221446
	mderrDifferentAggregationStructure = -2147221445
	mderrDifferentAggregationOLAPMode = -2147221444
	mderrDifferentAggregationDatasources = -2147221443
	mderrCannotCreatePartition = -2147221442
ServerStates State property	stateUnknown = 0 stateConnected = 1 stateFailed = 2
CloneOptions options for the Clone method	cloneObjectProperties = 0 cloneMinorChildren = 1 cloneMajorChildren = 2
ClassTypes ClassType property	clsServer = 1 clsDatabase = 2 clsDatabaseRole = 3 clsDatabaseCommand = 4 clsDatasource = 6 clsDatabaseDimension = 7 clsDatabaseLevel = 8 clsCube = 9 clsCubeMeasure = 10 clsCubeDimension = 11 clsCubeLevel = 12 clsCubeCommand = 13 clsCubeRole = 14 clsPartition = 19 clsPartitionMeasure = 20 clsPartitionDimension = 21 clsPartitionLevel = 22 clsAggregation = 23 clsAggregationMeasure = 24 clsAggregationDimension = 25 clsAggregationLevel = 26 clsCubeAnalyzer = 28 clsPartitionAnalyzer = 29 clsCollection = 30 clsMemberProperty = 31

Enumerator and Applies To	Values
SubClassTypes SubClassType property	sbclsRegular = 0 sbclsVirtual = 1
OlapStateTypes State property	olapStateNeverProcessed = 0 olapStateStructureChanged = 1 olapStateMemberPropertiesChanged = 2 olapStateSourceMappingChanged = 3 olapStateCurrent = 4
OlapLockTypes LockType parm of the LockObject method	olaplockRead = 1 olaplockExtendedRead = 2 olaplockProcess = 4 olaplockWrite = 8
ProcessTypes Open parm of the Process method	processDefault = 0 processFull = 1 processRefreshData = 2 processBuildStructure = 3 processResume = 4 processSuspend = 5
OlapStorageModes OlapMode property	olapmodeRolap = 15 olapmodeMolapIndex = 0 olapmodeHybridIndex = 1 olapmodeAggsRolap = 3 olapmodeAggsMolapIndex = 0

TABLE C-9 CLSSERVER METHODS

Method	Description
CloseServer	Releases all server resources acquired by the DSO server object.

Continued

TABLE **C-9 CLSSERVER METHODS** *(Continued)*

Method	Description
Connect([ServerName])	Connects to an OLAP server service. The server name is specified to connect to a specific server or use *LocalHost* to connect to a server running on the same machine as your DSO application.
CreateObject(ClassType[,SubClassType])	Creates an object of ClassType and optional SubClassType.
LockObject(object,LockType,LockDescription)	Locks a specified object.
Refresh	Reads the repository and refreshes all objects.
UnlockAllObjects	Removes locks from objects.
UnlockObject(object)	Removes a lock from a specified object.
Update	Updates an object in the repository.

TABLE **C-10 CLSSERVER SERVICESTATE VALUES**

Example Constant and Value	Description
SERVICE_CONTINUE_PENDING (5)	Service Continue is pending.
SERVICE_PAUSE_PENDING (6)	Service Pause is pending.
SERVICE_PAUSED (7)	Service is paused.
SERVICE_RUNNING (4)	Service is running.
SERVICE_START_PENDING (2)	Service Start is pending.
SERVICE_STOP_PENDING (3)	Service Stop is pending.
SERVICE_STOPPED (1)	Service is stopped.

TABLE C-11 DSO ERRORCODES ENUMERATION

ErrorCode	Description
mderrAggregationUsageNotCustom	The EnableAggregations property cannot be set for dimension levels where the AggregationUsage property has a value other than 3.
mderrBadParameterForServiceState	Invalid service state parameter.
mderrCannotAddVirtualDimension	Source dimension for virtual dimension is not in the database.
mderrCannotCloneObjectIntoItself	Object cannot be cloned into itself.
mderrCannotCommitDatabase	Database cannot be created on the OLAP server.
mderrCannotCreatePartition	No system partition is available for the operation. User-defined partitions are available only when running the Microsoft SQL Server OLAP Services, Enterprise Edition.
mderrCannotDeleteDimension	Dimension cannot be deleted because it is being used by a cube, and the cube is not temporary.
mderrCannotDeleteLastPartition	Cannot delete the last partition in a cube.
mderrCannotDeleteLevel	Cannot delete a level being used in a virtual dimension.
mderrCannotDeleteMemberProperty	Cannot delete a member property being used in a virtual dimension.
mderrCannotModifySharedObject	Cannot change a shared dimension property being used in a cube.
mderrCannotRemoveMeasureFrom DefaultAggregation	Cannot remove a measure from an aggregation created by clsPartitionAnalyzer.
mderrCannotRenameObject	DSO did not allow object to be renamed.
mderrCannotSaveInsideTransaction	Object cannot be saved inside a DSO transaction.
mderrCollectionItemNotFound	Item not found in collection.
mderrCollectionReadOnly	Objects cannot be added or removed from Read-Only collection.
mderrCouldNotLockObject	You attempted to lock an object already locked by another user session.

Continued

TABLE C-11 DSO ERRORCODES ENUMERATION *(Continued)*

ErrorCode	Description
mderrCouldNotOpenService	The OLAP service could not be opened.
mderrCouldNotOpenServiceControl Manager	The OLAP service control manager could not be opened.
mderrCouldNotQueryTheService	The OLAP service could not be queried.
mderrDifferentAggregationDatasources	Only for ROLAP partitions. Source and target partitions have different relational data sources. Merge of partitions is not allowed.
mderrDifferentAggregationNumber	Source and target partitions have different number of aggregations. Merge of partitions is not allowed.
mderrDifferentAggregationOLAPMode	Source and target partitions have different storage modes. Merge of partitions is not allowed.
mderrDifferentAggregationStructure	Source and target partitions have different structures or storage modes. Merge of partitions is not allowed.
mderrDimensionLockedByCube	Dimension is locked because it is being used in a cube.
mderrDimensionNotInUnderlyingCubes	Dimension cannot be added to a virtual cube because it is not in any of the cubes on which the virtual cube is based.
mderrDuplicateKeyInCollection	An item in the collection has the same name as an item being added to the collection.
mderrIllegalObjectName	An illegal name cannot be assigned to an object.
mderrInvalidLockType	Invalid LockType argument value.
mderrInvalidParent	An object not in a collection has no parent.
mderrInvalidPropertySetting	Property value is not valid.
mderrLockAccessError	Unable to lock an object that is already locked by another user session. Or, access denied when trying to lock an object.
mderrLockCannotBeObtained	Unable to acquire a lock from the server.

ErrorCode	Description
mderrLockDescriptionTooLong	Lock description exceeds maximum length.
mderrLockFileCorrupted	The server detected a corrupted lock file.
mderrLockFileMissing	The server cannot find lock file.
mderrLockNetworkDown	Network error detected.
mderrLockNetworkNameNotFound	Cannot find name on the network.
mderrLockNetworkPathNotFound	Cannot find network path.
mderrLockObjectNotLocked	Cannot unlock an object that is not locked.
mderrLockSystemError	A lock cannot be acquired due to an unknown error.
mderrMeasureDoesNotHaveValid SourceColumn	A measure cannot be added to a virtual cube when the name of the measure's source column is not in the correct format. The correct format is "[<underlying cube name>].[<measure name>]".
mderrNameCannotBeChanged	Only temporary objects can be renamed.
mderrNameCannotBeEmpty	An object cannot have an empty name.
mderrObjectChangedByAnotherApp	Object cannot be saved because it was not locked and was changed by another user session.
mderrObjectIsNotWriteLocked	Object cannot be updated because it is not write-locked.
mderrPropertyCannotBeChanged	Property cannot be changed in this context. Usually occurs if the parent of the member property is not a Database Level.
mderrRepositoryConnectionFailed	Cannot connect to repository. Object repository may be read-only.
mderrRepositoryIncompatible	Repository is incompatible with this version of DSO. Usually happens when you're opening repository created using a newer version of DSO, with an older version of DSO.
mderrSourceDoesNotExist	Source partition does not exist. Partitions cannot be merged.

Continued

TABLE C-11 DSO ERRORCODES ENUMERATION *(Continued)*

ErrorCode	Description
mderrTargetDoesNotExist	Target partition does not exist. Partitions cannot be merged.
mderrTooManyLevelsInDimension	The maximum number of levels in a dimension is 63 plus the All level.
mderrUnsuccesfullServiceOperation	The OLAP server service is not running on the specified computer.

TABLE C-12 DSO LOCK TYPES

OlapLockTypes Enumeration	Description
olapLockExtendedRead	Object properties can be read by other users but not changed or processed.
olapLockProcess	Other users can only read object properties until lock is released.
olapLockRead	Other users can read properties from the repository but cannot change them.
olapLockWrite	Other users cannot access the object properties.

TABLE C-13 DATATYPEENUM VALUES

Data Type	Value
Big Integer	AdBigInt
Binary	AdBinary
Boolean	adBoolean
Char	adChar
WChar	adWChar

Data Type	Value
Currency	adCurrency
Date	adDate
Time	adDBTime
DateTime	adDBTimeStamp
Decimal	adDecimal
Double	adDouble
Integer	adInteger
Numeric	adNumeric
Single	adSingle
Small Integer	adSmallInt
BSTR	adBSTR
Tiny Integer	adTinyInt
Unsigned Big Integer	adUnsignedBigInt
Unsigned Integer	adUnsignedInt
Unsigned Small Integer	adUnsignedSmallInt
Unsigned Tiny Integer	adUnsignedTinyInt

TABLE C-14 LEVELTYPES VALUES

Level	Value
Top level of a dimension	levAll
A level not related to time	levRegular
Day level	levTimeDays
Half-year level	levTimeHalfYears
Hour level	levTimeHours

Continued

TABLE C-14 LEVELTYPES VALUES *(Continued)*

Level	Value
Minute level	levTimeMinutes
Month level	levTimeMonths
Quarter level	levTimeQuarters
Second level	levTimeSeconds
Week level	levTimeWeeks
Year level	levTimeYears

TABLE C-15 PROCESS TYPES

Process Type	Description
processBuildStructure	Can be used on cubes only; causes the structure of the cube to be created, but no data is populated into it.
processDefault	Causes a refresh if the structure of the cube is up to date or a full process if the cube needs to be built.
processFull	Rebuilds the structure if necessary and repopulates the data into the partition.
processrefreshData	Refreshes the data in the partition but does not rebuild it.
processResume	Server should resume responding to user queries against the partition or cube.
processSuspend	Server should suspend responding to user queries against the partition or cube.

TABLE **C-16 SECURITY RULE CATEGORIES**

Rule Category (Permissions Key)	Description
Readable cells (CellRead)	The cell value is returned whenever a security rule for one of the user's roles in the cube evaluates True. When all rules evaluate False, access to the cell value is prohibited.
Contingent Readable cells (CellReadContingent)	Used for calculated members. Cell value is returned if rule evaluates True and derived cells are accessible by the user. When all rules evaluate False, access to the cell value is prohibited.
Write-Enabled cells (CellWrite)	Cell values can be changed and committed if the cell security rule evaluates True; otherwise, the change fails.

TABLE **C-17 SECURED CELL VALUE ARGUMENTS**

Value	Description
0	#N/A returned for failed access to a cell.
1	Same as 0.
2	HRESULT is an error code. Used in calls to OLE DB for OLAP IMDDataset::GetCellData.
3	Null is returned in Formatted Value and Value properties.
4	Zero is returned in Formatted Value and Value properties.
5	#SEC is returned in Formatted Value and Value properties.

Appendix D

The MDX Statement and Format String Specifiers

TABLE D-1 THE MDX STATEMENT SYNTAX

Statement Component	Defined As

`<MDX statement>`	`<select_statement>`
	  `| <create_formula_statement>`
	  `| <drop_formula_statement>`

`<select_statement>`	`[WITH <formula_specification>]`
	    `SELECT [<axis_specification>`
	`[, <axis_specification>...]]`
	  `FROM [<cube_specification>]`
	  `[WHERE [<slicer_specification>]]`
	      `[<cell_properties>]`

`<formula_specification>`	`<member_specification>` `| <set_specification>`

`<member_specification>`	`MEMBER <member_name> AS`
	    `<value_expression>`
	`[, <solve_order_specification>]`
	`[, <member_property_definition>...]`

`<member_name>`	`<member>.<identifier>` `| <cube_name>.<member>.<identifier>`
`<solve_order_specification>`	`SOLVE_ORDER = <unsigned_integer>`
`<member_property_definition>`	`<identifier> = <value_expression>`
`<set_specification>`	`SET <set_name> AS <set>`
`<set_name>`	`<identifier> |` `<cube_name>.<identifier>`

Continued

TABLE D-1 THE MDX STATEMENT SYNTAX *(Continued)*

Statement Component	Defined As
`<axis_specification>`	`[NON EMPTY] <set> [<dim_props>] ON` `<axis_name>`

`<axis_name>`	`    COLUMNS`
	`  | ROWS`
	`  | PAGES`
	`  | CHAPTERS`
	`  | SECTIONS`
	`  | AXIS(<index>)`

`<dim_properties>`	`[DIMENSION] PROPERTIES <property>` `[, <property>...]`
`<cube_specification>`	`[<cube_name> [,<cube_name>...]]`
`<slicer_specification>`	`{<set> | <tuple>}`
`<cell_properties>`	`[CELL] PROPERTIES <cell_property> [,` `<cell_property>...]`

`<cell_property>`	`<mandatory_cell_property>`
	`| <optional_cell_property>`
	`| <provider_specific_cell_property>`

`<mandatory_cell_property>`	`CELL_ORDINAL | VALUE` `| FORMATTED_VALUE`

`<optional_cell_property>`	`FORMAT_STRING`
	`| FORE_COLOR`
	`| BACK_COLOR`
	`| FONT_NAME`
	`| FONT_SIZE`
	`| FONT_FLAGS`

`<provider_specific_` `cell_property>`	`<identifier>`
`<create_formula_statement>`	`CREATE` `[<scope>]<formula_specification>`
`<drop_formula_statement>`	`<drop_member_statement>` `| <drop_set_statement>`
`<drop_member_statement>`	`DROP MEMBER <member_name>` `[, <member_name>...]`

Statement Component	Defined As
`<drop_set_statement>`	`DROP SET <set_name>` `[, <set_name>...]`
`<scope>`	`GLOBAL	SESSION`

TABLE D-2 FORMAT STRING SPECIFIERS

Specifier	Description
@	Character placeholder for displaying a character or space at the position in the expression where the @ character appears.
&	Character placeholder for displaying a character or nothing at the position in the expression where the & character appears.
<	Displays characters in lowercase.
>	Displays characters in uppercase.
!	Forces a fill of placeholder from left to right instead of the default right to left.
0	Digit placeholder for displaying a digit or zero at the position in the expression where the 0 appears. When fewer digits are contained in the expression than there are zeros in the format specifier, leading or trailing zeros are displayed. When there are more digits to the right of the decimal than there are zeros to the right of the decimal in the format specifier, the number is rounded to the number of zeros in the specifier. When there are more digits to the left of the decimal than there are in the format specifier to the left of the decimal, the extra digits are displayed without formatting.
#	Digit placeholder for displaying a digit or nothing at the position in the expression where the # appears. When fewer digits are contained in the expression than there are # symbols in the format specifier, leading or trailing zeros are not displayed. When there are more digits to the right of the decimal than there are # symbols to the right of the decimal in the format specifier, the number is rounded to the number of # symbols in the specifier. When there are more digits to the left of the decimal than there are in the format specifier to the left of the decimal, the extra digits are displayed without formatting.

Continued

TABLE **D-2** **FORMAT STRING SPECIFIERS** *(Continued)*

Specifier	Description
.	Decimal placeholder that determines the number of digits displayed to the left and right of the decimal when used with the 0 and # specifiers.
%	Percentage placeholder causing the expression to be multiplied by 100 and displayed with a percent character where the % symbol appears in the specifier.
,	Thousand separator to separate thousands from hundreds where the numeric expression contains more than three digits to the left of the decimal. When two thousand separators appear adjacent to each other, the number is divided by 1,000 and the result displayed rounded.
:	Time separator separating hours, minutes, and seconds for time values.
/	Date separator separating day, month, and year for date values.
E- E+ e- e+	Scientific format specifier displaying the expression in scientific format when a digit placeholder appears to the right of the specifier character. The number of digit placeholders to the right of the specifier character determines the number of digits in the exponent. Use − or + where appropriate to display negative and positive exponents.
- + $ ( )	Displays a literal character in the formatted expression. Other characters may be displayed if preceded by a \ character or enclosed in double quotes.
\	Displays the character following the backslash as is. Use double backslash to display the \ character.
"string"	Displays the characters inside the double quotes as is. To specify this string in Visual Basic code, use Chr(34) in place of the double quotes.
C	Displays date in the format ddddd and time in the format ttttt.
D	Displays the day without a leading zero.
Dd	Displays the day with a leading zero.
Ddd	Displays the day name abbreviated.
Dddd	Displays the day name fully spelled.

Specifier	Description
Ddddd	Displays the complete date formatted according to the system short-date format.
Dddddd	Displays the date serial number formatted according to the system long-date format.
W	Displays the day of the week as a number starting with 1 for Sunday.
Ww	Displays the week of the year as a number.
M	Displays the month as a number without a leading zero.
Mm	Displays the month with a leading zero.
Mmm	Displays the month name abbreviated.
Mmmm	Displays the month name fully spelled.
Q	Displays the quarter as a number.
Y	Displays the day of the year as a number.
Yy	Displays the year as a two-digit number.
Yyyy	Displays the year as a four-digit number.
H	Displays the hour without a leading zero.
Hh	Displays the hour with a leading zero.
N	Displays the minute without a leading zero.
Nn	Displays the minute with a leading zero.
S	Displays the second without a leading zero.
Ss	Displays the second with a leading zero.
Ttttt	Displays the complete time.
AM/PM	Displays uppercase AM for hours before noon and after midnight. Displays uppercase PM after noon up to midnight.
am/pm	Displays lowercase am for hours before noon and after midnight. Displays lowercase pm after noon up to midnight.
A/P	Displays uppercase A for hours before noon and after midnight. Displays uppercase P after noon up to midnight.
a/p	Displays lowercase a four hours before noon and after midnight. Displays lowercase p after noon up to midnight.

Continued

TABLE D-2 FORMAT STRING SPECIFIERS *(Continued)*

Specifier	Description
AMPM	Displays AM string literal as defined by your system for hours before noon and after midnight. Displays the PM string literal as defined by your system after noon up to midnight. The case of the literal displayed is dependent on the system setting.

Appendix E

The ADO MD Object Model

The ADO MD Catalog Model

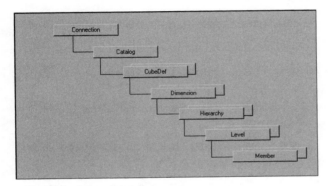

The ADO MD Cellset Model

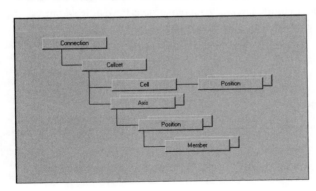

TABLE E-1 ADO MD OBJECTS

Object Name	Description
Axis (Axes Collection)	Contains a collection of tuples, each of which contains members selected from one or more dimensions.
Catalog	Contains the schema information for multidimensional structures.
Cell	The data at the intersection of axis coordinates in a cellset.
Cellset	A collection of cells resulting from a query.
Connection	An ADO connection open on a data source.
CubeDef (CubeDefs Collection)	The definition of a multidimensional structure containing dimensions and measures (also known as the measures dimension).
Dimension (Dimensions Collection)	Contains hierarchies of members at various levels by which measures are aggregated.
Hierarchy (Hierarchies Collection)	A parent-child relationship among levels by which measures are aggregated.
Level (Levels Collection)	A set of members in a hierarchy all of which have the same depth in the hierarchy. All dimensions have at least one hierarchy with at least one level.
Member (Members Collection)	A value associated with a dimension level.
Position (Positions Collection)	A coordinate of an axis containing a tuple of dimension members.

Appendix F

OLAP Services Specifications

TABLE F-1 SQL SERVER 7.0 OLAP SERVICES LIMITS

Item	Limit
Number of dimensions in a database	65,535
Number of levels in a database	65,535
Number of base cubes in a virtual cube	32
Number of measures in a cube	127
Number of dimensions in a cube	63
Number of levels in a cube	128
Number of levels in a dimension	64
Number of members in a virtual dimension	760
Number of members in a parent	64,000
Number of global calculated members in a cube	65,535
Number of session calculated members in a parent measure	32,700
Number of query calculated members in a parent measure	32,700
Number of session calculated members in a parent dimension	760
Number of query calculated members in a parent dimension	760
Number of aggregations per partition	65,535
Number of cells in a cellset returned by a query	2,147,483,647
Maximum record size for a source table	64 KB
Maximum length of object names not including dimension names	50 characters in OLAP server 24 characters in PivotTable service
Maximum length of dimension name	24 characters
Maximum length of aggregation prefix	22 characters

Appendix G

OLAP Services Function Reference

Table G-1 ARRAY, DIMENSION, HIERARCHY, LEVEL, AND LOGICAL FUNCTIONS

Category	Function Name	Syntax	Description
Array	SetToArray	**SetToArray** (<Set>[, <Set>]... [, <Numeric Expression>])	Converts Set arguments to an array. Number of dimensions in array equals number of sets. Array cell values are default members of Set or Numeric Expression.
Dimension	Dimension	<Hierarchy>.**Dimension** <Level>.**Dimension** <Member>.**Dimension**	Returns the dimension containing the specified Hierarchy, Level, or Member.
	Dimensions	**Dimensions** (<Numeric Expression>) **Dimensions** (<String Expression>)	Returns the dimension with position specified as Numeric Expression (zero-based) or Name.
Hierarchy	Hierarchy	<Level>.**Hierarchy** <Member>.**Hierarchy**	Returns the Level or Member hierarchy.
Level	Level	<Member>.**Level**	Returns the level associated with Member.
	Levels	<Dimension>.**Levels** (<Numeric Expression>) **Levels**(<String Expression>)	Returns the Level in Dimension with position specified as Numeric Expression (zero-based) or Name.
Logical	IsEmpty	**IsEmpty** (<Value Expression>)	Returns True if Expression is empty cell value.

TABLE G-2 MEMBER FUNCTIONS

Category	Function Name	Syntax	Description
Member	Ancestor	**Ancestor** (<Member>, <Level>)	Returns the ancestor of Member at Level.
	ClosingPeriod	**ClosingPeriod** ([<Level>[, <Member>]])	Returns the last sibling in the descendants of Level or Level Member.
	Cousin	**Cousin** (<Member1>, <Member2>)	Returns the member under Member2 with the same relative position as Member1.
	CurrentMember	<Dimension>. **CurrentMember**	Returns the member at current position in Dimension during an iteration.
	DefaultMember	<Dimension>. **DefaultMember**	Returns the dimension's default member.
	FirstChild	<Member>.**FirstChild**	Returns the first child of a member.
	FirstSibling	<Member>.**FirstSibling**	Returns the first child of a member's parent.
	Item	<Tuple>.**Item** (<Numeric Expression>)	Returns a member from a tuple.
	Lag	<Member>.**Lag** (<Numeric Expression>)	Returns a member that is <Numeric Expression> positions prior to the specified member along the member's dimension.
	LastChild	<Member>.**LastChild**	Returns the last child of a member.
	LastSibling	<Member>.**LastSibling**	Returns the last child of a member's parent.
	Lead	<Member>.**Lead** (<Numeric Expression>)	Returns a member that is <Numeric Expression> positions after the specified member along the member's dimension.

Category	Function Name	Syntax	Description
Member *(continued)*	Members	**Members** (<String Expression>)	Returns the member with name specified by <String Expression>.
	NextMember	<Member>**.NextMember**	Returns the next member at the same level as the specified member.
	OpeningPeriod	**OpeningPeriod** ([<Level>[, <Member>]])	Returns the first sibling among the descendants of a member at the specified level.
	ParallelPeriod	**ParallelPeriod** ([<Level>[, <Numeric Expression>[, <Member>]]])	Returns a member from a prior period in the same relative position as the specified member.
	Parent	<Member>**.Parent**	Returns the member's parent.
	PrevMember	<Member>**.PrevMember**	Returns the previous member at the same level as the specified member.
	ValidMeasure	**ValidMeasure**(<Tuple>)	Returns a valid measure in a virtual cube.

TABLE G-3 NUMERIC FUNCTIONS

Category	Function Name	Syntax	Description
Numeric	Aggregate	**Aggregate** (<Set>[, <Numeric Expression>])	Returns a calculated value using an aggregate function.
	Avg	**Avg** (<Set>[, <Numeric Expression>])	Returns the average of Numeric Expression over a set.

Continued

TABLE **G-3** **NUMERIC FUNCTIONS** *(Continued)*

Category	Function Name	Syntax	Description
Numeric *(continued)*	CoalesceEmpty	**CoalesceEmpty** (<Numeric Expression> [, <Numeric Expression>]...)	Coalesces an empty value to a Numeric Expression.
	Correlation	**Correlation** (<Set>, <Numeric Expression> [, <Numeric Expression>])	Returns the correlation of two series over a set.
	Count	**Count** (<Set> [, EXCLUDEEMPTY | INCLUDEEMPTY])	Counts the tuples in a set. EXCLUDEEMPTY eliminates empty cells from the count.
	Covariance	**Covariance** (<Set>, <Numeric Expression>[, <Numeric Expression>])	Returns the covariance (biased) of two series over a set.
	CovarianceN	**CovarianceN** (<Set>, <Numeric Expression>[, <Numeric Expression>])	Returns the covariance (unbiased) of two series over a set.
	IIF	**IIf** (<Logical Expression>, <Numeric Expression1>, <Numeric Expression2>)	Returns Numeric Expression1 if Logical Expression is TRUE; otherwise, returns Numeric Expression2.
	LinRegIntercept	**LinRegIntercept** (<Set>, <Numeric Expression>[, <Numeric Expression>])	Calculates the linear regression of a set and returns b in regression line y = ax + b.
	LinRegPoint	**LinRegPoint** (<Numeric Expression>, <Set>, <Numeric Expression> [, <Numeric Expression>])	Calculates the linear regression of a set and returns y in regression line y = ax + b.
	LinRegR2	**LinRegR2** (<Set>,	Calculates the linear regression of a set and

Category	Function Name	Syntax	Description
Numeric *(continued)*		<Numeric Expression>[, <Numeric Expression>])	returns the coefficient of determination R^2.
	LinRegSlope	**LinRegSlope** (<Set>, <Numeric Expression> [, <Numeric Expression>])	Calculates the linear regression of a set and returns a in the regression line y = ax + b.
	LinRegVariance	**LinRegVariance** (<Set>, <Numeric Expression>[, <Numeric Expression>])	Calculates the linear regression of a set and returns the variance associated with the regression line y = ax + b.
	Max	**Max** (<Set>[, <Numeric Expression>])	Returns the maximum of Numeric Expression over a set.
	Median	**Median** (<Set>[, <Numeric Expression>])	Returns the median of Numeric Expression over a set.
	Min	**Min** (<Set>[, <Numeric Expression>])	Returns the minimum of Numeric Expression over a set.
	Ordinal	<Level>.**Ordinal**	Returns the ordinal for the specified level. Ordinals are zero-based.
	Rank	**Rank**(<Tuple>, <Set>)	Returns the rank of a Tuple in Set. Rank is one-based.
	Stddev	**Stddev** (<Set>[, <Numeric Expression>])	Returns the standard deviation (unbiased) of Numeric Expression over Set.
	StddevP	**StddevP** (<Set>[, <Numeric Expression>])	Returns standard deviation (biased) of Numeric Expression over Set.
	Stdev	**Stdev** (<Set>[, <Numeric Expression>])	Same as Stddev.

Continued

TABLE G-3 NUMERIC FUNCTIONS *(Continued)*

Category	Function Name	Syntax	Description
Numeric *(continued)*	StdevP	StdevP (<Set>[, <Numeric Expression>])	Same as StddevP.
	Sum	Sum (<Set>[, <Numeric Expression>])	Returns the sum of Numeric Expression over Set.
	Value	<Measure>.**Value**	Returns the value of the specified measure.
	Var	Var (<Set>[, <Numeric Expression>])	Returns the variance (unbiased) of Numeric Expression over Set.
	Variance	Variance (<Set>[, <Numeric Expression>])	Same as Var.
	VarianceP	VarianceP (<Set>[, <Numeric Expression>])	Same as VarP.
	VarP	VarP (<Set>[, <Numeric Expression>])	Returns the variance (biased) of Numeric Expression over Set.

TABLE G-4 SET FUNCTIONS

Category	Function Name	Syntax	Description
Set	AddCalculated-Members	**AddCalculatedMembers** (<Set>)	Adds calculated members to Set.
	BottomCount	**BottomCount** (<Set>, <Count>[, <Numeric Expression>])	Returns the bottom Count items from a Set ordered by Numeric Expression.

Category	Function Name	Syntax	Description
Set *(continued)*	BottomPercent	**BottomPercent** (<Set>, <Percentage>, <Numeric Expression>)	Returns the bottom items whose total is at least Percentage of all items in Set ordered by Numeric Expression.
	BottomSum	**BottomSum** (<Set>, <Value>, <Numeric Expression>)	Returns the bottom items in Set whose sum is at least Value. The Set is ordered by Numeric Expression.
	Children	<Member>.**Children**	Returns the children of the specified member.
	Crossjoin	**Crossjoin** (<Set1>, <Set2>)	Returns the cross product of two sets.
	Descendants	**Descendants** (<Member>, <Level>[, <Desc_flag>])	Returns the descendants of a Member at the specified Level. Descendants from other levels can be included/excluded using Desc_flag.
	Distinct	**Distinct** (<Set>)	Eliminates duplicate tuples from Set.
	DrilldownLevel	**DrilldownLevel** (<Set>[, <Level>]) or **DrilldownLevel** (<Set>, <Index>)	Drills down the members of Set at the specified Level to one level below or drills down on a specified dimension in the Set.
	DrilldownLevel Bottom	**DrilldownLevelBottom** (<Set>, <Count>[, [<Level>][, <Numeric Expression>]])	Drills down the bottom Count members of Set at the specified Level to one level below.
	DrilldownLevel Top	**DrilldownLevelTop** (<Set>, <Count>[, [<Level>][, <Numeric Expression>]])	Drills down the top Count members of Set at the specified Level to one level below.

Continued

TABLE **G-4** **SET FUNCTIONS** *(Continued)*

Category	Function Name	Syntax	Description
Set *(continued)*	Drilldown Member	**DrilldownMember** (<Set1>, <Set2>[, RECURSIVE])	Drills down the members in Set1 that are present in Set2.
	Drilldown MemberBottom	**DrilldownMemberBottom** (<Set1>, <Set2>, <Count>[, [<Numeric Expression>][, RECURSIVE]])	Drills down the bottom Count child members in Set1 that are present in Set2.
	Drilldown MemberTop	**DrilldownMemberTop** (<Set1>, <Set2>, <Count>[, [<Numeric Expression>][, RECURSIVE]])	Drills down the top Count child members in Set1 that are present in Set2.
	DrillupLevel	**DrillupLevel** (<Set>[, <Level>])	Drills up the members of Set that are below the specified Level.
	DrillupMember	**DrillupMember** (<Set1>, <Set2>)	Drills up the members in Set1 that are present in Set2.
	Except	**Except** (<Set1>, <Set2>[, ALL])	Finds the difference between two sets.
	Extract	**Extract** (<Set>, <Dimension>[, <Dimension>...])	Returns a Set of tuples extracted from specified dimensions. This function is the opposite of Crossjoin.
	Filter	**Filter** (<Set>, <Search Condition>)	Returns a set resulting from filtering Set on Search Condition.
	Generate	**Generate** (<Set1>, <Set2>[, ALL])	Returns a set resulting from joining each member of Set1 with each member of Set2.
	Head	**Head** (<Set>[, < Numeric Expression >])	Returns the first Numeric Expression number of elements from Set.

Category	Function Name	Syntax	Description
Set *(continued)*	Hierarchize	**Hierarchize** (<Set>)	Orders the members of Set into a hierarchy.
	Intersect	**Intersect** (<Set1>, <Set2>[, ALL])	Returns the intersection of two sets.
	LastPeriods	**LastPeriods** (<Index>[, <Member>])	Returns a set of members prior to and including the specified member.
	Members	<Dimension>.**Members** <Hierarchy>.**Members** <Level>.**Members**	Returns the set of members in the specified dimension, Hierarchy, or Level.
	Mtd	**Mtd** ([<Member>])	PeriodsToDate function at the month level.
	Order	**Order** (<Set>, {<String Expression> | <Numeric Expression>}[, ASC | DESC | BASC | BDESC])	Arranges members of Set into specified order.
	PeriodsToDate	**PeriodsToDate** ([<Level>[, <Member>]])	Returns a set of members from the specified Level starting with the first period and ending with the specified Member.
	Qtd	**Qtd** ([<Member>])	PeriodsToDate function at the quarter level.
	StripCalculated Members	**StripCalculatedMembers** (<Set>)	Removes calculated members from a set.
	StrToSet	**StrToSet** (<String Expression>)	Constructs a set from String Expression.
	Subset	**Subset** (<Set>, <Start>[, <Count>])	Returns Count elements from Set starting with Start element.
	Tail	**Tail** (<Set>[, <Count>])	Returns Count elements from the end of Set.

Continued

TABLE G-4 SET FUNCTIONS *(Continued)*

Category	Function Name	Syntax	Description
Set *(continued)*	ToggleDrillState	ToggleDrillState (<Set1>, <Set2>[, RECURSIVE])	Toggles the drill state of members up or down. Combines DrillupMember and DrilldownMember.
	TopCount	TopCount (<Set>, <Count>[, <Numeric Expression>])	Returns Count items from the top of Set which is ordered by Numeric Expression.
	TopPercent	TopPercent (<Set>, <Percentage>, <Numeric Expression>)	Returns the top number of items from the ordered Set whose total is at least a specified Percentage.
	TopSum	TopSum (<Set>, <Value>, <Numeric Expression>)	Returns the top number of items from the ordered Set whose sum is at least a specified Value.
	Union	Union (<Set1> <Set2>[, ALL])	Returns the union of two sets.
	Visual;Totals	VisualTotals (<Set>, <Pattern>)	Dynamically totals child members in Set using a Pattern for the total label in the result set.
	Wtd	Wtd ([<Member>])	PeriodsToDate function at the week level.
	Ytd	Ytd ([<Member>])	PeriodsToDate function at the year level.

TABLE G-5 **STRING AND TUPLE FUNCTIONS**

Category	Function Name	Syntax	Description
String	CoalesceEmpty	**CoalesceEmpty** (<String Expression>[, <String Expression>]...)	Coalesces an empty cell into String Expression.
	IIIf	**IIf** (<Logical Expression>, <String Expression1>, <String Expression2>)	Returns String Expression1 if Logical Expression is TRUE; otherwise, returns String Expression2.
	Name	«Dimension».**Name** «Hierarchy».**Name** «Level».**Name** «Member».**Name**	Returns the name property value of the specified Dimension, Hierarchy, Level, or Member.
	SetToStr	**SetToStr** (<Set>)	Builds a string from the specified Set.
	TupleToStr	**TupleToStr** (<Tuple>)	Builds a string from the specified Tuple.
	UniqueName	<Dimension>.**UniqueName** <Level>.**UniqueName** <Member>.**UniqueName**	Returns the unique name of the specified Dimension, Level, or Member.
Tuple	Current	<Set>.**Current**	Returns the current tuple from Set during an iteration.
	Item	<Set>.**Item** (<String Expression>[, <String Expression>...] | <Index>)	Returns a tuple specified by String Expression or Index from the specified Set.
	StrToTuple	**StrToTuple** (<String Expression>)	Builds a tuple from the specified String Expression.

Index

A

access control
  cell-level, 191–193
  enabling, 189
  role privileges, 99
access control lists (ACLs), 189
Access 97 repository, migrating from, 109
Accounts dimension table, 25
  populating, 30
Accounts table, 22
ActiveConnection property, 114
  setting, 114–115, 120
ActiveScriptTask objects, 276
ActiveX Data Objects. *See* ADO
ActiveX Data Objects Multidimensional. *See* ADO MD
ActiveX DLL project, creating, 201
add-ins
  creating, 201. *See also* Property Inspector
  error values, 209
  extension, 196
  OLAP Manager, 195–196
  registering, 209
  Registry key values for, 273
  standalone, 196
AddCalculatedMembers function, 265
AddExistingAggregation method, 186
AddGoalQuery method, 187
Addins key, 273
AddNew method, 84
administrator privileges, 189
ADO, 19, 112–113
ADO MD, 19, 112–113
  cellsets, 119–124
  object model, 111–113
  OLAP Catalog, 113–119
ADODB library, DataTypeEnum enumeration, 173
Aggregate function, 264
AggregateFunction property, 174
AggregatesTypes enumerator, 103
aggregation tables, 90–91
AggregationDimension object, 184
aggregations, 3
  adding to collections, 186
  calculating on the fly, 95
  dimensions in, 184
  duplications of, 77
  estimated storage reaches, 55

in hierarchies, 9
of partitions, 183–188
performance gain reaches, 55
precalculated, 7–9
prefixes for, 198
storage of, 69
temporary, 252
Until I click stop option, 55
for virtual dimensions, 62, 225
Aggregations Options screen, 54
"All" level, 11
All member, as default, 145
analysis
  of partition aggregations, 186
  and virtual dimensions, 225–226
  what-if, 230, 239
analysis databases, 8
Ancestor function, 220
ancestor members, 212
Archive and Restore Databases Add-In, 198–200
archive files, 198–199
array functions, 153
authentication, 189
Average Investment calculation, 129, 149
  CoalesceEmpty function, 130
  filtering data for, 132
  formatting result, 150
  null values, counting, 130
  query scope, 150–151
Avg function, 128, 264
  Amount measure, 149
  arguments to, 149
  for Average Investment calculation, 131
axes
  index mapping for, 144
  in MDX statements, 144
  NON EMPTY specification, 224
  number of positions on, 121
  slicer, 145
  specifying, 120–121
  tuples in, 147
axes collection, 19
axes points
  correlation between, 262
  covariance of, 262–263
  linear regression of, 263
axes positions, 121–122
axis objects, 19

B

BackgroundInterval setting, 252
biased population formula, 262, 264
BottomCount function, 215
BottomPercent function, 215
BottomSum function, 216
BulkInsertTask objects, 277
Business Office level, members of, 212

C

CAB files, 200
caches
  WITH clause, specifying with, 151–152
  creating, 133–134
  Read-Ahead buffer size, 252
  scope of, 128
Calculated Member Builder, 63–65
Calculated Member Manager Add-In, 196–198
calculated members, 10, 63–65
  WITH clause, specifying with, 148–150
  creating, 128–130, 197
  current values, referencing, 132
  editing, 197
  Expression property, 118
  format string, 150
  importing, 198
  including in set, 265
  naming scheme for, 75
  query, dependence on, 131–132
  query scope, 150–151
  scope of, 128
  solve order specification, 150
  time series functions in, 262
Caption property, 117
Catalog objects, 19
  ActiveConnection property, 114
catalogs
  closing connection to, 115
  schema of, 115–119
CD-ROM (accompanying)
  aggregation dimensions code, 184
  Assign Aggregations button, 181
  ClientAdjustment function, 156
  COMPUTE and GROUP BY clause scripts, 14
  Create Local Cube sample, 138

349

Continued

CD-ROM *(continued)*
Create Roles button, 190
CREATE TABLE script, 25
CREATE TABLE statement
scripts, 23
drilling operations example,
259–261
DSO Inspector application, 247
DTSPackage folder, 135
File name: text box, 31
FundAccts database, 21
FundAcctsWH warehouse, 21
incremental update script,
74–75
Investment fact table, queries
against, 133
key values, 273
MDX statements samples,
143–144
Process Partitions button,
184–186
Property Inspector project, 267
Register User-Defined Functions
button, 154
role code, 190
Show Aggregations button, 184
Show Commands button, 188
simple MDX query, 120–121
SourceTableFilter code, 183
cells, 10–11, 19
access control for, 191–193
coordinate members, displaying,
122
empty. *See* empty cells
FormattedValue property, 122
positions collection, 122
retrieving, 121–122
Value property, 122
cellset Close method, 123
cellset Item method, 121–123
Cellset objects, 19
ActiveConnection property, 114
closing connection to, 115
cellset Open method, Source
argument, 121
cellset Source property, assigning
into recordset Source
property, 127
cellsets, 113, 119–124, 144
closing, 123–124
connections of, 120
creating, 119–124
data, viewing, 260
navigating, 122–123
opening, 120–121
releasing memory, 123
retrieving cells in, 121–122
ChangeDatabase function, 250

changes, update methods for, 70–71
charts, 236–237
type selection, 239
child members, 212–213
totaling, 265
Children property, 118
ClassName value, 273
ClassType property, 84
ClassTypes enumerator, 106–107
ClientAdjustment function, 156
CloneOptions enumerator, 106
clsAggregation objects, 85, 90
properties of, inspecting, 249
clsAggregationDimension objects
iterating, 91–92
Levels collection, 92, 94
clsAggregationLevels object, 95
clsAggregationMeasure objects, 97
clsCube Dimensions collection, 89
clsCube object, 86, 98
properties of, inspecting, 249
clsCubeAnalyzer class, 101
clsCubeCommand class, 188
clsCubeCommand collection, 98
clsCubeLevel object, 95
clsCubeRole objects, 99
clsDatabase Dimensions
collection, 89
clsDatabase object, 98
properties of, inspecting, 249
clsDatabase objects, 85
clsDatabaseCommand collection, 98
clsDatabaseLevels object, 95
clsDatabaseRole objects, 99
clsDatasource class, 101
clsMemberProperty class, 101
clsPartition objects, 90
clsPartitionAnalyzer class, 101
clsPartitionLevels object, 95
clsPartitionMeasure objects, 97
clsServer class, 101
clsServer object, 159–165
methods of, 160
clsServer.State property,
enumerations of, 161
cnn object, 114
CoalesceEmpty function, 130, 224
coefficient of determination, 263
collections, repository storage,
108–109
colon operator, 221
column, mappings between, 35
Column objects, 277
Columns objects, 277
ColumnType property, 173
COM interfaces, 195–196
Command interface, 85, 97–99
class properties, 99

commands, 188–189
CommandTypes enumerator, 102
complete processing, 75, 79–80
COMPUTE clause, 7, 14–17
conditional MDX expressions,
222–223
Connection objects, 277
Close method, 115
connecting to OLAP server
with, 113–114
Connection Properties page, 31–33
Connection property, 251
connection status, 161
Connections objects, 277
ConnectionString property,
113–114, 251
ContainedClassType property, 85
Copy and Paste Objects Add-In, 198
correlation coefficient, 263
Correlation function, 262
Count function, 224, 264
Cousin function, 220
cousin members, 212
Covariance function, 262–263
CPUs, thread allocation, 253
CREATE CACHE statement,
133–134
CREATE CUBE statement, 134–139
CREATE MEMBER statement,
128–129
CREATE statement, 148
CreateProcessTask objects, 277
Crossjoin function, 217
Cube Browser, 56–60
drilling down in hierarchies,
58–59
filtering measures with, 59–60
cube commands, 188–189
Cube Editor, 50–53
Calculated Members node, 64
cube-level member properties, 101
Cube Manager, adding dimensions
to grid with, 60
CUBE query, 81
Cube Wizard, 44–50
CubeDef Dimensions collection, 116
cubedef objects, 19
CubeDef Properties collection, 116
CubeDefs collection, 115–116
cubes, 3, 7, 84. *See also* local cubes
access restrictions, 99
browsing, 56–60
building, 44–50
complete processing of, 72–73
copying and pasting, 198
counts as measures in, 133
creating, in Excel, 240–243
dimensions, adding, 50–52

dimensions, creating, 45–48
dimensions, sharing, 47–48
dimensions of, 9–10
Excel access to, 233
fact table specification, 44
local versus server-based, 134, 139
navigating. *See* drilling operations
partitioning, 12–13. *See also* partitions
rebuilding, 79–80
role definition, 52–53
roles of, 189. *See also* Roles collection
security for, 189–193
storage for, 53–55
storage modes, 12–13
synchronizing with data warehouse, 68, 79–80
time relations, 221–222
virtual, 12
write-enabled, 166–167, 230–231
curly braces, as set delimiters, 131
CurrentMember function, 220
CurrentNode.LinkedObject property, 272

D

data
  drilling through, 58–59, 256–258
  transferring. *See* DTS
  for warehouses, 4
data buffer, size of, 252
data definition language. *See* DDL
Data Driven Query properties dialog box, 34
  Destination tab, 34
  Options tab, 36–37
  Queries tab, 36
  Transformations tab, 35–36
Data Link Properties dialog box, 43
data mappings, 4–5
  selecting type, 35
data points, 10
Data Pumps, 276
Data Source= parameter, 113–114
data sources, specifying, 43–44
data transfers. *See also* DTS
  with DTS Export Wizard, 25–30, 279–281
  with DTS Import Wizard, 278–279
Data Transformation Services. *See* DTS

Data Transformation Services folder, 31
Data Transformation Services Task Kit, 275, 283–285
data warehouses, 4–5
  defined, 4
  queries to, 3, 132
  schema of, 4–7
  synchronizing with cubes, 68, 79–80
  updating method, 70–71
database files, directory for, 253
database member properties, 101
database objects, 85. *See also* OLAP databases
DataDrivenQueryTask objects, 276
DataPumpTask objects, 277
datasets, 144
DataSource object, Connection property, 251
DataTypeEnum enumeration, 173
DDL, 143
  PivotTable Service support of, 127–128
debugging add-ins, 273–274
Decision Support Objects. *See* DSO
Depth property, 117
descendant members, 212–213
Description value, 273
DesignedAggregations collection, 186
destination connections, designing, 33–35
detail data, 8
Dimension Editor, members and properties, viewing, 61
dimension functions, 153
Dimension interface, 85, 89–94
  class properties, 93–94
dimension levels, collections and properties of, 101
Dimension objects, 116
  Hierarchies collection, 117
dimension properties, accessing, 157–158
dimension structure, rebuilding, 284–285
dimension tables, indexes on, 68
Dimension Wizard, 45–48
DimensionAddUsageTypes enumerator, 103
dimensions, 9–10. *See also* shared dimensions
  accessing, 6
  adding to cubes, 50–52
  adding to grid, 60
  in aggregations, 184
  (All) level in, 94

copying and pasting, 198
creating, 45–48, 168–172
defining, 45–46
DSO storage of, 89
hierarchies in, 89, 94, 212
members of, 212
private, 10, 47–48, 90, 172
shared, 10, 47–48, 90
slicer, 145–146
storage of, 69
type specification, 47
virtual, 10–11, 61–63
DimensionTypes enumerator, 103
Distinct function, 216
Dividends cube
  creating, with DSO, 167–174
  creating, with PivotTable Service, 135–139
Dividends fact table, 135
DrillDownLevel function, 258
DrillDownLevelTop function, 258
DrillDownMember function, 256, 260–261
DrillDownMemberTop function, 257
drilling operations, 256–258
  Cube Browser, 58–59
  displaying, 260
  sample operation, 259–261
DrillUpLevel function, 258
DrillUpMember function, 257
DROP statement, 133
DSO, 18
  cube creation with, 167–174
  dimension storage, 89
  in-process server DLL, 86
  interfaces of, 85
  lock types, 166
  MDStore interface, 85–88
  overview, 84–85
  partitions, creating, 180–181
  partitions, merging with, 181–183
  repository for, 19
  role creation, 190
  virtual cubes and dimensions, creating, 229
DSO enumerations, 102–107
  AggregatesTypes, 103
  ClassTypes, 106–107
  CloneOptions, 106
  CommandTypes, 102
  DimensionAddUsageTypes, 103
  DimensionTypes, 103
  ErrorCodes, 104–106
  LevelTypes, 102
  OlapClassTypes, 107
  OlapEditions, 103
Continued

DSO enumerations *(continued)*
   OlapStorageModes, 107
   OrderTypes, 102
   ProcessTypes, 107
   ServerStates, 106
   SubClassTypes, 107
   SupportLevels, 103
   ValidateErrorCodes, 103–104
DSO1 form, 249, 267, 271
DSO model
   hierarchy forms, 249–251
   property list box, 248, 250
DSO repository, 108–109
dsoClassTypesMap collection, 248
DSOInspector DLL, 247, 267–268
DSSAddInsManager library, 201
DTS, 5, 25, 275–278
   objects in, 276–277
DTS Export Wizard, 25–30,
   279–281
DTS Import Wizard, 278–279
DTS Package Designer, 30–39, 283
dtsrun utility, 282–283
dtswiz utility, 281–282

E

empty cells, 130
   averaging, 264
   counting, 264
   replacing value in, 224
   testing for, 224
   working around, 223–224
Enterprise Manager, 195
enumeration values, 102–107
Equal allocation, 240, 242
ErrDSSAddInErrorNumbers
   enumeration, 209
ErrorCodes enumeration, 104–106,
   162–165
errors, in large packages, 36
Excel, 233
   cube creation in, 240–243
   OLAP@Work for, 238–240
   PivotTable creation, 233–236
Excel function library, OLAP
   Services support of, 63
Except function, 149, 217
Execute method, 129
ExecuteMenuItem method, 203
   coding, 271
ExecuteSQLTask objects, 277
Executing Package dialog box,
   package run status, 38
exporting data, 25–30, 279–281
   authentication method for, 28
   destination specification, 27–28

query statement specification,
   26–27
type of copy specification,
   26–27
Expression property, 118
Extract function, 217
extraction, 5

F

fact tables, 5–6
   equi-joins between, 14–17
   indexes on, 68
   measures in, 9
   numeric measures
     representation, 97
field names, construction of, 127
field values, accessing by field
   name, 127
FillView function, 260
Filter function, 151, 216
FilterAxis property, 146
filters
   for measures, 59–60
   for partitions, 178
   for sets, 150–151
   slicer dimensions, 145–146
Find method, 84
FirstChild function, 219
FirstSibling function, 219–220
Flattened Dataset button, 127
flattening
   with MDX, 127–128
   with SQL, 124–127
foreign keys. *See also* fundacctno
   key; fund_cd key
   in fact tables, 6–7
   referential integrity,
     verifying, 68
format string, 150
function libraries
   Command interface
     references, 98
   registering, 63, 154
   unregistering, 157
functions, 152–153
   built-in, 153
   categories of, 153
   referencing, 155–156
   user-defined, 154–157
Fund dimension, 63
   Age property, 11
   "All" level, 11
   creating, 48
FundAccounts table, 22
fundacctno column, 22
fundacctno key, 22
FundAccts database, 21–23

data warehouse for, 23–25
exporting query results from,
   25–30
FundAcctSample database, 42
   virtual dimensions in, 225
FundAcctsWH Connection, 172
FundAcctsWH database,
   Investments fact table, 6
FundAcctsWH warehouse, 23–25
   destination connection to,
     33–35
   investment types, 24
   schema, 24
fund_age column, 25
   source of, 30
FundAge dimension, 60–61
   creating, 62–63
FundAgeUpdate package, 31
fund_cd key, 22
Funds dimension, 11
   fact table, joins to, 14
Funds dimension table, 25
   populating, 30

G

Generate function, 149, 218
GetClassTypes routine, 248
GetConnectionProps function, 251
GetDatabaseList function, 250
GetDataSourceProps function, 251
GetObject method, 203
GetRegSettings function, 252
GetServerProps function, 249–250
GlobalVariable objects, 277
GlobalVariables objects, 277
GoalQuery property, 186–187
grid
   adding dimensions to, 60
   filling values, 260
GROUP BY statement, 7, 14–17, 81
   PivotTable Service support of,
     125

H

hierarchies, 9
   "All" level, 11
   drilling down in, 58–59
Hierarchize function, 214–215
hierarchy functions, 153
Hierarchy objects
   Caption property, 117
   Depth property, 117
   Levels collection of, 117–118
   properties of, 117
HighMemoryLimit setting, 253
historical view, of warehouse, 70–71
Hybrid OLAP (HOLAP), 12–13, 69

I

IIF expression, 222–223
importing data, 278–279
IncludeEmpty argument, 224
incremental updates, 72, 74–78, 284–285
   recovering from, 77–78
   results of, 76–77
   running, 76
indexes, for fact and dimension tables, 68
Initial Catalog= parameter, 113–114
Initialize routine, 247–248, 268
InitializeDesign method, 186
INSERT INTO statement, 136–138
   ATTEMPT_DATA clause, 139
   DEFER_DATA clause, 138–139
   options of, 138–139
   PASSTHROUGH clause, 138
Insert menu, Tables, 50
Inspector, 247–248
   connection properties, inspecting, 251
   hierarchy forms in, 249–251
   methods in, 248
   object variables, initializing, 251
   property values, zooming, 251
   registry settings, inspecting, 252–253
   server connection, 248
Inspector class, 268
Intersect function, 216–217
Investments cube
   AgeOfFund virtual dimension, adding, 226
   aggregation tables in, 90
   calculated member for, 129
   command objects, 98–99
   commands of, 188–189
   library registration for, 154–155
   MDX statement for, 144–145
   member order, 213–214
   partitions for, 90, 176–179
   Read permission for values, 192
   referential integrity, 68
   write-enabling, 230–231
Investments fact table, 44
   foreign key for, 24
   importing query results to, 25–30
InvestUpdate table, 78
InvSummary table, 22
IOlapAddIn interface, 201, 268
   enumerations, 207–209
   implementing, 202–209
   methods of, 202–204
   Name property, 202
   objects and collections, 204–206
IsEmpty function, 132, 224
IsTemporary property, 167
Item function, 218–219

K

keys
   for add-ins, 273
   for menu items, 269

L

LastChild function, 219
LastPeriods function, 221–222
LastSibling function, 219–220
Lead function, 220
level functions, 153
Level interface, 85, 94–96
   class properties, 95–96
Level objects, Members collection of, 118–119
levels
   default members of, 145
   drilling operations, 258
   members of, 212
   time periods in, 221–222
Levels collection, properties of, 117–118
LevelType property, 174
LevelTypes enumerator, 102
libraries. *See* function libraries
LinRegIntercept function, 263
LinRegPoint function, 263
LinRegR2 function, 263
LinRegSlope function, 263
LinRegVariance function, 263
listener thread, wakeup interval for, 252
LoadClassTypesMap routine, 248
local cubes. *See also* cubes
   aggregations, on-the-fly, 139
   connecting to, 114
   creating, 134–139
   creating, from PivotTable, 241
   populating, 136–138
   scope of, 128
   storage mode, specifying, 138
   structure of, 136
   for what-if analyses, 240
locking, 165–167
LockObject method, 166–167
logical functions, 153
Lookups objects, 277
LowMemoryLimit setting, 252
lstProps list box, 250
   zooming property values in, 251

M

maintaining user state, 260
maintenance plan, 70–71
MakeServerConnection function, 87, 160, 248
Manager dimension
   creating, 52
   members of, 212
Manager role, 189
manager_num column, 22
Managers dimension table, 24
   populating, 30
Managers table, 22
Map The Column dialog box, 50–51
Max function, 264
MDStores collection, 84–85
MDStores interface, 85–88
   class properties, 88
MDX, 120, 143–147, 211–212
   conditional expressions, 222–223
   conditional functions, 222–223
   data drilling functions, 256–258
   and empty cells, 223–224
   flattened queries, 126–127
   member expressions, 219–220
   sample application, 11
   set expressions, 147, 212–219
   simple query, 120–121, 125
   time series functions, 221–222
   tuple expressions, 212–219
Measure interface, 85, 96–97
   class properties, 97
measures, 9
   aggregation type, 174
   filtering, 59–60
measures dimension, 10
   and CREATE CACHE statement, 133
Median function, 264
MEMBER clause
   property identification, 150
   solve order specification, 150
member functions, 153
Member objects, Properties collection of, 118
members, 9–10, 211
   adding, 81
   addressing, 218–219
   ancestor, 220
   calculated. *See* calculated members
   child, 219
   ChildCount property, 118
   cousin, 220
   current, 220
   drilling operations, 256–258
      Continued

members *(continued)*
  dropping, 133
  hierarchizing, 214–215
  input, 10, 63
  LevelDepth property, 118
  LevelName property, 118
  ordering, 213–214
  parallel time periods in, 222
  parent, 219
  previous, 219
  properties, accessing, 157–158
  properties, defining, 60–61
  properties of, 10–11
  referring to, 219–220
  siblings, 219–220
  time periods in, 221–222
  Type property, 118–119
Members collection, 118–119
menu items
  adding and removing, 205
  coding, 268–270
  enumerating, 207
  flags for, 269
  mode values, 208
  processing commands, 203
  providing, 202–203
menus
  for nodes, 272
  popup, 270
merging partitions, 175
metadata
  archiving, 199
  copying and pasting, 198
  inspection of, 267
Microsoft Data Shaping Service, 113
Microsoft Excel. *See* Excel
Microsoft Management Console (MMC), 195
  COM interfaces, 195–196
  snap-ins, 17
  snap-ins, adding, 42
Min function, 264
modal forms, 267
MOLAP, 69
  for local cube storage, 134, 139
MsgBox statements, for debugging, 274
msmdarch.exe program, 199–200
msmdrep.mdb database, 19
msmdrep.mdb file, 108
multidimensional data. *See also* cubes
  PivotTable Service support of, 111–124
multidimensional expressions. *See* MDX

Multidimensional OLAP (MOLAP), 12–13
mutual fund account database. *See* FundAccts database

N
Name value, 273
named sets, 131
Navigate Cellset button, 126–127
Net Asset Value (NAV), 128
NextAnalysisStep method, 186
NextMember function, 219
nodes, 272
NON EMPTY specifier, 144
NONNULLAMOUNTS set, 132
  query scope, 151
null values
  counting, 130
  for security rules, 192
numeric functions, 153, 264–265
  cube as context of, 132
  and empty cells, 224
  and null values, 130

O
Object Transfer tasks, 276
objects
  direct-access, 101
  locking, 165–167
  metadata storage, 108
  properties of, listing, 250
  temporary, 167
ObjList form, 250
office_num column, 23
Offices dimension
  creating, 50–51
  drilling down in, 58–59
  hierarchy of, 211–212
Offices dimension table, 24–25
  populating, 38–39
Offices table, 23
office_type column, 23
OLAP Add-In Manager, 268
  Registry key, 209
OLAP Add-In Manager Kit, 196
  Archive and Restore Databases Add-In, 198–200
  Calculated Member Manager Add-In, 196–198
  Copy and Paste Objects Add-In, 198
OLAP Add-In Manager library, 201
OLAP Administrators group, 159, 189
OLAP databases, 84
  archiving, 198–200

creating, 42–43
cubes, browsing, 56–60
cubes, building, 44–50
cubes, editing, 50–53
data source specification, 43–44
populating, 56
properties of, 249–250
restoring, 200
storage mode specification, 53–55
OLAP Manager, 17, 195
  add-ins for, 195–196
  Cube Browser, 56–60
  Cube Wizard, 44–50
  integrating with SQL Server Enterprise Manager, 41
  Merge Partitions screen, 179–180
  partitions, merging in, 179–180
  Registry settings, editing with, 253
  shortcut to, 42
  starting, 41–42
  tree view, 18, 201–209
  user interface, 201
OLAP Manager Calculated Member Builder, library registration, 154
OLAP Server, 18. *See also* server
OLAP server
  accessing, with clsServer, 159–165
  closing connection to, 115
  connecting to, 113–115
  DSO error codes, 162–165
  queries to, 119
OLAP server service, controlling, 101
OLAP Services
  empty cell rules, 224
  function libraries, 63, 153–154
  goal of, 3
  memory allocation for, 252–253
  Microsoft Excel function library support, 63
  multiple partitions capability, 175
  Visual Basic for Application Expression Services library support, 63
OLAP Services Processing Task dialog box, 283–284
OlapClassTypes enumerator, 107
OlapEditions enumerator, 103
OlapMenuFlags, 208, 269
OlapMenuItem class, 201
OlapMenuItem objects, 204–205
OlapMenuItems collection, 205, 269

OlapMenuTypes enumeration, 207
OlapObjects table, 108
    ObjectDefinition field, 108
OlapObjects_bak table, 108
OlapStorageModes enumerator, 107
OlapTreeNode
    adding child nodes, 202
    HTML file display, 203
    refreshing, 207
OlapTreeNode class, 201
OlapTreeNode object, 206
OlapTreeNodes collection, 206, 272
OLAP@Work for Excel, 238–240
    allocation methods, 240
    what-if analysis, 239, 241–242
Online Transaction Processing
    (OLTP) systems, 4
Open method, ConnectionString
    specification in, 114
Opening Period function, 222
OpenQueryLogReset method, 101
Order function, 213–214
OrderTypes enumerator, 102
ordinal positions, 121–122
    navigating by, 123

P

Package Designer window, 31
    Browse button, 31
    Column Delimiter dialog box,
        32–33
    Connection Properties page,
        31–32
    Source icon, 31
    text annotations in, 37
    Text File format dialog box, 32
Package objects, 276
packages, running, 282–283
ParallelPeriod function, 222
Parent function, 219
parent members, 212
ParentNode, 272
parent_office column, 23
partition-level member properties,
    101
Partition Wizard, 176–179
PartitionAnalyzer property, 186
partitions, 174–175
    aggregations of, 183–188
    aggregations storage in, 69
    analyzing, 101
    creating, with DSO, 180–181
    cube data storage in, 12–13, 90
    data slice specification, 183
    default, 172, 174
    filtering, 178, 183
    merging, 175–176, 179–183

Partition Wizard, 176–179
    processing, 178
    properties of, inspecting, 249
    prt files, 175
    refreshing data, 188
    storage mode for, 175
    write-back table conversion
        into, 231
performance
    and aggregation design, 188
    of aggregations, 186
    and caches, 133
    and cube partitioning, 12–13
    gains, calculating, 55
    of MOLAP cubes, 134
    and partition storage mode, 175
    and write-enabled cubes, 231
PeriodsToDate function, 221
permissions. *See also* access control
    for user groups, 99–100
Permissions property, 190
    security rules in, 191
PivotCharts, 236–237
PivotTable and PivotChart Wizard,
    234–235
PivotTable Service, 18
    as client to OLAP server, 111
    connecting with, 113
    cube creation, 138
    DDL support, 127–128
    Item method, addressing cells
        in, 121
    local cube support, 134
    SQL support, 124–127
    as stand-alone OLAP server, 111
PivotTables
    creating, in Excel, 233–236
    levels, collapsing, 235
    levels, displaying, 235
    levels, removing, 235–236
positions, 19
PrecedenceConstraint objects, 277
PrecedenceConstraints objects, 277
PrepareGoalQueries method, 187
PrevMember function, 219
Price, 128, 228–229
    charting, 236–237
Price calculated dimension, 98
Price calculated member, 189
    building, 64–65
primary keys, empty cells in, 68, 76
Print Report function, 267
Priority value, 273
Process method, 187–188, 284
Process window, 55–56
ProcessReadAheadSize setting, 252
ProcessReadSegmentSize setting,
    252

ProcessTypes enumerator, 107
program code, library registration
    for, 154–155
properties
    of members, 10–11
    repository storage, 108–109
properties collection, 19
properties sheet, 253, 273
    Debugging tab, 274
PROPERTIES specification, 157–158
Property Inspector, 267
    class initialization, 268
    debugging, 273–274
    ExecuteMenuItem method,
        coding, 271
    menu items, coding, 268–270
    nodes for, 272
    references for, 268
    registering, 273
    server connection method, 272
PropertyList property, 248, 250
ProvideChildNodes method, 202,
    272
ProvideHTML method, 203
ProvideIcon method, 203–204
ProvideMenuItems method,
    202–203, 268–269
provider, loading, 113

Q

queries. *See also* MDX
    data-driven, 36
    drilldown and drillup, 256–258
    against local cubes, 134
    parsing, 27
    processing time, 8
    specifying type, 36
query performance, 8
query statement, 26–27
QueryCube function, 259–260
QueryLogSampling setting, 252
Quick allocation, 240, 242

R

Rank function, 265
read-only access permissions, 190,
    192
read/write access permissions,
    99–100, 190
    for cubes, 230–231
ReadAheadBufferSize setting, 252
Recordset object, 119
recordset Source property, assigning
    cellset Source property into,
    127
referential integrity, verifying, 68
Refresh data task, 284

refresh methods, 77–79
RefreshTreeTypes enumeration, 207
RegionalOffices table, 23
Registry
    add-in key values in, 273
    settings, listing, 252–253
Registry key, 209
Relational OLAP (ROLAP), 12–13,
    54, 69
    for local cube storage, 134, 139
Remove method, 84, 191
repository, 19, 108–109
    adding objects to, 167
Role interface, 85, 99–101
    class properties, 100–101
roles
    adding, 100
    creating, 52–53, 190
    permissions for, 99–100, 191,
        230–231
    removing, 191
Roles collection, 189
    Remove method, 191
ROLLUP query, 81
RootDir setting, 253
rows, accessing, 119
rowsets, flattened, retrieving,
    124–127

S

sample database. See FundAccts
    database
scope, 128
    global, 128
scrubbing, 5
searched case expression, 223
Secured Cell Value parameter, 192
security, 189–191
    cell-level, 191–193
    for user groups, 99
    with virtual cubes, 12, 226, 228
security rules, cell-level, 191–193
Security Support Provider Interface
    (SSPI), 189
SELECT statement
    INSERT INTO statement options
        and, 138–139
    PivotTable Service support of,
        124
SendMailTask objects, 277
server
    connecting to, 42–43, 86–87,
        271–272
    enumerating databases known
        to, 87
    name specification, 161
    properties, inspecting, 249
    State property, 161

server-based cubes. See also
        Investments cube
    aggregation design, 139
server connections, security mode
    for, 43
server objects, 84
    properties, displaying, 267
server query log, sampling rate, 252
Server table, 109
ServerStates enumerator, 106
services, starting, pausing, and
        stopping, 162
ServiceState property, 161
    starting, pausing, and stopping
        services with, 162
set functions, 153
Set verb, 114
SetPermissions method, 99–100,
    191
sets, 147, 211
    axes points, correlation
        between, 262
    WITH clause, specifying with,
        150–151
    difference between, 217
    dropping, 133
    duplicates, removing, 216
    extracting dimension members
        from, 217
    filtering, 216
    generating, 218
    intersections of, 216–217
    joining, 217
    MDX expression, 147
    percentages, sorting on, 215
    specifying, 218–219
    sums, sorting on, 216
    top and bottom expressions,
        returning, 215
    uniting, 216
    user-defined. See user-defined
        sets
shared dimensions
    adding members, 73
    rebuilding structure, 73
    updating, 80–81
shortcut menus
    inserting items in, 268–269
    for tree-view nodes, 204–205
sibling members, 212
simple case expression, 223
slicer axis, 145
slicer dimensions, 145–146
    accessing, 145
snap-ins. See add-ins
snowflake schema, 5–7
source data, accessing, 189
Source property, 121

source systems, schema of, 4
sources, connection to, 31–32
SQL
    PivotTable Service support,
        124–127
    query with Group By clause,
        125–126
    query with Where clause, 126
    simple query, 125
SQL Server, migrating repository to,
    109
SQL Server Enterprise Manager,
    integrating with OLAP
    Manager, 41
SQL Server node, expanding, 30–31
SQL Server OLAP Services
    Enterprise Edition, 12
standard deviation, 264–265
star schema, 5–7, 24
Statements table, 22
Stdev function, 264–265
Step objects, 277
Steps objects, 277
Storage Design Wizard, 54–56
storage modes
    aggregation storage, 69
    defining, 53–55
    dimension storage, 69
string functions, 153
SubClassTypes enumerator, 107
Sum function, 264
summary information, separate
        database for, 8
summations. See also aggregations
    grouping, 14–17
SupportLevels enumerator, 103

T

tabular data, PivotTable Service
        support of, 124–127
Task objects, 276
Tasks objects, 276
TempDirectory setting, 252
text files, source connection to,
    31–32
tilde (/) character, 167
Time dimension, 24
    creating, 47
    levels of, 94
time series functions, 221–222,
    262–263
ToggleDrillState function, 257–258
Tools menu
    Design Storage, 54
    Select Manage Roles, 52
TopCount function, 215
TopPercent function, 215
TopSum function, 216

trandate column, 24
TranHistory table, 22, 24
Transact-SQL, 120
TransferObjectsTask objects, 277
Transferring Data dialog box, 29
transformation, 5
Transformation objects, 277
Transformations objects, 277
tree view, 18, 201–209
    nodes, adding, 272
tuple functions, 153
tuples, 121, 147, 211
    averaging, 264
    counting, 264
    empty, 224
    hard-coded, 218
    ranking, 265
    removing, 144
    and sets, 130

U

unbiased population formula, 264
und Shared dimension, 61
Union function, 216
UnlockObject method, 166–167
updates
    checking results, 81
    complete process, 72–73
    incremental, 72, 74–78,
        284–285
    methods, 70–71
    processing, 71–73
    rebuilds, 73
    refresh, 73
    for shared dimensions, 80–81
Usage-Based Optimization
        Wizard, 95
USE LIBRARY statement, 154–156
user authentication, 189

user-defined functions, 154–157
    registering library, 154
user-defined sets, 131
    creating, 130–133
    curly braces for, 131
    scope of, 128
user groups, maintaining, 99
user state, maintaining, 260
users
    adding to roles, 100
    list of, 190
    permissions of, 190. *See also*
        access control
UsersList property, 99, 190

V

ValidateErrorCodes enumerator,
        103–104
Var function, 264
variance, 264
verification, 4, 67–68
    of updates, 81
VEST (verification, extraction,
        scrubbing, and
        transformation), 5
virtual cubes, 12, 84, 225–229
    calculated member
        management, 196–198
    copying and pasting, 198
    creating, 227–228
    creating, with DSO, 229
    role for, 228
    for security, 226, 228
virtual dimensions, 10–11, 61,
        225–229
    copying and pasting, 198
    creating, 62–63, 225
    creating, with DSO, 229
Virtual Dimensions Wizard, 225

Visual Basic
    CREATE MEMBER, submitting,
        129
    cube object creation, 86
Visual Basic for Application
        Expression Services library,
        153
    OLAP Services support of, 63
VisualTotals function, 265

W

Weighted allocation, 240
what-if analysis, 230, 239
WHERE statement
    as data filter, 285
    default members, specifying
        with, 145
    PivotTable Service support of,
        124
WITH clause, 148
    cache specification with,
        151–152
    calculated member specification
        with, 148–150
    set specification with, 150–151
wonkies, 130
WorkerThreads setting, 253
write-back tables, 230
    backup of, 199
    committing changes to, 239
    converting to partitions, 231

Z

zooming, support for, 267
ZoomProperty method, 267

IDG Books Worldwide, Inc.
End-User License Agreement

4. <u>Restrictions on Use of Individual Programs</u>. You must follow the individual requirements and restrictions detailed for each individual program in Appendix A of this Book. These limitations are also contained in the individual license agreements recorded on the Software Media. These limitations may include a requirement that after using the program for a specified period of time, the user must pay a registration fee or discontinue use. By opening the Software packet(s), you will be agreeing to abide by the licenses and restrictions for these individual programs that are detailed in Appendix A and on the Software Media. None of the material on this Software Media or listed in this Book may ever be redistributed, in original or modified form, for commercial purposes.

5. <u>Limited Warranty</u>.

   (a) IDGB warrants that the Software and Software Media are free from defects in materials and workmanship under normal use for a period of sixty (60) days from the date of purchase of this Book. If IDGB receives notification within the warranty period of defects in materials or workmanship, IDGB will replace the defective Software Media.

   (b) IDGB AND THE AUTHOR OF THE BOOK DISCLAIM ALL OTHER WARRANTIES, EXPRESS OR IMPLIED, INCLUDING WITHOUT LIMITATION IMPLIED WARRANTIES OF MERCHANTABILITY AND FITNESS FOR A PARTICULAR PURPOSE, WITH RESPECT TO THE SOFTWARE, THE PROGRAMS, THE SOURCE CODE CONTAINED THEREIN, AND/OR THE TECHNIQUES DESCRIBED IN THIS BOOK. IDGB DOES NOT WARRANT THAT THE FUNCTIONS CONTAINED IN THE SOFTWARE WILL MEET YOUR REQUIREMENTS OR THAT THE OPERATION OF THE SOFTWARE WILL BE ERROR FREE.

   (c) This limited warranty gives you specific legal rights, and you may have other rights that vary from jurisdiction to jurisdiction.

6. <u>Remedies</u>.

   (a) IDGB's entire liability and your exclusive remedy for defects in materials and workmanship shall be limited to replacement of the Software Media, which may be returned to IDGB with a copy of your receipt at the following address: Software Media Fulfillment Department, Attn.: *SQL Server" OLAP Developer's Guide*, IDG Books Worldwide, Inc., 10475 Crosspoint Blvd., Indianapolis, IN 46256, or call 1-800-762-2974. Please allow three to four weeks for delivery. This Limited Warranty is void if failure of the Software Media has resulted from accident, abuse, or misapplication. Any replacement Software Media will be warranted for the remainder of the original warranty period or thirty (30) days, whichever is longer.

(b) In no event shall IDGB or the author be liable for any damages whatsoever (including without limitation damages for loss of business profits, business interruption, loss of business information, or any other pecunia-ry loss) arising from the use of or inability to use the Book or the Software, even if IDGB has been advised of the possibility of such damages.

(c) Because some jurisdictions do not allow the exclusion or limitation of liability for consequential or incidental damages, the above limitation or exclusion may not apply to you.

7. <u>**U.S. Government Restricted Rights**</u>. Use, duplication, or disclosure of the Software by the U.S. Government is subject to restrictions stated in paragraph (c)(1)(ii) of the Rights in Technical Data and Computer Software clause of DFARS 252.227-7013, and in subparagraphs (a) through (d) of the Commercial Computer – Restricted Rights clause at FAR 52.227-19, and in similar clauses in the NASA FAR supplement, when applicable.

8. <u>General</u>. This Agreement constitutes the entire understanding of the parties and revokes and supersedes all prior agreements, oral or written, between them and may not be modified or amended except in a writing signed by both parties hereto that specifically refers to this Agreement. This Agreement shall take precedence over any other documents that may be in conflict herewith. If any one or more provisions contained in this Agreement are held by any court or tribunal to be invalid, illegal, or otherwise unenforceable, each and every other provision shall remain in full force and effect.

my2cents.idgbooks.com

CD-ROM Installation Instructions

There is no set up or installation program provided on the CD for installing CD content. To be able to edit chapter samples or Visual Basic projects on the CD, complete the following steps:

1. the files from the CD to your hard drive.

2. Select all copied files in the Windows Explorer, right-click the selection and select Properties from the shortcut menu.

3. In the Properties dialog, uncheck the Read-only attribute.

To install software from the Third-Party folder on the CD, double-click the self-extracting executable or setup program and follow the onscreen instructions.

Please see Appendix A for information on CD content.

MICROSOFT PRODUCT WARRANTY AND SUPPORT DISCLAIMER

The Microsoft program on the CD-Rom was reproduced by IDG Books Worldwide, Inc. under a special arrangement with Microsoft Corporation. For this reason, IDG Books Worldwide, Inc. is responsible for the product warranty and for support. If your CD-Rom is defective, please return it to IDG Books Worldwide, Inc. which will arrange for its replacement. PLEASE DO NOT RETURN IT TO MICROSOFT CORPORATION. Any product support will be provided, if at all, by IDG Books Worldwide, Inc. PLEASE DO NOT CONTACT MICROSOFT CORPORATION FOR PRODUCT SUPPORT. End users of this Microsoft program shall not be considered "registered owners" of a Microsoft product and therefore shall not be eligible for upgrades, promotions, or other benefits available to "registered owners" of Microsoft products.

"There are many introductory textbooks available in social work, but *How to be a Social Worker* is unique because of how it manages to combine deep intelligence with practical relevance. It skilfully draws on a wide range of theories from sociology, pyschology, and social work itself and applies them in a highly accessible but never simplistic way to practice and the challenges of acquiring a professional identity in social work. It deserves to be an instant bestseller." – Harry Ferguson, Professor of Social Work, University of Nottingham, UK

"This is a highly readable and practical first-steps introduction to doing the job of social work. The content is eminently usable and digestible in a way that will equip students with essential ideas and knowledge and an appreciation of the importance of thought and reflection in doing social work." – Martin Sheedy, Programme Leader for Social Work, Liverpool John Moores University, UK

"This text provides students and practitioners with a critical account of the importance of self and professional identity within social work and offers valuable opportunities to challenge assumptions, reflect and review what it means to be an effective professional in the 21st century." – Steve Hothersall, Head of Social Work Education, Edge Hill University, UK

"A useful exploration of the development of the professional self in social work, particularly for students." – Sharlene Nipperess, Lecturer in Social Work, Deakin University, Australia

"This book will be a useful reference for those contemplating a career in social work through to those newly employed. In particular, the case studies used throughout are interesting and illustrate the complexity of social work and the dilemmas faced on a daily basis." – Louise Houston, Practice Educator in Social Work, University of Plymouth, UK:

"This is an extremely well laid out, easy to read book which came in particularly useful when I was writing an assignment on communication skills in social work. It was a valuable tool in helping me to understand the theories I was drawing on during my first placement setting, too." – Matthew Caunce, Year 2 BA Social Work student, Lancaster University, UK

Priscilla Dunk-West

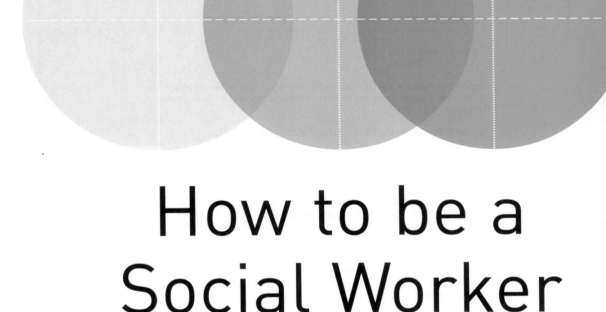

How to be a
Social Worker

A Critical Guide for Students

palgrave
macmillan

First published 2013 by
PALGRAVE MACMILLAN

Palgrave Macmillan in the UK is an imprint of Macmillan Publishers Limited,
registered in England, company number 785998, of Houndmills, Basingstoke,
Hampshire RG21 6XS.

Palgrave Macmillan in the US is a division of St Martin's Press LLC,
175 Fifth Avenue, New York, NY 10010.

Palgrave Macmillan is the global academic imprint of the above companies
and has companies and representatives throughout the world.

Palgrave® and Macmillan® are registered trademarks in the United States,
the United Kingdom, Europe and other countries

ISBN: 978–0–230–37016–6

This book is printed on paper suitable for recycling and made from fully
managed and sustained forest sources. Logging, pulping and manufacturing
processes are expected to conform to the environmental regulations of the
country of origin.

A catalogue record for this book is available from the British Library.

A catalog record for this book is available from the Library of Congress.

This book is dedicated to Penny:
sister extraordinaire

Contents

List of Figures   xi
Acknowledgements   xiii

Introduction   1

1 The Social Work Self   11
   Understanding social work   13
   Working with others   16
   What is the self?   21
   Social interaction or sociality   22
   The self, reflexivity and contemporary life   29
   Understanding the social work self   31
   Chapter summary   34
   Further reading   34

2 Human Development   35
   Life stages   40
   Generations   53
   Neglect, child abuse and developmental theories   53
   Working with others   54
   Chapter summary   56
   Further reading   57

3 Communication Skills   59
   Demonstrating listening   62
   Asking questions   64
   Reflecting   64
   Clarifying   65
   Summarising   66
   Probing   66
   Framing action   67
   Written communication   68
   The self, reflexivity and empathy   69
   Working with others   73

Chapter summary   73
Further reading   73

4   Social Work Theory   75
Social work theory: differing orientations   78
Cognitive behavioural therapy   81
Humanistic approaches   82
Strengths perspective/empowerment approach   82
Systems theory/ecological perspective   83
Feminist social work theory   84
Critical social work and structural approaches   85
Sociological social work   87
Chapter summary   89
Further reading   90

5   Everyday Ethics   91
Utilitarianism   97
Kantianism   98
Virtue-based ethics   99
Ethics of care   100
Bioethics   100
Human rights approach   101
Codes of practice, codes of ethics and other institutionalised
    ethical rules   102
Ethical dilemmas in social work: What to do?   103
Organisational ethical issues   104
The impaired worker   106
Dual role relationships   107
Working with others   108
Chapter summary   109
Further reading   110

6   Practice Learning in Organisational Settings   111
Learning and placements   113
Social work and the organisational setting   115
The professional self   116
Assessment   118
What about reflexivity on placement?   120
Supervision   122
Working with others   123

Chapter summary	125
Further reading	125

7 Research in Social Work — 127

Research mindedness	130
Research questions, aims and scope	132
Epistemology	133
Research methodology and methods	133
Ethics	138
Sampling	139
Data analysis	140
Dissemination	142
Literature reviews	143
How to use research in social work: working with others	144
How to find information	150
Chapter summary	151
Further reading	151

8 'Doing' Social Work: Constituting the Professional Self — 153

What happens once I'm a social worker?	157
Working with others	159
Periodisation and social work	160
Glossary of Key Terms	165
References and Further Reading	171
Index	189

List of Figures

0.1	The intersection: What happens when our rules are removed?	2
1.1	What and who do you see?	22
2.1	What is the relationship between the subjects in this photograph?	38
2.2	Trilby painting: How can theories of development be applied to this scenario?	40
4.1	Different social work theories focus on different areas of human experience, action, thoughts and social structure	79
4.2	Cognitive behavioural therapy relates to thoughts and behaviours	81
4.3	Humanistic approaches focus on individuals and the helping relationship	82
4.4	Strengths perspectives are interested in individual strengths	83
4.5	Systems approaches highlight the external environment and the individual's place within	84
4.6	Feminist social work highlights broader social inequalities	85
4.7	Critical approaches are interested in change at the structural level	86
4.8	Sociological social work seeks to understand the individual by looking at social and individual contexts	87
5.1	The bridge dilemma: What would you do?	98
5.2	Ethical dilemmas can be messy, complex and confusing	103
5.3	Asking pertinent questions can help to unravel an ethical dilemma	104
6.1	Making the connections between the everyday self and the professional self helps the professional to emerge	117
6.2	An insurmountable mountain? A range of professionals with whom social workers work	124
7.1	Narrowing down topics is an important step in research	132
8.1	Using knowledge in social work practice	156

Acknowledgements

This book has emerged from almost a decade of teaching social work to students in Australia and England and my subsequent desire to create a text that brought together the varying strands of the curriculum in a new way. This desire turned into a reality with the assistance of Lloyd Langman, Commissioning Editor at Palgrave Macmillan. Lloyd's enthusiasm has endured throughout this project and he has been a joy to work with. Similarly Katie Rauwerda, Assistant Editor at Palgrave Macmillan, has provided skilful and critical insights and support at crucial times throughout the writing process.

I have been incredibly fortunate to have taught so many inspiring students over the years: thank you to each and every one of you for helping me develop my teaching skills and knowledge. Students energise me to remain curious about the world of social work. Working with a diverse bunch of students over a number of years has highlighted the need for learning resources to be flexible and to offer various methods of knowledge delivery. I deliberately used visual methods and reflective prompts alongside traditional writing in the hope that this book opens up new opportunities for reflexivity and creativity and that it will appeal to former and future students of social work.

The central theoretical idea contained in this book comes from George Herbert Mead, an early figure in what we refer to as the symbolic interactionist tradition in sociology today. The idea that the self is 'made' through social interactions has been influential for me in that it has helped me better understand the professional world of social work. I first encountered G. H. Mead through my early studies in sociology. More recently, scholars in sociology have applied his work to intimacy studies, so my PhD research in the area of the everyday sexual self in sociology led me to think about his theory and its application to both my own research as well as to my profession of social work. It is therefore these shoulders upon which I stand in making the claim for the application of Mead to social work.

I have also been fortunate to work with a number of scholars whose wisdom and passion has inspired me and whom I wish to thank. These include: Professor Fiona Verity, Dr Trish Hafford-Letchfield, Dr Gill Cressey and Professor Lesley Cooper. Thanks are equally due to Elaine Bourne and Sue Maywald who shared their wisdom about practice learning and education and helped me to understand the world of placement learning in my initial years in the university setting. I have had institutional support in the writing of this book from the University of South Australia and my brilliant new colleagues, for which I am very grateful.

Andrew Dunbar, I sincerely appreciate you allowing your work to be reproduced and applied to social work learning. Thank you to the excellent Trilby and her folks for the child development photograph. Laura Varley, who helped with administrative tasks associated with this project, provided crucial, and timely, assistance and helped with the final push to get everything together in time. Veronica Gubbins has always, over a great number of years, encouraged the writer in me: thank you. Thanks are also due to Jan and Gary Dunk for their continuing support across continents. Last, but by no means least, Blake and Paxton: thank you for being two wonderful people in my life. Brad: thank you for everything, including for being you.

Priscilla Dunk-West

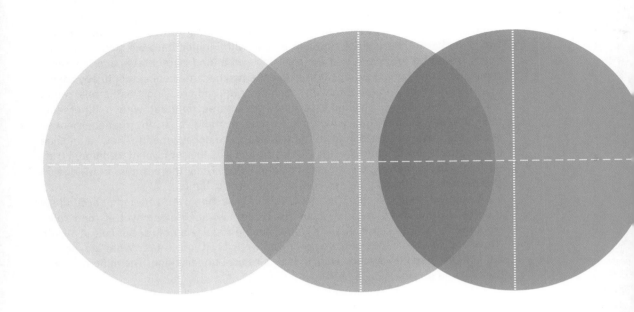

Introduction

During the conceptualisation of this book I held an academic post at Coventry University, England. Given the multiple roles the contemporary academic must fulfil, mundane tasks become opportunities for thinking, reflection and planning. It was a deliberate merging of a mundane task with intellectual work to use my time spent travelling to Coventry in the mornings as a kind of mental space for me to think about this book. Perhaps that's how the two became connected. In any case, I shall explain. The commute to work each day required crossing what is referred to as a 'shared space'. This is essentially an intersection but with a difference. Coventry City Council has adopted a European model of traffic management in which the travels of various forms of transport are encouraged to 'flow' alongside one another. Encouraging the 'flow' of traffic involves the removal of traditional traffic rules (Chris Young, pers. comm. 18 June 2012). Thus, there are no markings on this particular intersection, nor are there any traffic lights.

Having watched the construction of this intersection over a period of around six months, I grew more and more curious as to how such a removal of road rules would work. Would chaos ensue? Would people require a new set of rules? Would these apply to all modes of transport? Can we live without rules? What looked like a fairly standard intersection was, in fact, a radical undertaking. The appearance of the finished intersection is shown in Figure 0.1.

Aside from the physical connection between my journey into Coventry and my thinking about this book, what does traffic have to do with social work? Our everyday

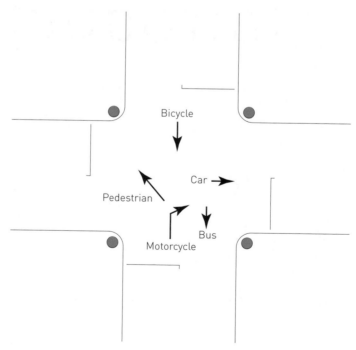

FIGURE 0.1 The intersection: What happens when our rules are removed?

activities, I believe, help us understand not only our external world, but our internal perceptions. Hopefully as you read this, the traffic metaphor will begin to make sense and will assist in providing some insight into the theoretical orientation upon which this book has been developed. But first, some overview as to how the book relates to social work students is needed.

In short, this book aims to teach the reader how to develop and establish their professional social work identity. This means not only learning how to be a social worker but also understanding how identity is made and appreciating how this self is related to its broader society. It is only through this awareness of the self that we can consciously fashion a *social work self*—and this is a process which continues throughout our careers. The ways in which we engage in this process shape the local, national and even international social work identity.

The book brings together the subjects studied during qualifying courses as well as engaging the reader in key debates and tensions in social work. A critical aware-ness of these, and their manifestations in practice, is vital to a positive social work identity. In this introductory chapter we will begin to examine how the social work identity is 'made'. In order to understand this it is crucial to examine the self.

From the very beginning of study to completing the award, social work students can find it difficult to connect up the subjects they study in university with the expe-riences they have in placement, and often this continues well into one's social work practice career. The subjects studied—which range from human development to communication skills to research—can feel somewhat separate from one another. This book aims to develop in the reader an understanding that the learning process is concerned with the construction or 'making' of the social work self.

Back to our traffic metaphor. The experimental intersection held my interest because, as a social scientist, I am curious about the ways in which everyday rules shape our behaviour. I watched others' reactions as they drove, cycled, walked into this new shared zone. I also drove and walked through the area.

What I noticed is that despite the absence of rules, people were required to enter the zone at a slower speed than on traditional roads. Generally speaking, the people I observed on my daily trek to work would approach the intersection as though diving into the unknown. When approaching a roundabout, for example, we have an understanding of the rules: giving way to traffic to one's right, waiting until there is a clear path, signalling direction through the use of indicators—these are all exam-ples of the expected rules which help us negotiate our path on traditional roads. A traffic light is a very clearly defined set of rules with colours signalling certain actions. So the shared space was very different from these other types of intersec-tions. The reduced speed on approach to the intersection was prompted by a lack of knowledge about what the rules were, and yet in the shared zone there are still rules. Motorists give way to others, people look to see if there is oncoming traffic, people allow others to proceed before them. There are rules in this system—they are just different from those on traditional roads.

Similarly, the beginning social work student enters university without an under-standing of the 'rules' of social work. On the surface, entering into the world of social work entails a letting go of previously held values, ideas, theories and knowl-edge. Learning about social work can feel like being in a space with unknown rules and boundaries. Being on placement, for example, can be enormously confronting for a person who has developed a successful career elsewhere, either in paid or non-paid work.

Studying social work can feel like starting all over again. Yet as the social work student progresses through their studies, they find some confidence in developing a social work self which incorporates knowledge and values that were previously held. Many social work students have a long-held interest in social justice, for example, and this value resonates through social work ethics, theory and practice. Making connections between the self who comes to social work and the social work self is inherent to the learning that occurs throughout the social work degree.

It is also the task of the social work student to try to navigate their way through their classroom social work education and the practice that occurs through placements. Although it can feel like drifting amongst oncoming traffic, this journey is one that occurs through navigating theoretical frameworks in the real world of practice. Your fellow learners are a source of support in your social work journey, and key ideas and theories enable the traveller to gain momentum in their journey to become a competent social worker.

Similarly, lectures, seminars and other facilitated learning assists in the process whereby the social work self is constituted. This book has been written as a support to all of these 'anchors' to learning in the hope that it will make navigating your path through the seemingly chaotic intersection a little easier and clearer.

There is another way the new traffic management model I have described is comparable to becoming a social worker. Our behaviour as motorists, motorcyclists, pedestrians in using traditional forms of management becomes, as George Herbert Mead might say, 'routinized'. We engage in routine behaviours in our everyday lives: these are formed through repetition over time until the behaviours become so familiar that you become unaware of them. If you have ever arrived at a destination and been unable to recall your journey in specific detail (Did you wait at that set of traffic lights, or were the lights green? Was it easy this morning to turn right on the usually congested road?), you have experienced an example of routinized behaviour. It can seem as though you were, for example, driving *without thinking* (Chris Young, pers. comm. 18 June 2012). The new model of shared traffic management seeks to interrupt this routinization by removing familiar cues and force active engagement with what is occurring within the shared space. It therefore becomes impossible to drive in this space passively, or *without thinking*. This is because the environment is constantly changing and there are multiple forms of modes of transport and directions travelled.

The underlying theoretical idea in this book is Mead's theory which argues that our selves are constructed through our interactions with others. Most of the time we are unaware of our selves or our identities when we engage in these interactions (Mead 1934).

In social work, we have long been concerned with reflexivity or the ability to think back or reflect on our behaviour and change our subsequent behaviour according to our desires. This book contains material to assist in this tradition of reflexive practice, and in particular how it relates to your emerging social work self. It is important in social work to disrupt practice with reflexivity so that our practice is constantly positively engaging in the dynamic terrain in which we find ourselves.

Subjects taught in social work curricula can feel disjointed. Although this book deals with each subject in a chapter format, there is a common approach to all of these seemingly separate topics. In order to develop the social work self, the learner is required to:

- Actively engage in critical reading, thinking, listening and talking about issues related to social work, including the broader social sphere
- Use personal biography and experiences in everyday life in making sense of social work topics. This, in turn, requires students to
- Engage in reflexive exercises based on theoretical material

In facilitating the above, this book is a little different from other social work text-books. The key idea in this book—that the self is constructed through social inter-action—is a forgotten idea in social work (Forte 2004a, 2004b). There is much to be gained through the application of such a theory of self to social work learning. In this vein, this book is an attempt to stimulate the reader's thinking—both about one's self and about one's everyday life—in new ways, and to relate this knowledge to social work. Theoretical material, reflexive exercises and active engagement in the curriculum enable students to surrender their 'routinized behaviour' so that new skills and knowledge may be developed.

The book is designed in such a way that chapters can be read either as stand-alone text, from beginning to end, or in an order which fits the reader's purpose. It is hoped it will be a book which accompanies students from the beginning of their course to the end of their course and into their social work career. I will now outline how the book is set out and then explore how the material in each chapter fits with the task of helping people to *be* social workers.

Chapter 1 examines the concept of selfhood and relates this to social work learn-ing and self-making. Social work is a profession which is committed to the under-standing that the social environment, including the cultural setting, has an enormous impact on individual experiences. In Chapter 1 we therefore spend some time exploring some of the automatic assumptions we make about others due to our socially situated knowledge. The 'self' is a central term used in this book so in Chapter 1 we explore how understanding professional practice through the analysis of self is important to social work as a profession as well as to one's emerging iden-tity as a social worker. The role of reflexivity is examined in relation to the self and social work. In social work, being able to progressively get 'better' in one's practice is an accepted outcome from reflexive engagement. Chapter 1 outlines what this means for one's own developing professional self.

With Chapter 1 laying the conceptual foundations for the book, Chapter 2 commences with an engagement with theoretical material which helps social work-ers make sense of individual circumstances. Thinking about individual problems through a life course or lifespan approach involves compartmentalising life stages. Generally speaking, the life stages are birth, early childhood, middle childhood, adolescence, adulthood, older age and death. This is a linear model of life: as one grows older, one moves on to the next category. Scholarship derived from the disciplines of developmental psychology, sociology and social work has contributed to our current knowledge of the life course. All of these approaches inform the knowledge-base discussed in Chapter 2. In this chapter we consider how knowledge about human development assists both in contextualising individual problems within broader social and age contexts and in helping to frame the different roles social work plays in helping to meet the age-related requirements which emerge in each life stage. In Chapter 2 the reader is encouraged to engage in thinking about one's own self and life stages. The key ideas which underpin Chapter 2 are that in order to be a competent social worker, one must understand the key developmental theories, be able to apply them to particular client scenarios and be able to understand and apply theories of normative development in the context of social and cultural norms.

Chapters 1 and 2 may describe knowledge new to the reader whereas in Chapter 3 we move on to consider one of the fundamental skills used in everyday life. Communication skills involve the exchange of information between one person and another. Since social work is a profession in which relationships are fundamental, knowledge about and abilities in communication are essential. Being able to 'read' situations, verbal and non-verbal cues, for example, is central to social work practice in all settings. In Chapter 3 the differing types of communication are outlined and the reader is encouraged to reflect on particular scenarios and think about how meaning is conveyed, and what the social work role might be. They are also invited to 'read' situations using their knowledge about communication. Invariably, students of communication skills tend to have a heightened awareness about the ways in which they and those around them communicate. This appreciation is encouraged in this book, for it is through everyday life—noticing the day-to-day events, exchanges and communications around us—that new insights emerge. In Chapter 3, communication and skills relating to communication are seen as occupying a central role in social work. Combining the social work purpose alongside communication skills enables students to practise how to be a social worker. As we shall see in Chapter 6, placement enables students to put their communication skills to use. But before these skills can emerge, a theoretical framework for practice needs to be developed.

Chapter 4 outlines some of the central theories used in contemporary social work practice. These include cognitive behavioural therapy, humanistic approaches, systems theory/ecological perspectives, feminist social work theory, critical and structural approaches and sociological social work. Each of these theories is outlined and placed in context compared with the others. For example, the view that individual thoughts affect behaviour influences some theoretical traditions whereas in other traditions, social and cultural values and institutions are seen to play a key role in limiting individual opportunities. Therefore the answer to the question: 'what is the role of the social worker?' will differ depending on which theoretical position is taken. Increasingly, organisations are aligning themselves with particular traditions, which has meant the dominance of a set of theories in particular areas of practice. For the social work student, this can be confusing. This chapter suggests choosing a theoretical tradition or approach which appeals to the reader and exploring why it fits. Social workers' development throughout their practice often means engaging with new theoretical traditions and evaluating one's own current ones. In this way, knowledge about theory can be 'scaffolded' or constructed upon a firm foundation. Chapter 4 begins this process through identifying groupings for theories and suggesting ways in which individuals can accommodate a tradition alongside their emerging professional self.

Just as with social work theories, the ethical basis of social work must be considered alongside the emerging social work self. Chapter 5 therefore explores values and ethics and notes that decisions we make in our everyday lives are derived from our own framework of values and ethics. Ethics relate to the rules we employ in making decisions about how we live. In social work, ethics are foundational for practice, alongside our theoretical perspectives. Chapter 5 outlines some of the key philosophical orientations used in social work. These include utilitarianism, Kantianism, virtue-based ethics, care ethics, bioethics and a human rights approach. The chapter examines governing bodies and their role in institutionalising and policing social work ethics. It looks at some ethical issues which can emerge in practice including ethical dilemmas, organisational ethical issues, impaired workers and dual role relationships. Just as with the material explored in Chapter 4 which related to theories, in Chapter 5 the reader is invited to consider: 'what roles do values and ethics play in one's everyday life?' Developing these alongside social work values and ethics is a key task in the emergence of the social work self.

In Chapter 6 we consider the complex world of placement. Field education, or placement, requires students to enter an organisational setting and begin to practise their social work skills and use their social work knowledge for purposeful action and interaction. Because this type of knowledge acquisition is derived through an experiential means—that is, students are 'doing' social work in a real setting—placement can feel separate from other types of knowledge acquired during social work study. In fact, placement is an opportunity to bring together learning from classroom-based subjects. We also discuss assessment. Assessment is a core social work skill and is evident in virtually all practice settings, and in this chapter we consider ways in which assessment skills can be applied to client scenarios. The role of the supervisor concludes Chapter 6.

As we see in Chapter 7, research is increasingly used in social work practice settings. The ability to think about issues as a researcher is first explored, through the concept of 'research mindedness'. For the social work student, it is essential to develop an understanding of research in the context of the profession. Therefore in this chapter the following are explored since they are foundational to carrying out research: research questions, aims and scope, epistemology, research methodology and methods, interviews, focus groups, questionnaires, observation and ethnography, ethics, sampling, data analysis and literature reviews. Not only is it important for social workers to consider research as a potential dimension to their social work role, but it is crucial that social workers understand how to apply social work research. This skill is encouraged using targeted exercises in Chapter 7.

Chapter 8 concludes *How to be a Social Worker*. In this final chapter there is some consideration of how, post qualification, social workers' identities are continually forged. Although the chapter brings the book to its conclusion it is also designed to assist newly qualified graduates to understand and continue to develop their social work selves. Positioning reflexive moments in the world of practice is argued to provide social workers with the tools to appreciate and grow the social work self. Finding the ethical and theoretical framework to carry social work practice into the future is also important to maintaining passion and interest in this profession. We consider some of the ongoing challenges in social work and how we can respond to the changing world around us. Understanding selfhood is argued to have important benefits to social work identity on a personal level as well as for the collective identity that we hold as a profession. In this final chapter we see that it is important to understand who we are and what we do in social work.

Now that we have briefly explored the content of the chapters, it will be useful to understand the ways in which the material comes together. The two common threads which tie all of the chapters together in this book are (i) the importance of relationships and (ii) the centrality of the everyday.

Firstly, relationships are central to social work. Social relations are also essential to selfhood, as we shall see throughout this text. Additionally, a student's engagement in learning about social work requires understanding the relationships between themselves and formal knowledge, themselves and their own values and those of the profession, as well as understanding how existing skills in communication are transferred into social work practice. Thus, those chapters which explore skills and values are oriented towards student engagement with the ways in which their own relationships have developed and are characterised. Understanding the ways in which one's own values and beliefs shape one's interaction with others, for example, helps to frame the ways in which social work values are central to social work practice, theory and research. A student's relationship with formal knowledge such as theoretical material is made stronger through reflexive engagement in the subject matter. For this reason, theory is outlined in relation to the social world and students are invited to consider the relationship between theories used in social work and the needs of others. Identifying the relationships—that is, the connections and synergies between practice, theory and the emerging social work self—is of central concern to this book.

Secondly, throughout this text the reader is encouraged to reflect upon their lived experience. Day-to-day or everyday life is used to help student engagement with social work. The everyday level of analysis, combined with the emphasis on relationships, promotes critical engagement with issues of central concern to social workers. Since social work is concerned with working with people, the ways in which we engage in the world around us prior to studying social work require reflection and analysis. It is through the engagement with the everyday that we can begin to unravel the embedded assumptions, values and social norms which characterise our social setting.

As we shall see throughout this book, becoming a social worker occurs through the intersection of one's life circumstances and experiences or biography, the broader scholarly ideas held by our profession, our own imagination and engagement in reflexivity. In order to participate in these interactions, we must understand the role of human interaction (Mead 1934). What brings social work students to social work differs greatly, but there is often a 'personal' experience which propels people into the work. This book offers opportunities to better understand the connections between who we are as a 'private' person and who we are as a professional and how these intersect and play out in the work that we do. At the beginning of studying social work it can be difficult to see what the future social work self will look like in everyday practice.

As a beginning social work student you are therefore entering a period of time and space where you will learn and fashion your social work self. The interaction between older ways of thinking and relating and newer ways which develop as you gain additional knowledge will be reflected upon. Your social work self is very much a part of who you already are. I leave you with the words of C. Wright Mills, who sums up this connection between our work and our selves. Here he urges students to view their intellectual endeavours as very much a part of their personal lives. In social work we bring our selves to our role and in this sense, the nexus between the personal, biographical, political and social holds the key to incorporating new knowledge about social work. Social work cannot be practised well without a personal commitment to fighting inequality and injustice.

It is best to begin, I think, by reminding you, the beginning student, that the most admirable thinkers within the scholarly community you have chosen to join do not split their work from their lives... What this means is that you must learn to use your life experience in your intellectual work: continually to examine and interpret it. In this sense craftsmanship is the centre of yourself and you are personally involved in every intellectual product upon which you may work. (Mills 1959, p. 196)

1

The Social
Work Self

This chapter:

- Introduces social work

- Explains what is meant by the term 'self'

- Promotes reflection about the self and assumptions

- Introduces the concept of reflexivity

- Outlines the theoretical orientation featured in this book

Imagine you are asked the question: 'who are you?' You might answer this by describing the way that you see yourself or you might imagine what others would say about you. The kinds of words you might use may well suggest a particular kind of 'personality'. Words such as 'easygoing' or 'shy' or 'kind' or even 'extrovert' or 'introvert' might spring to mind, for example. Yet the concept of a personality is just that: a concept. It is merely a theory to explain the self. Additionally, the ways in which we describe ourselves will change over time, alongside new and varied life experiences.

Think about how you would have been described when you were aged nine compared to your current age. Do you think you will use the same kinds of words to describe yourself when you are in your 80s? In this chapter we will critically challenge the notion of 'personality' through examining the idea that our self is always changing and in flux because it is produced through our interactions with others (Mead 1934). In social work, there is much to be learned about identity, or what we call 'the self', because the ways in which we think about our own identities help to shape how we approach others.

In this chapter we therefore begin to examine what this ongoing process of 'making' the social work self entails and specifically how identity is 'made'. In the same way that we can reflect upon and describe ourselves in everyday life, for example in the articulation of a 'personality' and its associated traits, so too can the professional social work self be described in specific terms. Whilst the ways in which we present ourselves as social workers will differ from person to person, there is also a broader social work identity which draws all social workers into a shared set of values, theory base and purpose. Before examining how individual social work identity is constituted, it is important to understand social work more broadly.

UNDERSTANDING SOCIAL WORK

The term 'social work' provokes varying responses, depending on the context within which the words are uttered. As Payne points out, 'there will never be a final answer that says social work is one thing' (2005, p. 11). This is due to a range of factors. For example, national policies can frame and determine the scope of social work roles and international social work practices vary markedly. Similarly, social work varies at certain temporal points in history. Social work in today's economic and social climate differs from the social work being practised decades ago. Exactly what I mean by social work may not be exactly what others mean. Yet despite all of these influences on social work, we can still make some general statements about what it entails. Social workers share similar professional values and work from a shared theory base. Social workers work to address inequality and injustice across a range of differing settings, roles and foci. Despite some differences in the ways social work is practised, experienced and even articulated, it does have a clear identity.

Social work involves working with people. Social workers see people in their social and cultural contexts and work to promote the well-being of others. This means that social workers share the view that inequality and oppression ought to be challenged and the rights of vulnerable people promoted. Yet what does this mean in practice? What do social workers *do*? The International Federation of Social Workers (IFSW) describes some of the *practices* that social workers engage in:

> Social work addresses the barriers, inequities and injustices that exist in society. It responds to crises and emergencies as well as to everyday personal and social problems. Social work utilises a variety of skills, techniques, and activities consistent with its holistic focus on persons and their environments. Social work interventions range from primarily person-focused psychosocial processes to involvement in social policy, planning and development. These include counselling, clinical social work, group work, social pedagogical work, and family treatment and therapy as well as efforts to help people obtain services and resources in the community. Interventions also include agency administration, community organisation and engaging in social and political action to impact social policy and economic development. The holistic focus of social work is universal, but the priorities of social work practice will vary from country to country and from time to time depending on cultural, historical, and socio-economic conditions. (IFSW: http://ifsw.org/policies/definition-of-social-work/)

Therefore some of the roles of a social worker entail: providing education; providing assistance to those in crisis; advocating for the rights of others; promoting the well-being of communities; providing clinical services such as individual, family and group therapeutic counselling services; working in partnership with others to advance political rights movements; designing services for communities based on needs; working with vulnerable persons to promote their safety and help them thrive; working in social policy and engaging in research.

There are some terms which help categorise the work which social workers undertake and these are primarily associated with particular groups of people. Therefore social workers often talk in a kind of 'shorthand' about their work. For example, a social worker may say they 'work in mental health'. Although the specific focus of their mental health work will depend on the type of organisation they work for (Is it government or non-government? Does the organisation work with people who self-refer or do people need a referral from another professional?), it is useful to understand the ways in which social work is divided according to themes or fields. Some of the key terms used to denote a particular social work focus are listed in Table 1.1.

TABLE 1.1 Some key terms used to denote a particular social work focus	
Field of practice	**Description**
Youth offending	Social work in youth offending involves working with young people who have committed criminal offences. Some organisations work with young people to try to prevent reoffending while others work to address broader issues such as safety, housing, employment and other needs.
Mental health	This area involves working with people with mental illness/mental health concerns. It can include those with diagnosed mental health conditions, those at risk of mental illness and their families and/or carers. Depending on the context, work can be with individuals, groups, families or communities. Services such as Child and Adolescent Mental Health Services (CAMHS) cater for mental health needs in children and teenagers whereas other services cater for adults.

TABLE 1.1 *continued*

Field of practice	Description
Substance misuse	This area involves working with people who have substance misuse issues such as drug and alcohol dependency/addiction. Work can be with a range of client issues/groups including individuals, families, groups and communities.
Older people	Social work with older people can include addressing health and/or accommodation needs, for example assessing and arranging residential aged care facilities. Depending on the organisational context, it can include working to prevent and/or protect against abuse ('safeguarding'), working with families, groups or communities.
Disability	Disability services can be divided according to age groups or for particular disabilities. For example, the needs of people with acquired brain injury will differ markedly from those of people with learning disabilities.
Children and families	Child protection, for example, involves working with children, young people and their caregivers towards protecting children and young people from harm, which includes abuse, violence and neglect. There are various services in this area, which determines the agency focus. Work can therefore span working with children, young people and their families, foster carers and carers, groups and communities. Work can be preventative, for example parenting programmes aimed at reducing child abuse, or can be in response to community need.
Sexual health	Sexual health services include specialist programmes such as those directed towards reducing teenage pregnancy, reducing sexually transmissible infections and issues relating to sexuality or sexual identity. Client groups can include school-based programmes, individual work and group work in community settings.
Domestic violence	Domestic violence involves control and the misuse of power through violence towards an intimate partner. Domestic violence can take the form of actual or threatened violence. This violence can be verbal, emotional, financial, sexual and/or physical. Services relating to domestic violence include shelters for people escaping domestic violence, counselling services, and programmes for perpetrators of domestic violence. Depending on the agency context, social workers can work with individuals, groups or communities.
CALD	This field of practice refers to working with people who are from Culturally And Linguistically Diverse backgrounds (CALD). The term NESB is also used for this client group (people from Non English Speaking Backgrounds). Some social workers describe their work according to this category, which can include work with refugees, particular ethnic communities, diaspora communities and people from particular cultural and religious groups.
Community	Community-based intervention targets a particular issue. For example, working towards prevention of stroke within the community might include encouraging smoking cessation, increasing community awareness about stroke symptoms and risk factors and working with other organisations to undertake early screening for risk factors. Community development encompasses work in national and international contexts and intervention occurs with the community rather than at an individual level.
Advocacy	Social workers in advocacy represent and work in partnership with clients so that they may gain access to services and opportunities. Rights-based intervention seeks to redress oppression. There are a number of client groups in this area, including the general population. Some organisations represent one particularly vulnerable and oppressed group of people. For example, the social model of disability recognises that the environment 'disables' people through its lack of design or accommodation for people with disabilities and this model can be used in individual, group and community work aiming for political and social change.

TABLE 1.1 *continued*	
Field of practice	**Description**
Health	Social workers within health can work towards preventing illness as well as alongside other health professionals on a range of programmes. Social models of health highlight the important contextual role that one's social setting, class, gender and other 'determinants' of health play in how well-being and health are experienced by individuals. Social work is well placed to work within a social model of health. Practitioners in this area may be employed in acute services such as hospitals and specialist clinics as well as in organisations working to prevent ill health.
International development	International development activities can encompass community work, individual work and group work. International development will involve a particular issue, such as reducing HIV transmission or assisting in peace-building. The work occurs in the country in which the development is targeted.
Policy	Policy refers to government-endorsed decisions about a particular issue. Working in policy can entail researching an issue and canvassing viewpoints from key individuals and groups about that issue. Policy working often involves communicating through written material such as reports, and work can be undertaken through both government and non-government organisations.
Research	Research entails a deeper understanding of a particular issue. Social workers who work in research can be employed in government and non-government organisations. They can carry out very large scale surveys as well as small scale studies such as those evaluating social work services.
Self-employed	Some social workers can work through consultancy. For example, those who have acquired particular expertise in an identifiable area of practice may offer services in such an area. Whether a social worker is able to sustain employment through working for themselves depends on the national context: social workers in some countries are more able to go into private practice than in other countries.

WORKING WITH OTHERS

Throughout this book we will explore some of the differing practice contexts and issues which relate to working with other professional groups. In understanding social work we also need to place the profession within its multidisciplinary context. Multidisciplinary, interdisciplinary or allied professionals working together all mean the same thing. These terms refer to the ongoing relationships between other professions and social workers. Multidisciplinary approaches entail working alongside, or in partnership with, various disciplines besides social work. The types of professions engaged in interdisciplinary working vary according to the field of practice. Table 1.2 takes the fields of practice from Table 1.1 and matches them to the key professions with whom social workers in the area may work.

Alongside these professionals, social workers can expect to work with carers and volunteers in a variety of settings. Social workers can also become specialised in their particular field, which differentiates them from other social workers whose work may be more generic. For example, mental health social

TABLE 1.2 The key professions with whom social workers in each field of practice may work

Field of practice	Working with others: Social workers work with...
Youth offending	Lawyers General practitioners (GPs) and specialists Teachers in educational institutions Youth workers Psychologists Interpreters
Mental health	Nurses Psychiatrists Psychologists General practitioners (GPs) Diversional therapists Interpreters
Substance misuse	Specialist medical professionals including nurses and doctors Interpreters Counsellors
Older people	Occupational therapists Speech therapists/speech pathologists Physiotherapists General practitioners (GPs) and specialists Podiatrists/chiropodists Psychologists Dieticians Exercise physiologists Interpreters
Disability	Occupational therapists Physiotherapists Speech therapists/speech pathologists General practitioners (GPs) and specialists Podiatrists/chiropodists Interpreters
Children and families	Teachers and educational institutions Police Community-based workers General practitioners (GPs) and specialists such as paediatricians Health Visitors Speech therapists/speech pathologists Lawyers Interpreters Family therapists Developmental psychologists
Sexual health	Nurses General practitioners (GPs) and specialists such as sexual health physicians, gynaecologists, obstetricians and midwives Community development workers Teenage pregnancy coordinators Health Visitors Interpreters

TABLE 1.2 *continued*	
Field of practice	**Working with others: Social workers work with...**
Domestic violence	General practitioners (GPs) and specialists Interpreters Counsellors Health Visitors
CALD	Interpreters Government and non-government workers Health professionals including general practitioners (GPs) and specialists
Community	Interpreters Government and non-government workers Community development workers
Advocacy	Interpreters Government and non-government workers Councillors/Members of Parliament (MPs)
Health	Occupational therapists Speech therapists/speech pathologists Physiotherapists General practitioners (GPs) and specialists Podiatrists/chiropodists Psychologists Health Visitors Dieticians Exercise physiologists Interpreters Diversional therapists
International development	Interpreters Policy-makers Epidemiologists Medical doctors and nurses Medical specialists such as obstetricians and gynaecologists Teachers Community workers
Policy	Government and non-government workers Advocacy groups Experts such as researchers Medical experts such as epidemiologists Interpreters
Research	Statisticians Social scientists Psychologists Interpreters Funders such as government and non-government employees

workers (also referred to as 'approved social workers/approved mental health practitioners') have particular roles within mental health and may be involved in the clinical assessment of people with mental health conditions. Similarly, social workers can work as counsellors and may gain further qualifications to specialise in therapeutic practice. Specialisms in social work can allow people to continue to develop their expertise in a particular area, which is an important aspect of professional self-development.

Although the idea that social workers work alongside or in partnership with other professionals can sound relatively straightforward, in fact there are many complexities relating to interdisciplinary working. Looking at Table 1.2, note in how many fields of practice social workers work alongside health professionals. What do you think might be the issues when working with other professions? For example, which professions are more respected or hold more power? Do social workers have less status than health professionals?

Recent research into the mental health field found that social workers were indeed worse off than other colleagues in relation to their professional identity and subsequent status (Bailey & Liyanage 2012). The researchers found that despite mental health social workers having gained expertise in the area, they have 'reduced status' (p. 1113) compared to other professional groups. This research resonates with earlier work which explored the relationship between medical doctors and social workers, and found that the respective world-views of each of these professions differed markedly (Huntington 1981). Yet differences can be productive, allowing each profession to bring new ideas which, when combined, benefit others (Lymbery 2006, p. 1122). Conflict as a result of interprofessional working can lead to creative responses to problems which might otherwise have been overlooked (Quinney & Hafford-Letchfield 2012). However, further complicating matters is the organisational context within which professions work together.

Broadly speaking, there are two aspects to interdisciplinary working. The first relates to the interpersonal relationships between professional staff. For example, some interdisciplinary team members are situated together in the work environment. The ways they communicate with one another will depend on a range of factors, but the portrayal of the profession of social work in that exchange depends on the profession's own identity as well as how that social worker understands and practises social work. Secondly, the funding models devised by governments and policy-makers along with the organisational settings, including the non-government or voluntary sector, impact on whether interdisciplinary work is effective and positive. This aspect to interdisciplinary working is more *structural* whereas the former is *interpersonal*. The structural setting and interpersonal relationships influence the service clients receive.

Bywaters (1986) argues that medical professionals and social workers cannot work together unless the medical profession adapts its world-view to include an appreciation of *social* models of health (Bywaters 1986, p. 663 cited in Lymbery 2006, p. 1122), rather than simply viewing work with others, as it has done historically (Lymbery 2006, p. 1125), through a strictly medical lens. Bywaters' position raises an important question: is it necessary to have shared world-views or epistemologies in order to work effectively together? This is something we will consider throughout the book. Importantly, what is the impact on the client of professions working alongside each other? Let's consider Case Study 1.1.

CASE STUDY 1.1 Samuel Carey

Imagine you are a social worker in a mental health hospital setting. As part of your role, each week you attend a case allocation meeting. This meeting is chaired by the medical Consultant who is the head of the medical team. Other attendees include other medical doctors, occupational therapists, physiotherapists, mental health nurses and social workers. You learn the following information:

> Samuel Carey is a white British male in his late 50s. He is in a long-term relationship with Sarah, aged 59, and they have two children who are both aged in their 30s. Samuel and Sarah live in a two bedroom flat in an upmarket area of town. Until recently, Samuel worked in the IT industry but he recently became retrenched. Sarah has Ehlers-Danlos syndrome which means that she has mobility problems. Sarah sees a physiotherapist privately for this condition, which is expected to worsen as she ages. Samuel has come to the attention of the unit after being arrested by the police one day prior to this referral. Samuel was reportedly seen damaging property after assaulting one of his former employees. The police reported that Samuel was 'psychotic' when he was incarcerated and they would like him to be detained and assessed by the unit. Although Samuel has been hostile since his contact with the police, he has no criminal history and has been described by former employees as 'a lovely guy who wouldn't hurt anyone'.

Consider what information might be important to take into account in deciding how to act. For example, consider:

- What might the physiotherapists be interested in learning more about?
- What might the mental health doctors and nurses be interested in learning more about?
- What might the social workers be interested in learning more about?

In this case study, it is somewhat easy to assume that the physiotherapists would be interested to hear more about the impact the Ehlers-Danlos syndrome is having on Sarah and how this will be managed in the future. Similarly, the occupational therapists may be interested in better understanding the limitations of mobility and related mental health issues and how these might be overcome in day-to-day life. Similarly, the mental health doctors and nurses may be interested in investigating further in order to undertake an assessment with a view to diagnosing Samuel so they can meet his needs through medication or therapies. The social worker might be approaching the situation wanting to understand how and why Samuel's behaviour has changed so markedly and what the impacts are for Sarah.

Yet all of the above are assumptions. The assumptions include that medical staff (including doctors, nurses and physiotherapists) are only interested in medical issues whereas the other professions are more interested in the social contexts (occupational therapists, mental health social workers). A more realistic and optimistic perspective is that each profession can apply their specialist knowledge in their work in order to help their client. In working with other professions, any one professional can recognise other areas where a client can benefit from others' expertise. Given the case study described a case allocation meeting, it is important to recognise that usually in these meetings a plan of action is decided. Consider, for example, that the medical doctor wanted to see Samuel immediately to make an assessment whereas the social worker wanted to see Samuel and Sarah together first. Both professions want to undertake their own assessment, but they will need to decide upon an agreed course of action. Similarly, the other professions will need to agree on what to do next. There are many potential ways to respond to this scenario. Assessing using some of the longer-term questions might consider: is there a risk of Samuel harming others? How will Sarah's mobility needs be met in the future? What are Samuel's needs and how will these be met?

Research has identified the tensions and complexities in interprofessional working (Bailey & Liyanage 2012; Bywaters 1986; Carpenter *et al.* 2003; Lymbery 2006). Multidisciplinary working may be more prevalent in the future, or it may become less common, but it is clear that the social work profession will need to continue to work with other professionals in the immediate future. One aspect which affects the status of a profession and its portrayal to other professional groups is the identity of social work itself. We now consider what is meant by identity, or *self*, and how this is relevant to becoming a social worker.

WHAT IS THE SELF?

Take a look at Figure 1.1 on page 22. What do you see? Take a few moments to really reflect upon this image and begin to think about the identity of the subject. Who do you think is featured in this image? Does the ear belong to a man or a woman? What makes you think about them as gendered? From this image are you able to draw any conclusions about the person's age? Do you think they are aged in their teens, for example, or are they in older age? What clues are there to help you decide their age group? Do you see the person as wealthy, or working class? What kind of house do they live in and are they employed? Can you tell what their cultural background is? Are they part of a large family, do they have siblings and how might you characterise their peer group?

Even though what is featured in the photograph is only a fragmented image of a person, when you first began to study the image you already began to connect the ear with an individual. Through looking at the image you started to piece together experiences unique to you—your life, the people around you such as your friends and family—and think about how you might categorise the person featured in the photograph in relation to these. For example, from studying this image you may imagine that the subject is male, that because of his piercing he is a young person and perhaps he is image conscious. You can then begin to create a mental image of the person by linking together your own experiences in everyday life with the imagined identity of the subject in the photograph. Perhaps you know a young man whom you are basing your image upon. Or maybe you are drawing your knowledge and inspiration from images you see in the media. Your experience of social interaction—or sociality—helps you to make some initial assumptions about the identity of the person featured in this image. Human interactions take place in everyday life and include conversations and communication with others in a range of daily activities.

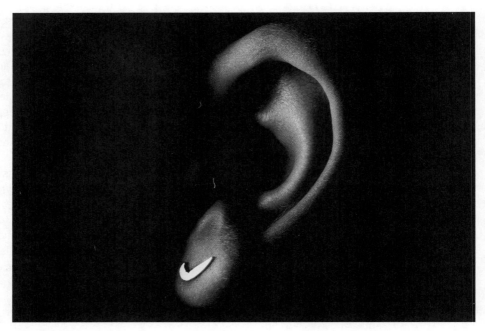

FIGURE 1.1 What and who do you see?

© Andrew Dunbar

Without these interactions, society would cease to function. Not only are these inter-actions central to a functioning society—sociality is also central to creating the self (Mead 1934). Let us take a closer look at sociality and what it means for selfhood.

SOCIAL INTERACTION OR SOCIALITY

George Herbert Mead's scholarship has provided a significant, and continuing, contribution to sociology (Alexander 1989; Joas 1997). His work is usually associ-ated with a particular tradition in sociology called symbolic interactionism. Symbolic interactionism 'directs our attention to the detail of interpersonal interac-tion, and how that detail is used to make sense of what others say and do. Sociologists influenced by symbolic interactionism often focus on face-to-face interaction in the contexts of everyday life. They stress the role of such interaction in creating society and its institutions' (Giddens 2005, p. 18). As we shall see, Mead (1934) argues that the self is created through social interactions.

There are strong historical links with Mead's theory-building about interpersonal relationships and social work, with Mead having been involved in many of the hous-ing and rights struggles of early social work figures such as Jane Addams (Forte 2004a, p. 393). For this reason, Mead is also associated with a type of early sociol-ogy in which social problems were not only theorised or thought about by scholars but were acted upon through social action and activism.

Mead's conception of self is useful for understanding the professional social work self. Broadly speaking, interactionism emphasises the power produced through relationships between people. Since social work is also focused on relationships and their meanings for individuals, groups and communities, it makes sense that person-to-person interaction and understanding the person themselves is an area of intellectual inquiry. Mead's theory of self resonates with early social work literature ranging from Mary Richmond's notion of self to Siporin's (1972) appreciation of the self in its social context (Forte 2004a, p. 394). As we will see throughout this book, Mead's theories are relevant to social work. Yet it is important to understand what we mean by social interaction. This involves understanding the link between social interaction and selfhood.

In *Mind, Self and Society* Mead (1934) argues that the self is 'made' through *sociality* which consists of social interactions and relationships with others. Thus we only create our identities or selves through these relationships. As we shall see, this idea is in direct contrast with psychoanalytic notions of the self, which primarily see identity as being complex and compartmentalised. For example, Mead rejects the notion that people have a mind—the only mind, he says, is that which is produced through external relationships with others. Mead says that the mind is not internal to individuals but is a concept which is reinforced through our interactions with others. This idea—that the mind is outside our selves rather than inside—goes against what is popularly accepted to be 'true'.

At the beginning of this chapter you were invited to think about how you would respond to the question: 'who are you?' Your response would have most likely drawn from the idea that people's identities can be defined through the notion of personality. Yet a personality is simply an idea in which the self is represented as an internal, quantifiable and descriptive entity. Mead's notion of self (1934) rejects the view that people have personalities and he argues that there is no such thing as a 'mind' beyond the idea shared between people. Instead, social interaction is central to 'producing' the self. There are some examples of ways people display a sense of self which is external to their thoughts or minds. Imagine you were to make a collage of images, for example on a pin board or a social media website, to represent yourself—this would be an example of how we like to pictorialise our selves and present this to others for them to see. Mead's idea about self being external to our minds is similar to this idea in that we describe ourselves to others and think about ourselves only in relation to others and the rest of society.

According to Mead (Mead 1934; Da Silva 2011), all social interactions—interactions involving more than one person engaged with another through gestures and language, conversations and behaviours—are constitutive of the self. Whereas in psychoanalytic theory the self is formed through internal thought processes and conflicts, Meadian sociality emphasises social processes, which are 'outside' the self, as constitutive.

It is often assumed that in order to understand ourselves we need to go back to think about our childhood, since that was the time we learned particular things and experienced particular things. In thinking about childhood, we can see the differences and similarities between psychoanalytic theories and interactionist theories. For both psychoanalytic theory as well as Mead's theory, childhood is important to the self (Crossley 2001, p. 145). However, precisely *how* it is important differs markedly between the two theories.

Mead argues that by social interaction through childhood games and play children learn about society's norms and values (Mead 1934, pp. 368–373) and in this way children learn about the 'generalized other'. Society's norms and values (which are called the 'generalized other' by Mead) are easy to forget since we are continuously using this knowledge automatically. Society's norms about how we conduct ourselves in a café include, for example, the assumption that we will sit on a seat, order a drink or food and talk to people at our table. Childhood learning about the generalized other enables people to pre-empt how others will respond to things. For example, imagine you were to stand up from where you are reading this book, throw the book into the air and start shouting. What would others around you do? We can say with a certain confidence that throwing books and shouting is not a generally accepted social act. Yet if we had been bitten by a wasp, this behaviour might be perfectly understandable. The reaction of those around us would depend on the social situation. If you are in a library or a crowded bus, others will respond with caution. If you are with family or friends they might be less reluctant to question you about why you are behaving in this way.

The fact that we can pre-empt others' behaviour is for Mead evidence that we are able to draw upon our knowledge of the generalized other. For Mead, fantasy or 'abstract thought' is the means through which the generalized other is manifest (Mead 1934, pp. 155–156). In psychoanalytic theory, fantasy symbolises the deeper tension that characterises the self, as we shall see in the following critical discussion. Because of the prominence of psychoanalytic theories of the self in everyday life it is crucial to critique these approaches and examine their differences to the social construction of the self.

Psychoanalytic scholarship about the self represents an established intellectual tradition and one which has been argued to apply to sociological understandings of the self (see, for example, Elliott 2001, 2005). Yet the contrast between the ways in which the self can be examined through Meadian analysis and psychoanalytic theory could not be more marked. Despite the historical emphasis and subsequent proliferation of therapeutic discourse in contemporary life (Furedi 2004) Mead's theoretical tradition better accounts for the ways in which the social work identity is forged. As we shall see, there is some common ground between the two approaches: the prominence of childhood in the formation of the self and the role of language and communication, for example, are central to both approaches.

Psychoanalytic theory influenced much of the theorising about the self until the 1960s social constructionist theory-building shifted the emphasis away from the Freudian self more towards the social self (Jackson & Scott 2010a, p. 9). Although the social self is prominent in scholarly literature, we are most familiar with psychoanalytic notions of identity. For example, in popular culture we uncritically accept the concept of personality—the idea that we can describe particular traits about ourselves—yet this is merely a theoretical concept that has gained popularity in contemporary culture. We explore this further in Chapter 4 in relation to social work theory.

In particular, ideas from psychoanalytic theory have had significant purchase in various disciplines since the 19th century and continue to be embedded in social work theory and practice. The idea that in order to resolve a problem one must engage in therapy or counselling is an example of the underlying assumptions from psychoanalytic theory. The 'therapeutic turn'—or the historically identifiable point at which we elevated therapy as important to our well-being—is not only a process involving individual subjectivities, but is argued to have become a ubiquitous aspect of contemporary social life in western societies (Furedi 2004; Lasch 1979; Reiff 1966).

Evidence for this is the comparatively recent rise in the number of self-help books, television shows and other media which promote the idea that through learning more about ourselves we are free to change things we do not like in us. Yet in this tradition, who we are—or the self—is splintered in that it contains a conscious, socially mediated self as well as an unconscious dimension to identity. Symbols connected to the self such as language, dreams and everyday interactions offer interpretations of this conflict between the unconscious and the conscious. Therefore the psychoanalytic self cannot ever be seen to be conflict-free. Accepting those theories that see desire and the unconscious as being problematically connected in time to stages of development from childhood would seem to mean that the adult self cannot be free from pathology.

The therapeutic application of psychoanalytic theory equates to what has been termed the 'talking therapies'. Here individuals can reflect upon and explore subjective issues. Although the ubiquity of therapeutic practices is utilitarian (Elliott 1996; Elliott & Lemert 2006)—they offer 'individuals a radical purchase on the dilemmas of living in the modern epoch' (Elliott 1996, p. 329)—it is the contribution made by George Herbert Mead that enables a richer and more socially orientated analysis of the self in contemporary times (Jackson 1999; Jackson & Scott 2010a, 2010b).

To understand individuals, one must look at their relationships with others and the broader society in which they are immersed. This idea differs from the focus on the *individual themselves*, an idea which dominates the public sphere due to its fascination with therapeutic discourse (Furedi 2004). In social work, as we shall see in Chapter 4, there has been a dual focus on psychology and sociology which is realised through the differing strands of social work theory.

For Mead, to understand individual action, one must see the action as part of an individual's *interactions*: 'Significance belongs to things in their relations to individuals. It does not lie in mental processes which are enclosed within individuals' (Mead 1922 [2011], p. 69).

Whereas in psychoanalytic theory the mind contains an 'unknowable unconscious' (Jackson 2007, p. 4), for Mead, the mind is only 'knowable' through social processes. Therefore in understanding the individual, one must understand their relationship to others in society and the role these relationships play in determining identity. Specifically, this means that the individual gradually learns how to interact and understand the role of others and the values of society. This learning occurs from birth onwards, with children learning about society's rules and values through interaction. Mead says:

In the process of communication the individual is an other before he [sic] is a self. It is in addressing himself in the role of an other that his self arises in experience. The growth of the organized game out of simple play in the experience of the child, and of organized group activities in human society, placed the individual then in a variety of roles, in so far as these were parts of the social act, and the very organization of these in the whole act gave them a common character in indicating what he had to do. He is able then to become a generalized other in addressing himself in the attitude of the group or the community. In this situation he has become a definite self over against the social whole to which he belongs. (Mead 1925 [2011], p. 199)

In social work it is vital to remain oriented to the role the social dimension plays in influencing human experience. The connection between the individual and the society within which they are embedded is central to social work, as we shall see throughout this book. Let's now consider the role of childhood in relation to the development of the self.

For Mead the period of childhood is of crucial importance to social competence as it enables individuals to learn the dominant norms and attitudes of society—'in the instance of the infant ... effective adjustment to the little society upon which it has so long to depend' (Mead 1934, p. 368). There is a more detailed examination of childhood play in Chapter 2, where it is discussed in relation to human development, but it is important to note the placement of childhood as central to Mead's sociality because for him it is a time when children undertake learning that helps them engage in social exchanges throughout their lives.

For Mead, sociality—which is the engagement in social interactions and processes—is constitutive of selfhood (Mead 1934). Being 'constitutive' of selfhood means that it constitutes, 'makes' or 'produces' the self. Put simply, Mead argues that *we can only become ourselves, and continue to be ourselves, by interacting with others.*

There are many examples of the ways in which our relationships with others reinforce our identity or self. Imagine the way you might greet a person with whom you might be working. A simple 'hello' might result in a particular set of gestures, dialogue and other ways of communicating such as through non-verbal activity. You might, for example, make eye contact with your colleague and smile. You might sit down across from them to begin your discussion. Your posture might be upright and formal. You might be holding on to stationery such as a pen and a pad of paper. Think about the differences between the 'you' in this context and the 'you' in another context. Think about, for example, greeting a family member or close friend in your home. You might not make eye contact with them and might walk past them to get to your chair, briefly saying 'hi' to them. Once you get to your chair you may slump down and watch television or start reading a book. Your friend or family member may not look up from their activity and may simply reply 'hi' back to you. The 'you' in both of these situations are examples of the different roles we play in everyday life. In both these examples, the interaction with others takes different forms. The familiarity which is embedded in the relationship and interaction at home means that the 'you' is reflected differently than in the interaction with the colleague. The tiny changes in mannerisms, bodily postures and movements as well as other forms of communication are all employed differently depending on the context. Both of these are examples of sociality—engagement with other people. In interacting with you, the social interactions reinforce your own identity as 'worker' or 'family member' or 'friend'. In my own research about selfhood I have found that the role that interaction with others plays is crucial to our ongoing identities (Dunk-West 2011). It is therefore crucial to understand the role that sociality plays in the context of people's everyday life worlds.

Yet so far we have been thinking about the self as an individual, and not so much about the broader social setting within which these interactions take place. Although the individual self has been given prominence in Mead's work, it is also important to understand how *society* is theorised in relation to the ways in which selfhood is argued to be produced. In particular, individual behaviour ought to be made sense of in the context within which it takes place. Is society just a collection of individuals? Are we free to choose our actions or are we influenced by other factors? The degree to which one person is able to exercise choice within this context is an historically enduring debate (Handel 2003, p. 133).

The tension between the individual and society is related to the so-called 'agency versus structure' debate. Put another way, this refers to the idea of individual will versus societal pressure. Ending this debate means reconciling the tension between seeing individuals as able to shape their lives through choice and seeing them as constrained by social circumstances and therefore less free to make choices. Are we free to act or are we following a script? There is no easy answer to this question.

Consider what assumptions underpin the idea that we can become 'better'. The notion of working hard to achieve particular means relies upon the idea that individuals are able to change their circumstances. Material wealth, for example, is something that some people strive to achieve. Having agency relates to the freedom to make changes in one's life or circumstances. To have unlimited agency means that everyone has the same opportunities to make changes and choices in their lives, whereas to believe that structure shapes society means supporting the view that individuals are less powerful than social institutions and that although individuals may try to achieve certain goals, their success is ultimately shaped by the influence of social structures.

Mead's approach is to argue that there is little use in making distinctions between individuals and society, since it is individuals who *make* society. A useful starting point to understand how Mead views the dynamic between the individual and the social emerges through the explanation in the following quote:

> The social act is not explained by building it up out of stimulus plus response; it must be taken as a dynamic whole—as something going on—no part of which can be considered or understood by itself—a complex organic process implied by each individual stimulus and response involved in it. (Mead 1934, p. 7)

Sociality is not only constitutive for the formation of the self—that is, social interactions do more than enable people's selves to be produced. Sociality exists through complex, dynamic interactional processes. Therefore the individual is part of a broader 'organic process' (Mead 1934, p. 7) in which other individuals interact. These interactions form what we might call 'society'.

Whilst Mead's conceptualisation of selfhood has achieved a great deal of attention in sociological literature, the ways in which he theorises 'society' have been of lesser interest to scholars (Athens 2005, p. 305). Yet Mead is clear about the relationship between the individual and society:

> Human society as we know it could not exist without minds and selves, since all its most characteristic features presuppose the possession of minds and selves by its individual members; but its individual members would not possess minds and selves if these had not arisen within or emerged out of the human social process. (Mead 1934, p. 227)

Social values relate to what Mead refers to as the 'generalized other' which, as we have seen, is the 'attitude of the community' (Mead 1934, p. 154). These attitudes are internalised to a greater and greater extent through the process of socialisation until individuals have intuitive knowledge of broader society's attitudes (Mead 1934, pp. 155–156) and social interaction becomes so familiar it is routine (Crossley 2001, p. 145). This process occurs from birth onwards, throughout childhood and into adulthood. It is a central question, then, to consider the role of changes in society, given the shifts and changes brought about by the contemporary world.

Scholars interested in late modern social life make links between broader forces such as globalisation and individualisation (see, for example, Giddens 1992) and the ways in which these are manifest in the decisions individuals make in everyday life. For example, the relatively recent trend in which people in committed intimate relationships live apart from one another, so called 'living apart together' (LAT) (see Holmes 2006), can be used as evidence of the increasingly detraditionalised (Giddens 1992, pp. 178–181) environment in which couples negotiate their lifestyles, jobs and relationships. The ways in which these changes in relationships fit with the life course are further discussed in Chapter 2. Detraditionalisation simply means that we have more choices available to us than when our roles were more clearly defined. For example, the traditional roles of 'male bread-winner' and 'wife' meant quite different things in the 1950s to today.

Mead notes the importance of communication in the ongoing interaction between people. In particular, communication is attained in the same manner as all knowledge which is required of social competence: through socialisation. Mead stresses that communicative action is a social process, yet it also links the individual with the means by which to reflect upon his or her self:

> The process of communication simply puts the intelligence of the individual at his [sic] own disposal. But the individual that has this ability is a social individual. He does not develop it by himself and then enter into society on the basis of this capacity. He becomes such a self and gets such control by being a social individual, and it is only in society that he can attain this sort of a self which will make it possible for him to turn back on himself and indicate to himself the different things he can do. (Mead 1934, p. 243)

For Mead, communication is intrinsically connected to the socialising process which, in turn, forms the ongoing social interaction which produces the self (Mead 1934, p. 257). Mead examines other forms of interaction—such as an individual reading a novel or a journalistic text—and demonstrates that although these are varying communicative forms which require knowledge about the generalized other they are forms of communication (Mead 1934, pp. 256–257). Social exchanges in which no personal interaction is required—say that which occurs through engagement in social networking sites or via email or instant messaging—meet the requirements for Mead's depiction of sociality. This is because (i) such exchanges draw from written forms of communication, (ii) they involve more than one person and (iii) they occur as part of existing networks between individuals. Technology both facilitates and replicates interaction that is similar to interaction in the social world (West *et al.* 2011). As Mead says:

> You cannot build up a society out of elements that lie outside of the individual's life-processes. (Mead 1934, p. 257)

In this way, forms of communication which utilise new technologies such as Web 2.0 (see Gauntlett 2007, 2011), including Twitter, Facebook and other social networking sites, can be considered as involving Meadian social interaction. These new forms of communication help to underline the importance we place on interacting with one another in social life (Gauntlett 2011).

THE SELF, REFLEXIVITY AND CONTEMPORARY LIFE

So far we have considered the role of others in helping us make relationships which produce our identities. Also significant is the role of reflexivity and reflexiveness, an area which has been the subject of sociological examinations of the self. In social work, reflexivity means a particular set of processes which help us know who we are as professionals. There is an explanation of the differences between these concepts in the theoretical and applied social sciences in the Glossary at the end of this book. We now consider the role of reflexivity in understanding the processes whereby our selves are 'made' through interaction with other people.

Reflexivity entails engaging in three interrelated processes. Firstly, we think about, or reflect upon, something specific. Secondly, we critically evaluate that activity. Thirdly, we change future relations of actions based on a conscious decision to change the particular activity. For example, I might reflect upon an incident in which I felt I did not get my point across to a colleague. I might think about one particular incident and decide that I was not assertive enough. Based upon my wish to be more assertive and taking into account my perceived failure to be assertive on a previous occasion, the next time I relate to that colleague, I will deliberately work at being more assertive and this will change my behaviour towards them. I might use different words, have different gestures or come across as 'rude'. These changes are brought about as a direct result of my reflexive engagement with my self and the ways in which I see myself (as non-assertive, for example). Reflexivity in social work is not new (see Schon 1983, for example) and relates to the idea that we reflect upon our social work practice to get better and better.

There is an argument in sociology that identity has become an 'ongoing project' (Giddens 1992, p. 30). This means that we are constantly reflecting upon who we are and who we want to be and making changes to realise this idealised version of ourselves. As Giddens (1992, p. 30) says, 'The self today is for everyone a reflexive project—a more or less continuous interrogation of past, present and future'.

Both Bauman (2003) and Giddens (1992) argue that the characteristics of the late modern world, such as globalisation, have 'transformed' ways in which individuals interrelate in personal relationships in their day-to-day lives. For example, because of greater communication across continents, we now have more opportunities to see how others live which may cause us to think about how we live. In western countries, television shows and other forms of technological communication expose us to new alternatives. This new type of 'extended reflexivity' (Adams 2003) means that reflexivity has been increased *because* of globalisation and other large social shifts. However, Giddens' 'extended reflexivity', in which complex social conditions are theorised to have provided new possibilities for self-fashioning, does not address the everyday social and cultural practices within which we are engaged (Adams 2003).

Whilst Giddens' extended reflexivity is viewed as a *product* of contemporary life, Mead argues that what he calls 'reflexiveness' is firmly embedded within social relations. It is not increasing because of new social conditions. Both Giddens and Mead highlight the importance of the social setting from the onset of human life (Adams 2003, p. 232). Mead's reflexiveness is merely a part of his broader theory of the self. It is a feature of the interaction between people. For Giddens, reflexivity is increasing because society is changing.

Mead argues that 'reflexiveness' means being an 'other' to oneself, only through continual interaction with social processes (1934, p. 134). Mead says that (what would be named) 'reflexivity' is not merely a tool for self-fashioning but is required for social functioning (Jackson 2007, p. 8). What people think of as their 'minds' are, in fact, firmly locatable outside their selves (in contrast to psychoanalytic notions of subjectivity which see identity as related to an 'inner' world of individual thoughts and reflections): minds arise only through social interactions. Mead (1934, p. 134) argues that 'reflexiveness, then, is the essential condition, within the social process, for the development of mind'.

The notion of reflexiveness, or reflexivity, is therefore a compulsory condition for sociality, which in turn 'makes' the self. It is a feature of human life and human action (Archer 2007). The term reflexivity has been simplified in both social work and the social sciences because of a failure to recognise the complex processes associated with sociality:

> Being reflexive is enormously complex because the actor has to think of many possibilities and many consequences not only for others, but for the constitution of the self. The pressure to select, to choose one of the many lines of action, increases the more you get into the public world... The task of the actor is to continually link and adjust and transform and stabilize the interpersonal and the

cultural while maintaining the plausibility of the self. (Gagnon 2011 in Gagnon & Simon 2011 [1973], p. 315)

The process of reflexiveness is central to sociality, which is in turn constitutive of the self and self-making, which is both an aspect of a broader identity and part of a more private sphere. The process of reflexiveness is central to making the social work self. Throughout this text, the exercises are designed to actively engage you in that reflexive process in order to make your social work self. You also do this through engagement with texts, discussions with fellow students and your lecturers as well as through your experiences on placement.

Why is all of this important in social work? It is somewhat of a truism in social work that we are not good at saying who we are or what we do. How do we describe our role to others? How do we distinguish our work from other professions? What value do social workers bring to multidisciplinary work? I believe that although we might not always be able to articulate our work, in practice, social workers develop creative and innovative ways which characterise their practice and identity.

In this book the focus is upon the social work self: how to be a social worker involves understanding one's self and how selfhood is theorised. I argue that the Meadian notion of the self is relevant and helpful to claiming the terrain that social work encompasses. Such a theoretical framework helps in social workers understanding themselves and their professional work. As we shall see, such an understanding relies upon having insights into one's own life experiences and characteristics.

Having a purchase on a theoretical model of selfhood helps social workers to approach knowledge accordingly. The subsequent chapters in this book therefore examine the contexts and material relevant to learning about social work and developing the social work self. Let us now move to consider more fully what this understanding entails.

UNDERSTANDING THE SOCIAL WORK SELF

The centrality of interaction to self-production in the professional context is what drives this book. In other words, becoming a social worker occurs through the intersection of biography, scholarly ideas, imagination and reflexivity: none of these are possible to engage in without human interaction (Mead 1934).

In Table 1.3 some of the key ideas we have examined in this chapter are related directly to social work.

The choice of words and the way we frame social work is influenced by historical, social, cultural and political contexts. The International Federation of Social Workers notes that our definition of social work is always in flux. They offer the following as a way to describe the work of social workers throughout the world:

The social work profession promotes social change, problem solving in human relationships and the empowerment and liberation of people to enhance well-being.

TABLE 1.3 The relation of some of the key ideas in this chapter to social work

General	Specific to social work
The self is not simply a 'personality', it is produced through social interactions	The social work self is dependent on broader social, economic and political contexts
Our experiences are shaped by broader social inequalities and there is a tension between 'agency and structure'	Social workers work with people to change individual behaviour but also to challenge oppressive systems and broader social inequalities
Reflexiveness or reflexivity is important in contemporary life	The social work self is produced through social interactions. Reflexivity is central to social interaction

Utilising theories of human behaviour and social systems, social work intervenes at the points where people interact with their environments. Principles of human rights and social justice are fundamental to social work. (IFSW 2012)

At the end of your studies, and throughout your social work career, it is important to remind yourself what social work means. You will find that your definition will evolve and shift. It is crucial that social workers define their own profession: policy and legislation should never dictate what social work entails. Instead, your social work self will be made through adherence to particular ethical obligations, through understanding the purpose of your work with others and through the ongoing interaction between yourself and those you work with, including your colleagues, employers and clients.

Exercises 1.1 and 1.2 are designed to help you begin to engage with your present understanding of what social work means.

EXERCISE 1.1

Put the following statements in order from most important (1) to least important (10).

Social workers ... need to change the world
Social workers ... need to work hard
Social workers ... are always on duty
Social workers ... should make people do things
Social workers ... are like the police
Social workers ... help people to change
Social workers ... work with communities
Social workers ... should be able to work anywhere in the world
Social workers ... need career goals
Social workers ... should be caring

Think about how you came to believe the statements above and note that we will revisit this activity at the end of the book.

EXERCISE 1.2

Begin to think about the interactions you engage in in your everyday life. For example, think about your interactions at university: has your attendance at university changed the way you view the world? This activity is designed for you to reflect upon who you interact with and how these interactions influence your sense of self. Map these out using the shapes in 1.2. Your self is at the centre and each cloud represents an institution. For example, one cloud may represent university. Draw a line towards your self and write a statement near the line which characterises the strength of its influence on who you are. Another cloud may be your family.

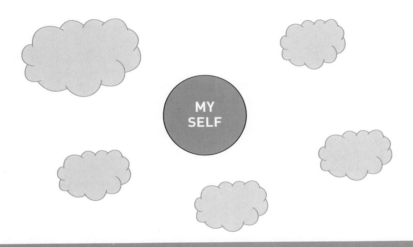

After completing Exercise 1.2 you will see that there are many ways in which you engage in sociality in your everyday life. This is how Mead would say your self is produced or made. Your understanding of the ways in which you come across to others and how you think others perceive you underpins these social exchanges. You learned about appropriate ways to interact with others in childhood and this knowledge is referred to as understanding the generalized other. For example, in lectures, there is an unspoken rule that you sit and listen to the lecturer: you and your fellow students understand that this is expected of you. In noting your relationship to your social work studies in Exercise 1.2, there is a lot of knowledge about relating to others that goes unnoticed. Engaging in these exercises has helped you begin the process of reflexivity in relation to producing your social work self, and you will continue to develop an increased awareness about your emerging social work self throughout this text.

In this chapter we have explored how the ongoing process of 'making' the social work self requires engagement with formal texts, one's sense of self and interaction with colleagues and class-mates alongside the learning that takes place at university and on placement. We have begun to highlight the significance of this interactionist way of viewing professional self-constitution through understanding how identity is 'made'. This chapter has therefore laid the foundations upon which this book is constructed. The interactionist social work self is one in process. It is the aim of this book to help students *engage* with this process. This can occur through the discussion of the formal learning material which is set out in each chapter alongside creative opportunities to extend such learning.

FURTHER READING

DA SILVA, F. C. (2011) *G. H. Mead: A Reader*. London: Routledge.

GRAY, M., WEBB, S. A. & MIDGLEY, J. O. (eds) (2012) *The Sage Handbook of Social Work*. London: Sage Publications.

MEAD, G. H. (1934) *Mind, Self and Society: From the Standpoint of a Social Behaviorist*. Chicago: University of Chicago Press.

QUINNEY, A. & HAFFORD-LETCHFIELD, T. (2012) *Interprofessional Social Work: Effective Collaborative Approaches*, 2nd edn. Exeter: Learning Matters.

SCHON, D. (1983) *The Reflective Practitioner: How Professionals Think in Action*. London: Temple Smith.

2

Human Development

This chapter:

- Introduces the lifespan approach

- Examines the socio-cultural aspect alongside developmental approaches

- Outlines the key developments in childhood, adulthood and older age

- Invites reflexive engagement with knowledge about the self and others

- Considers the role of social work in the context of human development throughout the lifespan

How old are you? Do you like being your current age, and if so, why? Do you wish you were older, or younger? What would you say is the best age to be? Whenever I have posed these questions to social work students the common answer I get is that the best age is older than adolescence and younger than, say, around 70 years of age. A large percentage of my students over the years have reported that childhood is a 'good age' because of its association with being 'carefree' and a time of little or no worry about those issues associated with adulthood such as career, income and other responsibilities.

Our notions of age and the way we feel about age are somewhat personal but, as we shall see in this chapter, there are common, general experiences that fall within specific age categories. Thus we can make fairly generalised statements about age, and these will hold true for the majority of people. Our favourite age is therefore not only a personal view. It is influenced by a number of forces, including the developmental milestones and socially derived attitudes associated with the age stage in question. How we think about age and the knowledge we have about development are central to our professional work with people in a variety of settings.

In social work we are purposefully developing ongoing relationships with individuals, families, groups and communities. To better understand those with whom we work, knowledge about life stages and human development is crucial. This is because, for example, such knowledge helps us to distinguish between 'normal' development and development that might require additional assistance or assessment. As we shall see in this chapter, knowledge about human development also assists us to help others make sense of their lives. Knowledge about human growth and development is relevant to all areas of social work practice, from the most obvious—working with children—to other areas such as the disabilities field or working with particular age groups such as younger people and older people as well as communities. Understanding broader demographic trends, for example the increasing number of older people as a percentage of the population, helps us plan better for social work services in particular communities.

Generally speaking, there are two main ways of thinking about age. The first—theorised through developmental psychology—relates to the view that our lives are characterised by a series of incremental, developmental stages, each of which brings its own challenges and achievements. The second is more sociological and enables an appreciation of the broader social experiences and the ways in which life stages are produced through social exchange. In this chapter we will examine the lifespan using knowledge from both psychological and sociological theories and research.

Take a look at Figure 2.1 on page 38. What do you notice in this photo of a man, a child and a dog? Is your immediate thought to assume the relationship between these characters? For example, do you see the older man as the grandfather of the younger boy who is there with his pet dog? Let's reflect upon the people in the photograph using the two approaches to human growth and development. Firstly, let's try to think about the ages of the man and the boy. Think about others you may know—these can be people in your family or friendship networks or people in the media—and try to place the subjects in the photograph alongside them. The boy

FIGURE 2.1 What is the relationship between the subjects in this photograph?
© Andrew Dunbar

looks too tall to be a toddler and not quite old enough to be an adolescent. If he were to be between these age ranges—that is, between toddlerhood or early childhood and adolescence—this would place him in the 'middle childhood' age range. The man in the photograph looks much older than the boy. We can see that the older man is wearing a wedding ring, suggesting that he is in a committed intimate relationship. He looks older than, say, someone in their 20s or 30s but not yet in older age. We could assume that the man is aged in his mid to late 50s. Given this information we can surmise that the man could be the boy's father or he could be his grandfather.

It is also important to understand the historical context in which we are viewing this image—this is because societal shifts change the ways in which our day-to-day relationships are lived out. There is clear evidence that in western cultures people are putting off having children until later in life. Couples and individuals who delay the onset of family life have to weigh up both biological and social factors (Stein &

Susser 2000) in a way that previous generations did not. Someone from the 1940s studying the photo would see it in a very different way from yourself, a citizen of the 21st century where older parents are becoming the norm.

In a moment we will begin to explore how these two life stages—middle childhood and adulthood—are theorised in relation to developmental psychology. In these, and other, life stages we can make general assumptions about social, emotional, cognitive and physical changes and milestones associated with each age. Before we discuss these in further detail, let's go back to the subjects in the image and approach how we understand them in a slightly different manner. We have established that the ages of the subjects are approximately late 50s and somewhere in middle childhood, say 7–10 years. If we think about a man in his late 50s then we might assume he is the father of the younger person. Or, we could assume he is his grandfather.

In this chapter we will examine both of these traditions in the context of the human lifespan and its associated development. There is a vast body of knowledge—mostly in the fields of developmental and social psychology—that has provided theories for understanding human development. In particular, childhood has been the subject of a great deal of research and theorising over the past five decades.

The work of Jean Piaget (1964, 1973), for example, draws upon his empirical work with children and has been advanced in recent years by followers of his tradition, called neo-Piagetians. Piaget is often studied in social work because, although criticised for its generalisations, his work continues to remain highly relevant to the ways in which we understand childhood. Piaget's central theory is that cognition—or thoughts—form differently for children than for adults. Based on his experiments with children, he believed that children make sense of the world around them differently than adults. He believed that children think differently than adults. This central tenet can be applied in direct work with parents who often—understandably—think about their children's behaviours in adult terms.

Piaget's reminder that children do not think in the same 'logical' ways adults do can help to more optimistically frame children's behaviour, and his stages are a kind of mapping of childhood cognitive development. Understanding children's behaviour through developmental theories helps social workers to understand the world of the child, and to see the world through their eyes involves a sophisticated application of theory to individual, social and cultural circumstances. As we shall see, Piaget argues that children progress through various stages during childhood in which their cognition, or thinking, changes according to their developmental stage.

In the same way that childhood is thought about in relation to key developmental milestones, so too can the entire lifespan be thought about in this way. The lifespan can be divided into key categories, and these are elucidated upon below.

FIGURE 2.2 Trilby painting: How can theories of development be applied to this scenario?

Figure 2.2 shows a little girl, called Trilby, painting. We can see that she is engaged in the activity and has mastered her hand and eye coordination, which enables her to successfully complete this activity. Trilby is three years old in this photograph. She is able to grasp the paintbrush and will probably have developed a preference for a particular hand by this age. She can move the paintbrush from the paint to the paper and sweep it across the paper with purpose. Though a seemingly mundane activity (by adult standards!), it is important to remember that Trilby was not always able to paint like this. Rather, her ability to successfully engage in this activity is the product of years of achieving specific developmental milestones. Meeting these milestones depended upon her engagement in the world around her and, in particular, her relationship with her caregivers, her environment, as well as her health which includes her physical, cognitive, emotional and social well-being.

In social work we are often interacting with families and developing an understanding of the individuals within the family as well as its functioning as a whole. It is important to understand both the family and the broader world from children's perspectives. This is referred to in social work literature as being 'child-centred' (see Munro 2011). Being able to see the world through a child's eyes requires the use of your imagination as well as an underpinning grasp on child development. Indeed, social workers must have a working knowledge of the key theoretical and empirical debates relating to human growth and development across the entire lifespan, starting with birth and ending with death. We shall now consider some of the key developmental milestones in childhood before moving on to later life stages of adolescence, adulthood and older age.

INFANCY TO TWO YEARS

Birth is the point at which the newborn baby leaves the mother's womb, and it is from this very early life stage that human interaction begins (Peterson 2004, p 98). Babies and their caregivers are able to look at one another and caregivers begin to interpret babies' gestures to better understand their wishes. A gentle stroke of a newborn baby's cheek encourages them to turn towards this touch and open their mouths as they look for the breast in order to feed. This so-called rooting response is one of a number of reflexes demonstrated by the newborn child. Another reflex behaviour central to communication between the newborn and their caregiver(s) is crying. Crying signals to the caregiver that the newborn is hungry, tired or uncomfortable. For example, the child may need his or her nappy changed or a layer of clothing removed to accommodate for a change in temperature.

In Chapter 1 we examined the importance of human interaction to one's identity through looking at the work of George Herbert Mead (1934). Even at this early life stage, human social interaction—specifically between the child and their caregivers—is crucial, not only for the development of the self but for survival. As we shall see, the central importance of social interaction to the development of identity continues throughout the lifespan.

During the time between birth and two years children's physical development progresses rapidly. Newborns are unable to roll or control their head movements, yet by around 12–14 months of age they are able to walk. Thus, the period between birth and one year is a time of rapid physical change, characterised by advances in the ways in which babies move and interact with others, and this continues into their second year of life and beyond. Children's caregivers often report that their child's physical development is a continual source of surprise. The ability to grasp a toy, to wave to others, to sit unaided and crawl: these are all examples of the ways that babies' physical strength and coordination come together to reach new physical milestones.

Given the rapid changes characterising physical development from birth, the perceived failure to achieve these milestones can be a cause of concern for parents and caregivers. Like other stages, there is much variation in the degree to which children fall neatly into achieving them.

Before the age of two, children develop what Piaget termed 'sensorimotor intelligence' (Piaget 1970), which involves behaving in an increasingly purposeful manner. For example, as babies grow from birth to two years, they develop different types of sucking—from the sucking of a dummy to a toy to a particular way of sucking at the breast or bottle to enable the optimum level of milk flow: the sucking behaviour differs, depending on the purpose (Peterson 2004, p. 58). As a child grows from a newborn to a two-year-old, their ability to act in purposeful ways depending on the environment also markedly increases. In the latter stages of sensorimotor development, babies begin to learn about cause and effect as they begin to anticipate the world around them. Piaget might describe a child thinking in the following way: 'If I roll this ball toward my mother, she will roll it back to me'. In this way, the world becomes increasingly predictable for children as they grow.

The interaction between a child and their environment or social setting is central to the theories of Erik Erikson (1968). Erikson is known for his notion of the 'identity crisis', which is often associated with the middle age life stage. Erikson argues, however, that at each life stage there is a tension between individual needs and the social expectations upon the individual. Erikson was thus concerned with the 'sociocultural environment' (Peterson 2004, p. 55) in which the child is embedded. At each stage, the individual must overcome the 'battle' between two states. These are:

- Basic trust vs mistrust (0–1 years)
- Autonomy vs shame and doubt (1–3 years)
- Initiative vs guilt (4–5 years)
- Industry vs inferiority (6–11 years)
- Identity vs role confusion (12–18 years)
- Intimacy vs isolation (early adulthood)
- Generativity vs self-absorption (middle adulthood)
- Integrity vs despair (older age)

We will discuss each of these at the life stages they occur.

Let's first explore what Erikson means by trust vs mistrust. For Erikson, the role of the caregiver(s) was central to whether the infant could develop trust:

> The quality of the parental care that infants receive during this stage largely determines the balance of trust vs mistrust in their budding psyches. Resolution of unconscious conflict entails finding a realistic compromise between blind faith in the primary caregiver, as the source of total pleasure, and an acceptance of the unavoidable pain of delay and frustration. The outcome of a satisfactory resolution brings babies their first 'psychosocial strength', which Erikson described as hope, and which will form a cornerstone for all manifestations of faith in later life. (Peterson 2004, p. 55)

There have been some theories that are reminiscent of Erikson's notion of trust and mistrust. For example, Giddens' notion of ontological security (Giddens 1992) argues that individuals carry their early experiences of relationships into their future selves, which affects the ways they view the world. Does this mean that individuals who do not have positive experiences in this life stage will then go on to mistrust the world and fail to form positive relationships? In short: no. Erikson's theory allows individuals to complete previously incomplete resolution in future life stages. Further, what we now know from studies in resilience is that some individuals are able to thrive *despite* negative early experiences (Ungar 2008).

Attachment

A great deal has been written about attachment, both in social work and within the discipline of psychology. So ubiquitous is this term that immediately it is recognisable as central to the relationship between a child and their caregiver. The central role played by caregivers in the development of children is a truism on many levels since children require to be fed, clothed, protected from danger and so on. Yet attachment specifically relates to the emotional dimension of human experience, and the foundational role that the caregiver plays in providing emotional stability for an infant.

Attachment theory was developed by John Bowlby and argues that children require 'secure' attachments to their mother in order for them to be 'stable' individuals in later life. A strong attachment is said to be foundational to a child in their first five years of life, thus it is the responsibility of the caregiver, or mother in Bowlby's terms, to give this much-needed stability from the onset of life. A strong attachment during childhood is argued to be central to happiness across the lifespan. This is summarised through the following statement, in which Bowlby famously argued:

> Mother love in infancy and childhood is as important for mental health as are vitamins and proteins for physical health. (Bowlby 1951, p. 182)

Bowlby's work remains important to child development literature and the theoretical notion that children require strong bonds with their caregivers continues to persist in contemporary childcare literature and practice. However, the application of attachment theory to issues in social work requires careful consideration of the ways in which attachment is conceptualised and placed within a clear theoretical and ethical framework. A critical awareness of gender and power and understanding the complex and contextual ways in which caregivers and their children interact are key to such work.

For example, Buchanan's (2008) research into domestic violence and the use of attachment theory in practice found there are specific ways in which practitioners ought to work with women. Practitioners should have 'knowledge about the impact of relationships on infants' attachment patterns' and should be

- experienced and knowledgeable about working with women and infants who have been subjected to domestic violence
- aware of the de-skilling that can affect women, as mothers, in domestic violence situations, and know that attachment may have been adversely affected
- very clear that the violence perpetrated against her and difficulties with attachment are not the fault of the woman. (Buchanan 2008, p. 11)

The historical and continuing role that gender plays in attachment theory has been highlighted as tending to blame women and serving a patriarchal system of power relationships (Bliwise 1999; Franzblau 1999; Morris 2008). Yet the ways in which family roles and daily routines are constructed have shifted dramatically since Bowlby's theory began to take shape 60 years ago.

Whereas in the 1950s women traditionally held the childrearing and caring roles within a family, in contemporary culture there have been a number of key shifts which have had an impact on the ways children are raised. These include:

- The detraditionalisation of gender roles: This relates to the increase of women's participation in the paid workforce from the 1960s onwards (Giddens 1992) and subsequent care arrangements for children, including nursery care, nannies, relative care (such as grandparents) and childminders. There has also been a greater awareness of the important role that fathers, as well as mothers, play.
- The recognition that culture and cultural relativism are relevant to theory-building: Bowlby's work requires a somewhat 'traditional' view of women whereas in contemporary life we have a broader appreciation of differing cultural views on

raising children, such as the central roles that close and extended relatives have in a child's life.

- Recent research into resilience and childhood: This has found no evidence that adults will be at risk of poor mental health if their childhood experiences are traumatic. Rather, research has demonstrated that some children are able to thrive *despite* adversity. This has meant there is a need to understand children in their contexts, for example in their cultural, social, emotional and biographical contexts.

In social work there is a great deal of literature relating to attachment which takes into account the shifts described above. Thus attachment remains a relevant concept which can help us better understand the child's world and the world from the child's perspective. Prescriptive and presumptive application of attachment theory to our clients should always be avoided: it is never appropriate to assume that a person's present behaviour or state of mind is 'because of poor attachment'. This simplistic application of attachment theory does little more than pathologise our clients and undervalue our profession.

TODDLERHOOD (TWO TO FOUR YEARS)

Piaget argued that, between the ages of two and seven years, children enter the 'preoperational stage' of cognition. This means that children:

- Use language and gestures to communicate and name the objects and people around them
- Are able to group objects together
- Continue to think in a way that can be described as 'egocentric'

If you have ever accompanied a child into a setting in which there are a lot of other people, you may have witnessed the effects of a child's egocentric thinking. For example, a two-year-old may begin screaming and crying in a quiet public space such as a church or a library, and may not understand that their behaviour is frowned upon by others who are attempting to keep quiet. For the child the world around them is merely a place in which feelings of, say, frustration or tiredness may be vented. Notoriously referred to as the 'terrible twos', toddlerhood sees egocentrism, a new emotional range, increasing agility, more stable gait and the increasing desire for independence all combining for some potentially difficult times for caregivers, who may struggle to understand the world from the child's perspective. Therefore some forms of child abuse may be more highly associated with this age stage than any other.

When children are learning to exercise their autonomy in this way during the toddler years, it can result in conflicts which can lead to confrontations between children and their caregivers. This can lead to child abuse. There are a number of ways that neglect and child abuse should be responded to in practice, and specialist training about how to work with children and families in statutory settings is contained within social work programmes. By understanding 'normal' development and the key milestones in each life stage, social work students become equipped with the tools to identify when children are not progressing at the pace expected. The impact of neglect, for example, can mean that children do not achieve their developmental milestones, and they are severely harmed as a result of not having their needs met (Minty & Pattinson 1994).

Positive relationships between parents and their children are central to development. Like Piaget, Vygotsky was interested in the ways in which children's development was dependent upon their relationship with others. Vygotsky's emphasis on the socio-cultural context to childhood development meant that communication was central to understanding how children learn. Vygotsky noted that children were sometimes able to complete particular tasks with the help of an adult. The 'zone of proximal development' is 'the distance between the actual developmental level as determined by independent problem solving and the level of potential development as determined through problem solving under adult guidance, or in collaboration with more capable peers' (Vygotsky 1978, p. 86). Again, the role of others in the development of children is highlighted. Being able to achieve a particular task, for example filling a cup with sand—even with the help of an adult—can serve to extend the child's interest into other tasks and help to advance their development.

Language develops during the toddler years. Caregivers often report that during this age it is a relief to begin to hear what the child wants instead of having to interpret their wishes through gestures and behaviours. Language is therefore the important means through which children are able to articulate their needs and place themselves in the world around them (Vygotsky 1978, p. 26). Language also enables better communication and interaction between a child and their caregivers. It is also important to others such as nursery staff and other professionals such as social workers, medical staff and specialist professionals because it can be the means through which the child's view can be better understood.

We now move on to consider the middle childhood life stage.

MIDDLE CHILDHOOD (FIVE TO ELEVEN YEARS)

For Piaget, the period between the ages of seven and eleven years signalled the 'concrete operational stage', which means that children are able to:

- Group objects according to rational 'rules' (for example, grouping all of the small pink beads in one pile and the large pink beads in another pile)

The ability to undertake tasks associated with grouping is argued by Piaget to be possible because children's thinking changes during these ages to accommodate more logical 'rules'.

The major social event to occur during middle childhood is entry into the schooling system. For children who had previously been at home with a caregiver, as well as those who had previously been at nursery, day-care or in the care of relatives or workers, school attendance signals a momentous shift. We have seen in previous life stages that the caregiver has a central role in influencing development. The socio-cultural setting within which the child is immersed has an impact on the ways in which they experience and respond to the world around them:

> According to those who take a sociocultural approach to development, the child should be seen not as a physical scientist seeking 'true' knowledge but as a newcomer to a culture who seeks to become a native by learning how to look at social reality through the lens of that culture. (Rogoff 2000 cited in Smith *et al.* 2003, p. 82)

The culture of the school system is largely institutionalised and regulated through variously structured and identifiable time periods. The emotional impact of school is often noted by parents, who may also feel that this life stage signals the end of the 'baby' years.

Erikson argues that this life stage brings with it the challenge of resolving the tension between 'industry vs inferiority'. Industry, which is the ability to work to complete a task, is embedded within the schooling system. Children are taught and assessed according to their ability to work diligently and achieve particular learning goals. Unlike in other environments such as nursery or the home setting, assessments are competitive processes. In the school setting the system of knowledge acquisition means that children can compare their achievements, or failures, with the other children around them. 'A satisfactory resolution requires the development of cooperation with other people, so that children can freely and successfully exercise their own unique competencies in contribution to a larger productive effort' (Peterson 2004, p. 56).

During this period of time children also learn to socialise together and understand the social rules of self and others. Because of their mastery over their bodily movements, they are able to fully participate in sporting activities and game playing. Engagement in these activities was manifest in Janet Lever's (1978) study into childhood socialisation of gender. Through ethnographic observation of childhood play at school, Lever found that the rules which dominated the boys' and girls' groups were reproduced in relation to gendered occupational 'rules' later in life. The children in her study were grouped according to gender and each group engaged in different games and activities. Additionally, each group learned to resolve conflict in idiosyncratic ways, regardless of individual attributes. Although Lever's study took place more than 30 years ago, the continuation of the dominant group's marked presence in particular professions and positions of power suggests that inequality based on gender and other markers of difference stems from childhood socialisation and still exists today. Thus, there is inherent power in the school environment in relation to learning social norms and rules including gender (as we have just seen) as well as other issues such as disability, culture and other markers of difference.

ADOLESCENCE

Piaget argues that during adolescence, individuals reach the ability to think in the same way as adults. This 'formal operational stage' is the final stage in his theory

of child development. Thinking associated with this stage follows on from the previous stage in which cognition based on logic dominates. Additionally, adolescents:

- Can think in abstract terms about things, for example they can hypothesise
  fantasy scenarios and outcomes
- Are able to conceptualise abstract concepts, theories and notions

For Erikson, the importance of self identification is evident in the conflict
between 'identity vs role confusion'. Central to this resolution is being able to negotiate a preferred identity amongst the many that are available:

> The problem is enhanced in contemporary society by the wide range of alterna-
> tive roles available and by their inconsistency with one another and with the
> traditions of the past. A satisfactory resolution of the identity conflict entails the
> development of a coherent sense of self that integrates all the essential features
> of the individual's past and sets the direction for further personal growth and a
> productive contribution to society. (Peterson 2004, p. 56)

Social interactions are central to the sense of self (Mead 1934), as we have explored
in Chapter 1. Adolescence brings changes through puberty, not only physical ones
to sex organs and other areas of the body but also various emotional and social
changes. These include:

- Increased self-consciousness
- Shifts in existing relationships, based on gender and sexuality
- Increased interest and/or social expectations around coupling/sexual activity
  and experimentation
- Increased importance of peer groups and friendships

Sexuality in social work is both a specialist and a general or 'everyday' area of work
(see Dunk-West 2011; Dunk-West & Hafford-Letchfield 2011). Often social workers
feel ill-equipped to talk to young people about their sexual relationships, but the
theories which underpin other practice apply equally to this area of work (Dunk
2007). Listening to young people's needs, understanding their biographies and relationships and working together to address inequality and oppression at the individual and social levels: all of these apply to working with a young person in a sexually
active relationship. Let us consider Case Study 2.1.

CASE STUDY 2.1 Seshni Patel

Seshni is 15 years old. Born in a small village in India, at age 5 she moved to London
with her parents and brother, Sanjay, aged 2. When Seshni was 14 years old both her
mother and father died in a car accident. As no other relatives could be located, Seshni
and her brother were placed into care and separated. Seshni did not settle at her
foster carers, who were a White British couple aged in their 50s, living in Bath. Seshni
ran away from the foster carers and made her way back to London. Once in London,
Seshni reunited with her friendship group and her friends gave her money to help her

support herself. Seshni told friends that she wanted to find her brother Sanjay but did not know where to begin. Seshni had been 'sleeping rough' for almost three months when she came to the attention of social services after being admitted to hospital, having been found unconscious in a park.

Imagine you are employed by social services as a social worker and you are going to meet with Seshni in the hospital. Think about the following questions:

- How do you think Seshni might be feeling?
- What do you think you could do to support Seshni?
- What is important in the work and why is it important?
- What theories of human development are helpful in understanding this situation?

There are numerous ways you may be able to assist Seshni but they will be dependent upon what Seshni would like to happen and whether you are able to establish a positive working relationship with her. The following is one possible area for social work intervention.

Living arrangements and reuniting Seshni and Sanjay

It is crucial that Seshni receive help with her living arrangements since being homeless places her 'at risk of harm'. Questions to ask include: why were Seshni and Sanjay separated? How was the loss of their parents accommodated for in relation to supports for the siblings? One way to make sense of Seshni's actions is to view her running away as a normal response to the situation. Given her parents died suddenly and she 'lost' her brother and was then removed from her friends and supports in London and accommodated with foster carers, is it surprising that Seshni returned to her community? Given that Seshni has said that she wants to find her brother, it is crucial to work from her 'perspective', to be 'client-centred' (Rogers 1951). Working from the client's perspective involves working with clients in such a way as to help them reach their goals (Egan 2006).

Other questions to ask could include: what are Seshni's needs around her health and education? How have these been met or not met and what can be done to achieve well-being? Are there cultural needs which are not being met? What can be done to respect her cultural background? It is crucial that social workers do not make assumptions about others' cultures but start from the perspective that we all have a culture. Race is a concept which is related to culture. Race refers to 'a set of social relationships which allow individuals and groups to be located, and various attributes of competencies assigned, on the basis of biologically grounded features' (Giddens 2005, p. 696). Culture is a 'historically transmitted pattern of meanings embodied in symbols, a system of inherited conceptions expressed by which men [sic] communicate, perpetuate, and develop their knowledge about and their attitudes towards life' (Geertz 1973, p. 89). Culture is an important kind of knowledge which is embedded in family relationships and practices and relationships and patterns of relating with others. Culture is an important part of identity and enables one to name a collective affinity with a particular group. It is also one of the central tasks of social work to fight oppression and inequality, and reflecting on social work's role in racism and discriminatory practices in day-to-day practice helps the profession maintain accountability towards others as well as towards social work values and ethics.

All of the questions about how the social work role might assist in this situation arise from thinking about Seshni and imagining what it might be like to see the world through her eyes (Lee 1994). Applying developmental theories to her situation helps to raise further questions. For example, what does Piaget say about adolescence? What does Erikson say? Let's briefly look at how these theories might be applied to Seshni. According to Piaget's theory of adolescence, Seshni will be able to think as an adult would—that is, she would be able to engage in thinking about issues more 'deeply' than a person aged, say, in their middle childhood. She would be able to conceptualise complexities. Erikson might say that Seshni is at a time when identity is central, and in particular, it is crucial for Seshni to 'find' her identity. Seshni's culture is an example of an aspect of her identity. Of course, only Seshni would be able to inform you as the social worker about whether these theories are relevant to understanding her current situation, but there are some indications that she feels attached to her peers since she moved back to London to see them. The loss of her parents may also fit with the theme of identity since her entire life has been upturned since their death. We shall consider some of the theories related to grief and loss later in this chapter.

ADULTHOOD

Adulthood is often simply conceptualised as being the period after adolescence and prior to older age. When we think about adulthood, we generally refer to the ages between 18 and 65. This is a large age range and some texts divide adulthood into early, mid and late adulthood. In this book we refer to adulthood to encompass the following general events: work, intimacy, children and separation.

For Erikson, early adulthood is concerned with achieving true intimacy with another person. The conflict between 'intimacy vs isolation' requires successful integration of the self into a loving partnership. Middle adulthood is characterised by an Eriksonian conflict between 'generativity vs self-absorption'. Generativity refers to the sense that one has left a legacy which will thrive in the world beyond one's lifetime. For some people this is a creative product, whilst having children, for some, means that they are contributing to 'future generations' (Peterson 2004, p. 57). Self-absorption is the opposite of generativity in that it means a lack of engagement with the future besides which the self is invested.

Adulthood is popularly associated with finding one's profession or identifying the main source of income generation through work. Yet the negotiation of employment in times of personal and economic hardship can prevent people from experiencing meaningful activity. Unpaid work such as domestic responsibilities and caring for relatives and children can too be unrecognised as legitimate in some countries. For Erikson, work can be associated with generativity which means that it must have some *broader meaning* coded into it by the individual engaging in it.

Shifts in intimacy have meant that the way individuals experience and display their romantic attachments has changed. From the late 1920s, researchers became interested in what was termed 'marital disenchantment' (Pineo 1961, p. 3). This concept captured the ways in which individuals within marriages felt about the marriage at various points. Pineo (1961) noted four stages which characterised research participants' experiences:

1. After marriage, people report feeling less happy with being married ('marital disenchantment).
2. The rate of physical intimacy drops.
3. Although there are changes in the marriage dynamic, individuals feel the same.
4. Interaction between people in a marriage changes. Sexual activity decreases. (Pineo 1961, p. 3)

In explaining the above, Pineo says that 'in any situation, such as marriage ... some process of disenchantment is to be expected' (1961, p. 7). For some theorists, the high divorce rates which have characterised the years following such studies into marital disenchantment signal a tendency for 'quick fixes' and a lack of commitment to the institution of marriage over individual desires (Bauman 2003).

Yet people continue to get married and enter into committed intimate partnerships despite the high failure rates of marriage (Giddens 1992). The nature of relationships has certainly changed since the studies into marital disenchantment, but the notion of disenchantment can be useful in capturing couples' experiences post-marriage. Here are some of the key shifts in relationships in contemporary life:

- There have been changes in women's roles through the entry of women into the workforce and changes in the ways in which the household is arranged (Giddens 1992).
- More people are living separately but still are in committed relationships. These couples are referred to in the literature as 'living apart together' (Holmes 2006).
- Same sex couples' friendships can constitute 'family'. This is referred to as 'families of choice' (Weeks *et al.* 2001).
- Shifts in technology and the way we interact with one another have impacted upon how individuals meet and form intimate relationships.

It is important for social work students to understand the shifts in relationships and the centrality of them to adulthood because such knowledge assists in understanding the world from our client's perspective.

OLDER AGE

Societies in the west are made up of increasing numbers of older people as a result of developments in nutrition, lifestyle awareness and medical and other technology. Sometimes referred to as 'grey power', older people are increasingly politically powerful. Erikson argues that, in older age, the task requiring resolution relates to 'integrity vs despair'. The knowledge that one has contributed to society in a positive way and reflecting positively on the life they have led leads to integrity. According to Erikson, people experiencing integrity understand 'that an individual life is the accidental coincidence of but one life cycle with but one segment of history, and that for him [sic] all human integrity stands and falls with the one style of integrity of which he partakes' (Erikson 1968, p. 140 cited in Peterson 2004, p. 57). Erikson's depiction of older age draws upon the assumption that in older age one is looking back at life retrospectively as opposed to looking forward. Yet in developed nations older age has changed, perhaps more rapidly than any other age stage, given technological advances along with increased health determinants.

Older age can signal the end of the employment cycle as people enter a period of retirement or semi-retirement. The age at which retirement occurs is generally around 65, but this will almost certainly increase to adjust for our longer lifespans. Rising costs of childcare alongside lower wages can mean that people entering retirement are engaging in caring roles for grandchildren and others in the family. This is a relatively recent shift which has come about through a combination of factors including longer lifespans, social policies relating to work and childcare provision, and economic conditions.

DEATH

Death, in short, is the end to life. Death is seen as an inevitable part of life and although it is viewed as normative after older age, the impact on loved ones is always great. We will therefore explore grief and loss briefly. It is important to acknowledge the broad scholarship which deals with death and its related issues. Much of the literature in philosophy, ethics, sociology, psychology and disciplines such as health have currency in social work. The application of literature from other disciplines to social work raises important questions. Some of the issues which emerge in other disciplines are summarised below, together with their relevance for social work:

- Issues relating to ethical issues about death. For example, assisted suicide or euthanasia is when a person 'chooses' to end their life. What is the role for social workers in these situations? Should social work as a profession have a view about whether euthanasia is 'right' or 'wrong'?
- Issues relating to ethical and medical issues about death. For example, when is someone classified as dead? Is a person kept 'alive' through technology such as a respirator 'living' or is a coma a state of being 'dead'? Should social workers have a role to play in determining some of the ethical impacts of decisions about these issues? How can social workers support families and others who are affected by these issues?
- Given the role that religion plays in death, for example in relation to the rituals which mark death, how can social workers work with others in a culturally and spiritually sensitive manner?
- How does society understand and deal with death? Is death taboo and if so, why? Should all social workers, irrespective of their practice, understand death and how to respond to others who are grieving?

We explore some of the complexities involved in making ethical decisions in social work in Chapter 5. Although there are no easy answers to the questions raised, there are some key issues which emerge. Highlighting the religious or spiritual beliefs associated with death uncovers the need for social workers to work in a way which invites dialogue about clients' religious beliefs across all work (Crisp 2010). Similarly, starting with the client's viewpoint and wishes and trying to understand how they are feeling about what is happening for them helps people feel supported and understood. This application of empathy is called 'tuning in' and having 'empathic presence' (Egan 2006, p. 49). Egan points out:

> At some of the more dramatic moments of life, simply being with another person is extremely important. If a friend of yours is in the hospital, just your being there can make a difference, even if conversation is impossible. Similarly, being with a friend who has just lost his wife can be very comforting to him, even if little is said. Your empathic presence is comforting, but tuning in is also important in the give-and-take of everyday life. Most people appreciate it when others pay attention to them. They feel respected. By the same token, being ignored is often painful: The averted face is too often a sign of the averted heart. (Egan 2006, p. 49)

In Chapter 3 we discuss some further communication skills which help us in our work with others and in Chapter 4 we explore the theories which underpin our interpersonal practice. In each of these chapters, a clearer social work role emerges. As we have begun to see throughout this chapter, theories about human development and life stages help shape the social work role. We now move on to briefly explore how individual and collective responses to death impact on the grieving process.

Grief and loss

In Shakespeare's *Macbeth*, grief is conceived as a state which can and must move actors to great action, thus the exclamation: 'Give sorrow words. The grief that does not speak whispers the o'er fraught heart, and bids it break'. In this context, grief is portrayed as so powerful and debilitating it can break the heart. The quote gives us some insight into the powerful ways that the emotional context of loss and grief can be so consuming, frightening and completely overwhelming. Grief has many aspects to it, both private and public. Private experiences of grief are tied up with the emotional dimension to human experience, which means that people can be unsure how to respond to loss. Public or socially recognised ways of mourning include funerals, wakes, burials and cremations, celebration of life events as well as various religious-inspired rituals and traditions. Thus, the socio-cultural as well as personal ways that people experience death are important to recognise in social work.

Yet there is also a *relationship between* the personal and the social. When a loss is not socially sanctioned as loss, this can result in the mourner experiencing what is termed as disenfranchised grief (Doka 1989, 2002). Disenfranchised grief is grief which is suppressed by society because of a stigma. For example, in societies where being in a same sex relationship is discriminated against, the same sex partner of someone who has died may not be involved in the deceased person's funeral arrangements, family events or other socially sanctioned rituals associated with death. This sends the message to the bereaved person that they were not as significant as would be an opposite sex partner. Disenfranchised grief means that the mourner, in this case the same sex partner of a deceased person, is personally affected as they are not able to resolve their grief through traditions involving interpersonal relationships and socially sanctioned events and rituals. This means they become isolated and left alone with their grief.

Since death is a part of human existence, social workers must know how to respond to death, grief and loss. Death affects us all and social workers' clients can, themselves, die. This can be difficult for the social worker, quite apart from others who are affected by the loss. In addition people can experience other types of losses throughout their lifespan which can be made sense of using theoretical models from the literature about loss, grief and dying.

GENERATIONS

So far, we have considered age through individuals' experiences which are dependent upon their numerical age. Another way of thinking about the lifespan is to consider the historical epoch within which the individual or group was born. Thus, a 10-year-old today will have a completely different experience than a 10-year-old who was born in 1912. The 10-year-old born 10 years ago will have entered a world with fewer infant mortalities (in developed countries), longer lifespans (in developed countries), internet technology, Web 2.0 and so on. The 10-year-old born in 1912 will have experienced their early years very differently (Plummer 2010). One of the problems with viewing age solely through developmental terms is that we do not get a picture of the broader social events and shifts which make up the landscape into which the person 'fits'. In terms of generations, we refer to each of these groups using terms such as baby boomer, generation X, generation Y and so on. In the historical period we are currently in, for example, a large number of so-called baby boomers are entering retirement. Thus, some general, population-based characteristics may be associated with this generation.

Generation-based ways of viewing the lifespan can assist in a more sociologically informed approach towards making sense of people's experiences. They can also usefully be combined with developmental psychological perspectives which already draw to a considerable degree on a socio-cultural context.

NEGLECT, CHILD ABUSE AND DEVELOPMENTAL THEORIES

Your knowledge of child development is crucial to responding to children in need of care and protection. In understanding normative child development, you will be able to respond to and raise concerns about children whose development is not progressing as expected. Children with undiagnosed disabilities and other difficulties and needs require early intervention. Here are some key points:

- Clearly articulate concerns. Knowledge of child development can assist in social workers understanding children's behaviours including raising concerns when development is 'abnormal' or not progressing as expected.
- Communicate in an age appropriate manner (Miller 2003). This means that your knowledge of child development can help in your work with children and their caregivers: toddlerhood can be a difficult time for parents and conveying information about child development can assist parents in better understanding the world through their child's eyes. Parents can become frustrated with the wilfulness associated with toddlerhood and believe that their child is 'deliberately winding them up' as opposed to understanding the challenging behaviour as a symptom of frustration or thwarted autonomy.
- The ways in which children live through the abuse and neglect they have experienced must be able to be understood through social workers' application of developmental theories, but importantly children must always be protected (Davies 2012).
- Social workers need to have a dual focus in protecting children and being guided by their needs and wishes (Lefebvre 2010). Both protecting children as well as involving them in decisions about their care is important since children do not feel involved enough in decisions about their care, despite this being a policy and practice requirement (for example, see Cleaver *et al.* 2007).

WORKING WITH OTHERS

Because this chapter explores life stages across the entire lifespan, there are many contexts, and professionals, with whom social workers can expect to work in varied environments. The health professions' engagement with the lifespan approach is, generally speaking, a strong one. This is because of the dominance of medical knowledge which is embedded within developmental theories.

Theories in which the lifespan is divided into clearly identifiable stages serve to reinforce the idea that there is a 'normal' way to develop. Since this is the case, there is also an 'abnormal' category within which people's development (or lack thereof) may be categorised. Of course, there is much variance in terms of whether individuals 'fit' with the ages and prescribed stages. There is also variance in relation to professions' engagement in social models of development. It is fair to say that in contemporary practice, the health professions have engaged in social models of health far more than in the past. In Chapter 1 we discussed the impacts of interprofessional working between social work and health and noted that social work's association with social models of health might be incompatible with other professions whose world-views are very different (Bywaters 1986). Yet professional values and priorities and theories are always in flux. Indeed, there is some evidence to suggest that health professionals are moving more towards collaborative working. For example, research which examined general practitioners' (GPs') views about their roles found they felt there had been a shift away from traditional power relationships where medical doctors were at the top of the hierarchy (Jones & Green 2006, p. 936). The authors of the study call this a 'new general practice' in which equal relationships between other professionals promotes a positive work environment which ultimately benefits the client. One respondent in the study, for example, reported that:

> The reason I like my practice so much is this really fluid sort of communication between doctors, nurses, receptionists, everything's sort of on a level, everyone's on first name terms and there aren't any doors that you can't knock on. (Helen, GP locum, in Jones & Green 2006, p. 937)

The study found that this 'new way' of working broke down traditional power relationships between GPs and others and was more in line with a 'patient-centred approach' (Jones & Green 2006, p. 937). Such an approach is, as we shall see in Chapters 3 and 4, compatible with a social work approach in which we work alongside our clients.

Yet how does interaction with other professionals look in relation to the material explored in this chapter? To better examine this, let's consider Case Study 2.2.

CASE STUDY 2.2 Carol Leblanc, Juliette Leblanc and baby Célia Leblanc

Carol is a 43-year-old woman who had recently moved from her native France to London. Carol is Célia's mother. Carol had relocated to be closer to Célia's father but after doing so, just over three years ago, the relationship broke down and they no longer have contact. A few months ago, Carol's sister Juliette, aged 47, came to live with her sister and niece as she was worried about Carol's mental state. Carol and Juliette have a strong, supportive relationship. They were raised in a small flat by their father who had mental health problems as well as a problem with alcohol. Carol and Juliette would often care for their father. Despite some difficulties, Carol and Juliette were able to attend school and go on to complete university studies— the first generation in their family to have done so. Before moving to London, Carol was employed as a journalist for a local newspaper, and Juliette is taking leave from her job as an accountant. Carol has been trying to find freelance writing work but she has not been successful in gaining paid employment. Carol cares for Célia full time.

Célia is aged $2\frac{1}{2}$ and was referred to the local social services by the Health Visitor and GP. Both feel Célia has not met her developmental milestones and, when concerns were raised with her mother, they felt she did not want to accept there would need to be further assessments of Célia. Specifically, there are concerns about Célia's language development, her gross motor skills and her lack of engagement with people around her. Although a happy child, Célia does not talk except to say 'ma ma'. She does not appear interested in communicating with others. Both the GP and the Health Visitor would like Célia to be assessed by a paediatrician.

- What developmental theories are relevant to this case study?
- What do you think ought to happen next?
- Are you concerned for Célia?
- What are the roles of the professionals? Are there any other professionals who could or should be involved?

In any situation where we do not have all of the information, application of theory must be tentative. However, there are some key pieces of information which can be noted at this stage. These are:

- There are concerns about Célia's development. These specifically relate to physical, social and language development.
- There are concerns about Célia's needs not being met.
- Little is known about Carol's mental health, but we do know that her sister, to whom she is reportedly close, has concerns about this.
- There are a number of social factors which provide context such as the recent relocation of the family, and problems with Carol finding paid work.

In relation to working with others, in this scenario the GP and Health Visitor have suggested that because Célia's development falls outside the *normal* range, a more detailed assessment would give a better picture about what is happening for this child. Some of the social issues which are relevant to this context include: exploring the supports for Carol, who is parenting by herself, has moved away from her home and has left her regular workplace to live in a different country; the language context to living outside the family's homeland and how this might affect Célia's presenting difficulties with language and communication; how much social interaction, connectedness and support is available to the family. The latter issues which relate to social support may alter the ways in which developmental theories are applied to the scenario. As noted previously, the application of developmental theory must be tentative and take into account the socio-cultural and broader social issues and contexts within which problems are presented.

CHAPTER SUMMARY

This chapter has explored lifespan development. We have examined the major theoretical traditions associated with this way of thinking and explored how these relate to social work. The socio-cultural context within which development occurs has been considered alongside the important influence of family and caregiver relationships on children and young people.

Using visual prompts, the reader has been invited to reflexively engage with their own reading of lifespan in relation to roles and social expectations or attitudes, as well as their own biographic associations with age. Throughout the chapter the central role of knowledge about human growth and development in social work practice in its many manifestations has been highlighted. In the following chapter we move on to consider how we relate to others, and the communicative skills required to form professional relationships with our clients.

FURTHER READING

BERK, L. (2010) *Exploring Lifespan Development*, 2nd edn. Boston: Allyn & Bacon.

BOYD, D. A. & BEE, H. L. (2011) *Lifespan Development*. Boston: Pearson Education.

GREEN, L. (2010) *Understanding the Life Course: Sociological and Psychological Perspectives*. Cambridge, UK: Polity Press.

LEFEVRE, M. (2010) *Communicating with Children and Young People: Making a Difference*. Bristol: The Policy Press.

PETERSON, C. (2004) *Looking Forward Through the Lifespan*. Frenchs Forest, NSW: Pearson Education.

3

Communication Skills

This chapter:

- Introduces key ideas in communication

- Outlines why communication is central to the social work role

- Describes specific types of communication through the use of examples

- Provides prompts to enable the reader to consider their own communication style

- Outlines how social workers use their communication skills in their work with clients

In social life, our interactions with others are guided by complex rules which, once broken, disrupt the flow of communication between people. Imagine acting as a houseguest in your own home, for example (Garfinkel 1984). How would your behaviours change? We might expect that you would be more polite and less relaxed than you would normally be in the comfort of your usual surroundings. How would the familiar people around you react if you adopted a formal tone in your interactions with them?

Sociologist Harold Garfinkel sought to uncover what would happen when the unwritten rules in everyday life were disrupted or 'breached'. He called upon his students to undertake experiments such as the one detailed above. (Although these experiments enabled new ways of theorising human interaction, experimenting on others without ethics approval is not recommended! See Chapter 7 for more information about ethics and research.) Amongst other key sociological contributions, Garfinkel's work drew attention to the *assumed* knowledge we draw upon when we interact with others. It was in breaking or 'breaching' the codes which rule our behaviour towards others in specific situations that their strength could be understood (Garfinkel 1984). Our knowledge of social rules forms the backdrop of our interactions with others during day-to-day life.

Unless we really think about it, we are unaware of the rules that govern our behaviour. In this chapter we will begin to explore some of the key communicative devices we draw upon in social work. Like social norms or rules of behaviour, some of the concepts relevant to communication such as 'listening' appear commonsense; however, as we shall see, successfully employing a range of verbal and non-verbal techniques helps us to engage well with others—and this is vital to good, competent social work practice.

Given that this chapter draws upon the skills you use in everyday life, exercises are designed to get you thinking about ways in which you currently communicate. As a social work student learning about social work *practice*, it is important to name and understand how particular techniques help us communicate. Practising and devoting time and imagination to understanding communication are key to learning.

How do you know you are being listened to? What happens when you are trying to communicate with another person and you feel they are not hearing what you are saying? In the following section we will consider various forms of communication and ways in which interpersonal interactions take place. As discussed in Chapter 1, interpersonal interaction is the means through which we realise and develop our selves (Mead 1934). Communication is also the central conduit through which we relate to our clients, and developing a reflexive awareness of how we come across to others is vital to our work, particularly as beginning practitioners.

Students out on placement often encounter practitioners who have 'practice-wisdom' and do not seem as reflexive as students of social work. Considering the role of reflexivity in the creation of the social work self, this is not surprising. It is therefore useful to think about reflexive engagement with one's own communication style and methods whilst recognising that with practice, this becomes more intuitive. In relation to this, thinking about types of questions to ask and statements to make in response to role play scenarios can often feel stilted and disingenuous.

Like all beginnings to learning, this phase soon passes as students develop confidence and learn from mistakes and insights from others.

As with all aspects of the social work curriculum, entering into the reflexive arena requires a deliberate engagement with the self. Once the foundational work in the area of communication skills has been achieved, through practice, reflexivity in relation to the social work self becomes more aligned with Mead's notion of 'reflexiveness' (1934) which we explored in Chapter 1.

In a recent study into communication skills learning and subsequent social work practice, for example, one participant reported that learning about communication 'was incredibly helpful in teaching me to routinely reflect my own thoughts, feelings and actions. I think that it is quite easy not to reflect unless you are taught to "get into the habit"' (account from Helen, in Dixon 2012, p. 11). 'Getting into the habit' is what Mead might see as 'routinized' behaviour and it is through practising particular styles of communication that the social work self is constituted.

Before we explore key concepts relating to communication it is important to ask the question: 'what is meant by communication?' Communication entails social *interaction*. It is a dialogical, spontaneous and complex process. For example, relating to others involves:

- Demonstrating that one is listening and hearing
- Actively communicating through verbal or spoken cues
- Communicating through body language and gestures
- Using external metaphors and tools such as visual art, literature, sculpture, object placement and other creative forms (Morgan 2000)
- Recognising barriers to communication and responding appropriately
- Taking action arising from communication

We now consider differing types of tools for verbal communication.

DEMONSTRATING LISTENING

There are many different cues which demonstrate that a person is listening to another. Sitting across from another person and demonstrating listening through non-verbal cues involves what is termed 'attending'. Attending involves recognising that geographical placement of one's self has an impact on communication. Sitting behind a desk or writing as another person is speaking can be off-putting to clients, for example (Nelson-Jones 2012). A social worker who adopts an open stance without barriers between themselves and clients can help the flow of conversation. Generally speaking other non-verbal cues which suggest that listening is occurring include nodding, maintaining eye contact and remaining physically still. Cultural traditions and norms, gender, age and class as well as religion all play a part in the ways in which listening is conveyed.

Techniques which assist in communication can feel artificial when first experimenting with them in role plays and other formal learning opportunities. Communicative techniques are not intended to be used to manipulate or belittle our clients. As with all interactions with clients, asking them for feedback, for example about whether they feel listened to, is the best way to monitor your effectiveness in communication. Above all, being genuinely curious (Rogers 1961; White & Epston 1990) and interested in our clients' selves, biographies and narratives is central to social work interaction which is respectful and responsive to individual needs.

Consider the following exchange:

Interior. Coffee shop. Buzzing with people. A man, Alexandro, aged 40s, and a woman, Nora, also 40s, sit opposite one another at a coffee table. They are siblings in mid conversation.

Nora (*animated, looking at Alexandro*): ... and I mean I could not believe it!
(*Alexandro looks around, gaze hovering on people around him.*)
Nora: The cheek of it!
Alexandro (*eyes still on those around him*): Mmmm.
Nora: Are you listening to me?
Alexandro: Huh (*finally looks at Nora quizzically*): What?
Nora: I just told you about what happened to me last time I went in there. Did you even listen?
Alexandro: Just because you had a bad experience once doesn't mean it will happen again.
Nora: I can't even bear the thought of stepping through those doors again. All those other mothers and babies. And the social workers... No, I can't go back. I'll manage.
Alexandro: Ok.
Nora: I mean the depression isn't as bad as last time, right?
Alexandro (*looking off into the distance again*): Did I lock the car?
Nora: Do you know this is the first time I've been out of the house in weeks?
Alexandro (*grabbing at his pocket, miming locking the car*): I'm sure I did this. Did I do this? (*as if talking to himself, nodding*). Yes, I did. I'm sure I did.
Nora: Feels kind of weird to be out. The noise.
(*Alexandro looks at his nails. Silent.*)
Nora: It's weird to be without Jack too, though I'm sure he's fine with Mum. He's just so completely connected to me as I'm his only source of food. It's overwhelming sometimes. (*Looking around the cafe*) So weird to be out. Maybe we should get back...?
Alexandro (*jumping up from his seat*): Ok.

The scene above involves Alexandro and Nora who are in a coffee shop. Did you notice the way that Nora's questions and comments are not answered and not responded to in any empathic way by Alexandro? We have some clues about how these are ignored both in his body language and gaze as well as in what he says and doesn't say. Nora is trying to open up about how she is feeling but the signals she receives from Alexandro does not make this possible. Being able to see an example of when communication does not work can help to understand the importance of good communication skills in the professions. Imagine that Alexandro had followed up on Nora's comments where she is beginning to disclose how she is feeling. We know through these comments that she has a history of depression and was treated or assessed at a mother and baby facility in the past. We also know that she is finding it strange to be out of the house. There is also a lot that we do not know. We don't know, for example, why she has not been out of the house, what age her son Jack is and whether she has other children, a partner or friends and family around her. We will now consider particular techniques which aim to maximise communication between professionals and their clients.

ASKING QUESTIONS

Asking questions when conversing can help to extend the conversation or end the conversation. We will explore two types of questions which can be used in varying ways when working with clients. Open-ended questions invite a long, explanatory response. Closed-ended questions require shorter answers. Here is an example of an open-ended question from Alexandro.

> **Nora**: It's weird to be without Jack too, though I'm sure he's fine with Mum. He's just so completely connected to me as I'm his only source of food. It's overwhelming sometimes. (*Looking around the cafe*) So weird to be out. Maybe we should get back…?
> **Alexandro**: Can you tell me more about what you mean by feeling overwhelmed?

In asking this question Alexandro is inviting Nora to tell him more about how she is feeling and the situation she finds herself in. Open-ended questions in this context help to demonstrate to Nora that he is listening to her and that he is interested in hearing more. This is quite a contrast to his earlier response when he stood up to leave. Given that we can assume that Nora is keen to talk about how she is feeling, using an open-ended question in this way is likely to have a positive impact on Nora who has been trying to raise the issue of her feelings since the beginning of the conversation.

REFLECTING

Reflecting involves mirroring what the person has just said. Sometimes the same words can be used or they can be *paraphrased*, which means to put the original phrase into other words whilst keeping the original meaning. For example, reflecting meaning in the context above produces the following dialogue:

> **Nora**: Do you know this is the first time I've been out of the house in weeks?
> **Alexandro**: This is the first time you've been out of the house for weeks.
> **Nora**: Yes! Can you believe it? Time is flying past.

Reflecting feelings involves reflecting back what has already been said in relation to emotions. Here Alexandro reflects the emotion Nora articulates:

> **Nora**: Feels kind of weird to be out. The noise.
> **Alexandro**: It's a weird feeling, being out. Different noises to home.
> **Nora**: Totally different. The house is just so quiet with just me and Jack.

Reflecting in conversation can help when people 'lose' where they are in the narrative. For example, if there is a gap in conversation which is due to the speaker losing their place, it can help to provide a reflective statement. Reflective questions and statements need to be used sparingly. Overusing them can make the conversation stilted or disingenuous.

CLARIFYING

Clarifying questions and statements help to 'check in' with clients that they are being understood. In social work, it is vital that we use empathy to imagine what it must be like to view the world through our client's eyes (Lee 1994). Clarifying questions must fit with our client's narrative. For example, using our two characters, here is an example of a clarifying question which is inappropriate:

> **Nora**: Do you know this is the first time I've been out of the house in weeks?
> **Alexandro**: Speaking of your house, did you say that you've been decorating?

It is clear from Alexandro's response that he is not responding to Nora's attempts to discuss her current situation. An example of a more appropriate clarifying question is as follows:

> **Nora**: Do you know this is the first time I've been out of the house in weeks?
> **Alexandro**: Do you mean you haven't been out without Jack, or do you mean you haven't been out by yourself in weeks?

Here Alexandro is asking a clarifying question because he is not sure about whether Nora means that she has not been out with other people or whether she has not been out at all, including with her newborn baby. In clarifying her meaning, he is demonstrating that he is listening and curious about what she is saying, and in better understanding why she has not been out of the house he is attempting to understand 'the problem' from Nora's perspective. Is Nora not getting out of the house related to her depression, for example, or is it more that life is busy with a young baby and she has not had the opportunity to go out? How does Nora feel about not being out of the house? Does she miss social interaction and feel isolated, for example, or is she instead making a comment about how busy she has been?

SUMMARISING

Summarising information from a whole conversation or segments of dialogue serves a few functions. For example, here is a social worker summarising a client interaction: 'Have I got this right? You've come here so that you can get some more support with your disability which leaves you unable to get your children to school on time', or 'You and your partner Sue would like help with your relationship'. Summarising helps to narrow down the specifics of why someone requires assistance. It also helps to demonstrate listening skills. It is important in summarising that we are tentative about our assessment of the issues. If we were to summarise the dialogue between Nora and Alexandro we would need to note the following issues:

- Nora and Alexandro are siblings, both in their 40s
- Nora has a young baby named Jack
- Nora is feeling 'weird' being out in public
- Nora has a history of depression and thinks perhaps that although she might be depressed she is 'not as bad' as in the past

Being able to summarise often complex information is a central task in social work. Although we might like to draw some preliminary assessments about Nora and Alexandro's relationship, this process is more of an analysis than a summary. Analysis involves synthesising information and knowledge and is the means through which social workers make assessments (we explore assessments in Chapter 6 which looks at placement and organisational settings).

PROBING

Probing invites people to comment more fully or in more detail about a particular issue or emotion. For example, probing questions ask things such as 'What effect has that had on you?' (Morgan 2000) or 'Can you tell me more about what that meant in terms of your previous relationship?' Probing requires attention to the whole of a person's narrative as it can involve bridging two or more themes together. For example, if someone has talked about 'anger issues' at the beginning of the session then towards the end of your meeting they tell you about a history of property damage, probing might entail asking more about 'anger' in those contexts. Note that probing is merely an interest in looking further or more deeply at our client's issues. It is not meant to be a confronting or obtrusive challenging. Probing is an invitation for clients to talk more about issues. In our example, probing might consist of asking Nora to talk more about her feelings of depression and checking with her about isolation and support. These issues are directed through our understanding of what Nora has told us about so far but are also drawn from our knowledge about human growth and development (see Chapter 2), social work theory (see Chapter 4) and mental health and postnatal depression. Here is an example of a probing question:

Nora: Do you know this is the first time I've been out of the house in weeks?

Alexandro: That sounds really difficult.

Nora: Yeah, it has been really hard. Some days I just don't feel like getting out of bed in the morning.

Alexandro: Do you think depression is making you feel like this?

Nora: I think it might be. Last time I got really depressed I had trouble getting out of bed. That, to me, is a bit of a sign.

FRAMING ACTION

It is important that the contact between a social worker and their client is *purposeful* (Compton & Galaway 1999). In hearing a narrative from a client, for example, it is a mutual expectation that this contact will produce positive change. Since social workers have various roles and functions which depend on their organisational context, the 'outcomes' from contact with a social worker will differ. Two of the roles that social workers fulfil are:

- Counsellor: in this case the client's interaction with the social worker may occur in order to produce insight and re-frame 'problems' (Morgan 2000).
- Specialist social worker: for example, Nora might require assistance from children and families or mental health organisations in government or non-government. Social workers in this role might respond to her needs through advocacy, referring her on to more appropriate services, linking her in with supports such as local groups and services, agreeing on a contract for direct work together, and so on.

Framing action often occurs at the beginning or ending of sessions with clients. For example, imagine that Nora presented to a social worker in a children and families non-government organisation. Nora and the social worker would have discussed her experiences and subsequent needs in their initial meeting. At the end of the session the social worker may frame action through identifying things that they have agreed upon. The social worker may say something like this: 'So Nora, I have agreed to find out what the waiting list is like for the postnatal group at the hospital. I will call you tomorrow around 3pm when Jack might be asleep to see how you are. And you said you are okay with thinking more about what we might be able to do to help you feel less isolated and that you had a good GP with whom you will make an appointment tomorrow. Does that sound okay? Have I left anything out?' This process of agreeing and framing action is known as *contracting* (Cournoyer 2010). Contracting occurs at the beginning of interaction with clients, but should also occur at various points during each contact with our clients.

WRITTEN COMMUNICATION

Many students are competent at writing assignments, essays and exams, and in social work practice those academic writing skills are essential to extend into good practice. Examples of written tasks social workers undertake are:

- Written assessments, case summaries, timelines, case reviews
- Case notes
- Letters of referral to other organisations/professionals/teams
- Court reports
- Online content, for example contributing to the organisation's website
- Refereed journal articles and media copy
- Research proposals, summaries, reports
- Grant applications and tenders
- Annual reports

With competent writing skills being so central to social work, it is crucial for students to work on any gaps in knowledge about writing. For example, if grammatical errors are due to confusion about the 'rules' of grammar, universities often provide academic writing courses, workshops and one to one sessions which would be worth considering. These help with general issues such as how to construct an essay, tips on building an argument successfully, how to write critically as well as some foundational skills in writing such as structure, content, referencing, sentence construction and so on. Similarly, there are many social work books dedicated to written skill development (Healy & Mulholland 2007) and free online learning activities which help participants learn about correct use of apostrophes, for example, and other grammatical rules. Attending to writing skills early on saves problems in later study and helps to build the skills required in social work.

Each type of writing activity requires a slightly different focus, but here are some general writing tips which apply across both academic and practice contexts:

- Re-read your work and make sure it makes sense.
- Think about the purpose of your written piece of work: is it to provide a critical argument? Is it to create a record of a meeting with a client? Knowing the purpose of your writing is central when reading back your work. Ask yourself: have I achieved the requirements of the task? Is it clear why I have written what I have?
- Stick to the 'facts'. Unless the piece requires reflection (you will likely have to use references in reflective accounts), it is important to present information as objectively as possible. In case notes, for example, say: 'Daniel told me: "I want Mum to leave me alone"' rather than: 'Daniel wants to be left alone by his mother'. This helps to identify where different types of information have originated and differentiate fact from opinion.

THE SELF, REFLEXIVITY AND EMPATHY

In Chapter 1 we explored what we mean by the 'self'. Mead's interactionist self requires social interaction and identity is formed not through internal traits but through unique biographical events (Mead 1934). How we communicate to others is of concern in social work. Being able to reflexively engage in how we come across to others is therefore important, as is the ability to empathise. All of these require us to 'know' or understand ourselves in relation to others. Rather than seeing your self through therapeutic discourse as fixed and unchanging (Furedi 2004), think about how different situations bring out different ways of expressing or 'being' your-self. Complete Exercise 3.1, thinking about how you might be talking, gesturing, relating to others. Would you be confident? In your comfort zone? Would you be playful or serious? Would you be able to relate easily to others in that environment?

EXERCISE 3.1

If I was in a temple, I would be...
If I was at home I would be...
If I was in a school I would be...
If I was at work at a restaurant I would be...
If I was at university I would be...
If I was in the library I would be...
If I was at a game of football I would be...
If I was at the beach I would be...

Although it is the same 'you' in all of the places suggested, these differing locations would have provoked varying anticipated behaviours and attitudes. These might have depended on your own previous experiences of similar or the same places, or how you might imagine the people and surrounding culture of the place in question. Knowing that you respond differently to different social and cultural contexts is important in social work. This is because different emotions and experiences come together to influence the ways in which you interact with others. Imagining yourself at a football match may be one person's idea of pure joy while for someone else such an environment may be experienced as extremely challenging. In differing contexts our behaviours change and how we appear to others also changes. Being interpreted by others as aggressive or rude, for example, may occur because of a lack of understanding about how one comes across to others. When you engage in role plays at university, other students and tutors can often offer helpful, critical yet sensitive insights into how others interpret your tone, manner, gestures and communication styles. It is important to be aware of these and to experiment through play in learning activities: this is key to learning (West et al. 2011).

Through using imagination and play, children learn about how to take the perspective of others (Mead 1934). Similarly, in adulthood, we use this skill to under-stand others (Mead 1934). Therefore empathy requires both emotional literacy and imaginative action which enables one to imagine the perspective of others. The statements in Exercise 3.2 represent accounts from various different people. Practise your empathic imagination by thinking about how the person making the statement is feeling.

EXERCISE 3.2

I'd met this girl and we stayed at hers. In the morning I was running for the bus when they got me. Everyone knows they are racists. I was in their turf. I should have known better.
EMOTION:

They hurt me. I can still feel their hands on me. It was my fault.
EMOTION:

When he was born he was exactly the same. I loved him then and I still love him. He's my son and yeah he's got a disability but stop discriminating against him. He was determined then and he's determined now. I couldn't ask for a better son.
EMOTION:

It's like I'm two people. When I've got the smack I'm loved up, you know. When I'm without it I'm so alone and scared. I love it but I hate it too.
EMOTION:

Some of the emotions you may have thought about when reading the different statements may have included, for example (in order of the accounts in Exercise 3.2), feeling regret, fear and terror, horror, pride and conflicted or torn. When we considered Nora's account earlier in the chapter we explored different ways we could better understand her views and experiences through using differing communicative devices. Understanding how someone feels requires empathy which requires imagination and knowledge about the world around us. It is important when discussing emotions with our clients not to assume or generalise about emotions. As ever, tentative and careful discussion about emotions helps people find their own words to describe and understand their experiences and the world around them.

Your own biography or life events will have exposed you to different experiences than your fellow students. Direct experiences of the impacts of discrimination, oppression and injustice, or an interest in social issues such as addiction, violence, abuse and ill health, often prompt people's interest in studying social work. Using one's own experiences of oppression or inequality can help in engaging in imaginative accounts whereby the task is to understand the world from another person's perspective.

Sometimes students feel they do not 'bring enough experience' to their social work studies. There are numerous ways students can engage with developing empathy besides first-hand experience. Being able to imagine others' perspectives and associated emotions is the key task in the arts. Watching films, reading fiction and non-fiction books, listening to music and looking at visual art all help to develop empathic understanding. Engaging in reading about theories can also assist in this process, as we shall see in Chapter 5 when we explore ethics and values.

USE OF SELF

In this book we have begun to explore how to 'be' a social worker through engagement in key social work ideas including theories. In order to become a social worker, one must work to encourage the ongoing development of the social work self. This occurs through interaction between formal and informal learning. Such learning can occur in both structured and less structured environments, the former, for example, occurring in the university setting and the latter on placement.

In scholarship relating to therapeutic interactions, particularly in counselling, the emergence of the 'professional' has conceptualised identity in a compartmentalised way (Dunk-West 2011). The self we are at home, for example, is meant to differ from the self we are at work. Aspects of the 'personal' self, for example, might be used in 'professional' work: is one's sense of humour to be used in professional life? There are no easy answers in the literature as the question of the 'use of self' in practice has continued to be debated in social work scholarship (Heydt & Sherman 2005; Mandell 2008; McTighe 2011; Reupert 2006, 2007, 2009; Urdang 2010).

Although the questions and theories which make up the 'use of self' literature have their roots in psychoanalytic theory (Mandell 2008, p. 236), some of the ideas from this area of scholarship are relevant to our discussions in this book. Yet it is important to see the distinction between the idea of the 'use of self' and the way this book conceptualises the self.

The theoretical foundation of this book is that Mead's theoretical work, in which the self is produced through social interactions (Mead 1934), is relevant to social work. This means that the self we are at work and the self we are at home *are* different—but this is not because we are holding back or deliberately forcing a persona, but rather because our surrounding environment and subsequent *interactions produce the self*.

The way we reflect upon our selves is relevant to this chapter because we are exploring communication and communicative techniques which help us engage with those around us in the professional setting. Therefore the literature which examines the 'use of self' can be used—albeit with a critical lens—to assist in making the connections between our methods of communication and the ways in which we have communicated with others in the past, in different contexts, and those in our emerging social work role. Mandell articulates this in the following way:

> When countertransference approaches to the use of self are trapped by their failure to address power, while anti-oppression approaches are reductive to oppressor/ oppressed relations, a gap is created. Neither the traditional use of self literature nor the developing work on critical reflection seems to adequately capture a process of combining insight into one's own personhood—comprising individual

developmental history and multiple social identities in the context of personal experience, education, socialization and political milieus—with a critical analysis of one's role as a social worker in the relations of power that constitute our practice. This kind of multi-layered process is ... what we should be aiming for. (Mandell 2008, p. 237)

Therefore it is vital that we focus on communication skills and practices as one level of social work interaction. These must be combined with a critical appreciation of the world around us and some of the 'bigger' systems within which we operate in our day-to-day lives. These bigger systems include organisations and institutions as well as social norms, attitudes and practices.

Before we move on to consider working with others, take some time to complete the five questions in Exercise 3.3 in light of the material covered in this chapter.

EXERCISE 3.3

1. I communicate verbally by (for example, use of hands to gesture, using animated facial expressions, sitting close to the person you are speaking to):

   ....
   ....
   ....

2. In terms of effective interpersonal communication, I think I am (choose which statement fits, you can choose more than one option):
   a. good at getting my point across
   b. not so great at getting my point across
   c. sometimes good at getting my point across; how I communicate depends on the context
   d. always effective at getting my point across
3. I am good at 'reading' people (choose which answer fits).
   a. True
   b. False
   c. Sometimes true/false
4. It is better that social workers do not force particular types of communicative devices (such as reflective questions and the like) because it patronises the people with whom we work.
   a. True
   b. False
   c. Somewhat true/false
5. It is always important to consider power and power inequality and how it has a bearing on communication between social workers and the people with whom they work. This awareness of power can be addressed through (suggest ways that you will address this in your work as a social work student and in your social work career):

   ....
   ....
   ....

WORKING WITH OTHERS

Making the link between broader theories of inequality and person-to-person inter-action enables social workers to communicate in ways that help to address power imbalances and inequalities. Therefore, the way in which we communicate as social workers is immensely powerful in itself. Addressing broader inequalities in 'micro' or person-to-person interaction has been highlighted in Jan Fook's theoretical work (Fook 1993, 2002; Hugman 2005, p. 1142). Equally it is important how we communicate with other professions, since this is the means through which we convey to others who we are as social workers and what social work means.

Working with other professionals requires high level communication skills. It can be difficult to articulate the underlying values and theoretical foundation upon which social work is built, particularly if other professions come from very different perspectives. We have discussed in previous chapters some of the tensions which can occur in multidisciplinary settings, but this quote from a participant involved in research into interprofessional identity sums up why it is important to connect with others on a 'human' level:

> Whether it's a manager of a ward or social services or a day centre, treat us as individuals, it doesn't matter whether you're a manic depressive, schizophrenic, got personality disorder ... or mental condition let's say, or whatever, or severely depressed, you're an individual, you're a human being with problems and address that person as an individual and not as a condition. (Reynolds 2007, p. 451)

Similarly, other professionals can help to increase our knowledge about the profession itself. Using effective communication can assist social workers in having their views heard by other professions and help to foster positive working relationships.

CHAPTER SUMMARY

This chapter has introduced communication in social work. We have examined some of the key ways in which verbal communication can be used to elicit client narratives, in particular: demonstrating listening; asking questions; reflecting; clarifying; summarising; probing and framing action. Written communication was also explored, with some key tips on how to develop written skills in the academic and practice contexts. Finally, we considered the use of self and working with others in relation to communicating as a social worker.

FURTHER READING

COURNOYER, B. R. (2010) *The Social Work Skills Workbook*, 6th edn. Florence: Cengage Learning Inc.
HEALY, K. (2012) *Social Work Methods and Skills: The Essential Foundations of Practice*. Basingstoke: Palgrave Macmillan.

HEALY, K. & MULHOLLAND, J. (2012) *Writing Skills for Social Workers*, 2nd edn. London: Sage Publications.

LISHMAN, J. (2009) *Communication in Social Work*, 2nd edn. Basingstoke: Palgrave Macmillan.

NELSON-JONES, R. (2012) *Basic Counselling Skills*. London: Sage Publications.

THOMPSON, N. (2011) *Effective Communication: A Guide for the People Professions*, 2nd edn. Basingstoke: Palgrave Macmillan.

TREVITHICK, P. (2012) *Social Work Skills and Knowledge: A Practice Handbook*, 3rd edn. Maidenhead: Open University Press.

4

Social Work Theory

This chapter:

- Introduces key social work theories

- Identifies the underlying orientation in each theory

- Encourages scrutinising theoretical approaches in relation to values, ethics and one's world-view

- Considers broadly conceived social work values such as anti-oppressive and social justice frameworks and how these apply to practice

- Explores the tension between the public and the private worlds of experience and how these apply to social work

Dear Dr Agony Aunt,

I am a woman in my late 30s and am at my wits' end, as I can never seem to find the right guy. I have had two significant relationships which both ended with them saying that they found me emotionally distant and more like a friend than a girlfriend. These comments at the time really hurt me but I know that they were true as I didn't like to kiss and cuddle very often. The guys were lovely people and I feel I really lost out when they dumped me.

Generally I find it hard to open up to people as I'm really shy which, as I said, has meant that I have only had a few long-term relationships. My friends are all so sexually confident but I find that I wear clothes to cover my body and don't go out as a result of feeling like I don't fit in. I want to be more like them but can't seem to feel comfortable with myself. I see television shows and read magazines like yours and find myself comparing—not so favourably—myself to others. I am successful in my work and have some really great friends whom I have confided in, though I am sure they don't realise the extent to which this gets me down. How can I find a partner for life when I'm so unhappy with the way I am? Will I ever be confident and self-assured?

Feeling Lonely, via email

...

Dear Feeling Lonely,

You have taken the first step in dealing with your problems. In reaching out for help, you have shown that you are willing to examine where these issues arise from and how you might be able to fix them. I will offer you some general advice and hope that you will seek out the expert help, which will assist you in your journey towards greater self-acceptance. It appears to me that your issues seem to stem from your inability to really confide in and connect with others—which you say is down to your shyness. Whilst people with introverted personalities do tend to find it difficult to act in an extroverted way, I don't feel that your problems with intimacy are because of your shyness. Consider instead why you might have subconsciously sabotaged your previous relationships. What is it that is scary about intimacy and closeness? In answering these questions you may wish to further understand how your childhood learning about relationships might have impacted upon the ways in which you behave in relationships. I recommend that you get in touch with a registered counsellor to help you resolve these issues.

Best of luck,
Dr Agony Aunt

The correspondence above, though fictionalised, represents similar columns which appear in newspapers and magazines throughout the world on a daily basis. As we saw in Chapter 1, the way in which we think about ourselves has been so shaped by psychological theories of the self that the tendency is to uncritically accept them.

Consider, for example, the response above from the 'expert'. The advice given is that the letter-writer seek professional help. Peppered through the response are important clues as to which sets of theories or discourses the expert is utilising. The mention of the subconscious, for example, presupposes that such a thing actually exists. Similarly, the elevation of childhood as an indicator of present behaviour is presupposed. As we saw in Chapter 1, such notions of childhood can be seen in psychoanalytic theories and have become a central part of the ways in which we understand the self in contemporary popular culture. Finally, the role of the expert is assumed to be beneficial if not *crucial* in helping the individual overcome their personal problems. Inherent in the account is the presumption that the following are real and objectively true:

- Personality
- The subconscious
- Childhood as a predictor of adult interactions
- That experts and therapy are required to 'fix' individual pathologies

Yet all of these assumptions need to be critically understood: whilst all are presupposed to be 'true' in contemporary western culture (Furedi 2004) it is only through examination of the theoretical world-view held by differing theories that social workers can be of better assistance to their clients. The uncritical acceptance of these notions does little to assist our clients. Consider, for example, that the person writing the letter may not require therapy or any assistance from professionals in order to overcome her articulated concerns. In their everyday work, social workers come into contact with individuals experiencing problems or wanting change so it can become second nature to assume that in order for change to occur, individuals require the assistance of experts. However, as we shall see, such a position does little to account for agency, which is the ability to bring about change in one's life. It is crucial that social workers reflect upon their understanding of the expert, and social work theories make this explicit.

The purpose of this chapter is to outline some of the key theories which underpin social work practice. Through a brief but critical discussion of differing approaches, we will better understand the underlying assumptions and challenge the role of the expert.

SOCIAL WORK THEORY: DIFFERING ORIENTATIONS

Figure 4.1 represents the ways in which social workers work to effect change through intervention at various levels. Social work theories examine how to assist others in making change which involves a shift in:

- Individual behaviours
- Thoughts or cognition
- Social interactions
- Social structures, systems, policies and institutional practices

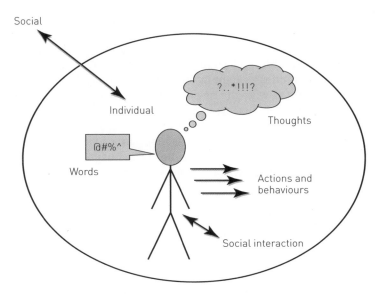

FIGURE 4.1 Different social work theories focus on different areas of human experience, action, thoughts and social structure

While many theories focus on changing individual patterns of behaviour or ways of thinking, others theorise that individual change does little to address broader social problems in which inequality is produced. Such approaches instead argue that social workers ought to focus on changing broader systems or structures (Mullaly 1997).

For example, if a client working with a social worker was experiencing poverty through unemployment the social worker's intervention could vary, depending on which theoretical perspective is informing their social work practice. Using theories in which change is individualised, the social worker might try to help the client gain employment, which would address the problem of poverty. The social work intervention might entail looking at individual 'blocks' to employment such as lack of experience or skills desired by employers. Assisting the client through referring them to community groups and services designed to help people into employment might be a course of action when taking an 'individual' approach. Yet this course of action relies upon the notion that employment is available to people who are willing to undergo personal transformation to get them 'work ready'. A more structural approach involves taking a broader view of the problem. Though the individual client's issue relates to poverty due to unemployment, a structural approach would entail understanding the client's problem in the context of their broader socio-cultural environment and arrangement of societal institutions, practices, policies and legislation. For example, the client may live in an area that is characterised by high unemployment and poverty. They may be ineligible for unemployment benefits or the benefits themselves may be inadequate to meet the rising costs of living, including food, housing, clothing, fuel costs such as electricity and gas, and costs associated with communication such as the internet and mobile telephone accounts.

The social worker using a structural approach may work with the individual along with other individuals in the community to lobby political figures to address the inequalities evident in their community such as the lack of access to employment. In this way, the social worker is assisting the client to form relationships with others with a view to bringing about change, not through a focus on the individual's circumstances, but through a focus on the shared experiences which are due to external factors such as lack of jobs. The social worker may try to raise public awareness about the issues facing people in the area and may do so through public education, writing letters to key community leaders, policy-makers and legislators.

Although each of the tasks relating to the individual and structural approaches differs, often in practice social workers will work towards *both* assisting others in making individual changes in their lives to increase well-being *and* promoting principles such as social justice through challenging oppressive social structures. Indeed it is vital that social work continues to assist in addressing problems identified by individuals, and that it distinguishes itself as a profession that is committed to bringing about social change (Fook 1991). We shall explore some of the key theoretical approaches used in social work. As we consider them it is important to distinguish between those which advocate for individual change and those advocating for social change.

In social work this tension between the individual and structural levels of disadvantage requires constant reflection and analysis on behalf of the social worker but it also requires personal commitment. Not only must social workers decide whether they intervene through individual or social action, they must also account for their own personal values and beliefs. For example, can a person be a competent social worker if they are abusive in their private lives? To believe in social justice requires a clear professional and personal value-base, and we will explore this further in Chapter 5 when we explore ethics. It is crucial to recognise and engage in this tension. Social work has long been concerned with the coming together of the ways in which individual experiences feed into broader society:

> The triangular discourse about the extent to which and the ways in which social work is personal, political or professional have always been present in social work. I have interpreted them as being about the struggle to achieve social work's claim of bringing together the interpersonal and the social. (Payne 2005, p. 186)

Despite the different foundations upon which theories are built, in social work across differing practice settings and differentiated theoretical applications, the process whereby we implement theories is very similar. The 'social work process' (Compton & Galaway 1989) involving the assessment of the 'problem', intervention and review requires collaboration, clearly defined timeframes and a belief that people are able to successfully 'address the challenges they face' (Healy 2012, pp. 56–57). We will now examine some of the key theoretical models which frame contemporary social work practice.

COGNITIVE BEHAVIOURAL THERAPY

Cognitive behavioural therapy (CBT) (Figure 4.2) is an approach that argues that in changing an individual's thoughts, or cognition, their behaviour will change. There is much empirical evidence to suggest that CBT is an effective intervention to address a range of issues such as anxiety and phobias, or substance misuse (Vasilaki *et al.* 2006; Witkiewitz & Marlatt 2004) for example. Because CBT has a high success rate and is a relatively inexpensive way to treat individual problems, it is increasingly used in practice, particularly in mental health settings. Internationally, CBT is practised by psychologists as well as social workers, and in social work the idea that thoughts affect behaviours is broadly accepted. The specific ways in which CBT can be utilised in social work are far reaching. The bene-fit of CBT to social work is that underpinning this approach is the belief that the self is able to shift and change previously unhelpful ways of thinking and acting (Ronen 1997, p. 204) without recourse to constraining notions such as personality 'types'. Using this broad conceptualisation of the self helps to frame individual pathology in terms of change. In this way:

> CBT ... is neither a strict implementation of learning theory, nor is it merely a collection of effectual techniques. Rather, CBT constitutes a holistic way of life, a way of thinking and perceiving human functioning and needs, and a way of operating within the environment in order to achieve the most effective means of accomplishing one's aims. (Ronen 1997, p. 202)

FIGURE 4.2 Cognitive behavioural therapy relates to thoughts and behaviours

HUMANISTIC APPROACHES

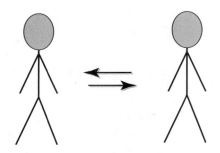

FIGURE 4.3 Humanistic approaches focus on individuals and the helping relationship

Humanistic approaches (Figure 4.3) emphasise the quality of the relationship between the client and the professional and it is therefore the interaction between the social worker and their client that is central to bringing about positive change. The key theorist in the application of humanistic approaches to social work is Carl Rogers (1951, 1961). Rogers argues that in order for the therapeutic relationship in counselling to be successful, the counsellor must have particular abilities. These include: empathy or the ability to understand the world from another's perspective, 'unconditional positive regard' which is the ability to think positively about people no matter what their circumstances, and to be congruent which means that there is a real connection between the values and beliefs of one's profession and those of one's true self (see Rogers 1951, 1961). Research consistently demonstrates, particularly in counselling, that the relationship, or *interaction*, between the professional and the client is crucial to successful outcomes for the client (Lambert & Barley 2001; Ribner & Knei-Paz 2002). Such findings underline that the relationship between social workers and their clients is of central importance in working together successfully. Using a humanistic approach entails interacting in a genuine, truthful and empathic manner, and social workers using such an approach thus need to be aware of their language, their communication style and the way in which they come across to others. More importantly, however, they need to build a relationship in which clients feel able to disclose information and work together towards a common goal. A Rogerian approach is often thought about in relation to counselling work, but in contemporary social work practice the underpinning values of this framework are just as important in casework or community work as they are in one-to-one interactions.

Motivational interviewing is a type of intervention used in social work, particularly in the substance use field, which similarly emphasises the Rogerian importance of the relationship between the social worker and the client. Rogers advocates for an approach which is led by the client: it is up to the client to direct the issues discussed, for example. In motivational interviewing the professional is a facilitator who helps their client 'examine and resolve ambivalence. The specific strategies of motivational interviewing are designed to elicit, clarify, and resolve ambivalence in a client-centred and respectful atmosphere' (Nelson 2011, p. 111).

STRENGTHS PERSPECTIVE/EMPOWERMENT APPROACH

Rather than seeing people in relation to what is going 'wrong' in their lives, the strengths perspective and empowerment approach instead takes a more positive angle in that the social worker's motivation is to work towards encouraging and

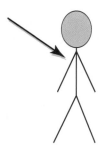

FIGURE 4.4 Strengths perspectives are interested in individual strengths

helping to facilitate change through the unconditional support of their client's capabilities (Figure 4.4). Such approaches are more interested in the future than in the past (Healy 2012, p. 14) and can therefore be seen as a counter to psychoanalytic approaches in which problems in childhood, for example, can be viewed as a barrier to current functioning (as discussed in Chapter 1). The strengths perspective argues that individuals have particular skills and strategies for coping with adversity and it is vital for social workers to work 'with' and 'for' client strengths (see Saleeby 1992, 1996, 2006). There are some similarities with other approaches such as solution-focused, problem-solving (Perlman 1957) and narrative approaches (Morgan 2000; White & Epston 1990) in that these all share an interest in separating the 'person from the problem' (Healy 2012, p. 71). Similarly, alongside the privileging of client strengths in social work practice, the notion of empowerment is often cited as being important. It is crucial to note however that social workers do not 'empower' individuals.

Rather, social workers work to assist in individuals' empowerment through working *alongside* their clients, consistently working to understand clients' struggles and challenges, advocating against constraining social structures and sharing information that assists in promoting change. Central to empowerment approaches is the understanding that there is unequal distribution of power which results in disempowered individuals. Social workers from this perspective must therefore work alongside clients in collaboration: 'we are partners against oppression, but in this dance, leading and following may be fluid and interchangeable. The concept of coteaching implies that clients and workers teach each other what they know about the presenting problem and about the oppression(s) faced' (Lee 1994, p. 29).

Both of these theoretical positions are useful in the problem-saturated landscape within which social work can take place because 'our focus on problems and work with disadvantaged populations creates the occupational hazard that workers will focus too much on client weakness and problems and fail to identify strengths' (Compton & Galaway 1989, p. 223).

SYSTEMS THEORY/ECOLOGICAL PERSPECTIVE

Systems theory and the ecological perspective or ecosystem approach argue that the individual is best understood only in relation to their environment (Figure 4.5). Although there are various traditions arguing that clients must be understood through analysis of their setting, they share some common ideas. Interactions in the world around us, including its people, geographical places, organisations and institutions, make up our ecology. Systems theory can be used with groups (Balgopal & Vassil 1983) and individuals (Rose 1962).

For example, social workers working with a young person having problems living at home with their family would be interested in the ways the young person

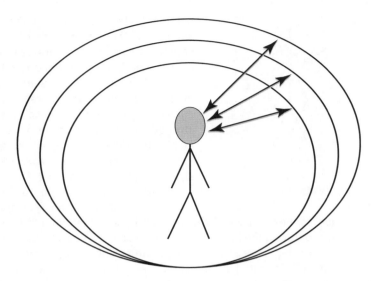

FIGURE 4.5 Systems approaches highlight the external environment and the individual's place within

is interacting in the broader family or family 'system' and the role they play within such a system. This is because 'the family as a larger system relies on each individual member to play his or her part if it is to function successfully as an entity in the community' and the family is connected to the community in varying ways (Compton & Galaway 1989, p. 120). In this way, individuals are connected to others through varying 'systems'. Social workers using these theories to underpin their practice must work to understand their client's ecological setting and which interactions become stressors (Germain & Gitterman, 1980).

Although this group of theories is rich in 'technical terminology' (Payne 2005, p. 157), historically social work has long been concerned with understanding the person in relation to their environment (Healy 2012, p. 13). In Chapter 1 we considered the role of psychological discourses in shaping the way we currently think about ourselves. Ecological perspectives tend to shift the focus away from the individual and are more concerned with how individuals' attempts to *interact* with particular systems or organisations become problematic. A social worker's role is to assist people in resolving problems in these interactions as well as to link people with others who may further assist in successfully realising their aspirations (Pincus & Minahan 1973, p. 9).

FEMINIST SOCIAL WORK THEORY

Feminist social work theory involves the critical analysis of power in relation to gender and understands it both in the context of broader social structures and through individual experiences in day-to-day life (Figure 4.6). The relatively recent

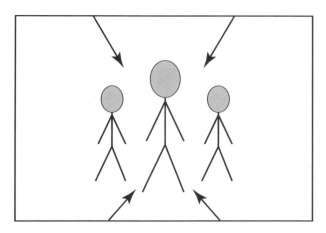

FIGURE 4.6 Feminist social work highlights broader social inequalities

shift in women's social roles has been the result of increased labour participation outside the family home and changes in traditional gender expectations due to contraceptives allowing women to choose when and whether to have children (Giddens 1992). Yet despite these changes, women continue to experience gendered oppression in contemporary social life. For example, women are more often diagnosed with depression than men. Further, 'racialized, "minoritorized" and immigrant women are more likely than British-born white women to enter the statistics of those experiencing mental illnesses' (Bondi & Burman 2001, p. 9). Women are subject to higher rates of sexual violence than their male counterparts. Domestic violence is overwhelmingly perpetrated by men towards women. All of these social issues, and more, are important to the ways in which social workers work with both women and men, adults and children:

> Women have been at the centre of the struggle to define the appropriate role for social work in rapidly changing societies. Although crucial policies and legislation are formulated by men, women undertake the bulk of the caring tasks carried out within the home, and dominate the basic grades of paid professions doing such work. Thus, arguments about the purpose of social work are intricately wound up with disputes over women's position in the social order. (Dominelli 2002, p. 17)

In social work it is vital to understand the sociological analysis of gender. The implications for practice are varied. Understanding differential power through the lens of gender means that social issues such as child sexual abuse in the family, for example, can be better theorised and responded to in practice (see Dominelli 1989).

CRITICAL SOCIAL WORK AND STRUCTURAL APPROACHES

Like feminist social work approaches, critical and structural approaches to social work practice entail awareness of and action towards the *external* causes of individual problems (Figure 4.7). At the beginning of this chapter we explored the issue of poverty and unemployment from both an individual perspective and a social perspective. The social perspective entailed understanding how external factors such as a community's high rate of unemployment or lack of jobs made it difficult for labour force participation. Thus, a social work focus on individual factors contributing to unemployment from a critical perspective does little to acknowledge

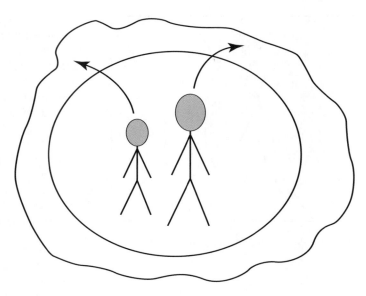

FIGURE 4.7 Critical approaches are interested in change at the structural level

or address the wider issues at stake. In this way, individual problems are always framed as being part of a broader community or social setting which constrains or oppresses individuals. Such an approach requires social workers' reflexive engagement with oppression:

> Critical social work demands that social workers reflect upon the ways in which social disadvantage and oppression shape our sense of purpose as practitioners. This perspective demands that a social worker should, at the very least, have a critical understanding of social disadvantage and how to respond to individuals living in oppressed or difficult circumstances ... it is often necessary for social workers to critically reflect on the broader societal attitudes that contribute to the discrimination and oppression experienced by service users. (Healy 2012, p. 12)

In Chapter 3 we examined the ways in which social workers develop the necessary skills to listen, empathise and act upon our clients' needs, and these skills are as central for structural work as they are for interpersonal work. Advocating on behalf of clients to external organisations, for example, requires many of the same communicative skills used in interpersonal exchanges. In Chapter 6 we will consider the organisational contexts in which social work intervention takes place. Social workers are required to challenge the ways in which institutions discriminate against others on the basis of gender, sexual identity, race, disability, class and other areas of difference (Mullaly 1997, p. 104). While it may seem intuitive that social workers challenge oppression, in practice this can feel risky. For example, a social worker in a statutory setting in which they work with young people may know that the closure of a local service for young people who are survivors of sexual assault will further oppress young women. The social worker's attempts to bring about structural change in their own organisation can be met with resistance and result in the worker feeling that their structural social work is curtailed by hierarchy and organisational culture. Yet it is also important to recognise the role that social work plays in the maintenance of oppressive systems, and ultimately social workers from this perspective are urged to take action:

> Social workers need to understand the nature of state power and the role of social work as an element of state control and oppression, and to construct an approach to practice which is underpinned by this understanding. Such practice must be directed at challenging and changing structures which oppress. (Davis 1991, p. 70 cited in Mullaly 1997)

SOCIOLOGICAL SOCIAL WORK

In Chapter 1 we examined our professional identity, through examining the theory of self developed by George Herbert Mead. In Chapter 2 we also saw the ways in which social models of self have influenced developmental psychology, for example, in relation to highlighting the importance of the social and cultural settings in which the individual develops. Historically, sociological theory has heavily influenced social work theory (see Forte 2004a, 2004b). The notion of sociological social work (Figure 4.8) is the means through which a broad application of sociological

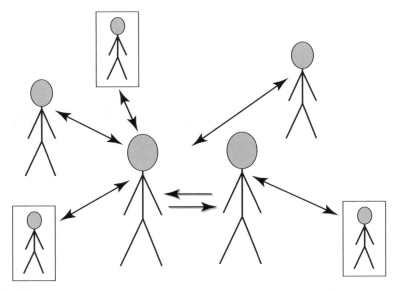

FIGURE 4.8 Sociological social work seeks to understand the individual by looking at social and individual contexts

theory can be translated into social work practice (Dominelli 2004), and sociological social work helps social workers respond to the challenges of contemporary life
(Dunk-West & Verity, forthcoming). Since interactions are central to Mead's self-
making, it follows that social work ought to be interested in the relationships
between people. The meaning of one's environment and relationships within that
environment are constitutive of selfhood: social work must always therefore origi-
nate from this understanding. In all of the theoretical traditions discussed in this
chapter, the importance of the social environment is clear. Although social work
theories can feel distinct from one another, in reality they share the same axis of
understanding about people as being understood in relation to their environment
(social, cultural settings) and relationships with others.

Similarly, a sociological lens helps social workers understand the broader
patterns of inequality and oppression which are experienced by particular groups
(Dominelli 2004; Cunningham & Cunningham 2008). Discrimination on the basis of
gender, age, culture, race, disability, sexual identity, gender identity, socio-
economic status, health status and other difference continues to occur in contemporary life. Institutions discriminate as well as individuals, and social workers must
take responsibility for practising in a way that counters inequality and actively advocates for and with people who are discriminated against. Anti-discriminatory
approaches (Thompson 1993) and anti-oppressive practice, pursuing social justice:
these are *foundational to all social work* interventions. The sociological analysis of
power and broader patterns of inequality are at the core of competent social work
practice and are threaded through all social work theories and methods. It is vital
that social work students engage in understanding power and its (unequal) distribution in society. This involves understanding how social workers and their organisational settings contribute to inequality. Developing an ethical framework for
oneself (see Chapter 5) helps to direct social work practice appropriately, with
inequality actively addressed in social work interventions.

Now take some time to complete Exercise 4.1, a reflexive exercise designed to
engage you with the material we have covered in this chapter.

EXERCISE 4.1

Think about a personal issue you have had in the past. Reflect on what the issues were
and whether others in your family, community or society have experienced similar
issues. What social work approaches help you in understanding this issue? What are
your favourite social work theoretical approaches? Do you think social workers should
use theories that help them understand social problems and injustices or individual
problems and injustices? Your answers to these questions will be personal to you, but
are worth noting at this stage and comparing at various points in your academic study
as well as into your social work career.

Map out how you see social work theory informing your practice. You can do this
visually using a diagram with arrows and shapes, or you could draw a picture. For
example, in the picture a river or stream could represent your work with clients and
the terrain beside could represent the foundations upon which such work is built.
Stones set on the terrain may represent your three preferred social work theories. In

particular, while you are completing this exercise, think about an issue using your sociological imagination. What are the implications for individuals and what does the issue mean in the broader historical and social context? Highlight which theories you think will assist you in your future role as a social worker. How do these theories differ from the perspectives of other professionals?

CHAPTER SUMMARY

As we have seen, different social work theories emphasise different things. As you continue your reading and social work studies, you will begin to develop a prefer-ence for certain theoretical frameworks, but you will probably have some prefer-ence already. In this chapter we have briefly examined some theories which argue that social workers ought to focus on the individual and others which argue it is more important to fight against oppressive structures and systems. Yet other approaches argue that individuals are best understood as relating to the world and people around them and social workers should aim to help individuals overcome difficulties in these interactions with systems. What makes social work distinctive is its concern with both the personal and the social.

Social work theories ought to be approached with a 'sociological imagination' (Mills 1959). Regardless of the theoretical orientation underpinning practice, social workers need to develop this imagination through the dual focus upon the individ-ual and the social setting (Schwartz 1974). Understanding a person requires being curious about their lives, their biography as well as the society in which they are embedded:

> The sociological imagination enables its possessor to understand the larger historical scene in terms of its meaning for the inner life and the external career of a variety of individuals. (Mills 1959, p. 5)

In our challenging social and economic landscape the tension between the public and the private, or the macro and the micro, is more important to resolve than ever. Social work needs to continue to highlight the dual focus on the individual and the environment if we are to realise our desire to effect positive and long-lasting change. At the beginning of the chapter we considered poverty and unemployment; to return to this issue, here is what C. Wright Mills—the scholar who invented the term 'sociological imagination'—had to say about it:

> When, in a city of 100,000, only one man [sic] is unemployed, that is his personal trouble, and for its relief we properly look to the character of the man, his skills, and his immediate opportunities. But when in a nation of 50 million employees, 15 million men are unemployed, that is an issue, and we may not hope to find its solution within the range of opportunities open to any one individual. (Mills 1959, p. 9)

FURTHER READING

ADAMS, R., DOMINELLI, L. & PAYNE, M. (2005) *Social Work Futures: Crossing Boundaries, Transforming Practice*. Basingstoke: Palgrave Macmillan.

BECKETT, C. (2006) *Essential Theory for Social Work Practice*. London: Sage Publications.

COMPTON, B. R. & GALAWAY, B. (1989) *Social Work Processes*. Belmont: Brooks/Cole Publishing Company.

HEALY, K. (2012) *Social Work Methods and Skills: The Essential Foundations of Practice*. Basingstoke: Palgrave Macmillan.

HOWE, D. (2009) *A Brief Introduction to Social Work Theory*. Basingstoke: Palgrave Macmillan.

MILLS, C. W. (1959) *The Sociological Imagination*. New York: Oxford University Press.

PAYNE, M. (2005) *Modern Social Work Theory*, 3rd edn. Basingstoke: Palgrave Macmillan.

5

Everyday
Ethics

This chapter:

- Explores personal and professional values and how these relate to social work

- Explains the importance of ethics in underpinning social work practice and theory

- Outlines the key ethical theories which inform social work

- Examines the ethical dimension in relation to particular scenarios

- Highlights ethical dilemmas within organisational contexts and professional roles

In our contemporary, everyday life we are faced with a number of ethics-related dilemmas each day (Singer 1993, 2004, 2009). Consider, for example, the myriad of product choices available in western cultures. Whether choosing from 12 different types of potatoes or selecting the best supplier for a service, it can be difficult to make choices about goods and services. Specifically, how much thought should go in to buying a product? Is it better to buy cruelty-free and organic? Should we buy food in glass containers which can be recycled or the cheaper, plastic version? Should we worry about giving our custom to companies whose ethics towards its employees are dubious? Should we buy products that have been tested on animals, subjecting them to suffering? Should we participate in meat eating or become vege-tarian or vegan in order to help the environment and avoid species' mass produc-tion, suffering and slaughter? Should we select locally grown and sourced food to reduce our 'carbon footprint'? Such questions may have come up in your purchas-ing of products in everyday life. Broader questions about how to live include: should we care for others or look after ourselves? Should children have 'rights'? Are social workers ever 'off duty'? In this chapter we will begin to examine the relationship between our personal and emerging professional self regarding ethics. We consider how to make ethical decisions and what is required in order to justify such deci-sions. The chapter concludes with an examination of some of the ethical issues in organisations.

Ethical decision-making involves 'the systematic exploration of questions about how we should act in relation to others' (Rhodes 1986, p. 21). Our values influence how we go about our everyday activities. Values are important in social work. There is even a suggestion that successful work between a social worker and their client is promoted when they have some shared values (Loewenberg *et al.* 2000). To begin to think about your own values, complete Exercise 5.1. This has been designed to help you firstly, notice where you stand on a particular issue and secondly, begin to reflexively engage with your values.

EXERCISE 5.1

Read the statements below. Mark a point on the spectrum that represents where you 'stand' on a particular issue. Try to answer honestly rather than putting down what you think are the 'right' answers.

The best place to raise children is within a family

Agree _____Disagree

All children need a mother and a father

Agree _____Disagree

Euthanasia (choosing to die) is wrong

Agree _____Disagree

Abortion should be freely available

Agree _____Disagree

Everyone should have access to education
Agree _____Disagree

If you work hard, you deserve wealth
Agree _____Disagree

Women and men are equal
Agree _____Disagree

Plastic surgery is wrong
Agree _____Disagree

Everyone should eat healthy food
Agree _____Disagree

Cultural diversity means tolerating difference
Agree _____Disagree

People living in England should know how to speak English
Agree _____Disagree

People who get good grades at university are clever
Agree _____Disagree

Women should not wear revealing clothing
Agree _____Disagree

Sexual behaviour should only commence once someone is married
Agree _____Disagree

ADHD is over-diagnosed
Agree _____Disagree

Older people are nice
Agree _____Disagree

Technology is important to young people
Agree _____Disagree

Life is riskier now than when my grandparents were young
Agree _____Disagree

Multinational companies are bad
Agree _____Disagree

Unemployed people need to get a job
Agree _____Disagree

People with a disability need special help with things
Agree _____Disagree

Monogamy (being faithful to one sexual partner) is not natural

Agree _____Disagree

It is healthy to have hobbies

Agree _____Disagree

Community is important to young people today

Agree _____Disagree

Social workers are powerful

Agree _____Disagree

Did you find you answered the questions in Exercise 5.1 quickly and were you surprised by any of your answers? Do you foresee that any of your values will get in the way of your development as a social worker? One person's personal values can clash with another's. Having completed this exercise, it is important to note that people's values are constantly changing. This means that your responses today may differ markedly from your responses to the same questions after you have completed your course and, again, in subsequent years. This is because our personal values are influenced by external factors which include, for example, those around us, our education, background and culture, and our life experiences. Your social work studies will likely change your values as well as the way you see the world around you.

Our values influence the ways in which we interact with our clients and those around us in everyday life. When we meet with clients, we must not only be aware of power and inequality, but also understand how our values can affect the service we provide (Shardlow 1995, p. 65). Values come together in practice in complex ways because:

> Social workers are not autonomous professionals whose guiding ethical principles are solely about respecting and promoting the self-determination of service users. They are employed by agencies, who work within the constraints of legal and procedural rules and must also work to promote the public good or the well-being of society in general. (Banks 2012, p. 31)

An example of how personal values come into our practice is when you believe something that a client has done is either 'wrong' or 'right'. This is not to be avoided; rather, acknowledging our personal values is an important process which should emerge during reflexive practice, and may be articulated in supervision, for example. Social work students often report that their values have changed throughout the course without them consciously trying to. It is fair to say that while it is important to 'notice' one's values, being open to new ways of thinking and being able to unravel values are perhaps most central to social work learning.

So far we have thought about values as they relate to ourselves, as influenced through our biography and broader socio-cultural context. In social work there are also professional values that we need to understand and integrate into our practice. In practice, our professional values can clash with one another. More specifically, this relates to what we call in social work an 'ethical dilemma'. As we shall see, an ethical dilemma occurs when there is a clash of ethical principles. Here Richard Hugman explains:

> [T]here are ... times when the professional ought to give conscious attention to the reasons why one choice seems better or worse than another, whether about the way in which something is done or about the objective that is being sought. In these circumstances the person is engaging with ethics. Ethics, in this sense, is the 'conscious reflection on our moral beliefs'. (Hinman 2003, p. 5 cited in Hugman 2005, p. 1)

In your everyday life you will have encountered ethical dilemmas. For example, imagine that you have first-hand evidence that your close friend's partner is cheating on them. As far as you are aware, they are in a monogamous relationship. Do you:

(a) Tell your friend.
(b) Say nothing.
(c) Tell the friend's partner that you know in the hope that they will 'come clean'.
(d) Tell another friend.
(e) ....

There are many options for how you might respond to that situation, and the choice you make will depend on what you think is important. For example, if you chose to tell your friend, you may have thought things such as:

• They have a right to know
• It's my responsibility as their friend to be honest
• Not being honest will hurt my friend
• Once they know all the facts then they can make the decision for themselves about how they respond
• It's the right thing to do

If you thought that saying nothing was the best option, then you may have felt this was justified for the following reasons:

• It's not my business as a relationship is private
• My friend may not believe me and I will lose them as a friend
• The information will hurt my friend
• It's not my responsibility to act since I wasn't the one who cheated
• It's the right thing to do

When we make decisions relating to ethical dilemmas we are weighing up the conflicting sides of the debate in question. Ethical decision-making requires us to understand the ethical principles underlying the situation and the responsibilities we have towards others.

In social work we encounter ethical dilemmas on a daily basis. Without the language and conceptual frameworks to make sense of these, we quickly lose our way.

In the following sections, we consider the ways in which social workers are expected to engage in their professional conduct with others through examining key ethical theoretical traditions. Yet ethics are not straightforward in social work, and merely learning about differing traditions is only half way to becoming an ethical practitioner. Your task in your practice as a social work student and throughout your career is to make your own decision in response to ethical dilemmas. Your decision must have its foundations in ethical scholarship and you must be able to clearly use these theoretical ideas to justify your chosen course of action. Examples of questions that emerge in social work practice include:

- What is the right thing to do?
- Should I go against my client's wishes?
- Should I obey the law?
- How should I respond to another worker whose practice is below acceptable standards?
- Should I breach my client's trust?

There are many disciplines interested in the pursuit of ethics. These include 'pure' disciplines such as philosophy and sociology (see, for example, Morris 2012) but also applied disciplines such as social work, medicine, nursing and other allied health professions. We now move on to consider the central traditions which are concerned with the question of ethical conduct.

UTILITARIANISM

There are many differing philosophers, such as Bentham and Mill, and subsequent philosophical traditions associated with utilitarianism. Broadly speaking, in utilitarianism the outcome of an action is considered in relation to its benefit, or utility, for the greatest number of people. Doing the 'greatest good for the greatest number' involves bringing about happiness and well-being for the majority of people. Dilemmas are therefore resolved through understanding that 'the right action is that which produces the greatest balance of good over evil' (Banks 2012, p. 50). Therefore the focus is upon the *outcome* of actions.

To give an example of the application of utilitarianism, consider the dilemma shown in Figure 5.1 on page 98.

Imagine the scenario. There are many people on a bridge which is about to fall down. There is one person standing under the bridge. Both the person under the bridge and the people on top of the bridge are in mortal danger. You can only send out a warning to either the person under the bridge or the people on the bridge. Do you warn:

Who do you warn?

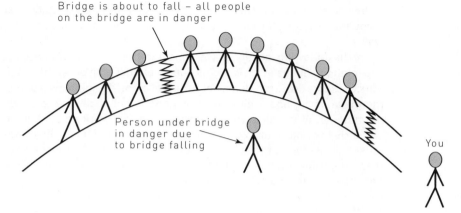

FIGURE 5.1 The bridge dilemma: What would you do?

- The people on the bridge *or*
- The person under the bridge?

A utilitarian approach would consider the dilemma in relation to outcomes. The people on the bridge are at risk of death and injury due to the falling bridge and the person under the bridge is at risk of death and injury due to the bridge falling on top of them. Applying the notion of the 'greatest good for the greatest number' to the scenario would mean that the warning would go out to the people on the bridge because there are more of them than the one person under the bridge.

There are many ways in which utilitarianism is applicable to everyday social work practice. For example, how does an organisation decide on whether to provide social work services to one client or to groups of clients? Providing the outcomes were equally beneficial to both an individual and a group, a utilitarian response to this question would argue for 'the greatest good for the greatest number'. Since a social worker can see more clients in a group setting than individually, the decision to run more groups than individual sessions would be made using this perspective.

KANTIANISM

Unlike utilitarianism's focus on outcomes, a Kantian approach to an ethical dilemma highlights one's *duty* towards others. Immanuel Kant, a philosopher from the 18th century, argued that there are moral principles that apply to everyone. He 'thought that a system he called the "categorical imperative" could produce rules for any situation. In its simplest form the categorical imperative says that each of us should always act in such a way that our actions could become a rule for everyone without creating a contradiction' (Bowles *et al.* 2006, p. 57). 'Respect for persons' is central to Kantian philosophy (Banks 2012, p. 51).

Consider the example of the ethical dilemma posed in Figure 5.1. A Kantian perspective would argue that failing to warn *everyone*, both the people on the bridge and the person below it, fails to respect everyone and would set an unworkable rule for future relations between people. Without the understanding that people have a duty to warn others of dangers, trust would be diminished. Without trust, relationships between others become strained.

Here is another example of the Kantian categorical imperative in action. Imagine that a client asked their social worker if they were planning on working for the organisation in the longer term. Imagine that the social worker does not like working at the organisation and is actively applying for jobs so that they can leave. The social worker has a choice about how to respond. Should they lie or tell the truth? If they tell the truth to their client will this undermine the service? If they lie, from a Kantian perspective they would be setting an undesirable precedent. Note in particular the way that lying is examined through the Kantian perspective in which rationality is central:

> ... if you want to lie in a particular situation you should assume that if you lie then everyone else will start lying too. But if this happened, then lying itself would be impossible because lying depends on trust. If everyone lied then no one would ever believe what anyone said and lying would not work. Successful lying requires other people to keep telling the truth. It involves the liar treating themselves as an exception, which violates what Kant thought of as a fundamental obligation, to treat all people as morally equal, a principle that social workers adopt under the banner of equal dignity and worth. (Bowles *et al.* 2006, p. 57)

Thus if they were to use this perspective the social worker may decide to be tactful but ultimately truthful in the likelihood of them being at the organisation long-term.

VIRTUE-BASED ETHICS

Virtue-based approaches argue that acting ethically requires a virtuous self. Virtues include temperance, courage, justice and being truthful (Cohen & Cohen 1999). The philosopher Aristotle is associated with this perspective:

> As defined by Aristotle ... moral virtues are states of character concerned with rational control and direction of emotions. Moreover, such states of character are ... habits acquired from repeatedly performing virtuous actions. A person who has acquired a habit of confronting life situations without being deterred by undue or irrational fears possesses the virtue of courage; and a person who has acquired a habit of rationally indulging—neither overdoing nor underdoing— bodily desires such as for food or sex possesses the virtue of temperance. (Cohen & Cohen 1999, p. 19)

Whereas other approaches highlight consequences of actions and rules for the way we ought to behave, a virtue-based ethical standpoint requires the individual to *become* virtuous. Being virtuous is particularly appropriate to professional roles such as social work (Rhodes 1986), where congruence is central to the helping relationship (Rogers 1961) and reflexive development is ongoing. Thus, using this approach would mean that as a social work student, when you reflect upon your work with clients, you would also consider your virtuousness. Thus, you might ask questions such as: did I promote justice in that exchange with my client? Was I honest with all concerned in my recent exchange with my clients? Have I shown courage to stand up to inequalities and oppression? These questions are important to prompt reflexive thinking and subsequent action. They would help not only in relation to one's ever-evolving social work practice, also with one's development as a virtuous professional (Cohen & Cohen 1999). As we shall see, there are some similarities between virtue-based ethics and ethics of care.

ETHICS OF CARE

Ethics of care, also referred to as care ethics, 'links morality to the concrete situation ... [and] perceives morality in terms of concrete interpersonal relationships that can be understood only by people who have compassion and empathy for the predicaments of other people' (Cohen & Cohen 1999, p. 14).

Since, in general, ethics is concerned with decisions about situations where there is some ambiguity about what is best, theories of moral development have been drawn upon to understand this process. Crucially, previously accepted theories of moral development have been legitimately challenged through the work of Carol Gilligan (1982). Whereas historically moral development had become associated with rational decision-making, Gilligan argues that the 'male oriented system of morality ... does not take account of approaches to ethics which tend to be adopted by women' (Banks 2001, p. 47). Gilligan's (1982) work emphasises the complex interaction between the individual, the situation and the context as well as highlighting the importance of the nature of an individual's relationship with others. Ethical conduct from a care ethics perspective therefore requires asking 'What rights and responsibilities accompany the caring relationship?'

BIOETHICS

Bioethics outlines a clear set of ethical principles which underpin the helping relationship. These can be applied to professions working with people, including the medical profession and allied health professionals including social workers. Each of the principles should be embedded in professional practice as they are foundational to the ways we respond in our work with others. The following is derived from Beauchamp & Childress (1989), who argue there are four principles important to medical ethics (and applicable to social work) as well as certain qualities which must characterise the relationship between a professional and their client(s).

Principles

1. Nonmalificence: avoiding harming people
2. Beneficence: doing good
3. Self-determination: promoting and respecting others' autonomy
4. Justice: those in need are provided for fairly, professionals understand power relations and act accordingly

Qualities for the professional's relationship with their client(s)

1. Veracity: being honest, telling the truth
2. Confidentiality and privacy: respecting clients' right to privacy, and to not disclose their information and biographies to others
3. Fidelity: being faithful to professional promises

Bioethical approaches are practical and clearly applicable to the helping relationship, yet this is also a source of criticism, as we shall see in our consideration of human rights approaches.

HUMAN RIGHTS APPROACH

In contemporary life a human rights discourse has become synonymous with concerns which broadly relate to people's rights and freedoms (Ife 2008, p. 4). The Universal Declaration of Human Rights was formally recognised by the United Nations Assembly in 1948. This declaration outlines the rights of citizens in relation to their governments, and came about because of the government-sanctioned abuses which took place during the Second World War. Since this time, the declaration has been applied to many international contexts. Although the ethical stance inherent to the declaration is focused on the rights of peoples as *citizens*, often people will refer to human rights as being relevant to a range of contexts including institutional and interpersonal interactions. As we shall see, there is a strong case that a human rights approach can inform both social work ethics as well as practice, theory and education (Ife 2008, p. 160).

Ife argues that a human rights approach in social work involves understanding that people ought to be treated with respect and dignity *as a fellow individual*. So often in social work clients' issues are externalised: the term 'service user', for example, identifies people who are clients as somehow different from social workers, as though social workers do not use services themselves! What makes social workers any different from others in our societies? Further, a human rights perspective rejects the notion that oppression and inequality due to differences in race, class and gender is best addressed in social work through specifically defined types of intervention. Social justice is still vital to social work (Ife 2001, p. 4) but awareness of and action to address oppression and inequality should be embedded in every approach to each individual, couple, family, community, group and society. Underpinning all interactions in social work with others ought to be recognition of a *shared humanity*:

> A human rights discourse ... is concerned with ideas of what it means to be human—what is the nature of our shared humanity that transcends culture, race, gender, age, class... From this perspective, moral principles for a social work based on human rights might be expressed simply this way:
> - Act so as to always affirm and realise the human rights of all people.
> - Do nothing to restrict, deny or violate the human rights of anyone. (Ife, 2001, p. 129)

The use of universal rights, which apply to everyone, is an 'alternative framing' of the individualised ethical frameworks usually applied in social work (Ife 2001, p. 121). When ethical dilemmas emerge in social work practice, a human rights approach enables the clients to be actively engaged in resolving the issues at stake. This is a radical departure from other ethical theoretical models in which the social worker has the power to resolve the dilemma (Ife 2001, p. 122) through their own action or inaction.

CODES OF PRACTICE, CODES OF ETHICS AND OTHER INSTITUTIONALISED ETHICAL RULES

Codes of ethics outline ethical conduct for professionals. Internationally, there are various codes of conduct/codes of ethics and other documents in social work which outline the core values for the profession and give some clarity about the ways in which professional conduct is expected to take place. Social workers must abide by their code of ethics and may face serious consequences if these are breached, from receiving formal warnings to being 'struck off' and prevented from practising again. Professional associations of social workers have committees who investigate and take action regarding breaches of ethics or professional conduct. Codes of ethics and ethics audits can be used in organisational settings to manage ethical concerns using a 'risk management' framework (Reamer 2001).

Some codes also offer general advice about what to do in the event of an ethical dilemma. In social work codes of ethics have a long history and have served as 'a public declaration of one's commitment and obligation to its rule over one's conduct' (Siporin 1972, p. 91).

Yet codes of ethics can also be criticised because they may be seen to detract from an individual's responsibility or obligation towards others, to reinforce professionals as powerful since the code 'belongs' to them, and to diminish the importance that everyday interactions have on the society as a whole (Bauman 1993; Ife 2001). Yet despite these criticisms, codes of ethics can be important in social work. As Ife argues, 'it is the morality of social work and social workers' actions that is at issue; ethical codes are merely a yardstick by which that morality can be measured and evaluated' (Ife 2001, p. 110).

It is vital to view codes of ethics through a critical lens. Take a look at your code of ethics, which you will be able to access through your professional association. Note what words or terms will be more important or less important in future years. Note also that ethical frameworks differ from legislative frameworks: at times in history social workers have played a role in implementing policies which are now viewed as abhorrent. For example, the systematic removal of Indigenous children from their families in Australia on the basis that white culture was preferable to Indigenous Australian culture created what is referred to as the 'stolen genera- tions'. Although perfectly legal, there is no justification for such action using the application of various ethical theoretical standpoints. It is important to analyse the ethical dimension to your own social work practice in contemporary times, as we shall see in the next section.

Finally, rapidly increasing technological advances changing the ways everyday life is lived (Lash 2001) mean social work will take differing forms in the future. Virtual services, online counselling and support, and shifts in the ways we assess individuals' identities will need to be accommodated (Dunk-West 2011): all of these affect the ways we imagine and articulate the ethics of the work. The important issue relating to ethics and social work is to understand, articulate and justify your actions using an ethical theory base.

ETHICAL DILEMMAS IN SOCIAL WORK: WHAT TO DO?

In social work, whether as a student or as a qualified worker, there are daily dilem- mas which one must contend with and bring to resolution. Ethical dilemmas involve making 'a choice between two equally unwelcome alternatives' (Banks 2001, p. 163). Students often report that being 'inside' an ethical dilemma feels confusing and although they may know what they want to do, they are unclear what the ethi- cal justification is for their course of action. It can feel so jumbled that, represented visually, it looks like Figure 5.2.

There are frameworks which can help social workers and social work students resolve ethical dilemmas (Reamer 1990). Common approaches entail 'breaking down' the problem or dilemma into differing compartmentalised areas. The process of gaining clarity about an ethical dilemma is represented in Figure 5.3 on page 104.

Although at first the dilemma can be seen as messy and without shape or form, in breaking it up into the key areas which are relevant to ethical decision-making it is easier to understand the key ethical prin- ciples which are in conflict. For example, consider the friend whose partner is cheating on them. Moving through the process of gaining clarity we can ask, and answer, the following questions. This is one suggested course of action:

Who is involved? What do they want to happen? Myself, my friend and her partner. To a lesser extent, the person who the partner was with. My friend's part- ner does not want me to say anything. I can only guess what my friend wants, but I would assume that she would want to know.

FIGURE 5.2 Ethical dilemmas can be messy, complex and confusing

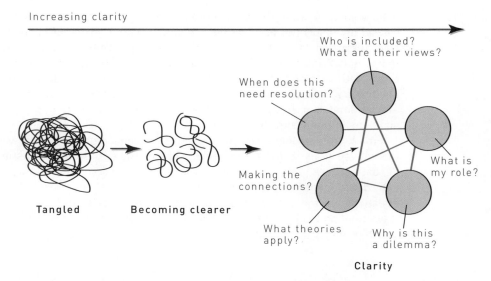

Increasing clarity

Tangled   Becoming clearer

Who is included?
What are their views?

When does this
need resolution?

Making the
connections?

What is
my role?

What theories
apply?

Why is this
a dilemma?

Clarity

FIGURE 5.3 Asking pertinent questions can help to unravel an ethical dilemma

What is my role?   Friend.

Why is this a dilemma?   If I tell my friend, it may cause her upset/harm. It may also mean the end of the relationship. If I don't tell my friend, then I will feel that I am not being honest or truthful with her. Is it doing good to cause harm? Is it worth causing harm for the sake of veracity (telling the truth)?

When does this need resolution?   As soon as possible.

What theories apply?   Any theoretical perspective could apply but I will choose care ethics to make sense of this dilemma because I feel that the relationship between myself and my friend is important. We have been friends since we were children and we have been through so much together. We have a mutual obligation towards one another to be honest and I feel very confident that my friend would want me to tell them.

The resolution/decision: To tell my friend. The harm caused by telling my friend is outweighed by my obligation as their friend to be honest and tell the truth.

ORGANISATIONAL ETHICAL ISSUES

In this chapter so far we have explored ethics in relation to the ways we choose to live as well as the ways we behave and respond to our clients in social work. In this section, we consider some of the key ethical issues which emerge out of working in an organisational context. Although ethical theory is more usually focused on clients in social work, complaints about ethical conduct are also often made by professionals about their colleagues' conduct (Loewenberg *et al.* 2000, p. 174).

As noted in our discussion of ethical theories, the manner in which power is exercised ought to be an enduring concern in social work practice. It is important to understand the ethical implications of the organisational context in which social work is practised.

In some countries such as England, for example, government employers of social workers arrange services based on client groups. Children and families statutory social work (services that are provided because of legislation and state funding), for example, caters for the care needs of children and their families. This organisation has a legislative mandate to use specific legal Acts to remove children from their families and place them into the care of others (including foster care, relative care, approved carers, residential care and adoptive families): social workers play a central role in this statutory action. Having a legal mandate, social workers removing children from their homes also need to have a clear *ethical* justification for their actions. Consider the following situation:

CASE STUDY

Mary and Veronica are aged 5 and 7 respectively. Their parents, Anika and Roberto, are heroin users and currently unemployed. Anika and Roberto have successfully managed to coordinate the care of their children, despite the challenges brought about by the recession which meant they lost their jobs. Recently there have been some highly concerning developments regarding the well-being of the children. With the recent scrutiny of welfare payments, Anika and Roberto have had their benefits cut as they were unable to provide enough evidence of their job search efforts. This has meant that Anika and Roberto have resorted to leaving the children home alone at night while they engage in criminal activity such as theft. When recently charged by police for burglary offences, it emerged that the children had been left all night alone. The parents do not wish to work with social workers.

Do you think the situation requires removal of the children from their home? Without adequate additional information such as the perspectives of the children, how the parents view the situation and an analysis of the issues at stake, it may be difficult to justify a particular type of intervention. What is clear, however, is that it is unsafe to leave a seven- and a five-year-old by themselves in the house overnight. The ethical dimension of social work intervention in this situation involves the following: the children's safety and well-being versus the autonomy of the family and parents. Promoting the autonomy of the parents places the children at risk of harm and promoting the safety and well-being of the children reduces the autonomy of the parents. Social workers in statutory roles such as this one make *paternalistic* decisions. Such decisions involve overriding another person's autonomy—the parents in this case—in order to prevent harm occurring to others—in this case, the children.

The scenario above has been created for the purposes of this book but illustrates some key themes relating to child protection and children and families work.

Working in this field can include encountering any or all of the following: poverty, oppression and disadvantage, substance misuse, violence including domestic violence, physical, sexual and emotional abuse and exploitation of children. Student social workers can often be reluctant to engage in this kind of work because it may not feel 'right' to remove children from their homes, for example, or they may believe that social work should only be involved with people who voluntarily engage in the services. The reality is that in working in children and families organisations, a great deal of other work aside from the removal of children takes place, such as preventing family breakdown, promoting and encouraging parenting, and direct work with children, young people and their parents and carers. Another ethical issue which can arise when working in this field is the sometimes limited way in which social workers and social work students feel they can undertake structural social work. Lobbying government as a government employee can be frowned upon by the organisation, which can provoke an ethical problem. Similarly, in adults work in England personalisation policies have assumed too much autonomy in some people who may require more assistance than is provided, and social workers may not wish to work in such ways. All of these concerns relate to what is referred to as the 'care or control' aspects of social work. Do we care for our clients or do we control them? Can we do both? What happens when our values conflict with those of our organisation? These are questions which social workers and social work students on placement must think through and come to some sort of resolution regarding.

The other major cause of ethical problems in organisational settings relates to workers who are either impaired or engaging in unethical practice.

THE IMPAIRED WORKER

In ethics literature 'the impaired social worker' (Reamer 1992) relates to social workers who are unable to carry out their normal responsibilities due to an identifiable reason:

> Impairment is '...interference in professional functioning that is reflected in one or more of the following ways: (a) an inability and/or unwillingness to acquire and integrate professional standards into one's repertoire of professional behaviour; (b) an inability to acquire professional skills in order to reach an acceptable level of competency; (c) an inability to control professional stress, psychological dysfunction, and/or excessive emotional reactions that interfere with professional functioning'. (Lamb *et al.* 1987, p. 598 cited in Reamer 1992, p. 166)

When working in an organisational context, it is important to recognise the potential for harm towards clients which can occur through worker impairment. Focusing on the needs of clients can help to disentangle competing obligations towards clients and colleagues, as we have seen earlier in the chapter. Yet speaking out against one's colleague or 'whistleblowing' brings with it various ethical and professional issues and much can be at stake. It is also important to recognise that working with particular client groups or contexts can provoke differing coping mechanisms for social workers. Recognising when one's own behaviours have the potential to cause unintended harm to clients is central to ethical practice. Literature which discusses issues of 'burnout' or vicarious traumatisation can be helpful in embedding policies into the organisation which assist in reducing the effects of difficult or emotive work on workers (Women's Health Statewide: www.whs.sa.gov.au/pub/draft_ VT_polic_1.pdf).

DUAL ROLE RELATIONSHIPS

Dual role relationships refer to the assuming of another role with clients in addition to the helper role:

> When a professional assumes at least one additional professional or personal role with respect to the same client, the relationship thus formed is termed a dual-role or multiple role relationship. (Cohen & Cohen 1999, p. 137)

Why are dual role relationships problematic in social work? The existence of roles subsequent to the helping role can prevent the worker from carrying out their duties in a professional manner. Further, social workers are in positions of power and should not abuse the trust of their clients. Here are some of the clearest examples of dual role relationships:

- Entering into sexual relationships with clients
- Entering into friendships with clients
- Personally accepting large gifts or money from clients
- Engaging in business relationships with clients
- Providing social work services to friends and family

There are some areas which are less clear however. For example, imagine you have been working with a man who has recently been diagnosed with a life threatening illness. Your role has entailed assessing his needs and providing him with information about relevant services for him and his family. At your final meeting, he brings in a handmade card and a pot plant for your office. Whether you accept this gift depends on the meaning and context of the gift being given. Organisations sometimes have a formal record of all gifts given as well as the context in which they are given, so that a transparent account is made regarding the circumstances surrounding the gift. Similarly, social work students often give a token gift to their placement supervisors or assessors to mark the end of their placement. Giving the gift after the final report is written separates the two processes—assessment and endings—which means ethical conflicts are lessened. What is important in these situations is that the application of ethical ideas is clearly stated to explain or justify a particular decision or set of decisions.

WORKING WITH OTHERS

The ethical perspectives discussed in this chapter demonstrate the breadth of this area of intellectual and professional debate and scholarship. The definition of social work from the International Federation of Social Workers, which we explored in Chapter 1 of this book, outlined the ethical dimension to our profession: 'social work addresses the barriers, inequities and injustices that exist in society. It responds to crises and emergencies as well as to everyday personal and social problems'. The consideration of 'barriers, inequities and injustices' is central to the concept of social justice. Social justice holds particular currency in our profession, and is a common theme in social work codes of ethics from many countries.

We have discussed the bioethical approach advanced by Beauchamp & Childress (1989). We shall now consider this again in the context of working with other professionals. In particular, read through the principles and qualities with the following questions in mind:

- Do these 'fit' for GPs?
- Do these apply to social work in all areas of practice?
- Can you imagine these would be useful for allied health professions such as physiotherapists, occupational therapists, dieticians and speech therapists?

Principles (Beauchamp & Childress 1989)

1. Nonmalificence: avoiding harming people
2. Beneficence: doing good
3. Self-determination: promoting and respecting others' autonomy
4. Justice: those in need are provided for fairly, professionals understand power relations and act accordingly

Qualities for the professional's relationship with their client(s) (Beauchamp & Childress 1989)

1. Veracity: being honest, telling the truth
2. Confidentiality and privacy: respecting clients' right to privacy, and to not disclose their information and biographies to others
3. Fidelity: being faithful to professional promises

Because of the generalised and applied nature of bioethics, the principles can be applied to a number of professions. What we have seen throughout this chapter is that the large scope of ethical approaches offers the potential to assist the social work student and practitioner to come to a decision or act in a particular way. Being able to take a particular perspective and think 'how would this perspective view the problem or situation?' is useful in coming to a resolution or offering a framework for analysing one's practice. Yet how does this relate to new collaborations in social work which might be different to the historical alignment with health?

Bronstein argues that 'interdisciplinary collaboration is an effective interpersonal process that facilitates the achievement of goals that cannot be reached when individual professionals act on their own (Bruner 1991)' (Bronstein 2003, p. 299). If we think about the interdisciplinary context within which social work is situated, using Bronstein's definition of such work means there are new ethical goals to be reached in social work. For example, some of the environmental issues which have surfaced in recent years, such as climate change, have impacts on social life (Lever-Tracy 2010). As the ways in which people live their day-to-day lives change because of these shifts, ethical issues related to 'climate justice' (Star 2008) will emerge. Interdisciplinary work in this area might therefore see social workers alongside environmental scientists, sociologists, biologists, urban planners and geographers, to name but a few. Each of these groups brings with them their theoretical orientations as well as their ethical perspectives. It is therefore plausible that social workers may be increasingly thinking about the following:

- What are the ethical considerations which relate to housing for people who have experienced extreme weather events?
- In the future, what kinds of social work services will people be entitled to?
- What is social work's ethical obligation to the environment?
- How can social work be sustainable?

There are many more questions which relate to this area and additional ones that will only become evident as we know more about our changing world and subsequent needs. Recent research identifies the need for social work to rise to meet the challenges being brought about by 'climate change ... [which is] widely recognised as one of the greatest threats facing society' (Evans *et al.* 2012, p. 746). The authors also note that 'the risks that climate change poses for the most vulnerable people in society in particular' have been addressed in government policy in England but ought to be central to social work more generally (Evans *et al.* 2012, p. 746).

CHAPTER SUMMARY

This chapter has explored personal and professional values and ethics. We have looked at some scenarios in which ethical dilemmas may surface. These include through direct social work practice with our clients as well as within the organisational setting. We have examined some of the key ethical theoretical perspectives in order to better understand the ways in which our actions can be applied to ethical theory and ethical theory can be applied to our actions. Ethics are central to any kind of social work practice, regardless of the setting. As social workers and social work students, we must always be able to articulate the ethical justification for our work with others. It is only through relationships with the people we work with and an ethical foundation for our practice that we can be accountable and help to promote individual and social change. This chapter has set out some of the key ideas which require consideration and adaptation to one's own practice and world-view.

FURTHER READING

BANKS, S. (2012) *Ethics and Values in Social Work*, 4th edn. Basingstoke: Palgrave Macmillan.

BEAUCHAMP, T. L. & CHILDRESS, J. F. (1989) *Principles of Biomedical Ethics*. New York: Oxford University Press.

COHEN, E. D. & COHEN, G. S. (1999) *The Virtuous Therapist: Ethical Practice of Counselling and Psychotherapy*. Belmont: Wadsworth Publishing Company.

HUGMAN, R. & SMITH, D. (eds) (2005) *Ethical Issues in Social Work*. Abingdon: Routledge.

IFE, J. (2008) *Human Rights and Social Work: Towards Rights-based Practice*, 2nd edn. Cambridge, UK: Cambridge University Press.

REAMER, F. (2006) *Social Work Values and Ethics*. New York: Columbia University Press.

6

Practice Learning in Organisational Settings

This chapter:

- Examines how practice learning fits with social work education

- Explores the ways the social work role is situated in its organisational setting

- Outlines suggestions about how to start on placement

- Highlights how social work skills, such as those used in assessing, are central to advancing practice learning

- Looks at the role supervision plays in developing the social work self on placement

Conversation, writing, talking, communicating and engaging with others: all of these skills that we use in our everyday life are the 'nuts and bolts' of activities in placement settings. Yet often these everyday actions become infused with meaning and cause trepidation when students are on their social work placement. This chapter outlines the knowledge and skills required for successful learning experiences in practice settings. It starts by exploring the spontaneous and complex world of social work practice through the lens of learning. Exploring learning in the practice context requires understanding the position of social work in its organisational context. Assessment in the context of client work across organisational specialisms is then examined. Reflexivity is discussed in relation to student learning. The chapter concludes with a discussion of supervision.

LEARNING AND PLACEMENTS

As noted in Chapter 1 in our discussion of identity, participation in social relationships and the external social environment are crucial to the ways in which we experience ourselves and develop our self (Mead 1934). The central idea in this book—which follows from this—is that through social interaction the professional self is constituted. In Chapter 1, Mead's foundational idea of the self as theorised through an interactionist tradition was explored. We have returned to this theme throughout our consideration of the key academic subjects social work students encounter during their studies. In this chapter the importance of relationships formed through professional practice is highlighted, and seen as foundational to successful practice learning experiences.

Often the social work placement is viewed differently than 'academic' subjects or modules. While there is a crucial difference between theory-rich topics and the experiential aspect to placement education, the interactionist notion of the production of the professional self is equally applicable to both types of knowledge acquisition. Placement is enormously important in the development of the professional self. In fact the movement of social work students into practice learning settings is the ultimate way in which the professional self is constituted.

In this sense, there is a difference between being in the 'field' and being in a controlled university environment. The physical relocation of students into the organisational setting exposes students to new and varied learning experiences which arise from interaction with clients, staff, volunteers, other professionals and fellow students. Learning how to combine the knowledge gained through immersion and reaction in the spontaneous, dynamic setting of the placement with the knowledge attained through engagement in academic modules is the task of the social work student.

Based upon previous experiences within educational settings you may be aware of the ways in which you like to learn. For example, some people prefer to learn through others' experiences, while for another person reading is a more effective way to gain knowledge. Here are just some examples of various types of learning activities which are relevant to 'academic' knowledge:

- Reading books, journal articles, non-fiction, online content and other text
- Hearing others' stories
- Audio listening to lectures
- Listening to lectures, watching lecturers and writing notes
- Revisiting lecture material online after physically attending a lecture
- Talking to other students about theories
- Engaging in conversation through facilitated classes such as seminars, workshops and tutorials
- Watching a documentary, film or other visual clip
- Writing notes about a particular topic after reading a book, attending a lecture or engaging in a learning activity
- Applying a theory to a practical situation through being presented with a problem (for example, a case study with questions about how you would act)
- Observing or listening to a debate or expert panel discussion

It is worth reflecting upon how you like to learn in these contexts. Your course is structured around providing various types of the above activities, as educators recognise that people learn in differing ways. Now think about a practical activity that you have learned that is connected with transport. This could involve thinking about how you learned to drive a car, roller skate, ride a scooter, ride a bike and so on. Reflect upon the following questions: Did you...

- Observe the mode of transport being used by others before attempting to try it yourself?
- Study the mode of transport, looking at the wheels and body, and understanding how it was powered before beginning to control the apparatus?
- Experiment through trying different techniques, making mistakes and learning along the way?
- Ask someone else to instruct you to help you learn through their instruction and feedback?

Unlike academic forms of learning, the knowledge required to operate a type of transport requires skills. The two types of learning differ: in the transport example, the practicality and physicality of the learning activity is evident. Moving away from the classroom into a new environment as a student social worker requires a level of reflexive knowledge, and it is helpful if students are aware of their preferred conditions of learning as well as the way they like to learn. Some students, for example, like to read about an organisation and understand the client and community needs, the organisational philosophy and mandate and get to know the staff before they begin to work with clients. Other students feel better experimenting from the beginning, for example, engaging with client work very early on and reflecting on this work together with the organisational setting as they go along.

There is no 'right or wrong' way to learn, but it is important to recognise that 'all students, irrespective of their experiences or cultural backgrounds, come to their first field placement with some trepidation, anxiety and excitement about this new learning challenge' (Cooper & Briggs 2000, p. 4). Practice teachers or supervisors therefore have a central role to play in facilitating a positive learning experience (we explore this later in the chapter). First, let's consider the organisational setting within which placements take place.

SOCIAL WORK AND THE ORGANISATIONAL SETTING

Amongst the professions, social work is uniquely suited to enormously varied contexts which can range from health settings to community development to policy, research and direct practice with either voluntary or involuntary clients. Internationally, social work's identity varies in that social work may have more of a presence in particular fields of practice. For example, in Australia, New Zealand and the USA it is common for social workers to have a clinical or therapeutic focus. Social policies, professional associations and social shifts all impact on employment opportunities for social workers as well as how social work is situated in broader culture. Social work students are often aware of how social workers are portrayed in the media—this is particularly the case for workers in, say, child protection. It is often only when students begin their course that they become aware of the vast opportunities for social work in traditional settings (such as in child protection, aged care, working with people with disabilities and so on) as well as in newer settings such as schools, doctors' surgeries and health practice settings. Social workers can also work in community settings such as in community development, population-based interventions and international settings. Table 1.1, on page 14, listed just some of the areas social workers are employed in throughout the world. Take some time to look through this table and note a few which you think would be of interest to you. Note areas in which you know you would *not* like to work. Finally, note which fields of practice you are open to learning more about.

Although there is a great deal of diversity in terms what social workers do in their organisational settings, all social work students on placement need to orient themselves to their particular settings. This is where Table 1.1 can be helpful. Choosing a 'box' in which to put the organisation can help at the beginning to compartmentalise the work.

Thinking about the organisational context helps to demarcate the work of the setting from other types of social work services. It can be helpful to begin to understand the organisational context through varying resources. Staff descriptions of the work undertaken can help social work students to orient themselves to the organisation. Similarly, policy documents and other written material can also assist in understanding the scope of the service. Usually when students are on placement, at the beginning it can feel as though there is too much information. Given time, however, students develop a sophisticated understanding of the organisational setting including the culture and history of the service. The following are suggestions about how to begin as a social work student on placement:

1. Develop a positive working relationship with your supervisor *as well as* with other colleagues. Other colleagues can help you gain a varied perspective on

the work and represent diverse practice experiences which can help broaden your knowledge and strengthen your developing practice.

2. Read policy, funding and other documents and study organisational charts. Attend organisational meetings. These activities will help you understand the scope of the work and the broader organisational culture.

3. Become both 'inward' facing as well as 'outward' facing. Engage in thinking or conversations to try to understand the organisation from clients' perspectives. Visit other organisations in the region to get a picture of the community needs the organisation fulfils. Ask: what are the tensions between the needs of clients and the provision of services? What is the role of social work? How do these contribute to the work I will undertake?

4. Connect with other students on placement. Compare your experiences. It is vital to continue to engage with your university through seminars, tutorials, visits from the university and other activities. Your informal networks with other students are equally crucial in helping to support your learning.

5. Record your learning (Cleak & Wilson 2004, p. 27). Through documenting your knowledge acquisition you can create a clear picture of the development of your professional self. Include pictures, clippings from articles, notes to yourself, drawings and other media.

6. With the support and knowledge of your supervisor, take risks. Try using a different theory, for example, and get feedback from clients about how they experienced your work with them. Push yourself to try new things and fully develop your social work self.

THE PROFESSIONAL SELF

As we have noted, there are 'boundaries' in the ways social workers relate to people and these are marked out depending on the nature of one's relationship. A social worker's *purpose* (Compton & Galaway 1999) informs *how* they relate to others in a professional setting. The ways we relate to others differ, depending on the context and nature of our relationships. As discussed in Chapter 3 when we examined communication skills, Garfinkel's research (Garfinkel 1984) found that we rely on unspoken 'rules' which dictate the way we conduct ourselves with others. In particular, Garfinkel argues that the *way* we interact depends on *with whom* the interaction takes place.

It is the task of the student social worker to develop newer ways of relating to others in the professional context of the placement. The 'discovery of "self"' through interaction with others on placement is often recorded in student journals as being a major achievement in their learning (Lam *et al.* 2007).

At first, interactions of the student social worker in their professional role can feel awkward. For example, students can think: is it okay to laugh with clients? Is it unprofessional to disclose personal information to my supervisor? Students on placement develop the professional self through engagement with their own learning in terms of theory and practice, supervision with their practice teacher and reflection about their emerging professional self. This can be depicted as a gradual coming together of the 'personal' along with the 'professional' self (Figure 6.1).

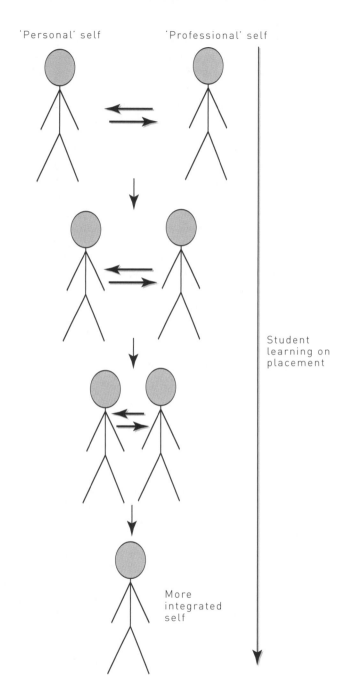

FIGURE 6.1 Making the connections between the everyday self and the professional self helps the professional to emerge

Developing the professional self in social work education includes learning through university-based topics as well as through placement experiences. During this process students gradually 'grow' their professional selves. Figure 6.1 illustrates the ways the existing self interacts with the professional self until a kind of integration occurs. This is because our actions, behaviours and communication change from a professional context to a personal context, as we examined in Chapter 3. As a refresher to the differing manifestations of self in varying contexts, imagine that a woman in her mid 30s says 'Yusef has left me'. How you respond to this depends on the relationship you have with the speaker. As her social worker, your response will be guided by your ethical and theoretical frameworks and the purpose of your role. You might say, for example, 'Are you okay?' or 'Do you want to tell me about that?' or even 'That must be awful!'. Your responses will depend on a number of factors, including your history with the client(s) and the purpose of your role and organisational setting which will define the scope of your work. Now imagine that your friend tells you 'Yusef has left me'. Like your professional response, your answer to your friend's disclosure will depend on the circumstances, but the difference will be that you can probably give advice, give her your opinion and communicate in a far less formal or structured way. Although there are similarities in the ways we respond to clients and to friends, there are marked differences because of the professional nature of social work. The professional self is therefore developed through interaction: placement is crucial to testing out and developing this self. The ways in which people make sense of this process are as unique as our selves, and reflection helps us notice and engage with the process.

ASSESSMENT

Despite the differing organisational contexts in which social work takes place internationally and nationally, the process and function of assessment is universally important to social work practice. Put simply, an assessment identifies need. Once need is identified, services and professional intervention can be matched (Taylor 2011, p. 2). Whether this process is undertaken formally through particular formats such as assessment proformas or informally through conversation with clients and groups, skills in assessment are vital to social work generally (Milner & O'Byrne 2002). Assessment skills are learned during placement. The process of assessment offers practitioners opportunities for identifying and responding immediately to need which can 'go beyond' traditional assessment (Mantle *et al.* 2008, p. 440). Although the issue of how social workers capture their identity is somewhat problematic (Dunk-West 2011), the process whereby social work students begin to understand the needs of their clients, groups and/or communities remains important to their developing skills and knowledge.

Exercise 6.1 is provided to help you develop your assessment skills with individuals, families, groups and communities. These 'levels' of assessment help to frame broader issues within the communities you may be working with in your placement setting and relate to the structural social work we discussed in Chapter 4.

EXERCISE 6.1

Case study: Jennifer Scanlon

Jennifer reminds you that she's 'fifteen and a half' and perfectly able to negotiate sexual activity with her boyfriend Daniel (who is 16 years old). You are a social worker in the Adolescent Team in a non-government organisation (NGO). Yesterday you were given referral details about Jennifer, a young woman who attends the local high school who had disclosed to a teacher that she was 'slapped across the face' by her mother. Social services are carrying out a mandated assessment. Your role is to work with Jennifer to support her and you are in close contact with the social worker from social services with Jennifer's consent. Jennifer tells you in an interview today that her mother hit her two nights ago due to finding out about Daniel and Jennifer's sexual relationship. Jennifer tells you that in her culture, bringing shame on the family is taken very seriously and if her father finds out she'll 'be dead'. Jennifer also says that her parents are 'behind the times' and, as they left India when Jennifer was a baby, she 'feels more British than Asian'.

Developing your assessment skills

1. What is your assessment of Jennifer? In one sentence, what is/are her need(s)? How might your role assist in meeting this/these need(s)?
2. What is your assessment of the family? In one sentence, what is/are the family's need(s)? How might your role assist in meeting this/these need(s)?
3. What is your assessment of the community? Imagine Jennifer's scenario was similar to others presenting at your placement setting. What would be the needs of the community? How might your role assist in meeting this/these need(s)?

Finally, reflect on the role of assessment in your organisational setting. Is assessment the means through which services are allocated? Who assesses and where does the information go? Identify your learning needs in relation to assessment and make a plan for addressing these needs during the course of your placement and beyond. Being able to understand the links between clients' needs, your own role and the organisational setting and broader community is central to sociological social work (Dunk-West & Verity, forthcoming) and structural social work as discussed in Chapter 4.

Although people's responses to the needs in the scenario in Exercise 6.1 will vary slightly, generally speaking there are some 'themes' which are present in Jennifer's situation. These are:

- Safety and family
- Relationships and cultural expectations
- Sexuality and 'shame'
- Cultures and organisations (school, social services and the NGO)
- Family relationships and differing expectations

This case study has enabled some thinking in relation to Jennifer's circumstances. It should be noted that in placement, the communication skills we discussed in Chapter 3 are required in order to successfully engage with clients for the purpose of assessment. We now move on to examine student learning on placement and how this is facilitated through reflexive engagement.

WHAT ABOUT REFLEXIVITY ON PLACEMENT?

Being reflective involves recalling prior events or sensations. Reflexivity is the active decision to act differently as a result of the analysis of the reflection. As we have discussed in Chapters 1 and 3, reflexivity is of interest to the social sciences (see Lash 2003) and there is some evidence that we are, in western cultures, becoming increasingly reflexive in our everyday lives (Beck & Beck-Gernsheim 2002) and relationships (Giddens 1992). In social work, reflexivity and reflective practice are well conceptualised and historically embedded within our profession (see, for example, Hamilton 1954). In placement settings, engaging in reflexive activities helps to conceptualise the learning and bring theories encountered within the university setting 'alive' in the spontaneous setting of the social work organisation.

Being reflexive in relation to placement experiences involves engaging in recalling one's practice and analysing the practice with a view to *changing future activity* based upon the analysis. One helpful model suggests that this process entails: **retrieval** (the social work student remembers the interaction, aided by activities such as a process recording or written summary) → **reflection** (thinking the issue through, aided by supervisor) → **linkage** (the student articulates the theories informing action and interaction) → **professional response** (anticipating future events through activities such as role plays and future client engagement) (Bogo & Vayda 1987, p. 71).

The spontaneous and sustained immersion in the placement experience (Kolb 1984) makes it possible for reflection-in-action to take place, yet tools must be utilised to make the connection between theory and practice (Argyris & Schon 1974). Many tools will be found in students' academic requirements for placement learning such as the activities contained within their portfolio or workbook. Exercise 6.2 is designed to reflexively engage with organisational and practice contexts alongside students' understandings of power (Fook 1999), inequality and the role of social work.

EXERCISE 6.2

For this activity, study the items shown opposite, which include a feather, a closed door, a rock, a winding road, a ring, a handshake and so on. Think about what these mean *to you*. Now look at each of the diagrams representing the client, the organisation, you and broader society. Select three of the items and draw these in the empty spaces labelled 1, 2 and 3. You can use an object for more than one person or organisation. For example, you might select a feather for both the client and broader

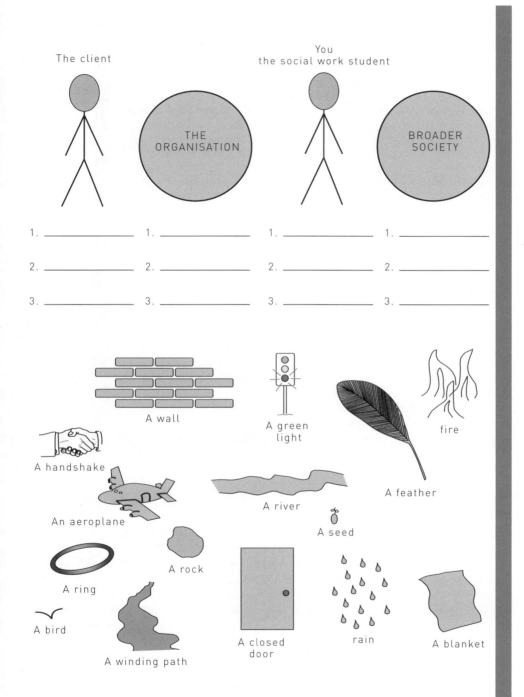

The client

You
the social work student

THE ORGANISATION

BROADER SOCIETY

1. _____   1. _____   1. _____   1. _____

2. _____   2. _____   2. _____   2. _____

3. _____   3. _____   3. _____   3. _____

A wall

A green light

fire

A handshake

A feather

An aeroplane

A river

A seed

A rock

A ring

A closed door

rain

A blanket

A bird

A winding path

society. Think carefully about your choice of object/item. The purpose of choosing a particular object is that it sums up your view about a particular issue. For example, if you chose a ring, a rock and a handshake as metaphors for the organisation you may explain this by saying that the ring represents fidelity or relationships and these are central to the organisation. The rock represents a solid history as the organisation has been in operation for over 30 years. It may also have been chosen because it is 'solid' and in your view, the organisation could do more to be receptive to change. The handshake may represent a move towards including clients and external organisations in the everyday running of the service. This is just one explanation for a choice of objects: your own choices are only limited to your imagination and your perceptions.

Once you have selected objects for each of the pictures, have a look at each of these. Reflect upon your meanings for the objects and the overall depiction of each given the three objects. Do you notice any patterns? Are you, for example, optimistic and generally positive about the organisation and broader society and negative or pessimistic about yourself as a social work student and the client? Or are you positive about the client and negative about the organisation? Think about power and inequality. Where are the tensions and symbioses? Are there some who have more 'powerful' objects and others are less powerful? What does this say about the distribution of power and manifestation of inequality? Take the time to really think these issues through: this activity can be a tool for supervision or discussion with your fellow students. Comparing your responses with others and discussing reasons for these can produce additional insights and reflection.

Finally, given your analysis of the client, the organisation, yourself as a social work student and broader society, what can you do to impact positively on each of these? If you have identified structural oppression with affects the ways in which your clients experience your service, what can you do to counteract this? Write three suggestions about ways *that you can change your practice* by being more aware of power, inequality and the social work role.

Engagement in this exercise and your changed views, insights, perceptions and behaviours as a result of it: this is social work reflexivity in action.

SUPERVISION

It can be particularly challenging for social work students to be on placement within an organisation where there is no social worker. Having supervision through an external supervisor who is a social worker helps to frame activity within a social work knowledge-base. Whilst some students can feel that being in a non-traditional setting is counter to their learning, the benefits of such a placement are varied. Shifts in the employment opportunities for graduates alongside increasing levels of multidisciplinary working reflect the creative opportunities available through non-traditional placements. As Bellinger notes:

> Placements are opportunities to develop new possibilities for practice in response to changing social conditions as increased regulation reduces opportunities for creative responses. Patterns of qualified social work

employment continue to change and services are increasingly provided by multidisciplinary teams and non-statutory agencies under contract. (Bellinger 2010, p. 2462)

Supervision is the means through which reflexive engagement with one's professional self and practice—as well as related issues—takes place. It serves a number of functions (Kadushin 1976) and has a particular meaning in social work. As Wilson explains:

> Supervision is both a series of *events*—regular formal meetings between a student and agency staff member—and a *process* of enabling students to learn and to deliver an appropriate standard of service to the client group. Students are expected to be taught experientially, learning by observing others, participating in the agency's work and reflecting on their own work. They learn about the practice context; about deriving knowledge to understand situations and create opportunities for advancement. Importantly, this learning is about themselves and their orientation to practice. (Wilson 2000, p. 26 (italics in original))

In the practice setting, social work supervision can make the difference between a student who feels overwhelmed by and unclear about the work and setting and a student who feels supported in a learning environment. Students often report feeling 'tired' and 'overwhelmed', particularly in the first few weeks of placement. This is often because they are absorbing a great deal of new information in an unfamiliar setting. Supervisors have a central role to play in mediating this environment with the processes through which social work students constitute their social work selves.

The differing ways that supervision takes place are often dictated by the organisational setting. For example, universities may need to appoint an external social work supervisor if the organisation does not employ social workers. Student engagement with the on-site supervisor can help to open up new opportunities for learning (Cleak *et al.* 2000, p. 165) since social work might be an allied profession in the organisational context, for example. Similarly, group supervision, whereby one supervisory session is held with a number of social work students, can also open up new opportunities for learning (Cleak *et al.* 2000; Maywald 2000). Supervision enables students to practise their emerging social work self as well as reflect upon this self. Thus supervision is an important place to consider the constitution of the professional self.

WORKING WITH OTHERS

Working with others in differing professions while on placement can be overwhelming, particularly at first. This can be partly due to the challenges of engaging in a new environment, including gaining an understanding of policy and of the nature of service provision. Additionally, students on placement can feel unsure about what a

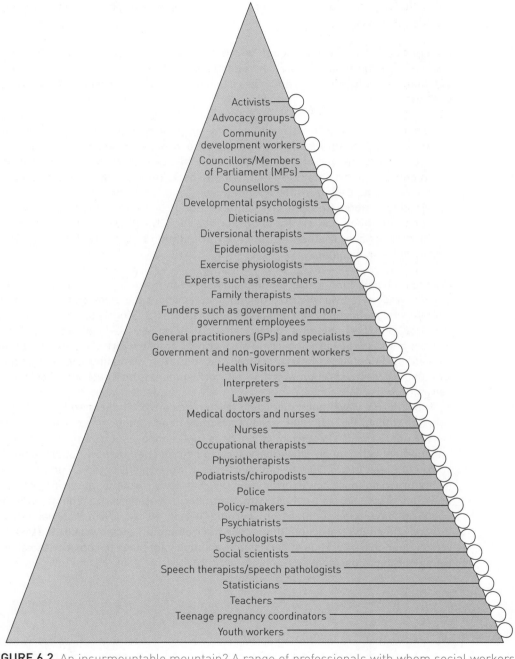

FIGURE 6.2 An insurmountable mountain? A range of professionals with whom social workers work

particular profession 'does' and how it differs, or is similar to, social work. Figure 6.2 captures in a visual way this seemingly insurmountable 'mountain'.

Conduct an audit of your knowledge about the professions shown in Figure 6.2. Next to each of them, note how much you know about the group/profession by assigning an icon as follows:

☺ I feel confident that I know enough about the work of this group
☺ I feel confident that I know a little about the work of this group
☹ I do not feel confident that I know about the work of this group

In evaluating existing knowledge, think about how you know about the profession. How has your knowledge originated? Did you have ideas about the professional grouping which have subsequently changed? If so, why did your ideas change? Have you had positive experiences? What connections are there to social work? What are the differences? It is highly likely that you have come into contact with many of these groups in your everyday life. You may have been a client or people you know such as relatives and friends may have told you about experiences they have had with a particular professional.

Entering an organisation in which individuals from varying professions are represented is an opportune time to broaden knowledge. Induction and orientation meetings with other staff, for example, can be excellent opportunities to ask of others: can you tell me about your profession? Such conversations can also be opportunities to reflect upon social work differences and similarities, and possibilities for collaboration. Like many aspects of practice, working interprofessionally requires confidence in one's own ability to make it work as well as trusting and positive relationships in the working environment (Quinney & Hafford-Letchfield 2012, p. 25). Thus it can be useful to see the placement setting as an opportunity to practise working interprofessionally.

CHAPTER SUMMARY

This chapter has explored learning in the practice context. I have argued that the social work self is constituted through interaction (Mead 1934) on placement. The organisational setting of social work placement learning was explored, and it was argued that despite the differing contexts for social work nationally and internationally, the core skill of assessment helps to frame initial work in placement. Reflexivity was explored as the means through which professional practice occurs. The chapter concluded with a short exploration of supervision and the various forms it can take, and a brief look at the nuances of the interprofessional landscapes in practice settings.

FURTHER READING

CHENOWETH, L. & MCAULIFFE, D. (2005) *The Road to Social Work and Human Service Provision: An Introductory Text*. Southbank: Thomson.

CLEAK, H. & WILSON, J. (2004) *Making the Most of Field Placement*. Sydney: Cengage Learning Australia Pty Limited.

DOEL, M. (2010) *Social Work Placements: A Traveller's Guide*. Abingdon: Routledge.

LOMAX, C., JONES, K., LEIGH, S. & GAY, C. (2010) *Surviving your Social Work Placement*. Basingstoke: Palgrave Macmillan.

7

Research in Social Work

This chapter:

- Demonstrates the ways in which research is relevant to the social work role

- Encourages research mindedness

- Outlines epistemology, research design and methodology, and explores some of the key methods employed in social work research

- Examines literature reviews, sampling, data analysis and dissemination

- Outlines how social work values and ethics can be applied to social work research

Research often makes it into media headlines. For example, print copy such as 'new study shows...' and 'researchers found...' or a statement of fact such as 'young people twice as likely to be at risk of sexual violence' pushes research into the public sphere through sharing researchers' findings with the broader public. News stories appear so definitive in the reporting of research findings that it becomes difficult to weigh up competing studies such as those with differing findings.

Yet there is little research that can be said to be categorically 'true', particularly from the perspective of social work in which we understand social issues as complex, subjective and historically grounded. If we take the final claim above relating to young people and sexual violence, can we assume that this figure is true? In order to assess the veracity of the claim we need to consider a number of questions, such as:

- How many people were involved in the research, or what was the research population?
- How was the research undertaken in terms of methods? For example, were people interviewed or were statistics such as the number of sexual assaults collated and matched alongside age? How were these 'data' collated to come to the findings?
- What definition of sexual violence was used?
- What about victims of sexual violence who do not report the crime to the authorities? How were these accounted for in the data?
- What was the profession of the researcher or research team?
- Why was the research undertaken?
- Who funded the research?
- Was the research ethical? For example, did people involved in the research give their consent?
- How do the findings compare with existing studies?
- Where was the research undertaken?

The answers to all these questions will help us to better understand the study's findings. The questions above relate to the research population and research design, ethical considerations, data analysis and findings in relation to existing knowledge. We shall explore all these concepts in this chapter. Despite research often being seen as 'marginal' to social work (MacIntyre & Paul 2012), empirical work, which is research in which the researcher 'does' research with others, has a clear application in this area. Research can both inform as well as reflect practice and theory, and can also help organisations understand and respond appropriately to the needs of the communities they serve. In addition research helps to bring previously individualised issues to the attention of others, including the general public, policy-makers and organisations.

In this chapter we begin to consider research by examining the process of research, from its design to the choice of methods to the ways in which research findings are communicated with others.

RESEARCH MINDEDNESS

In previous chapters we have considered the approach to understanding social and individual problems through the exercising of what C. Wright Mills (1959) calls the *sociological imagination*. In understanding and developing a passion for research, a similar imaginative sensibility is required.

Research mindedness is the ability to extend the curiosity about the world around us towards empirical ends. Research mindedness is central to social work—indeed, it is argued by some to be so compatible with social work itself that research and practice go hand-in-hand (Everitt *et al.* 1992; McLaughlin 2012, p. 11). The following account provides an example of the ways in which research and practice influence one another:

> I was working in a very deprived area and in my work with individuals and communities I was struck by the level of resilience to hardship these people demonstrated. In my work I had only come across research that talked about problems: problems of poverty, problems of relationships, poor health outcomes and so on. Though these problems were very real, there were also a lot of counters to all the negativity. My clients used to tell me that they didn't want me to see them as victims and although they needed some assistance in one area of their lives or relationships, this did not mean that they were not coping in other areas of day to day life. I firmly believe that requiring social work intervention is no different to medical intervention: it should not be seen as a sign of weakness but I didn't feel that this view was represented in the literature I had read. This prompted an interest in resilience and I discovered that quite a bit of research was going on to investigate resilience in individuals. Community based approaches such as the notion of capacity building helped frame a more positive way forward in my work with the communities. These emerging theories were examined in the social research at the time: luckily I stumbled upon the library that my organisation ran. Reading about research and new theory in journals and books changed my approach in my everyday practice. For example, when I worked with individuals, I shared the recent research about a particular issue, including research that said different things. Sharing this knowledge at appropriate times seemed to work well. I also wanted to know more about the community so I developed some questionnaires for clients of the service. These helped me further understand the issues relevant to the community which had been framed in their own words. This process also led me on to research non-problematic communities in my future work as an academic.

Other examples of the connection between practice and research are growing since many social workers go on to undertake research themselves to justify programmes or demonstrate social work effectiveness. Examples of social work research include:

- Finding out what the community needs are via questionnaires
- Evaluating programmes to see whether they are effective. This might entail running focus groups or interviews to understand how programmes are perceived and experienced by others
- Research specific to a client group, such as older people, young people, children or families, people with disabilities

Social work students sometimes find it difficult to see the relationship between their own everyday life, their social work identity and the world of research. Imagination and curiosity are vital to understanding research.

Research mindedness is developed through a genuine curiosity about the world. For example, think about the meaning behind the everyday activity of 'catching up' with friends or family members. 'Catching up' is the concept of getting together and communicating with someone you know. Indeed this notion of 'catching up'—which might entail going for a hot drink such as coffee or tea or going to a pub to drink alcohol—has no currency to people in varying cultures. There are also various types of 'catching up': from the conversations you might have with your fellow students after the summer break or placement to meetings with prospective employers or mentors. At first glance it would seem that 'catching up' is a social activity, shared between two or more people, and is a feature of contemporary life in developed nations. Curiosity about this social event might lead to ask questions such as:

- What purpose does 'catching up' have?
- Are the methods of 'catching up' similar across different
  - o age groups, or
  - o cultures, or
  - o genders, or
  - o sexual identities, or
  - o classes?
- Do problems emerge from these events and if so, how are they managed?
- What are the experiences of people who do not drink alcohol during 'catching up' activities at drinking venues?
- Why does 'catching up' involve food and/or drink?
- Does 'catching up' fulfil the need for social interaction?

These are just a few questions that might be asked when reflecting upon the everyday activity of 'catching up', and reading these may have prompted you to think of further questions. Questions emerge when curiosity is focused on the notion of 'catching up', which generates more and more questions. When beginning to exercise your research mindedness, try not to let yourself be too sure of the answers to the questions. If you feel unsure how to generate questions, it can be useful to imagine that you are explaining a concept, situation or social issue to someone who has no knowledge of it. For example, explaining homelessness might entail describing differing types of homelessness, how people become homeless, what can be done to help people who are homeless, how to prevent it and so on. These aspects to the issue of homelessness require curiosity and imagination which can lead to the generation of questions. These questions can then be narrowed down in a more focused manner in preparation for the empirical work ahead.

The task for the researcher, then, is to narrow down the questions and decide on usually just one aspect of them. It is important to avoid trying to 'solve' a particular issue through one piece of research. We shall explore this in the next section when we consider how to develop a research question.

RESEARCH QUESTIONS, AIMS AND SCOPE

There are various discrete stages or steps in research, and many researchers adopt a project management approach to the process. The stages include choosing a topic, deciding on methodology and methods, undertaking the research and analysing subsequent data and finally, disseminating the research findings (Sarantakos 2013, p. 104).

The first step in research involves opening up areas of inquiry using the imagination and curiosity, as we saw with our consideration of homelessness. The next stage is to narrow the focus, and devising a research question facilitates this process. Imagine a funnel into which all of your ideas about a particular issue are being poured (Figure 7.1). This process involves 'letting go' of some topics or areas that might be of interest.

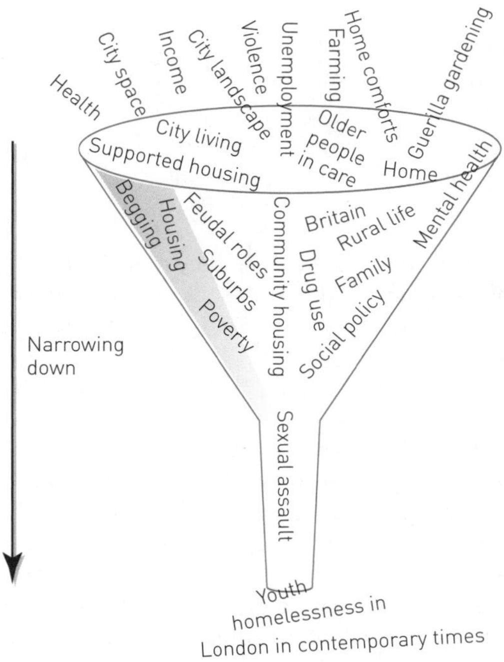

Research questions relate to the specific focus of the intended research. In this sense, it is useful to remember that 'research is about answering questions' (D'Cruz & Jones 2004, p. 15). In thinking about the research question and research design, the researcher will need to decide who the research is interested in, what the research will consist of, why the research is important and how the research will be carried out. All of these variables require careful consideration. Although it may appear that choices about the research are limitless, the choice of research question may also be affected by such factors as budgetary restrictions and availability of research participants (Sarantakos 2005, p. 131).

Once the research question has been formulated, it is time to consider how to go about answering it. In the following section we will examine the choices relating to methods, and what influences these choices.

FIGURE 7.1 Narrowing down topics is an important step in research

EPISTEMOLOGY

When you begin to think about your research, you may already have ideas about methods, for example interviews, focus groups and so on. Preferences for certain types of research reveal something about one's world-view. This is because your ideas about research are connected with your world-view or epistemology (Crotty 2007; Liamputtong & Ezzy 2006; Sarantakos 2013).

Epistemology relates to the way in which we approach knowledge. Crotty defines epistemology as 'the theory of knowledge embedded in the theoretical perspective and thereby in the methodology' (2007, p. 3). He argues that the epistemology affects the theoretical perspective employed which, in turn, influences the methodology and subsequent research methods (Crotty 2007).

For example, if you have a preference for large scale studies in which many participants are consulted using a traditional, scientific study design then you will likely believe that things can be proved or disproved. This kind of research is influenced by the belief that one can make general, *objective* assumptions about others. This perspective is referred to as objectivism, and positivistic research is connected to this theoretical tradition (see Crotty 2007, pp. 18–41). On the other hand, some people believe that statistics and research which claim that things are universally 'true' have little credibility because we all 'interpret the world' or *construct* in our subjective/unique ways (see Berger & Luckmann 1973; Crotty 2007, pp. 42–65; Mead 1934). This perspective is referred to as constructionism or subjectivism, and interpretivistic research is connected to this theoretical tradition. It is useful to think of these two competing views, objectivism and constructionism, as being at opposite ends of a spectrum. Many researchers would see themselves along the spectrum at particular points. Do you have a preference for objectivism or constructionism? Place a mark along the following spectrum to indicate your own preference.

OBJECTIVISM  CONSTRUCTIONISM

There are many theoretical traditions associated with both objectivism and constructionism. For the beginning researcher, it is useful to think about research relating to objectivism as being in the quantitative tradition and research relating to constructionism as being in the qualitative tradition. We now move on to consider research methodology and methods.

RESEARCH METHODOLOGY AND METHODS

In distinguishing between methodology and methods, it is useful to think about research methods as describing specifically *how* the research is *done*. The methodology includes the broader perspective which outlines the general approach in the research as well as the choice of research methods (Sarantakos 2005, p. 30). An example of a methodology is phenomenology. Phenomenology is a range of theoretical positions which are interested in the meanings individuals attach to particular situations, events and phenomena encountered in the course of everyday life (Schutz 1967). Schutzian (1954) phenomenology, for example, highlights individual meaning-making processes as important to understand through the research process. In understanding individual meanings, societal meanings—or 'social reality' (Schutz 1954, p. 492)—is discovered.

When considering research methods the most important thing is to make sure that the method 'fits' with the research question being answered, rather than choosing the method based on researcher preference (Stanley & Wise 1983, p. 724 cited in Letherby 2003, p. 86).

As a beginning researcher, it is helpful to have a sense of the scope of research methods available. The following are examples of some of the key research methods used in social research, but are by no means exhaustive. New research methods continue to emerge and researchers often use a combination of approaches, also called 'mixed methods', or they adapt a method to suit their research question. When considering the methods listed below, it may be helpful to think about them in relation to a particular issue you consider worthy of further research. This will assist in thinking through how a particular method might fit in with the research question being asked.

INTERVIEWS

Interviews are a very popular research method (Holstein & Gubrium 2011, p. 150; Silverman 2007, p. 39) and often preferred by social workers who are used to relating to others using dialogue (D'Cruz & Jones 2004, p. 111). There are various ways in which interviews can be designed to suit the overall research design. A key question to think about when designing research which uses interviews relates to the level of researcher involvement. For example, interviews can range from being highly structured with lots of predetermined questions, to more 'open-ended' or unstructured where the direction of the conversation between the researcher and the interviewee is free-flowing and spontaneous. Open-ended interviews are often preferred by researchers in the social sciences because they allow for the interviewer to check with the interviewee that they have understood them:

> ... data are valid when a deep mutual understanding has been achieved between interviewer and respondent. The practical consequence is that most interactionists reject prescheduled standardized interviews in favour of open-ended interviews. The latter allow respondents to use their own particular way of defining the world [and] assume that no fixed sequence of questions is suitable to all respondents. (Fielding 1996, p. 151)

In order to conduct interviews, it is necessary for the researcher to build a good relationship with the interviewee. Your social work skills in communication are vital in conducting this type of research (Hardwick & Worsley 2011, p. 77). As a researcher using interviews, you are asking that someone disclose or describe their experiences and life events. This can be challenging as the rapport necessary to achieve this has to be built at the beginning of the interview in a short space of time (Hardwick & Worsley 2011, p. 77).

Interviews enable 'sensitive' topics to be addressed on a one to one basis (Denzin 1978; Fielding 1996; Silverman 1985; Strauss & Corbin 1990). It is important to think about gender when designing research. For example, women are traditionally socialised to discuss matters through conversation rather than through action (see, for example, Lever's 1978 study about childhood socialisation). Calls for participant interviews may therefore be taken up more readily by women, who may have little opportunity for their experiences or voices to be heard (Reinharz & Chase 2002), and therefore take up the opportunity to be interviewed more enthusiastically than men (Dunk-West 2011).

FOCUS GROUPS

Like interviews, focus groups are very popular with social researchers. Focus groups are groups of people who are brought together by the researcher with the aim of discussing issues as a group. Henn *et al.* (2009) argue that the focus group's intention is to:

> ... stimulate discussion among people and bring to the surface responses that otherwise might lay dormant. Such discussions may enable participants to clarify their views and opinion positions or, on the basis of engaging with others, to articulate more clearly than they otherwise might. The interactive dynamic is therefore considered to be a crucial element of the focus group approach. (p. 190)

Given the dynamism of focus groups, it is vital for the researcher to facilitate the process whereby information is elicited. Again, social work skills are useful to the social work researcher. The researcher facilitating focus groups must understand group dynamics, be able to elicit the views of people whose voices might be less represented because of issues such as gender, class, disability, culture, sexual identity, age and so on and have the confidence to skilfully address these issues.

QUESTIONNAIRES

Most people reading this book will have come across an invitation to complete a questionnaire, whether you have been contacted directly by a researcher, through a site visited on the internet or by a telephone caller working for a market research company. Questionnaires can help researchers gain an overall view about a particular issue.

When designing your questionnaire, it is important to think very carefully about your wording: 'questionnaire construction is a very demanding task which requires not only methodological competence but also extensive experience with research in general and questioning techniques in particular' (Sarantakos 2013, p. 241). Ambiguous questions or those that lack specifics are likely to result in respondents becoming confused and filling out the questionnaire incorrectly (Neumann 2006, pp. 315–316). This will affect the outcome of your research because you may not be asking what you think you are asking. This phenomenon is known as *skewed data* and to avoid this it is important to think carefully about what you are asking and how it relates to your overall research question.

For example, imagine you are conducting research which critically examines the following: what do clients want in a social worker? Imagine you have decided that questionnaires will generate data to assist you to answer your question.

For one of the questions in your questionnaire, imagine you want to find out what clients think about their social worker. You will need to think about what kind of question or questions will elicit this information. If you ask 'Do you like your social worker?' the answer might be 'yes' or 'no' or 'maybe'. Is it important to understand 'maybe' or the reasons for selecting a particular response? If so, you may need a follow up question. You might think about re-framing the question because asking 'Do you like your social worker?' might elicit a different response than 'Do you think your social worker is competent?' Again, it is vital to think about what overall research question you are trying to answer. It may, for example, be better to give respondents a space to fill out their response to the following question:

> 'What do you think about your social worker?' Please use the space below to respond:
>
> ....
> ....
> ....
> ....

Whereas the question above generates qualitative data, that is, information that is descriptive, questionnaires can also measure using numbers. This means that they can be designed using quantitative approaches. For example, another way to measure how a client feels about their social worker is to provide a Likert scale (Sarantakos 2005, p. 250):

> When thinking about my relationship with my social worker, I feel:
>
> | | |
> |---|---|
> | Very positive | 5 |
> | Positive | 4 |
> | Neutral | 3 |
> | Negative | 2 |
> | Very negative | 1 |
>
> (Adapted from Sarantakos 2005, p. 250)

The answers to these interval levels of measurement would then be calculated and therefore measured.

OBSERVATION/ETHNOGRAPHY

There is a strong tradition of ethnography in the social sciences, particularly within sociology and anthropology. Ethnography is 'study through the observation of institutions, cultures and customs' (Henn *et al.* 2009, p. 196) and requires the researcher to be *immersed* in the culture or social setting. Ethnography is a research methodology (see Crotty 2007, p. 5) and its methods might include observation, participation and interviews, for example. Being immersed in a setting requires a clear decision by the researcher about whether they will be strictly observing the 'action' around them or whether they will be participating and observing. For example, if a researcher wanted to understand the organisational culture of statutory social work in London, an ethnographic method might be used. The researcher would need to think about whether they would engage in the 'action' of the organisation they were immersed in. Would they, for example, answer the telephone if staff were unable to attend to this task? Would they speak to clients of the organisation if they were accompanying a social worker on a home visit? (For an interesting ethnographic analysis about practitioners in child protection, see Harry Ferguson's (2011) book *Child Protection Practice*.)

In ethnographic studies where observation is occurring, it is important to think about how observations will be captured by the researcher. There are various ways to capture data, including:

- Recording interviews, conversations and/or the researchers' thoughts using a recording device
- Completing field notes at regular intervals (at the end of each day, or at various points during the day, for example)
- Keeping mental notes of the events/conversations which are then written down at a later date

The other issue related to this type of research is choosing which kinds of events of, in our example, organisational life are captured. For example, is it important to record the non-verbal communication between colleagues or clients and social workers or is it more important to focus on the events that occur within the setting? (see Sarantakos 2013, p. 229).

Internet ethnography is another means through which particular issues can be researched and 'in some cases the openness and flexibility of design that are hallmarks of ethnographic research can arguably be better achieved by conducting the research on-line' (Aull Davies 2008, p. 151). As with all research, it is vital to gain the consent of the research participant; in internet research this can be an area of uncertainty because of the publicly available information internet technology facilitates. As we shall see in the next section, all types of research involving others require careful consideration of ethical responsibilities.

Generally speaking, the ethical principles used in social work that we discussed in Chapter 5 are transferable to the research context.

Gaining ethical approval for any research involving others is crucial because it allows critical assessment of whether the proposed research conforms to ethical standards. Ethics committees are a common feature in organisational settings, government and non-government organisations, universities and the like. Such bodies require the researcher to submit a clearly articulated plan for their proposed research which will then be scrutinised and assessed for its suitability. Sometimes researchers are required to adjust their approach according to the judgement made by an ethics committee.

The guiding tenet in all research ought to be to 'do no harm'. This notion, also known in ethics literature as avoiding harm or 'non-maleficence', is a principle underpinning contemporary medical and social sciences research (for example, see Beauchamp & Childress' 1979 text on bioethics). Some researchers believe that research should do more than avoid harm and should, in fact, 'do good' which is the ethical principle of beneficence. Such research is called emancipatory research and has particular appeal to social workers. Researchers hold positions of power (Bloom 1998, pp. 34–36) and emancipatory research attempts to share that power more equally with others such as those being 'researched'.

Emancipatory research seeks to empower those with limited opportunities to exercise power because of, for example, gendered inequality (Letherby 2003, p. 114). Here is a basic example of emancipatory research:

- Research question: How does youth homelessness impact on relationships with their peers?
- Epistemology: Constructionism.
- Methodology: Phenomenology.
- Method: Interviews with 10 young people who are currently homeless, five men and five women.
- Specifics: The lead researcher will recruit three young people who are or have been homeless. They will be paid to be trained in qualitative research and will be employed as research assistants. These young people will conduct interviews with the research population (outlined above), lead in the design and analysis of data and take a key role in disseminating the research through publications and conference presentations/seminars. Interview participants will be paid for their time, invited to assist in the research design and dissemination and will be provided with access to housing or specialised agencies if appropriate/wanted.

The research described above seeks *to empower* others through providing:

- Training and skills acquisition for the research assistants recruited
- Financial and other support/resources for the research population

Confidentiality is an ethical concept and legal principle and is crucial to consider in any research involving others. Just as with social work practice, it is important that participants in studies understand the role of the researcher and the nature of involvement. Researchers often write a short summary of the research—a participant information sheet—in which the key aims of the study are laid out, and including how the information obtained from respondents will be used. It is important that people involved in research are able to withdraw their consent to take part in the study at any point.

SAMPLING

Sampling relates to the question: 'how many people should be involved in the research?' For example, if we decide that we would like to interview people to better understand the impacts of welfare cuts in England, how many people should we interview? In addition, who should we interview? Should we select a random section of the population or should we interview a small number of people who are affected by the government cuts to the public sector? How will we find our sample population? These are all questions which relate to sampling. In short, sampling refers to:

- Who is included in the research
- How many people are included in the research
- How participants will be found and selected

Generally speaking, research uses samples that are either representative or non-representative. Research which claims to have significance for the broader population is said to be *generalisable*. Generalisability means that based on the findings of a piece of research, general assumptions can be made about others who were not included in the study. If five hundred people from a range of *variables* such as class, gender, age, educational attainment and socio-economic status were surveyed about their attitudes towards the 2012 London Olympics, researchers may be able to generalise their findings to the rest of the population. This is because the researchers have included particular features in their research design which allow for them to see their participants as representing the general public.

A number of sampling methods can be used to recruit participants for research. For example, snowball sampling (Biernacki & Waldorf 1981) enables potential interviewees to hear about the study via word of mouth, for example via a forwarded email or in person from someone who was aware of the study. They can then tell others about the study and the sample increases or 'snowballs' in this way. This is similar to opportunistic sampling which utilises existing networks and spontaneous opportunities to meet others who may be interested in being part of research (Liamputtong & Ezzy 2006, p. 48). These kinds of sampling methods are suited to research which is non-representative, that is, it does not claim to represent the broader population. Like representative samples, non-representative samples can make a valuable contribution to existing theory and knowledge.

DATA ANALYSIS

Data analysis is required for the researcher to conclude the findings of the study. Data are the products of whichever research method has been used. For example, the narratives or dialogue from interviews or focus groups are data. Completed questionnaires contain data. Broadly speaking, there are two differing processes for data analysis, and these are dependent on whether research is quantitative or qualitative. We will now briefly consider each of these.

QUANTITATIVE DATA ANALYSIS

The ways in which surveys are collated in quantitative research enables numerical assessments to be made. For example, it is possible to add up and calculate differing aspects of data collected for the purposes of *measurement*. Measures include mode, median and mean.

> **Mode**: this is the highest frequency. For example, in the following list of measures, the number 3 appears the most, so 3 would be the mode.
>
> 1   3   3   5   8   9   10   11
>
> **Median**: the median is the middle score, and in this set of numbers is 6.5. When there is an odd number of scores the median is easy to identify, as being the middle score in the set. When there is an even number of scores the median is calculated by adding the two middle scores and dividing by 2. In this case the middle scores are 5 and 8. Adding those and dividing by 2 gives the median score.
>
> 1   3   3   5   8   9   10   11
>
> **Mean**: this is the average of the scores. Adding the scores and dividing them by the total number of scores gives the mean or average.
>
> 1   3   3   5   8   9   10   11

In this case the calculation would be

$$1 + 3 + 3 + 5 + 8 + 9 + 10 + 11 = 50 \div 8 = 6.25$$

Certain types of measurement are better suited to mean, median and mode respectively. As we can see above, the same set of numbers can have differing mean, median and mode scores. Imagine that almost all respondents to a question in a questionnaire said they ranked their social worker as number 5 which is the top category in a Likert scale from extremely unsatisfied to extremely satisfied. Some respondents, however, ticked the lower end of the scale, at number 1, which suggested they were extremely unsatisfied. When scoring the questionnaire and reporting on the findings, using median, mode or mean could each suggest different things.

Various statistical techniques can be applied to quantitative data. Standard deviation, for example, measures the distance a score is from the average, or mean, of scores in the study. Relationships between particular variables can also be measured. Data can be arranged into visual descriptors such as scatterplots, histograms and bar and pie charts, for example, and there are various computer programs that assist in both creating and computing statistics (for example SPSS). Now that we have introduced some of the ways in which quantitative data are analysed, let's move on to consider qualitative analysis.

QUALITATIVE DATA ANALYSIS

Qualitative data generated from focus groups and interviews, for example, can be analysed using various techniques. Depending on the research methodology used, analysis can vary from narrative analysis to discourse analysis to case studies. Many studies using qualitative data require transcription of verbal dialogue between the researcher and participants.

Here are some data generated through my research into everyday sexuality. In this research project I was interested in how people reflected upon and made sense of their sexualities. This involved interviewing 15 men and 15 women aged between 30 and 65 years. A constructionist epistemology, combined with a phenomenological methodology, influenced the ways in which data were analysed. I began the research by asking: 'can you tell me about your sexuality?' Here is what one respondent said in our interview:

> Ruth:
> It's difficult isn't it? Because I know like when I first um got that email I thought I wonder what it is, you know, what sort of... you're looking to explore and I thought... 'oh god... I don't know' (laugh). Um... I don't know ... I don't know if it's how you sort of think of yourself some people sort of certainly define their selves with their sexuality quite strongly. I've got a couple of friends who are very much like that. And then there are other people who maybe don't cause it much thought. And I probably sit in that category of not necessarily causing it much thought. Um. But I do think that there are... I mean there are elements of... I guess in my role um and where I've been and what I've done um, some of the, you know, whether it's power balance issues as... Having started out quite young in, um, in fairly senior positions.
>
> Ruth, 39-year-old CEO

How do we make sense of these kinds of accounts? The answer lies with the methodology being used. In some cases narrative or life story approaches help to frame people's stories with life events and the ways that they make sense of the world. Broadly speaking, a phenomenological approach, for example, is interested in the meaning people ascribe to particular phenomena.

In looking at the account from Ruth (not her real name), and comparing it to other accounts from the study, we can begin to separate out what are themes. This is called coding. Coding relates to themes which emerge from data and it is vital that the researcher immerse themselves in their data in order to find these. Often researchers will read, re-read and listen to their data. They can also check back with participants during this process, as a kind of triangulation to make sure they have understood the account in the way the interviewee, or group, for example, intended. Data analysis is a broad term which is used to mean many processes (Wolcott 1994). 'Analysis' suggests that this can be a straightforward, time-limited process. In some research designs, analysis occurs while data are being gathered whereas for other studies, analysis is a process whose boundaries are dictated by the timescale of the project. In any case, analysis in qualitative research involves being familiar with data, comparing data, drawing out themes or making some generalisations such as findings and thinking about the significance of the outcomes in relation to existing knowledge and research.

Qualitative researchers must also decide how much they are informed by their data. Do they, for example, privilege people's stories over theories? Or should people's accounts inform theory? Again, the chosen research methodology needs to fit with decisions made about such matters.

Like quantitative packages, computer programs such as NVIVO help to arrange qualitative data.

DISSEMINATION

Dissemination in relation to research concerns itself with how the research findings are shared with others. There are many ways for researchers to share their findings. The method used will reflect the purpose of the research, for example whether it was commissioned by a particular organisation to review a programme or whether the research was conducted by the government (for example, Censuses are large scale studies). Possible methods of dissemination include:

- Presenting the findings at a conference
- Writing a report which is given to organisations and others
- Issuing a media release
- Using social media such as Twitter, Facebook and other networking sites
- Writing a dissertation (for Honours, Masters or Doctor of Philosophy degrees, for example)
- Publishing the findings in peer reviewed journals
- Writing copy for publication in newspapers, magazines and other relevant print media
- Speaking on television, radio and/or digital media about the issue you researched
- Writing a book chapter for an edited book or a book
- Presenting findings to the community through seminars or workshops

LITERATURE REVIEWS

Literature reviews are written accounts which firstly, name relevant literature such as studies or theoretical contributions to the field being studied. Secondly, literature reviews enable the author to argue that their research fits and is important in this broader context of scholarly contributions. A well-written literature review details all of the important research and scholarship about a particular area, highlights what is missing and locates the present study or argument in this context. Considering how much information is contained within a literature review, they are surprisingly brief. It is therefore essential to be succinct and arrange information in a clear format when drafting a literature review.

Literature reviewing is a skill that takes time to develop because the task is to synthesise existing literature. With the current emphasis on evidence-based practice, being able to consult literature through finding and reading appropriate journal articles is a vital skill to social workers. When writing a literature review, it can be helpful to group articles into themes. These themes can be things such as dates, countries where research originates, particular types of theories, similar methodologies and methods used in studies or a myriad of other possibilities. Being able to read a large number of articles and summarise them all by grouping together those that have something in common is a skill well worth developing.

Social work students are required to write many assignments during their studies and it is helpful to learn how to access literature through database searching, using key terms to narrow the search. When reading journal articles, you will notice that they have a similar format. Journal articles in the social sciences usually have an introduction, a literature review, a methodology/method section, a findings section and discussion followed by a conclusion. When reading the literature review from a journal article, notice how the authors summarise existing studies and argue that theirs is important.

In summary, here are some techniques that can assist in writing a literature review for a dissertation:

- Group all your articles according to themes. These could be based on anything from the country where the studies originated, to the method being studied to any other criteria you notice while reading.
- Make notes on your paper copy of articles and summarise in dot points the three key points in the top right-hand corner of the article. This helps when you have a large number of articles.
- Begin writing. Edit, edit, edit. Experiment with moving text around to make your argument stronger.
- Read your work and ask: what is my argument? Is it clear?
- At the beginning of your literature review state what you are going to do. For example: 'The ways in which depression has been responded to in the past decade have shifted. This dissertation argues that depression has been medicalised which has marginalised the social model. In making this argument, the dissertation commences by providing a critical appraisal of the ways in

which the medicalisation of depression has occurred in relation to pharmaco-
logical intervention in England.'

- Avoid summarising literature, instead, critically appraise it: say what is good about it and what is neglected.
- Show others your work and ask them to summarise your argument. This helps to check if you have stated your argument clearly enough.
- Use signposting and summarising such as 'this chapter argues...', 'this chapter has...'. This makes it less likely that your examiner will be confused by your discussion.

HOW TO USE RESEARCH IN SOCIAL WORK: WORKING WITH OTHERS

Social workers in organisational settings who wish to do research sometimes work alongside institutions that specialise in research. For example, universities, govern-ment workers and people in private research consultancy may be brought in to an organisation to help it undertake primary research. This means that social workers can work with statisticians, qualitative researchers and analysts who may have qualifications in economics, sociology, history, mathematics, or more applied areas such as epidemiology, psychology and social work as well as many, many other disciplines. Social workers in the organisational setting who undertake such work need to clearly articulate what it is they would like to find out in the research. Some organisations have a great deal of input into the research design and execution while others commission the research and have little involvement aside from receiving the final report.

Once research is undertaken, how is it used in an organisational context? The answer is that it depends on the purpose of the research. Often, organisations providing social work services like to have evidence of the efficacy of particular programmes or interventions. This can help with funding, for example, because being able to demonstrate that a particular approach works can highlight its need. Similarly, being able to show tangible outcomes can help services choose which types of intervention are cost effective, meet the needs of clients and are effective. Findings of research that is commissioned is conveyed to the funding organisation through meetings, formal presentations and reports. Written reports usually summarise the literature in the area through a literature review in which the central research problem is contextualised. A summary of findings helps to break down the findings of the research into clearly worded, brief statements. When on placement, students often find themselves reading policy documents and may also read research reports which have been completed 'in house', that is, internal to the organisation, or externally.

Similarly, organisations may base their policies upon other research, such as research reported by the World Health Organisation which found that every six seconds someone around the world dies from tobacco smoking or exposure to second-hand smoke (www.who.int/research/en/). These kinds of statistics help to frame global problems and inform thinking about services for local communities and individuals. How might social work in a community organisation respond to this statistic? One possible response is to offer low cost or free smoking cessation classes and supports. Another response is to use advocacy and lobbying approaches to argue that legislators and policy-makers need to protect their citizens against this public health issue. These suggestions are based on existing public health approaches to address smoking in England, Australia and other nations. Social work in this context would aim to address such a 'problem' through understanding it in research terms and adopting a helping service according to the need of its clients and broader community.

Let us now consider other ways that research is used in social work practice by looking at a more individual situation (Case Study 7.1).

CASE STUDY 7.1 The Oscar family

Bob Oscar is 52 years old and lives with his two children, Ruby Oscar, aged 15, and Christopher Oscar, aged 13. Ruby and Christopher have a good relationship and are very close. They both attend the local school. The Oscar family live in private rental accommodation in central London. Bob is White British and Ruby and Christopher describe themselves as mixed race. The children's mother, Jane, died from a heroin overdose when both children were under the age of five years. Jane was from Zimbabwe and moved to London as a teenager. Bob is a housepainter and has a good reputation locally, but in the past few years the work has become less and less frequent. Things have become difficult financially and Bob visits the organisation you work for to see if they can help. He meets with you and tells you some more about his family.

Bob tells you that Ruby is a 'bright girl' but recently she has had health problems and has been having anxiety attacks at school which has made her want to avoid school altogether. Both Ruby and Christopher have asthma which is worse in the colder months. The central heating at the flat is not very effective and there is dampness in the building. Additionally, since money is tight, they are not able to run the heating for very long. Bob tells you that Christopher has started to ask about his mother more since becoming a teenager. He is not sure how much to tell the children about the death because when she died the children did not attend the funeral, nor were they told how she died. Bob would like to know if you can assist him. He's not sure where to start, but feels that the family are struggling.

HOW TO USE RESEARCH TO ASSIST THE OSCAR FAMILY

There are many issues which are present in the case study which could eventuate in different approaches, courses of action and outcomes. Your response would depend on the agreement between Bob and yourself and the children about what areas might be important to begin with and which areas require future work together. Here is a summary of some of the potential areas of work and how research can be used in varying ways in social work practice:

Bob's financial situation

Your organisation may already have information about how much parents are entitled to for a range of things such as housing assistance, support for electricity and/or gas costs, school related expenses and childcare benefit. Discussing with Bob the support he is entitled to could address and help to alleviate some of the problems with asthma that Ruby and Christopher have experienced because of the dampness and cold in the home. Discussing medical support with Bob is also relevant here since asthma is a potentially life-threatening condition if untreated or not managed appropriately.

A cursory glance at the research literature about this kind of financial hardship which impacts upon decisions about whether to use the heating (or cooling) shows that it has been named as a kind of poverty called 'fuel poverty'. In the UK, the Department of Energy and Climate Change define fuel poverty in the following way:

> A household is said to be in fuel poverty if it needs to spend more than 10% of its income on fuel to maintain a satisfactory heating regime (usually 21 degrees for the main living area, and 18 degrees for other occupied rooms). (www.decc.gov. uk/en/content/cms/statistics/fuelpov_stats/fuelpov_stats.aspx)

A search in the *British Journal of Social Work* highlights an article about health inequality in which fuel poverty is mentioned. This seems relevant to Bob's situation because the lack of income has affected whether he heats his home, which, in turn, has had consequences for his children's health. The article:

> ... presents arguments for recognizing and tackling health inequalities as a major new challenge for social work. Four underpinning points provide the building blocks for this case, that health inequalities are a matter of social justice and human rights, that the causes of health inequalities are primarily social, that poverty and poor health are common characteristics of social work service users and, that, therefore, health inequalities are a vital issue for social workers in all settings. A number of implications for social work practice and policy are outlined. The paper concludes that addressing health inequalities implies that social work has to become more actively engaged with critical global social, economic, environmental and political issues. (Bywaters 2009, p. 353)

This paper reports on a range of existing research which has taken place around health inequality and poverty. It makes the argument that social work ought to be more active in being aware of inequalities, such as those brought about by fuel poverty, in day-to-day practice. Yet what is the connection between this piece of research and Bob and his children? How might you use it as his social worker?

Being able to name Bob's situation and link it with the growing number of people who are under financial hardship because of rising costs of fuel can be a powerful thing for clients. That there is something called 'fuel poverty' can help to name individuals' experiences and highlight that this is a new phenomenon and something that needs to change. As a social worker, using this research to help to frame your search to find financial assistance for Bob, you will be more informed.

Similarly, you may recognise other clients in the organisation for whom this is an issue. Arranging a space for people to meet in order to frame a collective response is one way to help to address this problem. Facilitating social action, helping with advocacy activities—these too help to enable people to address the problems brought about by fuel poverty. In some countries certain groups of vulnerable people (such as very young and very old people with health conditions) have been highlighted as being particularly at risk of heat or cold related health problems as a result of the rising costs of fuel. Some countries have introduced financial relief for these groups in the form of credits and tariff reductions. Searching for information on behalf of Bob or providing him with the information about tariffs is an example of how research can be used in social work practice.

Anxiety

During your search into anxiety, you find that *The Medical Journal of Australia* evaluated studies which looked at the efficacy of programmes in schools to address anxiety. The finding was as follows:

> A number of schools programs produce positive outcomes. However, even well established programs require further evaluation to establish readiness for broad dissemination as outlined in the standards of the Society for Prevention Research. (Neil & Christensen 2007, p. 305)

You do not think this article is helpful to your direct practice with Ruby. However, reading this gives you an idea: you plan to talk to Bob about meeting with Ruby to talk about school and whether there are any supports in place at her school to help her deal with her anxiety. This plan of action could lead to you working alongside Ruby and the school to help reduce the impacts of the anxiety for Ruby.

What if Ruby asked you: 'what is the best way to treat anxiety?' A search of the literature in peer reviewed journals in which approaches are evaluated highlights some of the key ways anxiety is addressed in a clinical setting. Through reading this literature you begin to wonder about the role of health and whether Ruby has been assessed as having anxiety. Given her asthma and other recent events, you go back to Ruby and discuss whether there has been an involvement from health professionals. Your concern relates to the possibility that there could be an underlying health issue which has been self-diagnosed as anxiety. Ruby tells you she has looked it up on the internet and self-diagnosed anxiety. Her heart pounds and she feels sick. Following up with health might offer opportunities for working with other professions alongside Ruby. This means that any findings that are made can be responded to alongside other services, with Ruby at the centre of these relations.

Grief and loss in children and young people

After a further meeting with Bob and Christopher, Christopher tells you he would like to talk to you about his mother. You, Christopher and Bob all agree this is a good way forward. Before you meet with Christopher for the first time, you want to 'read up' about grief and loss in young people as it will help you frame your responses to him. Although you remember studying grief and loss at university, you do not feel that you are up to date with your knowledge in this area. You suspect that children ought to be included in rituals around death but wonder if this has changed since you studied.

After conducting a search of the literature you find that there is some debate surrounding grief that does not reach some sort of resolution in a timeframe which you might expect (Worden 1983). This, you find, is called 'complicated grief' or 'complicated mourning'. There is some research which suggests that complicated grief is not a social disorder but one characterised by negative thoughts about one's self. In this study:

> The data revealed a profile of processing in CG [complicated grief] characterized by significant relationships between CG symptoms or diagnosis and both self-devaluation and negative self-related cognitions about the future. (Golden & Dalgleish 2012)

You find an article written by American scholars published in a respected psychology journal. The paper summarises practice approaches to working with children who have lost a parent and the ideas fit with your theoretical and ethical social work perspective. Reading the following text from the article makes you curious about how Christopher must be feeling given that his father never speaks of his late mother and that he did not participate in the funeral or mourning rituals:

> Parental death is one of the most traumatic events that can occur in childhood ... several reviews of the literature have found that the death of a parent places children at risk for a number of negative outcomes. (Haine *et al.* 2008, p. 113)

The authors of the study outline specific ways to work positively with a bereaved child. These include helping to build the capacity of the child to feel positively about themselves, express emotion and communicate with their caregiver, and reducing stressors for the child (Haine *et al.* 2008, pp. 115–119). The same article also highlights some important factors which have been found in research to affect children who are grieving. These include (Haine *et al.* 2008, pp. 120–121):

- The child's developmental stage
- The child's gender
- The cause of death
- How long it's been since the death
- The cultural background of the family and child

This gives you a lot of material which will help to shape your work with Christopher. You plan to meet with him and discuss working together and you will 'check in' with the notes you have made about the research into children and grief. Although the research has been very helpful in terms of summarising studies into grieving children and the outcomes, you do not allow the research to let you leap to any conclusions about what is going on for Christopher. Rather, using a 'client-centred' approach (Rogers 1951), you wish to see how he is experiencing the problem and what he would like to happen. Although the research cannot speak for Christopher, he may be interested in some of the findings: this will be evaluated as the work with him progresses.

HOW WAS RESEARCH USED?

In this case study in which we considered the Oscar family, we looked at how research could be applied to the situation and to our practice. The ways in which research can be applied to social work can be summarised as follows:

- To inform about new terms, movements and phenomena
- To highlight shared problems and possible solutions
- To uncover more questions which help you and the client understand the problem more fully
- To uncover any hidden risks
- To frame practice; this is also referred to as 'evidence-based practice' or 'research-based practice'

The push for social work to be more 'evidence based' is part of a broader shift in which professions are increasingly asked to justify particular responses to their clients. Medical doctors use the evidence from research trials to pick the best medication for their clients. This is an example of the ways in which research *informs intervention*. However, the ways in which clinical trials have been reported on have come under scrutiny (Goldacre 2012). In the social sciences, however, often research does not claim to be generalisable. Research reporting on the positive evaluation of a group for young people who are at risk of homelessness may inform another social worker's work but the process is more than the logical application of 'what works' to a problem. This means that social workers must ask questions of the research they encounter and assess its suitability to the context in which they are interested in it. As we have seen in this chapter, there are many kinds of research approaches and without knowledge about such approaches, critical appraisal of research findings becomes impossible. Here are some suggestions about questions to ask when reading a research report or journal article or book which reports on research:

- Where did the research take place? Is it applicable to your context?
- Who undertook the research? What is the professional world-view of the researchers? Are they biologists or social workers? Is it a multidisciplinary team?
- Who published the research? Is the journal well-respected? Does the publisher review book proposals or do they publish them without review?
- Who was involved in the research? How many people?
- Do you understand how the researchers came to the findings? Are you convinced of the arguments being made in the piece?
- Do the authors cite other research? Are any of these references worth looking at? Are there any studies which have counter findings to this one?

There are many, many questions which can be asked when evaluating research. Fortunately, students of social work develop a critical eye for written material during their university studies: essays and the like enable students to develop these skills. It is crucial that these skills continue to be applied post qualification.

HOW TO FIND INFORMATION

In the university setting students are often taught how to use the library's databases. This is the most important skill to master early on in one's social work academic career. Students who are unable to access key pieces of research can struggle to make clearly supported arguments in their written work.

In this chapter there have been some references to 'peer reviewed journals'. Students are sometimes confused about what this means. Generally speaking, journals only agree to publish articles once others have read and critically evaluated them. Researchers, academics or practitioners who write an article—for example about some research into older people and intimate relationships—and would like this published submit it to a journal of their choice. The journal then sends the article to experts in the field. In our example, they will be experts in the field of older people and intimacy. These are the 'peers' who review the article (also known as referees). They read the article, which has been anonymised so they do not know who has written it, and decide if they think it should be published.

There are usually recommendations to do one of the following: reject the article as it is not suitable; accept the article provided the author(s) make major revisions to the paper; accept the article provided minor revisions are made; or accept the article for publication. Generally speaking, it is more likely that there will be changes required or a rejection than a straight-out acceptance. If the paper requires changes, the reviewers will outline what they think are the problems with the paper. When the authors have made the changes (either minor or major depending on what has been suggested), it is likely to go back to the referees for another round of reviews. Journals differ in how many people review but it is usually around three. Because of the 'peer review' process, authors must make sure their arguments are sound and supported by research or theory, and that they have structured the paper appropriately. Peer reviewed papers, having gone through this process, are therefore more respected than other forms of publication such as blogs, self-published material and other non-peer reviewed outputs.

Students who move from the university setting to the organisational setting can find it difficult to find information once their university library membership has expired. Some organisations have their own libraries which may have access to databases and journals and this can be an excellent resource for staff. There are online journals which do not require institutional or individual membership for access: the trick is to ensure that the material is peer reviewed. If it is not peer reviewed, this does not mean the contents are of no use, but that claims about research have not been through the peer review process.

As technology enables quick searching, it can be tempting to use a popular search engine to search for research. Although there are some gateways which contain scholarly articles, social work students and social workers need to be careful that the material they are accessing has been through peer review and that it is up to date. Other sources which contain information which might assist in social work practice can come from non-government organisations and government organisations. If accessing material, it is important to understand who the author is and how they are able to make the claims they make. Similarly, newspaper articles can be based upon opinion and public perception: if reading a newspaper report about new research, try to access the original research to assess for yourself.

CHAPTER SUMMARY

This chapter has introduced some of the key ideas in social research. Developing your own research mindedness is an important skill, particularly since increasingly social workers are undertaking their own research in organisational settings. We have begun to explore some of the key methods used in research such as interviews, focus groups and questionnaires and we have examined objectivism and constructionism as epistemological influences on research design, methodology and analysis (Crotty 2007). Throughout the chapter we have seen how important it is to be clear about methodology and reasons for making decisions about the design of research. The application of social work values and ethics was argued to be relevant to research decisions. We have also considered how to use research in social work. The critical application of research must occur in the context of our work with others: it is not a separate process. We have outlined the specific ways that research can assist in our work with others through the consideration of a case study. We now move on to Chapter 8 where the key ideas of the book are highlighted and the future social work self is explored.

FURTHER READING

ALSTON, M. & BOWLES, W. (1998) *Research for Social Workers: An Introduction to Methods.* Abingdon: Routledge.

BLANKSBY, P. E. & BARBER, J. G. (2005) *SPSS for Social Workers: An Introductory Workbook.* Boston: Pearson.

CROTTY, M. (2007) *The Foundations of Social Research: Meaning and Perspective in the Research Process.* London: Sage Publications.

D'CRUZ, H. & JONES, M. (2004) *Social Work Research: Ethical and Political Contexts.* London: Sage Publications.

DODD, S-J. & EPSTEIN, I. (2012) *Practice-based Research in Social Work: A Guide for Reluctant Researchers.* Abingdon: Routledge.

DYSON, S. & BROWN, B. (2006) *Social Theory and Applied Health Research.* Berkshire: Open University Press.

HENN, M., WEINSTEIN, M. & FOARD, N. (2009) *A Critical Introduction to Social Research*, 2nd edn. London: Sage Publications.

LETHERBY, G. (2003) *Feminist Research in Theory and Practice.* Buckingham: Open University Press.

LIAMPUTTONG, P. & EZZY, D. (2006) *Qualitative Research Methods*. South Melbourne: Oxford University Press.

MCLAUGHLIN, H. (2012) *Understanding Social Work Research*, 2nd edn. London: Sage Publications.

SARANTAKOS, S. (2005) *Social Research*, 4th edn. Basingstoke: Palgrave Macmillan.

SILVERMAN, D. (ed.) (2011) *Qualitative Research*, 3rd edn. London: Sage Publications.

WHITTAKER, A. (2012) *Research Skills for Social Work*, 2nd edn. Exeter: Learning Matters.

8

'Doing' Social Work: Constituting the Professional Self

This chapter:

- Summarises the key theoretical ideas in this book

- Articulates the purpose of the reflexive exercises

- Considers how learning continues post qualification

- Offers a summary of the chapters

- Outlines suggestions for the future about how to be a social worker

This book has examined the key knowledge required in social work education. We have explored this knowledge through various forms of learning. From reflexive thinking to active engagement with scenarios, case studies and other targeted activities, material relevant to social work has been presented to help you engage with your social work self. This book has also, hopefully, encouraged the reader to think about their emerging social work identity in a new way and to make the connection between new forms of relating and existing skills, knowledge and experiences.

In Chapter 1 the process of socialisation was examined by looking at the importance of childhood in the acquisition of social skills and learning about social rules. Similarly, social work students enter a period of rapid knowledge acquisition when they enter university and begin to engage with the vast array of materials which help them to *become* social workers.

Research shows that learning in contemporary life can occur through varying, seemingly unrelated contexts (West *et al.* 2011). Becoming a social worker occurs through the reflexive intersection of biography (one's own personal life history and experiences), scholarly ideas, traditional learning materials and imagination: none of which are possible to engage in without human interaction (Mead 1934). In the same way that childhood learning or socialisation occurs through interaction with others in games and play, so too can adult learning (West *et al.* 2011) about social work.

Therefore the activities contained within this book have been designed to:

- Help you engage creatively with the purpose of deeper learning
- Prompt reflexive engagement with your professional self
- Help you identify the social work theories, ethics and values which 'fit' for you
- Re-iterate, mirror and begin to challenge some of the key ideas encountered through traditional learning materials

The subjects brought together in this book will make sense to each social work student in differing ways at differing times. For example, the theories used in interaction with a client in a particular situation will differ to those which underpin practice in another setting or with another client or client group. Figure 8.1 shows one way for you to think about how the material contained within this book is brought together.

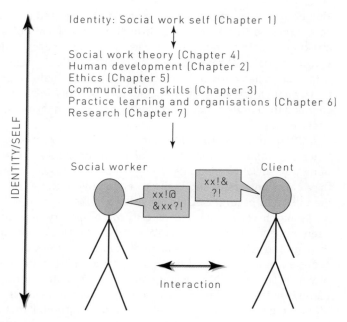

FIGURE 8.1 Using knowledge in social work practice

Think about how the information and knowledge contained in this text can be conceptualised and draw a map of this. You could use stick figures in the same way as in Figure 8.1 or you could come up with a different sort of diagram.

WHAT HAPPENS ONCE I'M A SOCIAL WORKER?

As we have seen in Chapter 1, socialisation is central to learning about empathising with others and understanding relationships in social life (Mead 1934). For the student of social work, the same kind of socialisation occurs. This socialisation process involves understanding the ways in which social workers interact with others, what theories they use and which values and ethical ideas are associated with the profession. Once students finish their course, this process of learning should not end, even though it can *feel* that it has.

Post qualification, social workers can often feel that they are, in fact, not ready to be social workers. Since social work students are engaging in a socialisation process during their studies, once the conditions for learning are removed, this feeling of 'not being ready' is understandable. Some social workers who have been working for some time insist that they do not 'use theory'. What happens once social workers qualify?

To understand, we must return to our traffic metaphor from the beginning of the book. In the same way that people can forget the specifics of a journey—'Did I cross that road? Was the light back there green or red? Which way did I travel to get here?'—so too does behaviour become routinized (Mead 1934). Similarly, social workers can wonder 'What did I say that really helped that client?', 'Did I let that client have enough "air time" in the group setting?', 'Did that session go well?' In social work, the way to periodically break routinization is through supervision and reflexive practice. Students learn the skills to reflexively engage with their learning and these are further developed through the placement experience and professional practice. Writing reflections, case studies, critical incidents, process recordings and more enable students to fully engage with their emerging professional selves.

While social work students interact in their practice learning they are trying out their professional identities—relating to clients, building professional relationships with colleagues and external organisations.— All of these social interactions help to reinforce student identities as student social workers. Once qualified, social workers will likely abandon the written requirements associated with university work. However, they may write reflections, present at conferences, engage in research for their organisation and review their practice with the help of clients. All of these involve a level of reflexivity and an external prompt for doing so. Supervision provides a space where some reflexive engagement with the work can take place and it is crucial for social workers to engage in this thinking. Organisational limitations can affect the frequency of supervision so developing one's own tools for reflection can be a useful strategy for maintaining the social work self. We will now return to a reflective activity which considers your broader view about social work.

At the very beginning of this book you were asked to reflect upon your beliefs about social work. How have these changed throughout your reading and practice experiences? Take some time now to complete Exercise 8.1.

EXERCISE 8.1

Put the following statements in order from most important (1) to least important (10).

Social workers ... need to change the world
Social workers ... need to work hard
Social workers ... are always on duty
Social workers ... should make people do things
Social workers ... are like the police
Social workers ... help people to change
Social workers ... work with communities
Social workers ... should be able to work anywhere in the world
Social workers ... need career goals
Social workers ... should be caring

You may find that the statements in Exercise 8.1 are no longer enough for you to articulate what social work means to you. Hopefully this is because you now see social work as a central part of your self or who you are. Your professional self will continue to change and respond to the shifts in your external environment and profession. Monitoring this can occur through increased opportunities for reflexive engagement with practice, as we discussed in Chapter 6.

This book has aimed to teach the reader how to understand their professional social work identity. This has meant not only learning about social work itself. How to *be* a social worker means understanding that the self is made through its relationships with others. Learning how to be a social worker requires engagement with:

* Formal knowledge through texts, readings, research and other reports
* Engagement in activities which assist in better understanding this knowledge
* Experimentation with social work skills such as communication
* Experimentation with practice as a social work student on placement working with clients (individuals, groups, communities, globally)
* One's self. This includes reflexive engagement with one's biography and the socio-cultural setting within which the self is constituted
* A political lens which enables power and inequality to be identified at interpersonal, local, national and global levels
* Other students, academic staff and practice teachers, colleagues

Crucially, it is only through the awareness of the interactionist nature of self production that we can consciously fashion a social work self. This is a process that must continue throughout our careers. The ways in which we engage in this process shape the local, national and even international social work identities. In the same way that our social work selves are constantly developing and changing, so too is our profession. Therefore the professional self *you* constitute becomes part of the future generation of social workers who are also constitutive of social work itself.

WORKING WITH OTHERS

Throughout this book we have examined some of the possibilities, limitations and positives to working with other professions. Interdisciplinary working can help to highlight what social work brings to the work. There is a long-held belief that social workers are not very good at articulating who they are. This may be because social work, since its inception, has searched for an ontology: the elusive, clearly articulated set of values, beliefs, theory base and skills has been present since social work began (Gibelman 1999, p. 299).

This book has focused on the social work self and in reading it and considering your own social work self, you take this knowledge with you into your work with others. Working with other groups can help to promote our individual and shared identity as social workers because, as we have seen throughout this book, interaction and relationships with others is central to self-making. George Herbert Mead says:

> A self is a composite or interaction of ... two parts of our natures—the fundamental impulses which make us cooperating neighbors [sic] and friends, lovers and parents and children, and rivals, competitors, and enemies; on the other side the evocation of this self which we achieve when we address ourselves in the language which is the common speech of those about us. We talk to ourselves, ask ourselves what we will do under certain conditions, criticize and approve of our own suggestions and ideas, and in taking the organized attitudes of those engaged in common undertakings we direct our own impulses. (Mead 1925 [2011], p. 316)

The power of language and communication help to promote—or even denigrate—the ways in which social workers view their profession. Our sense of self as a profession is projected upon those with whom we work and other professional groups. The ways in which we make the connection between who we are and what we do need to go beyond reflexivity (Reupert 2009, p. 775). It is a useful (and emancipatory!) exercise to try to move beyond our historical difficulties and 'have a go' at articulating in just one sentence what you think is social work.

SOCIAL WORK IS............

In thinking about the question: 'what is social work?' you may have reflected upon all that you have learned in your studies so far as well as the opportunities available through employment. A definition of social work can be found in Chapter 1 as well as in the Glossary at the end of this book. Each definition, including your own, is equally relevant. We bring our own meanings to the work and interpret our theory and ethical foundation in slightly differing ways: this promotes social work as a dynamic and ever changing profession. We now move on to think more about the key issues which have an impact on our social work selves and the ways in which we conceptualise the social work profession.

PERIODISATION AND SOCIAL WORK

Hopefully this book has highlighted the importance of viewing social work and the social work self through a sociological lens. Such a perspective highlights the ways in which various forces coincide to create a particular reality. What social work means today is not what social work meant 30 years ago. National and international contexts and events which occur serve to continuously shape and help to define what social work means. In the same way as our relationships with others shape who we are as a social worker, so too do these broader contexts have an impact on the profession as a whole.

In Chapter 1 we explored the historical context within which this text has been written. Some of the themes that occupy social work scholarship, practice and research are to do with risk; the role of the state; the shifting social and geographical landscape; global issues; ethical debates about the role of social work, and increased complexity to name but a few. Yet why are these things of concern to us?

As we have noted, late modernity—or contemporary life—has brought with it new challenges. The continuing improvement of technology and the speed with which it brings new products and services has had a massive impact on our lives. As little as a few generations ago, communicative technologies were very different to those used today. Email, the internet and mobile telephones have all had an impact on the ways we communicate. Such new technologies have changed the social landscape because they have led to an increase in the speed at which exchanges occur between cultural settings (for example, see Bauman 1998, 2000; Beck *et al.* 1994; Giddens 1991; Lash 1994b; Urry 2000). No longer constrained by different time zones, people are able to communicate with others around the clock: this has been argued to have an emotional and social cost (Elliott & Lemert 2006).

Additionally, increasingly people in wealthier nations have been able to travel internationally. This increase in mobility has been marked in recent years. The greater availability of affordable travel has led to a significant rise in global movements, and has earned this new social world the description 'borderless' (Urry 2000). Yet travellers do not disembed from their lived experiences once they are away from their homeplace, 'unmarked by the traces of class, gender, ethnicity, sexuality and geography' (Cresswell 1997, p. 377). The ability to travel can, on the one hand, be seen as liberating. Yet it is important to consider that increased mobility is more available to some people than to others. Additionally, people's lived experiences of the broader categories of class, gender, culture, sexual identity and geography do not disappear with travel.

As we discussed in Chapter 1, the late modern life is said to be detraditionalised. Our move away from traditional roles can be seen in the new ways we relate to one another and live out our intimate—and subsequently, family— relationships (Bauman 2003). No longer is social life regulated through tradition. This, coupled with the increased travel and global dimension which is evident in day-to-day life, has been argued to have reduced traditional boundaries. Therefore it is the very fabric of our lives which has been transformed. In this way, life is unstable. It is 'fluid' or 'liquid' (Bauman 1998, 2000) and unable to take a shape or form for very long. The 'scapes and flows' that characterise new 'mobile' lives (Urry 2000, p. 13) are in constant ebb and flow. In this scheme, '"everyday life" become[s] less clear cut' (du Gay 1993, p. 583).

Late modernity is important to consider in social work (Ferguson & Powell 2002). Yet what does this mean for social work and everyday social work practice? What impacts do increased communication, changing relationships and familial patterns and our new 'mobile' lives (Urry 2000, p. 13) have on social work? What relevance do these theories have to our work? The answers to these questions lie in how social work makes sense of the current historical period: it must both engage in debates about complexity, risk, global and environmental concerns, technology and economic shifts while at the same time being grounded by what social work is good at—fighting against inequality.

In social work we must continue to value the importance of everyday social life and understand the patterns in which our social and cultural environments shape the day-to-day level of experience. As Heaphy (2007, p. 4) notes:

> The reconstructivist theory of reflexive modernity proposed by Giddens and Beck, for example, has argued the emergence of new universalities and commonalities in global and individualized experience where there are no 'others'. This argument may be (relatively) convincing when it is focused on the abstract theoretical working out of the 'reflexivity' of modernity, but it fails to be convincing when the theory is brought down to earth and compared to other arguments about how otherness and difference are centrally important—locally and on a global scale—to shaping personal and day-to-day experience, and to strategies of power.

This means that in social work we need to engage in new movements and theories about the world around us (Dominelli 2010) and our relationships with others; we must seek to recognise that this concern fits within a particular historical point in time and therefore a critical lens helps us understand the reasons for these concerns, and finally, we must continue to address the causes of inequality and injustice in our work.

The increased use of technologies has enabled greater communication between social workers. The desire to come together as a profession and address the issue of inequality through a 'global' means has been expressed through a manifesto called 'The Global Agenda for Social Work'.

> As social workers, educators and social development practitioners, we witness the daily realities of personal, social and community challenges. We believe that now is our time to work together, at all levels, for change, for social justice, and for the universal implementation of human rights, building on the wealth of social initiatives and social movements. We, the International Federation of Social Workers (IFSW), the International Association of Schools of Social Work (IASSW), and the International Council on Social Welfare (ICSW), recognise that the past and present political, economic, cultural and social orders, shaped in specific contexts, have unequal consequences for global, national and local communities and have negative impacts on people. (www.globalsocialagenda.org)

This movement is an example of the ways in which social work is responding to the new 'liquid' environment. Following are the key areas to which this group is committing. It is useful to read through these to see how social work is responding to issues such as economic change, environmental concern, conflict and war, extreme weather events and changing social relationships and landscapes.

- The full range of human rights are available to only a minority of the world's population: unjust and poorly regulated economic systems, driven by unaccountable market forces, together with non-compliance with international standards for labour conditions and a lack of corporate social responsibility, have damaged the health and well-being of peoples and communities, causing poverty and growing inequality.
- Cultural diversity and the right to self-expression facilitate a more satisfactory intellectual, emotional, moral and spiritual existence, but these rights are in danger due to aspects of globalisation which standardise and marginalise peoples, with especially damaging consequences for indigenous and first nation peoples.
- People live in communities and thrive in the context of supportive relationships, which are being eroded by dominant economic, political and social forces; people's health and well-being suffer as a result of inequalities and unsustainable environments related to climate change, pollutants, war, natural disasters and violence to which there are inadequate international responses. Consequently, we feel compelled to advocate for a new world order which makes a reality of respect for human rights and dignity and a different structure of human relationships.

Therefore:

We commit ourselves to supporting, influencing and enabling structures and systems that positively address the root causes of oppression and inequality. We commit ourselves wholeheartedly and urgently to work together, with people who use services and with others who share our objectives and aspirations, to create a more socially-just and fair world that we will be proud to leave to future generations. We will prioritise our endeavours to these ends. (www.global socialagenda.org)

These kinds of movements demonstrate the creative ways in which the profession is moving forward and facing the challenges which present themselves, whilst remaining committed to a clearly articulated value and theory base. The commitment to social justice, eradicating systems and structures which continue to oppress others and working with and on behalf of vulnerable people is clearly articulated. However, importantly, community, social connectedness, health and well-being and self-expression are also stated as being important aspects of social life which enable individuals, families, groups and communities to thrive. Social work has a role to play not only in addressing inequality but also equally in highlighting and working to promote well-being.

Throughout this book we have seen that the answer to 'how to be a social worker' is to establish and develop one's social work self. The ways we engage in this process shape the local, national and even international social work identity. There is a school of thought within the literature about couples which argues that the ability to thrive in an intimate relationship requires people to 'hold on' to their own identities while committed to the 'couple' identity (Schnarch 1997). In this literature, 'differentiation involves balancing two basic life forces: the drive for individuality and the drive for togetherness' (Schnarch 1997, p. 55). Similarly, the ability to work with other professional groups requires social workers to 'hold on' to their own identity. The individual social work self—your individual social work self—realises the 'drive for individuality' and the collective identity of social work in its interprofessional context realises the 'drive for togetherness'. As we have seen throughout this book, this is no easy task, but one which is fraught with dilemmas, differences and points of division, as well as similarities and points of unity. The ways in which we work with other professions will continue to change. This means the trust we put in our own profession and our own practice must be present in our everyday interactions. Ultimately, it is the people we work with to whom we are committed and therefore any trust we put in our own practice and profession must be earned.

Additionally, being able to articulate the values and theories which help to propel the social work self into its role with clients helps in firming up the social work identity. In this book, the ways in which the social work self is constituted have been explored. Specifically, the following are examples of activities which help in the process of professional self-making:

- Use knowledge about one's self. This includes reflexive engagement with one's biography and the socio-cultural setting within which the self is constituted
- Acquire formal knowledge through texts, readings, research and other reports
- Engage in activities which assist in better understanding this knowledge
- Experiment in the classroom with social work skills such as communication
- Experiment (under supervision) with practice as a social work student on placement working with clients (individuals, groups, communities, globally)
- Develop one's political lens which enables power and inequality to be identified at interpersonal, local, national and global levels
- Engage with other students, academic staff and practice teachers, colleagues

How to be a Social Worker contains the idea that social workers must regain confidence in selfhood. This applies both to understanding the importance of self—how it is constituted, socially situated and contextual—as well as being able to answer the question: 'what is social work?' In answering this question, our ethical, value and theoretical foundations are revealed. Social work students beginning their studies and entry into the profession, equipped with this self-knowledge, are perfectly positioned to continue to positively shape the profession of social work and the important role it has in society.

The centrality of interaction to self-production in social work has been of key concern in this book. In other words, becoming a social worker has been argued to occur through the intersection of biography, scholarly ideas, imagination and reflexivity: none of these are possible to engage in without human interaction (Mead 1934). It is therefore imperative that social workers retain their social focus. Professional development, interaction with other professions and reflexive engagement with the self and social work itself: all of these are required in order to continue good practice and development in our field.

In this book we have seen that awareness of the interactionist nature of self is required so that we understand both who we are as a social worker and also who we are as a profession. Individuals do not come to social work with a 'clear slate'. Rather, social work students bring their own identities to their learning and to their profession. As a reminder, here is a final quote from C. Wright Mills who sums up this need to incorporate one's self into one's work:

> What this means is that you must learn to use your life experience in your intellectual work: continually to examine and interpret it. In this sense craftsmanship is the centre of yourself and you are personally involved in every intellectual product upon which you may work. (Mills 1959, p. 196)

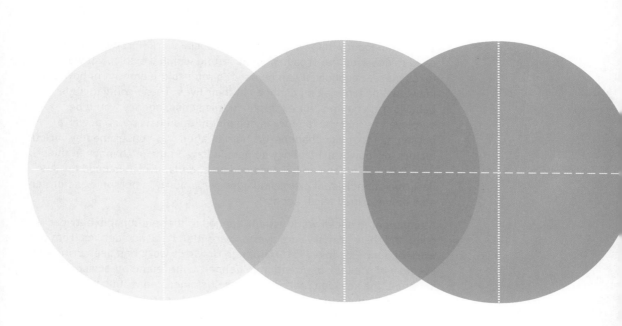

Glossary of
Key Terms

Actor
In sociology, the term 'actor' refers to individuals in society. The term is also used in social work to denote an individual.

Agency
The term 'agency' has two meanings in social work. Firstly, it can be used to describe the organisational setting within which social work takes place. Secondly, it can be used to refer to the amount of power an individual has in making changes in their lives. These could include behavioural changes, for example. In this sense, agency would be employed as follows: 'agency is dependent upon how much power a person has to make changes' or 'human agency is constrained by various factors' or 'how much agency do people have to make changes in their lives?' Social action can be classified as *agential*, which is used to describe an individual exercising agency. Similarly, a person or actor can also be described as an agent.

Attachment
Attachment in social work usually applies to the relationship between a child and their primary caregiver or parent(s). Its usage derives from the work of John Bowlby (1951). Although Bowlby's work has been criticised because of the lack of attention to gender, culture and other aspects of selfhood, the key idea that a deep and sustained connection with a caregiver is important to early life continues to persist. Giddens' (1991) concept of ontological security, for example, argues that intimate relationships formed in adulthood are affected by the level of personal security which is derived from early social interactions in the child–caregiver dyad. Theories such as this make the leap between early experiences in childhood and adult patterns of behaviour and interaction. Social workers need to be careful when applying theories about attachment. Having a nuanced understanding of the historical context within which Bowlby's empirical work and subsequent theorising was carried out helps to better understand how to apply notions of attachment to the needs of children.

Client
The term 'client' is used to depict the person or persons receiving a service from a social worker. There are various terms which mean the same as client, and these come in and out of fashion in social work. They include consumer, service user and customer. In some settings, particular language is used to describe a person receiving a service from a social worker. For example, a client of a hospital service might be referred to as a patient since this is the term used in health and allied professions.

Culture
Culture is notoriously difficult to define, and there are many social work and social science texts which discuss culture in great depth. It is important to recognise that everyone in society has a culture. Culture refers to historically significant, shared beliefs, patterns of behaviour, knowledge, customs, rituals and values. Culture is an important part of the self and is embedded in actions and social interactions. Because culture is so embedded in social interaction it can be difficult to discern and name, particularly for the dominant group in society. Recent

scholarship about culture therefore focuses on 'whiteness studies', which seek to uncover the hidden aspects of culture that are interlinked in existing systems and create inequality based on culture and race.

Detraditionalisation Detraditionalisation (Giddens 1991) refers to the gradual removal of tradition which results in people's roles, which were traditionally prescribed, being upturned. An example of detraditionalisation is the shift in gender roles in the family. Whereas a few generations ago it was common for women in western cultures to be at home raising children and participating in domestic chores, women's roles in relationships have now changed. For example, the increase in more women being in paid work has meant that the traditional role of 'housewife' has decreased. Detraditionalisation is a theory and opponents to this theory argue that society has always evolved and shifted and tradition has always been complex so this is not a new issue (Alexander 1989).

Epistemology Broadly speaking, epistemology can be described as a 'world-view'. Epistemology is a way of describing the attitude to knowledge which relates to the world around us. For example, imagine I took the view that there are universal truths and therefore believe that some things are true regardless of the context or situation or the people involved. This attitude might be summed up by saying that I had an *objectivist* epistemology. On the other hand, imagine I took the view that there are no universal truths and that people construct their own meanings in individual ways. Although these meanings may share characteristics, we all see the world in slightly—or markedly—differing ways. This way of viewing the world might be described as a *constructionist* epistemology.

Ethics A consideration of ethics means thinking about how we *should* act towards other people (Rhodes 1986, p. 21). Ethics entails thinking about what we think should occur in our behaviours towards other people. In social work, professional ethics are enshrined in our theoretical frameworks and outlined in professional codes of conduct and codes of ethics. There are many traditions which contribute to scholarship on ethics: these can come from philosophy or applied disciplines such as medical sciences and allied health.

Identity Generally speaking, 'identity' is a term used to describe who we are. The term came to prominence in the 1990s, and is used in varying disciplines (Jenkins 2000, p. 8). In contrast to the word 'self', the term identity is usually associated with a psychoanalytic or psychological tradition. Identity, for example, can be used to describe one's 'personality'.

Intimate relationship, Sexuality, Sexual identity Intimate relationships are varied but include marriages, couples living together or living apart and de facto relationships. Intimate relationships can be single sex relationships or opposite sex relationships. Couples can be committed to one another (monogamous) or not committed (non-monogamous). Sexuality refers to a range of emotions and behaviours and desires whereas sexual identity refers to particular categories which define attractions and behaviours and desires. Some sexual identities are bisexual, lesbian, gay, transgender, intersex, fluid and heterosexual.

Late modernity

Various disciplines interested in the study of social life employ periodisation which divides particular epochs into named, historically recognisable points in time. The names given to each of these periods signify particular forms of expression and resonate with a large audience. For example, the term 'postmodern' can be used to describe various things, from architecture to the design of a cereal box. The term 'late modernity' is used in this book to denote the current historical period. The term has been chosen because of its recognition within sociological literature about identity, but can just as easily be substituted with 'contemporary life' or something similar.

Norm

A norm is an unspoken social 'rule'. Norms govern the ways in which we behave towards others.

Reflexivity and reflexiveness

Reflexivity is a well-established concept in social work. Reflexivity relates to the idea that we reflect upon our social work practice to get better and better (see Schon 1983, for example). In social work, reflection is the act of thinking about an event whereas reflexivity relates to the change in action as a direct result of prior reflection. For example, a social worker may begin to facilitate a group for adult survivors of child sexual abuse. In the group the social worker is using art therapies for the first time. The session does not go well. In supervision, the social worker talks about her disappointment with using art. In thinking back and *reflecting* upon what went well and what did not go well, the social worker identifies a new approach to using the art which she plans to try in the next group. The social worker has therefore *reflected* upon her work. In a subsequent group, the social worker tries a new approach as a direct result of her supervision session in which she analysed her previous work. She changes the way she does things in the group and the way she uses art with the group members because of these insights. The social worker has therefore become *reflexive* since her present behaviour has been shaped by her *reflection*. Reflexivity involves three interrelated processes (Bogo & Vayda 1987; Schon 1983). Firstly, we think about, or reflect upon, something specific. Secondly, we critically evaluate that activity. Thirdly, we change future relations of actions based on a conscious decision to change the particular activity (Bogo & Vayda 1987). Although there is a clear difference between reflection and reflexivity in social work, there are complexities involved in the distinction between the terms in the work of George Herbert Mead and social theorists such as Anthony Giddens. Mead argues that 'reflexiveness' means being an 'other' to oneself, only through continual interaction with social processes. Mead says that 'reflexiveness', or what can be called 'reflexivity', is not merely a tool for self-fashioning but is required for social functioning (Jackson 2007, p. 8). What people think of as their 'minds' are, in fact, firmly locatable outside their selves (in contrast to psychoanalytic notions of subjectivity which see identity as related to an 'inner' world of individual thoughts and reflections): minds 'arise' only through social interactions. Mead (1934, p. 134) argues that 'reflexiveness' then, is the essential condition, within the social process, for the development of mind'. Giddens argues that in contemporary society people treat themselves as 'a project' which requires constant evaluation and improvement: this is said to occur through reflexivity (Giddens 1991). Whilst Giddens' 'extended reflexivity' (Adams 2003) means that reflexivity is linked as a product of late modernity, Mead argues that what he calls 'reflexiveness' is merely a feature of social relations. Both Giddens and Mead highlight the importance of the social setting from the onset of human life (Adams 2003, p. 232). Mead's conception of the self is neither the decentred postmodern depiction nor the psychoanalytic subject (Jackson 2007, p. 7): reflexiveness is a part of an overall process in which social interaction produces the self (Mead 1925 [2011]). Whilst it is important not to confuse or conflate these two concepts of reflexiveness and reflexivity, it can be noted for the purpose of providing a simple definition of what is meant by these in relation to sociology that they both suggest varying degrees of awareness of one's self and its relationship to the surrounding world. In social work the terms are more easily separated and distinct from one another.

Scripting

Just as a film or play is scripted, individuals may engage in acts of spontaneity akin to dramatic improvisation, but they are limited by the choices available to them. Thus, although actors can choose their scripts to some extent, their choices do not fall outside a predetermined set of actions and interactions. Scripting theory can help to make sense of the degree to which actors have agency. See also *Agency* and *Structure*

Self

Self is a way to describe who a person is. This can encompass one's attitudes, behaviours and biography and the term suggests that each person has uniqueness. Whereas 'identity can imply a fixity about who one is' (Jackson & Scott 2010a, p. 122), the term 'self' is less fixed. Thus, the use of the term self is associated with particular sociological theories such as those advanced in symbolic interactionism. The term self is primarily employed throughout this book because of its association with Meadian traditions (Mead 1934; Da Silva 2011) in which the changeable and dynamic process of sociality is central to self-making. Mead's notion of the self implies a changeable form of identity (Jackson & Scott 2010a, p. 123).

Self-making

The 'construction of the self' refers to the processes that make up or constitute the self. Throughout this book I use the term 'self-making' (Skeggs 2004) to mean this ongoing process of the constitution or 'making' of the self. These ongoing social processes are made up of various types of social interactions—from discussions with colleagues and communications with others through both verbal and non-verbal means to the intimate communications and actions between lovers.

Service user	See *Client*
Social constructionism	Social constructionism is the idea that individuals each construct the world around themselves. In this way, there is no universal 'truth' which is true for everyone.
Social work	There is much debate about what social work is and is not and this has endured throughout its history (Gibelman 1999). Social work is a broad term used to describe the professional grouping of a range of interventions at the following levels: individual, couple, family, group, community, nationally and globally/internationally. Social work is supported by clear theoretical and ethical foundations. Social work is generally conceived as being a profession which seeks to promote positive change. The particular type of work undertaken in social work is varied and depends on the context. Social workers may have skills in counselling or therapy, casework, group work, advocacy, community development, policy analysis and development and/or research.
Sociality	The notion of sociality is what is important in interactionist appreciations of the self. Sociality consists of the processes involved in social interactions. Sociality is theorised by George Herbert Mead (1934) as the process through which the self is constituted.
Socialisation	Socialisation is the process of learning about the rules which govern behaviour in a given society. Socialisation occurs primarily in childhood, but in some areas of life people become socialised in new ways. For example, social work students become socialised in social work during their studies: they learn the norms, ethics and theories which underpin the profession.
Structure	Structure, or social structure, is a concept which refers to identifiable patterns of relating in social life. In speaking about the relationship between social structure and society, Giddens (2005, p. 699) describes social structure as 'like the girders which underpin a building and hold it together'. See also *Agency*

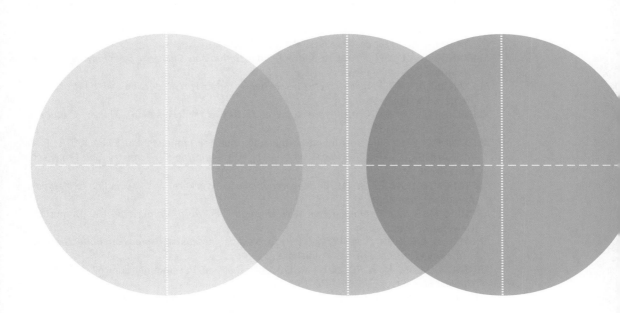

References
and Further
Reading

ADAMS, M. (2003) The reflexive self and culture: A critique. *British Journal of Sociology*, 54, 221–238.

ADAMS, R., DOMINELLI, L. & PAYNE, M. (2005) *Social Work Futures: Crossing Boundaries, Transforming Practice*. New York: Palgrave Macmillan.

ALEXANDER, J. (1989) *Structure and Meaning: Rethinking Classical Sociology*. New York: Columbia University Press.

ALEXANDER, J. (1995) *Fin-de-siecle Social Theory: Relativism, Reduction and the Problem of Reason*. London: Verso.

ALEXANDER, J. (1996) Critical reflections on 'reflexive modernisation'. *Theory, Culture & Society*, 13, 133–138.

ALEXANDER, P. (1988) Prostitution: A difficult issue for feminists. *In:* DELACOSTE, F. & ALEXANDER, P. (eds) *Sex Work: Writings by Women in the Sex Industry*. San Francisco: Cleis Press.

ALSTON, M. & BOWLES, W. (1998) *Research for Social Workers: An Introduction to Methods*. Abingdon: Routledge.

ARCHER, M. S. (2007) *Making Our Way Through the World*. Cambridge, UK: Cambridge University Press.

ARGYRIS, C. & SCHON, D. A. (1974) *Theory in Practice: Increasing Professional Effectiveness*. San Francisco: Jossey-Bass Publishers.

ARND-CADDIGAN, M. & POZZUTO, R. (2008) Use of self in relational clinical social work. *Clinical Social Work Journal*, 36, 235–243.

ATHENS, L. (2005) Mead's lost conception of society. *Symbolic Interaction*, 28, 305–325.

AULL DAVIES, C. (2008) *Reflexive Ethnography: A Guide to Researching Selves and Others*. London: Routledge.

BAILEY, D. & LIYANAGE, L. (2012) The role of the mental health social worker: Political pawns in the reconfiguration of adult health and social care. *British Journal of Social Work*, 42, 1113–1131.

BALGOPAL, P. R. & VASSIL, T. V. (1983) *Groups in Social Work: An Ecological Perspective*. New York and London: Macmillan/Collier Macmillan.

BANDURA, A. (1986) *Social Foundations of Thought and Action: A Social Cognitive Theory*. Englewood Cliffs: Prentice-Hall.

BANKS, S. (2012) *Ethics and Values in Social Work*, 4th edn. Basingstoke: Palgrave Macmillan.

BARKER, R., MILLER, S., PLACE, M. & REYNOLDS, J. (2003) Children with difficulties, parenting training and action research. *International Journal of Child and Family Welfare*, 6, 103–112.

BARNARD, A. M. (2011) The self in social work. *Work Based Learning e-Journal*, 2.

BAUMAN, Z. (1990) *Thinking Sociologically*. Oxford: Blackwell.

BAUMAN, Z. (1993) *Postmodern Ethics*. Oxford: Blackwell.

BAUMAN, Z. (1998) *Globalization: The Human Consequences*. Cambridge, UK: Polity Press.

BAUMAN, Z. (2000) *Liquid Modernity*. Cambridge, UK: Polity Press.

BAUMAN, Z. (2003) *Liquid Love: On the Frailty of Human Bonds*. Cambridge, UK: Polity Press.

BEAUCHAMP, T. L. & CHILDRESS, J. F. (1979) *Principles of Biomedical Ethics*. New York: Oxford University Press.

BEAUCHAMP, T. L. & CHILDRESS, J. F. (1989) *Principles of Biomedical Ethics*, 3rd edn. New York: Oxford University Press.

BECK, U. (1992) *Risk Society*. London: Sage Publications.

BECK, U. (1994) *Reflexive Modernization: Politics, Tradition and Aesthetics in the Modern Social Order*. Cambridge, UK: Polity Press in association with Blackwell Publishers.

BECK, U. & BECK-GERNSHEIM, E. (2001) *Individualization*. London: Sage Publications.

BECK, U. & BECK-GERNSHEIM, E. (2002) *Individualization [electronic resource]: Institutionalized Individualism and its Social and Political Consequences.* London and Thousand Oaks: Sage Publications.

BECK, U., GIDDENS, A. & LASH, S. (1999) *World Risk Society.* Malden, Mass.: Polity Press.

BECKETT, C. (2006) *Essential Theory for Social Work Practice.* London: Sage Publications.

BELLINGER, A. (2010) Talking about (re)generation: Practice learning as a site of renewal for social work. *British Journal of Social Work*, 40, 2450–2466.

BENKO, G. & STROHMAYER, U. (1997) *Space and Social Theory: Interpreting Modernity and Postmodernity.* Oxford, UK and Malden, Mass.: Blackwell Publishers.

BERGER, P. L. (1971) *The Social Construction of Reality: A Treatise in the Sociology of Knowledge.* Harmondsworth: Penguin.

BERGER, P. L. & LUCKMANN, T. (1973) *The Social Construction of Reality: A Treatise in the Sociology of Knowledge.* Middlesex: Penguin Books.

BERK, L. (2010) *Exploring Lifespan Development*, 2nd edn. Boston: Allyn & Bacon.

BHIMJI, F. (2009) Identities and agency in religious spheres: A study of British Muslim women's experience. *Gender, Place & Culture*, 16, 365–380.

BIERNACKI, P. & WALDORF, D. (1981) Snowball sampling. *Sociological Methods and Research*, 10, 141–163.

BLANKSBY, P. E. & BARBER, J. G. (2005) *SPSS for Social Workers: An Introductory Workbook.* Boston: Pearson.

BLIWISE, N. G. (1999) Securing attachment theory's potential. *Feminism and Psychology*, 9, 43–52.

BLOOM, L. (1998) *Under the Sign of Hope: Feminist Methodology and Narrative.* Albany: State University of New York Press.

BOGO, M. & VAYDA, E. (1987) *The Practice of Field Instruction in Social Work.* Toronto: University of Toronto Press.

BONDI, L. & BURMAN, E. (2001) Women and mental health: A feminist review. *Feminist Review*, 68, 6–33.

BOYD, D. A. & BEE, H. L. (2011) *Lifespan Development.* Boston: Pearson.

BOWLBY, J. (1951) *Maternal Care and Mental Health.* New York: Schoken.

BOWLES, W., COLLINGRIDGE, M., CURRY, S. & VALENTINE, B. (2006) *Ethical Practice in Social Work: An Applied Approach.* Crows Nest: Allen & Unwin.

BRONSTEIN, L. R. (2003) A model for interdisciplinary collaboration. *Social Work*, 48, 297–306.

BROWNMILLER, S. (1976) *Against Our Will: Men, Women and Rape.* Harmondsworth: Penguin.

BRUNER, C. (1991) *Ten Questions and Answers to Help Policy Makers Improve Children's Services.* Washington, DC: Education and Human Services Consortium.

BRYMAN, A. (1984) The debate about quantitative and qualitative research: A question or epistemology? *British Journal of Sociology*, 35(1) (March).

BUCHANAN, F. (2008) *Mother and Infant Attachment Theory and Domestic Violence: Crossing the Divide.* Sydney: Australian Domestic and Family Violence Clearinghouse.

BUDGEON, S. & ROSENEIL, S. (2004) Editors' introduction: Beyond the conventional family. *Current Sociology*, 52, 127–134.

BURR, J. (2009) Exploring reflective subjectivity through the construction of the 'ethical other' in interview transcripts. *Sociology*, 43, 323–339.

BUTLER, J. P. (1993) *Bodies that Matter: On the Discursive Limits of "Sex".* New York: Routledge.

BYWATERS, P. (1986) Social work and the medical profession: Arguments against unconditional collaboration. *British Journal of Social Work*, 16, 661–677.

BYWATERS, P. (2009) Tackling inequalities in health: A global challenge for social work. *British Journal of Social Work*, 39, 353–367.

CARMICHAEL, L. (1970a) *Carmichael's Manual of Child Psychology*, 3rd edn. New York: Wiley.

CARMICHAEL, L. (1970b) Piaget's theory. *In:* MUSSEN, P. H. (ed.) *Carmichael's Manual of Child Psychology*, 3rd edn. New York: Wiley.

CARPENTER, J., SCHNEIDER, H., BRANDON, T. & WOOFF, D. (2003) Working in multidisciplinary community mental health teams: The impact on social workers and health professionals of integrated mental health care. *British Journal of Social Work*, 33, 1081–1103.

CARROLL, J. (2007) *The Existential Jesus*. Carlton North, Vic.: Scribe Publications.

CHENOWETH, L. & MCAULIFFE, D. (2005) *The Road to Social Work and Human Service Provision: An Introductory Text*. Southbank: Thomson.

CHISHOLM, D. (2008) Climbing like a girl: An exemplary adventure in feminist phenomenology. *Hypatia*, 23, 9–40.

CLEAK, H. & WILSON, J. (2004) *Making the Most of Field Placement*. Australia, Brazil, Japan, Korea, Mexico, Singapore, Spain, United Kingdom, United States. Sydney: Cengage Learning Australia Pty Ltd.

CLEAK, H., HAWKINS, L. & HESS, L. (2000) Innovative field options. *In:* COOPER, L. & BRIGGS, L. (eds) *Fieldwork in the Human Services*. St Leonards: Allen & Unwin.

CLEAVER, H., NICHOLSON, D., TARR, S. & CLEAVER, D. (2007) *Child Protection, Domestic Violence and Parental Substance Misuse: Family Experiences and Effective Practice*. London and Philadelphia: Kingsley Publishers.

COHEN, E. (1992) Pilgrimage centers: Concentric and excentric. *Annals of Tourism Research*, 19, 33–50.

COHEN, E. D. & COHEN, G. S. (1999) *The Virtuous Therapist: Ethical Practice of Counselling and Psychotherapy*. Belmont: Wadsworth Publishing Company.

COLOMBO, M. (2003) Reflexivity and narratives in action research: A discursive approach. *Forum: Qualitative Social Research*, 4.

COMPTON, B. R. & GALAWAY, B. (1989) *Social Work Processes*, 5th edn. Pacific Grove: Brooks/Cole Publishing Company.

COMPTON, B. R. & GALAWAY, B. (1999) *Social Work Processes*, 6th edn. Belmont: Brooks/Cole Publishing.

COOPER, L. & BRIGGS, L. E. (eds) (2000) *Fieldwork in the Human Services: Theory and Practice for Field Educators, Practice Teachers and Supervisors*. St Leonards: Allen & Unwin.

COULSHED, V. & ORME, J. (2012) *Social Work Practice*, 5th edn. Basingstoke: Palgrave Macmillan.

COURNOYER, B. (2010) *The Social Work Skills Workbook*, 6th edn. Florence: Cengage Learning Inc.

CRESSWELL, T. (1997) Imagining the nomad: Mobility and the post modern perspective. *In:* BENKO, G. & STROHMAYER, U. (eds) *Space and Social Theory: Interpreting Modernity and Postmodernity*. Oxford: Blackwell.

CRISP, B. R. (2010) *Spirituality in Social Work*. Surrey: Ashgate.

CROOK, S. (1998) Minotaurs and other monsters: 'Everyday life' in recent social theory. *Sociology*, 32, 523–540.

CROSSLEY, N. (2001) *The Social Body: Habit, Identity and Desire*. London: Sage Publications.

CROTTY, M. (2007) *The Foundations of Social Research: Meaning and Perspective in the Research Process*. London: Sage Publications.

CUNNINGHAM, J. & CUNNINGHAM, S. (2008) *Sociology and Social Work*. Exeter: Learning Matters Ltd.

CURTIS, L., MORIARTY, J. & NETTEN, A. (2010) The expected working life of a social worker. *British Journal of Social Work*, 40, 1628–1643.

DA SILVA, F. C. (ed.) (2011) *G. H. Mead: A Reader*. London: Routledge.

DAVIES, M. (ed.) (2012) *Social Work with Children and Families*. Basingstoke: Palgrave Macmillan.

D'CRUZ, H. & JONES, M. (2004) *Social Work Research: Ethical and Political Contexts*. London: Sage Publications.

DENSCOMBE, M. (1998) *The Good Research Guide: For Small-scale Social Research Projects*. Buckingham: Open University Press.

DENZIN, N. K. (1978) *Sociological Methods: A Sourcebook*. New York: McGraw Hill.

DEWANE, C. (2006) Use of self: A primer revisited. *Clinical Social Work Journal*, 34, 543–558.

DICKENSON, D., JOHNSON, M. & KATZ, J. S. (eds) (2000) *Death, Dying and Bereavement*, 2nd edn. London, Thousand Oaks, New Delhi: Sage Publications in association with the Open University.

DIXON, J. (2012) Effective strategies for communication? Student views of a communication skills course eleven years on. *British Journal of Social Work*.

DODD, S. J. & JONES, M. (2004) *Practice-based Research in Social Work: A Guide for Reluctant Researchers*. Abingdon: Routledge.

DOEL, M. (2010) *Social Work Placements: A Traveller's Guide*. Abingdon: Routledge.

DOKA, K. J. (ed.) (1989) *Disenfranchised Grief: Recognizing Hidden Sorrow*. Lexington: Lexington Books.

DOKA, K. J. (ed.) (2002) *Disenfranchised Grief: New Directions, Challenges, and Strategies for Practice*. Champaign: Research Press.

DOMINELLI, L. (1989) Betrayal of trust: A feminist analysis of power relationships in incest abuse and its relevance for social work practice. *British Journal of Social Work*, 19, 291–307.

DOMINELLI, L. (2002) *Feminist Social Work: Theory and Practice*. Basingstoke: Palgrave Macmillan.

DOMINELLI, L. (2003) *Anti-oppressive Social Work Theory and Practice*. Basingstoke: Palgrave Macmillan.

DOMINELLI, L. (2004) *Social Work: Theory and Practice for a Changing Profession*. Oxford: Polity Press.

DOMINELLI, L. (2010) *Social Work in a Globalizing World*. Cambridge, UK: Polity Press.

DU GAY, P. (1993) 'Numbers and souls': Retailing and the de-differentiation of economy and culture. *British Journal of Sociology*, 44, 563–587.

DUNK, P. (2007) Everyday sexuality and social work: Locating sexuality in professional practice and education. *Social Work and Society*, 5, 135–142.

DUNK-WEST, P. (2011) Everyday sexuality and identity: De-differentiating the sexual self in social work. *In:* DUNK-WEST, P. & HAFFORD-LETCHFIELD, T. (eds) *Sexual Identities and Sexuality in Social Work: Research and Reflections from Women in the Field*. Surrey: Ashgate.

DUNK-WEST, P. & HAFFORD-LETCHFIELD, T. (eds) (2011) *Sexual Identities and Sexuality in Social Work: Research and Reflections from Women in the Field*. Surrey: Ashgate.

DUNK-WEST, P. & VERITY, F. forthcoming. *Sociological Social Work*. Surrey: Ashgate.

DUTTON, J. E., ROBERTS, L. & MORGANBEDNAR, J. (2010) Pathways for positive identity construction at work: Four types of positive identity and the building of social resources. *Academy of Management Review*, 35, 265–293.

DYSON, S. (2006) *Social Theory and Applied Health Research*. Maidenhead: Open University Press.

EGAN, G. (2006) *Essentials of Skilled Helping, Managing Problems, Developing Opportunities*. Canada: Thomson Wadsworth.

ELLIOTT, A. (1996) *Subject to Ourselves: Social Theory, Psychoanalysis and Postmodernity.* Cambridge, UK: Polity Press.

ELLIOTT, A. (2001) Sexualities: Social theory and the crisis of identity. *In:* RITZER, G. & SMART, B. (eds) *Handbook of Social Theory.* London: Sage Publications.

ELLIOTT, A. (2005) The constitution of the subject. *European Journal of Social Theory*, 8, 25–42.

ELLIOTT, A. & LEMERT, C. (2006) *The New Individualism: The Emotional Costs of Globalization.* Abingdon: Routledge.

ERIKSON, E. H. (1968) *Identity, Youth and Crisis.* New York: W. W. Norton.

EVA, K. W. & REGEHR, G. (2008) "I'll never play professional football" and other fallacies of self-assessment. *Journal of Continuing Education in the Health Professions*, 28, 14–19.

EVANS, S., HILLS, S. & ORME, J. (2012) Doing more for less? Developing sustainable systems of social care in the context of climate change and public spending cuts. *British Journal of Social Work*, 42, 744–764.

EVERITT, A., HARDIKER, P., LITTLEWOOD, J. & MULLENDER, A. (1992) *Applied Research for Better Practice.* Basingstoke: Macmillan.

FERGUSON, H. (2001) Social work, individualization and life politics. *British Journal of Social Work*, 31, 41–55.

FERGUSON, H. (2009) Driven to care: The car, automobility and social work. *Mobilities*, 4, 275–293.

FERGUSON, H. (2011) *Child Protection Practice.* Basingstoke: Palgrave Macmillan.

FERGUSON, H. & POWELL, F. W. (2002) Social work in late-modern Ireland. *In:* PAYNE, M. & SHARDLOW, S. (eds) *Social Work in the British Isles.* London: Jessica Kingsley.

FIELDING, N. (1996) Qualitative Interviewing. *In:* GILBERT, N. (ed.) *Researching Social Life.* London: Sage Publications.

FOOK, J. (1991) Is casework dead? A study of the current curriculum in Australia. *Australian Social Work*, 44, 19–28.

FOOK, J. (1993) *Radical Casework: A Theory of Practice.* St Leonards: Allen & Unwin.

FOOK, J. (1999) Critical reflexivity in education and practice. *In:* PEASE, B. & FOOK, J. (eds) *Transforming Social Work Practice: Postmodern Critical Perspectives.* St Leonards: Allen & Unwin.

FOOK, J. (2012) *Social Work: Critical Theory and Practice*, 2nd edn. London: Sage Publications.

FORTE, J. A. (2004a) Symbolic interactionism and social work: A forgotten legacy, Part 1. *Families in Society*, 85, 391–400.

FORTE, J. A. (2004b) Symbolic interactionism and social work: A forgotten legacy, Part 2. *Families in Society*, 85, 521–530.

FRANZBLAU, S. H. (1999) Historicizing attachment theory: Binding the ties that bind. *Feminism and Psychology*, 9, 22–31.

FREUD, S. (1914) *Psychopathology of Everyday Life.* [S.l.], [s.n.].

FREUD, S. (1949) *An Outline of Psychoanalysis.* New York: W. W. Norton.

FREUD, S. (1965) *Three Essays on the Theory of Sexuality.* [New York], Avon.

FRIEDAN, B. (1965) *The Feminine Mystique.* Harmondsworth: Penguin Books.

FUREDI, F. (2004) *Therapy Culture: Cultivating Vulnerability in an Uncertain Age.* London: Routledge.

GAGNON, J. H. (1999) Sexual conduct: As today's memory serves. *Sexualities*, 2, 115–126.

GAGNON, J. & SIMON, W. (1973) *Sexual Conduct: The Social Sources of Human Sexuality.* Chicago: Aldine.

GAGNON, J. & SIMON, W. (2011) *Sexual Conduct: The Social Sources of Human Sexuality*, 2nd edn, 3rd printing. New Brunswick, USA and London, UK: Aldine Transaction, A Division of Transaction Publishers.

GANZER, C. (2007) The use of self from a relational perspective. *Clinical Social Work Journal*, 35, 117–123.

GARDINER, M. (2004) Everyday utopianism. *Cultural Studies*, 18, 228–254.

GARFINKEL, H. (1984) *Studies in Ethnomethodology*. Cambridge, UK: Polity Press.

GARRETT, P. M. (2012) Re-enchanting social work? The emerging 'spirit' of social work in an age of economic crisis. *British Journal of Social Work*.

GAUNTLETT, D. (2007) *Creative Explorations: New Approaches to Identities and Audiences*. London: Routledge.

GAUNTLETT, D. (2011) *Making is Connecting: The Social Meaning of Creativity, From DIY to Knitting to YouTube and Web 2.0*. Cambridge, UK: Polity Press.

GAVRON, H. (1966) *The Captive Wife: Conflicts of Housebound Mothers*. London: Routledge & Kegan Paul.

GEERTZ, C. (1973) *The Interpretation of Cultures*. New York: Basic Books.

GERMAIN, C. B. & GITTERMAN, A. (1980) *The Life Model of Social Work Practice*. New York: Columbia University Press.

GIBELMAN, M. (1999) The search for identity: Defining social work—past, present, future. *Social Work*, 44, 298–310.

GIDDENS, A. (1976) *New Rules of Sociological Method: A Positive Critique of Interpretative Sociologies*. London: Hutchinson.

GIDDENS, A. (1979) *Central Problems in Social Theory: Action, Structure, and Contradiction in Social Analysis*. London: Macmillan.

GIDDENS, A. (1984) *The Constitution of Society: Outline of the Theory of Structuration*. Berkeley: University of California Press.

GIDDENS, A. (1990) *The Consequences of Modernity*. Stanford: Stanford University Press.

GIDDENS, A. (1991) *Modernity and Self-identity: Self and Society in the Late Modern Age*. Cambridge, UK: Polity Press.

GIDDENS, A. (1992) *The Transformation of Intimacy: Sexuality, Love and Eroticism in Modern Societies*. Cambridge, UK: Polity Press.

GIDDENS, A. (2005) *Sociology*, 4th edn. Cambridge, UK: Polity Press.

GILBERT, N. (2001) *Researching Social Life*, 2nd edn. London: Sage Publications.

GILLIGAN, C. (1982) *In a Different Voice: Psychological Theory and Women's Development*. Cambridge, Mass.: Harvard University Press.

GOLDACRE, B. (2012) *Bad Pharma: How Drug Companies Mislead Doctors and Harm Patients*. London: Fourth Estate.

GOLDEN, A.-M. J. & DALGLEISH, T. (2012) Facets of pejorative self-processing in complicated grief. *Journal of Consulting and Clinical Psychology*, 80, 512–524.

GOTT, M. (2006) Sexual health and the new ageing. *Age and Ageing*, 35, 106–107.

GRAHAM, J. R. & SHIER, M. L. (2010) The social work profession and subjective well-being: The impact of a profession on overall subjective well-being. *British Journal of Social Work*, 40, 1553–1572.

GRAY, M., WEBB, S. A. & MIDGLEY, J. O. (eds) (2012) *The Sage Handbook of Social Work*. London: Sage Publications.

GREEN, A. I. (2007) Queer theory and sociology: Locating the subject and the self in sexuality studies. *Sociological Theory*, 25, 26–45.

GREEN, L. (2010) *Understanding the Life Course: Sociological and Psychological Perspectives*. Cambridge, UK: Polity Press.

GREER, G. (1970) *The Female Eunuch*. London: MacGibbon & Kee.

GROSZ, E. A. (1994) *Volatile Bodies: Toward a Corporeal Feminism*. St Leonards: Allen & Unwin.

HAINE, R. A., SAYERS, T., SANDLER, I. N. & WOLCHIK, S. A. (2008) Evidence-based practices for parentally bereaved children and their families. *Professional Psychology: Research and Practice*, 39, 113–121.

HAMILTON, G. (1954) Self-awareness in professional education. *Social Casework*, 35, 371–379.

HANDEL, W. (2003) Pragmatic conventions: A frame for a theory of action and interaction. *Sociological Quarterly*, 44, 133–157.

HARDWICK, L. & WORSLEY, A. (2011) *Doing Social Work Research*. London: Sage Publications.

HAWKES, G. (2004) *Sex and Pleasure in Western Culture*. Cambridge, UK: Polity Press.

HEALY, K. (2012) *Social Work Methods and Skills: The Essential Foundations of Practice*. Basingstoke: Palgrave Macmillan.

HEALY, K. & MULHOLLAND, J. (2012) *Writing Skills for Social Workers*, 2nd edn. London: Sage Publications.

HEAP, C. (2003) The city as a sexual laboratory: The queer heritage of the Chicago School. *Qualitative Sociology*, 26, 457–487.

HEAPHY, B. (2007) *Late Modernity and Social Change: Reconstructing Social and Personal Life*. Abingdon: Routledge.

HENN, M. W., WEINSTEIN, M. & FOARD, N. (2009) *A Critical Introduction to Social Research*, 2nd edn. London: Sage Publications.

HEYDT, M. J. & SHERMAN, E. (2005) Conscious use of self: Tuning the instrument of social work practice with cultural competence. *The Journal of Baccalaureate Social Work*, 10.

HOLMES, M. (2006) Love lives at a distance: Distance relationships over the lifecourse. *Sociological Research online*.

HOLMES, M. (2007) *What is Gender? Sociological Approaches*. London, Thousand Oaks, New Delhi, Singapore: Sage Publications.

HOLMES, M., BEASLEY, C. & BROOK, H. (2011) Guest editorial. *Australian Feminist Studies*, 26, 3–7.

HOLSTEIN, J. A. & GUBRIUM, J. F. (2002) *Handbook of Interview Research: Context and Method*. Thousand Oaks: Sage Publications.

HOLSTEIN, J. A. & GUBRIUM, J. F. (2011) Animating interview narratives. *In:* SILVERMAN, D. (ed.) *Qualitative Research*. London: Sage Publications.

HOOKS, B. (1986) Sisterhood: Political solidarity between women. *Feminist Review*, 23, Socialist Feminism—Out of the Blue (Summer), 125–138.

HOUSTON, S. (2010) Beyond homo economicus: Recognition, self-realization and social work. *British Journal of Social Work*, 40, 841–857.

HUGMAN, R. (2005) *New Approaches in Ethics for the Caring Professions*. Basingstoke: Palgrave Macmillan.

HUGMAN, R. (2009) But is it social work? Some reflections on mistaken identities. *British Journal of Social Work*, 39, 1138–1153.

HUGMAN, R. & SMITH, D. (eds) (2005) *Ethical Issues in Social Work*. Abingdon: Routledge.

HUMPHREY, G. M. & ZIMPFER, D. G. (2008) *Counselling for Grief and Bereavement*, 2nd edn. London, Thousand Oaks, New Delhi, Singapore: Sage Publications.

HUNTINGTON, J. (1981) *Social Work and General Medical Practice*. London: George Allen & Unwin.

IFE, J. (2001) *Human Rights in Social Work: Towards a Rights-based Practice*. Cambridge, UK: Cambridge University Press.

IFE, J. (2008) *Human Rights and Social Work: Towards Rights-based Practice*. Cambridge, UK: Cambridge University Press.

IFSW (2012) *Definition of Social Work* [Online]. International Federation of Social Workers. Available at: http://ifsw.org/policies/definition-of-social-work/.

INHELDER, B. (1964) *The Early Growth of Logic in the Child: Classification and Seriation.* London: Routledge & Kegan Paul.

IRIGARAY, L. (1985) *This Sex Which is Not One.* Ithaca: Cornell University Press.

JACKSON, S. (1999) Feminist sociology and sociological feminism: Recovering the social in feminist thought. *Sociological Research Online*, 4.

JACKSON, S. (2007) The sexual self in late modernity. *In:* KIMMEL, M. (ed.) *The Sexual Self: The Construction of Sexual Scripts.* Nashville: Vanderbilt University Press.

JACKSON, S. (2008) Ordinary sex. *Sexualities*, 11, 33–37.

JACKSON, S. (2011) Material feminism, pragmatism and the sexual self in global late modernity. *In:* JONASDITTOR, A. G., BRYSON, V. & JONES, K. B. (eds) *Sexuality, Gender and Power: Intersectional and Transnational Perspectives.* New York: Routledge.

JACKSON, S. & SCOTT, S. (1996) *Feminism and Sexuality: A Reader.* Edinburgh: Edinburgh University Press.

JACKSON, S. & SCOTT, S. (2007) Faking like a woman? Towards an interpretive theorization of sexual pleasure. *Body & Society*, 13, 95–116.

JACKSON, S. & SCOTT, S. (2010a) *Theorizing Sexuality.* Maidenhead: Open University Press.

JACKSON, S. & SCOTT, S. (2010b) Rehabilitating interactionism for a feminist sociology of sexuality. *Sociology*, 44, 811–826.

JAMIESON, L. (1998) *Intimacy: Personal Relationships in Modern Societies.* Cambridge, UK: Polity Press.

JENKINS, R. (2000) Categorization: Identity, social process and epistemology. *Current Sociology*, 48, 7–25.

JOAS, H. (1997) *G. H. Mead: A Contemporary Re-examination of His Thought.* Cambridge, Mass.: MIT Press.

JONASDITTOR, A. G., BRYSON, V. & JONES, K. B. (eds) (2011) *Sexuality, Gender and Power: Intersectional and Transnational Perspectives.* New York: Routledge.

JONES, L. & GREEN, J. (2006) Shifting discourses of professionalism: A case study of general practitioners in the United Kingdom. *Sociology of Health & Illness*, 28, 927–950.

JORDAN, B. (2012) Making sense of the 'Big Society': Social work and the moral order. *Journal of Social Work*, 12, 630–646.

KADUSHIN, A. (1976) *Supervision in Social Work.* New York: Columbia University Press.

KATZ, J. (1976) *Gay American History: Lesbians and Gay Men in the U.S.A.: A Documentary.* New York: Crowell.

KESSLER, S. J. & MCKENNA, W. (1985) *Gender: An Ethnomethodological Approach.* Chicago: University of Chicago Press.

KIMMEL, M. (ed.) (2006) *The Sexual Self: The Construction of Sexual Scripts.* Nashville: Vanderbilt University Press.

KING, A. (2009) Overcoming structure and agency. *Journal of Classical Sociology*, 9, 260–288.

KINSLEY, A. C. (1953) *Sexual Behavior in the Human Female.* Philadelphia: Saunders.

KOLB, D. A. (1984) *Experiential Learning: Experience as the Source of Learning and Development.* Englewood Cliffs: Prentice-Hall Inc.

KONDRAT, M. E. (2002) Actor-centered social work: Re-visioning 'person-in-environment' through a critical theory lens. *Social Work*, 47, 435–448.

KRISTEVA, J. (1991) *Strangers to Ourselves.* New York: Harvester Wheatsheaf.

LAM, C. M., WONG, H. & LEUNG, T. T. F. (2007) An unfinished reflexive journey: Social work students' reflection on their placement experiences. *British Journal of Social Work*, 37, 91–105.

LAMBERT, M. J. & BARLEY, D. E. (2001) Research summary on the therapeutic relationship and psychotherapy outcome. *Psychotherapy: Theory, Research, Practice, Training*, 38, 357–361.

LASCH, C. (1979) *The Culture of Narcissism: American Life in an Age of Diminishing Expectations*. New York: W. W. Norton.

LASH, S. (1988) Discourse or figure? Postmodernism as a 'regime of signification'. *Theory, Culture & Society*, 5, 311–336.

LASH, S. (1994a) *Economies of Signs and Space*. London: Sage Publications.

LASH, S. (1994b) Reflexivity and its doubles: Structure, aesthetics, community. *In:* BECK, U., GIDDENS, A. & LASH, S. (eds) *Reflexive Modernization*. Cambridge, UK: Polity Press.

LASH, S. (2001) Technological forms of life. *Theory, Culture & Society*, 18, 105–120.

LASH, S. (2003) Reflexivity as non-linearity. *Theory, Culture & Society*, 20, 49–57.

LAURENTIS, T. (1991) Queer theory, lesbian and gay studies. *Differences: A Journal of Feminist Cultural Studies*, 3, iii–xviii.

LEE, J. (1994) *The Empowerment Approach to Social Work Practice*. New York: Columbia University Press.

LEFEVRE, H. (1992) *Critique of Everyday Life*. London: Verso.

LEFEVRE, M. (2010) *Communicating with Children and Young People: Making a Difference*. Bristol: The Policy Press.

LEMING, M. R. & DICKINSON, G. E. (2002) *Understanding Dying, Death and Bereavement*, 5th edn. Fort Worth: Harcourt College Publishers.

LETHERBY, G. (2003) *Feminist Research in Theory and Practice*. Philadelphia: Open University Press.

LEVER, J. (1978) Sex differences in the complexity of children's play and games. *American Sociological Review*, 43, 471–483.

LEVER-TRACY, C. (ed.) (2010) *Routledge Handbook of Climate Change and Society*. New York: Routledge.

LEYS, R. (1993) Mead's voices: Imitation as foundation, or, the struggle against mimesis. *Critical Inquiry*, 19, 277–307.

LIAMPUTTONG, P. & EZZY, D. (2006) *Qualitative Research Methods*. South Melbourne: Oxford University Press.

LILJEGREN, A. (2011) Pragmatic professionalism: Micro-level discourse in social work. *European Journal of Social Work*, 15, 295–312.

LISHMAN, J. (2009) *Communication in Social Work*, 2nd edn. Basingstoke: Palgrave Macmillan.

LOEWENBERG, F. M., DOLGOFF, R. & HARRINGTON, D. (2000) *Ethical Decisions for Social Work Practice*. Itasca: Peacock Publishers, Inc.

LOMAX, C., JONES, K., LEIGH, S. & GAY, C. (2010) *Surviving your Social Work Placement*. Basingstoke: Palgrave Macmillan.

LUHMANN, N. (1977) Differentiation of society. *Canadian Journal of Sociology/Cahiers canadiens de sociologie*, 2, 29–53.

LUHMANN, N. (1984) The self description of society: Crisis fashion and sociological theory. *International Journal of Comparative Sociology*, XXV, 59–72.

LUHMANN, N. (1986) *Love as Passion: The Codification of Intimacy*. Cambridge, UK: Polity Press.

LYMBERY, M. (2006) United we stand? Partnership working in health and social care and the role of social work in services for older people. *British Journal of Social Work*, 36, 1119–1134.

LYMBERY, M. (2012) Social work and personalisation: Fracturing the bureau-professional compact? *British Journal of Social Work*.

LYNN, R. (2010) Mindfulness in social work education. *Social Work Education*, 29, 289–304.

MACINTYRE, G. & PAUL, S. (2012) Teaching research in social work: Capacity and challenge. *British Journal of Social Work*.

MACKEY, R. A. (2008) Toward an integration of ideas about the self for the practice of clinical social work. *Clinical Social Work Journal*, 36, 225–234.

MACKINNON, C. (1982) Feminism, Marxism, method and the State: An agenda for theory. *Signs*, 7, 515–544.

MACKINNON, C. A. (1989) *Toward a Feminist Theory of the State*. Cambridge, Mass.: Harvard University Press.

MACLAREN, C. (2008) Use of self in cognitive behavioral therapy. *Clinical Social Work Journal*, 36, 245–253.

MAINES, D. R. & MARKOWITZ, M. A. (1979) Elements of the perpetuation of dependency in a psychiatric halfway house. *Journal of Sociology and Social Welfare*, 6, 52–69.

MALINOWSKI, B. (1927) *Sex and Repression in Savage Society*. London: Kegan Paul.

MALINOWSKI, B. (1929) *The Sexual Life of Savages in North-western Melanesia: An ethnographic account of courtship, marriage and family life among the natives of the Trobriand Islands, British New Guinea*. New York: Eugenics Publishing.

MANDELL, D. (2008) Power, care and vulnerability: Considering use of self in child welfare work. *Journal of Social Work Practice*, 22, 235–248.

MANGAN, J. A. & NAURIGHT, J. (eds) (2000) *Sport in Australasian Society: Past and Present*. London: F. Cass.

MANTLE, G., WILLIAMS, I., LESLIE, J., PARSONS, S. & SHAFFER, R. (2008) Beyond assessment: Social work intervention in family court enquiries. *British Journal of Social Work*, 38, 431–443.

MARTIN, J. (2006) Reinterpreting internalization and agency through G.H. Mead's perspectival realism. *Human Development*, 49, 65–86.

MAYWALD, S. (2000) Two pedagogical approaches to group supervision in the human services. *In:* COOPER, L. & BRIGGS, L. (eds) *Fieldwork in the Human Services*. Sydney: Allen & Unwin.

MCLAUGHLIN, H. (2012) *Understanding Social Work Research*, 2nd edn. London: Sage Publications.

MCNAY, L. (1992) *Foucault and Feminism: Power, Gender and the Self*. Cambridge, UK: Polity Press.

MCNAY, L. (1994) *Foucault: A Critical Introduction*. Cambridge, UK: Polity Press in association with Blackwell Publishers.

MCNAY, L. (2000) *Gender and Agency: Reconfiguring the Subject in Feminist and Social Theory*. Malden, Mass.: Polity Press.

MCTIGHE, J. P. (2011) Teaching the use of self through the process of clinical supervision. *Clinical Social Work Journal*, 39, 301–307.

MEAD, G. H. (1913) [2011]. The social self. *In:* DA SILVA, F. C. (ed.) *G. H. Mead: A Reader*. Abingdon: Routledge.

MEAD, G. H. (1922) [2011]. A behavioristic account of the significant symbol. *In:* DA SILVA, F. C. (ed.) *G. H. Mead: A Reader*. Abingdon: Routledge.

MEAD, G. H. (1925) [2011]. The genesis of the self and social control. *In:* DA SILVA, F. C. (ed.) *G. H. Mead: A Reader*. Abingdon: Routledge.

MEAD, G. H. (1934) *Mind, Self and Society from the Standpoint of a Social Behaviourist*. Chicago: Chicago University Press.

MELTON, J. G. (2007) Perspective: New new religions: revisiting a concept. *Nova Religio: The Journal of Alternative and Emergent Religions*, 10, 103–112.

MIEHLS, D. & MOFFATT, K. (2000) Constructing social work identity based on the reflexive self. *British Journal of Social Work*, 30, 339–348.

MILLER, W. R. (2003) Commentary. *Addiction*, 98, 5.

MILLETT, K. (1970) *Sexual Politics*. PhD 0265025, Columbia University.

MILLETT, K. (1972) *Sexual Politics*. London: Abacus.

MILLS, C. (1958) *The Causes of World War Three*. New York: Simon & Schuster.

MILLS, C. & SCHNEIDER, H. (1948) *The New Men of Power: America's Labor Leaders*. New York: Harcourt Brace and Co.

MILLS, C. W. (1951) *White Collar: The American Middle Classes*. New York: Oxford University Press.

MILLS, C. W. (1956) *The Power Elite*. New York: Oxford University Press.

MILLS, C. W. (1958) The structure of power in American society. *British Journal of Sociology*, 9, 29–41.

MILLS, C. W. (1959) *The Sociological Imagination*. New York: Oxford University Press.

MILLS, C. W. (1962) *The Marxists*. New York: Dell Publishing. Also Harmondsworth: Penguin (1962/63).

MILLS, C. W. (1963) *Power, Politics, and People*. New York: Ballantine Books.

MILLS, C. W. (1964) *Sociology and Pragmatism: The Higher Learning in America*. New York: Paine-Whitman Publishers.

MILLS, C. W. (2000) *The Sociological Imagination*. New York: Oxford University Press.

MILNER, J. & O'BYRNE, P. (2002) *Assessment in Social Work*. Basingstoke: Palgrave Macmillan.

MINTY, B. & PATTINSON, G. (1994) The nature of child neglect. *British Journal of Social Work*, 24, 733–747.

MITCHELL, J. (1974) *Psychoanalysis and Feminism*. London: Allen Lane.

MOON, D. (2008) Culture and the sociology of sexuality: It's only natural? *Annals of the American Academy of Political and Social Science*, 619, 183–205.

MORGAN, A. (2000) *What is Narrative Therapy? An Easy-to-read Introduction*. Adelaide, South Australia: Dulwich Centre Publications.

MORRIS, A. (2008) Too attached to attachment theory? *In:* PORTER, M. & KELSO, J. (eds) *Theorising and Representing Maternal Realities*. Newcastle: Cambridge Scholars Publications.

MORRIS, L. (2012) Citizenship and human rights: Ideals and actualities. *British Journal of Sociology*, 63, 39–46.

MORRISSEY, G. & HIGGS, J. (2006) Phenomenological research and adolescent female sexuality: Discoveries and applications. *The Qualitative Report*, 11, 161–181.

MULHOLLAND, M. (2011) When porno meets hetero. *Australian Feminist Studies*, 26, 119–135.

MULLALY, R. P. (1997) *Structural Social Work: Ideology, Theory and Practice*, 2nd edn. Toronto, New York: Oxford University Press.

MUNRO, E. (2011) *The Munro Review of Child Protection: Final Report – A Child-centred System*. London: Department for Education.

NAYAK, A. & KEHILY, M. J. (2006) Gender undone: Subversion, regulation and embodiment in the work of Judith Butler. *British Journal of Sociology of Education*, 27, 459–472.

NEIL, A. L. & CHRISTENSEN, H. (2007) Australian school-based prevention and early intervention programs for anxiety and depression: A systematic review. *Medical Journal of Australia*, 186, 305–308.

NELSON, A. (2011) *Social Work with Substance Users*. London: Sage Publications.

NELSON-JONES, R. (2012) *Basic Counselling Skills, A Helper's Manual*, 3rd edn. London: Sage Publications.

NEUMANN, I. B. (2006) Pop goes religion. *European Journal of Cultural Studies*, 9, 81–100.

NEWBURN, T. & STANKO, E. (1994) *Just Boys doing Business?: Men, Masculinities and Crime*. London: Routledge.

NICHOLSON, L. & SEIDMAN, S. (eds) (1995) *Social Postmodernism: Beyond Identity Politics*. Cambridge, UK: Cambridge University Press.

OAKLEY, A. (1981) Interviewing women: A contradiction in terms. *In:* ROBERTS, H. (ed.) *Doing Feminist Research*. London: Routledge & Kegan Paul.

O'DONNELL, M. H. (2003) Radically reconstituting the subject: Social theory and human nature. *Sociology*, 37, 753–770.

PARSONS, T. (1956) *Family: Socialization and Interaction Process*. London: Routledge & Kegan Paul.

PARTON, N. (2008) Changes in the form of knowledge in social work: From the 'social' to the 'informational'? *British Journal of Social Work*, 38, 253–269.

PATTON, M. Q. (2002) *Qualitative Research and Evaluation Methods*, 3rd edn. Thousand Oaks: Sage Publications.

PAYNE, M. (2005) *Modern Social Work Theory*, 3rd edn. Basingstoke: Palgrave Macmillan.

PAYNE, M., ADAMS, R. & DOMINELLI, L. (2005) *Social Work Futures: Crossing Boundaries, Transforming Practice*. New York: Palgrave Macmillan.

PEASE, B. & FOOK, J. (1999) *Transforming Social Work Practice: Postmodern Critical Perspectives*. St Leonards: Allen & Unwin.

PERLMAN, H. H. (1957) *Social Casework: A Problem-solving Process*. Chicago: University of Chicago Press.

PETERSON, C. (2004) *Looking Forward through the Lifespan: Developmental Psychology*, 4th edn. Frenchs Forest, NSW: Prentice-Hall.

PIAGET, J. (1964) *The Early Growth of Logic in the Child*. London: Routledge & Kegan Paul.

PIAGET, J. (1973) *The Child's Conception of the World*. London: Paladin.

PINCUS, A. & MINAHAN, A. (1973) *Social Work Practice: Model and Method*. Itasca: Peacock Publishers, Inc.

PINEO, P. C. (1961) Disenchantment in the later years of marriage. *Marriage and Family Living*, 23, 3–11.

PLANTE, R. F. (2007) In search of sexual subjectivities: Exploring the sociological construction of sexual selves. *In:* KIMMEL, M. (ed.) *The Sexual Self: The Construction of Sexual Scripts*. Nashville: Vanderbilt University Press.

PLUMMER, K. (1975) *Sexual Stigma: An Interactionist Account*. London: Routledge & Kegan Paul.

PLUMMER, K. (ed.) (1981) *The Making of the Modern Homosexual*. London: Hutchinson.

PLUMMER, K. (2008a) Queers, bodies, and postmodern sexualities: A note on revisiting the 'sexual' in symbolic interactionism. *In:* KIMMEL, M. (ed.) *The Sexual Self: The Construction of Sexual Scripts*. Nashville: Vanderbilt University Press.

PLUMMER, K. (2008b) Studying sexualities for a better world? Ten years of sexualities. *Sexualities*, 11, 7–22.

PLUMMER, K. (2010) Generational sexualities, subterranean traditions, and the hauntings of the sexual world: Some preliminary remarks. *Symbolic Interaction*, 33, 163–190.

QUINNEY, A. & HAFFORD-LETCHFIELD, T. (2012) *Interprofessional Social Work: Effective Collaborative Approaches*. Exeter: Learning Matters.

REAMER, F. (1990) *Ethical Dilemmas in Social Service: A Guide for Social Workers*. New York: Columbia University Press.

REAMER, F. (1992) *The Impaired Social Worker*. Faculty Publications, Paper 171. Available online at: http//digitalcommons.ric.edu/facultypublications/171.

REAMER, F. (2001) *The Social Work Ethics Audit: A Risk Management Tool*. Washington: NASW Press.

REED, K., BLUNSDON, B., BLYTON, P. & DASTMALCHIAN, A. (2005) Introduction, perspectives on work–life balance [online]. *Labour and Industry*, 16, 5–14.

REIFF, P. (1966) *The Triumph of the Therapeutic: Uses of Faith after Freud.* New York: Harper and Row.

REINHARZ, S. & CHASE, S. (2002) Interviewing women. *In:* HOLSTEIN, J. A. & GUBRIUM, J. F. (eds) *Handbook of Interview Research: Context and Method.* Thousand Oaks: Sage Publications.

REUPERT, A. (2006) The counsellor's self in therapy: An inevitable presence. *International Journal for the Advancement of Counselling*, 28, 95–105.

REUPERT, A. (2007) Social worker's use of self. *Clinical Social Work Journal*, 35, 107–116.

REUPERT, A. (2009) Students' use of self: Teaching implications. *Social Work Education*, 28, 765–777.

REYNOLDS, J. (2007) Discourses of inter-professionalism. *British Journal of Social Work*, 37, 441–457.

RHODES, M. L. (1986) *Ethical Dilemmas in Social Work Practice.* Boston: Routledge & Kegan Paul.

RIBNER, D. S. & KNEI-PAZ, C. (2002) Client's view of a successful helping relationship. *Social Work*, 47, 379–387.

RICH, A. (1980) Compulsory heterosexuality and lesbian existence. *Signs*, 5, 631–660.

RITZER, G. & SMART, B. (eds) (2001) *Handbook of Social Theory.* London: Sage Publications.

ROBERTS, H. (1981) *Doing Feminist Research.* London: Routledge & Kegan Paul.

ROGERS, C. (1951) *Client Centred Therapy.* London: Constable and Company Limited.

ROGERS, C. R. (1957) The necessary and sufficient conditions of therapeutic personality change. *Journal of Consulting Psychology*, 21, 95–103.

ROGERS, C. R. (1961) *On Becoming a Person: A Therapist's View of Psychotherapy.* Boston: Houghton Mifflin.

RONEN, T. (1997) *Cognitive Developmental Therapy with Children.* Chichester: Wiley.

ROSE, A. (ed.) (1962) *Human Behavior and Social Processes: An Interactionist Approach.* Boston: Houghton Mifflin.

ROSENAU, P. V. (1997) [untitled]. *Contemporary Sociology*, 26, 246–247.

RUBIN, G. (1992) Thinking sex: Notes for a radical theory of politics and sexuality. *In:* VANCE, C. S. (ed.) *Pleasure and Danger: Exploring Female Sexuality.* [New ed.] London: Pandora Press.

RUCH, G. (2009) Identifying 'the critical' in a relationship-based model of reflection. *European Journal of Social Work*, 12, 349–362.

RYAN, A. (2005) From dangerous sexualities to risky sex: Regulating sexuality in the name of public health. *In:* SCOTT, J. & GAIL, H. (eds) *Perspectives in Human Sexuality.* South Melbourne: Oxford University Press.

SALEEBEY, D. (1992) *The Strengths Perspective in Social Work Practice.* New York: Longman.

SALEEBEY, D. (1996) The strengths perspective in social work practice: Extensions and cautions. *Social Work*, 41, 296–305.

SALEEBY, D. (2006) *The Strengths Perspective in Social Work Practice*, 4th edn. Boston: Allyn & Bacon.

SANDERS, T. (2006) Sexing up the subject: Methodological nuances in researching the female sex industry. *Sexualities*, 9, 449–468.

SARANTAKOS, S. (2013) *Social Research*, 4th edn. New York: Palgrave Macmillan.

SCHNARCH, D. (1997) *Passionate Marriage: Keeping Love and Intimacy Alive in Committed Relationships.* Carlton North: Scribe Publications Pty Ltd.

SCHON, D. A. (1983) *The Reflective Practitioner: How Professionals Think in Action.* New York: Basic Books.

SCHUTZ, A. (1954) Concept and theory formation in the social sciences. *In:* THOMPSON, K. & TUNSTALL, J. (eds) *Sociological Perspectives.* Middlesex: Penguin Education.

SCHUTZ, A. (1967) *The Phenomenology of the Social World*. Evanston: Northwestern University Press.

SCHWARTZ, P. (2007) The social construction of heterosexuality. *In:* KIMMEL, M. (ed.) *The Sexual Self: The Construction of Sexual Scripts*. Nashville: Vanderbilt University Press.

SCHWARTZ, W. (1974) Private troubles and public issues: One social work job or two? *In:* KLENK, R. W. & RYAN, R. W. (eds) *The Practice of Social Work*, 2nd edn. Belmont: Wadsworth.

SCOTT, J. & GAIL, H. (eds) (2005) *Perspectives in Human Sexuality*. South Melbourne: Oxford University Press.

SCOTT, S. (2010) *Theorising Sexuality*. Maidenhead: Open University Press [Imprint].

SEDGWICK, E. K. (1990) *Epistemology of the Closet*. Berkeley: University of California Press.

SEIDMAN, S. (1993) Identity and politics in a 'postmodern' gay culture: Some historical and conceptual notes. *In:* WARNER, M. (ed.) *Fear of a Queer Planet: Queer Politics and Social Theory*. Minneapolis: University of Minnesota Press.

SEIDMAN, S. (1995) Deconstructing queer theory or the under-theorisation of the social and the ethical. *In:* NICHOLSON, L. J. & SEIDMAN, S. (eds) *Social Postmodernism: Beyond Identity Politics*. Cambridge, UK: Cambridge University Press.

SEIDMAN, S. (1997) *Difference Troubles: Queering Social Theory and Sexual Politics*. New York: Cambridge University Press.

SEIDMAN, S. (2004) *The Social Construction of Sexuality*. New York: W. W. Norton.

SHARDLOW, S. (1995) Confidentiality, accountability and the boundaries of client–worker relationships. *In:* HUGMAN, R. & SMITH, D. (eds) *Ethical Issues in Social Work*. Abingdon: Routledge.

SHAW, I. (2011) Social work research—an urban desert? *European Journal of Social Work*, 14, 11–26.

SHIER, M. L. & GRAHAM, J. R. (2011) Mindfulness, subjective well-being, and social work: Insight into their interconnection from social work practitioners. *Social Work Education*, 30, 29–44.

SHILLING, C. (1999) Towards an embodied understanding of the structure/agency relationship. *British Journal of Sociology*, 50, 543–562.

SILVERMAN, D. (1985) *Qualitative Methodology and Sociology: Describing the Social World*. Aldershot: Gower Publishing Co.

SILVERMAN, D. (2007) *A Very Short, Fairly Interesting and Reasonably Cheap Book about Qualitative Research*. London: Sage Publications.

SILVERMAN, D. (ed.) (2011) *Qualitative Research*. London: Sage Publications.

SINGER, P. (1993) *How are We to Live?: Ethics in an Age of Self-interest*. Melbourne: Text Publishing.

SINGER, P. (2004) *One World: The Ethics of Globalisation*. Melbourne: Text Publishing.

SINGER, P. (2009) *The Life You Can Save: Acting Now to End World Poverty*. New York: Random House.

SIPORIN, M. (1972) Situational assessment and intervention. *Social Casework*, 53, 91–109.

SKEGGS, B. (1997) *Formations of Class and Gender: Becoming Respectable*. London: Sage Publications.

SKEGGS, B. (2004) *Class, Self, Culture*. London: Routledge.

SMITH, D. E. (1987) *The Everyday World as Problematic: A Feminist Sociology*. Boston: Northeastern University Press.

SMITH, E. E., ATKINSON, R. L. & HILGARD, E. R. (2003) *Atkinson and Hilgard's Introduction to Psychology*. Belmont: Wadworth/Thomson Learning.

SMITH-ROSENBERG, C. (1975) The female world of love and ritual: Relations between women in nineteenth-century America. *Signs*, 1, 1–29.

STANLEY, L. (ed.) (1990) *Feminist Praxis: Research, Theory, and Epistemology in Feminist Sociology*. London: Routledge.

STANLEY, L. (1993) On auto/biography in sociology. *Sociology*, 27, 41–52.

STANLEY, L. & WISE, S. (1990) Method, methodology and epistemology in feminist research processes. *In:* STANLEY, L. (ed.) *Feminist Praxis: Research, Theory, and Epistemology in Feminist Sociology*. London: Routledge.

STAR, C. (2008) Locating justice in a warming world: Developing notions of climate justice in the UK and the USA. *Australasian Political Science Association Conference 2008*.

STEIN, Z. & SUSSER, M. (2000) The risks of having children in later life. *BMJ*, 320, 1681–1682.

STRAUSS, A. & CORBIN, J. (1990) *Basics of Qualitative Research*. London: Sage Publications.

TAYLOR, B. J. (2011) Developing an integrated assessment tool for the health and social care of older people. *British Journal of Social Work*.

THOMPSON, N. (2012) *Anti-discriminatory Practice*, 5th edn. Basingstoke: Palgrave Macmillan.

THOMPSON, N. (2011) *Effective Communication: A Guide for the People Professions*, 2nd edn. Basingstoke: Palgrave Macmillan.

TREVITHICK, P. (2012) *Social Work Skills and Knowledge: A Practice Handbook*, 3rd edn. Maidenhead: Open University Press.

UNGAR, M. (2008) Resilience across cultures. *British Journal of Social Work*, 38, 218–235.

URDANG, E. (2010) Awareness of self—a critical tool. *Social Work Education*, 29, 523–538.

URRY, J. (2000) *Sociology beyond Societies: Mobilities for the Twenty-first Century*. London: Routledge.

URRY, J. (2005) The complexities of the global. *Theory, Culture & Society*, 22, 235–254.

VASILAKI, E. I., HOSIER, S. G. & COX, W. M. (2006) The efficacy of motivational interviewing as a brief intervention for excessive drinking: A meta-analytic review. *Alcohol and Alcoholism*, 41, 328–335.

VYGOTSKY, L. S. (1962) *Thought and Language*, Cambridge, Mass.: MIT Press.

VYGOTSKY, L. S. (1978) *Mind in Society: The Development of Higher Psychological Processes*. Cambridge, Mass.: Harvard University Press.

WAGNER, G. (1998) Differentiation as absolute concept?: Toward the revision of a sociological category. *International Journal of Politics, Culture, and Society*, 11, 451–474.

WARNER, D. N. (2004) Towards a queer research methodology. *Qualitative Research in Psychology*, 1, 321–337.

WARNER, M. (ed.) (1993) *Fear of a Queer Planet: Queer Politics and Social Theory*. Minneapolis: University of Minnesota Press.

WEBB, S. A. (2010) (Re)assembling the Left: The politics of redistribution and recognition in social work. *British Journal of Social Work*, 40, 2364–2379.

WEBER, M. (1949) *The Methodology of the Social Sciences*. New York: Free Press.

WEEKS, J., HEAPHY, B. & DONOVAN, C. (2001) *Same Sex Intimacies: Families of Choice and Other Life Experiments*. London: Routledge.

WEINSTEIN, J. (2008) *Working with Loss, Death and Bereavement: A Guide for Social Workers*. London, Thousand Oaks, New Delhi, Singapore: Sage Publications.

WEST, B., PUDSEY, J. & DUNK-WEST, P. (2011) Pedagogy beyond the culture wars. *Journal of Sociology*, 47, 198–214.

WHITE, M. & EPSTON, D. (1990) *Narrative Means to Therapeutic Ends*. New York: W. W. Norton.

WHITTAKER, A. (2012) *Research Skills for Social Work*. Exeter: Learning Matters.

WILSON, J. (2000) Approaches to supervision in fieldwork. *In:* COOPER, L. (ed.) *Fieldwork in the Human Services: Theory and Practice for Field Educators, Practice Teachers and Supervisors*. St Leonards: Allen & Unwin.

WITKIEWITZ, K. & MARLATT, G. A. (2004) Relapse prevention for alcohol and drug problems: That was Zen, this is Tao. *American Psychologist*, 59, 224–235.

WOLCOTT, H. F. (1994) *Transforming Qualitative Data: Description, Analysis and Interpretation.* London: Sage Publications.

WORDEN, J. W. (1983) *Grief Counselling and Grief Therapy.* London and New York: Tavistock Publications.

WRIGHT, C. M. (1960) *Listen Yankee: The Revolution in Cuba.* New York: McGraw Hill.

YIP, K. (2006) Self-reflection in reflective practice: A note of caution. *British Journal of Social Work*, 36, 777–788.

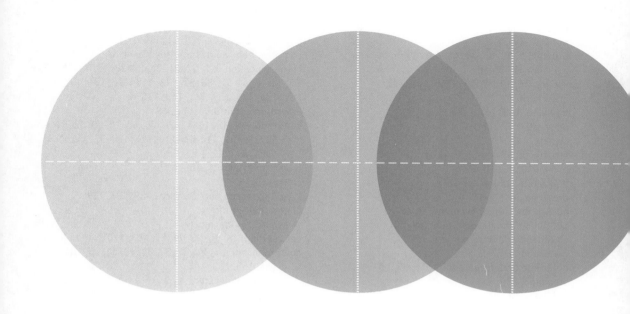

Index

actor, 30, 166, 168
adolescence, 5, 37–8, 40, 46–7, 49
   physical change, 47
   puberty, 47
adulthood, 5, 28, 37, 39, 40, 42, 49–50, 69, 166
   Erikson, 42, 49–50
advocacy, 15, 18, 67, 124, 145, 147, 170
   and client, 67
   lobbying, 145, 147
   political, 145, 147
   society, 147
   structural, 67
age, 5–6, 13, 21, 37–45
   and relationships, 38–40
   and the self, 13, 37
   adolescence and development, 47
   adulthood and development, 49–50
   childhood and development, 45
   generations, 37–9, 53
   older age and development, 15, 37, 50–51
   stages, 5, 37
   toddlerhood and development, 44
agency
   as an organisation, 14, 15, 123
   of self, 27, 32, 78, 166, 169, 170
   versus structure, 27, 32, 166
anti-discrimination/ anti-oppressive practice, 20,
    70–71, 86, 88
   see also disadvantage
Aristotle, 99
assessment, 7, 18, 20–21, 37, 46, 55–6, 66, 68, 80,
    107, 113, 118–20, 138
   and research, 140
attachment, 42–4, 166
autonomy, 42, 44, 54, 101, 105, 106, 108
   see also self-determination

birth, 5, 25, 28, 40–41
Bowlby, John, 42–3, 166
Burnout *see* vicarious traumatisation

child, 5–6, 13, 21, 37–45, 44, 45
   and psychoanalytic theory, 23–5, 78, 83, 167, 169
   and socialisation, 28, 46, 135, 155, 157, 170
child abuse, 15, 44, 53–4
   child-centred approach, 40
   child protection 15, 53, 105, 115, 137
class, 16, 21, 62, 86, 101, 102, 131, 135, 139, 145, 160
client, 6, 7, 15, 19–20, 32, 44, 48, 50, 52–3, 55–6,
    61–8, 70, 73, 78–80, 82–4, 86, 88, 93, 95,
    97–108, 113–23, 130–31, 136–7, 144–6, 148–9,
    155–8, 163, 166
code of ethics, 102–3
cognition, 39, 44, 47, 78, 81, 148
cognitive behavioural therapy (CBT), 81
communication 6, 8, 21, 24, 26, 27, 28–30, 41, 45, 52,
    55–6, 61–73, 80, 82, 116, 118, 120, 134, 137,
    156, 158, 159, 161, 163, 170
   written communication, 68
community, 9, 14, 15–17, 26, 28, 48, 79–80, 82, 84–6,
    88, 95, 101, 114–16, 119, 124, 130–32, 142, 144,
    145, 161, 162, 170
confidentiality, 101, 108, 139
consent, 119
   and research participation, 129, 137, 139
contemporary life
   see late modernity
counselling, 14, 15, 25, 71, 82, 103, 170
contemporary life, 24, 29, 30, 32, 43, 50, 88, 101,
    131, 155, 160, 168
   see late modernity
contracting, 67
couples
   and intimacy, 28, 50, 163, 167
   family, 38, 167
critical social work, 85–8
   feminist social work theory, 6, 84–5
culture, 54, 38, 43, 46, 48–9, 69, 78, 87–8, 93, 95,
    102–3, 115–16, 119–20, 131, 135, 137, 160,
    166–7
   popular culture, 24, 78

data, 129, 132, 134, 136, 137, 138, 140–42, 143, 148
   data analysis, 7, 132, 140–42
detraditionalisation, 28, 43, 167
developmental milestones, 37, 39, 40, 45, 55
   see also age
disadvantage, 80, 83, 86, 106
   see also anti-discrimination/anti-oppressive
     practice
discrimination *see* disadvantage, anti-
    discrimination/ anti-oppressive practice
dissemination, 138, 142, 147
dissertation, 142, 143
domestic violence, 15, 18, 43, 85, 106
dual role relationships, 7, 107

ecological perspective/eco-systems approach, 6,
   83–4
egocentrism and child development, 44

emancipatory research, 138
empathy, 52, 65, 69–71, 82, 100
empowerment approach, 31, 82–3
employment (and unemployment), 14, 16, 49, 51, 55, 79, 80, 85, 89, 115, 122, 123, 132, 159
epistemology, 7, 133, 138, 141, 167
    see also research epistemology
Erikson, Erik, 41–2, 46–7, 49–51
ethical decision making, 93, 96
    see also ethical dilemma
ethical dilemma, 7, 69–99, 102, 103–6
ethics
    Aristotle, 99
    bioethics, 100–1, 108, 138
    ethics of care, 100
    human rights, 32, 101–2, 146, 161–2
    Kantianism, 98–9
    utilitarianism, 97–8
    virtue based ethics, 99–100
    see also research ethics
Erikson, Erik, 41–2, 46–7, 49–51
ethnography, 7, 137
everyday life, 2, 4–9, 13–14, 21–30, 33, 47, 52, 61, 78, 93–6, 98, 102–3, 108, 113, 117, 120, 122, 125, 130–31, 134, 141, 161, 163

family, 14, 17, 21, 24, 26–7, 33, 37, 38, 40, 43, 48, 50, 51, 53, 55, 56, 64, 83–5, 88, 93, 101, 105–7, 119, 124, 131–2, 145, 148–9, 160, 167, 170
feedback, 63, 114, 116
feminist social work theory, 6, 84–5
    see also gender
focus groups, 7, 131, 133, 135, 140, 141, 151
Freud, Sigmund, 24–5
    see also psychoanalytic theory

Garfinkel, Harold, 61, 116
gender, 16, 21, 43, 46–7, 62, 84, 85–6, 88, 101, 102, 131, 135, 138, 139, 148, 160, 166, 167, 168
generalisability, 139
generations, 39, 49, 53, 55, 103, 132, 158, 160, 162, 167
Giddens, Anthony, 22, 28, 30, 42, 43, 48, 50, 85, 120, 160, 161, 166, 167, 168, 169, 170
globalisation, 28, 30, 162
government, 14, 16, 18, 19, 67, 101, 105, 106, 109, 119, 124, 138, 139, 142, 144, 151

human lifespan see lifespan
human rights, 32, 101–2, 146, 161–2
humanistic approaches, 6, 82

identity, 3, 5, 8, 13, 15, 19, 21, 23, 24–7, 30, 31, 34, 41, 42, 47, 48, 49, 69, 71, 73, 86, 87, 88, 113, 115, 118, 131, 135, 155, 156, 158, 159, 160, 163, 167, 168, 169
    see also self
interactionism see social interaction
    see also Mead, George Herbert
inequality, 9, 13, 46, 47, 48, 70, 72, 73, 79, 88, 95, 101, 120, 122, 138, 146, 158, 161, 162, 163, 167
    see also disadvantage, anti-discrimination/anti-oppressive practice
infancy see birth
internet see technology
interpersonal interaction see social interaction
intervention, 14, 15, 48, 53, 78, 79, 80, 81, 82, 86, 88, 101, 105, 115, 118, 130, 144, 149, 170
interviews, 7, 131, 134–5, 135, 138, 140, 141, 151

Kant see ethics
Kantianism see ethics

language, 23, 24, 25, 44–5, 55–6, 62–3, 82, 97, 159, 166
    see also communication and social interaction
late modernity, 160, 161, 168, 169
    see also contemporary life
life span, 5, 37, 39, 40, 41, 43, 51, 53–6
listening, 5, 47, 61–6, 71, 73, 114
    see also communication and social interaction
literature review, 7, 143–4
lobbying, 106, 145
    see also advocacy

Mead, George Herbert, 4, 8, 13, 22–3, 47, 61–2, 69, 71, 87–8, 113, 125, 155, 157, 159, 164, 168–9, 170
    see also social interaction/ sociality
motivational interviewing, 82
Mills, C. Wright, 9, 89, 130, 164
moral development, 100
Munro, Eileen, 40

neglect of children, 44, 45, 53, 54, 144
non-verbal communication, 137
    see also communication, social interaction
normative child development, 53

objectivism, 133, 151
organisational context, 15, 19, 67, 86, 105–6, 113, 115, 118, 123, 144

oppression *see* disadvantage
   see also anti-discrimination/anti-oppressive
      practice
open ended questions, 64

parenting, 15, 56, 106
paternalistic decisions, 105
   see also ethics
peer groups, 47
personality, 13, 24, 32, 78, 81, 167
Piaget, Jean, 39, 41, 44, 45, 46, 49
placement *see* practice learning
policy, 14, 16, 18, 32, 54, 80, 109, 115, 116, 123, 124,
   129, 132, 144, 145, 146, 170
popular culture, 24, 78,
population, 15, 37, 53, 83, 115, 129, 138, 139, 162
positivistic research, 133
practice learning/ placement, 4, 7, 26, 34, 61–2, 66,
   71, 106, 107, 113–25, 156, 157
professional self, 5, 7, 19, 34, 93, 113, 116–18, 123,
   155, 158
   see also social work identity
probing, 66, 73
   see also communication
problem solving, 31, 45, 83
professional conduct, 97, 102
protection, of children *see* child abuse
puberty *see* adolescence
psychoanalytic theory, 23–5, 71
psychosocial, 14, 42
puberty *see* adolescence

qualitative research, 138, 142, 144
   see also research
quantitative research, 133, 136, 140–42
   see also research
questionnaires, 7, 130, 131, 135, 136, 140, 151
   see also research

race, 48, 85, 86, 88, 101, 102, 145, 160, 167
   see also culture
reflexiveness, 29–32, 62, 168, 169
reflexivity, 4, 5, 8, 29–33, 41, 62, 69, 113, 120, 125,
   157, 159, 161, 164, 168, 169
   extended reflexivity, 169
religion, 51, 62
relationships, 6, 8, 22, 23, 25, 26, 29, 30, 31, 38, 43,
   48, 50, 53, 54, 80, 88, 99, 100, 113, 130, 138,
   157, 158, 159, 161, 162
   dual role relationships, 7, 107

family relationships, 43, 45, 56, 119, 160, 161,
   166
intimate relationships, 28, 42, 47, 50, 77, 120, 122,
   150, 161, 167
relationship between variables, 141, 148
relationships between social workers and clients,
   37, 80, 109, 113, 116, 119, 157, 160
relationships with other professionals, 16, 19, 55,
   56, 125, 157
   see also social Interaction
research, 3, 7, 9, 14, 16, 18, 19, 21, 27, 37, 39, 43, 44,
   49, 50, 54, 61, 68, 73, 82, 109, 115, 116, 124,
   129–51
dissemination, 142
evaluation, 147, 148, 149, 169
literature reviews, 143–4
methodology and methods, 133–7
research analysis, 140–42
research epistemology, 133
research ethics, 138–9
research mindedness, 7, 130–32
research question, 132
sampling, 139
snowball sampling, 139
use of research in practice, 144–51
resilience, 42, 44, 130
retirement, 51, 53
risk, 14, 15, 21, 44, 48, 86, 94, 98, 102, 105, 109, 116,
   129, 147, 148, 149, 160, 161
Rogers, Carl, 48, 63, 82, 100

sampling *see* research
school, 15, 45, 46, 55, 66, 69, 115, 119, 145, 146, 147,
   161
self, 3–9, 13, 19, 21–34, 39, 41, 42, 46, 47, 48, 49, 56,
   61, 62, 69, 71–2, 77, 78, 81, 82, 87, 88, 93, 95,
   99, 101, 108, 113, 114, 116–18, 123, 125, 130,
   148, 151, 155, 156, 157, 158, 159, 160, 161, 163,
   164, 166, 167, 168, 169–70
   see also social interaction/ sociality, identity
self determination, 95, 101, 108
   see also autonomy
sensorimotor, 41
sexual identity, 15, 86, 88, 135, 160, 168
   same sex relationships, 50, 52, 53, 167–8
   heterosexual relationships, 167–8
sexuality, 15, 47, 119, 141, 160, 167
snowballing *see* research
social constructionism, 170
sexual violence, 85, 129

social interaction / sociality 4–5, 7–9, 13, 21–34, 40–41, 45, 47, 50, 55–6, 61–7, 69, 71–3, 78–9, 82–4, 88–9, 100–2, 113, 116, 118, 120, 125, 131, 134, 155, 156, 157, 158, 159, 163, 164, 166, 168, 169, 170
   see also symbolic interactionism
social justice, 4, 32, 80, 88, 101, 108, 146, 161
social work identity, 3, 8, 13, 24, 131, 155, 158, 163
   see also professional self
social work values, 7, 8, 49, 151
statutory social work, 105, 137
sociological social work, 6, 87, 88
sociological imagination, 89, 130
statistics see research
strengths perspective, 82–3
structural social work, 87, 106, 118, 119
subjectivism, 133
summarising see communication
supervision, 95, 113, 116, 122–3, 125, 157, 163, 168
surveys, see research,
systems theory, 83–4

social work ethics see ethics
symbolic interactionism, 22–3, 169
   see also Mead, George Herbert
   see also social interaction

talking therapies, 25
technology, 29, 50, 51, 53, 94, 137, 150, 160, 161

unemployment (and employment), 14, 16, 49, 51, 55, 79, 80, 85, 89, 115, 122, 123, 132, 159
utilitarianism see ethics

values, see social work values
vicarious traumatisation, 107
   see also burnout
virtue based ethics see ethics
Vygotsky, Lev, 45

whistleblowing, 106–7
women see gender
written communication see communication